BRITAIN
THROUGH
AMERICAN
EYES

BRITAIN
THROUGH
AMERICAN
EYES

EDITED,

WITH AN INTRODUCTION

AND COMMENTARIES

by

Henry Steele Commager

McGRAW-HILL BOOK COMPANY

NEW YORK   ST. LOUIS   SAN FRANCISCO   DÜSSELDORF
MEXICO   TORONTO

123456789DODO7987654

Library of Congress Cataloging in Publication Data

Commager, Henry Steele.
    Britain through American eyes.

    1. National characteristics, English.   2. England—foreign opinion, American.   3. England—Social conditions.   I. Title.
DA118.C63 1974   301.15'43'91420385   73-8686
ISBN 0-07-012366-7

Acknowledgements

Excerpts from the following:

Volume 124 of Edward Everett papers. Courtesy Massachusetts Historical Society.

Reminiscences of William C. Preston, Minnie Yarborough, ed., published by University of North Carolina Press, 1933. Reprinted by permission.

Victoria, Albert, and Mrs. Stevenson, Edward Boykin, ed. Copyright (c) 1957 by Edward Boykin. Reprinted by permission of Holt, Rinehart and Winston, Inc.

The Journals of Bronson Alcott, Odell Shepard, ed. Copyright 1938 by Odell Shepard. Reprinted by permission of Little, Brown and Company.

"Henry Adams' 'Diary of a Visit to Manchester,'" Arthur Silver, ed. Reprinted by permission of *American Historical Review*, Washington, D.C.

A Cycle of Adams Letters, 1861–65, Volumes I and II, Worthington C. Ford, ed. Copyright 1926 by Worthington C. Ford; copyright renewed 1948 by Emily E. F. Lowes. Reprinted by permission of Houghton Mifflin Company.

The Letters of Bret Harte, Geoffrey Bret Harte, ed. Copyright 1926 by Geoffrey Bret Harte; copyright renewed 1954 by Geoffrey Bret Harte. Reprinted by permission of Houghton Mifflin Company.

Alice James: Her Brothers, Her Journal, Anna Robeson Burr, ed. Reprinted by Milford House, September 1971. Reprinted by permission.

Henry White, Thirty Years of American Diplomacy by Allan Nevins. Copyright 1930 by Harper & Row, Publishers, Inc., renewed 1958 by Allan Nevins. Reprinted by permission of the publisher.

The Pavilion by Stark Young. Copyright 1951 by Stark Young. Reprinted by permission of Charles Scribner's Sons.

Letters of Washington Irving to Henry Brevoort, George S. Hellman, ed., and *The Notebook of an American Parson in England* by George Monroe Royce. Reprinted by permission of G. P. Putnam's Sons.

A Backward Glance by Edith Wharton. Copyright 1933, 1934 by William R. Tyler; renewed 1961, 1962. Reprinted by permission of A. Watkins, Inc.

Autobiography by William Allen White. Copyright 1946 by Macmillan Publishing Co., Inc. Reprinted by permission of the publisher.

The Life and Letters of Walter Hines Page by Burton J. Hendrick. Copyright 1922, 1925; renewed 1948 and 1952. Reprinted by permission of the executors of the estates of Hobart J. Hendrick and Dr. Ives Hendrick.

*To
Storm Jameson
and to the memory of
Guy Chapman
with
admiration,
gratitude,
and
love*

Contents

1800–1820

1820–1830

1830–1840

1840–1850

1850–1860

1860–1870

1870–1880

1880–1890

1890–1900

1900–1910

1910–1920

1920–1948

Introduction

In September 1856 Henry James, Sr., wrote to his old friend Edmund Tweedy about Emerson's *English Traits,* which had just come to hand, a letter which takes on an ironic quality in the retrospective light of his son Henry's lifelong preoccupation with English traits:

Many thanks for Emerson! It came in most apropos to a great desire which I felt after it . . . I am disappointed now that I have read it; the appreciation is so overdone. The study has been too conscientious. The manners—the life—he was investigating, haven't the depth either for good or evil he attributes to them. His own standpoint is too high to do justice to the English. They are an intensely vulgar race, high and low; and their qualities, good or evil, date not from any divine or diabolic *depths* whatever, but from most obvious and superficial causes. They are the abject slaves of routine, and no afflatus from above or below ever comes, apparently, to ruffle the surface of their self-complacent quietude. They are not worth studying. The prejudices one has about them, even when they are unjust, are scarcely worth correcting. There is nothing better supplied by the actual truth of the case, to put in the place of them. They belong, all their good and their evil, to the past of humanity, to the infantile development of the mind, and they don't deserve, more than any other European nation, the least reverence from a denizen of the New World. They are a solider, manlier race than the French, according to the old ideas of manhood; that is, they do not lie, cheat, commit adultery and murder with half so much good will; but of the spiritual causes out of which these evil things proceed, pride and self love and the love of domineering, they have their full share, and perhaps more than most other people. They lack heart. Their love is clannish. They love all that wear their own livery, but they don't even *see* anyone outside of that boundary.[1]

"Worth studying"—that is itself a complicated phrase. Worth studying to whom, and for what purpose? Certainly the scores of commentators who are

1. Ralph Barton Perry, *The Thought and Character of William James,* I, pp.122–125.

somewhat surprisingly united in these pages by a single interest found the English worth studying for a wide variety of reasons ranging from filiopietism to a sense of outrage. Some studied England, and the whole of Britain, because they did indeed think English society and institutions interesting in themselves; some because they confessed a sentimental attachment to their "English cousins"; some—as with Henry James, Sr., in his long and penetrating essay on Carlyle—to justify, as it were, their distaste for things English; some, consciously and unconsciously, to discover their own identity in the choreography of their approach to and retreat from their social and cultural ancestors.

Certainly England (and it was almost always England rather than Scotland, Ireland, or Wales) troubled and confused America and Americans, from the time when John Adams resented royal slights but elaborately recommended—in three massive volumes—the British system of political balances to the attention of his fellow countrymen and Tom Paine called the English people "fools" but returned to England to persuade them to launch a revolution, down to the soul searchings of Henry James and William Dean Howells in the early years of the twentieth century.

This contrapuntal interaction of Americans and Englishmen over a period of a century and a half was indeed a reflection of a "special relationship." Americans have always been fascinated by the Old World—France, Italy, Spain, Germany, and more recently Russia, and the record of those fascinations is writ large in American literature, philosophy, and art. But until the First World War these miscellaneous relationships with the countries of Continental Europe differed not only in degree but even in kind from those with the "Mother Country." They were, in many respects, more interesting and more romantic; they were certainly less troubled and less exacting. If at times they seemed intellectually and artistically more rewarding than the complex relationships with England, they are psychologically less illuminating. And how suggestive it is that while Americans of all ethnic backgrounds have been fascinated by the problem of the American relationship to Britain, and have contributed richly to the discussion of that problem, there is no comparable body of literature by the Germans, Irish, Swedes, Italians, Russians, or Puerto Ricans exploring American—or even their own—cultural relationships to their countries. Clearly the break of Anglo-Americans with the Mother Country was political rather than cultural, while the rupture of European Americans with their mother countries was cultural rather as well as political.

From the beginning the nature of the American interest in Britain and in the continental countries has been vastly different. Americans who visited or lived in European countries have rarely allowed themselves to be absorbed into the political or social activities of those countries or even into their culture: there are a dozen expatriates to France or Germany or Italy who have never bothered to learn the language of their host countries for every Margaret Fuller Ossoli who flung herself into the Roman Revolution of 1849. Most Americans who committed themselves to expatriation to some Continental country did so for practical purposes—the study of painting or architecture or music—or perhaps for purposes that were wholly personal—fascination with the exotic, the amusing, the beautiful. Americans flocked to Florence and Rome to study sculpture rather than to study Italy, or perhaps merely for its "golden haze"—as Henry James made clear in his wonderful biography of William Wetmore Story. They turned to Germany for music, to Paris for painting and perhaps more, for life itself—for as Jefferson observed, France is everybody's second country—while Spain, anyway in the days of Irving, Ticknor, and Prescott, offered beauty and romance and perhaps a clue to the understanding of the New World, too. All in all there rarely seemed any necessity to come to terms with these countries morally and psychologically, as there was to come to terms with England, and Americans did not try to, but cheerfully set up their colonies in Florence or Dresden or Paris. The countries of Europe simply did not weigh on the American conscience or trouble the American mind.

England was from the beginning a special case. A good many American visitors and even some commentators—artists, scholars, students of medicine (who mostly headed for Edinburgh) or of law, who studied at the Temples —did visit England "on business," as it were, but the majority of those who visited and wrote about her did so in order to satisfy themselves about the character of the Mother Country, and about their own relationship with her.

How account for this interest, this anxiety, this passion? How account for the Niagara of commentary, much of it froth and foam but much of it living waters. Most of the explanations are obvious enough. There is, first, the elementary fact of a common language, certainly a common literary language, and that was what counted. With other nations there was almost always a language barrier which (except for those of Continental origin who had somehow retained their own mother tongue) operated at the very outset to cut Americans off from knowledge of or sympathy with other cultures —except perhaps those of Greece and Rome, whose history and literature they had learned in school. The Americans and the English knew each other from early childhood: how could they help themselves? American children read *Mother Goose* and *Alice in Wonderland* and, a bit later, *Tom Brown's Schooldays* and *The Jungle Book* as English children read *Little Women* and the *Leatherstocking Tales* and *Tom Sawyer* and when they grew up they continued to read each other's novels and poems without finding them in the least alien. How difficult *Il Paradiso* and *Faust* were to the average American, how familiar and almost domestic the plays of Shakespeare, the poems of Tennyson, the nonsense rhymes of Edward Lear. Indeed, many an American—especially those from the social groups which indulged in foreign travel and which produced most of the commentary on England—was more at home in the streets of Charles Dickens' London, or the cathedrals and parish churches of Trollope's Barchester, or the Highlands of Stevenson or John Buchan, than in the streets of New York City or the churches of Philadelphia or the mountains and valleys of the Catskills, and it is safe to say that more Americans feel at home in the zany quarters of Bertie Wooster's Drones Club than in George Apley's Somerset Club. They were, many of them, like Hawthorne's Edward Redclyffe, who felt

> the deep yearning which a sensitive American, his mind full of English thoughts, his imagination of English poetry, his heart of English character and sentiment—cannot fail to be influenced by, the yearning of the blood within his veins for that from which it has been estranged, the half-fanciful regret that he should ever have been separated from these woods, these fields, these natural features of scenery to which his nature was moulded.[2] . . .

What was true of literary relationships was scarcely less true of many others. Americans and English fought each other and made peace with each other in what came to take on, more and more, the aspect of family quarrels; and the two American daughters of Britain, the United States and Canada, lived peacefully side by side for a century and a half, taking each other for granted as Denmark and Norway took each other for granted after their separation. Americans and English read the same Bibles—the King James Version or the Douay —and they embraced, on the whole, the same religious precepts and moral values, and it is sometimes difficult to know whether Victorianism was more indigenous in America or in Britain. They shared each other's heroes and villains: every English schoolboy had read Thackeray's moving tribute to George Washington in *The Virginians,* and many of them knew "by heart," as Churchill did, "The Midnight Ride of Paul Revere" or "Barbara Fritchie," as almost every American schoolboy had read Macaulay's essay on Clive and could recite at least some of the lines of "The "The Charge of the Light Brigade."

All this is only part of the story. A common language and, for a long time, a

2. *Dr. Grimshawe's Secret,* pp.180–181.

common history encouraged but did not dictate this mutual preoccupation; it might have gone the other way. After all, no such preoccupation with each other animates the French in Paris and in Quebec, nor has Mexico or Chile produced anything like the literature of commentary on the Mother Country that the United States has showered on Britain. It is interesting, too, that though the conditions of a common language and history still obtain, the mutual interest of the Americans and British is far less compulsive now than it was in the nineteenth century.

In addition to language and history, there were cultural, sociological, and psychological forces which powerfully conditioned American relations with the British. The most powerful of these, particularly in that long stretch of years when the American population was still predominantly English in origin, was the "Mother Country" syndrome—a syndrome which, as with children and parents, revealed a pattern of tensions and ambiguities. Even after the large-scale German and Scandinavian immigration which set in at mid-century, the overwhelming majority of white Americans continued to think of Britain as the "Mother Country," and to be proud of a heritage which they assumed was American as much as it was British. The consciousness of that heritage weighed heavily on the American imagination. To this theme Hawthorne returned again and again. "Almost always," he wrote in *Our Old Home:*

> . . . in visiting such scenes as I have been attempting to describe, I had a singular sense of having been there before. The ivy-grown English churches were quite as familiar to me, when first from home, as the old wooden meeting-houses of Salem. . . . This was a bewildering yet very delightful emotion, fluttering about me like a faint summer wind, and filling my imagination with a thousand half remembrances, which looked as vivid as sunshine at a side glance, but faded quite away whenever I attempted to define and grasp them.

So James Russell Lowell, protesting in his review of Longfellow's "Kavanaugh" against the notion that Americans needed a "national literature of our own," burst out:

> As if we had been without one! As if Shakespeare had not also been ours! As if we had no share in the Puritan and republican Milton, we who had cherished in secret for more than a century the idea of the great puritan effort and at last embodied it in a living commonwealth.

And then he added one of those insights that occasionally surprise us in his otherwise commonplace observations: "The English mind has always been characterized by an emigrating tendency; its most truly national epic was the colonizing of America." It was a theme which fascinated Henry James, this of the American participation in the English past, and the narrator of *A Passionate Pilgrim*—clearly James himself—observed, of "the latent preparedness of the American mind for even the most delectable features of English life," that "the roots of it are so deeply buried in the virgin soil of our primary culture that, without some great upheaval of experience, it would be hard to say exactly when and where and how it begins."

England had indeed one inestimable advantage which was not so much a virtue as a condition: age. Almost everyone wants to associate himself with something bigger than himself, and the yearning for ancestry is as instinctive as the yearning for posterity is—or used to be—and has the added advantage that it can be contemplated more extensively. America, which had little past of her own, acquired one, vicariously but legitimately, through the Mother Country (and through the Mother Continent, too, as Thomas Paine and Washington Irving and Longfellow and others clearly showed). This vicarious past had the inestimable advantage that you were not required to burden yourself with the whole of it; you could reject whatever was discreditable or tiresome and claim all that was glorious and splendid and entertaining.

No need to elaborate on anything so elementary and so familiar, familiar especially in the first half of the nineteenth century. Thus Jefferson, who never really liked England or forgave her mistreatment of America, wrote in 1810 that "American laws, language, religion, politics and manners are so deeply laid in English foundations that we shall never cease to consider their history as part of ours, and to study ours in that as to its origins." Thus Washington Irving, who wrote "Europe," but meant "England," said in the introduction to his *Sketch Book:*

> My native country was full of youthful promise; Europe was rich in the accumulated treasures of age. Her very ruins told the story of times gone by, and every mouldering stone was a chronicle. I longed to wander over the scenes of renowned achievement, to tread, as it were, in the footsteps of antiquity . . . to escape from the commonplace realities of the present and lose myself among the shadowy grandeurs of the past.

Thus the sentimental novelist Catharine Sedgwick (author of *Hope Leslie*) confessed that "when I touched English ground I could have fallen on my knees and kissed it." Thus Benjamin Silliman, who went to England to learn the chemistry he was to teach, asserted bluntly that "to an American England is all 'classical.'" This starry-eyed attitude gradually evaporated in the latter part of the century; after all, it was pretty hard to be sentimental about the England that sympathized so ostentatiously with the Confederacy. And after the Civil War, politicians appealing to the Irish vote found it increasingly profitable to "twist the lion's tail." Yet even the irascible Henry Adams, who rejoiced, after all, in a hereditary quarrel with Britain, admitted after his seven-year stint in London that he too had succumbed to its seductions. "London had become his vice," he wrote in his *Education:*

> He loved his houses, his haunts, his habits and even his hansom cabs. He loved growling like an Englishman and going into society where he knew not a face and cared not a straw. . . . He had become English to the point of sharing their petty social divisions, their dislikes and prejudices with each other.

But it was not merely Irving, Sedgwick, Hawthorne, Adams, and others conscious of English ancestry who acknowledged an emotional attachment to "Our Old Home." Intellectual ancestry proved as powerful as genealogical, nor could intellectual involvement be divorced from emotional. Indeed, except in those somewhat rarified circles which cultivated filiopietism, it was often the intellectual commitment that was decisive. That commitment played a larger role in America than it might have elsewhere, because here so large a proportion of the population went to schools where they were exposed—indeed, where they could not avoid—that intellectual heritage. As children they rode a cock horse to Banbury Cross, asked Where has my Billy Boy gone?, and proclaimed that Charlie was their darling. From their mothers they learned about Dick Whittington, Alfred and the cakes, and Robert Bruce and the spider. When they were older they met Oliver Goldsmith and Charles Kingley and Lord Tennyson in the McGuffey Readers and their many imitators, and on their own they read *David Copperfield* and *Treasure Island.* Tom Brown taught them more about English schools than they knew about American, and the indefatigable George Henty gave them a sense of English history livelier than they had of any other, perhaps even of their own. If, when older, they studied law it was the common law; if they yearned to be statesmen they knew that England was the Mother of Parliaments, and that she had spread her political system—like her Empire—across the globe. If they were self-conscious about freedom—and most of our commentators were—they cherished those lines of Wordsworth,

> We must be free, or die, who speak the tongue
> That Shakespeare spake, the faith and morals hold
> Which Milton held,

and they knew that

> In everything we are sprung
> Of Earth's first blood, have titles manifold.

If they were literary-minded—and a passion for literature is the greatest single common denominator of the commentators—they made pilgrimages to the Poet's Corner in the Abbey, to Stratford, to Bath, or to Abbotsford, or somehow managed to breakfast with Byron, Carlyle, or Tennyson, or—the ultimate triumph—to dine at the Athenaeum. Happily, this harassment of famous authors died down in the twentieth century.

In the more sophisticated observers (and we do not on the whole draw on the unsophisticated), clergymen, journalists, scholars, diplomats, this sense of historical and intellectual heritage was more profound and inspiring than that kind of filiopietism displayed by the Passionate Pilgrim of Henry James's story who, in effect, died of a broken heart because he could not recover title to his ancestral estates. For the interest of the intellectuals was inspired by the study of history, literature, and law, and was directed to analyses of institutions and interpretation of character. No wonder that so much of the best American writing on England—*English Traits* is the most revealing example here—centers on institutions: Oxford and Cambridge, which were for long the only real universities in England, the Inns of Court, scientific establishments, hospitals, clubs, Church and Chapel, and the monarchy, which was both an institution and a pageant.

A third explanation of the American preoccupation with England is in a sense the obverse of the other two, and therefore, of course, part of them: resentment and hostility. Animus against Britain, overt or covert, was, as might be expected, a more complicated matter than either devotion or veneration. It was compounded of the recollection of hereditary quarrels—the Revolution and the War of 1812—and English sympathy for the Confederacy; of the transfer to the New World of Old World antipathies such as those of the Irish; of impersonal indignation at what appeared to be gross injustice or recurrent wrongdoing against other peoples; philosophical disapproval of the class system, the Established Church, and Imperialism (Bartholomew's maps showing half the world in British pink had something to do with creating this stereotype); resentment against what appeared to be, and often were, calculated snubs, slights, and discourtesies; and simple exasperation with the conventionality and complacency of the English mind—those qualities of which P. G. Wodehouse is perhaps the best historian. Animus and irritation ranged from the petulance of Fenimore Cooper to the amused vexation of Hawthorne, who wrote of the reaction to his *Our Old Home* that "the English critics seem to think me very bitter against their countrymen and it is perhaps natural that they should because their self-conceit can accept nothing short of indiscriminate adulation." It can be read in the moral indignation of Jack London against the conditions of the London poor; in the deep resentment of James Russell Lowell's "On a Certain Condescension in Foreigners," and the savage caricature of Mark Twain's *The Prince and the Pauper;* in Hawthorne's sad conclusion that "not an Englishman of them all ever spared America for courtesy's sake or kindness," and in Henry James's wry confession to Charles Eliot Norton: "Considering that I lose all patience with the English about fifteen times a day, and vow that I renounce them forever, I get on with them beautifully and love them very well"—a sentiment which few American visitors to England have failed to share.

Most of the criticism was serious and objective, and some of it was—for all its surface sharpness—flattering, for it confessed disillusionment with hopes that had been too high. This was most pronounced, perhaps, in Emerson, who had been prepared to believe that "England was the best of all actual countries," but whose final verdict was a good deal more qualified than that. In this Emerson was representative, for Americans who idealized or romanticized England were often disappointed, and tended to hold England herself responsible for their disappointment rather than their own high hopes.

What Americans disapproved of in British—and more particularly English—character and society was predictable, and there is a certain monotony in their strictures. Looming large on the English scene—and in the American vision—was the class system, ubiquitous and pervasive. It was what many Englishmen had immigrated to America to escape; it was by its very existence a challenge to what Tocqueville thought the most pervasive of all American Traits—equality; perhaps most awkward of all, it was something American visitors were simply unable to understand or unwilling to cope with. There were exceptions, to be sure: George Ticknor, who dearly loved a lord, comes to mind; and the silly Nathaniel Parker Willis, who made his living describing High Society; and the youthful Charles Sumner, who later learned better; and Walter Hines Page, who somehow persuaded himself that a class society was an element of strength in a nation; and the far more complex Henry James, to whom the English class structure was a subject of inquiry, elaboration, and fascination. But to most American visitors, including those who never thought of being outraged by the class societies of Germany, Italy, or Spain, the English class system was both a puzzle and an affront: one sometimes senses that it was a personal affront.

A second English trait to which many Americans were unable to accommodate themselves was the readiness to accept, quite uncritically, the authority and the power of the religious Establishment and—as a concomitant—the weakness and vulnerability of nonconformity; with this came the discovery that in Britain the Church was an integral part of the class structure, and that the difference between Church and Chapel was social as well as political.

Class was, of course, legal, social, and economic, but to American visitors its most ostentatious manifestation was economic. Nothing shocked Americans more than the contrast between the glittering wealth and abysmal poverty which they saw on every side, in the great cities and in the countryside. Landing in Ireland just after the close of the War of 1812, a great southern swell saw "beggary, starvation, and crime on every side," and a decade later the Reverend Henry McLellan reported that "the poor eat the bread of bitterness." Presumably this never happened in America, or if it did it was a temporary situation, one certain to be remedied. In Britain it seemed not temporary but permanent, built into the social and economic structure, as it were. Young Herman Melville's picture of the misery, crime, and vice which he saw on first landing in Liverpool is something of a literary classic; half a century later Jane Addams was revolted by the spectacle of the "hideous human need and suffering" in London; and a quarter-century later Jack London, viewing *The People of the Abyss,* concluded that "here was where the blood was being shed." How revealing that what Americans scarcely noticed in France or Germany, and thought merely picturesque in Italy and Spain, affronted and outraged them in Britain.

England was not, however, exempt from that moral rejection implicit in the larger theme of Old World depravity and New World innocence which so bemused the American mind from Jefferson to Henry James and beyond, a theme perhaps best—or anyway most crudely—expressed in Lowell's *A Fable for Critics* of 1848:

> Forget Europe wholly, your veins throb with blood,
> To which the dull current in hers is but mud;
> Let her sneer, let her say your experiment fails,
> In her voice there's a tremble e'en now while she rails.
> And your shore will soon be in the nature of things
> Covered thick with gilt drift-wood of cast-away kings. . . .
> O my friends, thank your God, if you have one, that he
> 'Twixt the Old World and you set the gulf of a sea . . .

It was a theme with numerous and, for the most part, respectable antecedents. In the beginning the argument was directed largely to England—France was, after all, our ally, and of other nations we knew little of. "Blest in their distance from that bloody scene, why spread the sail to pass the Guelphs between?" wrote the poet of the Revolution, Philip Freneau. Why indeed? Dr. Benjamin Rush—he had studied medicine at Edinburgh, but had no illusions about Britain—never ceased to argue the danger of moral contamination from Europe. "America," he said, "should be greatly happy by erecting a barrier against the corruptions in morals, government and religion which now pervades all the nations of Europe." Thomas Jefferson was the most cosmopolitan of all Americans of his generation, perhaps of all the men of the Enlightenment, but he could write from France in 1786 that the American people could not have "achieved that high ground which they occupied" had they not "been separated from their parent stock, and been kept from contamination either from them or from the other people of the Old World, by the intervention of so wide an ocean," and almost two decades later he could "bless the Almighty being who, in gathering together the waters under the heavens in one place, divided the dry land" of the European and the American hemispheres.

The argument came up again and again—in Emerson, Lowell, Melville, Whitman. Mark Twain, even, implicit rather than explicit, in William James and Henry Adams. Nowhere was it more elaborately adumbrated than in the stories and novels of Henry James, and it was James, too, who in *The Ambassadors* dramatically, and even tragically, foreshadowed its demise. The obsequies can be traced in Hemingway and Fitzgerald and Faulkner and Henry Miller and the many others who have chosen to elaborate on the theme not so much of Old World as of New World depravity. But this is another story.

Yet in the eyes of even the most censorious England was not really as abandoned to depravity as Continental countries. Indeed, in the matter of moral corruption it could not compete—in the eyes of Americans—with France, nor was it ever charged with that insidious spiritual malaise to which Henry James gave the name "golden haze." But no matter. France and Italy and doubtless other countries of Europe were merely acting according to character, and most Americans would have felt cheated had they not found France titillatingly immoral or Italy cultivating *la dolce vita*. The American judged Britain by higher standards—standards rather higher, indeed, than those he applied to himself or his own country—and was correspondingly more deeply affronted by British misdeeds and failings than by those of other countries.

Certainly the most interesting of the pressures and considerations which led Americans to focus their attention so heavily on Britain was that search for an American identity which looms so large on the horizon of our cultural history. Old World nations, except Germany, did not for the most part confess any identity problem; identity was simply a fact of nature and of history. No Englishman bothered to ask what it was to be English, for the English took themselves for granted (just as Hawthorne and Emerson saw), and all the best books on the English character are by the outsiders. No Frenchman worried about the Great French Novel or a French cuisine; the Italian's identity was fixed by the latitude of his particular state, Tuscany or Naples, and the longitude of Italy; even the Norwegians, who belonged to Denmark for a thousand years and Sweden for almost a hundred, do not wonder what it is to be Norwegian. It would of course be a mistake to suppose that Americans alone brood over the problem of their identity, for that problem has troubled Canadians from the beginning, as well as South Africans and Australians, and doubtless it troubles India and other nations that are culturally old but politically new. But from Crevecoeur to Henry James the question What is this New Man, this American? has bemused the American mind.

The problem was a real one: after all, *was* there an American identity distinct from the British; *was* there an American culture, an American language, law, music, painting, architecture; *was* there an American literature, religion, philosophy, education; *were* there American values? Our forefathers had brought forth a new nation, no doubt about that, but if all its cultural attributes from language to law, from poetry to painting derived from or merely reflected the English, how could they claim to have brought forth a national culture?

The search for an American identity was carried on chiefly at home, to be sure (a large story, this, to come to terms with a domain as large as the whole of Europe and a nature as varied), but overseas as well, for Americans had to discover their identity not in a cultural vacuum but in the macrocosm of Western civilization. No other nation, before the twentieth century, had a problem quite like this; eventually it was to be a problem familiar enough to those new nations which emerged out of the British Empire and Commonwealth, and even to new nations (and ancient peoples) such as the Arab states and Israel, to all of whom the American experience is now of compelling interest. In the nineteenth century the United States alone bore the weight of a Mother Country (for the new nations of Latin America did not really need to define themselves by a new culture, a new religion, or a new history) which appeared to have preempted the cultural field.

Curiously enough, the search for identity ignored all the Continental European mother countries and, until the mid-twentieth century, the African ones. Americans of German, Dutch, Scandinavian, even Irish origin, and later on of Italian, Polish, Russian, and Spanish, were for the most part untroubled by the problem of their identity vis-à-vis their own mother countries. Indeed, with most of them the problem often seemed quite the reverse. It was how to cast off as expeditiously as possible their heritage of language and culture (though not of religion) and to be absorbed into the great ocean of American society, culture, and mores, and even to adopt as their own an English heritage. This is the burden of a hundred diaries and autobiographies, from Crevecoeur's *Letters of an American Farmer* to Ole Rölvaag's *Giants in the Earth*—how to cast off the ancestral heritage and assimilate to the American.

An American identity was, of course, to be established in America itself. Crèvecoeur, who saw so much, saw that, but he saw too what came to be central to the whole inquiry—that the significance of the American experience could be discovered only by reference to the experience of the Old World. This too was a central theme in that greatest of all interpretations of the American character, Tocqueville's *Democracy in America*. To Americans, certainly to that self-selected group who traveled and recorded their impressions, that meant Britain. How, after all, determine the nature of the American language, or even if there was such a thing, except by comparison with the King's English; how understand the contributions of American law except in the context of Blackstone and the common law, or the significance of the American law school except by contrast with English legal education, all centered in London and controlled by the Inns of Court? How appreciate what was new and original in the American political system except by reference to the British parliamentary system, or of such innovations as separation of powers and judicial review except by comparison with the tradition of legislative supremacy in the Mother Country? Most American social institutions, too, traced their ancestry to Britain, and what was new and original about them could be best understood in terms of their adherence to or departure from the British originals. Americans took equality for granted, except for the Negro; let them then contemplate the social inequalities which persisted in Britain. They took for granted the separation of church and state, and voluntarism in support of religion; how instructive to study a society where the very opposite was taken for granted! Even in the intellectual arena the contribution of America—to the Enlightenment, for example, or to Romanticism—could be best understood in the context of European and British Enlightenment and Romanticism.

To be sure, there were even greater and more dramatic contrasts to be observed by comparing American institutions and practices with French,

Italian, German, but until the twentieth century, anyway, such comparisons and contrasts meant little to Americans. For here it was the contrasts that were taken for granted, just, indeed, as it was the contrasts with the French or the Spaniards that were taken for granted by the English themselves. It was Britain that provided Americans with a meaningful standard either for comparison or for contrast; it was in the approximation to or the departure from things British that the Americans discovered their character.

The search for an American identity was never wholly disinterested, except perhaps in an expatriate like Henry James (whose interpretation of the American identity in *The American Scene* was almost too acerbic to be considered disinterested), or perhaps in a citizen of the world like George Santayana who never really felt at home in America. Certainly it cannot be said that observation of Britain over a period of more than a century provided Americans with an identity in the sense that the frontier or the search for unity in heterogeneity did, or even with an infallible clue to that identity. But it can be said with some confidence that the search itself was an essential part of the process of self-identification, a process which finally concluded not with the discovery of a clear identity but rather with the realization that the matter was no longer of any great importance.

It is impossible to distinguish with any precision the changing patterns of the interpretation of Britain by successive generations of American observers, yet it is clear that the pattern did change, and that although the changes appear to be kaleidoscopic they do have a chronological pattern.

The first generation of Americans visited an England still smarting from defeat—a defeat which seemed to the English as contrary to nature as does defeat to Americans today, and one which was peculiarly bitter because it had been imposed upon her by her ungrateful offspring. It was an England whose ruling class reflected the sullen petulance of George III, the narrow greed of Sheffield, the reactionary philosophy of Burke; an England which had driven out Dr. Priestley and outlawed Tom Paine, and sent scores of critics of its political oppression to Botany Bay. Almost inevitably most American visitors of this generation came away from England confirmed in their conviction that they had indeed done well to separate from her; most, too, were gratified to confirm by observation what they had known by instinct, how fortunate was the average American by comparison with the average Englishman. That conviction was best put by Thomas Jefferson, who wrote shortly after his brief and unpleasant visit to England in the spring of 1786, a visit memorable for the snub which the insignificant George III saw fit to direct toward the greatest American of his time:

If all the sovereigns of Europe were to set themselves to work to emancipate the minds of their subjects from their present ignorance and prejudices, and that as zealously as they now endeavour the contrary, a thousand years would not place them on that high ground on which our common people are setting out. ... If anybody thinks that kings, nobles, or priests are good conservators of the public happiness, send him here. It is the best school in the universe to cure him of that folly.[3]

The Revolution had brought political independence to the American people, but it had not ended America's involvement in Old World rivalries and wars, nor cultural colonialism. Victory at New Orleans in 1815 put an end to both the involvement and the colonialism, and ushered in an era of self-confidence and self-sufficiency—an era in which most Americans could contemplate England more indulgently because no longer afraid of her. A billow of pride poured through the new nation, pride in its nascent culture and in its real achievements. In the cultural arena, indeed, the Second War for Independence was more decisive than the First; it ushered in a genuine American literature, the beginnings of a native art, important achievements in science, and spectacular contributions to law and politics. "In the four quarters of the globe, who reads an American book?" Sydney Smith had asked; one possible answer was that the captain of every English ship studied Nathaniel Bowditch's *The Practical Navigator*. The more amiable view of England found felicitous expression in essays by Washington Irving which at once introduced a healing note into Anglo-American relations, while the new self-confidence was reflected in the literature of commentary by Irving himself, by Cooper, by Hawthorne, best of all by Emerson. Thus Irving, celebrating "the matchless prosperity of America," could add that "the future destinies of that country do not admit of a doubt; over those of England there lower some shades of uncertainty." Thus Cooper could confidently predict that

should England give up her dependencies . . . she would sink to a second rate power in twenty years. Did we not exist the change might not be so rapid, for there would be less danger of competition; but we *do* exist . . . and in a quarter of a century more we shall number as many people as all the British Isles put together.

Thus Hawthorne, contemplating Westminster Abbey, "could not help" imagining

3. To George Wythe, 13 August 1786, *Works of Thomas Jefferson* (Memorial Edition), V, p. 396.

that this rich and noble edifice has more to do with the past than with the future; that it is the glory of a declining empire; and that the perfect bloom of this great stone flower growing out of the institutions of England, forebodes that they have nearly lived out their life.

When he left England for Italy Hawthorne entrusted his journals to an English friend with the instruction that he might break their seals in the year 1900, "by which time England will be a minor republic under the protection of the United States." It is Emerson, whose *English Traits* (for all Henry James's reservations) marks the end—for the time being anyway—of literary colonialism. How appropriate it was that the spokesman of American cultural independence should also provide the most judicious, illuminating, and persuasive argument for cultural equality with the Mother Country. What all these commentators discovered, each quite independently, was that though England may have been "the best of all actual nations," it was the United States that commanded the future. On this point the Emerson of *English Traits* was magisterial:

> I told Carlyle that I was easily dazzled, and was accustomed to concede readily all that an Englishman would ask. . . . They have everything and can do everything; but meantime, I surely know that as soon as I return to Massachusetts, I shall lapse at once into the feeling which the geography of America inevitably inspires, that we play the game with immense advantage; that there, and not here (in England) is the seat and centre of the British race; and that no skill or activity can long compete with the prodigious natural advantages of that country in the hands of the same race; and that England, an old and exhausted island, must one day be contented, like other parents, to be strong only in her children.

It was the Civil War and the postwar generation who presented the most complex pattern of responses to the spectacle of Britain—complex and almost paradoxical, for there was a curious combination, in these years, of fierce resentment and almost obsequious veneration. The resentment was inspired by the spectacle of the British aristocracy flaunting its preference for the Confederacy, and by the threat of formal intervention in the war over the *Trent* affair, when Captain Charles Wilkes halted the British ship and arrested two Confederate commissioners, Mason and Slidell. Anger at these affronts was deep and lasting. Nowhere did Yankee bitterness find more eloquent expression than in James Russell Lowell's biting protest, "Jonathan to John":

> It don't seem hardly right, John,
> When both my hands was full,
> To stump me to a fight, John—
> Your cousin, tu, John Bull . . .

Shall it be love, or hate, John?
It's you thet's to decide;
Ain't *your* bonds held by Fate, John,
Like all the world's beside?
  Ole Uncle S, sez he, I guess
  Wise men forgive, sez he,
But not forgit; an' some time yit,
Thet truth may strike J. B.,
Ez well as you an' me.

And Americans did not really forget; these grievances rankled in the American—or at least the Yankee—mind for more than a generation. Nor was resentment ameliorated by southern gratitude for British sympathy, for Southerners found little satisfaction in what they regarded as merely verbal gestures, but rather resented the failure to translate those gestures into policy. As the North Carolina agent, Lewis Peyton, said of the English reaction to the *Trent* affair, "It was not that they loved the Confederacy, but because they distrusted the Yankees."

Nor was this the whole burden of American displeasure with the Mother Country during the postwar years. It is less easy to forget a snub or a slight than an injury, and many Americans felt more keenly British animadversions on the pervasive corruption of American democracy, or on the endemic vulgarity of the American rich, than they did the depredations of the Confederate raider *Alabama* and its shelter in British ports. It was the bad manners of the British that Henry Adams excoriated, Adams who was something of an expert on bad manners; it was "a certain condescension in foreigners" that grated on the sensibilities of Lowell—Lowell who condescended easily enough to those so unfortunate as to live west of the Hudson.

Yet many Americans—those who traveled, those who preferred to live abroad—sympathized with the English point of view, adopted it themselves, and yearned for what Henry James called "the perfection of human society." These representatives of a new kind of colonialism shared that passion for the past so characteristic of European—and of Southern—romanticism, but very different from the romanticism of an Emerson or a Thoreau. They adored the Middle Ages and the Crusades, the Renaissance, and (with Miniver Cheevy) the Medici—everything that was exotic and picturesque. They rejoiced in the romanesque churches of Richardson or the Gothic of Renwick, and hired Richard Morris Hunt to duplicate on New York's Fifth Avenue or in the mountains of North Carolina the châteaux of the Loire. They flocked to Dresden for art and to Munich for music and to Bayreuth for Wagner, and studied architecture at the Ecole des Beaux Arts. They set up "public schools" on the English model and imported English schoolmasters, until it might almost be said that Groton was the model for Eton, and during summer vacations the masters would conduct the young men on edifying tours of the cathedrals of England and France while their sisters were being presented at court. They arranged international marriages—the Jeromes, the Vanderbilts, the Cuttings come to mind—and many of them bought stately homes in England and settled there permanently, safe from the vulgarity of American life. In Henry James they found their social historian, though not one they invariably approved.

Perhaps the best representatives of what we may call the new colonialism were those two New Englanders John Fiske and Thomas Bailey Aldrich; Fiske, who was so ecstatic over meeting all the great swells of the Athenaeum Club, Aldrich, whose diatribe against the "new" immigration—"Ungarded Gates," he called it—"a poem in which I mildly protest against America becoming the cesspool of Europe." It was of course Henry James himself who was the most sophisticated spokesman for this group of neo-colonials, or perhaps neo-romantics, though his own relationship with England, as with America, was always an ambiguous one. And it was James who made the classic observation that "it's a complex fate, being an American, and one of the responsibilities it entails is fighting against a superstitious evaluation of Europe," a responsibility he did not always fulfill.

The final era—final philosophically rather than chronologically—can be dated conveniently enough from the passing of the generation of Henry James and William Dean Howells, a long generation, to be sure, which lasted from the Civil War to the First World War. This era saw the evaporation of most of the issues which had agitated the minds of the Anglophiles, the Anglophobes, or those who were simply critics and observers of Britain, and it saw too a sharp decline in interest in the British character and in British institutions, with a corresponding increase in the scholarly, objective and impersonal concern for British history. The explanation is miscellaneous rather than complex. First is the vindication of Emerson's prophecy that America, not Britain, was to be the seat and center of the British race[4]—a vindication which came, astonishingly enough, within half a century, and not at all in the manner Emerson had hoped. Already by the turn of the century the center of

4. It is interesting that Gladstone should have been one of the first to acknowledge this shift. In 1878 he said that "while we have been advancing with portentous rapidity, America is passing us by as if in canter. There can hardly be a doubt as between America and England, of the belief that the daughter at no very distant time, will be unquestionably stronger than the mother."

gravity had shifted to America, which now boasted leadership in population, wealth, energy, and power, though not yet in science or literature or art. Yet even in these areas the tutelage was no longer to Britain but to the Continent, and that posed no serious psychological problems. For now that Americans could take for granted their own preëminence, actual or potential, interest in "identity" evaporated, and the problem which had agitated so many Americans for over a century ceased to have any genuine meaning or any vital interest. Thus was demonstrated once again the validity of Santayana's observation that Americans did not bother to solve problems, "they pleasantly bid them goodbye." The twentieth-century American concluded that the American character was not to be sought in the corridors of English history, but rather in the experiences and conditions of American life; he discovered —once more it is Santayana speaking—"that to be an American is of itself almost a moral condition, an education, and a career."

The inspiration, the stimulus, the vagaries of the American attitude toward the Mother Country provide us with the theme on which to arrange the selections which make up this volume. But it is the selections themselves which are substantive and central. Their interest to Americans is in a sense narcissistic; to the British it is, or should be, historical. And because Americans had a psychological and literary head start over other observers, what they had to say—the best of them—is more informed, perspicacious, and judicious than anything in French or German, or perhaps even in English, literature.

The fascination which the vast literature of travel from Herodotus to Sir Richard Burton has exercised over generations of readers is rooted in its exploitation of the wonderful, the astonishing, the exotic—and perhaps the perverse. With what excitement did the Romans read what Caesar and Tacitus had to say of the German tribes, or the Venetians listen to the report Marco Polo brought back from China; how famous were the Jesuit *Relations* from the Orient and the forests of Canada; how famous too those travel narratives so lovingly assembled by Richard Hakluyt and his successors; and the *Journals* of Captain Cook's voyages and of the expedition of Lewis and Clark still have the power to stir us.

In the early years of the Republic a good many British travelers wrote about America in this fashion, describing the United States as they might have described China or Peru; this was a passing phase and is now of only marginal interest. Nothing of this kind emerged in the literature of American visitors to Britain, certainly not in the writings of those whom we take seriously. The value of British reports on America and of American reports on Britain is in a sense just the opposite of that which inheres in classical travel literature of the Marco Polo or Hakluyt variety: it is in the familiar, not in the exotic. It was because the Americans and the British shared not only a common language and common institutions, but habits and values, that visitors from either country were so sensitive to variations on or departures from what they assumed to be the norm. Each saw what the other took for granted, and it is what is taken for granted that is perhaps the surest index to national character.

Examples come readily to mind. No American visitor to Russia or Spain would be astonished at the legal and juridical systems of those countries, for it was taken for granted that these would be vastly different from that which obtained back home. What arrested his attention in Britain was what the British themselves assumed to be the norm: that while Americans had but one class of lawyers, the British had barristers and solicitors, and that the differences were as much social as professional; that where Americans, at least on the Eastern Seaboard, generally studied law in formal law schools, the English read law in their undergraduate years at the University and then went up to the Inns of Court to read it with their seniors; that where the atmosphere of the American courtroom was informal the English judge still sported a wig and the barrister took the silk. Both the British and the American economy depended greatly on the new enterprise of advertising, but where the American does not expect advertising on the Continent to be like that with which he is familiar, he is taken aback to find that British advertising is directed to men rather than to women, and that where in the United States it is expected to be elaborate, irrelevant, titillating, vulgar, and misleading, in Britain it is (or was) mostly sober, simple, practical, respectable, and descriptive. Both people worship at the same altars but where in America church and state are sharply separated, in Britain they are interdependent; where Americans have carried denominationalism to its greatest extreme—three hundred sects, and more popping up all the time—the British are content with a score or so; and that where in America church affiliation follows no generally accepted social pattern, in England Church and Chapel are social as well as religious terms. Both peoples have pretty much the same educational structure, but where the college has long flourished in America, it did not until recently really exist in England except as a residential community at two of the ancient universities; where "democracy" in America has long dictated open admission to institutions of higher learning, access to British universities is limited and—until a century ago—access to the two great universities was limited to members of the Church of England; and where democratic America finds it necessary to exact tuition from most of its college and university students, class-conscious Britain now provides education—as it provides medicine—free.

What took the Americans to Britain—those who proposed, or were required or persuaded, to write up their experiences and their impressions? Some, like John and John Quincy and Henry Adams, were sent abroad to represent their country; some, like Ticknor and both Everetts, went to study; some, like Benjamin Silliman and Ticknor (a later visit, this), to buy books for university or private libraries. Some went as journalists, to cover elections or wars—thus Richard Harding Davis and Vincent Sheean; some went to enjoy fame and applause, like Harriet Beecher Stowe and General Grant; some went because they found life in England, all in all, more agreeable than life in America, thus Henry James, who gave us the most elaborate commentary we have from a single hand, and perhaps the best. Some went to lecture, and Emerson was doubtless the most distinguished of these; some, like Samuel Eliot Morison and Allan Nevins, to occupy chairs at great universities; some to take consular jobs—Hawthorne and Bret Harte come to mind—which would afford them an opportunity to see more of English life than was vouchsafed others. Many went for professional purposes: clergymen to observe the Church of England, or to deplore it; medical men to study and to work in hospitals; businessmen to knit more closely the economic ties of the two countries—few of these, alas, had time or inclination to write; artists, like John Singleton Copley or Whistler or Edwin Abbey to be at the center of the artistic world, or to pick up commissions. A good many—here almost wholly unrepresented—went as "innocents abroad," simply to see the Old World, to worship at historic shrines, to visit ancestral villages or towns, to broaden their horizons, social as well as intellectual, or quite simply to take a vacation. This generalization we can safely make: Those who not only visited Britain but wrote about her, went to learn something: to learn about the British political system, the class structure, the economy, the Church, the universities, painting or architecture or literature or history. Thus in a larger sense the Americans went as students, formal or informal, or (and the difference is negligible) as teachers.

Who are the commentators? They are, as might be expected, a more miscellaneous group than the English interpreters of America, those, for example, whom Allan Nevins drew upon in his invaluable *America Through British Eyes*. This miscellaneous character is largely a function of democracy, of a society, that is, where many people travel, and where everyone thinks he has a right to speak, and supposes that what he has to say is important. Where the British commentary on the United States was on the whole an upper-class affair (the lower classes could not afford to travel, nor did they have access to the journals and the publishers), American commentary on the Mother Country came from every segment of society. It may be of some significance that where Professor Nevins found only twenty-eight British travelers worthy of inclusion in his stout volume, I have levied on about one hundred American travelers: if all of them are not quite up to Emerson, neither were all the British observers quite up to Bryce. But in the United States no parson was too obscure, no spinster too timid, no scholar too modest to doubt that both the public and posterity would be interested in his or her impressions of the Old World. Two of our commentators—Warren Isham and Claudius Patten—are indeed so obscure or so elusive that every effort to identify them (except of course in terms of their books) has proved in vain, and they appear here without those credentials which their associates enjoy. Neither the optimism nor the vanity of the American travellers was wholly unjustified, for the nineteenth-century American was both unsophisticated and curious, and confessed to an almost insatiable appetite for comparing the world he knew with the world he wanted to know—just what you get in that classic of American Victorianism, *Innocents Abroad.*

The geographical distribution of the American commentators is not without interest. Of the hundred who speak here, almost half came from New England, and most of the remainder from other areas of the North; only a dozen or so came from the South. The imbalance is not a product of editorial astigmatism, but of the fact that New Englanders were, or seemed to be, more affluent, that with their long maritime history they had an ingrained habit of travel, that they were, on the whole, better educated than most of their countrymen, that they boasted, during the whole of the nineteenth century, the most distinguished colleges and universities, the most famous scholars, educators, and poets, and that they had in the *North American Review,* in the *Atlantic,* in Ticknor and Fields and Little, Brown, their own organs of publication.

There was something of a geographical pattern in the commentary as well—geographical and historical. London dominated England and England dominated Britain; Scotland was not neglected, but in all the ocean of literature how little there is of any value on Wales or on Ireland. After London it was Oxford and Cambridge that were most prominent on the literary horizon: not surprising, this, when we recall how many American visitors were scholars and men of letters, and what a spell those ancient universities cast on the imagination of the whole literary world; not surprising when we consider how many Americans, first and last, have studied or taught at these universities.

A word on the selection and organization of our material is relevant. The center of gravity is not so much the English scene as what Emerson so felicitously called English traits. On the whole, therefore, I have preferred interpretations of the English character to mere description, however lively. There are exceptions to be sure: Elkanah Watson's vivid picture of George III acknowledging the independence of his former colonies, George Ticknor delighting in the spectacle of High Society, George Smalley limning the Passing Show of London. But even description illuminates character, as with Herman Melville's bitter picture of poverty and misery in the slums of Liverpool, or Aldrich's portrait of "Smith," or Helen Hunt Jackson's wonderful tableau of the fishwives of Newhaven.

One may suggest but not delineate character in a few phrases or paragraphs, and I have tried to avoid the *disjecta membra* of literature and relied instead on more substantial analyses such as those by Hawthorne, Emerson, William Everett, Henry Adams, and Henry James. This has, of course, restricted the number of interpretations I could present, yet many remain to interest, to instruct, and perhaps to entertain us.

These essays appear in chronological form, with the chronology determined (whenever possible) by the date of writing rather than by the date of publication—which was sometimes half a century or more later. The only alternative to a chronological arrangement is a topical one, and material of the kind I have included simply does not lend itself to topical organization, in part because almost all the commentaries have the single theme of the English character, in part because most of the commentaries deal with many facets and manifestations of that character. Whatever its drawbacks, the chronological arrangement permits us to follow the changing pattern of the American response to Britain with some accuracy. The patterns, to be sure, are implicit rather than explicit: successive generations of American visitors to Britain did not organize themselves into battalions and march to appropriate tunes. Yet as we have already suggested, a pattern does emerge: from the resentment of the post-Revolutionary era to affection for Our Old Home; from the proud independence of the 1850s and early 1860s to the almost sycophantic veneration of the Brown Decades; from the practical disappearance of rivalry between the two great branches of the English-speaking peoples, and the long search for an American identity, to a decisive shift in the center of interest, away from Britain and to the Continent. No one was more perspicacious about this than Henry James—who was perspicacious about everything—and we may appropriately close with a passage from one of his letters to his brother William, written long before the later shift of American attitudes crystallized:

I can't look at the English-American world, or feel about them, any more, save as a big Anglo-Saxon total, destined to such an amount of melting together that an insistence on their differences becomes more and more idle and pedantic; and that melting together will come the faster and more one takes it for granted and treats the life of the two countries as continuous or more or less convertible, or at any rate as simply different chapters of the same general subject. Literature, fiction in particular, affords a magnificent arm for such taking for granted, and one may so do an excellent work with it. I have not the least hesitation in saying that I aspire to write in such a way that it would be impossible to an outsider to say whether I am at a given moment an American writing about England or an Englishman writing about America (dealing as I do with both countries) and so far from being ashamed of such an ambiguity I should be exceedingly proud of it, for it would be highly civilized.[5]

—*Henry Steele Commager*

Albany, London, 1971
Amherst, Mass., 1973

---

5. Henry to William James, October 29, 1888, in *Letters of Henry James*, (London, 1920).

BRITAIN
THROUGH
AMERICAN
EYES

1777-1800

SAMUEL CURWEN, LOYALIST,
LONGS TO RETURN TO SALEM

1777–82

The Loyalists should be heard from, for they had impressive credentials to Americanism, and none more respectable or more representative than Samuel Curwen of the ancient Massachusetts town of Salem. A graduate of Harvard College in 1735 who had participated in the glorious expedition against Louisburg during the French and Indian War, Curwen was a man of substance and, on the eve of the Revolution, a Judge of Admiralty and a supporter of the discredited Governor Hutchinson. At the outbreak of war Curwen fled to England, leaving his wife to stay on and take care of the family property in Salem. We have no better literary picture of the life of the American Loyalists in England than that furnished by Curwen's journal and his letters: in these pages we can read the anxiety, the boredom, the loneliness, the sense of neglect and disillusionment, the alternation between hopes and fears, with the fears steadily mounting, and with it all the deep nostalgia for America that so many of the Loyalists confessed. In the end, notwithstanding the savage character of the American anti-Loyalist laws, Curwen was able to return peacefully to Salem, where he found his property and his social position intact.

From *The Journal and Letters of Samuel Curwen, An American in England, From 1775 to 1783*, George A. Ward, ed. (Boston, 1864), pp. 174-283.

Exeter, Nov. 22.[1777] . . . By the papers, I learn the King in his speech takes notice of *"the obstinacy of his rebellious subjects in America,"* and promises himself *"all needful assistance from his faithful Commons."* It will be well if additional supplies, and an increase of foreign troops, do not prove a source of intolerable evil. Would to God an expedient could be devised to terminate this unnatural quarrel, consistent with the honor of both parties; but this I fear is a vain wish. The Dutch, from a sordid thirst of gain; the French, from their dread of the rising power of Great Britain, united with the Colonies; and Spain, from an attachment to the Court of Versailles, are too deeply concerned to permit a re-union. . . .

Dec. 14. This day General Burgoyne's mortifying capitulation arrived in town. Nothing could be more disgraceful and humiliating, unless a submission to the victor's power without terms. The loss of the military chest, estimated at seventy-five thousand pounds; the finest train of artillery ever sent out of this kingdom before; all the boasted acquisitions of the year's campaign gone at a blow, and Canada on the point of joining the grand American alliance.

In the House of Commons, on the 12th inst., after Lord Barrington's report of army estimates, Col. Barré rose and called on Lord George Germaine to inform the house whether the report of the surrender of General Burgoyne with his army and artillery was true or false; which Lord George did in a short narrative, and said intelligence had been received of the capture by the way of Quebec, which struck the House with astonishment; . . .

Dec. 18. From a correspondent at the west of the town, I learn that the language about the Court is nowise lowered by the last news from America; *"delenda est Carthago."* The old politicians, neither biassed by hatred to Americans, nor interested in the destruction of the Colonies, shake their heads at this language.

Dec. 25, Christmas. Service at Cathedral. No shops opened entirely, nor business publicly or generally carried on—though the day is otherwise negligently enough observed, nor indeed can more be expected, considering the low ebb of religion here.

Soon after the surrender of Burgoyne was announced by Lord George Germaine in Parliament, an adjournment took place till after the holidays, whereupon Sir George Young, Mr. Baring, the Exeter member, and Mr. Barré, hurried down, and it was suspected that this foreboded a new Parliament, a new ministry, new measures, and that the most active opposition is coming into play; a few days will undeceive the public, however. On confirmation of the American news, Manchester offered to raise a thousand men at their own expense, to be ready for service in America in two months, and was followed soon after by Liverpool. It is said there are to be proposals for raising two thousand men out of each parish through the kingdom; that the American Secretary will resign, and Lord Hillsborough succeed him.

Dec. 31. The lenity shown to General Burgoyne and his army is allowed on all hands to do more honor to America, than the laurels, reaped by the Howes, can bring to this distracted country. God knows what is for the best, but I fear our perpetual banishment from America is written in the book of fate; nothing but the hopes of once more revisiting my native soil, enjoying my old friends within my own little domain, has hitherto supported my drooping courage; but that prop taken away leaves me in a condition too distressing to think of; however, amidst the increasing evils of old age I have this consolation, that, mortifying as my lot is, severe as my sufferings may be, their continuance cannot be lasting. . . .

To Rev. Isaac Smith, Sidmouth

Exeter, Jan. 17, 1778

Dear Sir:

The account of Gen. Burgoyne's surrender is confirmed, and what think you of the Congress now? Of American independence? Of laying the Colonies at the ministers' feet? Of Lord S[andwich]'s boast of passing through the continent from one end to the other with five thousand British troops; and with a handful of men keeping that extensive continent in subjection? Of the invincibility of the said troops? Of the raw, undisciplined, beggarly rabble of the northern colonies? Of the humiliating surrender of a British General, five thousand troops, seven thousand small arms, and thirty-six pieces of brass artillery, to the aforesaid rabble? What think you of the pompous proclamation of the said General? Of the figure he is now making in the streets of Boston, compared to his late parading there, accompanied by his vainly fancied invincible cohorts, now, alas! rendered as harmless and inoffensive animals as you and I? Of the condition General Howe is now or soon may be in, should the combined army of Washington and Gates, numerous as it may be, perhaps exceeding his own in the proportion of two to one, elated with success, inflamed with an enthusiastic ardor, invest Philadelphia, defended by an army almost worn out by incessant labor, having, as the papers say, the shovel and firelock always in their hands, and greatly weakened by losses? What think you of the twenty thousand men voted in Parliament a few days since, in addition to the army now in America? Where are they to be raised? Is not Russia on the verge of a war with the Turks? Have not the two great potentates of Germany refused to suffer their country to be further drained of its inhabitants? ... Have not the Switzers too strong a sense of liberty themselves to engage against a cause wherein civil liberty is pretended to be invaded?

Pray what resources, then, has Great Britain, without allies able or willing to afford the needed help? Can her own country furnish the requisite numbers? Can the manufacturers spare, without essential injury to its commerce, a supply from thence? Does she abound in laborers? Are there not, rather, complaints that men of the lower classes are wanting? Have not the recruiting parties found great difficulty in raising men? And is it not well known that business goes on slowly and heavily at this day? Would not an Act of Parliament to press men for the American service, (and without it, it cannot be done,) raise disturbances and insurrections think you? Would not raising new regiments from among the Catholics of Ireland disaffect the bulk of the nation? In this sad dilemma, which way can Administration turn to extricate themselves? How can they escape out of this labyrinth wherein they are intricated? What measures can be adopted consistent with the honor and dignity of this late mighty empire—alas, how fallen!—that gave law but a few years ago to two of the most powerful, politic, and wealthy States in Europe, and thereby peace to almost all the world? ... The language of the Court, the papers say, is, as it ever has been, *"delenda est Carthago"*; if this be not slander, woe betide my poor country. I confess I feel too strongly the *amor patriae* not to wish it may be slander; its enemies will never, I hope, exult over its ruins; but its inhabitants be timely brought to a just sense and sight of their real interest and security, which in my view consists only in a close connection with this country.

Vigorous measures are talked of there; but in Parliament the language held by the ministers seems mild, leaning toward an adjustment of matters otherwise than by the *ultima ratio regum;* the out-door talk is just the reverse; unhappy the state of society and government that renders such conduct in any regard expedient. ... I will add a few lines to fill the sheet. Newspapers are crowded with articles of the offers of towns and counties to enable his Majesty's Government to carry on the war against America, which by some means is now become to be considered as less a ministerial affair than some time ago; should the proposed numbers, however, be taken out of the manufactories, I dare engage trade will sensibly feel it. Would to God, that moderate and just views of the real interests of both countries might possess the minds of those who direct the public measures here and there. That peace may again take place, and trade and agriculture and commerce be established on a lasting basis, is the most ardent wish of your friend,

S. Curwen

To WILLIAM BROWNE, ESQ., LONDON

Exeter, Jan. 30, 1778

Dear Sir:

General Burgoyne's defeat will, I think, prove a prelude to a succession of fatal events. The rapid increase of military skill and courage that enthusiasm produces, and the great numbers of European commanders and engineers of experience now incorporated amongst the Americans, are considerations that extinguish my expectation of the success of the following campaign, even should Great Britain send over in season the number of troops ordered by Parliament. . . . May those evils my gloomy mind forebodes, exist only in imagination; but I must confess I see, perhaps through a false vista, the expedition already ended in the disgrace of this powerful and wealthy kingdom, and in the ruin of that once singularly happy, but now, alas! deluded, wretched America; for, disconnected from this country, wretched it must necessarily be, if anarchy and the most grievous oppressions and taxes can make a people so. How weak, inconsistent, and dangerous is human conduct, when guided by lawless ambition, or any false or wrong motives! Into what dreadful evils are communities often plunged by hearkening to the declamations of pretended patriots, of crafty, selfish, unprincipled demagogues of this and many other countries, history furnishes us a present mortifying proof and example . . . noble exertions as her critical situation seems to demand: for which this people have in times past been famed, as the disaster you mention formerly produced among the Romans, and as heretofore within my own memory, has been the case with this very people. But the breast of every Roman was warmed with the *amor patriae* at that period, and with this principle he could brave dangers, and even death, to bring honor to his country. When riches poured in upon them from all quarters of the world, when manners degenerated, and selfish regards succeeded to the love of country; when luxurious tables and effeminacy among the higher ranks took the place of frugal meals, and manly fortitude, with the sense of honor sunk into venality and court dependence, they then became abject, desponding, cowardly, and were exposed to every invader, and instead of bravely defending, abandoned even their lands and wealth to be possessed by their courageous army; and such will always be the condition of every people in similar periods of its state. But away with politics. . . .

Believe me, with real regard, yours,

S. Curwen

To George Russell, Esq., Birmingham

Exeter, March 16, 1778

Dear Sir:

The dark and threatening cloud hanging over this island calls aloud for a more serious turn of mind than seems to characterize the present period; but how sadly true is the reverse of such a state of mind amongst us at this day; thoughtlessness, levity, frivolous manners, mirth and music, seem to have seized and engross the upper ranks; attention to business and a supine disregard to national danger and honor, do they not too justly characterize the middle ranks? As for the *canaille,* they are here, as they ever have been, and will be in all states and times, stupidly indifferent and unconcerned in the midst of impending destruction. If the features of this ill-favored portrait are in your opinion too harsh, believe me, it was not drawn by a pencil dipped in gall, nor dictated by envious misanthropy; I am no cynic, nor cursed with the spirit of a cloistered monk. The warmest regards to the country, which by long residence has become an *altera patria,* and holds the second place in my affection, few and faint as my connections with individuals are,—the most earnest wishes of my heart for its safety, and foreboding apprehensions of its danger and dishonor, occasion the painful reflections that cease not hourly to distress my mind. . . .

To Judge Sewall, London

Exeter, March 23, 1778

Dear Sir:

I was meditating an answer to your favor, when the alarming intelligence of the French Court's perfidious dealings, and the hourly expectation of war against her, arrived here. The *dénouement* of the plot, by the French Ambassador's declaring in form to Lord

Weymouth his Court's interference and engagement to support the claims of Congress, seems at present to render all speculation on the subject of Great Britain's further attempts to reduce her late deluded subjects in America needless: presuming all thoughts in regard to vigorous efforts being to be laid aside, superseded, at least for the present, as the papers inform us no more troops are to be sent out.

These events my fears have been long predictive of; not that I pretend to the spirit of prophecy, or the gift of second sight. States, like individuals, are liable to so many sudden and unlooked for vicissitudes, disappointments, untoward accidents, and evils that neither wisdom can foresee, nor power nor prudence prevent; he whose mind, not however to the increase of his enjoyment, leans towards doubts, fears, and apprehensions of evils, generally finds more events corresponding to his forebodings than he whose attention is turned to the brighter and more pleasing views that hope presents.

. . . I am not vain enough to wish myself in the King's councils, but I ardently wish that imaginary principle of National honor, the King's honor, might in this critical and dangerous condition the nation seems to be in, be dispensed with and given up to infinitely more important considerations, notwithstanding the clamors and reproaches to be expected from discontented, interested party men. That the war, should it unfortunately soon commence, to vindicate the King's honor or Nation's, must produce disgrace and irreparable losses to the nation, a review of the present force Great Britain has, her foreign dominions, etc., and the force requisite to secure her right, may perhaps convince: nor less so, Great Britain's inability at present to force a compliance or convince them by military exertions that it is their interest to accept her reasonable offers. The lucky minute for such an offer is past, irretrievably past, and a series of surprising events, owing to ill-concerted plans, interested views, a total disregard to the public weal, or, if you please, a certain fatality, has taken place, by which Colonies of inestimable value are lost to this country; and I wish the loss may end there. . . .

TO WILLIAM PYNCHON, ESQ.

Bristol, July 15, 1780

Dear Sir:
. . . Since my last, the political state of affairs seems in many people's opinion to have taken a more favorable turn for this coun-

try, but good and ill often succeed each other in the whirl of human affairs in quick succession; for amidst a deal of good news daily pouring in from abroad, a most tremendous cloud suddenly and unlooked-for arose and covered our horizon, threatening instant destruction even to the very being of Government itself. For some days it was feared the city of London would be laid in ashes, during which the most abandoned and profligate miscreants that were ever nourished by, or have proved the curse of society, were to have availed themselves of the conflagration and terror occasioned thereby, and plundered what the less cruel felons might have spared, perhaps murdering those against whom their spite might have been levelled. On the day that the petition of the Protestant Associators, as they denominated themselves, was to be presented to the House, the subscribers were by an advertisement of Lord George Gordon, their president, desired to meet in St. George's Fields; the reason alleged was, that no building in London was large enough to hold the expected numbers, and from thence to accompany him with the petition to the house—meaning by so numerous an appearance to give weight to it, or enforce it more effectually. The rabble, many of whom were signers, likely enough for the most villanous purposes, for with such the more mischief the better sport, joined, making no less a number, it is credibly said, than forty thousand; a number of such characters, and under such circumstances, truly alarming; from hence they paraded through the borough of Southwark and along London streets, at first it is said orderly, but no sooner had they reached palace yard than they filled that and all the avenues leading to the House. Throwing off the mask, they bawled aloud for liberty and the Protestant religion; and now their insolence began, for many members of both houses undistinguishingly received marks of their indignant rage; some were stopped and threatened, otherwise abused and assaulted, pulled out of their carriages, and glad to get off without hats, wigs, with lacerated garments and flesh-wounds; whilst many were happy to retreat unhurt and absent themselves from the House for that day at least. The distinguishing badge they wore was a blue cockade, which the president, Lord George, had the boldness to wear in his hat to the House, but being espied, he was desired, nay, even menaced, and with reluctance suffered it to be taken out. The most sober, and many such, doubtless, there were among them, retired peaceably and in good order; but the rabble, by far the greater number, having raised themselves into a frenzy, for fire you know is kindled by collision, adjourned, resolving to plunder and destroy the houses of those who from liberal principles had promoted a relaxation of the supposed too great rigor of the Act of William and Mary against papists, that had been for many months the occasion of a paper war on the subject, and excited a real or pretended terror in the minds of many who were, or affected to be, afraid of the increase and prevalence of popery. The houses of these and some unoffending Roman Catholics fell a sacrifice the first day to their rapine and malice; what became not plunder, was destroyed, or devoted to the flames. In the number were Sir George Saville's, a most worthy character, a steady whig, and an anti-ministerialist; but being a friend to taxation, and a man of property, was a suitable subject, and worthy of these sons of liberty and supporters of the Protestant cause to exercise their patriotism upon.

The second day, Lord Mansfield's house employed their patriotic labor; his valuable library, pictures, and household goods, to the amount of near thirty thousand pounds, were plundered, broken, destroyed, and devoted to the flames;—among other things was a large collection of manuscripts on various subjects, of immense loss to the world, it is said. In short, as Lord Loughborough, late Mr. Wedderburne, says, seventy-two houses and four prisons are now lying in ruins; of the latter, the fine new building of Newgate-street Prison, King's Bench, Clerkenwell, and Surry Bridewell; from whence were let loose all the debtors and felons who assisted in promoting those atrocious crimes, for which they were soon to have suffered the justice of the laws. Had they directed their aim at the Bank the first or second day of their rage, it is to be feared they might have annihilated the books, papers, and records: a blow that might have shaken Government to its centre, and involved the nation in evils too horrid to mention. The third day it was attacked; providentially, the fate of a score or two, and a strong party of dragoons and light-horse surrounding the palladium, saved it from the merciless claws of these ravening wolves. For three or four days, ten to fifteen houses were seen at one time in the centre of the metropolis lighted up by design; and to complete this most abhorred plan of destruction, a design was formed to cut off the new river pipes, but, in the moment of execution, it was most happily prevented.

Thus this great city and the Government are still preserved, monuments of Divine forbearance: it hath pleased Him who saith to the boisterous waves of the sea, "hitherto shalt thou come, and no further," to put a stop to the rage and madness of the people, and for the present to control the malicious designs of our inveterate enemies; for, that the ravages of the late banditti took their rise from abroad, has a face of probability. Though I cannot take upon me to warrant the following or any paragraph in the newspapers to be the word of Apollo, it is yet confidently asserted in them, that "a gentleman lately arrived from Holland has affirmed that he heard the French ambassador there declare openly, that London would be laid in ashes within a month." So deep was the plan, and so seriously in earnest to ensure complete destruction, that such situations and kinds of business were pitched upon, as afforded the most combustible materials for supplying a fierce flame, as oil-dealers, distillers, warehouses, &c.; but a kind interposing Providence stopped the devouring fire, and all is now once again settled, quiet, and, it is to be hoped, safe. To secure which, and overawe the profligate and daring, enough of whom all great cities abound in, a large encampment is still continued in Hyde Park of light-horse, dragoons, and foot; and are to be kept up during the summer; besides a party (notwithstanding the city mayor and patriotic gentry's remonstrance about city rights,) patrolling and keeping guard in London, to the great annoyance and terror of the turbulent and dangerous.

Bath and Bristol were intended to have been theatres whereon to have exhibited the future acts of the same tragedy. At the former, the Roman Catholic chapel and the priest's house were purged of all their effects that fell within the claws of these destructive harpies, and the combustibles they committed to the unrelenting flames; but a party of the Hereford Militia, and a troop of dragoons, being at callable distance, seasonably arrived to prevent further mischief. The latter city, by a vigorous internal police taking early precautions, dispersed a threatening storm; three or four hundred banditti, collected in St. James's parish in this city for the patriotic purpose of rapine and burning, were, by a well-timed early association, scattered and driven back to their dens; all the well-disposed arming and patrolling through the streets for several nights. During this miscreantic insurrection, Judge Sewall, Samuel Sewall, and myself, were on an excursion in the country, wherein we dropped on the abode of our townsfolks, Samuel Porter and Captain Poynton; the former carrying indelible marks of personal identity, the latter of an amazingly increased bulk and gouty habit; their present abode is Shrewsbury. I rather envy than lament our worthy friend, Mr. McGilchrist, who is now in a more peaceable neighborhood, I dare say, than that he has quitted, and I fancy without regret; would that you and I were with him, resting, perhaps, in undisturbed quiet till the last grand tribunal scene shall open, and restore the sleeping dust to life and activity; or, perhaps, roving in the unbounded fields of immensity, exploring and admiring the astonishing operations of Omnipotence. . . .

ELKANAH WATSON HEARS
GEORGE III RECOGNIZE THE
INDEPENDENCE OF THE
UNITED STATES

1782

It is appropriate to begin with the reluctant recognition of American independence by George III. That stubborn monarch, who at one time had threatened to abdicate rather than concede independence to the American colonies, was now forced to acquiesce in what had long seemed intolerable. We do not have the Earl of Oxford's answer to the King's anxious question, "Did I lower my voice when I came to that part of my speech?" but young Elkanah Watson records, perhaps too dramatically, that the King was embarrassed, that he hesitated and choked when he came to the admission that the Americans had won their case. Elkanah Watson, not quite twenty-five when he had the good fortune to hear the King's speech, had already lived a life of adventure and danger. Born on Cape Cod, he had as a mere boy explored Georgia and Florida. He had sailed to France with dispatches to Benjamin Franklin and engaged, profitably, in business at Nantes. When he visited England in 1782 it was to carry dispatches to the Earl of Shelburne, and to open a London branch of his commercial house. After his return to the United

From *Men and Times of the Revolution; or, Memoirs of Elkanah Watson,* Winslow C. Watson, ed. (New York, 1861), pp. 203-206.

States in 1784 he made and lost several fortunes, promoted canal companies and banks, farmed in North Carolina and Massachusetts, staged a series of "cattle shows"—the precursors of county fair—wrote widely on farming, and compiled the *Memoirs* from which this extract is taken.

At an early hour on the 5th of December, 1782, in conformity with previous arrangements, I was conducted by the Earl of Ferrers to the very entrance of the House of Lords. At the door he whispered, "Get as near the throne as you can; fear nothing." I did so, and found myself exactly in front of it, elbow to elbow with the celebrated Admiral Lord Howe. The Lords were promiscuously standing, as I entered. It was a dark and foggy day; and the windows being elevated, and constructed in the antiquated style, with leaden bars to contain the diamond-cut panes of glass, increased the gloom. The walls were hung with dark tapestry, representing the defeat of the Spanish Armada. I had the pleasure of recognizing, in the crowd of spectators, Copley, and West the painter, with some American ladies. I saw also some dejected American royalists in the group.

After waiting nearly two hours, the approach of the King was announced by a tremendous roar of artillery. He entered by a small door on the left of the throne, and immediately seated himself upon the Chair of State, in a graceful attitude, with his right foot resting upon a stool. He was clothed in royal robes. Apparently agitated, he drew from his pocket the scroll containing his speech. The Commons were summoned; and, after the bustle of their entrance had subsided, he proceeded to read his speech. I was near the King, and watched, with intense interest, every tone of his voice, and expression of his countenance. It was to me a moment of thrilling and dignified exultation. After some general and usual remarks, he continued:

"I lost no time, in giving the necessary orders to prohibit the further prosecution of offensive war upon the continent of North America. Adopting, as my inclination will always lead me to do, with decision and effect, whatever I collect to be the sense of my Parliament and my people, I have pointed all my views and measures, in Europe, as in North America, to an entire and cordial reconciliation with the colonies. Finding it indispensable to the attainment of this object, I did not hesitate to go to the full length of the powers vested in me, and offer to declare them."—Here he paused, and was in evident agitation; either embarrassed in reading his speech, by the darkness of the room, or affected by a very *natural emotion*. In a moment he resumed:—"and offer to declare them *free and indepen-*

dent States. In thus admitting their separation from the crown of these kingdoms, I have sacrificed every consideration of my own, to the wishes and opinions of my people. I make it my humble and ardent prayer to Almighty God, that Great Britain may not feel the evils which might result from so great a dismemberment of the Empire, and that America may be free from the calamities which have formerly proved, in the mother country, how essential monarchy is to the enjoyment of constitutional liberty. Religion, language, interests and affection may, and I hope will, yet prove a bond of permanent union between the two countries."

It is remarked, that George III. is celebrated for reading his speeches, in a distinct, free, and impressive manner. On this occasion, he was evidently embarrassed; he hesitated, choked, and executed the painful duties of the occasion, with an ill grace that does not belong to him. I cannot adequately portray my sensations, in the progress of this address; every artery beat high, and swelled with my proud American blood. It was impossible, not to revert to the opposite shores of the Atlantic, and to review, in my mind's eye, the misery and woe I had myself witnessed, in several stages of the contest, and the wide-spread desolation, resulting from the stubbornness of this very King, now so prostrate, but who had turned a deaf ear to our humble and importunate petitions for relief. Yet, I believe that George III acted under what he felt to be the high and solemn claims of constitutional duty.

The great drama was now closed. The battle of Lexington exhibited its first scene. The Declaration of Independence was a lofty and glorious event in its progress; and the ratification of our Independence by the King, consummated the spectacle in triumph and exultation. This successful issue of the American Revolution, will, in all probability, influence eventually the destinies of the whole human race. Such had been the sentiment and language of men of the profoundest sagacity and prescience, during and anterior to the conflict, in all appeals to the people. In leaving the house, I jostled Copley and West, who I thought were enjoying the rich political repast of the day, and noticing the anguish and despair depicted on the long visages of our American Tories.

The ensuing afternoon, having a card of admission from Alderman Wool, I attended in the gallery of the House of Commons. There was no elaborate debate, but much acrimony evinced in the incidental discussions. Commodore Johnstone assailed Lord Howe's late expedition to Gibraltar, because he had not gained a decisive victory, alleging that, with proper effort, he might have done so;

when Mr. Townshend defended him with zeal and spirit. Captain Luttrell, a naval officer, then attacked Fox with much severity, accusing him of treating the Navy, in some of his speeches, with disrespect. Fox replied, with his wonted keen and sarcastic style, in a short and rapid speech. Mr. Burke at length arose, and attacked the King's Address, of the day before, in a vein of satire and ridicule; he said "it was a farrago of nonsense and hypocrisy." Young Pitt, the newly-created Chancellor of the Exchequer, replied to Mr. Burke, and handled him with dignified severity, imputing to him buffoonery and levity. General Conway said —"The recognition of American Independence was explicit and unconditional."

JOHN ADAMS: "THE KING LISTENED WITH DIGNITY, BUT WITH AN APPARENT EMOTION"

1785

We come now to the first of the Adamses—that family which has the most distinguished record of any American family in the realm of politics and diplomacy and which has, incidentally, provided us with a larger body of commentary on Britain than any other family. Nor does any family, or "connection" better illustrate the ambivalence of the American towards the Mother Country over the years—the mixture of hostility and affection, of repulsion and attraction, of alienation and understanding, than does four generations of Adamses—John, John Quincy, Charles Francis, and Henry.

Congress had sent John Adams abroad as "commissioner" in 1778; he was later made Minister to the Hague—where he succeded both in getting recognition and money. He was one of the Commissioners to negotiate the Treaty of Paris that recognized American independence. In the light of his long record as a trouble-maker for England it was perhaps a bit tactless of Congress to appoint him the first Minister to the Court of St. James's—a position which both his son and his grandson were to hold with distinction, a record unprecedented in the annals of diplomacy.

From *The Works of John Adams*, Charles Francis Adams, ed., VIII, pp. 255–259.

The auspices were not favorable. Adams had already written, in 1780, that there were "natural causes of animosity between England and America" and that Britain and America were "natural rivals in commerce, shipbuilding, fisheries, etc." Though he was graciously received by King George, he found it impossible to negotiate a commercial treaty or to settle any of the outstanding problems that lingered on after the Treaty of Paris. Perhaps his only accomplishment in London was writing (or compiling) the three-volume *Defense of the Constitutions of the United States* which, in a curious way, was a tribute to the philosophy which he imagined animated the British constitution.

To Secretary Jay

Bath Hotel, Westminster, 2 June, 1785

Dear Sir:

During my interview with the Marquis of Carmarthen, he told me that it was customary for every foreign minister, at his first presentation to the King, to make his Majesty some compliments conformable to the spirit of his letter of credence; and when Sir Clement Cottrell Dormer, the master of the ceremonies, came to inform me that he should accompany me to the secretary of state and to Court, he said that every foreign minister whom he had attended to the Queen had always made a harangue to her Majesty, and he understood, though he had not been present, that they always harangued the King.

On Tuesday evening, the Baron de Lynden called upon me, and said he came from the Baron de Nolken, and they had been conversing upon the singular situation I was in, and they agreed in opinion that it was indispensable that I should make a speech, and that that speech should be as complimentary as possible. All this was conformable to the advice lately given by the Count de Vergennes to Mr. Jefferson; so that, finding it was a custom established at both these great Courts, and that this Court and the foreign ministers expected it, I thought I could not avoid it, although my first thought and inclination had been to deliver my credentials silently and retire.

At one, on Wednesday, the master of ceremonies called at my house, and went with me to the secretary of state's office, in Cleveland Row, where the Marquis of Carmarthen received me, and introduced me to his under secretary, Mr. Fraser, who has been, as his Lordship told me, uninterruptedly in that office, through all the changes in administration for thirty years, having first been appointed by the Earl of Holderness. After a short conversation upon the subject of importing my effects from Holland and France free of duty, which Mr. Fraser himself introduced, Lord Carmarthen invited me to go with him in his coach to Court. When we arrived in the antechamber, the *oeil de boeuf* of St. James's, the master of the ceremonies met me and attended me, while the secretary of state went to take the commands of the King. While I stood in this place, where it seems all ministers stand upon such occasions, always attended by the master of ceremonies, the room very full of ministers of state, lords, and bishops, and all sorts of courtiers, as well as the next room, which is the King's bedchamber, you may well suppose I was the focus of all eyes. I was relieved, however, from the embarrassment of it by the Swedish and Dutch ministers, who came to me, and entertained me in a very agreeable conversation during the whole time. Some other gentlemen, whom I had seen before, came to make their compliments too, until the Marquis of Carmarthen returned and desired me to go with him to his Majesty. I went with his Lordship through the levee room into the King's closet. The door was shut, and I was left with his Majesty and the secretary of state alone. I made the three reverences,—one at the door, another about half way, and a third before the presence,—according to the usage established at this and all the northern Courts of Europe, and then addressed myself to his Majesty in the following words:

"Sir: The United States of America have appointed me their minister plenipotentiary to your Majesty, and have directed me to deliver to your Majesty this letter which contains the evidence of it. It is in obedience to their express commands, that I have the honor to assure your Majesty of their unanimous disposition and desire to cultivate the most friendly and liberal intercourse between your Majesty's subjects and their citizens, and of their best wishes for your Majesty's health and happiness, and for that of your royal family. The appointment of a minister from the United States to your Majesty's Court will form an epoch in the history of England and of America. I think myself more fortunate than all my fellow-citizens, in having the distinguished honor to be the first to stand in your Majesty's royal presence in a diplomatic character; and I shall esteem myself the happiest of men, if I can be instrumental in recommending my country more and more to your Majesty's royal benevolence, and of restoring an entire esteem, confidence, and affection, or, in better words, the old good nature and the old good humor between people, who, though separated by an ocean, and under different governments, have the same language, a similar religion, and kindred blood.

"I beg your Majesty's permission to add, that, although I have some time before been intrusted by my country, it was never in my whole life in a manner so agreeable to myself."

The King listened to every word I said, with dignity, but with an apparent emotion. Whether it was the nature of the interview, or whether it was my visible agitation, for I felt more than I did or could express, that touched him, I cannot say. But he was much affected, and answered me with more tremor than I had spoken with, and said:

"Sir: The circumstances of this audience are so extraordinary, the language you have now held is so extremely proper, and the feelings you have discovered so justly adapted to the occasion, that I must say that I not only receive with pleasure the assurance of the friendly dispositions of the United States, but that I am very glad the choice has fallen upon you to be their minister. I wish you, sir, to believe, and that it may be understood in America, that I have done nothing in the late contest but what I thought myself indispensably bound to do, by the duty which I owed to my people. I will be very frank with you. I was the last to consent to the separation; but the separation having been made, and having become inevitable, I have always said, as I say now, that I would be the first to meet the friendship of the United States as an independent power. The moment I see such sentiments and language as yours prevail, and a disposition to give to this country the preference, that moment I shall say, let the circumstances of language, religion, and blood have their natural and full effect."

I dare not say that these were the King's precise words, and, it is even possible, that I may have in some particular mistaken his meaning; for, although his pronunciation is as distinct as I ever heard, he hesitated some time between his periods, and between the members of the same period. He was indeed much affected, and I confess I was not less so, and, therefore I cannot be certain that I was so cool and attentive, heard so clearly, and understood so perfectly, as to be confident of all his words or sense; and, I think, that all which he said to me should at present be kept secret in America, unless his Majesty or his secretary of state, who alone was present, should judge proper to report it. This I do say, that the foregoing is his Majesty's meaning as I then understood it, and his own words as nearly as I can recollect them.

The King then asked me whether I came last from France, and upon my answering in the affirmative, he put on an air of familiarity, and smiling, or rather laughing, said, "there is an opinion among some people that you are not the most attached of all your countrymen to the manners of France." I was surprised at this, because I thought it an indiscretion and a departure from the dignity. I was a little embarrassed, but determined not to deny the truth on one hand, nor leave him to infer from it any attachment to England on the other. I threw off as much gravity as I could, and assumed an air of gayety and a tone of decision as far as was decent, and said, "that opinion, sir, is not mistaken: I must avow to your Majesty, I have no attachment but to my own country." The King replied, as quick as lightning, "an honest man will never have any other."

The King then said a word or two to the secretary of state, which, being between them, I did not hear, and then turned round and bowed to me, as is customary with all kings and princes when they give the signal to retire. I retreated, stepping backward, as is the etiquette, and, making my last reverence at the door of the chamber, I went my way. The master of the ceremonies joined me the moment of my coming out of the King's closet, and accompanied me through the apartments down to my carriage, several stages of servants, gentlemen-porters and under-porters, roaring out like thunder, as I went along, "Mr. Adams's servants, Mr. Adams's carriage, &c." I have been thus minute, as it may be useful to others hereafter to know.

The conversation with the King congress will form their own judgment of. I may expect from it a residence less painful than I once expected, as so marked an attention from the King will silence many grumblers; but we can infer nothing from all this concerning the success of my mission.

There are a train of other ceremonies yet to go through, in presentations to the Queen, and visits to and from ministers and ambassadors, which will take up much time, and interrupt me in my endeavors to obtain all that I have at heart,—the objects of my instructions. It is thus the essence of things is lost in ceremony in every country of Europe. We must submit to what we cannot alter. Patience is the only remedy.

With great respect,&c.
John Adams

ABIGAIL ADAMS: "I SHALL NEVER HAVE MUCH SOCIETY WITH THIS KIND OF PEOPLE"

1785–87

The wonderful Abigail Adams shared most of her husband's prejudices against the English but had a livelier wit, a more resilient spirit. Her experience in London was not a happy one. "Some years hence," she wrote, "it may be a pleasure to reside here in the character of American minister; but . . . no one need envy the embassy. There would soon be fine work, if any notice was taken of their billingsgate and abuse; but all their arrows . . . fall harmless to the ground." Brilliant and vivacious Mrs. Adams would have graced any court; it was a measure of English resentment that the court treated her with frigid politeness. "Studied civility and disguised coldness," she wrote, "cover malignant hearts." Needless to say she was happy to return to Braintree (and then to New York as wife of the Vice-President) in 1788. Her letters are prophetic in their implicit indication of two major themes of American commentary: that it is in England that one discovers the true America, and that by comparison with America the Old World (for she included France in this) was hopelessly corrupt.

From *Letters of Mrs. Adams, the Wife of John Adams,* Charles Francis Adams, ed. (Boston, 1840), II, pp. 96-108, 120-124, 129-134, 180-190.

To Mrs. Cranch

London, Bath Hotel, Westminster, 24 June, 1785

My Dear Sister:

. . . The ceremony of presentation, upon one week to the King, and the next to the Queen, was to take place, after which I was to prepare for mine. It is customary, upon presentation, to receive visits from all the foreign ministers; so that we could not exchange our lodgings for more private ones, as we might and should, had we been only in a private character. The foreign ministers, and several English lords and earls, have paid their compliments here, and all hitherto is civil and polite. . . .

The Tory venom has begun to spit itself forth in the public papers, as I expected, bursting with envy that an American minister should be received here with the same marks of attention, politeness, and civility, which are shown to the ministers of any other power. When a minister delivers his credentials to the King, it is always in his private closet, attended only by the Minister for Foreign Affairs, which is called a private audience, and the minister presented makes some little address to his Majesty, and the same ceremony to the Queen, whose reply was in these words; "Sir, I thank you for your civility to me and my family, and I am glad to see you in this country"; then she very politely inquired whether he had got a house yet. The answer of his Majesty was much longer; but I am not at liberty to say more respecting it, than that it was civil and polite, and that his Majesty said he was glad the choice of his country had fallen upon him. The news-liars know nothing of the matter; they represent it just to answer their purpose. Last Thursday, Colonel Smith was presented at Court, and to-morrow, at the Queen's circle, my ladyship and your niece make our compliments. There is no other presentation in Europe, in which I should feel so much as in this. Your own reflections will easily suggest the reasons. . . .

The ceremony of presentation here is considered as indispensable. There are four minister-plenipotentiaries' ladies here; but one ambassador, and he has no lady. In France, the ladies of ambassadors only are presented. One is obliged here to attend the circles of the Queen, which are held in summer once a fortnight, but once a week the rest of the year; and what renders it exceedingly expensive is, that you cannot go twice the same season in the same dress, and a Court dress you cannot make use of anywhere else. I directed my mantuamaker to let my dress be elegant, but plain as I could possibly appear, with decency; accordingly, it is white lutestring, covered and full trimmed with white crape, festooned with lilac ribbon and mock point lace, over a hoop of enormous extent; there is only a narrow train of about three yards in length to the gown waist, which is put into a ribbon upon the left side, the Queen only having her train borne. Ruffle cuffs for married ladies, treble lace ruffles, a very dress cap with long lace lappets, two white plumes, and a blonde lace handkerchief. This is my rigging. I should have mentioned two pearl pins in my hair, ear-rings and necklace of the same kind.

Friday Morning [*July, 1785*]

Congratulate me, my dear sister, it is over. I was too much fatigued to write a line last evening. At two o'clock we went to the circle, which is in the drawing-room of the Queen. We passed through several apartments, lined as usual with spectators upon these occasions. Upon entering the ante-chamber, the Baron de Lynden, the Dutch Minister, who has been often here, came and spoke with me. A Count Sarsfield, a French nobleman, with whom I was acquainted, paid his compliments. As I passed into the drawing-room, Lord Carmarthen and Sir Clement Cotterel Dormer were presented to me. Though they had been several times here, I had never seen them before. The Swedish and the Polish ministers made their compliments, and several other gentlemen; but not a single lady did I know until the Countess of Effingham came, who was very civil. There were three young ladies, daughters of the Marquis of Lothian, who were to be presented at the same time, and two brides. We were placed in a circle round the drawing-room, which was very full, I believe two hundred persons present. Only think of the task! The royal family have to go round to every person, and find small talk enough to speak to all of them, though they very prudently speak in a whisper, so that only the person who stands next you can hear what is said. The King enters the room, and goes round to the right; the Queen and Princesses to the left. The lord in waiting presents you to the King; and the lady in waiting does the same to her Majesty. The King is a personable man, but, my dear sister, he has a certain countenance, which you and I have often remarked; a red face and white eyebrows. The Queen has a similar countenance, and the numerous royal family confirm the observation. Persons are not placed according to their rank in the drawing room, but promiscuously; and when the King comes in he takes persons as they stand. When he came to me, Lord Onslow said, "Mrs. Adams"; upon which I drew off my right-hand glove, and his Majesty saluted my left cheek; then asked me if I had taken a walk today. I could have told his Majesty that I had been all the morning preparing to wait upon him; but I replied, "No, Sire." "Why, don't you love walking?" says he. I answered, that I was rather indolent in that respect. He then bowed, and passed on. It was more than two hours after this before it came to my turn to be presented to the Queen. The circle was so large that the company were four hours standing. The Queen was evidently embarrassed when I was presented to her. I had disagreeable feelings too. She, however, said, "Mrs. Adams, have you got into your house? Pray, how do you like the situation of it?" Whilst the Princess Royal looked compassionate, and asked me if I was not much fatigued; and observed, that it was a very full drawing-room. . . . The queen was in purple and silver. She is not well shaped nor handsome. As to the ladies of the Court, rank and title may compensate for want of personal charms; but they are, in general, very plain, ill-shaped, and ugly; but don't you tell anybody that I say so. If one wants to see beauty, one must go to Ranelagh; there it is collected, in one bright constellation. There were two ladies very elegant, at Court,—Lady Salisbury and Lady Talbot; but the observation did not in general hold good, that fine feathers make fine birds. I saw many who were vastly richer dressed than your friends, but I will venture to say, that I saw none neater or more elegant. . . .

The Tories are very free with their compliments. Scarcely a paper escapes without some scurrility. We bear it with silent contempt; having met a polite reception from the Court, it bites them like a serpent, and stings them like an adder. As to the success the negotiations may meet with, time alone can disclose the result; but, if this nation does not suffer itself to be again duped by the artifice of some and the malice of others, it will unite itself with America on the most liberal principles and sentiments. . . .

TO MRS. SHAW

London (Grosvenor Square), 15 August, 1785

My Dear Sister:
. . . Polite circles are much alike throughout Europe. Swift's *Journal of a Modern Lady*, though written sixty years ago, is perfectly applicable to the present day; and, though noted as the changeable sex, in this scene of dissipation they have been steady. I shall never have much society with this kind of people, for they would not like me any more than I do them. They think much more of their titles here than in France. It is not unusual to find people of the highest rank there, the best bred and the politest people. If they have an equal share of pride, they know better how to hide it. Until I came

here, I had no idea what a national and illiberal inveteracy the English have against their better behaved neighbours, and I feel a much greater partiality for them than I did whilst I resided among them. I would recommend to this nation a little more liberality and discernment; their contracted sentiments lead them to despise all other nations. Perhaps I should be chargeable with the same narrow sentiments, if I give America the preference over these old European nations. In the cultivation of the arts and improvement in manufactures, they greatly excel us; but we have native genius, capacity, and ingenuity, equal to all their improvements, and much more general knowledge diffused amongst us. You can scarcely form an idea how much superior our common people, as they are termed, are to those of the same rank in this country. Neither have we that servility of manners, which the distinction between nobility and citizens gives to the people of this country. We tremble not, either at the sight or name of majesty. I own that I never felt myself in a more contemptible situation, than when I stood four hours together for a gracious smile from majesty, a witness to the anxious solicitude of those around me for the same mighty *boon*. . . .

As to politics, the English continue to publish the most abusive, barefaced falsehoods against America that you can conceive of; yet, glaring as they are, they gain credit here, and they shut their eyes against a friendly and liberal intercourse. Yet their very existence depends upon a friendly union with us. How the pulse of the ministry beats, time will unfold; but I do not promise or wish to myself a long continuance here. Such is the temper of the two nations towards each other, that, if we have not peace, we must have war. We cannot resign the intercourse, and quit each other. I hope, however, that it will not come to that alternative. Adieu.

Your sister,
A. A.

TO MRS. CRANCH

London, 1 October, 1785

My Dear Sister,

. . . Some years hence it may be a pleasure to reside here in the character of American minister; but, with the present salary and the present temper of the English, no one need envy the embassy. There would soon be fine work, if any notice was taken of their billingsgate and abuse; but all their arrows rebound, and fall harmless to the ground. Amidst all their falsehoods, they have never insinuated a lisp against the private character of the American minister, nor in his public line charged him with either want of abilities, honor, or integrity. The whole venom has been levelled against poor America; and every effort to make her appear ridiculous in the eyes of the nation. How would they exult, if they could lay hold of any circumstance, in either of our characters, to make us appear ridiculous.

I received a letter to-day from Mr. Jefferson, who writes me that he had just received a parcel of English newspapers; they "teem," says he, "with every horror of which nature is capable; assassination, suicide, thefts, robberies, and, what is worse than thefts, murder, and robbery, the blackest slanders! Indeed, the man must be of rock who can stand all this. To Mr. Adams it will be but one victory the more. It would illy suit me. I do not love difficulties. I am fond of quiet; willing to do my duty; but irritable by slander, and apt to be forced by it to abandon my post. I fancy," says he, "it must be the quantity of animal food eaten by the English, which renders their character unsusceptible of civilization. I suspect that it is in their kitchens, and not in their churches, that their reformation must be worked, and that missionaries from hence would avail more than those who should endeavour to tame them by precepts of religion or philosophy."

But he adds, "What do the foolish printers of America mean by retailing all this stuff in our papers, as if it was not enough to be slandered by one's enemies, without circulating the slanders amongst one's friends too?"

I could tell Mr. Jefferson that I doubt not there are persons in America equally gratified with them as the English, and that from a spirit of envy. But these open attacks are nothing to the secret and subtile enemies Mr. Adams has had heretofore to encounter. In Mr. Jefferson he has a firm and faithful friend, with whom he can consult and advise; and, as each of them has no object but the good of their country in view, they have an unlimited confidence in each other; and they have only to lament that the Channel divides their more frequent intercourse. . . .

To Miss Lucy Cranch

London, 2 April, 1786

. . . Perhaps there is no country where there is a fuller exercise of those virtues than ours at present exhibits, which is in a great measure owing to the equal distribution of property, the small number of inhabitants in proportion to its territory, the equal distribution of justice to the poor as well as the rich, to a government founded in justice and exercised with impartiality, and to a religion which teaches peace and good will to man; to knowledge and learning being so easily acquired and so universally distributed; and to that sense of moral obligation which generally inclines our countrymen to do to others as they would that others should do to them. Perhaps you will think that I allow to them more than they deserve, but you will consider that I am only speaking comparatively. Human nature is much the same in all countries, but it is the government, the laws, and religion, which form the character of a nation. Wherever luxury abounds, there you will find corruption and degeneracy of manners. Wretches that we are, thus to misuse the bounties of Providence, to forget the hand that blesses us, and even deny the source from whence we derived our being.

But I grow too serious. To amuse you, then, my dear niece, I will give you an account of the dress of the ladies at the ball of the Comte d'Adhémar; as your cousin tells me that she some time ago gave you a history of the birth-day and ball at Court, this may serve as a counterpart. Though, should I attempt to compare the apartments, St. James's would fall as much short of the French Ambassador's, as the Court of his Britannic Majesty does of the splendor and magnificence of that of his Most Christian Majesty. I am sure I never saw an assembly room in America, which did not exceed that at St. James's in point of elegance and decoration; and, as to its fair visiters, not all their blaze of diamonds set off with Parisian rouge, can match the blooming health, the sparkling eye, and modest deportment of the dear girls of my native land. As to the dancing, the space they had to move in gave them no opportunity to display the grace of a minuet, and the full dress of long court-trains and enormous hoops, you well know were not favorable for country dances, so that I saw them at every disadvantage; not so the other evening. They were much more properly clad;—silk waists, gauze or white or painted tiffany coats decorated with ribbon, beads or flowers, as fancy directed, were chiefly worn by the young ladies. Hats turned up at the sides with diamond loops and buttons of steel, large bows of ribbons and wreaths of flowers, displayed themselves to much advantage upon the heads of some of the prettiest girls England can boast. . . .

Thus, my dear girl, you have an account which perhaps may amuse you a little. . . . Do not fear that your aunt will become dissipated, or in love with European manners; but, as opportunity offers, I wish to see this European world in all its *forms* that I can with decency. I still moralize with Yorick, or with one more experienced, and say "Vanity of vanities, all is vanity."

Adieu, and believe me yours,
A. Adams

To Mrs. Cranch

Grosvenor Square, 15 September, 1787

. . . This whole town is the property of a widow lady. Houses are built by the tenants, and taken at life-rents, which, upon the decease of the lessees, revert back again to the owner of the soil. Thus is the landed property of this country vested in lordships and in the hands of the rich altogether. The peasantry are but slaves to the lord, notwithstanding the mighty boast they make of liberty. Sixpence and sevenpence per day is the usual wages given to laborers, who are to feed themselves out of the pittance. In travelling through a country, fertile as the garden of Eden, loaded with a golden harvest, plenty smiling on every side, one would imagine that the voice of Poverty was rarely heard, and that she was seldom seen, but in the abodes of indolence or vice. But it is far otherwise. The money earned by the sweat of the brow must go to feed the pampered lord and fatten the greedy bishop, whilst the miserable, shattered, thatched-roof cottage crumbles to the dust for want of repair. To hundreds and hundreds of these abodes have I been a witness in my late journey. The cheering rays of the sun are totally excluded, unless they find admittance through the decayed roof, equally exposed to cold and the inclement season. A few rags for a bed and a jointstool comprise the chief of their furniture, whilst their own appearances is more wretched than one can well conceive. During the season of hay and harvest, men, women, and children are to be seen laboring in the fields; but, as this is a very small part of the year, the little they then acquire is soon expended; and how they keep soul and body together the remainder of the year is very hard to tell. It must be owing to this very unequal distribution of property, that the poor-rate is become such an intolerable burden. The inhabitants are very thinly scattered through the country, though large towns are well peopled. To reside in and near London, and to judge of the country from what one sees here, would be forming a very erroneous opinion. How little cause of complaint have the inhabitants of the United States, when they compare their situation, not with despotic monarchies, but with this land of freedom! The ease with which honest industry may acquire property in America, the equal distribution of justice to the poor as well as the rich, and the personal liberty they enjoy, all, all call upon them to support their government and laws, to respect their rulers, and gratefully acknowledge their superior blessings, lest Heaven in wrath should send them a——.

THOMAS JEFFERSON:
"THE INVETERATE HOSTILITY OF
GEORGE III"

1786

Though Jefferson was by no means as belligerent—or as petulant—as his friend John Adams, he was more hostile to and critical of Britain. The explanation is to be found in differences of philosophy as well as temperament. Where Adams was irremediably provincial but quite ready to embrace much of Old World, especially British political philosophy, Jefferson was cosmopolitan, happy in the society and the beauty of France and Italy, but philosophically hostile to whatever the Old World stood for. In the spring of 1786 Jefferson, then Minister to France, joined his old associate in London in an effort to speed up negotiations for a commercial treaty. In vain. In letters to Richard Henry Lee and John Jay he blames his frustration on the "inveterate hostility" of the King and the ruling classes to America.

From *Works of Thomas Jefferson* (Memorial Edition), V, pp. 292–293, 296–297.

31

To Richard Henry Lee

London, April 22, 1786

The Marquis of Lansdowne spoke to me affectionately of your brother, Doctor Lee, and desired his respects to him, which I beg leave to communicate through you. Were he to come into the ministry (of which there is not the most distant prospect), he must adopt the King's system, or go out again, as he did before, for daring to depart from it. When we see, that through all the changes of ministry which have taken place during the present reign, there has never been a change of system with respect to America, we cannot reasonably doubt, that this is the system of the King himself. His obstinacy of character we know; his hostility we have known, and it is embittered by ill success. If ever this nation, during his life, enter into arrangements with us, it must be in consequence of events of which they do not at present see a possibility. The object of the present ministry is to buoy up the nation with flattering calculations of their present prosperity, and to make them believe they are better without us than with us. This they seriously believe; for what is it men cannot be made to believe! I dined the other day in a company of the ministerial party. A General Clark, a Scotchman and minis-terialist, sat next to me. He introduced the subject of American affairs, and in the course of the conversation told me that were America to petition Parliament to be again received on their former footing, the petition would be very generally rejected. He was seri-ous in this, and I think it was the sentiment of the company, and is the sentiment perhaps of the nation. In this they are wise, but for a foolish reason. They think they lost more by suffering us to partici-pate of their commercial privileges, at home and abroad, than they lose by our political severance. The true reason, however, why such an application should be rejected is, that in a very short time, we should oblige them to add another hundred millions to their debt in unsuccessful attempts to retain the subjection offered to them. They are at present in a frenzy, and will not be recovered from it till they shall have leaped the precipice they are now so boldly advancing to.

To John Jay

London, April 23, 1786

... With this country nothing is done; and that nothing is in-tended to be done, on their part, admits not the smallest doubt. The nation is against any change of measures; the ministers are against it; some from principle, others from subserviency; and the King, more than all men, is against it. If we take a retrospect to the beginning of the present reign, we observe that amidst all the changes of ministry, no change of measures with respect to America ever took place; excepting only at the moment of the peace; and the minister of that moment was immediately removed. Judging of the future by the past, I do not expect a change of disposition during the present reign, which bids fair to be a long one, as the King is healthy and temperate. That he is persevering, we know. If he ever changes his plan, it will be in consequence of events, which, at present, neither himself nor his ministers place among those which are probable. Even the opposition dare not open their lips in favor of a connection with us, so unpopular would be the topic. It is not that they think our commerce unimportant to them. I find that the merchants here set sufficient value on it. But they are sure of keeping it on their own terms. No better proof can be shown of the security in which the ministers think themselves on this head, than that they have not thought it worth while to give us a conference on the subject, though, on my arrival, we exhibited to them our commission, observed to them that it would expire on the 12th of the next month, and that I had come over on purpose to see if any arrangements could be made before that time. Of two months which then remained, six weeks have elapsed without one scrip of a pen, or one word from a minister, except a vague proposition at an accidental meeting. We availed ourselves even of that, to make another essay to extort some sort of declaration from the court. But their silence is invincible. But of all this, as well as of the proceedings in the negotiation with Portugal, information will be given you by a joint letter from Mr. Adams and myself. The moment is certainly arrived, when the plan of this court being out of all doubt, Congress and the States may decide what their own measures should be.

JOEL BARLOW WATCHES
THE WESTMINSTER ELECTION
OF 1788

1788

Joel Barlow, one of the now almost forgotten "Connecticut Wits," made his reputation as author of the immense and pretentious *Vision of Columbus,* today universally unread. In 1788 he was made agent for the Scioto Land Company in France. In the summer of that year he joined the Scioto agent in London to further the misguided scheme. After the collapse of that land speculation Barlow stayed on in France, doing odd jobs for the American government, speculating shrewdly in assignats, befriending Tom Paine, and acting as a kind of cultural clearing house for his fellow countrymen. It was he who rescued *The Age of Reason* from the hands of the French authorities when Paine was hurried off to prison, and it was in his house that Paine recovered after his release. Eventually Barlow returned to the United States, built himself a stately home (Kalomara) outside Washington, revised the *Vision of Columbus,* and went off on a diplomatic mission for President Madison which ended with his death in an obscure Polish village in 1812.

This election, as Barlow explains, was a contest between the government and the Foxites, which Fox's candidate Lord John Townsend won.

From Charles Burr Todd, *Life and Letters of Joel Barlow* (New York, 1886), pp. 78–80.

This day (August 4) ended the long contested Westminster election. It has lasted 15 days, and a scene of more curiosity to an American cannot well be exhibited. . . . Mr. Fox and Lord Hood were the members for Westminster. Hood is lately created a Lord of the Admiralty. His acceptance of this office vacates his seat in Parliament, but leaves him again eligible. Hood, being a ministerial man, was opposed in his re-election by Fox and his party, who set up Lord John Townsend. It was astonishing to behold the whole nation, from the king to the cobbler, engaged in this business. It was really no less than a contest between Charles Fox and George the Third, and to the satisfaction of every disinterested beholder, the former has won the day and Townsend is elected. On this occasion the Treasury was opened, and orders were drawn directly on it for the expense on the royal side. It is computed that the money spent on the king's side was 30,000 pounds; that on the opposition actually 20,000. Of this latter sum the Whig Club subscribed 10,000 pounds beforehand, and on the tenth day of the election, finding there would be a lack of money, the Duke of Bedford drew on his banker for 5000, and sent word that 50,000 more would be at the service of the opposition if needed. The other 5000 is supposed to have come from the Prince of Wales, and others less open in the cause of the opposition. This extraordinary expense will not appear strange when it is known that the simple article of ribbons for the cockades of the Townsend party cost 4000 pounds; that about 100 "bludgeon-men," as they are called, were hired at five shillings per day to out-mob the mob upon the other side, and that two thirds of the voters (the whole of which in this poll were 12,000) were actually paid for their votes. Add to this that, for 15 days, 200,000 people are constantly kept in an uproar. Not a tradesman, if he is disposed, can carry on business, for he is every day haunted by both parties, and his journeymen every day drunk for the honor of the candidates. Several persons have been killed on the spot, and many more languish under broken heads or legs, and it was as much as a man's pockets were worth to come within 200 yards of the hustings. The way of conducting the business is for the canvass to begin some time before the election begins and continue till it is closed. The first nobility of both sexes employ themselves in canvassing: they go to every house, stall, shop, and dock-yard and solicit the vote and interest of every person in favor of their candidate. Then comes a card in the newspapers requesting the voters in such a street or parish to breakfast with such a duke or lord and proceed with him to the polls. Thus he puts himself upon a level with the most ragged, vile, and worthless of creation, who move in a tumultuous procession through the streets, reeling and huzza-ing, with His Grace or the candidate at their head. The candidates meantime advertise in the papers their wishes to be elected, and request the votes and interest of all the *worthy and independent electors* in their favor. . . . When we hear, in common language, that such a duke *sends 16 members to Parliament,* and that such a gentleman *has bought a borough,* what shall we think of the political freedom of this people. A gentleman of my acquaintance, who has been an eminent merchant, has lately bought a borough for ten thousand pounds —that is, he has obtained the right of securing the election of the two members of that borough on all future occasions. He proposes to return himself as one member and sell the other place for three hundred pounds each election. As these recur but once in seven years it must be considered as a bad mercantile speculation unless there are secret profits arising from the place.

GOUVERNEUR MORRIS:

KITE-FLYING TO TEST

THE DIRECTION OF THE WIND

1790

Gouverneur Morris of New York was the "Founding Father" to whose skill we owe the final literary form of the Constitution. The French envoy Louis Otto described him as "perhaps the most eloquent and ingenious man of his country" but added that "his countrymen themselves distrust his talents." Not, however, Washington, whose confidence in Morris was unabated. In 1788 Morris sailed for France and England to see about tobacco contracts and other investments, carrying with him letters from Washington which gave him a semiofficial status; later he was promoted to a kind of unofficial minister to discuss with the British the possibility of a commercial treaty and the settlement of the still outstanding controversies about debts, compensation for deported slaves, and the British retention of Northwest frontier posts. In all of this he made a very good impression, but nothing was accomplished. Nevertheless Washington appointed him minister to France in 1792. As conservative in his instincts and his philosophy as Edmund Burke, he was soon deeply involved in French politics, attempting to save the King and to

From Gouverneur Morris, *A Diary of the French Revolution*, Beatrix Davenport, ed. (London, 1889), I, pp. 520–524.

37

impede the advance of the Terror. When Washington asked for the dismissal of Genêt, the French minister to the United States, Paris retaliated by demanding the recall of Morris. He traveled for four or five years on the Continent and in England and then returned to his home, Morrisania, where in his old age he joined the right wing of the Federalist Party, supported the Hartford Convention of 1814, and advocated the repudiation of that part of the national debt acquired for purposes of the war against Britain. We have here extracts from his *Diary* during a stay in England.

Friday 21 [*May, 1790*]. This Morning Mr. Payne calls and breakfasts with me. He enquires whether I have seen the Duke of Leeds. I tell him that I have and am to see him again. After he is gone I write, and at one o'Clock wait upon the Duke. After waiting some Time in the Antichamber I am introduced to where he and Mr. Pitt are sitting together. He presents me to the latter & we enter into Conversation. The first Point is that of the Impress, and upon that Subject Mr. Pitt approves the Idea of a Certificate from the Admiralty of America. I mention that it might be proper for the King's Servants to order that Certificates of a certain Kind should be Evidence of an American Seaman without excluding however other Evidence, and that in Consequence the Executive Authority in America could direct the Officers of the Admiralty Courts to issue such Certificates to those applying for them. We then proceed to the Treaty of Peace &c. They both mention that I had misapprehended the Letter of the Duke of Leeds respecting a Treaty of Commerce. I observe that it may easily be set right as to that Mistake but that it is idle to think of making a new Treaty untill the Parties are satisfied about that already made. Mr. Pitt says that the Delay of a Compliance on our Part has rendered that Compliance now less effectual, and that Cases must certainly exist where Injury has been sustained by the Delay. I observe generally that Delay is always a Kind of Breach, being as long as it lasts the nonPerformance of Stipulations. But descending a little more into Particulars I endeavor to shew that the Injury in fact sustained has not been great, and that on the other Hand Injury is complained of by the Americans for the nonPayment of Money due by this Government to the Owners of Slaves taken away. On the whole I observe that Enquiries of this Sort may be very useful if the Parties mutually seek to keep asunder, but that if they mean to come together it would be best to keep them entirely out of Sight, and now to perform on both Sides as well as the actual Situation of Things will permit. After many Professions, Mr.

Pitt mentions that it might be well to consider in general the Subject and on general Ground to see whether some Compensation could not be made mutually. I reply that if I understand him rightly he means to make a new Treaty instead of complying with the old one. He admits this to be in some Sort his Idea. I answer that I do not see even on that Ground what better could be done than to perform the old one. That the Compensation for Negroes is too trifling an Object for them not to make a specific Performance, and that Nothing will then remain in Contest but the Posts. That I suppose therefore they wish to retain those Posts. He says that perhaps they may. I tell him that they are not worth keeping, for that the only Ground on which they can be desired is for the Sake of the Fur Trade, and that such Trade will come to this Country let who will carry it on in America; and I give him the Reasons for that Opinion. He says that if I consider them as an Object of trivial Consequence there is the less Reason for requiring them. I tell him that it is useful to both Countries if they wish to live on Terms of Amity, that their Citizens should be seperated by a wide Water, and therefore that the Posts should be ceded to us. That for our Part, they are of particular Importance only because the national Honor is interested. They have held them with the avowed Intention of forcing us to comply with what they should dictate. He says that they can on the other Hand suppose their national Honor to be concerned in the Delay and Obstacles respecting other Articles of the Treaty. I tell him no, that the natural Course was to comply fully, and then if on Demand we had refused, they would have a Right to give Letters of Marque and Reprisal to their Subjects who were injured. That the Sentiment naturally arising in our Bosoms from the Conduct they had pursued, was Resentment. That we did not think it worth while to go into a War for the Posts, but we reserved our Rights and would certainly make Use of them when Time & Circumstances should suit. I then suggested that if they offered to deliver up those Posts whenever we should send thither Garrisons sufficient to protect the Trade against the Savages, they would probably be left a long Time in Possession. Mr. Pitt asked me if I had Powers to treat. I told him no, and that we could not appoint a Minister, because they had so much neglected the Minister formerly appointed. He asked if we would appoint a Minister if they did. I told him we should. We then converse loosely about the Manner of communicating on that Subject. In the Course of it I tell him that we cannot take Notice of their Consuls or any Thing which They may say, because they are not Characters known to or acknowledged by us. He observes that he should suppose

Attention might as well be paid to what they said as a Conference be held by the Duke of Leeds and himself with me. I tell him by no Means, for I should never have thought of asking a Conference if I had not possessed a Letter from the President of the United States upon the Subject, which I had shewn to the Duke. He says that they can in like Manner write to one of their Consuls. I tell him Yes, and the Letter will be attended to, not the Consul, who is in no wise different from any other british Subject. He says that Etiquette ought not to be pushed so far as to injure Business and keep the Countries asunder. I tell him the Rulers of America have too much Sense to care much for Etiquette but that they (the british) have hitherto kept us at a Distance rather than made any Advances, & the President had gone as far as could be expected in writing the Letter which he had done, but that in Consequence of what had passed, which as he might naturally suppose I had transmitted, we could not but consider them as wishing to avoid an Intercourse. He took up this Point and exprest a Hope that I would remove such an Idea. He assures me that they are disposed to cultivate a Connection, etc. To this I reply that any written Communications which may be made by his Grace of Leeds shall be duly transmitted. That I do not like to transmit meer Conversation, because it may be misconceived and disagreable Questions may arise, but that written Things remain and speak for themselves. That as to the Disposition for having a good Understanding between the two Countries, it is evidenced on our Part not only by the Step which the President has taken but also by the Decision of the Legislature, in which a considerable Majority were opposed to the laying extraordinary Restrictions upon british Vessels in our Ports. Mr. Pitt observes that on the contrary we ought to give them particular Privileges in Consequence of those which we enjoy here. I tell him that I really know of no particular Privilege we enjoy except that of being imprest, which of all others we are least desirous to partake of. Finally they promise to consult together and give me the Result.—Go hence to Mr. Boinville's but he is abroad. Return Home and write. Mr. Cutting calls and I ask the Event of his Application for the Seamen. He gives me a vaunting Account of his Services on this Occasion and of his Disinterestedness. He says he has transmitted an Account of the Affair to Mr. Jefferson. I ask if any other Americans are in the same Situation; he thinks there are, is to let me know if he hears of any. In the Conversation with Mr. Pitt he said they had evidenced Good Will towards us by what they had done respecting our Commerce and that this should have excited favorable Dispositions in us. I tell him that their Regulations have been made with a View to their own Interest meerly, so that if they had given us any Preference over others we felt no Sense of Obligation because we knew the Motive, and that it would be Nonsense even in forming a Treaty to stipulate Terms which it would not be the Interest of the Parties to abide by, because otherwise the Treaty itself would become a Cause of War as the Party aggrieved could not otherwise liberate himself from the onerous Conditions.—I incline on the whole to the Opinion that if France should put thirty Ships of the Line into Commission we may settle a Treaty with this Country upon such Terms as we may think proper. But if the present Clouds break away they will become again intractable. Dine at Home and after Dinner examine some Accounts between John and Richard Penn to see their Situation in Respect to each other. Visit Mrs. Rd. Penn and shew her the State which I have made for her Use. Take Tea and return Home.

DR. WARREN:

"THE PEOPLE HERE LOOK FOR FACTS: THEY TRUST NO THEORY"

1799

John Collins Warren was the eldest son of Dr. John Warren, hero of Bunker Hill and progenitor of the most famous of all American medical families. After graduation as valedictorian of the Harvard class of 1799, Warren headed for England and France to study medicine and surgery; he describes for us here opportunities at Guy's Hospital in London unavailable in the United States at that time. After his return to the United States Dr. Warren attached himself to the Harvard Medical School, where he succeeded his father as Professor in 1815. During the next thirty years he became one of the most distinguished medical teachers in the country; in 1846 he performed one of the first and most famous operations with the use of ether.

Once, I remember, you asked whether I intended to become a surgeon. The question remains unanswered. At that time, I had seen enough to have an idea of the difficulties of an operation, but

From Edward Warren, *The Life of John Collins Warren, M.D.* (Boston, 1859), I, pp. 31–34, 46–47.

none of its pleasures: now I see a good operation with the pleasure I used to feel at the successful solution of Euclid's problems—a pleasure greater than almost any I know. I have acquired that taste, that high relish, for these, without which no man can exert himself for the attainment of any art; and am only surprised that I was so long blind. There are operations almost every day—the stone, hydrocele, cataract, and amputations innumerable; but Mr. Cline's operations for aneurism or hernia are grand. It is pleasure to see him take up or turn his knife. There are some observations respecting these matters which I have not now sufficient time to communicate, but shall take the first opportunity. The lectures have gratified me very much: they have such immense advantages from the preparations. Not a part but is elegantly prepared; some injected with quicksilver, some with wax; dried and wet. Every morbid appearance is here preserved. You well know how much clearer an idea is conveyed by these specimens than can be done by a dead, flaccid body. If I had time, I should make many myself; but I despair of doing a quarter of what I wish, here. Dissection is carried on in style: twelve or fifteen bodies in a room; the young men at work on them in different ways. The people called resurrection-men supply us abundantly. An odd circumstance happened some time since. A hungry beggar had got some bread, and ate with so much avidity as to suffocate himself and fall down in the street. One of the resurrection-men, passing, immediately claimed the man as his brother, took him to the dissecting theatre of St. Thomas, and secured a good price. The man's trachea is now made into a preparation. The surgeons here, considering themselves at the head of their profession, dare to differ from everybody else, if they think they have truth with them. No authority is believed sufficient to prevent inquiry: thus, much of the rubbish left by Haller is cleared away, and even some of his own works overturned. A new theory of generation is brought forward; but what is infinitely more important than the best-wrought theory, are the discoveries respecting the absorbents. Much has been done, and all the able anatomists and physiologists are employed upon the subject. In this and every other research, the people here look for facts: they trust no theory, but experiment is the only creed. Go to Edinburgh for theory! I have much to say on many of these particulars, but must defer it to another time. I receive so much pleasure from the pursuits in which I am absorbed, that I hardly have time to think of my disconnected situation. . . .

You have no idea, sir, what a shocking place this is in winter. No cold weather, for the grass is perfectly green; but a constant drizzling, that keeps the town dirty as a kennel, notwithstanding all that can be done. The air is thickened with smoke and vapors, so that it is scarcely respirable; and as for the sun, no one can tell when he was seen. The days are five hours long; or, more strictly speaking, there are five hours of twilight: for, while I have been writing, I have, within this week, been obliged to stop almost every day, at some part of it, so totally dark was it. Many have already cut their throats; and, if the present weather lasts (which it will), a terrible slaughter will take place, I dare say. They have, however, plenty of amusements here: in truth, there is amusement at every step through the streets of London. I constantly meet something new and interesting in this wonderful place. Mrs. Siddons is now playing; but, the theatre being at a great distance, I cannot go there so often as I wish. I have not, therefore, yet seen this celebrated woman; but shall take the first opportunity. I have but this day learnt that a ship sails for Boston tomorrow; and must, therefore, say less than I wished to. I shall, however, soon write again to you, and to some of my friends. Gurley will, I hope, write to me by every opportunity. I cannot refrain from thanking you for the length of your letter, engaged as you are at every moment. Sir, I beg you will spare me as much time as you can. Please to tell my dear mother that her letters are short and sweet; but I cannot think they would be less sweet were they longer. Will none of my brothers or sisters write? It would be useless to enumerate all the friends I would be remembered to. Tell them, I think of them all particularly, and would write to them had I time; but I have already written to more than have returned it, and more than I ever will again. Wish my Aunt Polly joy for me. I am rejoiced that H. is so well recovered from the accident. Give my love to every one of them, and, most of all, to my mother. The *Minerva* is every day expected. After receiving my letters by her, I shall write by a ship to sail at the end of this month.

Most respectfully,
Your affectionate son,
J. C. Warren

. . . One evening, in going from my lodgings to the West End of the town, I fell in with a mob, which was raised on account of a scarcity of bread. Instead of keeping clear of it, as would have been wise, I entered into it, and talked with the people, to ascertain what their views and objects were. At this time, a charge was made upon the mob by a body of dragoons; and every one was obliged to save himself as he could. This attack irritated me among others; and we rallied, and made preparations for defence. Soon after, we were assailed by a body of police. Sympathizing with the people, who were in a state of starvation, and irritated by the attacks, I got on the edge of the sidewalk, and began to address the crowd on their unhappy condition. They were highly delighted to find a person, dressed like a gentleman, haranguing in their favor; and loudly cheered, and demanded a repetition of the harangue. At this moment, a gentleman spoke to me, drew me aside, and represented the dangerous position I was taking; and that, although the people were in a suffering state, they were not likely to get any remedy in this way. I readily understood this, of course; and, having no great desire to be apprehended as the leader of a mob, I walked off with him in the direction I had been going: and he, having ascertained what course I was taking, offered to show me the way; for it so happened, that, in following the mob, I had been drawn entirely away from the usual route from the east to west, into the complicated streets and lanes of the northern part of London. However, this gentleman went with me a good distance, told me he was an officer in the army, that he had no connection with the police, and that his speaking to me was accidental. I then as freely told him who I was, and made him understand I had no desire to overturn the British government. By a long and perilous route, I reached my destination, and walked back to the borough the same evening.

1800-1820

WILLIAM AUSTIN:

TO UNDERSTAND THE ENGLISH

ONE SHOULD BE A PLEBEIAN,

A GENTLEMAN AND A NOBLEMAN

1803

Almost all Americans in England during the years of strained relations that culminated in the War of 1812 must have felt some antipathy for the British. William Austin, son of a prominent Massachusetts family, had already trained himself in faultfinding before he went. As a student at Harvard he had written some well-deserved strictures on the administration of the college, and before graduation in 1798 he had refused membership in the honorary Phi Beta Kappa Society. But he wanted to study in England badly enough to earn money for it by teaching school and then by serving, quite improbably, as chaplain on the frigate *Constitution,* whose wartime fame was yet to come. He read law and ate his dinners at Lincoln's Inn in 1802–03, making good use of his time both professionally and socially. His *Letters from London,* published in Boston soon after his return, attracted immediate attention.

Notwithstanding Austin's pervasive antagonism to England and things English, his observations are not only sharp but judicious. Scorning the tendency of visitors to "lie boldly and speak the truth only by chance," he nevertheless confessed his difficulty in understanding the English—a confes-

From William Austin, *Letters from London* (Boston, 1804), pp. 45–65, 182–186.

49

sion which was to echo down the decades. "To understand the English," he wrote perspicaciously, "one should be a plebeian in the morning, a gentleman in the afternoon, and a nobleman by night. Otherwise the various grades of society are so fortified in peculiar habit that you are in danger of mistaking honest John for a different animal." After his return to the United States Austin had a long and not undistinguished career in law and politics, and wrote what is perhaps the best novel in early American literature, *Peter Rugg, the Missing.*

London, September 25th [*1802*]

The English have not that esteem for the citizens of the United States, which might naturally be expected from the various relations which obtain between them: in truth, they are partial to nobody. They hate all whom they do not despise, while the latter can only render hatred for contempt. Machiavel would probably think it a national virtue, to hate or despise all other people: but the English have improved on this. They undervalue their own fellow subjects, as much as they do foreigners. A poor Scotchman, who is necessitated to take the main road to England, because Sir John Sinclair has deprived him of the means of subsistence, by converting thirty six small farms into one, in order to try an experiment in raising sheep, is thought to be a very selfish fellow, if he comes to London, to shun the curse of Scotland. The Irishman too, tired at home of sour buttermilk and potatoes, is considered a poor vagabond, the moment he crosses the channel in search of roast beef and plumb pudding. Had the United States continued under the British government, we should have been the most contemptible of mankind. The English would have been the first to despise us: at present, they regard the United States with a sentiment far more honourable, than that of contempt.

It is very easy for these people to tell you what they do not respect; on the contrary, what they do respect, is not so evident. They differ wonderfully from the Scotch, in one particular: a Scot is partial to his fellow-Scotchmen, with very little fondness for Scotland: an Englishman is still more partial to England, with very little fondness for Englishmen—One might suppose such a people must be insufferably haughty; yet he would greatly mistake their character. I have never seen a haughty Englishman. They could not live within a mile of each other, were they both proud and haughty: but being only proud, they mutually respect each other; whereas, it is the property of haughtiness to be arrogant. Now the English admit not such claims. He who is haughty will inevitably render himself ridiculous to all who despise his airs: I do not recollect an instance of having seen an Englishman ridiculous on this account; hence, though their characters are extremely angular, they are rather defensively, than offensively, proud.

Nor are they more vain, than haughty: they dress, conduct, think as they please, and set every body at defiance. At the same time, if they know you esteem them, and feel conscious they have not demeaned themselves in obtaining your estimation, none can be more happy in possessing your good opinion. This carelessness of the opinion of other people shows itself among all ranks, especially the lowest. The swing of the arm, the incautious step, the rolling of the body, tell you plainly "They care for nobody, no not they": but this, in part, may be owing to a desperate majesty which they assume; for which the very lowest of the English are remarkable. Those, who are more immediately dependent on others for a livelihood, have a mixed character of servility and independence. They cherish the estimation of those on whom they are dependent; but seem utterly regardless of the good opinion of other people. The middling ranks follow their own inclinations, and are the original of their own manners; hence they form a motley picture, diversified, from quaker simplicity, to an appearance of studied artifice: but this appearance seldom arises from affectation, they are above that, but rather from whim. The nobility, judging at a distance, appear to me to build their characters much more on the populace, than do the populace build theirs on the nobility. But I am disposed to believe it policy and affectation which so frequently induce the nobility to dress more meanly, than many among the lower orders: policy, to conciliate; affectation, of seeming to attach no consequence to their rank. The king is liable to the same remark; he has much more of the external appearance of John Bull, than of the German; he is frequently seen not better dressed than one of our farmers, with an old hat not worth sixpence—But I was speaking of the nationality of this people.

It is a happy circumstance that this attachment is so deeply rooted in the great mass of the English. It serves a substitute for real patriotism. The rich, in every country, if they retain those sentiments for which an honest man ought to blush, may be tolerably happy, whether they happen to live at Constantinople, Venice or Madrid: but by far the greater part of every nation in Europe, and that part, to which a nation looks for support in the moment of emergency, is *fortunately* retained in the wizard spell of prejudice.

I will give you one . . . instance of this national partiality, which has already passed under my notice. . . .

The . . . instance occurred over a *pot of porter,* between a

French emigrant and a full blooded Englishman, whose pedigree had not probably been crossed, since the days of Canute. The Frenchman thought porter was too gross for those who led an idle life, and generally rendered those, who drank much of it, dull and stupid. This, in the opinion of the Englishman, amounted to an attack on the national character: and calling for another pot, like another Lord Peter, he endeavoured to persuade the Frenchman that, in a pot of porter was contained the quintessence of the best wines of every climate. The Frenchman thought there was not so much vivacity in it, as in Champaigne. "True," said John Bull, "there is not so much *evaporation,* but it has more *heart."* . . .

London, October 30th

I have lately made a most important discovery, which has displayed one of the great secrets of English rank. You, in the United States, knowing nothing of this, will consider the following authentic history of rank a singular curiosity.

They have confined the several species of man within such definite limits, in this country, that the moment they hear a knocking at their doors, they can tell you whether it be a servant, a postman, a milkman, a half or whole gentleman, a very great gentleman, a knight, or a nobleman.

A servant is bound to lift the knocker once: should he usurp a nobleman's knock he would hazard his situation. A postman knocks twice, very loudly. A milkman knocks once, at the same time, sending forth an artificial noise, not unlike the yell of an American Indian. A mere gentleman usually knocks three times, moderately: a terrible fellow feels authorized to knock thrice, very loudly, generally adding to these, two or three faint knocks, which seem to run into each other: but there is considerable art in doing this elegantly, therefore it is not always attempted: but it is a valuable accomplishment—A stranger who should venture at an imitation would immediately be taken for an upstart—A knight presumes to give a *double knock,* that is, six raps, with a few faint ones at the end. I have not yet ascertained the various peculiarities, which distinguish the degrees between the baronet and the nobleman; but this I know, too well, that a nobleman, at any time of night, is allowed to knock so long and loud, that the whole neighbourhood is frequently disturbed; and although fifty people may be deprived of their night's rest, there is no redress at law nor equity. Nor have I learnt how long and loud a prince of the blood presumes to knock, though, doubtless, he might knock an hour or two, by way of distinction. . . .

You may imagine it a very easy matter to pass from the simple *rap* of the servant, to that of the nobleman: but let me inform you these little monosyllables stand in the place of Alpine mountains, which neither vinegar nor valour can pass. . . . They have, by prescription, risen nearly to the dignity of Common Law, of which strangers as well as natives are bound to take notice. I was lately placed in a pleasant position through ignorance of this: soon after my arrival, I received an invitation to dine with a gentleman, and in my economical way, with the greatest simplicity, I gave one reasonable rap: after a considerable time, a servant opened the door, and asked me *what I wanted!* I told him Mr.——. He replied, "his *master* had company, but he would see if he could be spoken with." In the mean time, I was left in the entry. Presently Mr.—— came, who, a little mortified, began to reprove the servant; but it appeared in the sequel he was perfectly right, for on telling Mr.——, *"I knocked but once,"* he burst into a laugh, and said he would explain that at dinner.

London, April 29th [1803]

The English ordinaries and eating houses offer an inexhaustible source of observation on the national character and manners. You meet not only with all descriptions of London people, but likewise with French, Irish, Scotch and country people; and you may choose your company, from the most humble to the most exalted; that is, you may choose the price of your dinner, from sixpence to a guinea. You are not troubled with the least ceremony; if you wish for nothing more than a dinner, you have only to enter these places, hang up your hat, or keep it on your head, sit down, look at your *bill of fare,* call for your dinner, pay for it, and walk off.

A Londoner, generally, enters the room and observes nobody, plants himself at table in a dead position, breaks his bread in halves, *with an air,* falls to, says not a word during his dinner, which he eats rather slowly, yet swallows too quickly for his health, rises from table in resolute reserve, and retires from the room as he would from a cavern. . . .

If you wish to know how the petty cooks can afford to give you a dinner for sixpence or less, I will inform you what I learnt at Wapping, where I dined for four pence halfpenny including a farthing to the waiter, who was very much obliged to me. I was told it was the custom of the more respectable ordinaries and eating houses to sell their *leavings* to the next less great houses; these in their turn sell again, so nothing is lost: but part of that dinner which is eaten at a high price, at the west end of the town, perhaps, a fortnight after, is eaten at Wapping for four pence. Thus the delicious viands of the rich, degenerate at length into two penny broth for the poor. This may offend a delicate stomach, but hunger never reasons, and as the sailors say, "poison is killed by boiling, and what will not poison you, will fatten you." Some of these cook shops boast of more liberality than others. They give you a table cloth, and pewter plate, and spoon, and do not demand your money until you have dined; while others will make you pay before you eat a mouthful, and will trust you with nothing but a wooden plate, wooden bowl, and wooden spoon.

The different sorts of men with whom you meet at these places are remarkable. If it did not excite the most debasing ideas, it would be humourous to converse sometimes with a class of men whom you find at these places, whose stupid ignorance would disgrace a Hottentot. If they have half an idea, they know not enough of the English language to convey even that. They seem to have been born in a cockle shell, and have never burst their confinement. Locke, possibly got his opinion that the human mind was like a blank sheet of paper, from his knowledge of this description of men, whom you may find in every cook's shop. They are so profoundly stupid, they scarcely know whence they came, where they are, or whither they are going. Yet they frequently possess a remarkable sagacity in whatever is directly connected with their occupation; a fair proof that they once had minds capable of discernment. Therefore they ought not to be classed, by naturalists, as a distinct species, though they are generally considered such, by certain politicians.

As you know not who your company are, you may be as likely to dine with a pick pocket as a saint. One day, after a genteel person, whose conversation was very intelligent, had retired from table, I was asked, "If I knew him?" Answering in the negative, I was informed, he was a *reputed* highwayman. This will probably surprise you, but it ought not. In such a city as this, and in such a country, where, if a man is willing to brave suspicion, the law waits upon him until he affords full proof, a person may possibly pass the greater part of his life, a highwayman, and parade the public walks every day, and even affect the highest style of splendour, under the strongest suspicions, yet no one will venture to arrest him, or dare charge him with his crimes. Although a thousand witnesses should testify they were robbed, and could *almost* testify they were robbed by the prisoner, yet they must more than *almost* identify his person, which is extremely difficult, on account of his mask; otherwise, he would assuredly be acquitted. . . . The same person who informed me of this reputed highwayman, observed, "Most of them were well known to the Bowstreet Runners, that they frequently assembled together at known public houses, like other associated bodies, and that the Bowstreet Runners were on tolerable civil terms with them." For instance, if one of these Runners should demand admittance to their assemblies, which is frequently the case, he would be admitted, though treated in the most laconic style. Thus; *"Who do you want?"* The Runner names the person if he sees him, who replies, *"He will wait on him directly."* If the Runner says the person whom he wants is not there, *"Well then, off and be damned."* All those of their society whom they *lose,* they call *Flats.*

BENJAMIN SILLIMAN:
A YOUNG YALE PROFESSOR
PREPARES HIMSELF FOR
A SCIENTIFIC CAREER

1805

Benjamin Silliman was in many ways the representative scientist of his generation. Born in Connecticut in 1779, he graduated from Yale College at the age of seventeen and then studied law under the great jurist David Daggett. With that charming audacity which characterized American colleges of his generation, Yale appointed him, at the age of twenty-one, to teach chemistry, and in 1823 made him a professor of that subject. He promptly went to Philadelphia to learn something about it, then in 1805 to Britain and the Continent to buy scientific apparatus and books: his *Journal* is the record of that visit so important in the annals of American science. Yale's judgment was right, just as later Harvard's judgment in appointing Edward Everett Professor of Greek at twenty-one was right; Silliman rapidly became the leading chemist in the country, and perhaps the leading geologist to boot. He taught at Yale altogether some fifty-five years; helped found the Medical School there; laid the foundations for the later Sheffield Scientific School; and became the Grand Old Man of Yale and of American science. He was active,

From Benjamin Silliman, *A Journal of Travels in England, Holland and Scotland* (New Haven, 1820), I, pp. 292–296; II, pp. 18–21, 25–34; III, pp. 90–91, 105–109.

too, in the popularization of science, through his editorship of the *American Journal of Science and Arts,* his famous Lowell Lectures, and lectures throughout the United States; in this realm he was for his generation what John Fiske was for the next. In the 1850s he made another prolonged visit to the Continent which he once again recorded in three volumes, but the record of his first visit has about it the freshness of the discovery of a new world.

Sir Joseph Banks' Conversatione

June 30 [1805]. There are a number of literary assemblies in London, for the purpose of conversation, where a stranger has a better opportunity than he can enjoy in any other way, of seeing the distinguished men of the metropolis, and of forming an estimate of the English character in its most improved, intelligent, and polished form. The most distinguished of these meetings is held at Sir Joseph Banks', and I found that the gentlemen with whom I was walking, were going to attend it. When Mr. Watt inquired whether I had been introduced at this meeting, I informed him that I had supposed myself precluded from calling on Sir Joseph Banks, as I had left a letter of introduction with my card, on my first arrival in London, and had never heard any thing farther on the subject. He assured me that it would be perfectly in order to call again, as Sir Joseph, in consequence of the numerous demands on his time, was, by the universal consent of society, excused from the common obligations of civility with respect to returning visits and sending invitations, and every stranger who had been introduced to him, was expected to call again as a matter of course. I had learned the same thing, a day or two before, from Mr. Greville, and had accidentally heard that inquiry had been made by Sir Joseph whether I had called. I was therefore very happy to put myself under Mr. Watt's patronage, and to accept the offer which he kindly made to introduce me.

My reception was such as to make me regret that my mistake had not been sooner corrected, and every embarrassment was removed by the courteous behaviour of this celebrated man.

Sir Joseph Banks is verging toward old age; he is now afflicted with the gout, and from this cause, is so lame as to walk stooping, with the aid of a staff. His head is perfectly white, his person tall and large, and his whole appearance commanding though mild and conciliating.—From his being President of the Royal Society, and from his having been long distinguished by active and zealous exertions to promote the cause of science, especially in the various departments of natural history, he has become, by common consent, a kind of monarch over these intellectual dominions. We found Sir Joseph in his library, surrounded by a crowd of the literati, politicians, and philosophers of London. These constitute his court, and they would not dishonour the King himself. Mr. Watt was so good as to make me easy in this assembly, by introducing me to such of the gentlemen present as I had a curiosity to converse with.

Major Rennel is probably the first geographer living. In Asiatic geography particularly he has distinguished himself very much, and has given the world an excellent map of Hindustan.

The geographical illustrations at the end of Park's Travels in Africa were written by him.

Although few men have equally well founded claims to superiority, no man indicates less disposition to arrogate it than Major Rennel. His manners are perfectly modest, and so mild and gentle, that he makes even a stranger his friend. He thought that notwithstanding the efforts of the French to make their language the polite tongue of Europe, the English would ultimately become the most prevalent language in the world. This he inferred from the immense countries in Asia and America which were already settled or fast settling with English people. While conversing on this subject, he uttered the following extraordinary sentiment. He said, that *the Americans had improved the English language, by the introduction of some words and phrases very energetic and concise, instead of diffuse circumlocution.* To my remark that his sentiments were much more favorable to us than those of the English reviewers, he replied that they were not always the most candid men.

Among other distinguished men who were present, was Dr. Wollaston, a chemical philosopher of eminence, and Secretary of the Royal Society; Dr. Tooke, the historian of Catharine of Russia; Mr. Cavendish, who has done as much towards establishing the modern chemistry as any man living; Dalrymple, the marine geographer; Windham, the Parliamentary orator; and Lord Macartney, famous for his embassy to China.

Besides these there were many others among those who have distinguished themselves in science, politics, or literature, and whom it was gratifying to a stranger to see.

In this assembly the most perfect ease of manners prevailed; there was no ceremony of any kind. They came and departed when they pleased, without disturbing any body, and those present sat or stood, or walked or read, or conversed or remained silent, at pleasure. Eating and drinking formed no part of the entertainment, nor was any thing provided for this purpose.

Every person who had been introduced to Sir Joseph Banks, is at liberty to breakfast at his house at 10 o'clock, and to frequent his library and museum at any time between that hour and 4 o'clock P.M. every day in the week except Sunday. I shall doubtless avail myself of the privilege of the library frequently, although I may not perhaps make so much use of the breakfasts as a French loyalist is said to have done.

This man, having fled from the guillotine in France, found access at Sir Joseph Banks', and met that liberal reception which is known to characterize the house. Having understood that a public breakfast was ready every morning, at which Sir Joseph was always happy to see his friends, he construed the invitation in the most literal and extensive sense, and actually took up his board there for one meal a day, and came to breakfast regularly, till the sly looks and meaning shrugs of the servants taught him that in England, as well as in France, more is often said than is meant.

Sir Joseph Banks' library is very extensive, for a private one, and is freely consulted by all persons who have been properly introduced. Sir Joseph lives in all the dignity of science; he has a librarian constantly attending in the library: he is a Swede and himself a man of learning. There are also, I believe, two secretaries. Sir Joseph can well afford all this, for his income is seven thousand pounds sterling, or nearly thirty-three thousand dollars; a sum much larger than the salary of the President of the United States.

Sir Joseph Banks' efforts in favour of science, have not been those of a mere student. You will remember he accompanied the celebrated Captain Cook in one of his voyages, and in the narrative is mentioned under the name of Mr. Banks. Dr. Solander, a learned Swede, was also with him.

The same gentlemen also visited the Island of Iceland, and we have an account of their observations in the letters on Iceland, drawn up by Van Troil, who was also of the party, more than thirty years since.

On the whole, there is no man in England better entitled to lead in science, than this eminent veteran, and I imagine the august assembly at his levees, would give a stranger a more favourable idea of the intelligence and urbanity of the English than any other which he could frequent. . . .

Royal Institution

July 11 [1805]. Mr. Accum, to whom I have been indebted for many instances of kindness, since I came to London, this morning conduced me to see the royal institution. This institution was set on foot a few years ago for the purpose of encouraging useful knowledge in general, and for facilitating the introduction of useful mechanical improvements. Now, public lectures are delivered in the institution on different branches of science, and particularly on natural philosophy and chemistry. The establishment was munificently endowed, and Count Rumford was placed at its head, where he had opportunity to give full scope to his culinary and other experiments. The institution has become quite celebrated, and for two or three years past, has made more noise than any other in Europe. It is on a very extensive scale: for, the English, whenever any favourite object is in view, never spare money, and indeed, as the patrons of such institutions are generally rich, they commonly prefer the most expensive establishments, because there is a gratification derived from the distinction, as well as from the consciousness of doing good.

A number of contiguous houses in Albemarle-street have been so connected as to form one building, and this contains the numerous apartments of the royal institution. There are rooms for reading the journals and newspapers; others, devoted to the library, which is already considerably extensive; others to the philosophical apparatus, the lectures, the minerals, the professors, the cookery, servants, &c. In the lowest apartment they pointed out a great number of culinary utensils, consisting of stew pans, boilers, roasters, and other similar things, which Count Rumford has, at various times, invented, for reducing the humble processes of the kitchen to philosophical principles. The experiments were carried *quite* through, for, one of the objects of the institution was to give *experimental* dinners, at which the Count presided, and the patrons of his experiments attended, to judge of the merits of any newly invented mode of cooking, or of any new dish. It was probably not very difficult to *recruit* a sufficient number of men for this service, in a country where good living is so much in fashion, and could philosophical pursuits always come furnished with equal attractions, they would never want devotees.

Do not understand me however as meaning any reflections on Count Rumford. His labours have been highly meritorious, and useful to mankind, and I would be the last to throw an air of ridicule around those men who strive to make philosophy the handmaid of the arts.

They shewed me also the system of boilers and pipers, by means of which the Count has contrived to carry steam through his extensive edifice, and effectualy to warm the theatre by diffusing through it the air which has become heated by contact with the pipes containing the steam.

The theatre is the room where the lectures are given. It is a superb apartment, and fitted up with great convenience. It is semicircular, and contains a pit and gallery, in which the seats rise row behind row. It is lighted from above, through a circular orifice, which, whenever the lecturer wishes to darken the room, can be shut at pleasure by a horizontal screen connected with a cord. This theatre has often contained a thousand persons. It is so fashionable a resort, that the ladies of Westminster are in the habit of coming to the royal institution to derive instruction from the rational pursuits of philosophy. Surely every one would commend this preference, when the competition lies between routs and masquerades, and the delightful recreations of experimental science.

But, as one object of the institution has been to attract an audience, of course every thing has worn a popular air, and the amusing and the brilliant have been studiously pursued as well as the useful. The apparatus is by no means so extensive as I expected to find it.

Very recently two new institutions have been projected in London, on principles similar to this. They are patronised by the people of *the city,* as distinguished from Westminster, and are designed to rival the Royal Institution. There is a spirit of jealousy and rivalry subsisting in the city towards the people of fashion in Westminster. In the former, people accumulate fortunes by industry and spend their lives in business; in the latter, they live to be amused, and to enjoy their fortunes. Although there can be no hesitation in deciding which class is really most deserving, and which ought to be honoured and applauded, some how or other, the world has always been so *wrong-headed* as to permit elegant and fashionable idleness to give the ton to every thing, while less polished but more useful industry has stood in the back ground. It must be acknowledged that the citizens have taken a very laudable way to assert their dignity.

Besides these institutions there is still another of very recent origin, the object of which is to hold forth encouragement for the cultivation of the fine arts, particularly those which are connected with the manufacturing interests of Great Britain. The encouragement contemplated is not merely that of honorary distinctions, but of substantial pecuniary aid, and that sufficiently liberal to answer the purpose. . . .

Old Bailey

July 13. I dined with a friend, and in the afternoon went with him to the Old Bailey, a court which I need only name, to *you*, who are familiar with English jurisprudence. It is under the same roof with the famous Newgate prison. The cells which separate the unhappy felons from the rest of mankind; the court that furnishes their death warrant, and the fatal apparatus which launches them into eternity, are all here upon one spot. Tyburn is no longer the scene of execution; that distressing, although necessary act of justice, is now performed at the door of the Newgate prison, in one of the most public streets in London. In the back yard of the Old Bailey, we saw the scaffold. It is a stage erected on runners, and furnished with a gallows, beneath which is a trap-door, that falls from under the culprit; when an execution is to take place, the machine is dragged out from the yard into the street, and placed before one of the prison doors, through which the prisoner is conducted to the scaffold. There he is suffered to hang, sometimes for an hour. Although several executions have happened since I have been residing in London, it has not been my misfortune to pass by Newgate, in time to see a kind of tragedy of which I would not willingly be a spectator.

At the Old Bailey, a man was under trial for his life, on an indictment for burglary. I witnessed the issue of the trial. Judge Lawrence summed up the case to the jury, with perspicuity and humanity. Without leaving their seats, the jury acquitted the man of burglary, but found him guilty of a common larceny. Influenced by the commisseration which we are too prone to feel for one in his circumstances, I was gratified to find that his life was not forfeited, especially as he appeared like a forlorn, distressed man. He seemed to be half starved, and when called upon by the court for his defence, he said that he was without witnesses and without friends.

Immediately after, a woman was brought to the bar, and indicted for crimes, for which, if convicted, she must loose her life. As we did not stay to hear this trial through, I do not know her fate. Judge Lawrence had retired, and the Recorder now presided. I was disgusted with the captiousness and imperiousness which he displayed. Surely, while an upright judge asserts, with firmness, the dignity of the laws, he should bear himself with all possible humanity towards the trembling wretch who stands before him.

Last evening a young girl of sixteen or seventeen years of age was condemned to death in this court for forgery. In the same place, and for the same crime, stood convicted the famous Dr. Dodd, whose singularly distressing case called forth the pen of Johnson, and excited your friend Mr.—— with a warmth of friendship which we must admire, while we cannot but censure its interference with the laws—to exert himself, although unsuccessfully, for his rescue.

In the course of this week, an old man of about eighty years of age, has been tried for the sixty-first time at the Old Bailey, and this, after having been fifty-seven times publicly whipped, and otherwise ignominiously punished, and after being once condemned to death, the infliction of which was prevented by a pardon. I questioned whether the annals of criminal law can furnish a parallel. The old man was condemned again, at this trial, but not capitally, so that he may yet make the number of his convictions equal to three score and ten.

There is a great number of debtors confined in Newgate and the adjoining prisons, and most of them are immured for small sums, and have very little hope of escaping, because they are miserably poor. They are crowded, in great numbers, into small apartments, and I have never heard more piteous cries of distress, nor more moving entreaties for relief, than from the grates of the Fleet prison, as I have been passing along between it and Fleetmarket. . . .

Mr. Nicholson

July 16. I had an interview this morning with Mr. Nicholson, the conductor of the Philosophical Journal, and author of several works on Natural Science. He is so well known to the scientific world, and has long held a distinguished place in it both as a writer and teacher. It is always gratifying to find distinguished men amiable and attentive to civility in private life.

Mr. Nicholson is so in an eminent degree, and in several instances in which I have consulted him on subjects connected with his peculiar pursuits, he has exhibited a degree of urbanity and intelligence, which could not fail of making an advantageous impression. He holds a conversazione at his house: I was present at one.

I believe few men in Britain would, at the present time, be considered as higher authority in any thing relating to science, than Mr. Nicholson. I had long respected and admired him at a distance. But he is one of those men whose mental magnitude does not diminish by a nearer view. Great men, like islands seen through a mist, usually appear the largest at a distance; this misty magnitude is very apt to vanish as we approach them; like the islands, what seemed vast in extent and to the imagination stored with the finest productions, but turn out sometimes barren in soil, mean in cultivation, and inconsiderable in size. In preparing to decide what artist or artists to employ in constructing the philosophical apparatus for Yale College, I had frequent occasion to consult Mr. Nicholson, and he gave me the following wise advice. "Seek (said he) for a man who has both skill and reputation, but one who is still ambitious of rising, and who still has, in some good degree, his fortune and name to acquire; with such a man, it will be a great object to serve you faithfully, and especially to gain a name abroad; but some of those who have already gained great celebrity and grown rich, are less careful that their articles should be excellent, than that they should be showy."

When I apologized to Mr. N. for the trouble I was giving him by such frequent applications, he replied that I need feel no delicacy on that point, for he had always, through life, made it a principle to afford cheerfully, every assistance in his power, whenever called upon, and that in his opinion this was the wisest course, for it would procure a similar return. In his own experience he said he had ever found this expectation verified.

If it be a matter of some delicacy to *praise* living men, it is certainly a much more difficult task to pursue the opposite course; were it not for this, it would not be difficult to find in London, originals among men of great name, and high self-consideration, of whom the most faithful portrait would bear every appearance of a caricature. I could make you laugh and I could make you angry by a portrait of this kind taken from the life. I must not however proceed in this strain but will turn to a subject of an opposite character.

Dr. Hooper and the Mary le Bone
Establishments

I went with Mr. Accum this morning to the west end of London, to hear a lecture from Dr. Hooper, a medical gentleman of great respectability and author of several valuable professional works. He has a fine lecture room, in a quiet street, and although his class like those of most private lecturers in London was small, it was attentive and decorous. Dr. Hooper lectured with dignity, perspicuity and ease, and seemed perfectly to understand his business.

By invitation, I went with him to the Mary le Bone Infirmary, of which he is the resident physician. This infirmary is an appendage of the Mary le Bone Work House, and both are situated on the North

Western angle of London, quite on the confines of the city and country, where the verdure and fine air of the latter, are united with the accommodations of the former. These establishments were formed in 1775, and sometimes contain more than one thousand of "the helpless poor." They are very fine things of their kind. "The work-shops, wash-house, laundry, wards, kitchen, bake-house, chapel and officers' rooms are excellently suited to their different purposes." I have seen nothing in England of the kind more cleanly and desirable. Dr. Hooper, with that civility for which he is celebrated, made my visit interesting and instructive, and particularly so, by the exhibition of a great number of very fine drawings, and finished pictures of various diseased parts of the human body, done by himself from actual cases, which have occurred during a residence of fifteen years in this Institution.

Dr. Hooper informed me that he was a fellow student with our distinguished countryman Dr. Physic of Philadelphia, whose professional eminence, especially as a surgeon, would probably place him on a level with the most distinguished in London. . . .

The Royal Institution and
Professors Davy and Allen

I have esteemed it no small misfortune that Professor (Humphry) Davy, who although a very young man, has already filled Europe with his well earned fame, has been absent from London, during the whole time of my residence in it, till within a day or two. He has been travelling abroad, and recently, in Ireland. This morning, under the guidance of a scientific friend, I went to the Royal Institution on purpose to see Professor Davy, and found him in his laboratory, surrounded by apparatus, and in the midst of the occupations of his profession. He received me with much ease and affability; his manners are perfectly polite, easy and unassuming. He enquired concerning Dr. Woodhouse of Philadelphia, who visited London in 1802, and whose pupil I had since been. I was not less pleased with Professor Davy, as a man, than I had before been interested in him as a chemist and philosopher. We spent a short time, in conversing on chemical topics and on his late tour in Ireland, and he shewed me a new article of apparatus which he had then recently invented. He is about twenty five, and his appearance is even more youthful than would be expected from his years. His reputation is very high here, and without doubt deservedly.

The obscure town of Penzance in Cornwall where you may

remember I was on the 6th and 7th of September has the honour of giving him birth. Without a University education, he has, as I am informed, risen to his present eminence from a humble situation; he is now very much caressed by the great men of London, and by the fashionable world, and it is certainly no small proof of his merit, that he has so early attained such favour and can bear it without intoxication. ·

In the afternoon I heard at the Institution a perspicuous and interesting lecture from Professor William Allen, on the general properties of matter. This gentlemen, whom I had before met in private society is much distinguished for talent, science and worth, and is highly esteemed in the Metropolis.

The audience was composed of people of all ages, and of both sexes; about half were females and most of these were young ladies. There seems to be at present in London, a disposition to encourage a taste for the sciences, by giving them a popular air; there can be no danger that the dignity of science will be degraded so long as this duty is committed to able hands, and it would certainly be happy if the attractions of literature and scientific recreation could effectually decoy the fashionable people of London away from scenes of amusement, where delicacy is perpetually violated, all serious impressions are banished, and frivolity and thoughtlessness take their place. . . .

Booksellers and Philosophical Instrument Makers

You need not be informed that in London the bookselling trade is very extensive, and, as happens with other kinds of business, where the state of society has attained great maturity, it is divided in many instances, into distinct departments. Thus one establishment is devoted to the classics—another to medicine—another to juvenile books, &c. Most however are miscellaneous. The highest example of this kind is Lackington & Allen's, Finsbury Square, where the successive stories of a great house are thrown into one vast room, and books occupy the entire sides from the ground to the garret, and are seen at one view in this mighty quadrangle. They are approached by galleries with suitable stairs, and the sight is enough to make one dizzy, and to fill him with despair, considering how short is life and how extensive is knowledge.

This collection is said to contain fifty thousand volumes—not very select probably, but embracing much that is valuable, and affording often the convenience of completing broken setts. Their sales, exchanges, &c. are said to amount to five hundred thousand volumes per annum.

A stranger who visits London to collect books, and has formed his ideas solely from the London catalogues, will be much disappointed, when he examines the actual establishments. He will be very far from finding at once all that is advertised. In collecting about one thousand five hundred volumes of select books, during the summer, and with the aid of a very active and intelligent man deeply versed in the mysteries of the trade, I have found much difficulty in discovering no small number of books. In some instances they have not been found at last on the shelves of the booksellers, but in stalls in the streets, or in neglected garrets.

The prices are by no means uniform, in different establishments, and still less is a uniform discount afforded for large orders and cash payments. One man perhaps allows but ten per cent. from his retail prices; another tempts you with twenty-five; but, on comparing the prices minutely, it is very possible the latter may be the least advantageous offer. It is necessary for a stranger to be very circumspect, and not to be in haste to form his contracts, till by a good deal of examination and comparison, he has ascertained the actual state of things.

This remark is still more applicable to the philosophical instrument makers, among whom there is a strong spirit of rivalry, and among some of them no small spirit of detraction. Establishments of this kind are numerous in London, and I have found few of those engaged in them who allowed much merit to rival artists. Some, whose shops are not showy, make excellent instruments, and others, whose catalogues are much more extensive, and whose names sound more abroad, are less confided in at home. One very distinguished artist, to whom science has been much indebted, I found in a very plain shop, with no appearance of show about him; he is conspicuous for accurate instruments, such as extremely sensible balances. I enquired of him what he would charge for one that would turn with one-thousandth part of a grain; after some hesitation he replied sixty guineas. A stranger coming to London with expectations founded on the catalogues of apparatus, which he may have seen at home, will be much disappointed. He will find only a small proportion of the instruments ready made, and he will not find their quality in every instance the best. If he needs many instruments, and especially the more accurate—the more complicated and costly ones, he must, in general, wait for them to be made, and if he does not almost daily visit the artists, and inspect the progress of the work, and push it forward strenuously, he will wait till his patience is exhausted. I obtained in my own name some instruments for a philosophical man resident in London, because he said that he being known to reside there, could not get them done within perhaps a year or two, but that a stranger who must leave the country within a limited time, would much more readily command the services of the artists. This delay and want of punctuality, arise principally from the fact, that the heads of these establishments are dependant upon workmen who work at different shops in London, and are sometimes very faithless and profligate. A distinguished artist said to me: "my best workmen are drunkards: I pay them off on Saturday night—they are drunk on Sunday—on Monday they are good for nothing, and it is well if they return soberly to their work by Tuesday; and if there are holidays of any description, and they can obtain money, they are sure to have a drunken frolic. Thus I am always, more or less, in their power, and cannot pledge myself for punctuality." We must not however infer, that they are all drunkards. Some of them are very sober and worthy, and it is from this description that the heads of new establishments arise.

Our venerable countryman, the Rev. Dr. Prince, of Salem, is well known among the London artists, and his talents and skill appear to be appreciated highly. Both the air-pump and the lucernal microscope, with his alterations and improvements, are constructed in London.

London probably contains some of the best philosophical artists in the world. Orders are received here for philosophical apparatus, from every part of Europe, as well as of America, and even as I have been assured on good authority from Paris itself.

LYDIA SMITH:

"TWO OF THE MOST CELEBRATED
CHARACTERS OF THE DAY"

1805–06

Lydia Smith was a young girl when she visited London in 1805 and kept a diary which she faithfully sent back to her friend Miss Anna Lothrop of Boston. A few years later she married Thomas Motley and in 1814 became the mother of John Lothrop Motley, the historian of the Dutch Republic.

December, 1805. . . . I have determined if ever I go in the City again to go in disguise. Now imagine me with my Trafalgar Robe and Yeoman's Cap, so new and so gay, splashing along such a crowd as here. I will tell you exactly what a walk thro' the Strand resembles, it is just like one of the Country dances at our Assemblies, there is as much confusion, crowding, shoving, etc., in the one as in the other, tho I certainly give the preference to Concert Hall, because there you stand a chance of being clean and the danger is generally at your feet and here your head runs the continual hazard of fractures etc.

From "Lydia Smith's Journal, 1805-06," in *Proceedings of the Massachusetts Historical Society*, XLVIII (June, 1915), pp. 516–517, 531.

from the impudent porters who carry on their heads what our cartmen carry in handcarts. It was an observation of my own that these Anglois had pretty thick skulls for it. I call'd at Clementi's to see his harps, they were extremely elegant. I intend as soon as we are settled to commence taking lessons, at present I am very eager for it, it is very fashionable here and considered one of the most elegant accomplishments. I did not in my excursion meet with any great adventures, but 'tis impossible to pass thro London streets without meeting many things to interest the curiosity. As I pass(ed) along I was much struck with the appearance of a tall and elegant woman. She was supported upon crutches, there was something extremely excentric in her appearance. I inquired who it was and found her to be quite a celebrated character here. She is the sister of Mrs. Siddons. She leads this vagrant life from choice. Mrs. S. and Kemble have offered her a handsome support but she has refused it, it is supposed she gets more from the charity of transient passengers than they would give her. She is known perfectly all over London. It is a kind of tribute I think to the fame of Mrs. Siddons that ensures her the liberality of the public. She is extremely elegant in her form, her features are fine, she is not very old and has no more claim upon the charity of the publick than any other idle beggar, her picutre is in all the print shops and you will see it amongst all collections of waxworks; indeed one need not wish a better establishment in London than to be a celebrated beggar, they live in style excepting particular hours, *levee hours* which they appropriate to receiving their friends. I would never give to any such an one as her, it is mere ostentatious vanity and there are so many real objects to whom we owe a tribute that it is defrauding them to give to such as her. This woman is always dres'd as neat and *tasty,* she varies her dress according to the season, in summer a green jacket and in winter a long cloth cloak. 'Tis a droll idea that she should parade herself thro London for charity; however, she never asks anything, not she she is above that and will not take notice of anyone unless they particularly address her and then she will condescend to accept a guinea or so to keep her from starving. And I met another of the Popular Paupers, this fellow is the most expert and practis'd of any you ever imagined, he is one of the most celebrated characters of the age and when he dies he may, for aught I know, claim a place in Westminster Abbey, he will be the hero of all the wonderful magazines, excentric biographies for a century after him, he has lost both of his legs, his knees are fasten'd on to a little sled and he wheels himself about. He never asks for charity, he sometimes extends his hat, but if you look at him not all the stoicism of philosophy can resist him, there is an irresistible demand upon your sensibility in his look, his eye turns towards you so full of eloquence, with such an imploring air, that the passion that is not moved by him is not human and were your purse strings in a Gordian knot he would unwind them, and this same fellow—who every day takes his stand amidst the bustle of the City—a few months ago only he married one of his daughters with a portion of £ 7000, some say per annum, but I think it was enough to sound pretty well if it was *only* seven thousand pounds. I esteem myself quite fortunate in thus seeing two of the most celebrated characters of the day. I know no names for either of them, they are never mention'd but with their respective qualifications, so is there no name necessary. To give to the one is a tribute to Mrs. Siddons, and to the other is a tribute to Nature, who seems to have given this Pauper letters patent as her alms gatherer. But all the beggars about here are not so civil as these, some of the sturdy, healthy wretches will follow you a mile to extort a few pence from you and another to thank you for it. It is a great tax upon a person's feelings to pass thro the streets here, there are so many objects, miserable objects, and there are so many that it precludes the possibility of relieving them all. . . .

January, 1806. . . . The Opera House is much more splendidly ornamented than Drury Lane Theatre, but I do not admire it so much nor think it so elegant tho more gay. There is a great deal of gilding about it and a great deal of painting, but I thought not with so much taste. The boxes are entirely parted from each other by thick partitions. They are all of them private property and no one has a right to enter them more than a private house, they all generally take upon a lease, some of ten years, fifteen, and some for life, so that strangers, unless they have acquaintance with some of the possessors, are obliged to sit in the pit, which is by far the best place unless the front boxes, because in the side rows only three in front can see the stage, the partition being in the way of the others. In their boxes they feel as much at home as in their houses. The most fashionable generally talk and laugh so loud that they disturb the whole audience which is a source of infinite sport and delight to them. It is a fine sight to see the beauty and elegance of the English women at the Opera, they can nowhere be seen to so much advantage, every one appears there in full dress and displays as much taste and expense as possible. I have always observed that where there is a large assemblage of ladies they appear to a disadvantage, too much beauty cloys; but here there seemed to be an uniformity of beauty, a characteristic trait of elegance throughout the house, almost every one was beautiful and almost every one had a peculiar attraction. The English, take them as a nation, are extremely handsome, the men are generally elegant and the women beautiful. We were very much disturbed in the midst of the opera by the entrance of the Prince of Wales and Mr. Sheridan, they always attract particular notice. The Prince is known by his beauty and Mr. Sheridan by his great red nose! a la Tom Paine. I had a fine opportunity of seeing the Prince as he bent forward for a long time to converse with a gentleman in the pit. He is very elegant but is growing very *embonpoint* and I think that all the great characters of the age are rather inclined thus. Genius is no longer starved but fattens upon the smiles of fools, and is fostered from starvation into comfort. So will this century of 1800 be one of the most flourishing most brilliant the world has known—at least it should be so.

SAMUEL F. B. MORSE:

"THE ONLY WAY TO PLEASE

JOHN BULL IS TO GIVE HIM

A GOOD BEATING"

1812

Samuel Finley Breese Morse, son of the great Jedidiah Morse who compiled the first *American Geography* and provided some of the intellectual, or rhetorical, ammunition in the bitter Federalist campaign against Jefferson, went to England to study painting in 1811. Except for two long jaunts to Bristol, he stayed in London studying under Benjamin West and Washington Allston for four years—three of them a period of war between Britain and America. Morse's paintings were good enough to win him both acclaim and reward; on his return to America he moved to New York, where he became perhaps the most successful painter in that city and founded, in 1826, the National Academy of Design, of which he was long president. As a portraitist he was the successor to the remarkable trio of Copley, Stuart, and Peale, and fully the equal of Sully and Harding; his portrait of Lafayette is one of the triumphs of American art. In the 1830s he turned from art to invention, and finally worked out a method of electrical communication and a code—the still used Morse Code—to facilitate that form of telegraphy. His letters to his

From *S. F. B. Morse, His Life and Letters*, Edward L. Morse, ed. (Boston, 1914), I, pp. 76–77, 87–89, 152–153, 163–165.

father illuminate at once the unregenerate conservatism of the New England Federalists and—in the son—the emergence of an American patriotism which fed, quite naturally, on hostility to England. Later in life Morse himself became deeply conservative; his conservatism assumed, almost predictably, the form of isolationism and hostility to foreigners.

June 8, 1812

. . . What Lord Castlereagh said at a public meeting a few days ago ought to be known in America. Respecting the Orders in Council, when some one said unless they were repealed war with America must be the consequence, he replied that, '*if the people would but support the Ministry in those measures for a short time, America would be compelled to submit, for she was not able to go to war.*' But I say, and so does every American here who sees how things are going with this country, that, should America but declare war, before hostilities commenced Great Britain would sue for peace on any terms. Great Britain is jealous of us and would trample on us if she could, and I feel ashamed when I see her supported through everything by some of the Federal editors. I wish they could be here a few months and they would be ashamed of themselves. They are injuring their country, for it is *their* violence that induces this Government to persist in their measures by holding out hope that the parties will change, and that then they can compel America to do anything. If America loses in this contest and softens her measures towards this country, she never need expect to hold up her head again. . . .

November 1, 1812

. . . Your last letter was of October 2, via Halifax, accompanying your sermon on Fast Day. The letter gave me great pleasure, but I must confess that the sentiments in the sermon appeared very *strange* to me, knowing what I, as well as every American here does, respecting the causes of the present war. . . . 'Tis the character of Englishmen to be haughty, proud, and overbearing. If this conduct meets with no resistance, their treatment becomes more imperious, and the more submissive and conciliating is the object of their imperiousness, the more tyrannical are they towards it. This has been their uniform treatment towards us, and this character pervades all ranks of society, whether in public or private life.

The only way to please John Bull is to give him a good beating, and, such is the singularity of his character that, the more you beat him, the greater is his respect for you, and the more he will esteem you. . . .

If, after all I have now written, you still think that this war is unjust, and think it worth the trouble in order to ascertain the truth, I wish papa would take a trip across the Atlantic. If he is not convinced of the truth of what I have written in less than two months, I will agree to support myself all the time I am in England after this date, and never be a farthing's more expense to you. . . . I was glad to hear that Cousin Samuel Breese is in the navy. I really envy him very much. I hope one day, as a painter, I may be able to hand him down to posterity as an American Nelson. . . . As to my letters of introduction, I find that a painter and a visitor cannot be united. Were I to deliver my letters the acquaintance could not be kept up, and the bare thought of encountering the English reserve is enough to deter any one. . . . This objection, however, might be got over did it not take up so much time. Every moment is precious to me now. I don't know how soon I may be obliged to return home for want of means to support me; for the difficulties which are increasing in this country take off the attention of the people from the fine arts, and they withhold that patronage from young artists which they would, from their liberality, in other circumstances freely bestow. . . .

Postscript. I have just read the political parts of this letter to my good friend Mr. Allston, and he not only approves of the sentiments in it, but pays me a compliment by saying that I have expressed the truth and nothing but the truth in a very clear and proper manner, and hopes it may do good.

January 1, 1813

. . . Last Thursday week I received a very polite invitation from Henry Thornton, Esq., to dine with him, which I accepted. I had no introduction to him, but, hearing that your son was in the country, he found me out and has shown me every attention. He is a very pleasant, sensible man, but his character is too well known to you to need any eulogium from me.

At his table was a son of Mr. Stephen, who was the author of the odious Orders in Council. Mr. Thornton asked me at table if I thought that, if the Orders in Council had been repealed a month or two sooner, it would not have prevented the war. I told him I thought it would, at which he was much pleased, and, turning to Mr. Stephen, he said: "Do you hear that, Mr. Stephen? I always told you so."

Bristol, October 11, 1814

Your last letters mention nothing about my going to France. I perceive you have got my letters requesting leave, but you are altogether silent on the subject. Everything is in favor of my going, my improvement, my expenses, and, last though not least, *the state of my feelings.* I shall be ruined in my feelings if I stay longer in England. I cannot endure the continued and daily insults to my feelings as an American. But on this head I promised not to write anything more; still allow me to say but a few words— On second thoughts, however, I will refer you entirely to Dr. Romeyn. If it is possible, as you value my comfort, see him as speedily as possible. He will give you my sentiments exactly, and I fully trust that, after you have heard him converse for a short time, you will completely liberate me from the imputation of error. . . .

Do write me soon and do give me leave. I long to bury myself in the Louvre in a country at least not hostile to mine, and where guns are not firing and bells ringing for victory over my countrymen. . . . Where is American patriotism,—how long shall England, already too proud, glory in the blood of my countrymen? Oh! for the genius of Washington! Had I but his talents with what alacrity would I return to the relief of that country which (without affectation, my dear parents) is dearer to me than my life. Willingly (I speak with truth and deliberation), willingly would I sacrifice my life for her honor.

Do not think ill of me for speaking thus strongly. You cannot judge impartially of my feelings until you are placed in my situation. Do not say I suffer myself to be carried away by my feelings; your feelings could never have been tried as mine have; you cannot see with the eyes I do; you cannot have the means of ascertaining facts on this side of the water that I have. But I will leave this subject and only say *see Dr. Romeyn.* . . .

London December 22, 1814

My dear Parents: .

I arrived yesterday from Bristol, where I have been for several months past endeavoring to make a little in the way of my profession, but have completely failed, owing to several causes. . . .

Secondly, the virulence of national prejudice which rages now with tenfold acrimony. They no longer despise, they hate, the Americans. The battle on Champlain and before Plattsburgh has decided the business; the moans and bewailings for this business are really, to an American, quite comforting after their arrogant boasting of reducing us to unconditional submission.

Is it strange that I should feel a little the effects of this universal hatred? I have felt it, and I have left Bristol after six months' perfect neglect. . . .

With respect to peace, I can only say I should not be surprised if the preliminaries were signed before January. My reasons are that Great Britain cannot carry on the war any longer. She may talk of her inexhaustible resources, but she well knows that the great resource, the property tax, must fail next April. The people will not submit any longer; they are taking strong measures to prevent its continuance, and without it they cannot continue the war.

Another great reason why I think there will be peace is the absolute *fear* which they express of us. They fear the increase of our navy; they fear the increase of the army; they fear for Canada, and they are in dread of the further disgrace of their national character. Mr. Monroe's plan for raising 100,000 men went like a shock through the country. They saw the United States assume an attitude which they did not expect, and the same men who cried for "war, war," "thrash the Americans," now cry most lustily for peace.

The union of the parties also has convinced them that we are determined to resist their most arrogant pretensions.

Yours very affectionately,
Saml. F. B. Morse

MORDECAI M. NOAH:

MONEY IS "AN INFALLIBLE MANTLE,

WHICH COVERS EVERY DEFECT"

1813

Noah, like Morse and like Joseph Ballard, was highly critical of the British. His animus was perhaps sharpened by his personal misfortunes. A Jew, he had applied for the post of United States consul in Tunis, in order to study "the situation, character, resources and numerical force of the Jews in Barbary." The ship which was to take him to France was captured by a British man-of-war and Noah himself deposited in Plymouth. With considerable generosity, however, the British allowed him to live in London and, eventually, to leave for his Tunisian post. As with so many observers of his generation he was particularly concerned to establish differences between the English and the Americans rather than to discover similarities. After the war Noah had a long and varied career in public life: editor of the *National Advocate*, sheriff of New York, surveyor of the Port of New York, and eventually a judge of the New York Court of Sessions. Although Noah admitted that he left Britain "with a more favorable impression of the people, their customs, habits, and manners, than I had hitherto been taught to anticipate," he did not abate his conviction that the two nations were natural enemies.

From Mordecai Noah, *Travels in England, France, Spain and the Barbary States in the Years 1813–14 and 1815* (New York, 1819), pp. 51–54.

There are no very strong traits of character, which mark the difference between the Englishman and the American; speaking the same language, possessing the same religion, pursuing the same habits, and boasting of the same origin, they are only distinct in peculiarities; national feelings, and the etherial spirit, may be said to be more fully enjoyed by the Americans than by the English. This, in part, may be attributed to the difference of climate, and an elasticity of mind; together, with a greater familiarity with public affairs, and enjoying a greater portion of rational liberty; for, though the English boast of being the only free people on earth, the greatest portion of this liberty, is enjoyed in imagination. Where representation is shackled, and incquality distributed, as it is in England; where the people cannot lighten the burdens imposed upon them, and where the press shrinks from the oppression of the law; the liberty spoken of, is empty and evanescent. Personal rights, however, are securely protected and enjoyed, and when an Englishman boasts of his liberty, he alludes to his individual liberty, and his privilege of speaking his mind freely, and going where he pleases.

There is no spirit, which prevails with so much force, as an attachment to wealth; not that sordid attachment, which hoards up riches without their enjoyment; but a blind passion, a diseased infatuation, which considers money as the sole desideratum—the only constituent to happiness—the only harbinger of rank and talents. In England, the poor man is the poorest creature in existence, the mere cypher in society. The cultivated and accomplished mind, and the splendid genius, receive no deference if clothed in rags; hence, persons are induced to assume appearances, that they can ill afford, to keep alive the countenance of the world: talent is no doubt encouraged, but it passes first through the ordeal of fashion, or is ushered into existence, through the aid of patrons; men assume an independence in circumstances, that they do not feel, they continue to court the smiles and good opinion of their neighbours, by a display which their circumstances do not warrant; led on by a false pride, and false maxims of society, they continue to consume their means gradually, and in the decline of life, they are left to penury and want. If you are introduced to the friendship of a man, his eye keenly and rapidly passes over your dress, examines each ornament, and calculates from appearances, on your wealth, and capability to become his equal. In every rank of life, this scrutiny will be found, and the sacrifices made to appearances in society, the false grounds on which fame and credit are established in England, are ever objects of animadversion. Money, therefore, in London is indispensible, and you require more of it for mere comforts, as well as pleasures of life, than in any other city; but at the same time, money there compensates for many defects in mind and person; it brightens a stranger's talent, and gives force and character to his genius; it converts stupidity into fancy and imagination, dulness into wit; in short, it is an infalliable mantle, which covers every defect. Money, in London, passes for more than its value, though it produces less of the real pleasures and benefits of life.

The Englishman, fortified by insurmountable habits, views every other nation with cold indifference; there is no freedom, no institutions, no mode of life so perfect and agreeable, he will tell you, in any other country. Reserved and frequently haughty, they keep foreigners of equal, and sometimes of better mind and qualifications, at a distance, and are deficient in those soft traits, which distinguish a people at once urbane and polite. There is, nevertheless, a sincerity in the friendship of an Englishman, which covers many of his defects; his acts of kindness are extensive and permanent, and when friendship is formed, it is generally predicated on a basis of unlimited confidence; they make but few professions, but their actions are frequently worthy of admiration; to acquire this friendship, you must be long known, thoroughly tested, and go through all the formalities of coldness, repulsion, and haughtiness, before smiles, cordiality, or favour arrives. The English never give credit by anticipation, they must know you well, and you must be content to undergo a probation, if you are desirous of securing their friendship and good will.

English women, have not received from foreign writers, that credit due to their mind, virtues, and person: and although they do not command equal influence with the French, Spaniards, and Italians; although they cannot boast of extraordinary interest at court, they are not less qualified to counsel and controul. With minds generally well cultivated, which are sound without brilliancy, sentimental without affectation, and liberal without prejudice, they may be considered as superior to the men in many of the relations of life. An English woman prides herself upon her domestic qualities, which however humble, are indispensable to real happiness; they seem to know their sphere, and are more than respectable in the bosoms of their family. To complexions the most dazzling, and faces generally beautiful, they unite a disproportion of figure, an awkward gait, and ungraceful mode of dress; they read, principally, light desultory works, and the age of great women in England, may be considered as having passed away; a few celebrated novel writers are all they can now boast of. In London, we live much in the same way as in America, and habits and manners do not differ essentially. To an American, therefore, after visiting the principal objects of curiosity, this city ceases to be interesting; an overgrown capital, with a population equally overgrown; a climate humid, but not unwholesome; crowded streets; and bustle of business; present variety, without producing interest. The approach of night, introduces a new, and the worst portion of its inhabitants, who shun the day, and give evidence of that depravity, long known to exist in London; and this portion of residents neither the severity of law, nor the rigid surveillance of the Police, prevents from pursuing a general course of turpitude and crime. There are several walks and promenades, which are exceedingly beautiful; and among the gardens, it may be questionable, whether one equal to Vauxhall, in taste and splendour, is to be found in any part of the world. To view Vauxhall on a gala evening, filled with a numerous and fashionable audience, illuminated by thousands of variegated lamps, and full and effective orchestras, the scenes of enchantment seem realised. Among the theatres, those of Drury Lane and Covent Garden, have long held a distinguished rank; they are splendid buildings, highly ornamented and embellished, though I was compelled to see them in the day, and consequently to some disadvantage. To give a detailed account of every object of curiosity in London, would of itself occupy a volume, and require no inconsiderable time in visiting. Among the last places of curiosity, which occupied my attention, was Saint Paul's Church, one of the most beautiful specimens of architecture in this city, and probably, next to St. Peter's Church at Rome, the finest in the world; but placed in a narrow space, without the advantage of perspective, and crampt in its position and situation. Here are several well executed monuments, particularly two of Dr. Johnson and Howard; as usual, we paid to see the curiosities, in this Cathedral, and without the talisman, every door would have been closed upon us.

I took my departure from London, after a few weeks residence, not highly pleased, nor yet dissatisfied. With several prejudices eradicated, and with a more favourable opinion of the people, their customs, habits, and manners, than I had hitherto been taught to anticipate; there is much for disapprobation, much to admire, and much to respect, and withal something to disgust; yet on the whole, an American who visits London, with a desire to be pleased with the people, and the city, will not come away disappointed; he will see a moral industrious community, with many honorable institutions, indulging a spirit of intolerance towards every other nation, and in part to their own citizens; he will see a government, powerful in itself, and calculated to make the people happy, pursuing a system in relation to foreign affairs, at once injudicious and impolitic, and wasting their resources in trying times, to liberate continental powers, who intend to be their commercial rivals; he will perceive with regret, that a spirit of commercial and manufacturing monopoly, is undermining the constitution of state and people, and altogether, will feel satisfied, that Great Britain at the present day, has reached the zenith of her glory, and every attempt to add to her present stock, will diminish her resources, and create a decay of her power. With less continental influence, and more domestic efforts, she would find her independence and happiness strengthened, and a decrease of their great national debt, would be the first step, towards securing domestic tranquillity, and internal prosperity.

GEORGE TICKNOR
CULTIVATES LORD BYRON
AND OTHER GREAT SWELLS

1815

Of all American cultural ambassadors to Britain none was more success-ful, or more warmly received, than George Ticknor of Boston. Born with a silver spoon in his mouth, he was able to devote his life to scholarship and philanthropy. He was the first of that remarkable band of Argonauts who after the War of 1812 sought scholarship and culture in the Old World. In 1815, fired by accounts of higher learning in Germany, he left Boston for studies at Göttingen; while he was there Harvard appointed him to the Smith Professor-ship of French and Spanish Literature, and he spent two more years in Italy, Spain, and France preparing himself for that post. He was, when he first arrived in England in 1815, young, handsome, amiable, and rich; he carried with him letters to all the right people; he captivated his hosts and was handed from country house to country house, from club to club. The famous Mrs. Grant of Laggan, who had lived for many years in New York before she returned to Scotland, expressed her delight in the young Americans who were visiting Scotland: "They were the most distinguished representatives of your

From *Life, Letters and Journals of George Ticknor*, George Hillard, ed. (Boston, 1877), I, pp. 57–66.

new world, Mr. Ticknor preeminently so." After his return to Boston in 1819 Ticknor took up his professorship at Harvard and tried, in vain, to remake that university over into an American Göttingen. Retiring in 1835 to devote himself to travel, scholarship, and society, he set up Boston's most famous salon, wrote a three-volume *History of Spanish Literature* that was for long the magisterial work on that subject, and helped found the Boston Public Library. Ticknor defined his purpose in travel as "seeing many different persons, learning their opinion, modifying my own, collecting that sort of undefined and indefinite feeling respecting books and authors, the electric principle that gives life to the dead mass of indifferent knowledge and vigor and spirit to inquiries," and this purpose he amply fulfilled. We give here journal entries from his 1815 and 1819 visits to England.

June 13 [1815]. I breakfasted this morning with Sir Humphry Davy, of whom we have heard so much in America. He is now about thirty-three, but with all the freshness and bloom of five-and-twenty, and one of the handsomest men I have seen in England. He has a great deal of vivacity,—talks rapidly, though with great precision,—and is so much interested in conversation, that his excitement amounts to nervous impatience, and keeps him in constant motion. He has just returned from Italy, and delights to talk of it,—thinks it, next to England, the finest country in the world, and the society of Rome surpassed only by that of London, and says he should not die contented without going there again.

It seemed singular that his taste in this should be so acute, when his professional eminence is in a province so different and remote; but I was much more surprised when I found that the first chemist of his time was a professed angler; and that he thinks, if he were obliged to renounce fishing or philosophy, that he should find the struggle of his choice pretty severe.

Lady Davy was unwell, and when I was there before, she was out, so I have not yet seen the lady of whom Mad. de Staël said, that she has all Corinne's talents without her faults or extravagances.

After breakfast Sir Humphry took me to the Royal Institution, where he used to lecture before he married a woman of fortune and fashion, and where he still goes every day to perform chemical experiments for purposes of research. He showed me the library and model-room, his own laboratory and famous galvanic troughs, and at two o'clock took me to a lecture there, by Sir James Smith, on botany,—very good and very dull. . . .

June 20. I called on Lord Byron to-day, with an introduction from Mr. Gifford. Here, again, my anticipations were mistaken. Instead of being deformed, as I had heard, he is remarkably well built, with the exception of his feet. Instead of having a thin and rather sharp and anxious face, as he has in his pictures, it is round, open, and smiling; his eyes are light, and not black; his air easy and careless, not forward and striking; and I found his manners affable and gentle, the tones of his voice low and conciliating, his conversation gay, pleasant, and interesting in an uncommon degree. I stayed with him about an hour and a half, during which the conversation wandered over many subjects. He talked, of course, a great deal about America; wanted to know what was the state of our literature, how many universities we had, whether we had any poets whom we much valued, and whether we looked upon Barlow as our Homer. He certainly feels a considerable interest in America, and says he intends to visit the United States; but I doubt whether it will not be indefinitely postponed, like his proposed visit to Persia. I answered to all this as if I had spoken to a countryman, and then turned the conversation to his own poems, and particularly to his "English Bards," which he has so effectually suppressed that a copy is not easily to be found. He said he wrote it when he was very young and very angry; which, he added, were "the only circumstances under which a man would write such a satire." When he returned to England, he said, Lord Holland, who treated him with very great kindness, and Rogers, who was his friend, asked him to print no more of it, and therefore he had suppressed it. Since then, he said, he had become acquainted with the persons he had satirized, and whom he then knew only by their books,—was now the friend of Moore, the correspondent of Jeffrey, and intimate with the Wordsworth school, and had a hearty liking for them all,—especially as they did not refuse to know one who had so much abused them. Of all the persons mentioned in this poem, there was not one, he said, with whom he now had any quarrel, except Lord Carlisle; and, as this was a family difference, he supposed it would never be settled. On every account, therefore, he was glad it was out of print; and yet he did not express the least regret when I told him that it was circulated in America almost as extensively as his other poems. As to the poems published during his minority, he said he suppressed them because they were not worth reading, and wondered that our booksellers could find a profit in reprinting them. All this he said without affectation; in fact, just as I now repeat it. He gave great praise to Scott; said he was undoubtedly the first man of his time, and as extraordinary in everything as in poetry,—a lawyer, a fine scholar, endowed with an extraordinary memory, and blessed with the kindest feelings.

Of Gifford, he said it was impossible that a man should have a better disposition; that he was so good-natured that if he ever says a bitter thing in conversation or in a review he does it unconsciously!

Just at this time Sir James Bland Burgess, who had something to do in negotiating Jay's Treaty, came suddenly into the room, and said abruptly, "My lord, my lord, a great battle has been fought in the Low Countries, and Bonaparte is entirely defeated." "But is it true?" said Lord Byron,—"is it true?" "Yes, my lord, it is certainly true; an aide-de-camp arrived in town last night; he has been in Downing Street this morning, and I have just seen him as he was going to Lady Wellington's. He says he thinks Bonaparte is in full retreat towards Paris." After an instant's pause, Lord Byron replied, "I am d—d sorry for it"; and then, after another slight pause, he added, "I didn't know but I might live to see Lord Castlereagh's head on a pole. But I suppose I sha'n't, now." And this was the first impression produced on his impetuous nature by the news of the battle of Waterloo. . . . .

As I was going away, he carried me up stairs, and showed me his library, and collection of Romaic books, which is very rich and very curious; offered me letters for Greece; and, after making an appointment for another visit, took leave of me so cordially that I felt almost at home with him. . . .

While I was there, Lady Byron came in. She is pretty, not beautiful,—for the prevalent expression of her countenance is that of ingenuousness. "Report speaks goldenly of her." She is a baroness in her own right, has a large fortune, is rich in intellectual endowments, is a mathematician, possesses common accomplishments in an uncommon degree, and adds to all this a sweet temper. She was dressed to go and drive, and, after stopping a few moments, went to her carriage. Lord Byron's manner to her was affectionate; he followed her to the door, and shook hands with her, as if he were not to see her for a month. . . .

June 21. At three o'clock, I went to the literary exchange at Murray's bookstore. Gifford was there, as usual, and Sir James Burgess, who, I find, is the man of whom Cumberland so often speaks, and in conjunction with whom he wrote the Exodiad; and before long Lord Byron came in, and stayed out the whole party. I was glad to meet him there; for there I saw him among his fellows and friends,—men with whom he felt intimate, and who felt themselves equal to him. The conversation turned upon the great victory at Waterloo, for which Lord Byron received the satirical congratulations of his ministerial friends with a good-nature which surprised me. He did not, however, disguise his feelings or opinions at all, and maintained stoutly, to the last, that Bonaparte's case was not yet desperate.

He spoke to me of a copy of the American edition of his poems, which I had sent him, and expressed his satisfaction at seeing it in a small form, because in that way, he said, nobody would be prevented from purchasing it. It was in boards, and he said he would not have it bound, for he should prefer to keep it in the same state in which it came from America.

He has very often expressed to me his satisfaction at finding that his works were printed and read in America, with a simplicity which does not savor of vanity in the least. . . .

June 23. We spent half the forenoon in Mr. West's gallery, where he has arranged all the pictures that he still owns. . . . He told us a singular anecdote of Nelson, while we were looking at the picture of his death. Just before he went to sea for the last time, West sat next to him at a large entertainment given to him here, and in the course of the dinner Nelson expressed to Sir William Hamilton his regret, that in his youth he had not acquired some taste for art and some power of discrimination. "But," said he, turning to West, "there is one picture whose power I do feel, I never pass a paintshop where your 'Death of Wolfe' is in the window, without being stopped by it." West, of course, made his acknowledgments, and Nelson went on to ask why he had painted no more like it. "Because, my lord, there are no more subjects," "D—n it," said the sailor, "I didn't think of that," and asked him to take a glass of champagne. "But, my lord, I fear your intrepidity will yet furnish me such another scene; and, if it should, I shall certainly avail myself of it." "Will you?" said Nelson, pouring out bumpers, and touching his glass violently against West's,—"will you, Mr. West? then I hope that I shall die in the next battle." He sailed a few days after, and the result was on the canvas before us.

After leaving Mr. West, I went by appointment to see Lord Byron. He was busy when I first went in, and I found Lady Byron alone. She did not seem so pretty to me as she did the other day; but what she may have lost in regular beauty she made up in variety and expression of countenance during the conversation. She is diffident,—she is very young, not more, I think, than nineteen,—but is obviously possessed of talent, and did not talk at all for display. For the quarter of an hour during which I was with her, she talked upon a considerable variety of subjects,—America, of which she seemed to know considerable; of France, and Greece, with something of her husband's visit there,—and spoke of all with a justness and a light good-humor that would have struck me even in one of whom I had heard nothing.

With Lord Byron I had an extremely pleasant and instructive conversation of above an hour. He is, I think, simple and unaffected. When he speaks of his early follies, he does it with sincerity; of his journeys in Greece and the East, without ostentation; of his own works he talks with modesty, and of those of his rivals, or rather contemporaries, with justice, generosity, and discriminating praise. In everything, as far as I have seen him, he is unlike the characters of his own "Childe Harold" and "Giaour," and yet, those who know him best and longest, say that these stories are but the descriptions of his early excesses, and these imaginary characters but the personification of feelings and passions which have formerly been active, but are now dormant or in abeyance. Of this, of course, I know nothing, but from accounts I have received from respectable sources, and the internal evidence, which I have always thought strongly in favor of them.

This morning I talked with him of Greece, because I wished to know something of the modes of travelling there. He gave me a long, minute, and interesting account of his journeys and adventures, not only in Greece, but in Turkey; described to me the character and empire of Ali Pacha, and told me what I ought to be most anxious to see and investigate in that glorious country. He gave me, indeed, more information on this subject than all I have before gathered from all the sources I have been able to reach; and did it, too, with so much spirit, that it came to me as an intellectual entertainment, as well as a valuable mass of instruction. . . .

June 26. I passed the greater part of this morning with Lord Byron. When I first went in, I again met Lady Byron, and had a very pleasant conversation with her until her carriage came, when her husband bade her the same affectionate farewell that struck me the other day. Soon after I went in, Mrs. Siddons was announced as in an adjoining parlor. Lord Byron asked me if I should not like to see her; and, on my saying I should, carried me in and introduced me to her. She is now, I suppose, sixty years old, and has one of the finest and most spirited countenances, and one of the most dignified and commanding persons, I ever beheld. Her portraits are very faithful as to her general air and outline, but no art can express or imitate the dignity of her manner or the intelligent illumination of her face. Her conversation corresponded well with her person. It is rather stately, but not, I think, affected; and, though accompanied by considerable gesture, not really overacted. She gave a lively description of the horrible ugliness and deformity of David the painter; told us some of her adventures in France, a year ago; and, in speaking of Bonaparte, repeated some powerful lines from the "Venice Preserved," which gave me some intimations of her powers of acting. She formed a singular figure by Lady Byron, who sat by her side, all grace and delicacy, and this showed Mrs. Siddons's masculine powers in the stronger light of comparison and contrast. Her daughter, who was with her, is the handsomest lady I have seen in England. She is about twenty.

EDWARD EVERETT PREPARES
FOR HIS GREAT POSITION

1815

Edward Everett was generally regarded as the most gifted young man in America, and perhaps he was; his career seemed to bear out this early promise yet was somehow, in the end, a disappointment. Graduating from Harvard College in 1811 at the head of his class, he became minister of Boston's fashionable Unitarian Brattle Street Church and then, at the age of twenty-one, was made Eliot Professor of Greek at his university. It was to prepare himself for this position that he went abroad with his friend Ticknor to Göttingen in 1815; there, two years later, he took the first Ph.D. granted to an American student at that famous university. On his return to Boston in 1819 he became editor of the newly founded *North American Review,* and a few years later entered public life with election to the House of Representatives. In 1835 he was elected for the first of four terms as governor of his state; in 1841 he went to Britain as the American Minister; on his return from London he became president of Harvard University; in 1852 he was Secretary of State and went from there to the United States Senate. Like E. A. Robinson's Richard

From MSS. in Massachusetts Historical Society, Everett Papers, Vol. 124.

Cory he glittered when he walked; but he is probably remembered today chiefly as the man who also spoke at Gettysburg. We give here three excerpts from his diary while he was in England in 1815.

He Hears the Charity School Children at St. Paul's

Thursday, June 1 [1815]. I went today to an interesting exhibition, viz.—the assembling of all the charity children from the different schools, in St. Paul's. When it is said all the children, I do not know whether those of the different dissenting schools are included. Very possibly not. The occasion seemed to be one of great publick interest, and the floor of the cathedral, under the dome and the nave of the principal front, to its very remotest part, were early filled and crowded. The spectators were numbered, at from seventeen to twenty thousand, and certainly were a vast multitude to be brought together in one room. I cannot say that the part of the assembly, in which I happened to be cast, was very respectable. The number of the children was from 8 to 10,000, all dressed in an uniform, though each school appeared to have a different one. They came in at different times, each school headed by a boy, carrying the banner of the school, on which generally was emblazoned its name with some emblematical device. Their seats were arranged in the form of an amphitheatre, around the sides of the hall, and the whole aspect of so many children of both sexes; for the number was about equal of each; neatly and uniformly clad, assembled to exhibit in one view at once the sum of want and benevolence, which the great city contains, and to make one great appeal to the humane, was truly powerful. Such was the aspect; but when the services began, and so many children arose at once in the act of devotion, and a concert of so many youthful voices was heard, in prayer and praise, the effect was great and touching. The children had been trained extremely well, and performed the various portions of singing and chanting, that were allotted to them, with remarkable precision and concert. The accommodations for them however were quite inadequate, and very many fainted and were taken out. The quire of singers was large, and the organ apparently fine, but at the opposite entrance of the dome, where I stood, the musick was but faintly heard. Not a word of the prayers or service reached my ear, and we withdrew before the sermon. I do not know that there was more than one thing, which abated the pleasure with which I witnessed the scene. It was the hearing so many infant lips singing praises to God, under a distinction of three persons: a distinction, which whatever ideas of the divine nature it may carry to the minds of those, who are used to refined and metaphysical conceptions and terms, could give none to these children but that of three Gods; and I am well persuaded that all the common people who do not, as I trust multitudes do, secretly and unconsciously hold the strict unity of God, are led by the very name of Trinity, and by those portions of the service where the supposed different persons are separately named or addressed, to conceive of three distinct Gods.

He Meets Sir Joseph Banks, President of the Royal Society

Monday, June 12. George and myself rode out to dine, with Sir Joseph Banks, at his place at Spring Grove, about nine miles from town. . . . (The party consisted only of Sir J. and Lady Banks, the Countess Rumford, our countrywoman; Mrs. Banks, Sir J.'s sister, Sir C. Blagden, Mr. Salisbury, Secretary of the Horticultural Society . . . G. and myself. The present time of year, is that at which Sir J. leaves town for this residence: at the end of August he quits it for his estates in Lincolnshire (which by his success in draining the fens have added £ 8000 a year to his fortune) and returns in November to town. His whole property is said to amount to £ 20000 a year, including £ 5000 a year by his wife, which he resigns entirely to her disposal. His father was an attorney, and having married into the Exeter family obtained the professional patronage of many of the nobility and gentry; till he was able to leave his only son Sir J. the property, which under the economical management of the latter, has grown up to its present size. Sir J. is said to have acquired his first taste for natural science at Eton, where having been on some occasion deserted by his playfellows, he declared that if they could do without him, he could without them, and fell to culling weeds and grasses, and amusing himself by seeing how they were made. He has been married 35 years, and is without children; & when he dies it is supposed his large fortune will go to Sir——Hawley his heir-at-law, a country baronet as old as himself with whom he has only an intercourse of kindred and civility. Sir Joseph received us kindly, and having expressed great regret that Mr. and Mrs. Perkins could not come, proposed a walk. We entered his grounds by a noble manifold towering cedar of Libanus, by far the best specimen, we were informed, in the kingdom. We were taken next to a little pool, quite grown up with the American river-grass, and filled with gold and silver fishes, scarcely less than our tom-cods, which were perfectly tame and fearless. From this we passed to a noble bank of Rhododendrons, that great American favourite in England. Among them was what is commonly called the American Azalia, and what is mentioned as such in the preceeding part of this journal, but which Mr. Salisbury declared to be quite distinct from it and as yet anonymous. He proposed to call it by the name of some great American naturalist, and mentioned Mr. Peck, who spent a day or two at Spring Grove. Sir Joseph Banks spoke of Mr. Buckminster's having been there. A long border of these Azalias, which line it seems the shores of the Black Sea, took us to a splendid assortment of Kalmias; of many kinds and most luxuriant growth and bloom. By their side stood two beautiful——, and when I asked whether the Saracenia could not be gotten to bear them company, it was answered that the Saracenia, did not succeed well in the open air. We saw a Magnolia Conspicua—a large Chinese plant, which was pointed out as unique in the kingdom. This took us to the cranberry bed, formed with great skill, and what is better great success, for growing our cranberry. It is a spot of ground nearly insulated, by a ditch, a foot or two wide, and two or three deep, fed by a spring which bubbles up in the center, and flowing over a marine shell of two or three feet in length, waters the cranberries, and fills the ditch. We passed in succession by the pineries, where a great abundance of pineapples are perfectly matured; flowering in February and coming in rich and fine at the end of August: the melon-beds, laid out on the richest manures, and covered with a hot-house, for the sake of ripening those melons, which we get in the open air: the mushroom-beds, consisting of two or three tiers of cribs, like the berths of a ship, filled with a very strong compost, and kept entirely secluded from the light, and which yield a constant supply of mushrooms to the family; the apricot, peach, and orange houses, the graperies and fruit walls, in all which we saw the choicest productions of the remotest climates, cultivated in perfection side by side. The dairy and china, where centers the pride and beams the taste of Lady Banks, were the next objects to which we were admitted. We entered by a little winding avenue of privet, terminated by a grove of orange shrubs, at once in fruit and flower. The chinaroom presented a show on several shelves, around the four sides, of every grotesque and singular fabrick of China ware, that man could imagine or fabricate. The fine slate coloured marble dresser passed round the room, & a table of the same stood in the middle; and on these were deposited butter and cream of the most tempting appearance. The cows reared on the farm, we understood, to be of what is called the Normandy breed, whose milk, though smaller in quantity, is preferred to that of the common herds. Opening from the chinaroom is the dairy and the universal neatness and nicety were conspicuous, though I was loth to agree with Countess Rumford, that we saw nothing so nice in America. The churn was of a construction resembling the one lately introduced at home, inasmuch as it was a rectangular case; and turned with a crank: but differed from ours, in having within it, a kind of waterwheel, to accelerate the coagulation of the cream. The dairy maid told us it took her a half hour to churn twenty four pounds. I long for an opportunity of attaching a little machinery to one of these churns, by which it should go by water. I cannot but think the butter would be mighty fresh and cool, and on any farm, where there was a fall of a foot or two, in a brook, the thing might be done with all ease. In large dairies it is a great profligacy of labour to churn the butter by hand. We saw little in the remaining kitchen-garden, but a new species of artichoke, existing in three varieties from the Crimea. It was armed with formidable spines, and pronounced by Sir Joseph, "the prickliest divel he had ever seen." This brought about the dinner hour; and dinner was served up in excellent style. Another walk of wider circuit helped us to digest it, and in passing through a hay-field, we were told that as long as Sir J. was able to go about, he had his hay cut as soon as the (pollen) dusted his shoes, in walking through it. Another walk after tea completed our excursion. We admired the rapid growth and luxuriant foliage of the Irish Ivy, which covered a little shady summerhouse in the grounds, cast a farewell glance at the river-grass, and golden fish, and with very many regrets and kind remembrances to Mr. and Mrs. Perkins, together with a magnificent posy for the latter, returned in company with Mr. Salisbury to town.

He Calls Upon Lord Byron

Friday, June 16. Being very anxious to see Lord Byron, and without any immediate prospect of introduction, I determined to introduce myself. I accordingly wrote a letter to him, enclosed a copy of my poem, asking leave to do in a single case, what he had done in such multitudes, to introduce myself, by means of my poem. I then told him, who I was, and asked leave to pay my respects to him, requesting him after all, if the application were too abrupt to be granted, to have the goodness to forget that it was made, as I did not yet despair of becoming a *friend* of his Lordship, in the *regular way*. Having sent this despatch, which I felt of as much importance, as ministers did the last from Lord Wellington, I went to Mr. Vaughan's to dine. . . .

Sunday, June 18. I called at the appointed hour upon Lord Byron, whom I found in a very pleasant situation No. 13 Picadilly Terrace. He was in a parlour, but surrounded with the apparatus for writing. His countenance, though certainly not so beautiful as some of the pictures have represented it, is very fine. His hair short, jet black and closely curled over his head: his complexion entirely white, without the least bloom: his forehead not uncommonly high, but erect and manly, his eye not black but inexpressibly mild and soft; and his mouth very sweet, especially when smiling, are the most obvious traits in his appearance. His usual tone of voice is very low, and even indistinct, at the close of sentences: but yet when expressing some idea, that has just occurred to his mind, or in which he feels particular interest, his voice rises two or three octaves, to a very shrill and piercing note. Some gentlemen were just leaving his room, as I entered, and notwithstanding the irregularity of my introduction to him, or rather my want of introduction, he received me with great kindness. "Your lordship is very kind," said I, "to indulge me with this interview." "I am very happy," said he, "to have the pleasure of making your acquaintance," and immediately commenced a conversation upon the subjects most natural—how long since I had left home—how soon I would go to the continent—and what parts of it I hoped to visit. He recommended Greece very strongly: he had lived among them, in their own way, wearing their own dress, speaking their language, and having all his servants of the country; and besides all the objects of interest connected with the history of the country, he was fond of the freedom of their private life—its frankness and unceremoniousness. He would not have left it, he said, but for domestick affairs; and would rather go there again, than to any other foreign place, which he had not seen. He inquired of the American expedition against Algiers, and said he knew the barbarians well, and hoped we should exterminate them. He asked about the habits of our people, with respect to the interest they took in politicks and literature—and discovered considerable acquaintance with the state of our society. He said he had been a schoolfellow at Harrow with C. King. He was surprised, he said, at the virulence, with which Moore had attacked the Americans, for that he was one of the sweetest tempered, and best humoured men, he had ever known; he was very much attached to him, and was sorry he was not in town, for he should have been very happy to have made me acquainted with him. Scott he knew quite well, and when I asked if he was a reviewer, meaning an Edinburgh Reviewer, he replied in a laugh, "They are all reviewers." Scott was formerly an Edinboro' and now a Quarterly: there are twenty or thirty Reviews—and who is so poor as to be beneath them all? He corresponded, he said, with Jeffrey, although he had never seen him: nor had he been to Scotland since his boyhood. He observed that I looked very young for a professor, and asked how long I had preached; and if it were a fair question, what my opinions were. When I said, "Unitarian,"—"Ah," said he, "we have them here—a terrible heresy; they are thought worse than Socinians." I then explained in what respect those in England differed from us: and in what different publick estimation they are held. I asked him whether his poem, which he speaks of as "printed but not published," in the notes to the *Corsair,* would ever be given to the world. "Oh, no," he replied, "it was a satire on Lord Elgin, which a particular friend of each had begged him to suppress." I mentioned Lord E's petition to Parliament to buy his marbles, and Lord B. said, "You have been then to Parliament: whom have you heard—Grattan? Plunkett?" "No, but I have heard Whitbread."—"He's good."—"I have heard Horner." "Horner's very good."—"Lord Castlereagh." A terrible shrug of the shoulders was the reply, followed by, "I trust to live to see his head upon a pike yet, and if Lord Wellington should be defeated in Holland, as it is very problematical, whether he be or not, we should have woeful scenes in England." He said that Southey's *Don Roderick* was thought his best piece and that though he was not a favourite in England, his works regularly rose in reputation from year to year. He added that he had changed his politicks and was a mere courtier. Campbell he said had lately received a legacy of £5000 and was much improved in his circumstances by it. When I rose to go, Lord B. said he would furnish me with any letters in his power, particularly to M. Fauvel, Lusieri, and Ali Pacha—to which last, he wished, he said, to send some presents in return, for what he had lately received from him, and should be very glad to do it by my hands. I am to call upon him again next Thursday, and hope I shall have an opportunity of seeing Lady Byron. She is represented as a beautiful young woman—the daughter of a country member of Parliament, heiress of a fortune, and upon the death of her mother, viscountess in her own right. She is mistress of Latin, and a little acquainted with the Greek, and it is said that her acquirements in mathematicks are very great. To all these she unites the manners and graces which become her sex and rank.

Sunday, June 25. I called in the P.M. upon Lord Byron who was very kind and agreeable. He told me that he was twenty-seven years old last February; that he had found his opinions and feelings wonderfully altered since his youth upon all subjects; and said I should experience a similar change. He thought his *English Bards and Scotch Reviewers*—though he had endeavoured to suppress it and was professedly reconciled to the persons mentioned in it—would never be really forgiven by them: men do not get over things so easily. He suppressed it upon the representation of Rogers that it was an unnecessary injury to Lord and Lady Holland. He repelled the suggestion that he had done it to conciliate Jeffrey, adding that it was done before the *Edinburgh Review* of *Childe Harold.* He spoke in very high terms of Jeffrey, as a man of independence and magnanimity. After the review of *Childe Harold* had been published, Jeffrey sent a verbal message to Lord B., telling him that he was not the author of the original review, and thought their hostility unbecoming them both. Lord B. wrote to him upon this, explaining the feelings and impressions with which he had written the satire, and informing him that he had already suppressed it. Since then they have corresponded. He showed me some of the Athenian hemlock, and a cross given him by the Superior of the convent at Athens where he resided. I remarked upon the splendour of his seal which lay by us upon the table, and he inquired if it was not too aristocratic for a republican taste. Upon my saying that though a Republican myself, I thought there were advantages in a privileged order, that they were the sources of a patronage which could not otherwise exist; he quoted Johnson's couplet "See what ills &c." I said I supposed if I lived in a country, where there was a nobility, I should wish to be a nobleman: he said laughing that there was no advantage in it, but getting called "My Lord," and added seriously that the principal privelege of nobility was the seat in Parliament. He had never spoken he said but twice, once on the Catholic question: they accused him of saying saucy things. He gave me a written order for admission the next day—which however an engagement prevented me from using. He spoke of my poem and said if I wrote anything while in Germany, and would send it to him, he would get it published, without causing any delay or interruption on my travels.

mother, viscountess in her own right. She is mistress of Latin, and a little
Upon my mentioning the copy of his works, which he had given me,
he said he was sorry that he had not a copy of the second edition of
English Bards and Scotch Reviewers, to add to them. Having given me
the letters for T. and myself to Greece, he expressed the hope of
more acquaintance hereafter, and I bade him goodbye.

JOSEPH BALLARD:

"HERE WERE IMPRISONED

FIFTY WRETCHED BOYS

AND GIRLS"

1815

Here we have the first of many impressions of outraged shock at the spectacle of child labor and the wretched conditions of life among the working classes of Britain. It was a note that was to persist down to such books as Jack London's *People of the Abyss,* and to constitute, in a sense, the American counterpart to the animadversions of British travelers on American slavery. Yet Ballard is more ready than most travelers to confess shortcomings in his judgments. "Business," he says, "was my only object in visiting England. In my leisure moments I noted down the observations which I wish considered as the casual ones of a stranger . . . I am sensible that many things appeared to me different from what they otherwise would have done had I sufficient leisure to make further researches." Ballard, who had joined the English mercantile firm of Standrast Smith in 1803, eventually became its Boston partner.

Warrington is a manufacturing town. The manufactures consist of glass-houses, iron foundries, cotton works, breweries, &c. It has a

From Joseph Ballard, *England in 1815 as Seen by a Young Boston Merchant* (Boston, 1913), pp. 13–15, 24–25, 69, 76–79.

gloomy dirty appearance in consequence of these works and the quantity of coal used in them. A large part of its inhabitants subsist by their daily labor in these manufactories. It was late in the evening when I arrived. Opposite the inn were assembled a vast crowd of these workmen having (as it was Saturday night) received their weekly wages. This they were spending in ale which soon intoxicated a greater part and such a scene of riot ensued as I shall not attempt to describe. These men are generally intemperate: were it not for this habit they might live quite comfortably on their wages. As it is, their families are starving for food while they are spending all they can in drink. Saturday night does not satisfy them. Sunday and Monday which is called "blue" or "St. Monday" is kept the same, nor can any emergency of business whatever call them to resume their work if their last week's wages are not all spent. The old women seen in the streets are the most shocking looking creatures I ever beheld. I have seen them clothed in a man's hat and a short jacket over their gowns driving a little jackass through the town shewing such a countenance as to bring immediately to one's mind Shakespeare's scene of the witches in Macbeth. There is also an incredible number of children from two to four years of age swarming the street in such a state of nudity and uncleanliness as is quite disgusting. These wretched little beings are at quite an early age buried in the manufactories. I saw some in one who were not seven years of age. They had scarcely a rag to cover them. These poor little wretches earn sixty-seven cents a week! Could but the advocates of the manufactures of our country but witness the misery attached to those in Warrington, Sheffield, & Leeds, I am sure they would not so strenuously argue that it is for our national welfare that they should be established in America. . . .

At dusk arrived at Sheffield and sat myself down a solitary being in the travellers' room. I should have preferred the society of a favorite dog or cat to have passed away the "lagging moments" which were to me almost unsupportable. The next day visited some manufactories of cutlery, &c. &c. The manufactories of steel are brought to wonderful perfection. I saw twenty pairs of scissors so small that they were kept in a quill of the common size. The town is surrounded by hills, and were it not for its almost infernal smoke and fire, it would be quite pleasant. The inhabitants of this place partake of the misery resulting from manufactures. The poorer classes are worse off for the articles which they immediately manufacture than the inhabitants of the American back settlements are. Many children not eight years of age are at work in these cursed holes, deprived of education; they consequently grow up in ignorance, and all the comfort or pleasure they have is in drunkenness and sensuality. Many of these little wretches are sent from London workhouses to these manufacturing towns. Often has my heart bled to see a poor little sickly being hard at work, deprived of liberty and fresh air, when its situation demanded the indulgent care of a tender nurse. . . .

At a manufactory I saw the different operations from the beginning to the finishing of a piece of cloth. The whole machinery was put in force by a steam engine which cost the proprietor one thousand guineas. Here also were imprisoned about fifty wretched boys and girls, the eldest not over ten years of age. They were all besmeared with dirt and grease arising from the wool. The proprietor observed in reply to my asking him if they never went to play, that they were there at six in the morning and never left off work, except for dinner, until seven at night. Thus these poor little wretches are confined in these hells—for I cannot find a more appropriate name—deprived of education and buried in these dark, noisy and unwholesome dens. They either pass a quick but miserable existence or furnish turbulent, ignorant and vicious members of society.

May 22. Departed this morning in the coach for Manchester. The passengers were three agreeable ladies and a clever loquacious Scotsman. The last person was a great admirer of Doctor Franklin, whose works he had by heart and most liberally quoted from. . . .

At a small village before we entered Rochdale it was their market day. The streets were crowded with women, men and children, the ugliest, dirtiest wretches I ever beheld! The women in particular were the most shocking. Old and young had on large caps with two flaps at each side which hung down to their shoulders. On our appearance in the coach a mob of children were immediately let loose to chase after us to beg a penny. When we entered the suburbs of Manchester the atmosphere underwent a total change; from its being very clear weather it became dull and foggy. The smoke which perpetually overhangs this city is the cause of it. The next day it rained incessantly. It seems as if this were forever the case. An anecdote is related of a foreigner asking a person from Manchester whether or not it had done raining yet! This city like almost all the large towns in Great Britain has an infirmary for the reception of the indigent sick. The building is placed in a fine situation and is a handsome structure. The people of this country are renowned for their charities. There is scarcely a place where there is not some institution supported by private munificence for the relief of the poor. They first are compelled to give largely by the "poor laws"; to this are added immense voluntary contributions. Were it not for these donations the streets would swarm with beggars; as it is, there are in the large towns a great many. I remarked an advertisement stuck upon the walls by the civil authority offering two guineas reward each for the apprehension of thirty-seven men who had absconded and left their families upon the parish! This is one of the blessings of manufactories!

WILLIAM PRESTON:
"BEGGARY, STARVATION,
CRIME AND PUNISHMENT
WERE ON EVERY SIDE"

c. 1816

William Preston was one of the "distinguished" young men who won the approbation of Mrs. Grant of Laggan. He had graduated from Washington College in Virginia at the age of fourteen, and later studied law with the great William Wirt. In 1816 he went abroad in search of health and education, rooming with Hugh Legaré at Edinburgh University; he returned to the practice of law and to a distinguished career in state and national politics and became, eventually, president of the University of South Carolina. Preston was about twenty years old when he made the visit to Britain which he here recalls.

In May I sailed for England, in the good Quaker ship Amité one of (a) line owned by a company of Quakers, Lawrence and Co. The passengers were numerous, of all countries and entirely uninteresting. I don't believe I remember the name of one. A

From *The Reminiscences of William C. Preston*, Minnie Yarborough, ed. (Chapel Hill, 1933), pp. 23–28, 31–34.

run of 30 days brought us to the coast of Ireland, off the Cove of Cork. On a bright fair summer morning we hastened to the deck to rejoice our eyes with the sight of land, and in a few minutes came alongside a fishing smack to sell fish. While the Captain was bargaining for them, I was ready to get aboard, had engaged the fisherman to carry me up to Cork, and taking what coin I had or could borrow, with a single trunk of clothes, and leaving my letters and everything aboard, I determined to run thro Ireland, and meet my companions of the voyage at Liverpool.

There is hardly in the world anything more beautiful than the Cove of Cork, with its sloping banks of grass down to the water's edge. To my sea wearied eyes, it affected me with rapturous delight. One of the boatmen had lost an eye, another a leg, and all the four were as rough and squalid a set as I had ever seen, but they were animated by a certain quizzical good temper, which seemed amused at my raptures and delight and the eager questions I put about every object seen on the shore as we passed. Seeing a little boat house with a painted boat lying near it, I asked to be put ashore that I might look at it. The man at the helm said, "Our time, your honour, is valuable to us." "Then," said I, "here's half a crown. Give me that much of it." "That's an hour," said he, "and you may have as many as you please at that price." So we drove up beside the little wharf and stepping on the earth, I reeled off, nearly falling, the boatmen exclaiming, "Take care of your sea legs." I threw myself upon the rich sod and wallowed in it with delight. Such a sod. Soft, thick, and of pure emerald green, I had never seen any thing like it, nor as I think since. As we neared the City I asked where they would recommend me to put up. They answered—"The Captain told us to take you to the 'Duke's Arms' and get a receipt for me." So to the Duke's Arms I went, and as I handed a couple of crown pieces, One Leg said, touching his hat, "It is your honour's generosity, not our charge. God bless you. I wish I was in your free country with you." . . .

From my windows the next morning, looking upon the public square I found it covered with a dense crowd of sturdy and stalwart peasants, with a patient but surly air. They filled the enclosure of the square like cattle in a pound. Upon going down to ascertain the meaning of the assembly I found they were labouring countrymen from the surrounding neighborhood who had come in to see if they could get employment in the then approaching harvest. Some were provided with scythes and others with other implements of labour. They stood there all day. Some seemed to be provided with a scant allowance of food, many apparently without any. I went in amongst them. Several were employed by gentlemen, who came and inspected them and took such as they fancied. There was, as I could perceive, no bargaining. The gentleman said, "I will take you and you." I suppose the hire was fixed and known. Those selected stepped forward with an air of alacrity and followed the employer. Many of them said they were hungry, and all looked so. A cart of bread passed by. I told one with whom I was talking to buy it for me and divide the bread amongst them. He stepped forward and said, "What will you take for the bread in the cart?" The driver hesitated to answer, and my man perceiving it, pointed to me. Upon seeing me the driver said, "a guinea." My man said, "I will give you 15 shillings which is more than you and your bread, and scrawny cattle are all worth." "The bread is yours," said the driver. "I would not take it from you, you scalper, but from the gentleman," bowing to me. So the bread was distributed, and my man said, "I have saved your honour six shillings which I will buy for you in beer, from yonder shop as sure, your honour, the bread is very dry." The beer was brought in three tin buckets, with a couple of tankards. As he took the first draught he said, "Here's to your honour, and to your noble Country of America. Long life to you." All round the square were crowds of women and children, most importunate beggars. I was glad to retreat when my last copper was exhausted.

Late in the evening I got into the Clonmel coach, on my way for Dublin. It was a superb vehicle drawn by four spanking horses. Besides the coachman, a great fat man rolled up in a drab great coat, there was on the rear of the coach an equally fat man in a bright red wescoat with metal buttons; he I understood was the guard. He had two large pistols in his belt and a carbine lying on the coach before him. The lamps were lighted and as we left the City a file of dragoons rode up on either side. Thus attended, we proceeded at a moderate pace of about five miles an hour. The closing in of dusk gave me an opportunity of reflecting upon the novelty of my situation. From my fellow passengers I learned that the reason of the military escort, was for protection through a country of extreme disorganization and turbulence which had been recently put under the ban of the insurrection law, called the Peel Act. Curious to see a population in this condition of turbulence and enforced suppression, I left the coach at Clonmel that I might in the first place visit Cahir Castle and Cahir Cottage in the neighborhood and then traverse leisurely the disaffected territory. Cahir Cottage is an exquisite exhibition of taste and luxury, built on the summit of a rock, round which is made earth for shrubbery and gardens, the rock is perforated through and through by galleries and grottos—and the gem of a house finished and furnished with whatever the wantonness of wealth could buy. The neighborhood was in a state of starvation and necessarily so demoralized that there were daily shooting and hanging. There were several gibbets from which bodies were dangling, one having as many as three. By the Peel Act, as I understand, a military police was stationed in the country with power to arrest and try summarily before a court-martial persons suspected of crime or misdemeanor, with power to shoot, hang or transport them. One of the provisions of the act was that a person found out of his prescribed bounds between Sun and Sun, without a satisfactory excuse should be transported. Cahir Castle was the first I saw of those large stone monuments of feudal times, which had always filled my imagination with wonder and romance. This specimen is a very fine one, a noble wreck in ruinous perfection. I never passed near one of these old monuments without turning aside to contemplate it. Passing thro the counties of Limerick and Tipperary, I often saw peasants flying from the approach of my carriage and when I visited a hut the man slipped out the back way and the surly women would pretend not to understand English. An assurance that I was not a *Peeler,* but an American, generally restored confidence, which was confirmed when I gave a sixpence. The interior of the huts was of indescribable squalor, revolting and horrid—in one corner generally a pile of half rotted potatoes, at the door sill a mud hole, piles of filthy rags in the corners, children naked, and not one article of comfort or necessity. Thro such scenes I passed on to Tipperary and Limerick and then took my way to Dublin. My route lay thro a fine country, the lands were rich and highly cultivated, and the landscape beautiful. Beggary, starvation, crime, and punishment were on every side.

As I got into Dublin on an evening the drunken postilion had so exhausted his horses that at the head of the street they refused to go and when beating was obviously ineffectual I got out, upbraided him and refused to give him the customary fee, as by his misconduct he put me down in the street instead of taking me on to the hotel. We of course had a controversy, in which I was like to get the worse when there drove up two gentlemen in a jaunting car, who chid the ruffian with an air of authority, and offered me a seat in the car down to the Hibernian hotel. To my lavish expression of thanks they replied it was only what was due to a stranger, a gentleman, and that they were more than repaid by making the acquaintance of an American. That evening I went to the theatre and heard Braham sing, "Scots Wha Hae with Wallace" and "Love's Young Dream." In Dublin I had no acquaintances, and no letters to make any as it had not been in the project of my route. After breakfast next morning as I was walking in a somewhat disconsolate mood thro the reading room, to my utter surprise and unbounded delight I met my friend and kinsman Mr. Edward Coles, who, as it turned out, was going on a secret mission from the President to the Czar of Russia to accommode some recent offence given to that court. Coles had letters of introduction and money, both of which I wanted, for the small quantity of coin I had brought from the ship had been drawn from me by the beggary and want along the road. My letters of credit were upon Liverpool. . . .

When I got to the wharf to take the packet for Holyhead, a piteous spectacle was presented. It was a jam of poor and sturdy peasants, trying to get on board for going over to England, to get work in the harvest. The owner of the packet had put the passage at half price and at the instant that the bar was removed enough to cover the whole deck rushed on, many who were not able to pay and when notice being given that such should not be landed at Holyhead, many struggled back. As it was the crowd aboard was prodigious and squalid. The pay passengers bought all the bread in the vessel for their use, and I was drained of my money so as to leave barely enough for me to get to Liverpool on the outside of the coach. When I got there I had but two and sixpence in my pocket. It rained heavily and incessantly the whole way and before we got to the City I was seized with a chill which shook me with great violence. The Coachie seeing it, proposed at one of his drinking places that I should have a glass of hot negus, which may have been a wrong prescription but it gave me presence of mind to tell him that when we got to the City I desired to be driven to the King's Arms and that I was an American. This was a lucky communication for me, for a fever coming on I was somewhat delirious when we got to the King's Arms and lost all consciousness when I was carried into the house, nor had I the slightest recollection for some days. When my delirium passed off at length it was suddenly, and rising on my elbow in bed, I saw standing near me a rosy cheeked, tidy looking girl. Looking at her a moment, and endeavoring to recall my consciousness, I said, "Rosebud, who are you?" She dropped a little curtsey and said in a startled voice, "I am not Rosebud, your honour. My name is Betty," and she left the room. While I was trying to find out if I were not dreaming, the girl returned with a small gentleman dressed in black, (who) said to me in a kind tone: "The doctor said if the anodyne had its expected effect you would probably awake relieved. I hope it is so." "I do not know," said I. "I know nothing about it. Where am I?"

He said, "I am your countryman, Washington Irving," and gave me to understand that being ill and delirious at the King's Arms, they had sent for the United States Consul, who, opening my trunk, found my letters one of which was an introduction to him from Mr. Jefferson,—he took possession of me and my effects, employed a Doctor and had me transferred to private lodgings, where he with Mr. Irving and Mr. Brown the banker had been in attendance on me. While we yet talked, Mr. Maury the venerable old gentleman, came in, having been sent for. He extended his arms over me, and said, "Thank God, young man, I hear you are recovered, but I must continue to have jurisdiction over you until you grow strong. For the present you must lie still until the Doctor gives permission." A day or two brought the permission. The excellent old gentleman took me to his own house where I was under the care of his family and had daily visits from Mr. Irving and other Countrymen. . . .

The tenderness and attention which I received from Mr. Irving were consistent with his kind and generous nature. I found him a man of grave, indeed a melancholy aspect, of very staid manners, his kindness rather the offspring of principle and cultivated taste than of emotion. There was an unfailing air of moderation about him, his dress was punctilious, his tone of talking, soft and firm, and in general over subdued, until a natural turn would occasionally run into humour, and laughable delineation of character or events. During my convalescence, which was somewhat tedious, our acquaintance ripened into some degree of intimacy and I freely disclosed to him my condition, my plans, and my purposes. He was eight years my senior, had seen a good deal of society and had made for himself an honourable name. He was then eminently fit to exercise a large influence over me,—especially in restraining the exuberance of my national and natural temper. Of that characteristic of our country he had great dread and distaste. It was foreign to his peculiar idiosyncrasy—he called it whether in conduct or in conversation or in writing *Americanizing* and in himself pushed his opposition to this tendency to the extent almost of affectation. He had a great deal of the English reticence. With them it is, as it was not with him, a surly and ill mannered and unsympathyzing manner. It is a national character resulting from the false and foolish notion that true dignity is to be always on the watch for aggression and that *nihil admirari* is elegant and aristocratic. All emotion is vulgar and ardor horrible. Towards this Anglicism there was some little tendency in Irving—propriety, fitness, retention were what he admired. His great kindness to me made him sensible of my defects in these particulars, and he was free in his animadversions after we had become familiar. I vindicated myself upon the ground that they were nationalities, but he replied that they were wrong nationalities and ought to be suppressed in a gentleman,—that to suppress such things was one object of travel. Although in the warmth of such discussions Mr. Irving occasionally grew warm, and I did not seem to yield, yet he soon became cool and upon subsequent reflection I saw much truth in what he said. . . .

JOHN QUINCY ADAMS
DISCUSSES REFORM
AND REVOLUTION
WITH JEREMY BENTHAM

1817

John Quincy Adams is too well known to require any elaborate introduction. As a mere boy he had been with his father, John Adams, in Holland and Paris at the time of peacemaking with the Mother Country. He returned to the study and practice of law, and was then appointed Boylston Professor at Harvard University. Soon thereafter he was elected Senator from Massachusetts but in 1808 resigned in protest against the policies of his party and in time became an accepted member of the Republican-Democratic party. Madison sent him as Minister to St. Petersburg and in 1811 nominated him for the Supreme Court, a position which he refused. In 1813 he was appointed head of the American delegation to negotiate peace with Britain and at the end of the next year he and his fellow commissioners, Gallatin, Clay, Bayard, and Russell, concluded what must be considered one of the most successful peace negotiations in history, for the British surrendered all their demands and conceded every American demand. A grateful President promptly named Adams Minister to the Court of St. James's, a post which, like his father before him and his son after him, he occupied unwillingly and left with relief.

From *Memoirs of John Quincy Adams, Comprising portions of his Diary from 1795 to 1848,* Charles Francis Adams, ed. (Philadelphia, 1874), III, pp. 534–539, 562–563.

Adams—again it was a family trait—was an indefatigable diarist. Instead of his elaborate comments on diplomacy, we read here his report of conversations with Jeremy Bentham. Bentham's Utilitarian philosophy never commanded much attention in America (perhaps because it was the common sense of the matter), but his contributions to ethics, jurisprudence, and penal reform did.

[May] *20th* [1817]. I went to the House of Commons, and heard the debate upon Sir Francis Burdett's motion for the appointment of a committee to consider and report a plan for a reform in the mode of election for the Commons House of Parliament. It was with some difficulty that I obtained admission for my son George. Mr. Patterson came under the gallery. We went in about eight o'clock, and found Sir Francis drawing towards the conclusion of his speech, which was temperate and much less animated than I had expected. He appeared as if overwhelmed by the majority which he knew there would be against his motion in that House, and as if the suspension of the Habeas Corpus Act had been passed purposely for him. The motion was seconded by Mr. Brand, who made a short speech in support of it, in no wise remarkable. . . . The most vehement and bitterest speech was made by Lord Cochrane in favor of reform, and the most splendid and eloquent one against it by Mr. Ward. Cochrane's consisted of little more than sarcasm and invective. Ward's was in its principal parts prepared, and doubtless composed beforehand. He was two hours in delivering it, and has certainly no natural fluency. He speaks slow, repeats the greater part of almost every sentence, utters the whole with much hesitation, makes wry faces, and sucks oranges. His speech, however, was as powerful an argument as the cause which he supports could produce. He gave a just and very severe character of the Whigs, or, as they style themselves, the Moderate Reformers in Parliament, who, he observed, were utterly disavowed and contemned by the Radical Reformers without-doors. The real object of the Radical Reformer, he said, was a revolution, the very idea of which was his abhorrence. To prove that revolution was the object of the Radical Reformers, he pulled from his pocket the book published last Saturday by Mr. Jeremy Bentham, called the Catechism of Reform, and read several passages from it, which excited great laughter in the House. He observed that the book having been put into his hands only this morning, he had not had time to read it, and the quotations which he had read were adduced only to show the tendency of the doctrines in the book. He spoke in very respectful terms of Mr. Bentham, both in regard to his abilities and his integrity. But this very book is the boldest and most vehement argument for radical reform that has yet appeared in print. Bentham told me that he had found some difficulty in getting it printed, and was finally obliged to put his name to it, which he had not intended. Mr. Ward could not have chosen his proof better than by quoting this book to show that revolution is the real object of the Radical Reformers. He read particularly one passage, where the author insists that the Reformers ought to be satisfied with nothing less than the *ascendency* of the democratic part of the Constitution. Ward declared himself satisfied with the Constitution as it is. He deprecates all experimental innovation. He is willing to judge of the tree by its fruits. He finds that this Constitution has raised England to greatness and glory; that it has led to the triumphs of her navy and the victories of her armies: that it has raised her to high consideration and influence among the nations of the earth; and so riveted is he to all her institutions that in the system of her elections he considers Old Sarum as essential as Yorkshire. Sir Samuel Romilly and Mr. Tierney answered Ward, principally by personal reflections. Ward is what they call a rat. He was formerly a Whig, and has turned Tory. Romilly said no other answer was necessary to his speech than a reference to his own speeches in former sessions of Parliament. Romilly complained that it was unfair in Ward to read quotations from Bentham's book, but he did not show why. I thought them very much to the purpose. With a high panegyric of Bentham, Romilly said he regretted exceedingly his having published that book. Tierney was also sarcastic upon Ward's premeditated speech, and its inconsistency with his speeches in former times; but he did not answer it. He declared himself in favor of moderate reform, and of the present motion, though he had no hopes it would succeed, and he greatly lamented the excesses of the deluded Radical Reformers, because their effect was to render all reform impracticable. Sir Francis Burdett made no reply. The House was cleared for taking the question about two in the morning, when I came home. The motion was rejected by a majority of four or five to one.

22d. I took a walk this morning with J. Bentham through Hyde Park and Kensington Garden, in the course of which I had much conversation with him upon his political opinions and views, and upon the situation and prospects of this country. I mentioned to him the notice taken in the House of Commons of his Catechism of

Reform the evening before last, the quotations and comments of Mr. Ward, and the remark upon it of Sir Samuel Romilly. Bentham writes in a very peculiar style, and uses a multitude of words of his own coining. Ward said it was a sort of lingua franca—no language of itself, but a compound from various tongues, in which, however, an approximation of meaning was to be obtained.

Bentham said that was a fair joke, with which he was very well pleased, but he always took the privilege of coining words when they were necessary to express his ideas. He was much obliged to Mr. Ward, both for the respectful manner in which he had spoken of his personal character, which from him he had no right to have expected, and for the quotations which he had read from his book, because that would bring it more immediately into public notice. It was singular that the reference to the book should have been made from that quarter, which was totally unexpected to him, while it had not been even mentioned by Sir Francis Burdett, from whom he had expected that something of it would have been said. But Sir Francis himself was not an efficient Reformer. He was rich. His education had been bad. He was, above all, indolent. There was no steady reliance to be placed upon him. As to Sir Samuel Romilly, who was his intimate friend, he (Bentham) knew that he would not be pleased with the book. Romilly was a Whig, and the Whigs, as a party, were just as corrupt and just as averse to reform as their adversaries. I told him with how much keenness and severity they had been characterized by Mr. Ward, and he said they deserved it all.

I then remarked to him upon the force with which Mr. Ward argued that the real object of the Radical Reformers was revolution, and intimated to him my impression that it was so. And, recurring particularly to the passage of the book where the Reformers are exhorted to be satisfied with nothing short of democratic ascendency, I asked him how he could reconcile that even with the sound theory of the British Constitution, which I conceived to be a balance between the monarchical, aristocratical, and democratical branches, forbidding the ascendency of either of them. . . . He said the ascendency of one part did not necessarily imply the destruction of the others; that in regard to religious affairs, Protestant ascendency was established by law, yet the Roman Catholic religion was tolerated. As to the ascendency of one branch of the Government over the others, that existed in the present state of things, or rather the combination of the Crown and the aristocracy overpowered the democracy to such a degree that the popular check upon them was a mere name.

The liberties of the country were utterly gone—gone forever, unless the ascendency of the democracy could be substituted for that which now predominated.

I told him I thought this neither demonstrated nor necessary to the cause of reform; that the only principle upon which reform could be pursued distinctly from revolution appeared to me to be that of restoring democracy to its equal share of power, or removing the existing ascendency, but without substituting the other in its stead. I asked him whether he thought it possible for the monarchy and aristocracy to subsist at all with his democratic ascendency. . . .

I said that was very well so far as his own opinion and conduct were concerned; but, whatever might be the advantages of reform, it must, in the most favorable of all contingencies, be introduced by intrenching upon the principle of "uti possidetis." It must take franchises or property from somebody. The disfranchisement of Old Sarum itself could not be effected without violating the principle of "uti possidetis." He, to be sure, would stop at the point where democratic ascendency should be established, and then would let in the principle of "uti possidetis" to guard the remnant of power left to the Crown and the Peers. But let him suppose a Parliament assembled, with a reformed House of Commons, possessing the ascendency which his book recommends. Did he think that House of Commons would feel themselves restrained from encroachments upon their co-ordinate, but not coequal, authorities by his international principle of the "uti possidetis"?

He did not maintain that they would. And what if they should put down the Crown and the Peerage? said he. Is your Government in America the worse for having neither King nor Lords? Or are you exclusively entitled to the enjoyment of good government, and must you begrudge it to others? I said he was joking to escape from the consequences of his own argument. The question was not between the comparative merits of the British and American Governments, but whether a radical reform in England does not involve an inevitable revolution. I considered him now as having conceded that reform, with his democratic ascendency, would lead to the abolition of the Crown and Peerage. But these institutions were too powerful and too deeply rooted to perish without a struggle; and what would be the consequences of that?

He said, probably a civil war. Upon the whole, it was likely that no great and real reform could be effected in England without a civil war. Corruption had so pervaded the whole mass of the Government, and had so vitiated the character of the people, that he was afraid they could be purified only by fire. But anything was better than the present state of things, and that in which it must terminate, unless a vigorous effort on the part of the people should rescue them from that absolute despotism under which they are sinking.

From this conversation the inference is tolerably clear that Mr. Ward was not mistaken in the views of the Radical Reformers. . . .

[June] *7th*. . . . When I left Castlereagh it was too late for the walk with Mr. Bentham, and instead of going to his house I called upon his friend Place, the tailor and Republican. He keeps a shop in Charing Cross, and is quite prosperous in his trade, notwithstanding his dabbling with politics. Place, who was unwell, received me in his library, two pair of stairs up from his shop. He had a very considerable library, all the shelves of which, that I noticed, were full of books of history and political economy. He told me he was very glad I had rejected that ridiculous proposal of Sir Richard Phillips's to set up and pay for an American newspaper in London. Place asked me where he could procure a volume of the Constitution of the United States, and I promised to send him one. I had given mine to Bentham. Place was much interested about a man named Wooler, a printer, who had just been tried for a libel upon Lord Castlereagh and Mr. Canning in a weekly periodical publication called *The Black Dwarf*. Wooler was tried at the Old Bailey, before Judge Abbott, of the King's Bench. He pleaded his own cause, and astonished a crowded auditory by his eloquence. He was tried upon two informations, upon both of which the Judge strongly charged the jury against him. One of the jurymen of the first jury asked the Judge what they must do if they found the matter charged as libellous true. He said that by the law truth was no justification of a libel. The jury were out several hours without being able to agree. There were three talesmen who stood out for the defendant against nine special jurors still more stiff for the crown. At last the talesmen agreed to a verdict in this form, "As truth has been declared to us to be by law a libel, we of the jury are compelled to find the defendant guilty," but they stipulated that if the Court refused to receive the verdict in that form, the jury should go out again. Instead of this verdict, Abbott, the Judge, ordered a general verdict of guilty to be recorded, and refused to receive the affidavit of the talesmen as to the agreement about the terms in which the verdict was to be delivered. The next day, upon a statement of the facts by Abbott himself in the Court of King's Bench, Lord Ellenborough, in a manner, compelled Chitty, whom Wooler had in the mean time employed as his counsel, to say that he asked for a new trial, and immediately granted it. Subsequently, however, Chitty moved that the defendant should be discharged, which motion still remained to be argued when we left London. Bentham told me that it was a general opinion among the lawyers that Abbott had lost his reputation by his conduct on this occasion. He also told me that if a vacancy should occur in the election for Westminster it was intended to set up Wooler as a candidate. Place told me that if Wooler had not argued his own cause he would certainly have been convicted; that no lawyer would have dared or been suffered to put the cause upon its real and strong point of defence; that Lord Ellenborough, by his overbearing and browbeating control over the Bar, had annihilated the spirit of all the lawyers; that if any lawyer had a pretension to independence, Ellenborough would harass and persecute him till the suitors found out he was not well with the Court, and then no soul would give him a brief. He had in this manner ruined the practice of Brougham and many others. Place said he had often served as a juryman in Courts where Ellenborough presided, and seen much of him, but never without having his most vehement indignation excited by his despotic and insolent control over the lawyers. In all causes of mere property between man and man, he was an able and upright Judge, but in every case where the Court had an interest he was an unprincipled and unblushing despot and oppressor; and they had rewarded him for it by making him a Privy Councillor. It was somewhat curious that, after receiving this character of Ellenborough, Smith and I were on the same day received by him when we went our round of official visits.

RICHARD RUSH:

"THE PARADOXES AND

ANOMALIES OF ENGLISH SOCIETY"

1818

Richard Rush was the son of the more famous Dr. Benjamin Rush, one of the "Signers," one of the Founding Fathers, and the most influential medical teacher in the history of the nation. Young Richard Rush achieved both success and fame on his own: attorney general of Pennsylvania at the age of thirty-one, attorney general of the United States at thirty-four, and successor to John Quincy Adams at the Court of St. James's. Unlike so many of his predecessors, Rush liked England, the Court, and high society, and though he had none of the brilliance or profundity of his immediate predecessor he was successful in solving a number of outstanding diplomatic problems over slavery, the fisheries, the Northwest territories, and in negotiating the important Rush-Bagot agreement for disarmament on the Great Lakes. After his term at London he was sent as Minister to France. Rush, who had been born in 1780, may be said to represent a new generation which found it possible to forget the animosities of the Wars of Independence and of 1812, and to accept England with admiration and pleasure. "Her fame," he wrote of the American

From Richard Rush, *A Residence at the Court of London* (London, 1833), pp. 177–180, 195–203.

in England, "is constantly before him. He hears of her statesmen, her orators, her scholars, her philosophers, her divines, her patriots. In the nursery he learns her ballads. Her poets train his imagination. Her language is his. In spite of political differences her glory allures him."

April 16, 1818. Went to the Court of King's Bench to hear the argument in the case of wager of battle. The parties were present. Through the courtesy of the Judges, I had a seat on the bench, next to Mr. Justice Bayley. On his left was Lord Chief Justice Ellenborough, occupying the seat of the Cokes, the Hales, the Mansfields. To the left of Lord Ellenborough were Mr. Justice Abbot and Mr. Justice Holroyd. If at Lord Hardwicke's I was awake to the associations which the great legal names of England call up, the feeling could not be less here. The room was extremely full. The case was so remarkable as to have become a topic in general society.

By the ancient law of England, when a person was murdered, the nearest relative of the deceased might bring what was called an appeal of death, against the party accused of the murder. Under this proceeding, the accuser and accused fought. The weapons were clubs. The battle began at sun-rise, and was in presence of the Judges; by whom also the dress of the combatants, and all other formalities were arranged. Part of the oath was, that neither combatant would resort to witchcraft. If the accused was slain, it was taken as a proof of his guilt; if the accuser, of his innocence. If the former held out until star-light, that also attested his innocence. If either yielded whilst able to fight, it worked his condemnation and disgrace. Those who wish a full description of the proceedings, may seek it in Sully, or continental writers of an earlier day, as Froissart, the custom having been imported into England by the Normans. My summary will give the general idea.

It was a mode of trial for dark ages. Ashford the appellor, had accused Thornton the appellee, of the murder of one of his relations, and the later desired to fight. In the highest tribunal of the most enlightened country in Europe, I was listening to a discussion whether or not this mode of trial was in force in the nineteenth century! It was difficult to persuade myself of the reality of the scene. . . . Mr. Chitty, a lawyer of eminence, argued against the right of battle. Mr. Tindall had argued on the other side, on a former day. Fleta, Bracton, the Year-books, and other repositories of ancient law, were ransacked. Abundant ability was displayed on both sides. The greatest order prevailed; even gravity. The Judges were in their robes. About seventy lawyers sat in front of them; all in gowns and wigs. Finally, the Judges decided that trial by battle was in force. It had never, it seems, been repealed.

To repeal laws, belongs to the legislature. Courts expound and apply them. Free government is complex, and works slowly; tyranny is simple, and does its work at once. An absurd law may sleep in a free code, because overlooked; but, whilst there, it is the law. It is so, I suppose, that we must reason; and generally the reasoning would be right. Yet it might have been thought, that, in a case like this, long disuse added to obvious absurdity, would have worked the silent repeal of the law; according to the doctrine of *desuetude* under the Roman code.

In the end, no battle was fought. A technical flaw interposed to prevent it, and Parliament passed a repealing statute. But the case marks an incident in English jurisprudence, having come near to converting the Court of King's Bench into another Lyceum of Mendoza. . . .

April 29, 1818. A country is not to be understood by a few months' residence in it. So many component parts go to make up the grand total, where civilization, and freedom, and power, are on a large scale, that the judgment gets perplexed. It pauses for reexamination. It must be slow in coming to conclusions, if it would be right. Often it must change them. A member of the diplomatic corps, an enlightened observer, said to me a few days ago, that, at the end of his first year, he thought he knew England very well. When the third had gone by, he began to have doubts; and that now, after a still longer time, his opinions were more unsettled than ever. Some he had changed entirely; others had undergone modification, and he knew not what fate was before the rest.

There was reason in his remark. If it be not contradictory, I would say, that he showed his judgment in appearing to have at present no judgment at all. The stranger sees in England, prosperity the most amazing, with what seems to strike at the roots of all prosperity. He sees the most profuse expenditure, not by the nobles alone, but large classes besides; and, throughout classes far larger, the most resolute industry supplying its demands and repairing its waste; taxation strained to the utmost, with an ability unparalleled to meet it; pauperism that is startling, with public and private charity unfailing, to feed, clothe, and house it; the boldest freedom, with submission to law; ignorance and crime so widely diffused as to appal, with genius and learning and virtue to reassure; intestine commotions predicted, and never happening; constant complaints of poverty and suffering, with constant increase in aggregate wealth and power. These are some of the anomalies which he sees. How is he at once to pass upon them all? he, a stranger, when the foremost of the natives after studying them a lifetime, do nothing but differ!

One of the things that strike me most, is their press. I live north of Portman Square, nearly three miles from the House of Commons. By nine in the morning, the newspapers are on my breakfast-table, containing the debate of the preceding night. This is the case, though it may have lasted until one, two, or three in the morning. There is no disappointment; hardly a typographical error. The speeches on both sides are given with like care; a mere rule of justice, to be sure, without which the paper would have no credit, but fit to be mentioned where party-feeling always runs as high as in England.

This promptitude is the result of what alone could produce it; an unlimited command of subdivided labour of the hand and mind. The proprietors of the great newspapers employ as many stenographers as they want. One stays until his sheet is full. He proceeds with it to the printing-office, where he is soon followed by another with his; and so on, until the last arrives. Thus the debate as it advances, is in progress of printing, and when finished, is all in type but the last part. Sometimes it will occupy twelve and fourteen broad closely-printed columns. The proprietors enlist the most able pens for editorial articles; and as correspondents, from different parts of Europe. Their ability to do so may be judged of from the fact, that the leading papers pay to the Government an annual tax in stamps, of from twenty to fifty thousand pounds sterling. I have been told that some of them yield a profit of fifteen thousand sterling a-year, after paying this tax, and all expenses. The profits of the *Times,* are said to have exceeded eighteen thousand a-year. The cost of a daily paper to a regular subscriber is about ten pounds sterling a-year. But subdivision comes in to make them cheap. They are circulated by agents at a penny an hour in London. When a few days old, they are sent to the provincial towns, and through the country at reduced prices. In this manner, the parliamentary debates and proceedings, impartially and fully reported, go through the nation. The newspaper sheet is suited to all this service, being substantial, and the type good. Nothing can exceed the despatch with which the numerous impressions are worked off, the mechanical operations having reached a perfection calculated to astonish those who would examine them.

What is done in the courts of law, is disseminated in the same way. Every argument, trial, and decision, of whatever nature, or before whatever court, goes immediately into the newspapers. There is no delay. The following morning ushers it forth. I took the liberty of remarking to one of the Judges, upon the smallness of the rooms in which the Courts of King's Bench and Chancery sit, when the proceedings were so interesting that great numbers of the public would like to hear them. *"We sit,"* said he, *"every day in the newspapers."* How much did that answer comprehend! What an increase of responsibility in the Judge! I understood from a source not less high, that the newspapers are to be as much relied upon, as the books of law reports in which the cases are afterwards published; that, in fact, the newspaper report is apt to be the best, being generally the most full, as well as quite accurate. If not accurate, the newspaper giving it, would soon fall before competitors. Hence, he who keeps his daily London paper, has, at the year's end, a volume of the annual law reports of the kingdom, besides all other matter.

In the discussions of the journals, editorial or otherwise, there is a remarkable fearlessness. Things that in Junius's time would have put London in a flame, pass almost daily without notice. Neither the Sovereign nor his Family are spared. Parliament sets the example, and the newspapers follow. Of this, the debates on the royal marriages in the course of the present month, give illustrations. There are countries in which the press is more free, by law, than with the English; for although they impose no previous restraints, their definition of libel is inherently vague. But perhaps nowhere has the press so much latitude.

Everything goes into the newspapers. In other countries, matter of a public nature may be seen in them; here, in addition, you see perpetually even the concerns of individuals. Does a private gentleman come to town? you hear it in the newspapers; does he build a house, or buy an estate? they give the information; does he entertain his friends? you have all their names next day in type; is the drapery of a lady's drawing-room changed from red damask and gold to white satin and silver? the fact is publicly announced. So of a thousand other things. The first burst of it all upon Madame de Stael, led her to remark that the English had realized the fable of living with a window in their bosoms. . . .

Some will suppose that the newspapers govern the country. Nothing would be more unfounded. There is a power not only in the Government, but in the country itself, far above them. It lies in the educated classes. True, the daily press is of the educated class. Its conductors hold the pens of scholars, often of statesmen. Hence you see no editorial personalities; which, moreover, the public would not bear. But what goes into the columns of newspapers, no matter from what sources, comes into contact with equals at least in mind among readers, and a thousand to one in number. The bulk of these are unmoved by what newspapers say, if opposite to their own opinions; which, passing quickly from one to another in a society where population is dense, make head against the daily press, after its first efforts are spent upon classes less enlightened. Half the people of England live in towns. This augments moral as physical power; the last, by strengthening rural parts through demand for their products—the first by sharpening intellect through opportunities of collision. The daily press could master opposing mental forces, if scattered; but not when they can combine. Then, the general literature of the country, reacts against newspapers. The permanent press, as distinct from the daily, teems with productions of a commanding character. There is a great class of authors always existent in England, whose sway exceeds that of the newspapers, as the main body the pioneers. Periodical literature is also effective. It is a match at least for the newspapers, when its time arrives. It is more elementary; less hasty. In a word, the daily press in England, with its floating capital in talents, zeal, and money, can do much at an onset. It is an organized corps, full of spirit and always ready; but there is a higher power of mind and influence behind, that can rally and defeat it. From the latter source it may also be presumed, that a more deliberate judgment will in the end be formed on difficult questions, than from the first impulses and more premature discussions of the daily journals. The latter move in their orbit by reflecting also, in the end, the higher judgment by which they have been controlled. Such are some of the considerations that strike the stranger, reading their daily newspapers. They make a wonderful part of the social system in England. Far more might be said by those having inclination and opportunity to pursue the subject.

GEORGE TICKNOR MEETS
EVERYBODY WHO IS ANYBODY

1819

Ticknor had lived the life of a student at Göttingen; thereafter he lived the life of a grand seigneur. On his travels in Italy, Spain, and France he met everybody—everybody in literature, everybody in politics, everybody in society; in the end one has the impression that he would scarcely condescend to anyone less than a marquis, a lord, or a princess unless the alternatives were picturesque. It was all harmless enough, but it did confirm Ticknor in those habits of exclusiveness and superciliousness which were somewhat less profitable in Boston than they had been in Europe and England.

[*January 18, 1819*] Sir James Mackintosh is a little too precise, a little too much made up in his manners and conversation, but is at the same time very exact, definite, and logical in what he says, and, I am satisfied, seldom has occasion to regret a mistake or an error, where a matter of principle or reasoning is concerned, though, as he is a little given to affect universal learning, he may sometimes make a

From *Life, Letters and Journals of George Ticknor*, George S. Hillard, ed. (Boston, 1877), I, pp. 265–270, 282–284.

mistake in matters of fact. As a part of a considerable literary society, however, he discourses most eloquent music, and in private, where I also saw him several times, he is mild, gentle, and entertaining. But he is seen to greatest advantage, and in all his strength, only in serious discussion, to which he brings great disciplined acuteness and a fluent eloquence, which few may venture to oppose, and which still fewer can effectually resist.

Allen, who is a kind of secretary to Lord Holland, and has lived in his family many years, is a different man. He has a great deal of talent, and has written much and well, in the *Edinburgh Review;* he has strong feelings and great independence of character, which make him sometimes oppose and answer Lady Holland in a curious manner. He has many prejudices, most of them subdued with difficulty, by his weight of talent and his strong will, but many still remaining, and, finally, warm, sincere feelings, and an earnest desire to serve those he likes. Sir James Mackintosh said of him to me, that, considering the extent of his knowledge, he had never known anybody in whom it was so accurate and sure; and though there is something of the partiality of an old friendship in the remark, there is truth in it, as the "Review of Hallam's Middle Ages" and many others will prove. Mr. Allen, however, was not a man to contribute a great deal to such general conversation as that at Lord Holland's. It was necessary to sit down alone with him in a corner, or on a sofa, and then his conversation was very various and powerful, and showed that he had thought deeply, and made up his mind decisively, upon a great many subjects.

Sydney Smith, who then happened to be in London, was in one respect the soul of the society. I never saw a man so formed to float down the stream of conversation, and, without seeming to have any direct influence upon it, to give it his own hue and charm. He is about fifty, corpulent, but not gross, with a great fund of good-nature, and would be thought by a person who saw him only once, and transiently, merely a gay, easy gentleman, careless of everything but the pleasures of conversation and society. This would be a great injustice to him, and one that offends him, I am told; for, notwithstanding the easy grace and light playfulness of his wit, which comes forth with unexhausted and inexhaustible facility, and reminded me continually of the phosphoric brilliancy of the ocean, which sparkles more brightly in proportion as the force opposed to it is greater, yet he is a man of much culture, with plain good-sense, a sound, discreet judgment, and remarkably just and accurate habits of reasoning, and values himself upon these, as well as on his admirable humor.

This is an union of opposite qualities, such as nature usually delights to hold asunder, and such as makes him, whether in company or alone, an irresistibly amusing companion; for, while his humor gives such grace to his argument that it comes with the charm of wit, and his wit is so appropriate that its sallies are often logic in masquerade, his good-sense and good-nature are so prevalent that he never, or rarely, offends against the proprieties of life or society, and never says anything that he or anybody else need to regret afterwards.

Brougham, whom I knew in society, and from seeing him both at his chambers and at my own lodgings, is now about thirty-eight, tall, thin, and rather awkward, with a plain and not very expressive countenance, and simple or even slovenly manners. He is evidently nervous, and a slight convulsive movement about the muscles of his lips gives him an unpleasant expression now and then. In short, all that is exterior in him, and all that goes to make up the first impression, is unfavorable. The first thing that removes this impression is the heartiness and good-will he shows you, whose motive cannot be mistaken, for such kindness can come only from the heart. This is the first thing, but a stranger presently begins to remark his conversation. On common topics, nobody is more commonplace. He does not feel them, but if the subject excites him, there is an air of originality in his remarks, which, if it convinces you of nothing else, convinces you that you are talking with an extraordinary man. He does not like to join in a general conversation, but prefers to talk apart with only two or three persons, and, though with great interest and zeal, in an undertone. If, however, he does launch into it, all the little, trim, gay pleasure-boats must keep well out of the way of his great black collier, as Gibbon said of Fox. He listens carefully and fairly—and with a kindness that would be provoking, if it were not genuine—to all his adversary has to say, but when his time comes to answer, it is with that bare, bold, bullion talent which either crushes itself or its opponent. . . . . Yet I suspect the impression Brougham generally leaves is that of a good-natured friend. At least, that is the impression I have most frequently found, both in England and on the Continent. . . .

I went, however, at first, no farther than Bedfordshire, where I passed three days at the splendid seat of the Duke of Bedford. The entrance to Woburn Abbey is by a Roman gateway opening into the park, through which you are conducted, by an avenue of venerable elms, through fine varieties of hill and dale, woodland and pasture, and by the side of streamlets and little lakes, above three miles. . . . . . I arrived late in the afternoon. . . . . At half past six Lord John Russell, who had just returned from shooting, made me a visit, and carried me to the saloon and introduced me to his father and family. I was received with an English welcome, and a few minutes afterwards we sat down to table. There were about twenty guests at the Abbey, the Marquess and Marchioness of Woodstock, Earl and Countess Jersey, Earl Spencer, Marquess Tavistock, Lord and Lady Ebrington, Lord and Lady William Russell, Mr. Adair, etc. The dinner was pleasant,—at least it was so to me,—for I conversed the whole time with Mr. Adair, formerly the British Minister at Vienna, and a man of much culture, and Lady Jersey, a beautiful creature with a great deal of talent, taste, and elegant knowledge, whom I knew a little on the Continent. . . . .

In the evening the party returned to the great saloon, called the Hall of State, and every one amused himself as he chose, either at cards, in listening to music, or in conversation, though several deserted to the billiard-room. For myself, I found amusement enough in talking with Lady Jersey, or Lord John Russell, or the old and excellent Earl Spencer, but I think the majority was rather captivated with Lady Ebrington's music. . . . .

The next morning, at ten o'clock, found us mustered in the breakfast-room. It was a day of no common import at a nobleman's country-seat, for it was the last of the shooting season. The Duke was anxious to have a quantity of game killed that should maintain the reputation of the Abbey, for the first sporting-ground in Great Britain; and therefore solemn preparations were made to have a grand battue of the park, for it was intended, in order to give more reputation to the day's success, that nothing should be shot out of it; nor, indeed, was there any great need of extending the limit, for the park is twelve miles in circumference. Mr. Adair, Lord John, and myself declined, as no sportsmen, and so the number was reduced to eleven, of whom seven were excellent shots. The first gun was fired a little before twelve, the last at half past five; and when, after the dinner-cloth was removed in the evening, the game-keeper appeared, dressed in all his paraphernalia, and rendered in his account, it was found that four hundred and four hares, partridges, and pheasants had been killed, of which more than half were pheasants. The person who killed the most was Lord Spencer, though the oldest man there. This success, of course, gave great spirits to the party at dinner, a good deal of wine was consumed,—though nobody showed any disposition to drink to excess,—and the evening passed off very pleasantly. It was certainly as splendid a specimen as I could have hoped to see, of what is to be considered peculiarly

English in the life of a British nobleman of the first class at his country-seat. I enjoyed it highly.

The next day was much more quiet. Several of the party went to town, and, though Lord Auckland and one or two others came down to the Abbey, the number was seriously diminished. I had the more time and opportunity to see the establishment and become acquainted with its inhabitants. Considered as a whole, Woburn Abbey is sometimes called the finest estate in England. As I went over it, I thought I should never find an end to all its arrangements and divisions. Within—besides the mere house, which is the largest and most splendid I have seen—is the picture-gallery, containing about two hundred pieces, many of which, of the Spanish and Italian schools, are of great merit; and the library, which is a magnificent collection of splendid books, composed of beautiful editions of the best authors, in all languages, besides a mass of engravings and maps. I could have occupied myself in these apartments for a month. Outside, there are the aviary, fish-ponds, greenhouses, the gardens, tennis-court, riding-school, etc., and a gallery containing a few antiques that are curious, especially the immense Lanti vase, which has been much talked about, and well deserves it. . . . .

The Duke of Bedford is now about fifty-five, a plain, unpretending man in his manner, reserved in society, but talking well when alone, and respectable in debate in the House of Peers; a great admirer of the fine arts, which he patronizes liberally; and, finally, one of the best farmers in England, and one of those who have most improved the condition of their estates by scientific and careful cultivation. . . . . Lord John is a young man of a good deal of literary knowledge and taste, from whose acquaintance I have had much pleasure. . . .

On Monday, March 15, early in the morning, I left Edinburgh. I was not alone, for Cogswell came with me, and we had a pleasant drive of six or seven hours down into the Border country, and finally stopped at Kelso, a pleasant town on the beautiful banks of the Tweed. We went immediately to see the ruins of the old abbey. . . .

March 16. Two miles farther on [beyond Melrose] is the magician's own house,—Scott's, I mean, or the "sherrie's,' as the postilion called him, because he is sheriff of the county,—as odd-looking a thing as can well be seen, neither house nor castle, ancient nor modern, nor an imitation of either, but a complete nondescript. The situation is not very good, though on the bank of the Tweed and opposite the entrance of the Gala, for it is under a hill and has little prospect; but there is a kindness and hospitality there which are better than anything else, and make everything else forgotten. We had come down on an invitation to pass as much time with him as we could, and were received with the simple good-nature and good spirits which I have constantly found in his house. Mrs. Scott was not there, nor either of the sons. .... The establishment, therefore, consisted of Mr. Scott, his two girls, Sophia and Anne, and Mr. Skeene, to whom he has dedicated one of the cantos of *Marmion.*

Mr. Scott himself was more amusing here than I had found him even in town. He seemed, like Antaeus, to feel that he touched a kindred earth, and to quicken into new life by its influences. The Border country is indeed the natural home of his talent, and it is when walking with him over his own hills and through his own valleys, ... and in the bosom and affections of his own family, that he is all you can imagine or desire him to be. His house itself is a kind of collection of fragments of history; architectural orna-ments,—copies from Melrose in one part, the old identical gate of the Tolbooth, or rather the stone part of it, through which the Porteous mob forced its way, in another,—an old fountain before the house, and odd inscriptions and statues everywhere, make such a kind of irregular, poetical habitation as ought to belong to him. Then for every big stone on his estate, as well as for all the great points of the country about, he has a tradition or a ballad, which he repeats with an enthusiasm that kindles his face to an animation that forms a singular contrast to the quiet in which it usually rests.

Sophia shares and enjoys these local feelings and attachments, and can tell as many Border stories as her father, and repeat perhaps as many ballads, and certainly more Jacobite songs. She is, indeed, in some respects, an extraordinary person. There is nothing romantic about her, for she is as perfectly right-minded as I ever saw one so young; and, indeed, perhaps right-mindedness is the prevailing feature in her character. She has no uncommon talent, and yet I am sure he must have little taste or feeling who could find her conversa-tion dull; she is not beautiful, though after seeing her several times in company with those handsomer than herself, I found my eye at last rested with most pleasure on the playful simplicity and natural openness of her countenance. .... Anne is younger, no less natural, and perhaps has more talent, and is generally thought prettier; but nobody, I think, places her in competition with her sister. ....

Nobody came to Abbotsford while we stayed there, and of course we had a happy time. The breakfast-hour was nine, and after that we all walked out together and heard any number of amusing stories, for Mr. Scott has a story for everything; and so we continued walking about and visiting till nearly dinner-time, at half past four. As soon as we were seated the piper struck up a pibroch before the windows, dressed in his full Highland costume, and one of the best-looking and most vain, self-sufficient dogs I ever saw; and he continued walking about, and playing on his bagpipes until the dessert arrived, when he was called in, received his dram, and was dismissed. Mr. Scott likes to sit at table and talk, and therefore dinner, or rather the latter part of it, was long. Coffee followed, and then in a neighboring large room the piper was heard again, and we all went in and danced Scotch reels till we were tired. An hour's conversation afterwards brought us to ten o'clock and supper; and two very short and gay hours at the supper-table, or by the fire, brought us to bedtime.

I delighted to talk with these original creatures about themselves and one another, for they do it with simplicity, and often make curious remarks. Mr. Scott gave me an odd account of the education of his whole family. His great object has always been, not to over-educate, and to follow the natural indications of character, rather than to form other traits. The strongest instance is his son Walter, a young man with little talent; "and so," said Mr. Scott, "I gave him as much schooling as I thought would do him good, and taught him to ride well, and shoot well, and tell the truth; and I think now that he will make a good soldier, and serve his country well, instead of a poor scholar or advocate, doing no good to himself or anybody else" Sophia, however, did not seem to be quite well satisfied with her father's system of education in some respects. "He's always just telling us our faults," said she, with her little Scotch accent and idiom, "but never takes such very serious pains to have us mend. I think sometimes he would like to have us different from other girls and boys, even though it should be by having us worse." . . . .

But the visit that began so happily, and continued for two days so brightly, had a sad close. During the second night Mr. Scott was seized with violent spasms in his stomach, which could be controlled neither by laudanum nor bleeding. A surgeon was sent for, who continued with him all night, ... and the next morning the family was filled with the most cruel apprehensions, for though he has been subject to such attacks, none had come on with such violence. We therefore abruptly ended our visit a day sooner than we intended, and crossed to the main road at Selkirk, where I had a very sad parting from Cogswell.

JOHN GRISCOM VISITS
ROBERT OWEN'S MODEL TOWN
OF NEW LANARK

1819

"When you see John Griscom," wrote a Virginian, "tell him that Mr. Thomas Jefferson said that his book gave him the most satisfactory view of the literary and public institutions of England, France and Switzerland that he had ever read." Many others shared Jefferson's estimate of Griscom's *A Year in Europe*. Griscom himself was a man of parts. He was by profession a chemist, taught chemistry at Queen's College (now Rutgers University), discovered the medicinal value of cod-liver oil and was the first to use iodine in the treatment of goiter. One of the first educational statesmen, he founded the New York High School for Boys as early as 1807, and on his return from Europe tried to introduce the ideas of Pestalozzi, Fellenberg, and others of the new school of educational thought; indeed, the greatest value of his *Year in Europe* was in the chapters devoted to the new ideas about education then sweeping Germany and Switzerland. An ardent Quaker, Griscom was something of a philanthropist and reformer, serving as director of the New York Society for the Prevention of Pauperism and the Society for the Reformation of Juvenile

From John Griscom, *A Year in Europe* (New York, 1824), I, pp. 375–379, 383–387.

Delinquents. It is not surprising that he was sympathetic to Robert Owen's experiment in industrial Utopianism at New Lanark. Owen himself visited the new nation, and his son, Robert Dale Owen, had a long career in American politics.

As my visit here was to the noted establishment of Robert Owen, I repaired to Braksfield-house, his residence, and being informed he was at the mills, I immediately took the direction, and met him at New Lanark, in the centre of its busy population.

I know no man of equal celebrity, whose manners are less imposing, and who has more of the candour and openness of a child.

This manufacturing village, of which R. Owen is almost the sole director, has become famous throughout Great Britain. A brief description of it will, I am confident, be agreeable to you; and I shall proceed in it, in the same regular order of occurrences, which I have hitherto observed.

The village presented, upon my entering it, a very neat and interesting appearance, affording, in this respect, a remarkable contrast with old Lanark, about two miles distant, where the coach stopped. It is beautifully situated, on the right bank of the Clyde, which is here a small but romantic stream. It has grown entirely, and recently, out of the manufactory, which is exclusively that of spinning cotton. The whole population is about 2500, 1600 of whom are employed in and about the mills; the rest being mothers, engaged in their domestic affairs, or children too young for labour. The houses are mostly uniform in their structure, built of stone, with a roof of slate, and kept, to all appearance, in great decency, attention being evidently paid to cleanliness throughout the whole establishment. The people were returning from their work, as we approached the mills; and in passing us, they showed a cheerfulness and courtesy of demeanour, which evinced their content; and indeed, their general appearance bespoke health and satisfaction. Two of the boys fell into a dispute as they moved along, and one of them struck the other. Owen reproved them for this misconduct, and told me it was the first blow he had seen struck for years. The avowed principle upon which this large concern is regulated and conducted, is that of humanity to the labourers, in the most extensive and philosophical application of the term. It includes of course the consideration of their welfare, physical, intellectual, and moral. The whole is subjected to a strict discipline; but this discipline is studiously adapted to their wants, and is intended to produce the greatest possible share of cheerfulness and contentment, which their situation will admit of.

No one can converse with Robert Owen half an hour on this subject, without perceiving that his views are, in some respects, original; and without hearing him announce principles, which appear to be at variance with all established notions of the fundamental doctrines of genuine philanthropy. His theory, judging from his writings, as well as his conversation, appears to be that of a visionary schemer; destitute of the principles which we are accustomed to consider as lying at the root of all true benevolence. His practice, however, is obviously the reverse of all this. No man, perhaps, ever took more pains, or exerted himself more successfully, to promote the happiness of his own family, than Owen has done to render his 2500 villagers, harmonious, contented, and happy. The materials he had to work with were very discordant. When he first introduced his particular schemes of reformation, he was regarded by almost every body with distrust; and so strong was the prejudice against his measures, that he found it difficult to procure, even among the half starving population of the district, labourers, who would consent to fall in with his regulations. At present, he has applications from far and near, to a greater amount than he can possibly furnish with employment. But to proceed with the description.

After taking coffee in the house of one of his clerks, we awaited the hour of school. A neat and commodious building has been erected for the purpose of instruction, in a pleasant spot near the centre of the village. The manufactories close uniformly at half past six; hence none of that overstraining by which the health of children and young people are so much injured in other manufacturing towns, is here permitted. The evenings of the youth are devoted to the schools, and as many of the adults as choose, may also avail themselves of the instruction of the teachers. The first room we entered was a singing school, in which were both boys and girls, arranged on benches, and singing in chorus, under the direction of an instructer. On listening to the words of the song, judge my surprise on finding, that, instead of a hymn, it was a love song, beginning with,

> And will you love me, deary.

Passing into the next room, I found there a music-school. Half a dozen or more little fellows had each a flute, and were piping it away in notes that did not preserve the strictest accordance. The next apartment we entered, was a large room for reading, writing, and arithmetic. Some of the pupils in this room were pretty well advanced in age. From this we went into a large room above-stairs, where were fifty or sixty young people, both boys and girls, attending to the lessons of a dancing-master. These young students of the "merry mood," were not equipped in all the gaiety of a fashionable ball-room; though there was, probably, as great a diversity of costume as would be seen in a "belle assemblée" of Paris or Edinburgh. In fact, they were in much the same style as that in which they had left the manufactory,—some with shoes, and others barefoot. The dancing-master, too, was the painter and glazier of the village; who, after handling the brush all day, took up the fiddle in the evening, and instructed his motley group in the profound mysteries of the highland reel.

Owen's aim in all this is to make his villagers a *moral* and happy people. He wishes to relieve their minds and bodies as much as possible from the fatigues of labour, and he goes to work in his own way. He does not, I believe, compel any of his subjects to dance; but, if they choose it, he gives them the opportunity of learning how. Human nature, he says, is not understood by any class of society, and he has discovered that dancing is one of the means of reforming vicious habits. This he thinks it effects by promoting cheerfulness and contentment, and thus diverting the attention from things that are vile and degrading. Before the evening school closes, the pupils all collect into one room, and sing a hymn.

After leaving this singular school of moral reformation, he took me home with him, and gave me a kind introduction to his wife and family. He is so zealotte in his wishes to benefit society, and so confident of the soundness of his views, and the importance of his plans of improvement, that if his visiters are inclined to hear, he will entertain them as long as they please, with the details of his system. His manners, as I have already remarked, are altogether unobtrusive. He wishes to gain his point by illustration and persuasion; but as it is impossible to listen to him without objecting to some of his fundamental positions, argument becomes unavoidable. We sat up till twelve, engaged in a wordy warfare upon the best means of correcting the abuses of society, and making the whole world a band of brothers. He is confident that this would be the happy result, were his measures universally adopted. Pauperism would become unknown; for every individual would be at liberty to exert his faculties of body and mind, in such a way, as to provide most efficaciously for all his natural wants. Wars would cease, because no one would have the inclination to invade the rights of another. Idleness would vanish, because every man would find more pleasure in useful activity. The turbulent and angry passions would subside, for every one would find it his interest to treat others rationally and kindly. The pursuit of gain and the thirst for riches would disappear, because every man, finding himself perfectly comfortable, would have no wish to be richer than his neighbour. Ambition, as a passion of the human breast, would die a natural death; for, in this happy state of things, it would find no aliment to subsist upon. In short, such would be the just and equal balance between the wants of mankind, and the means of supply—between rational desire, and the power of gratification, that discontent and distress would become unknown. . . .

After breakfast we went to the mills, and spent the interval till a late dinner hour, in viewing the improvements and in walking to the falls of the Clyde, about a mile above the village, and surveying the delightful scenery of that region. The buildings of the factory are very large, and the machinery is in excellent style. The whole of it is made on the premises, by workmen skilled in all the complicated operations of metal and wood, connected with the fabrication and erection of the extensive apparatus of such an establishment. The hours of labour are from six till nine, when they breakfast; from ten to two, when they dine; and from three to half past six; making in the whole ten and a half hours. The wages of the spinners vary from 10s. to 1s. 6d. per week, according to age and ability. The education of their children is given to them without cost, or at least upon very moderate terms, though its expense to the establishment is not less than £ 700 per annum. At present, every family cooks its own provision, but a building is nearly completed which is designed as a kitchen for the whole village; and a refectory in which about one-fourth of them may take their meals at a time. Owen believes, that from four to five thousand pounds a year will be saved by this arrangement, besides the superior training and improved habits it will produce. The second story of this large building will contain a reading and lecture room, and a ball room for all the adult fashionables of the village; for I am told, that were I to see these people in their "Sunday decorations," I should be astonished at the contrast. A library is also nearly in readiness for the use of the villagers. All the principal buildings are warmed by steam, and a plan is on foot to extend this mode of warming to the dwelling houses, after the necessity of cooking in these shall be superseded by the general kitchen. There are four distinct religious societies among the labourers; viz. the National Kirk, the Gaelic, Methodists, and Independents. . . .

Such assiduous and expensive efforts to ameliorate the condition of labourers, as have been made at New Lanark, have occasioned manufacturers in other places, to prophesy its dissolution, from a belief that such heavy expenses could not be supported by the profits. The whole concern belongs to a few proprietors (in addition to Robert Owen), who joined in the enterprize, from a wish to give a fair trial to a lenient and benevolent system of management; and so far from its having proved a loss to the company, it has yielded them an interest of twelve and a half per cent on the original stock.

Large manufactories, in which young people, of various ages, and of both sexes, are indiscriminately employed, are considered as unfriendly to morals; but it would appear from the results of New Lanark, that the superior instruction here bestowed and the more elevated tone of social intercourse which arises from it, tend to counteract the vulgar propensities and to prevent the evils which so commonly prevail in those crowded establishments.

We visited the schools again to-day. The children are not allowed to go into the factories, till they are about ten years of age, but are kept till that time steadily at the day schools. One apartment of the school afforded a novel and pleasing spectacle. It consisted of a great number of children, from one to three or four years of age. They are assembled in a large room, under the care of a judicious female, who allows them to amuse themselves with various selected toys, and occasionally collects the oldest into a class, and teaches them their letters. They appeared perfectly happy, and as we entered, the little creatures ran in groups, to seize their benefactor by the hand, or to pull him by the coat, with the most artless simplicity. This baby school is of great consequence to the establishment, for it enables mothers to shut up their houses in security, and to attend to their duties in the factory, without concern for their families. . . .

There is not, I apprehend, to be found in any part of the world, a manufacturing village, or a community of equal extent, composed of persons indiscriminately brought together, without any peculiar bond of fraternity, in which so much older, good government, tranquillity and rational happiness prevail. It affords an eminent and instructive example of the good that may be effected by well directed efforts to promote the real comforts, and I may add, the morality of the indigent and labouring classes. No person, I am persuaded, can retire from this charming village, without a renewed conviction of the vast influence which an enlightened philanthropy may exert over the destinies and happiness of mankind.

WASHINGTON IRVING
INTRODUCES
THE ROMANTIC NOTE

1816–20

Irving and Cooper, the first two truly national figures in American literature, were both preoccupied with England and with the complex relationship of Americans to "Our Old Home." Both emerged in the post-Revolutionary era and both won their literary spurs in the first decade of the new century; both were powerfully influenced by the new waves of romanticism coming out of Europe and represented in Britain by Scott, in Germany by Schiller, in France by Chateaubriand and Victor Hugo; both wrote voluminously on Europe and turned increasingly to the American scene. Where Cooper was severely critical of Britain, Irving was charmingly sympathetic: the difference was rooted not so much in experience as in temperament. Irving had made his literary reputation with the *Knickerbocker's History of New York* in 1809; he was not as yet committed to literature but rather involved in law and business. At the close of the War of 1812 he sailed for England to engage in the family business, which promptly went on the rocks, and Irving turned back to literature in part to make a living. His first English book, *The Sketch Book*

From *Letters of Washington Irving to Henry Brevoort*, George S. Hellman, ed. (New York, 1918), pp. 194–197; *The Sketch Book of Geoffrey Crayon* (New York, 1819, London, 1820), pp. 55-61.

136

(1820), which contained such famous stories as "Rip Van Winkle" and "The Legend of Sleepy Hollow," was an immediate success; *Bracebridge Hall*, which followed two years later, won him an even greater public. It was in some ways prophetic, for it was inspired by the principle that animated so much of the American view of Britain for the next century. "England" wrote Irving, "is as classic ground to an American, as Italy is to an Englishman, and old London teems with as much historical association as mighty Rome." Irving was in literature what Ticknor was in social intercourse; his amiability, his charm, his liveliness, his sympathy, and, withal, his sturdy independence, won the affection of the English as later these same qualities won the admiration and affection of the Spaniards. William Cullen Bryant put it well when he rejoiced that we had "such a writer as Irving to bridge over the chasm between the two great nations—that an illustrious American lived so long in England and was so much beloved there, and sought so earnestly to bring the people of the two countries to a better understanding with each other and to wean them from the animosities of narrow minds."

In 1826 Irving was appointed to the legation in Spain, and there found material for his *Life and Voyages of Columbus, The Alhambra,* and *Granada;* in 1842 he was appointed American Minister to Madrid. A few years later he retired to his home, Sunnyside, on the Hudson—the name and the architecture are both eloquent of his romanticism—and there lived out the twilight of his life writing his immense biography of Washington and breathing the incense his countrymen burned for him.

To Henry Brevoort

Birmingham, November 6, 1816
... At the hotel where we put up we had a most singular & whimsical assemblage of beings. I don't know whether you were ever at an English watering place, but if you have not been, you have missed the best opportunity at studying English oddities, both moral and physical. I no longer wonder at the English being such excellent caricaturists, they have such an inexhaustible number & variety of subjects to study from. The only care should be not to follow fact too closely for I'll swear I have met with characters & figures that would be condemned as extravagant; if faithfully delineated by pen or pencil. At a watering place like Buxton where people really resort for health, you see the great tendency of the English to run into excrescences and bloat out into grotesque deformities. As to noses I

say nothing of them, though we had every variety. Some snubbed and turned up, with distended nostrils, like a dormer window on the roof of a house—others convex and twisted like a Buck handled knife & others magnificently efflorescent like a full blown cauliflower. But as to the persons that were attached to their noses, fancy every distortion, tuberance & pompous embellishment that can be produced in the human form by high and gross feeding, by the bloating operations of malt liquors, by the rheuming influence of a damp foggy vaporish climate. One old fellow was an exception to this, for instead of acquiring that expansion and sponginess to which old people are prone in this country from the long course of internal & external soaking they experience, he had grown dry & stiff in the process of years. The skin of his face had so shrunk away that he could not close eyes or mouth—the latter therefore stood on a perpetual ghastly grin; and the former on an incessant stare. He had but one serviceable joint in his body which is at the bottom of the back bone, and that creaked & grated whenever he bent. He could not raise his feet from the ground, but skated along the drawing room carpet, whenever he wished to ring the bell. The only signs of moisture in his whole body was a pellucid drop that I occasionally noticed on the end of a long dry nose. He used generally to shuffle about in company with a little fellow who was fat on one side and lean on the other. That is to say, he was warped on one side as if he had scorched before the fire; he had a wry neck, which made his head lean on one shoulder—his hair was snugly powdered and he had a round, smirky smiling apple face with a bloom on it like that of a frost bitten leaf in Autumn. We had an old fat general by the name of Trotter who had, I suspect, been promoted to his high rank to get him out of the way of more able and active officers, being an instance that a man may occasionally rise in the world through absolute lack of merit. I could not help watching the movements of this redoubtable Old Hero, who, I'll warrant had been the champion & safe guard of half the garrison towns in England, and fancying to myself how Bonaparte would have delighted in having such toast & butter generals to deal with. This old lad is doubtless a sample of those generals that flourished in the old military school—when armies would manoeuvre & watch each other for months; now and then have a desperate skirmish and after marching & countermarching about the "low countries" through a glorious campaign, retire on the first pinch of cold weather, into snug winter quarters in some fat Flemish town, and eat & drink & fiddle through the winter. . . .

Edinburgh, August 28, 1817

. . . I set off for Wilson and reached Selkirk that evening from whence on Saturday morning early I take chaise for the Abbey.

On my way I stopped at the gate of Abbotsford & sent in my letter of introduction to Walter Scott, with a card & request to know whether it would be possible for him to receive a visit from me in the course of the day. Mr. Scott himself came out to see me and welcomed me to his home with the genuine hospitality of the olden-times. In a moment I found myself at his breakfast table, and felt as if I was at the social board of an old friend. Instead of a visit of a few hours I was kept there several days—and such days! You know the charms of Scott's conversation but you have not lived with him in the country—you have not rambled with him about his favorite hills and glens and burns—you have not seen him dispensing happiness around him in his little rural domain. I came prepared to admire him, but he completely won my heart and made me love him. He has a charming family around him—Sophia Scott who must have been quite a little girl when you were here, is grown up, and is a sweet little mountain lassie. She partakes a great deal of her father's character—is light-hearted ingenuous, intelligent, and amiable. Can tell a whimsical story and sing a border song with the most captivating näivete.

Scott was very attentive in showing me the neighboring country. I was with him from morning to night and was constantly astonished and delighted by the perpetual and varied flow of his conversation. It is just as entertaining as one of his novels, and exactly like them in style, point, humour, character & picturesqueness. I parted with him with the utmost regret but received a cordial invitation to repeat my visit on my way back to England, which I think I shall do. I should not forget to mention that he spoke of you in the most friendly terms; and reproached himself for not having written to you; but says he is extremely remiss in letter writing.

Rural Life in England

> Oh! friendly to the best pursuits of man,
> Friendly to thought, to virtue, and to peace,
> Domestic life in rural pleasures past!—Cowper.

The stranger who would form a correct opinion of the English character, must not confine his observations to the Metropolis. He must go forth into the country; he must sojourn in villages and hamlets; he must visit castles, villas, farm-houses, cottages; he must wander through parks and gardens; along hedges and green lanes; he must loiter about country churches; attend wakes and fairs, and other rural festivals; and cope with the people in all their conditions, and all their habits and humours.

In some countries the large cities absorb the wealth and fashion of the nation; they are the only fixed abodes of elegant and intelligent society, and the country is inhabited almost entirely by boorish peasantry. In England, on the contrary, the Metropolis is a mere gathering-place, or general rendezvous of the polite classes, where they devote a small portion of the year to a hurry of gaiety and dissipation, and having indulged this kind of carnival, return again to the apparently more congenial habits of rural life. The various orders of society are therefore diffused over the whole surface of the kingdom, and the most retired neighbourhoods afford specimens of the different ranks.

The English, in fact, are strongly gifted with the rural feeling. They possess a quick sensibility to the beauties of nature, and a keen relish for the pleasures and employments of the country. This passion seems inherent in them. Even the inhabitants of cities, born and brought up among brick walls and bustling streets, enter with facility into rural habits, and evince a tact for rural occupation. The merchant has his snug retreat in the vicinity of the Metropolis, where he often displays as much pride and zeal in the cultivation of his flower-garden, and the maturing of his fruits, as he does in the conduct of his business and the success of a commercial enterprise. Even those less fortunate individuals, who are doomed to pass their lives in the midst of din and traffic, contrive to have something that shall remind them of the green aspect of nature. In the most dark and dingy quarters of the city, the drawing-room window resembles frequently a bank of flowers; every spot capable of vegetation has its grass-plot and flower-bed; and every square its mimic park, laid out with picturesque taste, and gleaming with refreshing verdure.

Those who see the Englishman only in town are apt to form an unfavourable opinion of his social character. He is either absorbed in business, or distracted by the thousand engagements that dissipate time, thought, and feeling, in this huge metropolis. He has, therefore, too commonly a look of hurry and abstraction. Wherever he happens to be, he is on the point of going somewhere else; at the moment he is talking on one subject, his mind is wandering to another; and while paying a friendly visit, he is calculating how he shall economise time so as to pay the other visits allotted in the morning. An immense metropolis, like London, is calculated to make men selfish and uninteresting. In their casual and transient meetings they can but deal briefly in common-places. They present but the cold superficies of character—its rich and genial qualities have no time to be warmed into a flow.

It is in the country that the Englishman gives scope to his natural feelings. He breaks loose gladly from the cold formalities and negative civilities of town; throws off his habits of shy reserve, and becomes joyous and free-hearted. He manages to collect round him all the conveniences and elegancies of polite life, and to banish its restraints. His country-seat abounds with every requisite, either for studious retirement, tasteful gratification, or rural exercise. Books, paintings, music, horses, dogs, and sporting implements of all kinds, are at hand. He puts no constraint either upon his guests or himself, but in the true spirit of hospitality provides the means of enjoyment, and leaves every one to partake according to his inclination.

The taste of the English in the cultivation of land, and in what is called landscape gardening, is unrivalled. They have studied nature intently, and discover an exquisite sense of her beautiful forms and harmonious combinations. Those charms, which in other countries she lavishes in wild solitudes, are here assembled round the haunts of domestic life. They seem to have caught her coy and furtive graces, and spread them, like witchery, about their rural abodes.

Nothing can be more imposing than the magnificence of English park scenery. Vast lawns that extend like sheets of vivid green, with here and there clumps of gigantic trees, heaping up rich piles of foliage: the solemn pomp of groves and woodland glades, with the deer trooping in silent herds across them; the hare, bounding away to the covert; or the pheasant, suddenly bursting upon the wing: the brook, taught to wind in natural meanderings, or expand into a glassy lake: the sequestered pool, reflecting the quivering trees, with the yellow leaf sleeping on its bosom, and the trout roaming fearlessly about its limpid waters, while some rustic temple or sylvan statue, grown green and dank with age, gives an air of classic sanctity to the seclusion.

These are but a few of the features of park scenery; but what most delights me, is the creative talent with which the English decorate the unostentatious abodes of middle life. The rudest habitation, the most unpromising and scanty portion of land, in the hands of an Englishman of taste, becomes a little paradise. With a nicely discriminating eye, he seizes at once upon its capabilities, and pictures in his mind the future landscape. The sterile spot grows into loveliness under his hand; and yet the operations of art which produce the effect are scarcely to be perceived. The cherishing and training of some trees; the cautious pruning of others; the nice distribution of flowers and plants of tender and graceful foliage; the introduction of a green slope of velvet turf; the partial opening to a peep of blue distance, or silver gleam of water: all these are managed with a delicate tact, a pervading yet quiet assiduity, like the magic touchings with which a painter finishes up a favourite picture.

The residence of people of fortune and refinement in the country has diffused a degree of taste and elegance in rural economy, that descends to the lowest class. The very labourer, with his thatched cottage and narrow slip of ground, attends to their embellishment. The trim hedge, the grass-plot before the door, the little flowerbed bordered with snug box, the woodbine trained up against the wall, and hanging its blossoms about the lattice, the pot of flowers in the window, the holly, providentially planted about the house, to cheat winter of its dreariness, and to throw in a semblance of green summer to cheer the fireside: all these bespeak the influence of taste, flowing down from high sources, and pervading the lowest levels of the public mind. If ever Love, as poets sing, delights to visit a cottage, it must be the cottage of an English peasant.

The fondness for rural life among the higher classes of the English has had a great and salutary effect upon the national character. I do not know a finer race of men than the English gentlemen. Instead of the softness and effeminacy which characterise the men of rank in most countries, they exhibit a union of elegance and strength, a robustness of frame and freshness of complexion, which I am inclined to attribute to their living so much in the open air, and pursuing so eagerly the invigorating recreations of the country. These hardy exercises produce also a healthful tone of mind and spirits, and a manliness and simplicity of manners, which even the follies and dissipations of the town cannot easily pervert, and can never entirely destroy. In the country, too, the different orders of society seem to approach more freely, to be more disposed to blend and operate favourably upon each other. The distinctions between them do not appear to be so marked and impassable as in the cities. The manner in which property has been distributed into small estates and farms has established a regular gradation from the nobleman, through the classes of gentry, small landed proprietors, and substantial farmers, down to the labouring peasantry, and while it has thus banded the extremes of society together, has infused into each intermediate rank a spirit of independence. This, it must be confessed, is not so universally the case at present as it was formerly; the larger estates having, in late years of distress, absorbed the smaller; and, in some parts of the country, almost annihilated the sturdy race of small farmers. These, however, I believe, are but casual breaks in the general system I have mentioned.

In rural occupation there is nothing mean and debasing. It leads a man forth among scenes of natural grandeur and beauty; it leaves him to the workings of his own mind, operated upon by the purest and most elevating of external influences. Such a man may be simple and rough, but he cannot be vulgar. The man of refinement, therefore, finds nothing revolting in an intercourse with the lower orders in rural life, as he does when he casually mingles with the lower orders of cities. He lays aside his distance and reserve, and is glad to waive the distinctions of rank, and to enter into the honest, heartfelt enjoyments of common life. Indeed, the very amusements of the country bring men more and more together; and the sound of hound and horn blend all feelings into harmony. I believe this is one great reason why the nobility and gentry are more popular among the inferior orders in England than they are in any other country; and why the latter have endured so many excessive pressures and extremities, without repining more generally at the unequal distribution of fortune and privilege.

To this mingling of cultivated and rustic society may also be attributed the rural feeling that runs through British literature; the frequent use of illustrations from rural life; those incomparable descriptions of nature that abound in the British poets, that have continued down from *The Flower and the Leaf* of Chaucer, and have brought into our closets all the freshness and fragrance of the dewy landscape. The pastoral writers of other countries appear as if they had paid Nature an occasional visit, and become acquainted with her general charms; but the British poets have lived and revelled with her—they have wooed her in her most secret haunts—they have watched her minutest caprices. A spray could not tremble in the breeze—a leaf could not rustle to the ground—a diamond drop could not patter in the stream—a fragrance could not exhale from the humble violet, nor a daisy unfold its crimson tints to the morning, but it has been noticed by these impassioned and delicate observers, and wrought up into some beautiful morality.

The effect of this devotion of elegant minds to rural occupations has been wonderful on the face of the country. A great part of the island is rather level, and would be monotonous, were it not for the charms of culture: but it is studded and gemmed, as it were, with castles and palaces, and embroidered with parks and gardens. It does not abound in grand and sublime prospects, but rather in little home scenes of rural repose and sheltered quiet. Every antique farm-house and moss-grown cottage is a picture; and as the roads are continually winding, and the view is shut in by groves and hedges, the eye is delighted by a continual succession of small landscapes of captivating loveliness.

The great charm, however, of English scenery is the moral feeling that seems to pervade it. It is associated in the mind with ideas of order, of quiet, of sober, well-established principles, of hoary usage and reverend custom. Everything seems to be the growth of ages of regular and peaceful existence. The old church of remote architecture, with its low, massive portal, its Gothic tower, its windows rich with tracery and painted glass, in scrupulous preservation, its stately monuments of warriors and worthies of the olden time, ancestors of the present lords of the soil; its tombstones, recording successive generations of sturdy yeomanry, whose progeny still plough the same fields, and kneel at the same altar—the parsonage, a quaint, irregular pile, partly antiquated, but repaired and altered in the tastes of various ages and occupants—the stile and footpath leading from the churchyard, across pleasant fields, and along shady hedge-rows, according to an immemorial right of way—the neighbouring village, with its venerable cottages, its public green sheltered by trees, under which the forefathers of the present race have sported—the antique family mansion, standing apart in some little rural domain, but looking down with a protecting air on the surrounding scene: all these common features of English landscape evince a calm and settled security, and hereditary transmission of home-bred virtues and local attachments, that speak deeply and touchingly for the moral character of the nation.

1820-1830

CHESTER HARDING:
"THE DUKE HONORED ME
WITH A SHAKE OF HIS HAND"

1824

From Benjamin West to John Singer Sargent, American artists have lived and painted in England, and even made their reputations there. Benjamin West—one of George III's favorites—succeeded Reynolds as president of the Royal Academy, and over the years patronized many of his young countrymen—among them Cooley and Peale and Trumbull and Morse. An American painter could not expect to bring his reputation with him to Britain, but one with a British reputation could count on carrying it back home with him. Chester Harding was, as he himself says, an untaught painter from the American backwoods. Like many American painters, he began as a sign painter and graduated from that to portraits. He went to England in 1823 and was an immediate success—as he tells us with some elaborateness. Returning to his native country in 1827, he became a rival of Morse and Sully; eventually he painted over a thousand portraits, some of them good. In his old age he wrote an eccentric autobiography which he entitled *My Egotistography*.

From *A Sketch of Chester Harding,* by Margaret E. White, ed. (Boston, 1890), pp. 91–93, 112–114, 116–117, 123–127.

147

To His Wife

January 14 [1824]. Began the portrait of His Royal Highness the Duke of Sussex. This was the first time that I ever had the honor of seeing one of the royal family; and, of course, my approach to this august personage was marked by some little palpitations of the heart: but his affable manners placed me entirely at my ease. In the course of the sitting, His Royal Highness spoke warmly of America, and said he felt a pleasure in being painted by an American artist. In this country, it is looked upon as a mark of great distinction to be allowed to paint one of the royal family. For this honor I am indebted to my friend Hunter. The duke is a prodigiously fat man, above six feet high, of very uncommon features, but not intellectual.

Monday, January 19. Finished the portrait of the duke. He seems well pleased with it, and seems to take considerable interest in my success. All who have seen the portrait think it the best that ever was taken of His Royal Highness.

His Highness gave me a ticket to the Highland Society's dinner, an annual jubilee from time immemorial. This was the grandest affair I ever had the pleasure of witnessing. Some two hundred of the Highland chiefs and lairds, all in their appropriate costume were assembled. Every man wore the plaid of his clan. There were five or six of us in black coats: we were placed at the foot of one of the long tables, and had a fine view of the company. Old and young were splendidly dressed, and a gorgeous sight it was. After the regular toasts, such as "The King," "The Royal Family," "The Ministers," and so on, volunteer toasts were given. The Duke of Sussex was the president, and was addressed as the Earl of Inverness; the clans considering that title higher than his English one.

At intervals, I tried to make some conversation with my black-coated neighbors; but their attention was apparently too much absorbed by what was going on at the other end of the table. Presently I saw the duke's servant coming down to our end of the table, and, approaching me, said, "His Royal Highness will take wine with you." I rose, and His Royal Highness half rose and bowed. Such a mark of distinction was felt by my taciturn neighbors. I found them sociable and very respectful after that. As soon as the dinner was dispatched, the bagpipes were introduced, and the first note started the company to their feet, and nearly the whole assembly joined in the "Highland Fling." Many songs were sung: Miss Payton, afterward Mrs. Wood, sang some Scotch songs from the gallery. It was an exciting scene, and continued till a late hour. Some were "fu'," and all were "unco Happy." As the duke retired, he honored me with a shake of his hand.

June 7

Dear Wife:

... Yesterday I, with a friend, got on a coach and went to Richmond, a place about seven miles from here, which has long been celebrated for its beauty of scenery. But, upon my soul, I could not find anything particular to admire but the cultivation and the appearances of comfort in the dwellings, as we walked about them. You are now living in a place a thousand times more beautiful (Northampton, Mass.), and as to grandeur of scenery there is no comparison. But art has made up the dificiencies of nature. Cultivation is brought to a very great degree of perfection here. It will be many years before we can vie with this country in that particular, and I must say it will be a long time before I shall wish to do so. This show is at the expense of nine tenths of the inhabitants, perhaps ninety-nine hundredths. Yet if contentment be riches, the lower order of peasantry are rich. I never saw any wrangling in all the various mobs which I have seen collected on different occasions. There seems to be in these lower orders a social and friendly disposition, which I am sorry to say does not exist in our country. There, on such days as an Election or General Review, the lower classes of society consider themselves licensed to get drunk, and render themselves as beastly as possible; and I hardly remember an instance of a holiday of the kind to pass over, without a fight and sometimes a dozen of them. I have not, while I have been in this country, seen anything in the streets, at the fairs, or any other place of amusement for the peasantry, that looked like ill-will toward each other. If I, in passing the crowd in the streets, happen to run against a boy, or tread upon his foot (which you know not to be a gentle pressure), he directly pulls off his hat and begs pardon, or at least makes no complaint. Not so at home. If one happens to encroach upon the rights of one of our republican boys in any degree, he lets fly a volley of mud rockets at you, and damns your eyes up and down. ...

Your affectionate husband,
C. Harding

Monday, June 14. ... I have already excited a warm interest with many friends in my behalf: to fail, therefore, would be painful beyond description. To return to Boston, and receive a cold welcome where I have been so warmly patronized would be a sore wound to my pride and ice to my ambition. Yet it is but fair to count upon this in some degree. Public favors and opinions are capricious. There was something novel, perhaps, in my history that contributed more to my unheard -of success than any merit I possessed as a painter. The fact of a man's coming from the backwoods of America, entirely uneducated, to paint even a tolerable portrait, was enough to excite some little interest. That source of interest will be cut off on my return. I shall be judged of as one having had all the advantages of the best schools of art in Europe; and the probability is, that more will be expected of me than is in the power of almost any man to perform.

To S.F.L.

Monday, August 16. Set off for Hamilton. Stayed at the inn. Tuesday morning, sent my letter with my address to the palace; but it was soon returned, with directions from the footman that "all letters to his Grace must come through the post-office." This, I afterwards learned, was to avoid refusing more directly, admittance to the gallery, as there were so many applicants that the family was constantly annoyed. I took the letters, and went to the palace with the resolve to see his Grace, if possible. After waiting half an hour, the duke came out from the breakfast-table, and very politely asked me into the breakfast-room, and invited me to take breakfast; but I declined the honor, and made my business known to him, which was to request the duke to sit for a picture for the Duke of Sussex. He readily complied, and asked me to send for my portmanteau, and take up my residence with him.

I soon commenced the portrait. The day passed off very happily in looking at the pictures of the old masters, of which here are hundreds. Five o'clock came, and I began to dress for dinner. . . . wished the ordeal of dinner well over. Six o'clock came at last, and I was ushered into the dining-room. In a short time I began to realize that my titled companions were very like other people; and in a short time more, my nerves became steady, though I could not entirely refrain from moving my knife and fork a little, or playing with my bread, or in some other awkward way betraying my want of ease. There was a display of great magnificence; servants all in livery, splendid plate. The duchess and her daughter retired early; and about nine, the gentlemen followed them. The duchess made tea with her own fair hand, and was, besides, very agreeable. At half past eleven, I set off for bed; and, on my way, thanked my stars that it was all over, and matters stood no worse.

The palace is two hundred and sixty-five feet long by two hundred broad. The picture gallery is a hundred and thirty-five long, full of old cabinets and other curious furniture. I am obliged to own myself that this style of living is very charming: everything around one savors strongly of title, wealth, and antiquity. We breakfast at ten, lunch at two, and dine at six. The duchess is pretty, witty, and sociable. Lord Archibald Hamilton is staying here at this time, and is a very clever man. I think I shall succeed very well. All the household servants have been in to look at the picture, and say it could not be more like. As I walk about the grounds, the laborers, old and young, lift their hats as I pass them. This respect and reverence sit but ill on me, who have been all the early part of life in as humble a sphere as those who pay it. What freak of fortune is this which has raised me from the hut in my native wilds to the table of a duke of the realm of Great Britain! By another freak, I may be sent back to the hovel again, but not to enjoy those innocent pleasures that were mixed with the toils of boyhood. . . .

Sunday night. After dinner, took leave of the family. The duke urged me to stay a few days longer. The duchess wished me every success, and Lord Archibald pressed me to call on him in London. The duke said if it was at any time in his power to serve me, he should be happy to do so. He ordered a portrait of his Royal Highness, the Duke of Sussex. He advised me not to think of returning to my own country for the present. Thus ended a visit of ten days that I shall long remember with delight and gratitude, but no honor which a royal duke or any one else in this country can confer upon me will ever make me feel that pleasure which the remembrance of the kindness of the people of Boston has done.

JOHN NEAL CONCLUDES THAT
BENTHAM IS THE GREATEST MIND
OF THE MODERN AGE

1827

John Neal is one of those figures who once loomed large on the literary horizon but is now universally forgotten. An editor, poet, and novelist, he was in his day considered something of a rival to Cooper, but the haste and carelessness and profusion of his writings forfeited his reputation. Lowell has hit him off neatly in his *A Fable for Critics:* he

> Might have been poet, but that, in its stead, he
> Preferred to believe that he was so already;
> Too hasty to wait till Art's ripe fruit should drop,
> He must pelt down an unripe and colicky crop. . . .

Outraged by British slurs on America, Neal betook himself to Britain in 1823 with the object of defense—and counterattack. His talent for journalism stood him in good stead, and he was soon contributing to a dozen English journals. Meantime he had made the acquaintance of the aged Jeremy Bentham, who gave him quarters in his house; he later wrote a memoir of Bentham, one of

From John Neal, *Wandering Recollections of a Busy Life, An Autobiography* (Boston, 1869), pp. 300–308.

the first in our literature. On his return to America he continued his literary and journalistic career but with ill success; fortunate investments in Maine quarries, however, compensated for the decline in his literary fortunes.

Before I went abroad, I was familiar with Mr. Bentham's published works, but supposed him to be a Frenchman, as all I had met with, except his "Morals and Legislation," and the "Defence of Usury," were written in French. Nobody to whom I applied, not even Professor Hoffman, of the Maryland University, nor John Pierpont, who were among his most enthusiastic admirers, could give me any information worth having, about the man himself, or his works.

After my arrival in England, I continued my inquiries, but found the "Philosopher of Queen-Square Place" little better than a myth. Nobody knew him, nobody had seen him, and nobody knew where to find him; nobody, that is, of whom I inquired. Judge of my surprise, therefore, when I received an invitation from Mr. R. Doane, his secretary, to a dinner at the "Hermitage," as they called it, on Queen-Square Place, Westminster, opening into St. James's Park.

I went; and the consequence was, after two or three capital dinners had been digested, that I was installed, without ceremony, though with decided emphasis, in the apartments occupied not long before by Aaron Burr, and then by Fanny Wright.

"Why are most of your works"—all I had been acquainted with in America, except the earliest issue of his Morals and Legislation, and the Defence of Usury—"published in French?" I asked, one day, when we were talking about his Théorie des Peines et des Récompenses, taken from the manuscripts of Jeremy Bentham, by Et. Dumont, which I had proposed to translate into English before I left America, . . .

"Because," he answered, "I wrote most of them in French."

"But why in French?"

"Because, in writing French, I was not so painfully sensible of the inadequacy of language, as when writing English." And this, from the man who had written a "Defence of Usury," so wonderful for its clearness, beauty, and precision, that it was attributed to Lord Mansfield himself, when it first appeared; and a "Fragment on Government," wherein he took not a few of the Law-Magnates by the ears, and fairly *boned* Blackstone, till there was little or nothing left of him, but the stuffing.

But who was Dumont? And how came he to be rummaging Bentham's manuscripts and other treasures, until he had produced no fewer than eight large octavos, of the highest authority over all Europe, in the most beautiful French, and so logically arranged, that every new volume seemed to be naturally evolved from the foregoing, like the banyan tree, which no sooner touches the soil, than it takes root and springs up anew. . . .

Dumont was born and educated at Geneva. He was also in process of time, pastor of a Protestant Church at St. Petersburgh. Lord Lansdowne applied to Romilly, a stranger at the time, about sending for Dumont to become the tutor of his son, Henry, the youngest, afterward Marquis of Lansdowne, . . .

Such was Dumont; the man, above all others, to whom the great and good Bentham is chiefly indebted for the prodigious reputation he now enjoys, throughout the world, among rulers, philanthropists, statesmen, lawgivers, and lawyers. "Nothing." Dr. Parr used to say, "nothing since the appearance of Bacon's 'Novum Organum,' is to be compared with Bentham's 'Morals and Legislation.'" And Dr. Parr was right; although even his "Morals and Legislation," as it first appeared in English, would never have been studied or cared for, but for Dumont's admirable translation into French, and his rearrangement of the whole in three large octavos, whereby the system, and laws of mind regulating that system, as first announced by Bentham, in language not easily understood by the common reader, became as clear as crystal, and compact as adamant.

The jokes of Sydney Smith, the fibs and laughable exaggerations of Captain Parry, and the wicked fun of Christopher North, had got such possession of the public mind, that nothing was too strange for belief, when told of the "whitehaired Sage," as Bowring called him. That he did much, and said more, to justify some of the notions that prevail, cannot be denied. His whimsies and extravagances were so out of the common way, that, really, it is no wonder sometimes, that he passed for a "gray-haired lunatic," out for exercise, or trying to escape from his keepers, when the simple truth was, that instead of taking his "post-prandial vibration," as he called it, in his "workshop," or up and down, and hither and thither in his garden, which was the largest that opened into the Park, he cantered off, with his white hair flying in the wind, and his secretary following, on his way through Charing-Cross and Fleet-Street, to the annuity-office, where he had to report himself, in person, and account for having outlived all their calculations. He was now in his seventy-eighth year, and lived till June 6, 1832; being past eighty-five at the time of his death. . . .

People who have heard of Jeremy Bentham, only through *Blackwood,* the *Edinburgh,* Francis Jeffrey, Professor Wilson, and that wittiest of reviewers, Sydney Smith, can have no idea of the wonderful changes in legislation and jurisprudence and in the administration of justice, throughout the world, of which he was the originator. . . .

Since the times of Aristotle and Lord Bacon, it may be said with truth, and here I have the opinion of Dr. Parr to strengthen me, there has been no such reforms brought by any mortal man in logic, in morals and legislation, in civil and criminal jurisprudence, in the administration of justice, or in the treatment of criminals, as by this extraordinary man, and his disciples and followers. The legislation of the world—it is not saying too much, of the whole world—has been modified, or completely revolutionized, by the tremendous, though quiet energy of that old man's mind. . . .

But how came this man to undertake so much, and to persevere so long, against all combinations and misrepresentations, for a lifetime?

"I am naturally a weak mind," said he to me, one day, as we sat over our tea, talking this matter over. "All that can be said of me is, that I have made the most of it."

"I have sometimes thought," said he, at another time, with a look of great solemnity, "whether or no I was not mad. If I am not—such things will come across our thoughts, now and then—all the rest of the world must be so."—"No, no," said I: "their not believing as you do, in cases which are abundantly clear to you, proves, not that they are mad, but that they have not considered the matter as you have."—"True, true," he said; "yes, yes, to be sure; besides, for forty years there was nobody to attack me, except with ridicule and misrepresentation."

"What did your father think of these works?" I inquired, as he took down the "Defence of Usury," from a shelf, and mentioned that the copy had belonged to his father. It was crammed with letters, and a review from the "Old Monthly" was wafered into it. "I'll tell you," said he, with great eagerness. "'Jerry,'" said he, on his deathbed, 'Jerry, you have made a philosopher of me.' . . . He made another will," added Mr. Bentham, "and left out the name of Christ." I did more than smile now; I laughed outright. The idea of taking that for a measure of improvement in philosophy was yet more diverting than the other. But he was perfectly serious. And, by the way, this reminds me that Mr. Solicitor Parkes, author of the "History of Chancery," who married an American wife, the daughter of Dr. Priestley, told me, one day, when we were canvassing the past of Benthamism, and casting his horoscope for the future, that, when he was a boy, Dr. Parr told him to read the works of Bentham, as the greatest man that ever lived.

JOHN J. AUDUBON: "I KNOW NOW THAT I HAVE NOT WORKED IN VAIN"

1826—28

John J. Audubon—originally Jean Jacques—is one of the most romantic figures in the history of American art and American exploration. Born in Santo Domingo, the natural son of a French planter, Audubon spent his boyhood in the West Indies and in Nantes. He early discovered a special talent for painting flowers and birds, studied for a short time under the great David, and when he moved to America in 1803 he found—as had the earlier ornithologist Alexander Wilson—an incredibly rich field for his talents. By good fortune he was a failure in trade, and began to apply himself exclusively to his art, roaming the American wilderness from Pennsylvania to New Orleans and, eventually, from Labrador to the Missouri, in his search for birds. In 1826, unable to find a publisher or even an engraver in America, he betook himself to England, where he found not only a great engraver, Robert Havell, but numerous subscribers to his projected work. Audubon stayed some years in Britain—chiefly in Edinburgh—doing the plates for his *Birds of America,* one of the great works of art, and of natural science, of his generation. Wholly

From Maria R. Audubon, *Audubon and His Journals* (London, 1898), pp. 110–111, 179–180, 206–207, 251–255, 277–278, 287–289.

without scientific training, he nevertheless prepared a five-volume *Ornithological Biography* and, in his old age, did substantial work on a *Quadrupeds of North America.*

August 6, Sunday [1826]. When I arrived in this city [Liverpool] I felt dejected, miserably so; the uncertainty as to my reception, my doubts as to how my work would be received, all conspired to depress me. Now, how different are my sensations! I am well received everywhere, my works praised and admired, and my poor heart is at last relieved from the great anxiety that has for so many years agitated it, for I know now that I have not worked in vain. This morning I went to church; the sermon was not to my mind, but the young preacher may improve. This afternoon I packed up Harlan's "Fauna" for Mr. E. Roscoe, and went to the Institution, where Mr. Munro was to meet me and escort me to Mr. Wm. Roscoe, Jr., where I was to take tea. Mr. Munro was not on hand, so, after a weary waiting, I went alone to Mr. Roscoe's habitation. It was full of ladies and gentlemen, all his own family, and I knew almost every one. I was asked to imitate the calls of some of the wild birds, and though I did not wish to do so, consented to satisfy the curiosity of the company. I sat between Mr. Wm. Roscoe and his son Edward, and answered question after question. Finally, the good old gentleman and I retired to talk about my plans. He strongly advises me not to exhibit my works without remuneration. Later more guests came in, and more questions were asked; they appeared surprised that I have no wonderful tales to tell, that, for instance, I have not been devoured at least six times by *tigers,* bears, wolves, foxes; no I never was troubled by any larger animals than ticks and mosquitoes, and that is quite enough. At last one after another took leave. The *well bred* society of England is the perfection of manners; such tone of voice I never heard in America. Indeed, thus far, I have great reason to like England. My plans now are to go to Manchester, to Derbyshire to visit Lord Stanley (Earl of Derby), Birmingham, London for three weeks, Edinburgh, back to London, and then to France, Paris, Nantes, to see my venerable stepmother, Brussels, and return to England. I am advised to do this by men of learning and excellent judgment, who say this will enable me to find where my work may be published with greatest advantage. I have letters given me to Baron Humboldt, General La Fayette, Sir Walter Scott, Sir Humphry Davy, Miss Hannah More, Miss Edgeworth, Sir Thomas Lawrence, etc., etc. How I wish Victor could be with me; what an opportunity to see the best of this island; few ordinary individuals ever enjoyed the same reception. Many persons of distinction have begged drawing lessons of me at a guinea an hour. I am astonished at the plainness of the ladies' dress; in the best society there are no furbelows and fandangoes. . . .

December 10, Sunday. My situation in Edinburgh borders almost on the miraculous. With scarce one of those qualities necessary to render a man able to pass through the throng of the learned people here, I am positively looked on by all the professors and many of the principal persons here as a very extraordinary man. I cannot comprehend this in the least. Indeed I have received here so much kindness and attention that I look forward with regret to my removal to Glasgow, fifty miles hence, where I expect to go the last of this month. Sir William Jardine has been spending a few days here purposely to see me, and I am to meet Mr. Selby, and with these two gentlemen discuss the question of a joint publication, which may possibly be arranged. It is now a month since my work was begun by Mr. Lizars; the paper is of unusual size, called "double elephant," and the plates are to be finished in such superb style as to eclipse all of the same kind in existence. The price of each number, which will contain five prints, is two guineas, and all individuals have the privilege of subscribing for the whole, or any portion of it. The two plates now finished are truly beautiful. This number consists of the Turkeycock, the Cuckoos on the pawpaws, and three small drawings, which in the centre of the large sheet have a fine effect, and an air of richness, that I think must ensure success, though I do not yet feel assured that all will go well. Yet on the other hand, all things bear a better aspect than I expected to see for many months, if ever. I think that if my work takes in Edinburgh, it will anywhere. I have strong friends here who interest themselves in me, but I must wait patiently till the first number is finished. Mr. Jameson, the first professor of this place, and the conductor of the *Philosophical Journal,* gives a beautiful announcement of my work in the present number, with an account, by me, of the Turkey Buzzard. Dr. Brewster also announces it, with the introductory letter to my work, and Professor Wilson also, in *Blackwood's Magazine.* These three journals print upwards of thirty thousand copies, so that my name will spread quickly enough. I am to deliver lectures on Natural History at the Wernerian Society at each of the meetings while I am here, and Professor Jameson told me I should soon be made a member of all the other societies here, and that would give my work a good standing throughout Europe. Much as I find here to enjoy, the great round company I am thrown in has become fatiguing to me in the extreme, nor does it agree with my early habits. I go out to dine at six, seven, or even eight o'clock in the evening, and it is often one or two when the party breaks up; then painting all day, with my immense correspondence which increases daily, makes my head feel like an immense hornet's-nest, and my body wearied beyond all calculations; yet it has to be done; those who have my interests at heart tell me I must not refuse a single invitation. . . .

January 22, Monday [1827]. I was painting diligently when Captain Hall came in, and said: "Put on your coat, and come with me to Sir Walter Scott; he wishes to see you *now*." In a moment I was ready, for I really believe my coat and hat came to me instead of my going to them. My heart trembled; I longed for the meeting, yet wished it over. Had not his wondrous pen penetrated my soul with the consciousness that here was a genius from God's hand? I felt overwhelmed at the thought of meeting Sir Walter, the Great Unknown. We reached the house, and a powdered waiter was asked if Sir Walter were in. We were shown forward at once, and entering a very small room Captain Hall said: "Sir Walter, I have brought Mr. Audubon." Sir Walter came forward, pressed my hand warmly, and said he was "glad to have the honor of meeting me." His long, loose, silvery locks struck me; he looked like Franklin at his best. He also reminded me of Benjamin West; he had the great benevolence of Wm. Roscoe about him, and a kindness most prepossessing. I could not forbear looking at him, my eyes feasted on his countenance. I watched his movements as I would those of a celestial being; his long, heavy, white eyebrows struck me forcibly. His little room was tidy, though it partook a good deal of the character of a laboratory. He was wrapped in a quilted morning-gown of light purple silk; he had been at work writing on the *Life of Napoleon*. He writes close lines, rather curved as they go from left to right, and puts an immense deal on very little paper. After a few minutes had elapsed he begged Captain Hall to ring a bell; a servant came and was asked to bid Miss Scott come to see Mr. Audubon. Miss Scott came, black-haired and black-dressed, not handsome but said to be highly accomplished, and she is the daughter of Sir Walter Scott. There was much conversation. I talked little, but, believe me, I listened and observed, careful if ignorant. I cannot write more now—I have just returned from the Royal Society. Knowing that I was a candidate for the electorate of the society, I felt very uncomfortable and would gladly have been hunting on Tawapatee Bottom. . . .

London, May 21. . . . I should begin this page perhaps with a great exclamation mark, and express much pleasure, but I have not the wish to do either; to me London is just like the mouth of an immense monster, guarded by millions of sharp-edged teeth, from which if I escape unhurt it must be called a miracle. I have many times longed to see London, and now I am here I feel a desire beyond words to be in my beloved woods. . . .

May 29. I have been about indeed like a post-boy, taking letters everywhere. In the evening I went to the Athenaeum at the corner of Waterloo Place, expecting to meet Sir Thomas Lawrence and other gentlemen; but I was assured that about eleven or half-past was the fashionable time for these gentlemen to assemble; so I ι eturned to my rooms, being worn out; for I must have walked forty miles on these hard pavements, from Idol Lane to Grosvenor Square, and across in many different directions, all equally far apart.

Tuesday, May 30. At twelve o'clock I proceeded with some of my drawings to see Mr. Gallatin, our *Envoy extraordinaire.* He has the ease and charm of manner of a perfect gentleman, and addressed me in French. Seated by his side we soon travelled (in conversation) to America; he detests the English, and spoke in no measured terms of London as the most disagreeable place in Europe. While we were talking Mrs. and Miss Gallatin came in, and the topic was changed, and my drawings were exhibited. The ladies knew every plant, and Mr. Gallatin nearly every bird. I found at home that new suit of clothes that my friend Basil Hall insisted upon my procuring. I looked this remarkable black dress well over, put it on, and thus attired like a mournful Raven, went to dine at Mr. Children's. On my return I found a note from Lord Stanley, asking me to put his name down as a subscriber; this pleased me exceedingly, as I consider Lord Stanley a man eminently versed in *true* and *real* ornithological pursuits. Of course my spirits are better; how little does alter a man. A trifle raises him, a little later another casts him down. Mr. Bentley has come in and tells me three poor fellows were hanged at Newgate this morning for stealing sheep. My God! how awful are the laws of this land, to take a human life for the theft of a miserable sheep.

June 1. . . . I was invited to dine with Sir Robert Inglis, and took a seat in the Clapham coach to reach his place. The Epsom races are in full activity about sixteen miles distant; and innumerable coaches, men on horseback, barouches, foot passengers, filled the road, all classes from the *beau monde* to the beggar intent on seeing men run the chance of breaking their necks on horses going like the wind, as well as losing or gaining pence, shillings, or guineas by the thousand. Clapham is distant from London five miles, and Sir Robert invited me to see the grounds while he dressed, as he came in almost as I did. How different from noisy London! I opened a door and found myself on a circular lawn so beautifully ornamented that I was tempted to exclaim, "How beautiful are Thy works, O God!" I walked through avenues of foreign trees and shrubs, amongst which were tulip-trees, larches, and cypresses from America. Many birds were here, some searching for food, while others gave vent to their happy feelings in harmonious concerts. The house itself was covered with vines, the front a mass of blooming roses exuberant with perfume. What a delightful feast I had in this peaceful spot! At dinner there were several other guests, among them the widow of Sir Thomas Stanford Raffles, governor of Java, a most superior woman, and her conversation with Dr. Horsfield was deeply interesting. The doctor is a great zoologist, and has published a fine work on the birds of Java. It was a true *family* dinner, and therefore I enjoyed it; Sir Robert is at the head of the business of the Carnatic association of India.

Friday, June 2. At half-past seven I reached Sir Thomas Lawrence, and found him writing letters. He received me kindly, and at once examined some of my drawings, repeating frequently, "Very clever, indeed!" From such a man these words mean much. During breakfast, which was simple enough and *sans cérémonie,* he asked me many questions about America and about my work. After leaving him I met Mr. Vigors by appointment, who said everything possible to encourage me, and told me I would be elected as a foreign member to the Athenaeum. . . .

January 20 [1828]. Oh! how dull I feel; how long am I to be confined in this immense jail? In London, amidst all the pleasures, I feel unhappy and dull; the days are heavy, the nights worse. Shall I ever again see and enjoy the vast forests in their calm purity, the beauties of America? I wish myself anywhere but in London. *Why* do I dislike London? Is it because the constant evidence of the contrast between the rich and the poor is a torment to me, or is it because of its size and crowd? I know not, but I long for sights and sounds of a different nature. Young Green came to ask me to go with him to see Regent's Park, and we went accordingly, I rather an indifferent companion, I fear, till we reached the bridge that crosses the waters there, where I looked in vain for water-fowl. Failing to find any I raised my eyes towards the peaceful new moon, and to my astonishment saw a large flock of Wild Ducks passing over me; after a few minutes a second flock passed, which I showed my young friend. Two flocks of Wild Ducks, of upwards of twenty each! Wonderful indeed! I thought of the many I have seen when bent on studying their habits, and grew more homesick than ever. . . .

[Cambridge] *March 5*. Since I left Edinburgh, I have not had a day as brilliant as this in point of being surrounded by learned men. This morning I took a long walk among the Colleges, and watched many birds; while thus employed, a well dressed man handed me a card on which was written in *English*, "The bearer desires to meet with some one who speaks either French, Italian, or Spanish." I spoke to him in Spanish and French, both of which he knew well. He showed me a certificate from the consul of Sweden, at Leith, which affirmed his story, that he with three sailors had been shipwrecked, and now wished to return to the Continent, but they had only a few shillings, and none of them spoke English. I gave him a sovereign, just as I saw Professor Sedgwick approaching; he came to my room to see my birds, but could only give me a short time as he had a lecture to deliver. I returned to my rooms, and just as I was finishing lunch the Vice-Chancellor made his appearance,—a small old man, with hair as white as snow, dressed in a flowing gown, with two little bits of white muslin in lieu of cravat. He remained with me upwards of two hours; he admired my work, and promised to do all he could. I was delighted with his conversation; he is a man of wide knowledge, and it seemed to me of sound judgment. Professor Henslow invited me to dine on Friday, and just as I finished my note of acceptance, came in with three gentlemen. At four I went to Mr. Greenwood's to dine; as I entered I saw with dismay upwards of thirty gentlemen; I was introduced to one after another, and then we went to the "Hall," where dinner was set. This hall resembled the interior of a Gothic church; a short prayer was said, and we sat down to a sumptuous dinner. Eating was not precisely my object, it seldom is; I looked first at the *convives*. A hundred students sat apart from our table, and the "Fellows," twelve in number, with twenty guests constituted our "mess." The dinner, as I said, was excellent, and I thought these learned "Fellows" must have read, among other studies, Dr. Kitchener on the "Art of Cookery." The students gradually left in parcels, as vultures leave a carcass; we remained. A fine gilt or gold tankard, containing a very strong sort of nectar, was handed to me; I handed it, after tasting, to the next, and so it went round. Now a young man came, and as we rose, he read a short prayer from a small board (such as butchers use to kill flies with). We then went to the room where we had assembled, and conversation at once began; perhaps the wines went the rounds for an hour, then tea and coffee, after which the table was cleared, and I was requested to open my portfolio. I am proud *now* to show them, and I saw with pleasure these gentlemen admired them. I turned over twenty-five, but before I had finished received the subscription of the Librarian for the University, and the assurance of the Secretary of the Philosophical Society that they would take it. It was late before I was allowed to come away.

Thursday, March 6. A cold snowy day; I went to the library of the University and the Philosophical Society rooms, and dined again in "Hall," with Professor Sedgwick. There were four hundred students, and forty "Fellows;" quite a different scene from Corpus College. Each one devoured his meal in a hurry; in less than half an hour grace was read again by *two* students, and Professor Whewell took me to his own rooms with some eight or ten others. My book was inspected as a matter of courtesy. Professor Sedgwick was gay, full of wit and cleverness; the conversation was very animated, and I enjoyed it much. Oh! my Lucy, that I also had received a university education! I listened and admired for a long time, when suddenly Professor Whewell began asking me questions about the woods, the birds, the aborigines of America. The more I rove about. the more I find how little known the interior of America is; we sat till late. No subscriber to-day, but I must not despair; nothing can be done without patience and industry, and, thank God, I have both. . . .

Sunday, March 9. Cambridge on a Sunday is a place where I would suppose the basest mind must relax, for the time being, from the error of denying the existence of a Supreme Being; all is calm —silent—solemn—almost sublime. The beautiful bells fill the air with melody, and the heart with a wish for prayer. I went to church with Mr. Whewell at Great St. Mary's, and heard an impressive sermon on Hope from Mr. Henslow. After that I went to admire Nature, as the day was beautifully inviting. Professor Heath of King's College wished me to see his splendid chapel, and with a ticket of admission I resorted there at three. We had simple hymns and prayers, the former softly accompanied by the notes of an immense organ, standing nearly in the centre of that astonishing building; the chanters were all young boys in white surplices. I walked with Mr. Heath to Mr. Whewell's, and with him went to Trinity Chapel. The charm that had held me all day was augmented many fold as I entered an immense interior where were upward of four hundred collegians in their white robes. The small wax tapers, the shadowy distances, the slow footfalls of those still entering, threw my imagination into disorder. A kind of chilliness almost as of fear came to me, my lips quivered, my heart throbbed, I fell on my knees and prayed to be helped and comforted. I shall remember this sensation forever, my Lucy. When at Liverpool, I always go to the church for the blind; did I reside at Cambridge, I would be found each Sunday at Trinity Chapel.

JAMES FENIMORE COOPER
CASTS A JUDICIOUS EYE
ON ENGLISH SOCIETY

1826

James Fenimore Cooper was perhaps the first distinguished man of letters to reveal that curious ambivalence about the relations of the New World and the Old that has been so persistent a theme in American literature, and in American politics too. Deeply rooted in American soil, and in American history, his devotion to his country was almost a religion, yet he was not happy in it nor could he come to terms with what it appeared to be during and after the Jackson Administration. Deeply suspicious of the Old World—and particularly of Britain (in 1839 he published a history of the naval war of 1812)—he much preferred life abroad to life at home, and spent years in Paris, Florence, Dresden, and other European cities. All this Cooper confessed readily enough in his writings: compare *Notions of a Traveling Bachelor* with *The American Democrat* or *Homeward Bound* with *Home as Found*. When Cooper sailed for Europe in 1826 he was already world-famous, his books, as S. F. B. Morse wrote, "in the windows of every bookshop . . . published, as soon as he produces them, in thirty-four different places in Europe." He spent less time in Britain than in any other European country, and was less at home

From James Fenimore Cooper, *England, With Sketches of Society in the Metropolis* (London, 1837), III, pp. 121–133, 171–202.

in it than anywhere else (except perhaps the United States). Yet he did enjoy his popularity there, and his association with the poet Samuel Rogers, the Holland House clique, and the Marquis of Lansdowne. And if his comments on the English class system are acidulous, his comparison of the social and moral qualities of the English and the Americans is judicious.

Servant Classes

To James Stevenson, Esq.

The question is often asked, in what do the poor of England suffer more than the poor of any other country? I am not sufficiently versed in the details connected with the subject, to speak with authority, but I can give you the impressions received, as a looker-on.

In comparing the misery of England with that of the continent of Europe, one must remember the great difference of climate. A man suffers less at Naples, without a coat or a fire, and with three *grani* for his daily pittance, than is undergone in England, beneath woollen, with ten *grani* to furnish the "ways and means." These facts make a great moral difference in favour of England, when we come to consider the merits of systems, though the physical consequences may be against her.

The poor of this country appear to me to be over-worked. They have little or no time for relaxation, and instead of exhibiting that frank, manly cheerfulness, and heartiness of feeling, that have been so much extolled, they appear sullen, discontented, and distrustful. There is far less confidence and sympathy between classes, than I had expected to see, for, although a good understanding may exist between the great landholder, and the affluent yeoman who pays him rent and farms the soil, the social chain appears to be broken between those below the latter and their superiors. I do not mean that the rich are obdurate to the sufferings of the poor, but that the artificial condition of the country has choked the ordinary channels of sympathy, and that the latter, when known at all, are known only as "the poor." They are the objects of duties, rather than fellow-creatures living constantly within the influence of all the charities, including those of communion and rights, as well as those which are exhibited in donations.

There is one large class of beings, in England, whose condition I should think less enviable than that of Asiatic slaves. I allude to the female servants of all work, in the families of those who keep lodging-houses, tradesmen, and other small house-keepers. These poor creatures have an air of dogged sullen misery that I have never seen equalled, in any other class of human beings, not even excepting the beggars in the streets. In our lodgings at Southampton there was one of these girls, and her hand was never idle, her foot seemed to know no rest, while her manner was that of wearied humility. We were then fresh from home, and the unmitigated toil of her existence struck us all most painfully. When we spoke to her kindly, she seemed startled, and looked distrustful and frightened. A less inviting subject for sympathy could scarcely be imagined, for she was large, coarse, robust, and even masculine, but even these iron qualities were taxed beyond endurance.

I should not draw a picture like this, on the authority of a single instance. I have seen too much to corroborate the first impressions, and make no doubt that the case of the woman at Southampton was the rule, and that instances of better treatment make the exceptions. In one of my bachelor visits here, I had lodgings in which there was a still more painful example. The mistress of this house was married and had children, and being a lazy slattern, with three sets of lodgings in the house, her tyranny exceeded all I had ever before witnessed. You are to understand that the solitary servant, in these houses, is usually cook, house-maid, and waiter. When the lodger keeps no servant, she answers his bell, as well as the street door knocker, and goes on all his errands that do not extend beyond a proper distance. The girl was handsome, had much delicacy of form and expression, and an eye that nature had intended to be brilliant and spirited. She could not be more than twenty-two or three, but misery had already driven her to the bottle. I saw her only at the street door, and on two or three occasions when she answered my own bell, in the absence of my man. At the street door, she stood with her eyes on the carpet, and when I made my acknowledgments for the trouble she had taken, she curtsied hurriedly, and muttered the usual "Thankee, sir." When she came into my room it was on a sort of drilled trot, as if she had been taught a particular movement to denote assiduity and diligence, and she never presumed to raise her eyes to mine, but stood the whole time looking meekly down. For every order I was duly thanked! One would think that all this was hard to be borne, but, a day or two before I left the house, I found her weeping in the street. She had disobliged her lazy, exacting mistress, by staying out ten minutes too long on an errand, and had lost her place. I took the occasion to give her a few shillings as her due for past services, but so complete was her misery in being turned away without a character, that even the sight of money failed to produce the usual effects. I make little doubt she took refuge in gin, the bane of thousands and tens of thousands of her sex, in this huge theatre of misery and vice.

The order, method, and punctuality of the servants of England are all admirable. These qualities probably contribute quite as much to their own comfort as to that of their masters and mistresses. It is seldom that well bred persons, any where, are unkind to their menials, though they are sometimes exacting through ignorance of the pain they are giving. The tyranny comes from those who always appear to feel a desire to revenge their own previous hardships on the unfortunate creatures whom chance puts in their power. I do not know that the English of condition are unkind to their domestics; the inference would fairly be that they are not; but there is something, either in the system that has unfortunately been adopted, or in the character of the people, which has introduced a distance between the parties that must be injurious to the character of those who serve.

On the continent of Europe the art of managing domestics appears to be understood much better than it is here. A body servant is considered as a sort of humble friend, being treated with confidence but without familiarity, nor can I say I have often witnessed any want of proper respect on the part of the domestics. The old Princesse de ——, who was a model of grace and propriety in her deportment, never came to see my wife, without saying something kind or flattering to her *femme de chambre*, who usually admitted her and saw her out. A French servant expects to be spoken to, when you meet on the stairs, in the court, or in the garden, and would be hurt without a *"bonjour"* at meeting, or an *"adieu"* at parting. A French duke would be very apt to take off his hat, if he had occasion to go into the porter's lodge, or into the servant's hall, but I think very little of this courtesy would be practised here. It is our misfortune to try to imitate the English in this, as in other things, and I make little question, one of the principal reasons why our servants are so bad is owing to their not being put on the proper footing of confidential dependants.

The comparison between the condition of the common English house-servant, and that of the American slave, is altogether in favour of the latter, if the hardship of compelled servitude be kept out of view. The negro, bond or free, is treated much more kindly and with greater friendship, than most of the English domestics; the difference in colour, with the notions that have grown up under them, removing all distrust of danger from familiarity. This is not said with a view to turn the tables on our kinsmen for their number-less taunts and continued injustice; for, with such an object, I think something more original and severe might easily be got up; but simply because I believe it to be true. Perhaps the servants of no country have more enviable places than the American slaves, so far as mere treatment and the amount of labour are concerned.

One prominent feature of poverty, in England, is dependent on causes which ought not to be ascribed to the system. If a man can be content to live on a few grapes, and a pound of coarse bread, and to go without a coat, or a fire, in a region like that of Naples, it does not necessarily follow, that another ought to be able to do the same things in a country in which there are no grapes, in which a fire is necessary, and a coat indispensable. The high civilization of England unquestionably contributes also to the misery of the very poor, by augmenting their wants, though it adds greatly to the comforts of those who are able to sustain themselves. As between the Americans and the English, it is not saying much, under the peculiar circum-stances of their respective countries, that the poor of the former are immeasurably better off than the poor of the latter; but, apart from certain advantages of climate in favour of the south of Europe, I am not at all certain that the poor of England, as a body, do not fare quite as well as the poor of any other part of Christendom. I know little more of the matter, however, than meets the eye of an ordinary traveller; but, taking that as a guide, I think I should prefer being a pauper in England, to being a beggar in France. I now speak of physical sufferings altogether, for on all points that relate to the feelings, admitting that the miserable still retain sentiment on such points, I think England the least desirable country, for a poor man, that I know.

The notion that so generally prevails in America, on the subject of the independence and manliness of the English, certainly does not apply to the body of the poor, nor do I think the tradesmen, in general, have as much of these qualities, as those of France. The possession of their franchises, at a time when such privileges were rare, may have given some claims to a peculiar character of this nature, but while the pressure of society has been gradually weigh-ing heavier and heavier on the nation, creating the dependence of competition and poverty, in lieu of that of political power, the other countries of Europe have lessened their legal oppression, until, I think, the comparison has got to be in their favour. I should say there is quite as little manly independence, in the intercourse between classes, here, as in any country I have visited. . . .

Comparative Merits of the English and the Americans

TO RICHARD COOPER, ESQ.

It would be an occupation of interest to note the changes, moral and physical, that time, climate, and different institutions have produced between the people of England, and those of America.

Physically, I do not think the change as great as is usually imagined. Dress makes a sensible difference in appearance, and I find that the Americans, who have been under the hands of the English tailors, are not easily distinguished from the English themselves. The principal points of distinction strike me to be these: we are taller, and less fleshy; more disposed to stoop; have more prominent features, and faces less full; are less ruddy, and more tanned; have much smaller hands and feet, anti-democratical as it may be, and are more slouching in gait. The exceptions, of course, are numerous, but I think these distinctions may be deemed national. The American, who has become Europeanized by dress, however, is so very different a looking animal, from what he is at home, that too much stress is not to be laid on him. Then the great extent of the United States is creating certain physical differences in our own population, that render all such comparisons liable to many qualifications.

As to stature, and physical force, I see no reason to think the animal has deteriorated in America. As between England and the old Atlantic states, the difference is not striking, after one allows for the disparity in numbers, and the density of the population here, the eye always seeking exceptions; but, I incline to believe that the southwest will turn the scale to our side. I believe it to be a fact, that the aborigines of that portion of the Union were larger than those of our section of the country. . . .

Morally, we live under the influence of systems so completely the converse of each other, that it is matter of surprise, so many points of resemblance still remain. The immediate tendency of the English system is to create an extreme deference in all the subordinate classes for their superiors, while that of American is to run into the opposite feeling. The effects of both these tendencies are certainly observable, though relatively, that of our own much less, I think, than that of England. It gives good models a rather better chance here, than they have with us.

In England, the disaffected to the government are among precisely those who most sustain government in America; and the disaffected in America (if so strong a word can properly be used, as applied to natives) are of a class whose interests it is to sustain government in England. These facts give very different aspects to the general features of society. Walking in Regent-Street, lately, I witnessed an attempt of the police to compel some hackney coachmen to quit their boxes, and go with them before the magistrate. A crowd of a thousand people collected immediately, and its feeling was decidedly against the ministers of the law; so much so, indeed, as to render it doubtful, whether the coachmen, whose conduct had been flagrantly criminal, would not be rescued. Now, in America, I think the feeling of such a crowd would have been just the other way. It would have taken an interest in supporting the authorities of the country, instead of an interest in opposing them. This was not the case of a mob, you will remember, in which passion puts down the reason, but an ordinary occurrence of the exercise of the power of the police. Instances of this nature might be multiplied, to show that the mass of the two people act under the influence of feelings diametrically opposed to each other.

On the other hand, Englishmen of the higher classes are, with very few exceptions, and these exceptions are usually instances of mere party opposition, attached to their system, sensitive on the subject of its merits or defects, and ever ready to defend it when assailed. The American of the same class is accustomed to sneer at democracy, to cavil at its fruits, and to colour and exaggerate its faults. Though this latter disposition may be, to a degree, accounted for by the facts, that all merit is comparative, and most of our people have not had the opportunities to compare; and that it is natural to resist most that which most annoys, although the substitution of any other for the actual system would produce even greater discontent; still, I think, the general tendency of aristocratical institutions on the one hand, and of democratical on the other, is to produce this broad difference in feeling, as bctwccn classes.

Both the Americans and the English are charged with being offensively boastful and arrogant, as nations, and too much disposed to compare themselves advantageously with their neighbours. I have visited no country in which a similar disposition does not exist, and as communities are merely aggregations of men, I fancy that the disposition of a people to take this view of their own merits is no more than carrying out the well known principle of individual vanity. The English and ourselves, however, well may, and probably do, differ from other nations in one circumstance connected with such a failing. The mass in both nations are better instructed, and are of more account than the mass in other countries, and their sentiments form more of a public opinion than elsewhere. When the bulk of a people are in a condition to make themselves heard, one is not to expect much refinement or delicacy, in the sentiments they utter. The English do not strike me as being a vainer nation than the French, although, in the way of ordinary intercourse, I believe that both they and we are more boastful.

The English are to be particularly distinguished from the Americans, in the circumstances of their being a proud people. This is a useful and even an ennobling quality, when it is sustained by facts, though apt to render a people both uncomfortable and unpleasant, when the glory on which they pique themselves is passed away. We are almost entirely wanting in national pride, though abundantly supplied with an irritable vanity, that might rise to pride, had we greater confidence in our facts. Most intelligent Englishmen are ready enough to admit the obvious faults of their climate, and even of their social condition, but it is an uncommon American that will concede any thing material, on such points, unless it can be made to bear on democracy. We have the sensitiveness of provincials, increased by the consciousness of having our spurs to earn, on all matters of glory and renown, and our jealousy extends even to the reputation of the cats and dogs. It is but an indifferent compliment to human nature to add, that the man who will join, complacently, and I may say, ignorantly, in the abuse of foreigners against the institutions of the country, and even against its people, always reserving a saving clause in favour of his own particular class, will take fire if an innuendo is hazarded against its beef, or a suggestion made that the four thousand feet of the Round Peak are not equal to the thirteen thousand of the Jungfrau. The English are tolerably free from this weakness, and travelling is daily increasing this species of liberality, at least. I presume that the insular situation of England, and our own distance from Europe, are equally the causes of these traits, though there may be said to be a "property qualification" in the very nature of man, that disposes him to view his own things with complacency, and those of his neighbours with disgust. Bishop Heber, in one of his letters to Lord Grenville, in speaking of the highest peaks of the Himalayas, throws into a parenthesis, "which I feel some exultation in saying, is completely within the limits of the British empire," a sort of sentiment, of which, I dare say, neither St. Chrysostom nor Polycarp was entirely free.

On the subject of sensibility to comments on their national habits and national characters, neither France nor England is by any means as philosophical or indifferent as one might suppose. As a rule, I believe all men are more easily enraged when their real faults are censured, than when their virtues are called in question; and, if the defect happen to be unavoidable, or one for which they are not fairly responsible, the resentment is two-fold that which would attend a comment on a vice. The only difference I can discover between the English and ourselves, in this particular, is easily to be traced to our greater provincialism, youth, and the consciousness that we are obliged to anticipate some of our renown. I should say that the English are *thin-skinned,* and the Americans *raw.* Both resent fair, frank, and manly comments with the same bad taste, resorting to calumny, blackguardism, and abuse, when wit and pleasantry would prove both more effective and wiser, and, perhaps, reformation wisest of all. I can only account for this peculiarity, by supposing that the institutions and political facts of the two countries have rendered vulgar-minded men of more account than is usually the case, and that their influence has created a species of public opinion which is less under the correction of taste, principles, and manners, than is the case in nations where the mass is more depressed. Of the fact, itself, there can be no question. . . .

The English are to be distinguished from the Americans, by greater independence of personal habits. Not only the institutions, but the physical condition of our own country has a tendency to reduce us all to the same level of usages. The steamboats, the over-grown taverns, the speculative character of the enterprises, and the consequent disposition to do all things in common aid the tendency of the system in bringing about such a result. In England a man dines by himself in a room filled with other hermits, he eats at his leisure, drinks his wine in silence, reads the paper by the hour; and, in all things, encourages his individuality and insists on his particular humours. The American is compelled to submit to a common rule; he eats when others eat, sleeps when others sleep, and he is lucky, indeed, if he can read a paper in a tavern without having a stranger looking over each shoulder. The Englishman would stare at a proposal that should invade his habits under the pretence of a common wish, while the American would be very apt to yield tacitly, though this common wish be no more than an impudent assertion of some one who had contrived to effect his own purposes, under the popular plea. The Englishman is so much attached to his independence that he instinctively resists every effort to invade it, and nothing would be more likely to arouse him than to say the mass thinks differently from himself; whereas the American ever seems ready to resign his own opinion to that which is made to seem to be the opinion of the public. I say *seems* to be, for so manifest is the power of public opinion, that one of the commonest expedients of all American managers is to create an impression that the public thinks in a particular way, in order to bring the common mind in subjection. One often renders himself ridiculous by a foolish obstinacy, and the other is as often contemptible by a weak compliance. A portion of what may be called the *community* of character and habits in America is doubtless owing to the rustic nature of its society, for one more easily maintains his independence in a capital than in a village, but I think the chief reasons are to be found in the practice of referring every thing to the common mind.

It is usual to ascribe the solitary and unsocial habits of English life to the natural disposition of the people, but I think unjustly. The climate is made to bear the blame of no small portion of this peculiarity. Climate, probably, has an influence on us all, for we know that we are more elastic, and more ready to be pleased, in a clear bracing air, than in one that is close and *siroccoish*, but, on the whole I am led to think, the English owe their habits to their institutions, more than to any natural causes.

I know no subject, no feeling, nothing, on which an Englishman, as a rule, so completely loses sight of all the better points of his character, on which he is so uniformly bigotted and unjust, so ready to listen to misrepresentation and caricature, and so unwilling to receive truth, on which, in short, he is so little like himself in general, as on those connected with America.

As the result of this hasty and imperfect comparison, I am led to believe, that a national character somewhere between the two would be preferable to either, as it is actually found. This may be saying no more than that man does not exist in a condition of perfection; but were the inequalities named pared off from both people, an ingenious critic might still find faults of sufficient magnitude, to preserve the identity with the human race, and qualities of sufficient elevation, to entitle both to be considered among the greatest and best nations of modern, if not of any other, times.

In most things that pertain to taste, the English have greatly the advantage of us, though *taste* is certainly not the strong side of English character. On this point, alone, one might write a book, but a very few remarks must now satisfy you. In nothing, however, is this superiority more apparent, than in their simplicity, and, particularly, in their simplicity of language. They call a spade, a spade. I very well know, that neither men nor women, in America, who are properly educated, and who are accustomed to its really better tone, differ much, if any, from the English in this particular, but, in this case, as in most others in which *national* peculiarities are sought, the better tone of America is overshadowed by its mediocrity. Although I deem the government of this country the very quintessence of hocus pocus, having scarcely a single practice that does not violate its theory, I believe that there is more honesty of public sentiment in England, than in America. The defect at home, I ascribe, in common with the majority of our national failings, to the greater activity, and greater *unresisted* force of ignorance and cupidity, there, than here. High qualities are nowhere collected in a sufficient phalanx to present a front to the enemy, in America.

The besetting, the degrading vice of America, is the moral cowardice by which men are led to truckle to what is called public opinion, though this opinion is as inconstant as the winds, though, in all cases that enlist the feelings of factions there are *two* and sometimes twenty, each differing from all the others, and though, nine times in ten, these opinions are mere engines set in motion by the most corrupt and the least respectable portion of the community, for unworthy purposes. The English are a more respectable and constant nation than the Americans, as relates to this peculiarity; probably, because the condensed masses of intelligence and character enable the superior portion of the community to produce a greater impression on the inferior, by their collective force. In standing prejudices, they strike me as being worse than ourselves; but in passing impressions greatly our superiors.

For the last I have endeavoured to account, and I think the first may be ascribed to a system that is sustained by errors that it is not the interest of the more enlightened to remove, but which, instead of weakening in the ignorant, they rather encourage in themselves.

1830-1840

CALVIN COLTON
VIEWS THE CHURCH OF ENGLAND:
"THERE IS LESS OUTRAGE
THAN IN IRELAND;
BUT THE SYSTEM IS THE SAME

1831

A graduate of Yale and of the Andover Theological Seminary, Calvin Colton joined first the Presbyterian, then the Episcopal church. In 1831 the *New York Observer* sent him to England as correspondent. He stayed there four years, immersing himself in the life of the country, but retaining some of his American notions—it is hard to call them prejudices—about an established church. Sensitive to English criticism of America from such visitors as Basil Hall and Mrs. Trollope, he answered, in 1833, with a book on *The Americans*. After his return to the United States Colton abandoned the church for journalism and politics, wrote a biography of Henry Clay, and in 1852 took the chair of political economy at Trinity College, in Hartford, Connecticut.

The Church of Ireland surely is bad enough. The present state of things there is probably a fair development of the tendencies of the system: Bring a powerful Christian heirarchy into alliance with the state; make it a part of the political fabric; withdraw all power

From Calvin Colton, *Four Years in Great Britain* (New York, 1836), pp. 238–239, 255–257.

relating to church economy from the people, and concentrate it in the hands of a few, who sympathize with the head of the nation —who is also constituted head of the church and who will, of course, use his influence as such, for political ends. If the church be wealthy, as in Great Britain, let the disposal of its benefices, in other words, the nomination of its priesthood, be divided among the chief dignitaries, high corporations, wealthy and powerful individuals, civil and ecclesiastical, who are interested, first, in providing places for their sons and family connexions, and next, in bringing the entire ecclesiastical economy to bear on their political designs. Let all the treasures of the church be regarded as the property of the government, and all dues to the church of tithes, or in whatever form, as a demand of government, for government purposes. And then, by a moral certainty, the church, thus allied to the state, will have a secularized clergy, and it will be no scandal, on the principles of such a church, to support its rights at the point of the bayonet, and by the mouth of the cannon, as in Ireland. It is perfectly consistent; it is the legitimate tendency and natural result of the system. The public may be shocked at the occasional outbreakings of some of these more palpable enormities, such as the recent slaughter of Rathcormac; the authors of the mischief may be startled for fear of a reaction on themselves; but they do not give up the principle; they do not confess that there is anything wrong, or even improper, in all this. They say, the state has a right, first, to make these exactions; and next, to support its authority—that its authority must be respected; and if anybody, with an unsubmissive temper, comes in the way of it, and falls before the bayonet or the cannon, it is his own fault. They have no sympathy and no regret on account of these disasters, except as it injures themselves.

And how is it in England? It must be acknowledged, that these affairs are managed more decently there than in Ireland—that there is less outrage; but the system is the same; and upon all dissenters, as well as upon thousands who have not dared to dissent, it operates in numberless forms, directly and indirectly, most oppressively and cruelly.

"How do you do, Mr. ——?" said the rector of ——, within fifty miles of London, to a dissenting clergyman, whose chapel, dwelling-house, and garden happened to be in the rector's parish. "You have a fine garden here, sir."

"Oh, yes, sir, I am very fond of a garden. Come, walk through, and see it."

"Indeed, it is not only very pretty, but I should think it might be profitable," said the rector, as he surveyed the premises in company with his dissenting brother, and while the latter took great pleasure in displaying all, and giving the history of his improvements.

"There is about half an acre here, as you see," said the dissenting minister. "Half of it is ornamental, where I take pleasure with my thirteen children; and the other half furnishes vegetables to feed them. You would hardly believe it, but this little patch, under the culture of my own hand, goes a great way towards supplying the table of my numerous family."

"Indeed, sir. And how many years has it been so productive?"

"Some half dozen or more."

It was a morning call of the rector, for a purpose best known to himself, as he had never condescended to visit his dissenting brother before. Having seen and been told all appertaining to the beauty and profitableness of the garden, from the open and unsuspecting communications of the owner, the rector said—"Good morning," and retired.

The next day, or soon afterward, the rector's steward sent in a bill for tithes on the said garden, of £ 6, or nearly $29, per year, for six years previous, and the same for the then current year —amounting in all to £ 42, or about $200; to continue, as I suppose, at £ 6, or nearly $29, a year, on a quarter of an acre of land!

The rector has a wife, but no children, on a living of some hundreds of pounds a year, which he can augment at pleasure by these modes. The dissenting clergyman had a family of thirteen children, and a small congregation, which could afford him only a slender support—by no means adequate for the demands of his family. He was astounded at this bill! For it was positively and unavoidably distressing.

"But you did not pay it?" said I, when he narrated to me the facts.

"Your ignorance of this country, sir, as manifested by this question, is very excusable. There is no redress for such an imposition —no tribunal for defence, to which a poor man will dare to appeal. The ecclesiastical courts, which have the supervision of all such matters, will always defend the rights of clergymen of the established church. Clergymen of this establishment, as this instance will show, have great powers, and a wide reach of discretion, in regard to tithes and other church dues. The law supposes them to be good men and reasonable; and a hundred or a thousand to one of those, who appeal to the law for protection against these extortions, return saddled with the enormous expense of English law. Remedy at law in such cases is absolutely and utterly discouraging; and few but the wealthy and influential, who can afford to fight for principle and justice, venture upon it. Ordinarily, the oppressions light on those who are not likely to show such resistance." . . .

It is no scandal in England—at least, it seems not to operate as such—that benefices, or livings in the churches, are sold at public auction to the highest bidder, over the heads of incumbents, by which means a wealthy man can at any time make a future provision for his son, and establish him in the world by anticipation; or a Jew may be the purchaser in his way of speculation on stocks, and nominate the preacher of a Christian pulpit. . . .

The following is a curious, and, it may be added, instructive advertisement on this point. It is from the London *Morning Herald*, April 15th, 1830:

"To be sold, the next presentation to a vicarage, in one of the midland counties, and in the immediate neighbourhood of one or two of the first packs of fox-hounds in the kingdom. The present annual income about £580, subject to curate's salary. The incumbent in 60th year."

"In the immediate neighbourhood of one or two of *the first packs of fox-hounds in* the kingdom." And this is a motive—a charm—a lure, to draw clerical bidders! Do those who speculate in public stocks which they offer for sale, understand this business? Did they in this case know, that those clergymen who want church livings would generally be attracted by such a lure as the "best pack of fox-hounds"? If not generally, and if it was not well known, would they run the risk of defeating their own object, as speculators, by putting it in? . . .

In the course of *one* month, I observed the following public notices in the London journals, in the usual style of reporting public amusements, or after the manner of a court circular: First, of a dramatic fête at the Bath Theatre, with dancing through the night, and on the list of names of the persons present were those of *twelve* clergymen. The next was an animated account of a public ball at Windsor, where the "iced champaign was flying about like water, and contributed to the friskiness of the light fantastic toe;" where "quadrilling, waltzing, and gallopading continued till 3 o'clock, and much fun at a later hour," with the names of *eleven* clergymen among the rest. Another begins thus: "The Rev. Arthur Mathews gave a grand ball at the Swan Hotel, in the town of Ross, &c., at which the following clergymen were present:" Then follows the list of their names, in number *nine*—among which were four high dignitaries, one belonging to the king's household.

What do these notices prove?

"I want you to speak at my grave," said a dying woman in London last spring to her dissenting pastor, but immediately recollecting that no dissenting clergyman would be admitted to a church burying-ground for the burial of the dead, she added, lifting her hand, expressive of her regret, "But, no, you cannot." She turned her head, burst into tears, and soon expired.

Sometimes the stranger in London and in England may witness, as he passes a churchyard, the remarkable scene of a clergyman standing without the paling in the street or highway, performing funeral obsequies by stealth, and in evasion of the law, over one of his own people, whose friends are assembled around the grave within. It is the dissenting minister, who is not permitted to enter that ground for this purpose, and who, as a Christian pastor, has complied with the urgent solicitations of surviving friends of the deceased, to perform this office in these humiliating circumstances.

Dissenting clergymen cannot celebrate marriage; they are prohibited performing funeral rites over their own dead in the churchyard, notwithstanding they and their people are taxed for all the expenses of that ground. Dissenters must pay the rector a special, and no trifling fee, for a place to lay their dead; another for the privilege of setting up a monument; another to the curate for reading the burial-service; and how many more I do not know. They are excluded from all the privileges of the universities, except that by long and hard fighting they have now a university of their own in London. Besides building and maintaining their own chapels, and supporting their own ministers, they are forced to do their part towards all the expenses of the establishment. There is no respect or delicacy shown towards dissenting clergymen, in exempting them from the common burdens of the established church; but as in the case I have noticed, they are often visited with special imposts from the very fact that they are dissenting ministers. Even the best of the established clergy, who might be expected to sympathize with their dissenting brethren on account of the many disadvantages they labour under, have so long enjoyed their high and prescriptive prerogatives, as apparently not to imagine that there is an obligation or propriety in dispensing with them in any matter or degree towards dissenting ministers.

THE REVEREND HENRY MC LELLAN:

IN LIVERPOOL:

THE POOR EAT "THE BREAD

OF BITTERNESS"

1832

Mc Lellan graduated from Harvard College and, at the age of twenty-one, from Andover Theological Seminary. He then embarked for further study at Edinburgh. Sharp and thoughtful in his observations, he was neither obtuse nor unsympathetic. His reaction to the abysmal poverty of the working classes, and to the subtle gradations of the class system, is typical of American reactions during these years. Mc Lellan gathered material for a large book on Britain, but died before he could write it: his *Journal* was taken from the voluminous manuscripts he left.

As far as we could see all was bustle. Heavy drays and large wagons drawn by huge horses loaded with cotton, thundered over the pavements; and a thousand blended sounds assailed our ears as we reached our landing place. A grim crowd awaited us there—forty or fifty drivers held up their whip handles to engage our attention. "Coach, your honor," "Coach, sir," were reiterated by as many voices from persons whose dirty hands and faces and ragged garb did not

From Henry B. Mc Lellan, *Journal of a Residence in Scotland* (Boston, 1834), pp. 94–98.

184

offer a flattering promise for the beauty and cleanliness of their vehicles. Their claim to our notice was disputed by about a hundred or two other persons ranging far beneath them in personal cleanliness.

Such a set of characters were perhaps never collected in our country. A dozen thrust themselves forward, "Shall I carry your baggage, your honor," "your umbrella;" "Shall I show you to the Adelphi, to the Mersey Hotel," &c., cried others; here were women ready to sell the "gemmen" oranges, and here the suspicious children of the wandering nation ready to buy "old clothes;" in all a motley group. This was not so painful. But to regard the group of ragged, wretched, lame and miserable creatures that had collected round us, as if we had been the last resource upon which their hopes rested, this was enough to rend one's heart. For such piteous tones and fearful accounts of their famishing condition I never before heard faltered forth from the tongues of human beings. It was the first phalanx of a class, that I afterwards found eating the bread of bitterness in large numbers through all the cities of Great Britain. Trained as our eyes are to see only well fed—decent and comfortable persons, even in the lowest rank in America, walking amongst the grim assemblage of an English crowd, even what is really elegant and neat is for a period almost unnoticed, until the first shock which so much distress and poverty makes on the feelings has subsided. An Englishman, so far as respects his enjoyment of what is beautiful, is disciplined into an entire disregard for these elements, which enter into the texture of their social system, to dim its glory. He only sees what is splendid; all the meanness thrown over it by surrounding want, he is accustomed to disregard, as much as if it did not exist. If it was not so he would be continually miserable. But it stares an American in the face in every street. This dark veil hides for a period all the grandeur that stands towering up behind it. I found it precisely so in my case.

We succeeded in separating ourselves from nearly all the rabble that had at first surrounded us, though one or two of the more professional or more hungry beggars harassed our march through several of the shorter streets. Three things struck me, in particular, as soon as I entered Liverpool, viz: the large size and powerful appearance of the dray horses; the vast extent and prison-like aspect of the ware houses, and the convenience and stability of their docks. But while the ware houses were so immense, the streets were narrow and choked up; the side walks by men, women and children, nearly all of whom were clothed in wretched garments, whilst the pavement was thickly covered with carts and wagons heavily laden with cotton and merchandize. A narrow strip of sky gray with smoke shone dimly above, lighting up the street, it is true, but not with that transparent brightness which cheers even the purlieus of our towns. The shops in these streets had a contracted and indigent air. We decided to go to the "Adelphi," one of the best houses in Liverpool. On the way we passed through two handsome streets, much like parts of Broadway in New York, or Washington Street in Boston. In the coffee room I had the pleasure of meeting a gentleman, who had been a fellow student with me at Andover.

There is no place where one is more independent than in an English hotel. If he has money enough he can command everything. We might have such houses if we desired them; perhaps they would be frequented and be profitable, but they are not suited to, at least they do not grow out of, our national character. They are the legitimate germ of English feeling. In England, condition, title and wealth are everything; character, person, humanity comparatively nothing. All yields to the dazzle of wealth and hereditary influence. This aristocracy predominates everywhere. Its spirit communicates itself to everything. See its genius in a Hotel. You are met at the door by the waiter. He measures at a glance your condition. He looks out to see whether you have come in your own carriage with livery, or post it in style. He watches the postilions to estimate the height of your dignity by the profoundness of their obeisance. And they do not leave the house till they have told him what you have paid them, and all other things which they know about you. In short he looks at the hack that you have come in; at the silver you pay for it; at your baggage, dress, and deportment, and scores you down accordingly; or, in the pithy language of an Englishman, "he sets you down as a porter, port-wine and water, or champaigne customer at once; and treats you at that rate, until you have fixed your own standard, by what you call for." If you do not immediately ask for the "travellers' room," or for the "coffee room," he inquires, "Will you see your chamber, sir." The bell is pulled; the chamber-maid appears, and you are conducted to an apartment suited to their estimate of your rank. If you do not like it, you are shown to another of higher price, and you are sure to get a very complaisant smile from the chamber-maid if you move like one that intends to pay well. They do not like too many "thank you's," thinking that when courtesy is too current, coin is rare. And if you have many needs, coats to be dusted, shoes to be cleaned, and trifles to be done, even if you pay no more for it, it purchases their respect, and satisfies them that you intend giving them their fees. Of such a person their opinion is, "he's a gentleman, he will pay for our services." . . .

The "coffee room" is arranged in the same style. After seeing my room I descended to it. It was a large and handsome apartment, with about ten or twelve tables, capable of accommodating four persons each; these were all covered with elegant white cloths, with knives and silver forks and spoons. . . . You are perfectly independent; you may have all, if you are rich enough to pay for all. There you sit alone; eat your dinner, pick over your nuts and raisins, and read the newspapers; no one thinks of you, speaks to you, or even looks at you. All keep aloof. They don't know you. Perhaps you are lower in the scale of importance than themselves. Such persons would of course feel uncomfortable at Bunker's or the Tremont's elegant table, with so many persons brought into juxtaposition with them, of whom they were ignorant. They would esteem it almost the compromise of their dignity to speak. It is not strange then that their public room differs from ours. It is not a matter of caprice, but it arises from the character of the people. It is a germ from the spirit of their constitution. Both the English and Americans are generous by nature; but English laws and institutions very naturally confine their courtesy to the circle of their acquaintance; whilst ours, on the contrary, give us a freedom of manner towards all men, which no circumstances ever disturb.

NATHANIEL PARKER WILLIS
HAS BREAKFAST WITH
CHARLES AND MARY LAMB
AND TAKES THE MEASURE
OF ENGLISH GENTLEMEN

1835

"Before he was twenty-five," the journalist-historian Samuel Goodrich wrote of N. P. Willis, "he was more read than any other American poet of his time; being possessed of an easy and captivating address he became the pet of society and especially of the fairer portion of it." Probably no American author of his day was more widely read than Willis, few have been more completely forgotten. He made his reputation as a kind of glorified society reporter in foreign lands. An inveterate tuft-hunter, he was able to give his large newspaper public the vicarious thrill of being at receptions of earls and dukes, visiting ancient castles, penetrating to remote villages in picturesque spots, visiting with celebrities—the kind of thrill that is obtained today via television "celebrities." He was important enough to find a place in Lowell's *A Fable for Critics,* but only as an object of satire:

> There is Willis, all natty and jaunty and gay,
> Who says his best things in so foppish a way. . . .
> For some to be slightly shallow's a duty,

From Nathaniel Parker Willis, *Pencillings by the Way* (London, 1835), III, pp. 117–121, 192–194.

And Willis's shallowness makes half his beauty
His prose winds along with a blithe, gurgling error,
And reflects all of Heaven it can see in its mirror.

Willis compiled a dozen or so travel books in his day; his most sprightly things are to be found in the oft-republished *Pencillings by the Way*.

There was a rap at the door at last, and enter a gentleman in black small-clothes and gaiters, short and very slight in his person, his head set on his shoulders with a thoughtful, forward bent, his hair just sprinkled with gray, a beautiful deep-set eye, aquiline nose, and a very indescribable mouth. Whether it expressed most humour or feeling, good-nature or a kind of whimsical peevishness, or twenty other things which passed over it by turns, I cannot in the least be certain.

His sister, whose literary reputation is associated very closely with her brother's, and who, as the original of "Bridget Elia," is a kind of object for literary affection, came in after him. She is a small, bent figure, evidently a victim to ill-health, and hears with difficulty. Her face has been, I should think, a fine and handsome one, and her bright gray eye is still full of intelligence and fire. They both seemed quite at home in our friend's chambers; and as there was to be no one else, we immediately drew round the breakfast-table. I had set a large arm-chair for Miss Lamb. "Don't take it, Mary," said Lamb, pulling it away from her very gravely, "it looks as if you were going to have a tooth drawn."

The conversation was very local. Our host and his guest had not met for some weeks, and they had a great deal to say of their mutual friends. Perhaps in this way, however, I saw more of the author, for his manner of speaking of them, and the quaint humour with which he complained of one, and spoke well of another, was so in the vein of his inimitable writings, that I could have fancied myself listening to an audible composition of new Elia. Nothing could be more delightful than the kindness and affection between the brother and the sister, though Lamb was continually taking advantage of her deafness to mystify her with the most singular gravity upon every topic that was started. "Poor Mary!" said he, "she hears all of an epigram but the point." "What are you saying of me, Charles?" she asked. "Mr. Willis," said he, raising his voice, "admires *your Confessions of a Drunkard* very much, and I was saying it was no merit of yours that you understood the subject." We had been speaking of this admirable essay (which is his own) half an hour before.

The conversation turned upon literature after a while, and our host could not express himself strongly enough in admiration of Webster's speeches, which he said were exciting the greatest attention among the politicians and lawyers of England. Lamb said, "I don't know much of American authors. Mary, there, devours Cooper's novels with a ravenous appetite, with which I have no sympathy. The only American book I ever read twice, was the *Journal of Edward Woolman,* a quaker preacher and tailor, whose character is one of the finest I ever met with. He tells a story or two about negro slaves, that brought the tears into my eyes. I can read no prose now, though Hazlitt sometimes, to be sure—but then Hazlitt is worth all modern prose-writers put together."

Mr. R. spoke of buying a book of Lamb's a few days before, and I mentioned my having bought a copy of *Elia* the last day I was in America, to send as a parting gift to one of the most lovely and talented women in our country.

"What did you give for it?" said Lamb.

"About seven and sixpence."

"Permit me to pay you that," said he, and with the utmost earnestness he counted out the money upon the table.

"I never yet wrote any thing that would sell," he continued. "I am the publisher's ruin. My last poem won't sell a copy. Have you seen it, Mr. Willis?"

I had not.

"It's only eighteen pence, and I'll give you sixpence toward it;" and he described to me where I should find it sticking up in a shop-window in the Strand.

Lamb ate nothing, and complained in a querulous tone of the veal-pie. There was a kind of potted fish (of which I forget the name at this moment) which he had expected our friend would procure for him. He inquired whether there was not a morsel left perhaps in the bottom of the last pot. Mr. R. was not sure.

"Send and see," said Lamb, "and if the pot has been cleaned, bring me the cover. I think the sight of it would do me good."

The cover was brought, upon which there was a picture of the dish. Lamb kissed it with a reproachful look at his friend, and then left the table and began to wander round the room with a broken, uncertain step, as if he almost forgot to put one leg before the other. His sister rose after a while, and commenced walking up and down very much in the same manner on the opposite side of the table, and in the course of half an hour they took their leave.

I have been struck every where in England with the beauty of the higher classes, and as I looked around me upon the aristocratic company at the table, I thought I never had seen "Heaven's image double-stamped as man, and noble," so unequivocally clear. There were two young men and four or five young ladies of rank—and five or six people of more decided personal attractions could scarcely be found; the style of form and face at the same time being of that cast of superiority which goes by the expressive name of "thoroughbred." There is a striking difference in this respect between England and the countries of the Continent—the *paysans* of France, and the *contadini* of Italy, being physically far superior to their degenerate masters; while the gentry and nobility of England differ from the peasantry in limb and feature, as the racer differs from the dray-horse, or the greyhound from the cur. The contrast between the manners of English and French gentlemen is quite as striking. The *empressment,* the warmth, the shrug and gesture of the Parisian; and the working eyebrow, dilating or contracting eye, and conspirator-like action of the Italian, in the most common conversation, are the antipodes of English high breeding. I should say a North American Indian, in his more dignified phase, approached nearer to the manner of an English nobleman than any other person. The calm repose of person and feature, the self-possession under all circumstances, that incapability of surprise or *dereglément,* and that decision about the slightest circumstance, and the apparent certainty that he is acting absolutely *comme il faut,* is equally "gentlemanlike" and Indianlike. You cannot astonish an English gentleman. If a man goes into a fit at his side, or a servant drops a dish upon his shoulder, or he hears that the house is on fire, he sets down his wine-glass with the same deliberation. He has made up his mind what to do in all possible cases, and he does it. He is cold at a first introduction, and may bow stiffly (which he always does) in drinking wine with you, but it is his manner; and he would think an Englishman out of his senses, who should bow down to his very plate, and smile, as a Frenchman does on a similar occasion. Rather chilled by this, you are a little astonished when the ladies have left the table, and he closes his chair up to you, to receive an invitation to pass a month with him at his country-house; and to discover, that at the very moment he bowed so coldly, he was thinking how he should contrive to facilitate your plans for getting to him, or seeing the country to advantage on the way.

THE REVEREND ORVILLE DEWEY
VISITS WORDSWORTH:
THE EXAMPLE OF AMERICA
DOESN'T COUNT

1836

The Reverend Orville Dewey—the thirties was the decade of prominent clergymen—belonged (like Willis) to what would today be called the "gee whiz" school of travel. "If I were asked what is the charm about this Old World," he wrote," I should say it is *antiquity*—antiquity in its castles, its cathedrals, its cities." A Unitarian minister, he visited Britain in the early thirties, and like so many American Unitarians, made a pilgrimage to the Lake Country to visit Wordsworth and Coleridge. The passion of the American transcendentalists for Wordsworth and for Carlyle was both humorous and pathetic; Wordsworth and Coleridge had long abandoned their earlier romantic enthusiasms for creating newer and more perfect worlds, and as for Carlyle it can be said that his American friends (always excepting Henry James, Sr.) never did understand him.

From Ambleside I took a pony and rode to Rydal Mount, the residence of Mr. W [ordsworth].
I was so much disappointed in the appearance of Mr. W——that

From Orville Dewey, *The Old World and the New* (London, 1836), I, pp. 104–112.

I actually began to suspect that I had come to the cottage of one of his neighbours. After ten minutes' common-place talk about the weather, the travelling, &c., had passed, I determined to find out whether I was mistaken; and aware of his deep interest in the politics of England, I availed myself of some remark that was made, to introduce that subject. He immediately left all common-place, and went into the subject with a flow, a flood almost, of conversation that soon left me in no doubt. After this had gone on an hour or two, wishing to change the theme, I took occasion of a pause to observe that in this great political agitation, poetry seemed to have died out entirely. He said it had; but that was not the only cause; for there had been, as he thought, some years ago an over-production and a surfeit.

Mr. W—— converses with great earnestness, and has a habit, as he walks and talks, of stopping every fourth or fifth step, and turning round to you to enforce what he is saying. The subjects, the first evening I passed with him, were, as I have said, politics and poetry. He remarked afterward that although he was known to the world only as a poet, he had given twelve hours' thought to the condition and prospects of society, for one to poetry. I replied that there appeared to me to be no contradiction in this, since the spirit of poetry is the spirit of humanity—since sympathy with humanity, and with all its fortunes, is an essential characteristic of poetry—and politics is one of the grandest forms under which the welfare of the human race presents itself.

In politics Mr. W—— professes to be a reformer, but upon the most deliberate plan an gradual scale; and he indulges in the most indignant and yet argumentative diatribes against the present course of things in England, and in the saddest forebodings of what is to come. The tide is beating now against aristocracy and an established religion, and if it prevails, anarchy and irreligion must follow. He will see no other result; he has no confidence in the people; they are not fit to govern themselves—not yet certainly; public opinion, the foolish opinion of the depraved, ignorant, and conceited mass, ought not to be the law; it ought not to be expressed in law; it ought not to be represented in government; the true representative government should represent the *mind* of a country, and that is not found in the mass, nor is it to be expressed by universal suffrage. Mr. W—— constantly protested against the example of America, as not being in point. He insisted that the state of society, the crowded population, the urgency of want, the tenures of property, in England, made a totally different case from ours. He seemed evidently to admit, though he did not in terms, that hereditary rank and an established priesthood are indefensible in the broadest views of human rights and interests; but the argument for them is, that they cannot be removed without opening the door to greater evils —to the unrestrained license of the multitude—to incessant change, disorder, uncertainty, and finally to oppression and tyranny. He says the world is running mad with the notion that all its evils are to be relieved by political changes, political remedies, political nostrums—whereas the great evils, sin, bondage, misery, lie deep in the heart, and nothing but virtue and religion can remove them; and upon the value, and preciousness, and indispensableness of religion, indeed, he talked very sagely, earnestly, and devoutly.

The next evening I went to tea to Mr. W——'s, on a hospitable invitation to come to breakfast, dinner, or tea, as I liked. The conversation very soon again ran upon politics. He thought there could be no independence in legislators who were dependent for their places upon the ever-wavering breath of popular opinion, and he wanted my opinion about the fact in our country. I replied, that as a secluded man and accustomed to look at the *morale* of these matters, I certainly had felt that there was likely to be, and probably was a great want of independence—that I had often expressed the apprehension that our distinguished men were almost necessarily acting under biasses that did not permit them to sit down in their closets and examine great political questions and measures, in a fair and philosophical spirit. Then, he said, how can there be any safety? I answered, as I had frequently said before, that our only safety lay in making the people wise: but I added that our practical politicians were accustomed to say, that there was a principle of safety in our conflicts, in the necessarily conflicting opinions of the mass—that they neutralised and balanced each other. I admitted, however, that there was danger; that all popular institutions involved danger; that freedom was a trust, and a perilous trust. Still I insisted that this was only an instance of a general principle; that all probation was perilous; that the greatest opportunity was always the greatest peril. I maintained, also, that think as we might of political liberty, there was no helping it; that in the civilized world, the course of opinion was irresistibly setting towards universal education and popular forms of government; and nothing was to be done but to direct, modify, and control the tendency. He fully admitted this; said that in other centuries some glorious results might be brought out, but that he saw nothing but darkness, disorder, and misery in the immediate prospect, and that all he could do was to cast himself on Providence.

I ventured to suggest that it seemed to me that all good and wise men had a work to do. I said that I admitted, friend to popular institutions as I was, that the world was full of errors about liberty; that there was a mistake and madness about popular freedom, as if it were the grand panacea for all human ills, and that powerful pens were needed to guide the public mind; and that the pen of genius could scarcely be more nobly employed. But he has no confidence in the body of the people, in their willingness to read what is wholesome, or to do what is right; and this, I took the liberty to say, seemed to me the radical point on which he and I differed. I told him that there were large communities in America in whom I did confide, and that I believed other communities might be raised up to the same condition; and that it appeared to me that it should be the grand effort of the world now, to raise up this mass to knowledge, to comfort, and virtue—since the mass was evidently ere long to rule for us.

After this conversation, Mr. W—— proposed a walk to Grassmere Lake, to see it after sunset; and in that loveliest of all the scenes I ever witnessed on earth, were lost all thoughts but of religion and poetry. I could not help saying, with fervent sincerity, "I thank you, sir, for bringing me here, at this hour;" for he had evidently taken some pains, pushing aside some little interferences with his purpose, to accomplish it. He said in reply, that so impressive was the scene to him, that he felt almost as if it were a sin not to come here every fair evening. We sat by the shore half an hour, and talked of themes far removed from the strife of politics. The village on the opposite side lay in deep shadow; from which the tower of the church rose, like heaven's sentinel on the gates of evening. A single taper shot its solitary ray across the waters. The little lake lay hushed in deep and solemn repose. Not a sound was heard upon its shore. The fading light trembled upon the bosom of the waters, which were here slightly ruffled, and there lay as a mirror to reflect the serenity of heaven. The dark mountains lay beyond, with every varying shade that varying distance could give them. The farthest ridges were sowed with light, as if it were resolved into separate particles and showered down into the darkness below, to make it visible. The mountain side had a softness of shadowing upon it, such as I never saw before, and such as no painting I ever saw approached in the remotest degree. It seemed, Mr. W—— said, as if it were "*clothed* with the air." Above all, was the clear sky, looking almost cold, it looked so pure, along the horizon—but warmed in the region a little higher, with the vermilion tints of the softest sunset. I am persuaded that the world might be travelled over without the sight of one such spectacle as this—and all owing to the circumstances—the time—the hour. It was perhaps not the least of those circumstances influencing the scene, that it was an hour, passed in one of his own holy retreats, with Wordsworth!

SALLIE STEVENSON:
VICTORIA BECOMES QUEEN
AND TURNS THE HEADS OF
YOUNG AND OLD

1837–38

Sallie Cowles was a member of one of the First Families of Virginia. One of her brothers was secretary to Jefferson, another secretary to Madison and later governor of the Territory of Illinois; she was a "kissing cousin" to Dolley Madison and a frequent guest in the White House. At the somewhat advanced age of twenty-seven she married a widower, Andrew Stevenson, who had early attached himself to the rising star of Andrew Jackson. In 1836 Jackson named him to the Court of St. James's, and Jackson's successor, Van Buren, allowed him to stay there. He was a successful, if not a distinguished, minister; his wife was a general favorite with the diplomatic corps and with the new and lovely young Queen. Among other things she introduced the Albemarle pippin to the English cuisine; Queen Victoria was so fond of this apple that Parliament passed an act permitting Virginia apples to enter duty free. Mrs. Stevenson had a large family connection whose members she bombarded with gossipy letters.

From *Victoria, Albert and Mrs. Stevenson,* Edward Boykin, ed. (London, 1957), pp. 76–77, 148–150.

. . . Lady Bagot mentioned an instance of her firmness & decision. She ordered her master of the horse to put in training some horses for her use as she meant to review her troops on horseback. The Duke of Wellington ventured to suggest to her Majesty that she had better review them in an open carriage to which she replied, "I shall review them on horseback, as Queen Elizabeth did." This is a Tory picture of her, the other side speaks of her as something almost superhuman. That she is an extraordinary person I think cannot be doubted—only imagine, a young creature just eighteen brought up in retirement & seclusion suddenly finding herself sovereign of the greatest Kingdom of the Earth. It is said that on the death of the old King, the Queen Dowager wrote her by the Arch-Bishop of Canterbury that she was Queen, & the poor thing was waked up at day break to receive the intelligence. She replied immediately in a letter of condolence & addressed it to the "Queen." The Arch-Bishop said to her, Your Majesty has omitted the "Dowager" when she replied with a feeling & readiness that speaks volumes for the goodness of her heart—"I will not be the first to give her that title." On the same day she met her Counsel & behaved with a dignity & self-possession that amazed them all. They say it was impossible for any thing to have been more what it ought to have been than her deportment but when she left the Counsel chamber she forgot that it was a glass door through which she had retired & the moment it closed upon her she rubbed her hand's & skipped off with a step as light & girlish as tho' she had just escaped from her school mistress. Again they say when her Uncle the Duke of Sussex presented himself to pay her homage as a subject she rose, threw herself into his arms—kissing both cheeks, & the same with her governess the Duchess of Northumberland, whom she was told she must receive sitting. She refused to do so, unless the Duchess was informed that she obeyed the laws of etiquette, but the moment she appeared she forgot all laws but those of feeling. She also appointed as maid of honour a young girl with whom she had gone to school. When she was told, this would not do, she had not rank, she replied, "I can give her rank, & will do it." Thus it is she wins all hearts by the union of goodness, sweetness & gentleness, with dignity, firmness & decision. She seems to have turned the heads of the young & old & it is amazing to hear those grave & dignified ministers of state talking of her as a thing not only to be admired but to be adored.

London, July 15, 1838

Imagine this immense building adorned with the richest draperies of crimson & gold & covered with costly carpeting, & filled in every part with persons in the most brilliant dresses—The peers and peeresses glittering in all the pomp of velvet & ermine, and the ladies sparkling with diamonds, the peers occupying the South, & the peeresses the North transept when the sun shone upon the latter it was realy dazzling to look upon them—It was really a gorgeous scene and one which no eye could witness without calling up in the heart mingled sensations of pleasure and astonishment. Mr. Stevenson and myself entered together, Van Buren, Rush, Vaux & Livingstone following close behind, with the eyes of 1000 persons upon us. My husband never looked better or moved with more dignity & grace. I cannot tell you how many have told me since, that he was the finest looking man in the Abbey, his countrymen & women say they felt proud of their Representative, and even Van Buren & his taciturne friend Mr. Clark, speak in high praise both of his appearance in the procession & in the Abbey—we ascended the Tribune, & took our seats Mr. Stevenson on the right hand of Marshal Soult, (Duke of Dalmatia) & I just by him—The Ambassadress' were blasing in diamonds & Prince Esterhazy was literally covered with precious stones, it is said he never wears this dress without losing 100 pounds worth of jewels. . . .

The Queen entered with a flourish of trumpets, proceeded by all her officers of State and accompanied by the beautiful Duchess of Sutherland mistress of the Robes, Lady Lansdowne Barham &c and her train borne by 6 young girls of her own age, dressed all alike in white satin with lace over it and bunches of pale pink roses up before, on their heads a string of diamonds with blush roses—these young ladies were of the highest rank in the Kingdom—The Queen advanced up the nave untill she reached the first chair where she Knelt, at her private devotions—The most Striking part of the Ceremony was the Crowning, when the superb crown was put on her head, at the very moment, a roar of canon announced it to her people, by signal I suppose, and at the same instant all the peers and peeresses put on their Coronets, it was really magnificent, but the most touching part, to me, of this great national pageant was when this fair young creature knelt at the Alter before receiving the Sacrement, with her head uncovered looking so young, so innocent, & so helpless, that involuntarily my heart was raised to Heaven in supplication to the great giver of all good, that, the little head which then bowed down in such seeming humility before the foot-stool of His mercy, might at last receive a Crown such as no mortal hands could bestow upon her—She was crowned in St Edwards Chair . . . it was covered with crimson & gold and I should not have recognised my old acquaintance in its new dress—In the Center of the Abby immediately under the central Tower, a platform was erected of a circular form with five steps, the summit of the platform, & the highest step leading to it, was covered with the richest cloth of gold, and in the centre a chair was placed in which she received the homage of the peers—The Royal Dukes first, knelt, kissed her hand & touched the side of her crown, I was struck with the manner of the Duke of Sussex, he kissed her hand repeatedly & when he touched her crown it was more the caressing action of a Father than the homage of a subject—a little incident occured during the ceremony of the homage which created quite a sensation, an old peer, Lord Rolle, vy infirm, in attempting to ascend, the weight of his robe, & his own feebleness caused him to fail & roll down the steps, when The Queen half rose from her seat as by a sudden impulse, & when he was put upon his feet, & attempted again to ascend she rose & met him—The House cheered, & all felt the action as indicative of her amiable disposition, some one in speaking of it afterwards, said, it was the only good action of his life, to tumble down in order to give the Queen an opportunity to show the kindness and benevolence of her heart—It is said she exhibited great sensibility on her arrival at the Abbey when she went into the Robing room on her arrival, that she wept so passionately that her attendants were alarmed lest she should be unable to go through the Ceremony. I remarked when she entered, that she was vy pale, but calm dignified, & self-possessed throughout the whole trying ceromonial—I thought she seemed much effected, when a hundred instruments and more than twice that number of voices united in, "God save the Queen!—Long live the Queen! May the Queen live forever!" The loud anthem, and then the applauding shouts of the multitude of spectators had a most thrilling effect even upon my democratic nerves, & I dare sy drew loyal tears, from loyal eyes. After the Queen retired, the rush to get out was immense, and I thought I should stand some chance of being crushed in the Squeeze when suddenly a Stentorian voice proclaimed, "Not a peer or peeress can leave the Abby untill the foreign Ambassadors have passed out" in an instant I found myself passing quietly along an avenue made for us, close along side of Marshal Soult & the procession returned as it had come, the patient Spectators still waiting to behold again the gorgeous show.

CHARLES SUMNER
IS IMPRESSED BY
THE ELEVATED CHARACTER OF
THE LEGAL PROFESSION

1838

Charles Sumner was still in his twenties when he borrowed (or raised) enough money to pay for a year of travel in the Old World. The son of "Sheriff" Sumner, he had graduated from Harvard College in 1830 and then studied at the Law School which Justice Joseph Story was even then making famous; after he had his law degree he taught for a few years in a law school. It was Story who provided the young man with the letters which opened all doors to him—Story who was even then acknowledged the greatest of American legal luminaries. On his return to Boston Sumner joined the ranks of the antislavery and reform forces. He achieved national attention—perhaps notoriety—by his Fourth of July Address on The True Grandeur of Nations in 1845, in which he proclaimed that there "is no war that is honorable, no peace that is dishonorable." Now a hero of the reform forces, he was sent to the Senate in 1851, and remained there much of the rest of his life, becoming, in time, one of the most distinguished and most powerful figures in American political life. He had early won the esteem and affection of many English

From *Memoir and Letters of Charles Sumner*, Edward L. Pierce, ed. (London, 1878), I, pp. 321-335.

statesmen and men of letters, and these he retained until, smarting from the recollection of British aid to the Confederacy, he proposed that Britain cede Canada to the United States in compensation for the injuries inflicted upon her during the war.

TO JUDGE STORY

Alfred Club, June 27, 1838

My Dear Judge:

I cannot recount (time and paper would both fail) the civilities and kindness which I have received in London. You know I have learned by your example and by some humble experience to husband time; and yet, with all my exertions, I can hardly find a moment of quiet in which to write a letter or read a book. But I cannot speak of myself: my mind is full of the things I hear of you from all quarters. There is no company of lawyers or judges, where your name is not spoken with the greatest admiration. Mr. Justice Vaughan feels toward you almost as a brother. He has treated me with distinguished kindness; invited me to his country seat, and to go the circuit with him in his own carriage; he placed me on the bench in Westminster Hall—the bench of Tindal, Eldon, and Coke—while Sergeants Wilde and Talfourd, Atcherley and Andrews argued before me. He has expressed the greatest admiration of your character. At dinner at his house I met Lord Abinger, the Vice-Chancellor, Mr. Justice Patteson, &c. With the Vice-Chancellor I had a long conversation about you and your works; he said that a few days ago your *Conflict of Laws* was cited, and he was obliged to take it home, and to study it a long evening, and that he decided a case on the authority of it. Shadwell is a pleasant—I would almost say—jolly fellow. With Mr. Justice Patteson I had a longer conversation, and discussed several points of comparative jurisprudence; he is a very enlightened judge, the most so, I am inclined to think, after Baron Parke, who appears to be *facile princeps*. Patteson spoke of your works, with which he is quite familiar. Abinger is not a student, I think. Coltman was an ordinary barrister with a practice of not more than five hundred pounds a year, and his elevation gave much dissatisfaction; but he has shown himself a competent judge. Only last evening I met Baron Parke at a delightful party at the poet Milman's; there was Taylor, the author of "Philip Van Artevelde," Babbage, Senior, Lord Lansdowne, Mrs. Lister, Spring Rice's family, and Hayward of the *Law Magazine*. Parke inquired after you, and said that in the Privy Council your work was of great resort. Baron Parke is a man with a remarkable countenance, intellectual and brilliant. The Solicitor-General honored me with a dinner, where I received the kindest attentions. He inquired about you, and Mr. Rand, as did the Attorney-General. With the latter I had a great deal of conversation (for several hours), and he has asked me to dinner ten days ahead; all invitations are for a long time ahead. I have just been obliged to decline a subsequent invitation from Lord Denman for the same day.

It would be impossible for me to give you a regular account of the persons I see. I may say that I am in the way of seeing everybody I desire to meet; and all without any effort on my part. Most of the judges I personally know, and almost all the eminent barristers. When I enter Westminster Hall, I have a place (I decline to sit on the bench) in the Sergeants' row of the Common Pleas, with Talfourd and Andrews and Wilde; or in the Queen's Counsel row of the Queen's Bench, with Sir F. Pollock, and the Attorney-General. Then I know a vast number of younger men, whom I meet familiarly in the court room or at the clubs. Not a day passes without my laying up some knowledge or experience, which I hope to turn to profit hereafter. In another walk of life, I am already acquainted with many literary men. Among the peers I have received great kindness from Lords Wharncliffe (with whom I have dined), Bexley, Fitzwilliam, and Lansdowne. I have just been with Lord Lansdowne in his study; I met him last evening at a party. He had previously been kind enough to call upon me, and presented me with a card for his great ball in honor of the Coronation, and also with a card of admission to the Abbey; the latter I gave away to a friend as I was already provided with a better ticket, being that of a privy-councillor. A few nights ago I was at the great ball at Lord Fitzwilliam's; I started from my lodgings at eleven o'clock, and such was the crowd of carriages that I did not reach the door till one o'clock in the morning. When I first saw Lord Fitzwilliam, he was leading the Duchess of Gloucester on his arm; the Duc de Nemours came in immediately after me. As I stood in the hall, waiting for the carriage (it rained torrents), I seemed in a land of imagination, and not of reality; carriages drove up to the door in quick succession, and twenty servants cried out the name of the owner. There was the *élite* of England's nobility—it was all "lord" or "lady," except "Spring Rice;" the only untitled name I heard pronounced was that of the Chancellor of the Exchequer. I stood there an hour with dowager duchesses pressing about me, and Lady John Russell, in delicate health, and beautiful, waiting with submission as great as my own.

If other engagements allow me, I go the House of Lords or Commons. In the former I have had a place always assigned me on the steps of the throne, in the very body of the house, where I remain even during divisions. I was present at a most interesting debate on the 20th June, on the affairs of Spain. I heard Lyndhurst; and I cannot hesitate to pronounce him a master orator. All my prejudices are against him; he is unprincipled as a politician, and as a man; and his legal reputation has sunk very much by the reversal of his judgment in the case of Small *v.* Attwood, in which it is said Brougham exerted himself with superhuman energy: notwithstanding all this, Lyndhurst charmed me like a siren. His manner is simple, clear, and direct, enchaining the attention of all; we have nobody like him: he is more like Otis than any other, with less *efflorescence,* if I may so say, and more force. Wellington is plain and direct, and full of common-sense; all listen with the greatest respect. Brougham is various—always *at home,* whether for argument or laughter. The style of debate is different in the Lords and in the Commons; in the latter I have heard the two discussions on the Irish Corporation Bill.

I have alluded to my opportunities of seeing various shades of life and opinion. I may add that I know men of all parties. With Lord Wharncliffe I have talked a great deal about toryism and the ballot; while Lord Lansdowne expressed to me this morning his strong aversion to the King of Hanover as King of England. Sir Robert H. Inglis one of the best men I ever met, has shown me great kindness; I breakfasted with him, and then partook of a collation with the Bishop of London. At the Solicitor-General's I heard politics much discussed; and Mr. Duckworth of the Chancery Bar, in going home with me, told me in so many words that he was a *republican.* Opportunities I have also of meeting the best and most philosophical of the radicals. And now, my dear Judge, do not believe that I have given this long detail of personalities and egoism, from vanity; but in the freedom of friendship, and because I have no other way of letting you know what I am about. I must reserve for conversation after my return my impressions of the bench and bar, of politics and society. Let me say, now, that nothing which I have yet seen has shaken my love of country, or my willingness to return to my humble labors. I am grateful for the opportunities afforded me, and congratulate myself that I have come abroad at an age when I may rank among men, and be received as an equal into all society; and also, when, from comparative youth, I may expect many years of joyous retrospection, and also of doing good. Your advice and friendship I rely upon; and you know that your constant kindness has been my greatest happiness. I hope Mrs. Story is well; I shall write her an account of something that may be interesting; but imagine that every moment of my time is absorbed, and my mind almost in a *fever*. I have averaged, probably, *five* invitations a day. To-morrow is the Coronation. [of Queen Victoria]. That I shall see. Unsolicited on my part, I have received two tickets; and kind offers of others. Thanks for William's letter.

As ever, affectionately yours,
C. S.

TO PROFESSOR SIMON GREENLEAF, CAMBRIDGE

Travellers' Club, July 1, 1838

My Dear Friend:

I have thought of you often, but particularly on three occasions lately; and what do you think they were? When, at a collation, the Bishop of London asked me to take wine with him; when I was placed on the bench of the Court of Common Pleas in Westminster Hall; and lastly, when, at the superb entertainment of the Marchioness of Lansdowne, I stood by Prince Esterhazy and tried in vain to count the pearls and diamonds on the front of his coat and in his cap. You will not remember it; but it was you who first told me of the extravagant display of this man. That I should call you to my mind on the two other occasions you will readily understand. And so here I am amidst the law, the politics, the literature, and the splendors of London. Every day teems with interests; and I may say, indeed, every moment. Minutes are now to me as valuable as Esterhazy's diamonds. Imagine me in Westminster Hall where I sit and hear proceedings and converse with the very counsel who are engaged in them. I hardly believe my eyes and ears at times; I think it is all a cheat, and that I am not in Westminster Hall, at the sacred hearthstone of the English law. With many of the judges I have become personally acquainted, as well as with many of the lawyers. I have received cordial invitations to go most all the circuits; which I shall take I have not yet determined. Mr. Justice Vaughan says that I shall take the coif before I return. I cannot express to you how kind they all are. You know that I have no claims upon their attentions; and yet wherever I go I find the most considerate kindness. They have chosen me as an honorary member of three different clubs, in one of which I now write this letter.

I know nothing that has given me greater pleasure than the elevated character of the profession as I find it, and the relation of comity and brotherhood between the bench and the bar. The latter are really the friends and helpers of the judges. Good-will, gracious-ness, and good manners prevail constantly. And then the duties of the bar are of the most elevated character. I do not regret that my lines have been cast in the places where they flagged. Forster was there, whom you well know as the great writer in the *Examiner* and the author of the *Lives*. He is a very able fellow, and is yet young. Landor takes to him very much. His conversation is something like his writing. I had a good deal of talk with him. You must know, also, that our host, Mr. Kenyon, is a bosom friend of Southey and Wordsworth, and is no mean poet himself, besides being one of the most agreeable men I ever met.

Dining at Lord Lansdowne's a few evenings since, I met another literary man, whom I saw with the greatest pleasure. There was Lord Lansdowne, with the blue ribbon of the garter across his breast and the star on his coat,—kind, bland, amiable; Lady Lansdowne—neat, elegant, lady-like. Next me was the daughter, about nineteen—pale and wan, but, I am glad to say, extremely well-informed. I conversed with her during a long dinner, and we touched topics of books, fashion, coronation, &c.; and I found her to possess attainments which certainly do her honor. She was kind enough to mention that she and her mother had been reading together the work of a countryman of mine, Mr. Prescott; that they admired it very much, and that the extraordinary circumstances under which it was written made them take a great interest in the author and desire to see him. During the dinner, I was addressed across the table, which was a large round one, by a gentleman with black hair and round face, with regard to the United States. The question was put with distinct-ness and precision, and in a voice a little sharp and above the ordinary key. I did not know the name of the gentleman for some time; till, by and by, I heard him addressed by some one—"Macaulay." I at once asked Lord Shelburne, who sat on my right, if that was T. B. M., just returned from India; and was told that it was. At table, we had considerable conversation; and, on passing to the drawing-room, it was renewed. He is now nearly or about forty, rather short, and with a belly of unclassical proportions. His conversation was rapid, brilliant, and powerful; by far the best of any in the company, though Mr. Senior was there, and several others of no mean powers. I expect other opportunities of meeting him. He says that he shall abandon politics, not enter Parliament, and addict himself entirely to literature.

I may say here, that among acquaintances you never hear the word "Mr." Lawyers at the bar always address each other without that prefix. It is always "Talfourd," "Wilde," "Follett;" and at table, "Landor," "Forster," "Macaulay," "Senior," &c. I did not hear the word "Mr." at Lord Lansdowne's table, except when he addressed me—a stranger. My time is hurried and my paper is exhausted, but I have not told you of the poet Milman, and the beautiful party I met at his house—Lord Lansdowne, "Van Artevelde" Taylor, Babbage, Senior, Mrs. Villiers, and Mrs. Lister, who talked of Mrs. Newton with the most affectionate regard; nor of the grand *fête* at Lansdowne House, where I saw all the aristocracy of England; nor of the Coronation; nor of Lord Fitzwilliam's ball; nor of the twenty or thirty interesting persons I meet every day. This very week I have declined more invitations than I have accepted; and among those that I declined were invitations to dinner from Lord Denman, Lord Bexley, Mr. Senior, Mr. Mackenzie, &c.

As ever, affectionately yours,

C. S.

To Judge Story

London, July 12, 1838

My Dear Judge:

I have now been in London more than a month; but have not seen the Tower or the Tunnel, the British Museum or the theatres, the General Post-Office or Westminster Abbey (except as dressed for the Coronation): I have seen none of the sights or shows at which strangers stare. How, then, have I passed this time, till late midnight? In seeing society, men, courts, and parliaments. These will soon vanish with the season; while "London's column" will still point to the skies, and the venerable Abbey still hold its great interests, when men and society have dispersed. In a few days, this immense city will be deserted; the equipages which throng it will disappear; and fashion, and wealth, and rank, and title will all hie away to the seclusion of the country. Have I not done well, then, to "catch the Cynthia of the minute"? One day, I have sat in the Common Pleas at Westminster; then the Queen's Bench and Exchequer; then I have visited the same courts at their sittings at Guildhall; I have intruded into the quiet debate at Lincoln's Inn before the Chancellor; have passed to the Privy Council (the old Cockpit); have sat with my friend, Mr. Senior,[1] as a Master in Chancery; with Mr. Justice Vaughan at Chambers in Serjeants' Inn; and lastly, yesterday, I sat at the Old Bailey. This last sitting, of course, is freshest in my mind; and I must tell you something of it. Besides the aldermen, there were Justices Littledale, Park (James Allan), and Vaughan. I was assigned a seat on the bench, and heard a trial for arson, in which Payne (Carrington & Payne) was the counsel in defence. I was waited upon by the sheriff, and invited to dine with the judges and magistrates, at the Old Bailey. I was quite dull, and really ill (beaten out by dining in society, and often breakfasting and lunching in the same way every day for more than a month); but they treated me very kindly: and Sir Peter Laurie, the late Lord Mayor, proposed my health in a very complimentary speech, in the course of which he "hoped that he might have the honor of calling me his friend," &c. I rose at once, and replied in a plain way, without a single premeditated thought or expression, and found myself very soon interrupted by "hears;" and Littledale and Park and Vaughan all gave me more hearty applause. As I sat down, Vaughan cried to me: "Sumner, you've hit them between wind and water!" I should not omit to mention that I simply expressed, in my remarks, the deep affection which all educated Americans owe to England; that we look upon her with a filial regard; that in her churchyards are the bones of our fathers: and then I touched upon the interest which I, a professional man, felt in being permitted to witness the administration of justice here; and concluded by proposing the health of the judges of England—"always honorable, impartial, and learned." Mr. Charles Phillips (the notorious Irish orator), was at the table. I wish I were at home, to give you personal sketches of the lawyers and judges. My heart overflows when I attempt to speak of them; their courtesy and high sense of honor you have never overrated. The bench and the bar seem to be fellow-laborers in the administration of justice. Among the judges for talent, attainment, and judicial penetration,

[1]Nassau William Senior, 1790–1864. He was appointed Master in Chancery, in 1836. His writings, on topics of political economy, are various; and he was for several years professor of that science at Oxford. Among his publications was one upon "American Slavery," which reviewed Sumner's speech, of May 19 and 20, 1856, on "The Crime against Kansas," and the personal assault which followed it, being a reprint with additions of his article in the *Edinburgh Review*, April, 1855, Vol. CI., pp. 293–331. In 1857 they met, both in Paris and afterwards in London, and enjoyed greatly each other's society. Mr. Senior invited Sumner to dine several times in 1838-39.

the palm seems to be conceded to Baron Parke—a man of about fifty or fifty-five, with a very keen, penetrating, chestnut eye, and an intellectual countenance. At his table I met the chief barristers of the Western Circuit—Erle, Manning, Bompas, Rogers, Douglas, &c.; and they have invited me, very kindly, to visit their circuit. At table, after Lady Parke had left, I put to the Baron and the bar the question on which you have expressed an opinion, in the second volume of my Reports, with regard to the power of a jury to disobey the instructions of the court on a question of law in rendering a general verdict; and on which, you know, Baldwin has expressed an opinion opposite to yours. Parke at once exclaimed, and Erle and Bompas chimed in, that there was no possible ground of question; that a court should instruct a jury to take the law absolutely as it is laid down from the bench; and that a jury should not presume, because it has the physical power, to pronounce upon the law. I was quite amused to see how instantaneously they all gave judgment in the matter, and what astonishment they expressed when I assured them that some persons held otherwise in America.

I have recently breakfasted with Lord Denman, as I was so engaged as not to be able to accept his invitation to dinner. Bland, noble Denman! On the bench he is the perfect model of a judge —full of dignity and decision, and yet with mildness and suavity which cannot fail to charm. His high personal character and his unbending morals have given an elevated tone to the bar, and make one forget the want, perhaps, of thorough learning. In conversation he is plain, unaffected, and amiable. I talked with him much of Lord Brougham. He assured me that Brougham was one of the greatest judges that ever sat on the woolsack, and that posterity would do him justice when party asperities had died away. (Of Lord B. by-and-by.) I told Lord Denman the opinion you had formed of Lord B., from reading his judgments; and his Lordship said that he was highly gratified to hear it. Denman called the *wig* "the silliest thing in England," and hoped to be able to get rid of it. He is trying to carry a bill through the Lords, allowing witnesses to *affirm* in cases of conscientious scruples, and inquired of me about the practice in America; but he said he could not venture to allude to any American usage in the Lords, for it would tell against his measure. Think of this! I must not omit to mention that Lord Denman has invited me to visit him on the Home Circuit, where I shall certainly go, as also to the Western; and to the North Welsh Circuit—perhaps also the Oxford; and, the greatest of all, the Northern. To all of these I have had most cordial invitations.

I have heard Lord Brougham despatch several cases in the Privy

Council; and one or two were matters with which I was entirely familiar. I think I understand the secret of his power and weakness as a judge; and nothing that I have seen or heard tends to alter the opinion I had formed. As a judge, he is electric in the rapidity of his movements: he looks into the very middle of the case when counsel are just commencing, and at once says, "There is such a difficulty (mentioning it) to which you must address yourself; and, if you can't get over that, I am against you." In this way he saves time, and gratifies his impatient spirit; but he offends counsel. Here is the secret. I have heard no other judge (except old Allan Park) interrupt counsel in the least. In the mean time, Brougham is restless at table, writes letters; and, as Baron Parke assured me (Parke sits in the Privy Council), wrote his great article in the *Edinburgh Review* for April last at the table of the Privy Council. I once saw the usher bring to him a parcel of letters, probably from the mail—I should think there must have been twenty-five—and he opened and read them, and strewed the floor about him with envelopes; and still the argument went on. And very soon Brougham pronounced the judgment in rapid, energetic, and perspicuous language—better than I have heard from any other judge on the bench. I have quoted the opinion of Denman. Barristers with whom I have spoken have not conceded to him the position accorded by the Lord Chief-Justice, but still have placed him high. Mylne, the reporter, an able fellow, says that he is infinitely superior to Lyndhurst, and also to Lord Eldon, in his latter days. In the Lords I have heard Brougham—with his deep, husky notes, with his wonderful command of language, which keeps you in a state of constant excitement. I found myself several times on the point of crying out "Hear!"—thus running imminent risk of the polite attentions of the Usher of the Black Rod!

I am astonished at the reputation which is conceded to Follett (I have not yet met him, except in court). He is still a young man for England—that is, perhaps, forty-five—and is said to be in the receipt of an immense income, much larger than that of any other lawyer at the bar. I have heard Sir William Alexander and Mr. Justice Vaughan, who remembers Lord Mansfield, say that Follett reminds them of him; but, with all the praise accorded to him from judges, lawyers, and even from Sir Peter Laurie (ex-mayor), who thought him the greatest lawyer he ever knew, it does not seem to be thought that he has remarkable general talents or learning. They say he has "a genius for the law;" but Hayward, of the *Law Magazine*, says he is "a kind of law-mill; put in a brief, and there comes out an argument," without any particular exertion, study, or previous attainment. I have heard him several times. He is uniformly bland, courteous, and conversational in his style; and has never yet produced the impression of *power* upon me; in this last respect, very unlike Serjeant Wilde—who is, however, harsh and unamiable. Wilde has an immense practice. The Solicitor-General is one of the kindest and most amiable of men, with a limited practice, and is a *bachelor*. The Attorney-General is able, but dry and uninteresting. I have been more pleased with his wife, than with any other lady I have met in England. You know she is the daughter of Lord Abinger, and is a peeress in her own right, by the title of Lady Stratheden. She is beautiful, intelligent, and courteous. The Attorney-General has invited me to meet him at Edinburgh, when he goes down to present himself to his constituents.

This morning, Lord Bexley was kind enough to invite me to "Foot's Cray," his country seat. Many invitations of this kind I already have; one from Lord Leicester (old Coke), which I cannot neglect; also from Lord Fitzwilliam, Sir Henry Halford, Mr. Justice Vaughan, Lord Wharncliffe; and besides, from my friend Brown in Scotland, Mr. Marshall at the Lakes, Lord Morpeth in Ireland; and this moment, while I write, I have received a note from the greatest of wits, Sydney Smith, who says, "If your rambles lead you to the West of England, come and see me at Combe Florey, Taunton, Somersetshire." Thus you see that there is ample store of means for passing an interesting two months, when you consider that I shall take the circuits, with all these.

Mr. Justice Littledale is a good old man, simple and kind, but without any particular sagacity. Patteson, who appears to stand next after Baron Parke in point of judicial reputation, is still young—that is, near fifty; he is about as deaf as Mr. Ashmun was, and yet Lord Denman says that he would not spare him for a good deal. Patteson was much annoyed by the report some time ago of his intended resignation.

Travellers', Sunday, July 15

Have I told you the character of Mr. Justice Vaughan? He is now seventy, and is considerably lame from an accident; and is troubled with rheumatism, possibly with gout. Otherwise he is in a green old age; is tall and stout; in his manners, plain, hearty, and cordial; on the bench bland, dignified, and yet familiar—exchanging a joke or pleasantry with the bar on all proper occasions; in book-learning less eminent than for strong sense and a knowledge of the practice of courts, and of the human character. Yet I have always found him apt in apprehending legal questions when raised, and in indicating which way he should instruct the jury. His wife is Lady St. John, the origin of whos title I do not remember, though I think he explained it to me. She is of the family of Sir Theodosius Boughton, whose murder by Captain Donellan makes such a figure in the history of crime. I have met at dinner the present Sir William Boughton, who is the successor of Sir Theodosius. Sir Charles Vaughan is living quietly, as a bachelor, quite at his ease. I expect to meet him at dinner to-night with Serjeant D'Oyly.

Tindal is a model of a *patient* man. He sits like another Job, while the debate at the bar goes on. I may say the same of the Lord Chancellor, who hardly moves a muscle or opens his mouth during the whole progress of a cause. But turning from the bench to the bar (you see how I jump about in my hasty letters), a few days ago I strayed into a committee room of the House of Lords. Several counsel were busily engaged. I observed one with a wig ill-adjusted, with trousers of a kind of dirty chestnut color, that neither met the waistcoat nor the shoes; and I said to myself, and then to my neighbor, "That must be Sir Charles Wetherell." "Yes," was the answer; and very soon a reply of the witness under examination confirmed all. The witness (a plain farmer) had been pressed pretty hard, and was asked by the counsel whether he thought many articles of *fashion* would be carried on a proposed railway; to which the witness promptly replied, "As to articles of *fashion*—I do not think they much concern either *you* or I, Sir Charles." The whole room was convulsed with laughter, in which Sir Charles most heartily joined.

Hayward, of the *Law Magazine,* I know very well. Last evening I met at dinner, at his chambers in King's Bench Walk, some fashionable ladies and authors, and M. P.'s. There we stayed till long after midnight, and—shall I say with Sir John?—"heard the chimes of midnight in this same inn"—though it was Clifford's Inn and not the Temple, which was the scene of Falstaff's and Swallow's mysteries. Hayward is a fellow of a good deal of talent and variety. He is well known as the translator of *Faustus,* and as one of the constant contributors to the *Quarterly Review,* in which he wrote the articles on "Gastronomy" and "Etiquette." I have talked with him very freely about his journal, and hope before I leave England to do something in a quiet way that shall secure a place in it for American law. He has acknowledged to me that "the Americans are ahead of the English in the *science* of the law." He speaks well of you, but evidently has only glanced at your works. It seems that his friend Lewis, who is the author of some of the best articles in his journal, as that on Presumptive Evidence, had undertaken to review your works, but has since gone to the Continent.

And thus I have rambled over sheets of paper! Do you, my dear judge, follow me in all these wanderings? ... Then think of my invading the quiet seclusion of the Temple; looking in upon my friends in King's Bench Walk; smiling with poetical reminiscences as I look at the "No. 5" where Murray once lived; passing by Plowden Buildings, diving into the retirement of Elm Court to see Talfourd, or into the deeper retirement of Pump Court where is Wilkinson, or prematurely waking up my friend Brown from his morning slumbers, at two o'clock in the afternoon, in Crown-Office Row.

You may gather from my letters that I have seen much of the profession, and also of others. Indeed, English lawyers have told me that there are many of their own bar who are not so well acquainted with it already as I am. And if I am able to visit all the circuits, as I intend, I think I shall have a knowledge and experience of the English bar such as, perhaps, no foreigner has ever before had the opportunity of obtaining. I shall be glad to tell you further that since I have been here I have followed a rigid rule with regard to my conduct: I have not asked an introduction to any person; nor a single ticket, privilege, or any thing of the kind from any one; I have not called upon anybody (with one exception) until I had been first called upon or invited. The exception was Mr. Manning of the Temple; the author of the *Digest,* and the translator of the newly found *Year-Book* I met him at Baron Parke's. He is a bachelor of about fifty, of moderate business, of very little conversation, who lives a year without seeing a soul that takes any interest in his black-letter pursuits. I took the liberty, on the strength of meeting him at Baron Parke's, to call upon him; and was received most cordially.

HERMAN MELVILLE: LIVERPOOL

1839

Melville's father, at one time a prosperous merchant in New York City, went bankrupt when his son was eight and died when he was twelve, leaving the boy to shift for himself. He worked briefly in a bank, and as a schoolmaster. At nineteen he shipped as a cabin boy on the *St. Lawrence* for Liverpool: that voyage formed the basis for the only quasifictional *Redburn: His First Voyage,* published a decade later. The Liverpool chapters of Redburn are factual enough: there was more to Liverpool than a poor sailorboy was permitted to see but what Melville describes he did indeed see. The Liverpool of 1839 was the second port in England, and perhaps the most depressing, vicious, and poverty-stricken of all English cities. It had the highest infant mortality rate in the whole of Britain, and the average length of life of its inhabitants was seventeen; it had shared for many years almost a monopoly on the slave trade; it confessed over three thousand prostitutes. Young Melville found it strangely like New York, outwardly, but wholly unlike New York in its class structure, its poverty, and its vice. The voyage to Liverpool was the beginning of Melville's career as a sailor; it was followed by those journeys to

From Herman Melville, *Redburn, His First Voyage* (New York, 1849), pp. 53–101.

the South Seas immortalized in *Typee, Omoo* and *Mardi,* and by his service on the U.S. frigate to which he gave the name *White Jacket.* Melville returned briefly to Britain in 1849 and again in 1853, but nothing of literary importance came out of these tamer visits.

The Dock-wall Beggars.

I might relate other things which befel me during the six weeks and more that I remained in Liverpool, often visiting the cellars, sinks, and hovels of the wretched lanes and courts near the river. But to tell of them, would only be to tell over again the story just told; so I return to the docks.

The old women described as picking dirty fragments of cotton in the empty lot, belong to the same class of beings who at all hours of the day are to be seen within the dock walls, raking over and over the heaps of rubbish carried ashore from the holds of the shipping.

As it is against the law to throw the least thing overboard, even a rope-yarn; and as this law is very different from similar laws in New York, inasmuch as it is rigidly enforced by the dockmasters; and, moreover, as after discharging a ship's cargo, a great deal of dirt and worthless dunnage remains in the hold, the amount of rubbish accumulated in the appointed receptacles for depositing it within the walls is extremely large, and is constantly receiving new accessions from every vessel that unlades at the quays.

Standing over these noisome heaps, you will see scores of tattered wretches, armed with old rakes and picking-irons, turning over the dirt, and making as much of a rope-yarn as if it were a skein of silk. Their findings, nevertheless, are but small; for as it is one of the immemorial perquisites of the second mate of a merchant ship to collect and sell on his own account, all the condemned "old junk" of the vessel to which he belongs, he generally takes good heed that in the buckets of rubbish carried ashore there shall be as few rope-yarns as possible.

In the same way, the cook preserves all the odds and ends of pork-rinds and beef-fat, which he sells at considerable profit; upon a six months' voyage frequently realizing thirty or forty dollars from the sale, and in large ships even more than that. It may easily be imagined, then, how desperately driven to it must these rubbish-pickers be, to ransack heaps of refuse which have been previously gleaned.

Nor must I omit to make mention of the singular beggary practised in the streets frequented by sailors; and particularly to record the remarkable army of paupers that beset the docks at particular hours of the day.

At twelve o'clock the crews of hundreds and hundreds of ships issue in crowds from the dock gates to go to their dinner in the town. This hour is seized upon by multitudes of beggars to plant themselves against the outside of the walls, while others stand upon the curb-stone to excite the charity of the seamen. The first time that I passed through this long lane of pauperism, it seemed hard to believe that such an array of misery could be furnished by any town in the world.

Every variety of want and suffering here met the eye, and every vice showed her its victims. Nor were the marvellous and almost incredible shifts and stratagems of the professional beggars wanting, to finish this picture of all that is dishonourable to civilization and humanity.

Old women, rather mummies, drying up with slow starving and age; young girls, incurably sick, who ought to have been in the hospital; sturdy men, with the gallows in their eyes, and a whining lie in their mouths; young boys, hollow-eyed and decrepit; and puny mothers, holding up puny babes in the glare of the sun, formed the main features of the scene.

But these were diversified by instances of peculiar suffering, vice, or art in attracting charity, which, to me at least, who had never seen such things before, seemed to the last degree uncommon and monstrous.

I remember one cripple, a young man rather decently clad, who sat huddled up against the wall, holding a painted board on his knees. It was a picture intending to represent the man himself caught in the machinery of some factory, and whirled about among spindles and cogs, with his limbs mangled and bloody. This person said nothing, but sat silently exhibiting his board. Next him, leaning upright against the wall, was a tall, pallid man, with a white bandage round his brow, and his face cadaverous as a corpse. He, too, said nothing; but with one finger silently pointed down to the square of flagging at his feet, which was nicely swept, and stained blue, and bore this inscription in chalk:

> "I have had no food for three days;
> My wife and children are dying."

Further on lay a man with one sleeve of his ragged coat removed, showing an unsightly sore; and above it a label with some writing.

In some places, for the distance of many rods, the whole line of flagging immediately at the base of the wall, would be completely covered with inscriptions, the beggars standing over them in silence.

But as you passed along these horrible records, in an hour's time destined to be obliterated by the feet of thousand and thousands of wayfarers, you were not left unassailed by the clamorous petitions of the more urgent applicants for charity. They beset you on every hand; catching you by the coat; hanging on, and following you along; and, *for Heaven's sake,* and *for God's sake,* and *for Christ's sake,* beseeching of you but *one ha'penny.* If you so much as glanced your eye on one of them, even for an instant, it was perceived like lightning, and the person never left your side until you turned into another street, or satisfied his demands. Thus, at least, it was with the sailors; though I observed that the beggars treated the town's-people differently.

I cannot say that the seamen did much to relieve the destitution which three times every day was presented to their view. Perhaps habit had made them callous; but the truth might have been that very few of them had much money to give. Yet the beggars must have had some inducement to infest the dock walls as they did.

As an example of the caprice of sailors, and their sympathy with suffering among members of their own calling, I must mention the case of an old man, who every day, and all day long, through sunshine and rain, occupied a particular corner, where crowds of tars were always passing. He was an uncommonly large, plethoric man, with a wooden leg, and dressed in the nautical garb; his face was red and round; he was continually merry; and with his wooden stump thrust forth, so as almost to trip up the careless wayfarer, he sat upon a great pile of monkey-jackets, with a little depression in them between his knees, to receive the coppers thrown him. And plenty of pennies were tossed into his poor-box by the sailors, who always exchanged a pleasant word with the old man, and passed on, generally regardless of the neighbouring beggars.

The first morning I went ashore with my shipmates, some of them greeted him as an old acquaintance; for that corner he had occupied for many long years. He was an old man-of-war's-man, who had lost his leg at the battle of Trafalgar; and singular to tell, he now exhibited his wooden one as a genuine specimen of the oak timbers of Nelson's ship, the Victory.

Among the paupers were several who wore old sailor hats and jackets, and claimed to be destitute tars; and on the strength of these pretensions demanded help from their brethren; but Jack would see through their disguise in a moment, and turn away, with no benediction.

As I daily passed through this lane of beggars, who thronged the docks as the Hebrew cripples did the Pool of Bethesda, and as I thought of my utter inability in any way to help them, I could not but offer up a prayer, that some angel might descend, and turn the waters of the docks into an elixir, that would heal all their woes, and make them, man and woman, healthy and whole as their ancestors, Adam and Eve, in the garden.

Adam and Eve! If indeed ye are yet alive and in heaven, may it be no part of your immortality to look down upon the world ye have left. For as all these sufferers and cripples are as much your family as young Abel, so, to you, the sight of the world's woes would be a parental torment indeed.

The Booble-alleys of the Town

The same sights that are to be met with along the dock walls at noon, in a less degree, though diversified with other scenes, are continually encountered in the narrow streets where the sailor boarding-houses are kept.

In the evening, especially when the sailors are gathered in great numbers, these streets present a most singular spectacle, the entire population of the vicinity being seemingly turned into them. Hand-organs, fiddles, and cymbals, plied by strolling musicians, mix with the songs of the seamen, the babble of women and children, and the groaning and whining of beggars. From the various boarding-houses, each distinguished by gilded emblems outside —an anchor, a crown, a mortal among tens of thousands of rags and tatters. For in some parts of the town, inhabited by labourers, and poor people generally, I used to crowd my way through masses of squalid men, women, and children, who at this evening hour, in those quarters of Liverpool, seem to empty themselves into the street, and live there for the time. I had never seen anything like it in New York.

Often I witnessed some curious, and many very sad scenes; and especially I remembered encountering a pale, ragged man, rushing along frantically, and striving to throw off his wife and children, who clung to his arms and legs; and, in God's name, conjured him not to desert them. He seemed bent upon rushing down to the water, and drowning himself, in some despair, and craziness of wretchedness.

In these haunts beggary went on before me wherever I walked, and dogged me unceasingly at the heels. Poverty, poverty, poverty, in almost endless vistas: and want and woe staggered arm in arm along these miserable streets.

And here I must not omit one thing that struck me at the time. It was the absence of negroes; who in the large towns in the "free states" of America, almost always form a considerable portion of the destitute; but in these streets not a negro was to be seen. All were whites; and with the exception of the Irish, were natives of the soil: even Englishmen; as much Englishmen as the dukes in the House of Lords. This conveyed a strange feeling; and more than anything else reminded me that I was not in my own land. For *there*, such a being as a native beggar is almost unknown; and to be a born American citizen seems a guarantee against pauperism; and this, perhaps, springs from the virtue of a vote.

Speaking of negroes recalls the look of interest with which negro-sailors are regarded when they walk the Liverpool streets. In Liverpool, indeed, the negro steps with a prouder pace, and lifts his head like a man; for here, no such exaggerated feeling exists in respect to him, as in America. Three or four times I encountered our black steward, dressed very handsomely, and walking arm in arm with a good-looking English woman. In New York, such a couple would have been mobbed in three minutes; and the steward would have been lucky to escape with whole limbs. Owing to the friendly reception extended to them, and the unwonted immunities they enjoy in Liverpool, the black cooks and stewards of American ships are very much attached to the place, and like to make voyages to it.

Being so young and inexperienced then, and unconsciously swayed in some degree by those local and social prejudices that are the marring of most men, and from which, for the mass, there seems no possible escape; at first I was surprised that a coloured man should be treated as he is in this town; but a little reflection showed that, after all, it was but recognising his claims to humanity and normal equality; so that, in some things, we Americans leave to other countries the carrying out of the principle that stands at the head of our Declaration of Independence.

During my evening strolls in the wealthier quarters, I was subject to a continual mortification. It was the humiliating fact, wholly unforeseen by me, that upon the whole, and barring the poverty and beggary, Liverpool, away from the docks, was very much such a place as New York. There were the same sort of streets pretty much;

the same rows of houses with stone steps; the same kind of sidewalks and curbs; and the same elbowing, heartless-looking crowd as ever.

I came across the Leeds Canal, one afternoon; but, upon my word, no one could have told it from the Erie Canal at Albany. I went into St. John's Market on a Saturday night; and though it was strange enough to see that great roof supported by so many pillars, yet the most discriminating observer would not have been able to detect any difference between the articles exposed for sale, and the articles exhibited in Fulton Market, New York.

I walked down Lord-street, peering into the jewellers' shops; but I thought I was walking down a block in Broadway. I began to think that all this talk about travel was a humbug; and that he who lives in a nut-shell, lives in an epitome of the universe, and has but little to see beyond him.

His Adventure with the Cross Old Gentleman

My adventure in the News-Room in the Exchange, which I have related in a previous chapter, reminds me of another at the Lyceum, some days after, which may as well be put down here, before I forget it.

I was strolling down Bold-street, I think it was, when I was struck by the sight of a brown stone building, very large and handsome. The windows were open, and there, nicely seated, with their comfortable legs crossed over their comfortable knees, I beheld several sedate, happy-looking old gentlemen reading the magazines and papers, and one had a fine gilded volume in his hand.

Yes, this must be the Lyceum, thought I; let me see. So I whipped out my guide-book, and opened it at the proper plate; and sure enough, the building before me corresponded stone for stone. I stood awhile on the opposite side of the street, gazing at my picture, and then at its original; and often dwelling upon the pleasant gentlemen sitting at the open windows; till at last, I felt an uncontrollable impulse to step in for a moment, and run over the news.

I'm a poor, friendless sailor-boy, thought I, and they cannot object; especially as I am from a foreign land, and strangers ought to be treated with courtesy. I turned the matter over again, as I walked across the way; and with just a small tapping of a misgiving at my heart, I at last scraped my feet clean against the curb-stone, and taking off my hat while I was yet in the open air, slowly sauntered in.

But I had not got far in that large and lofty room, filled with many agreeable sights, when a crabbed old gentleman lifted up his eye from the *London Times,* which words I saw boldly printed on the back of the large sheet in his hand, and looking at me as if I were a strange dog with a muddy hide, that had stolen out of the gutter into this fine apartment, he shook his silver-headed cane at me fiercely, till the spectacles fell off his nose. Almost at the same moment, up stepped a terribly cross man, who looked as if he had a mustard plaster on his back, that was continually exasperating him; who, throwing down some papers which he had been filing, took me by my innocent shoulders, and then, putting his foot against the broad part of my pantaloons, wheeled me right out into the street, and dropped me on the walk, without so much as offering an apology for the affront. I sprang after him but in vain; the door was closed upon me.

These Englishmen have no manners, that's plain, thought I; and I trudged on down the street in a reverie.

WILLIAM GIBSON:

A PHILADELPHIA DOCTOR

REVISITS THE HOSPITALS OF EDINBURGH

AND HIS OLD MENTOR,

SIR CHARLES BELL

1839

A distinguished surgeon, and professor of medicine at the University of Pennsylvania, William Gibson had studied medicine first in Baltimore and Philadelphia and then, in 1809, in Edinburgh and London, where he had the good fortune to work under Ashley Cooper and John Bell at the famous Guy's Hospital. At the age of twenty-three he became professor of surgery at the University of Maryland, and in 1819 succeeded Dr. Philip Physick at the University of Pennsylvania, where he occupied the chair of surgery for thirty-six years. A prolific scholar and writer, he was well known in both the United States and England for his *Institutes and Practice of Surgery*. In 1815 he had returned to England, visited the Continent, and was present at the Battle of Waterloo. *Rambles in Europe* was the product of a second visit to Britain and Europe, in 1839, and so too was an interesting volume of *Sketches of Prominent Surgeons of London and Paris*. In the tradition of the Philadelphia surgeons, from Benjamin Rush to S. Weir Mitchell, Gibson had far-ranging interests in classical literature, music, and painting. He gives us here not only fascinating glimpses of the idiosyncratic Dr. Bell, but some evidence of the high respect accorded American medicine in Britain.

From William Gibson, *Rambles in Europe in 1839* (Philadelphia, 1841), pp. 135–140, 147–154.

It would be impossible to describe my sensations upon thus being suddenly dropped into the midst of a people, among whom years of my boyhood had been passed; whom I had left as a stripling, and to whom I returned a "gray-head sire." My first impulse, however, I may say, was to cast about, and see if I could discover no familiar good-natured face with which to claim acquaintance; but, alas, no such face could be found. I saw the same houses standing where I left them, but their old tenants had disappeared and others occupied their place; I saw the same strange-looking, uncouth, figures, the cadie's, the fish-women, and others of various occupations, parading the streets, and listened to their well-remembered, discordant, cries; I saw them eyeing me, from head to foot, with the same inquisitive glances, and wondering, apparently, from what strange land I had come. The story of Rip Van Winkle flashed across my mind, and I involuntarily repeated to myself "Does nobody here know Rip Van Winkle?" I began to consider whether I could have slept in the mountain for twenty years, and suddenly awoke with a gun upon my shoulder, when my reverie was disturbed by the touch of the coachman's finger, reminding me of his fare. I dropped the fellow a shilling, stepped into Waterloo Hotel, engaged rooms, deposited my luggage, and the next moment found myself on the North Bridge, stretching towards the college, in quest, instinctively, of my old lodgings and my old landlady. The college which from Scotch pride had been commenced on a grand scale, some fifty years ago, and from Scotch economy left unfinished for a long time, had, during my absence, been built up, and so changed the aspect of the adjoining streets as to render it somewhat difficult, at first, to thread my way to a spot, which in former times I could have found, though blindfold, or at any hour of the night. I got, however, at last, upon the right scent, ascended the winding staircase, not, as formerly, with hop skip and jump, but by slow degrees, and after many a halt, and blow, and wheeze, reached the *garret high, with cobweb hung,* summoned, by a thundering knock, the lazy inmates, and entered, without ceremony, the very den, where as a youngster, I had consumed, over the midnight lamp, many a weary hour, and, at times, enjoyed many a merry prank with a score of Virginia lads—most of whom, poor fellows, have since passed away. I looked about and found that here, at least, I was at home; for I saw the same hooks I had driven into the wall to support my anatomical preparations, the same nail-holes I had made, by mistake, still open and staring me in the face, and above all, what can no where be found, except in a Scotch country, the same pane of glass upon which I had scratched with a flint, my name thirty years before, as safe and sound as the day it was fixed by putty in the sash. But where was the good old tabby, the kind-hearted soul that had administered so often to my wants, as landlady, and counsellor, and friend? Gone to her long home, to her final account and resting-place, to receive the reward of her "exceeding honesty," her pure, disinterested, benevolent actions. I found, upon inquiry, that the rooms had, ever since my occupancy, been devoted to the same purposes—a lodging for students. It so happened they were disengaged, and nothing but the great distance from the new town, where most of the friends I expected to meet resided, prevented me from resuming my old quarters.

Having satisfied my curiosity and promised the new landlady to send her, if I could, for *"auld lang syne,"* some of my young countrymen as lodgers, I returned to Waterloo, dined on haggis and sheep's-head, swallowed mouthfuls of singed wool, which I washed down with the best ale in the world, and then sallied forth in quest of my preceptor and friend—*Sir Charles Bell.*

In every large town certain streets remain as permanent avenues, and particular buildings are preserved and serve as landmarks for ages; it was not, therefore, surprising as I passed in the coach through Clerk and Nicholson and South and North Bridge streets—one continued line, under different names, of the principal entrance to the old town—I should have recognised many buildings quite familiar to me in former days. But I soon found when I attempted to avail myself of previous information, and applied the rule to the new town, and particularly that portion which, in my time, embraced the suburbs, I was almost as much a stranger as I should have been in Bagdad; for *streets* and *squares,* and *terraces,* and *crescents,* and *places* had multiplied without end or number, and Calton Hill had been partly cut down and paved and built upon; and, in short, I found what had long been considered the most beautiful city in Europe, now so extended and changed, so transcendently magnificent and superior to itself, as to hear without surprise of its having doubled in less than a quarter of a century. Still I was not prepared to believe I could lose my way in any part of *"Auld Reekie,"* and was only undeceived upon finding I had walked for two hours in search of *Ainslie Place*—the residence of Sir Charles—a place, upon the site of which woodcock and snipe were formerly shot, now covered by some of the finest houses and quite in a central part of the town. It may be proper, perhaps, to premise I had been, for months, the house pupil of Sir Charles, in London, and ever after his correspondent; that in 1837 he accepted the professorship of surgery in the University of Edinburgh, left London and returned to his native city, where he now resides and still holds his appointment.

He was aware of my being in Europe, and had been expecting me, daily, in Edinburgh. When my name, therefore, was announced, he came out of his study with alacrity, bounding into the hall like a young stag, full of life, animation, and vigour, and so little altered that I should have known him, instantly, had we met, in any part of the world. He was overwhelmed, however, at that moment with business—being engaged in reviewing theses, upon which he was to examine candidates the next day at the public commencement or "Capping." I insisted, therefore, upon his leaving me to range over his gallery of ancient masters, and still better collection, by his own hand, of spirited water-coloured sketches and finished drawings, with which large and numerous portfolios were filled, embracing almost every subject. In ascending together the hall stairs, my attention was instantly drawn to a very striking and spirited sketch, in oil, of the head of a lion, of full size, with the mouth widely expanded, the tongue and teeth finely displayed, and the whole features expressive of great energy and excitement. It was, indeed, an old acquaintance, and the first picture Sir Charles ever attempted in oil. I reminded him of my having procured, for dissection, the body of a large lion from Pidcock's menagerie, and, with the assistance of fellow-students, lugged it, at night, upon my shoulders, to his house; of his coming into the anatomical room next morning, and exclaiming, "My dear Doctor, I *must* have a sketch of that fine fellow's head before you cut him up;" of the great artists, Haydon and Eastlake, then his pupils in anatomy, determining, also, to try their skill in the same way, and of some other circumstances. He replied: "I had forgotten some of the things you mention, but remember enough to know you are fairly entitled to the picture, and if you think it worth carrying across the Atlantic, can only say it will gratify me, exceedingly, if you will accept it"—adding, it had been much admired by artists and amateurs, and even offers made for it by dealers, and had once actually been carried off, temporarily, by a friend, who seemed determined to possess it. I need hardly say, I was too happy to receive such a boon, and would almost as soon lose an eye as part with it.

From that moment I was a daily, almost hourly, visitor at Sir Charles's, saw him under all circumstances, met him at Lord Jeffrey's, of whom he is a bosom friend, and other places, and had great pleasure in hearing him spoken of everywhere, as entitled to the highest honours for superiority of intellect and excellence of heart; and, in short, found him, wherever personally known, honoured and beloved beyond measure. I was exceedingly struck with the tenacity of his memory, especially for *events;* for he told me many circumstances concerning myself I had entirely forgotten. Among others, he said, "You must have a very large and valuable library, by this time, if you have continued to collect with the same spirit you evinced while residing with me; and then mentioned the greater number of old, scarce, and valuable works I had picked up, commencing with the large and splendid volumes of Sandifort and of Chesselden on the Bones, and descending in the list until he almost enumerated my library. . . .

In person Sir Charles is rather below the medium height, stout, muscular, and admirably proportioned, quick and energetic in his movements, when roused or under the influence of mental excitement, the result of thought or study; but in moments of relaxation is singularly calm, placid, and unostentatious. His head is large, forehead lofty and expanded, his eye full, and prominent, very expressive, and of gray colour, his features animated and agreeable, and his voice soft and melodious in the extreme. His hair is perfectly white on the sides and top of the head, but grayish behind. It would be impossible, however, to form any idea of the man from the prints published by Pettigrew and others—so miserably deficient are they in drawing and expression. The same may be said of the oil pictures, one of which, nearly a full length, hanging in his own house, bears little or no resemblance, and is hard and disagreeably vulgar. The only print; indeed, I have ever seen at all approaching his physiognomy, is that of the celebrated *Vesalius*—from a picture by Titian —in his frontispiece to his large work on Anatomy and Surgery. He is now above sixty, having been born in 1778, but might easily pass, from his fine complexion and good health, for fifty. His father was an eminent Scotch Episcopal divine, all of whose sons were men of distinguished talent, especially the celebrated John Bell, by whom Sir Charles was educated. The only surviving brother of Sir Charles is *George Joseph Bell,* professor of law in the University of Edinburgh, successor in the Court of Session to Sir Walter Scott, and author of very celebrated works on Law—well known all over the world. There is no relationship between this family and that of the late surgeon, Benjamin Bell—erroneously supposed by many to exist.

The traits of character in the mind of Sir Charles Bell are eminently striking, and yet not easily understood or appreciated. His genius is of very high and commanding order, combined with inordinate powers of application, and perseverance so unflinching as to enable him to master any subject, and by unravelling its complexities, make each position as clear, and each statement as distinct, as the noon-day sun. So great, indeed, is his concentrativeness as to exclude, at will, all extraneous matters, and neither see objects around him, nor be roused by what would startle or enforce the attention of a common man. By many persons, unacquainted with this peculiarity, he has been considered cold, haughty, and supercilious, and has experienced, accordingly, ill usage for supposed slights and affronts, and has even suffered heavy losses by the jealousy and ill will of professional men and others, thus engendered and kept alive by most mistaken and unfounded impressions. And yet there is no one possessed in a more eminent degree of the milk of human kindness, no one who takes a deeper interest in the fate of a patient, whether of low or high degree, who studies the case with more unremitting diligence, and conscientiously gives his opinion, or applies his remedies with more perfect disinterestedness. But if I were to select, from his various merits, the trait most conspicuous in his pure, upright, honourable, blameless, character, I should say it was deep, most affectionate, and unquenchable regard for his family, relations, and friends, such as would induce him to run all hazards for their benefit, and sacrifice his comforts and interests, and even life, for their welfare and reputation. This, I am aware, may seem high praise, extravagant eulogy, nevertheless the picture is perfectly true to nature, and only to be overshadowed, perhaps, by the commanding qualities of mind that have enabled him, through some of the most brilliant discoveries which have ever adorned the annals of our profession, to place himself upon an eminence so exalted as to entitle him, beyond all question, cavil, or doubt, to the enviable prerogative of being considered the best anatomist, the best physiologist, the best pathologist, and one of the best medical and operative surgeons in the British empire, and, perhaps, in the world.

How does it happen, then, he has not enjoyed the extensive practice, and become so enormously rich as some of the European surgeons we hear of? This is easily understood, when recollected, that the facility of gaining practice does not, invariably, depend upon amount of intellect or extent of individual qualification; that many persons, of very limited capacity and meager acquirements, possess, inherently, the faculty of pleasing, and even fascinating the public—who are no judges of professional merit—to a great degree; that others cultivate, as a business, the means of obtaining professional livelihood, independently of professional knowledge, and resort to every stratagem and device which self-preservation suggests, in order to place them on a level, or force themselves above their intellectual rivals. So that many a man, with only the manners of a waiter and the intellect of a mouse, has obtained enormous business, whilst his talented brother has actually starved, or, perhaps, been thrown into prison. Such is well known to be the case, not only in our profession, but in law and divinity, and more or less, perhaps, in every other vocation, not only in Europe but in this country, and, indeed, throughout the world. Now Sir Charles, from early life, has been employed, most laboriously, in studying and teaching his profession; in writing and publishing large and valuable works; in hospital practice; in making collections of human and morbid anatomy, and pictures for class demonstrations, so expensive, as to absorb most of his professional receipts, and leave little time for playing the fine gentleman, for bowing, and scraping, and flattering old maids, and young maids, and old women, and noblemen, and gentry; and withal, has been too scrupulously honest, upright, and independent in sentiment, to stoop to any measures, however well calculated to advance his fortune, between which and strict professional dignity and honour he found vast incompatibility. I do not mean to infer, however, from what I have just said, that all who obtain extensive practice must, necessarily, resort to unworthy means. The reverse I know to be the case, in many instances; nor do I wish to be understood to say, that Sir Charles had not succeeded, at all, in obtaining business; but only to imply, that his private professional calls, though numerous and important, were much fewer than if he had laid himself out for practice, by cultivating the arts of obtaining and securing it. This much, however, is certain, that any man of moderate capacity, who, for years, has been a hospital surgeon, will see more, in two or three months, than any one, engaged in private practice only, in a year; and will often reap more, from close investigation of a single case, than another from fifty; so that, after all, it is not the number of cases a medical man may have attended, but the use made of them, which will establish for him the character of a bad or good practioner.

Of Sir Charles's talents as a *professor* or *teacher*, of his exquisite taste and skill as an *artist*, and of his numerous and very diversified writings, I have as yet said very little. As regards the first, if I may be allowed to judge from attending his lectures, formerly; from his present style of elocution; and from a very spirited, extemporaneous address to the graduates of the University of Edinburgh, at the public commencement, I attended . . . ; I should say, he had lost none of the plain, easy, enviable mode of elocution, so characteristic of a great and successful lecturer—none of the animation, sparkling vivacity, and enthusiasm, so indicative of genius—none of the substantial and effective power of reasoning, so essential to satisfy the understanding—none of the interest in communicating information, without which knowledge becomes dry and tasteless—none of the warm and sympathizing affection and playfulness towards his pupils which induced them to treat him more as a friend and beloved companion than as a stranger—none of those resources which enabled him to lay open, at pleasure, his vast storehouse of facts and boundless information—none of the authority and respect which maintained lenient order and indulgent supremacy over all around him—none of the ingenuity and felicity of illustration, and vigour of mathematical demonstration, that irresistibly carried conviction to the minds of his hearers—and none of the unbounded goodness of heart, sincerity, and self-dereliction, for which he has always been so remarkable. That this is no idle exaggeration, no groundless panegyric, no overweening partiality, no undue bias on the part of a friend and pupil, much higher authority than my humble name is ready to attest. "The Discourses of Sir Charles Bell," says the venerable *Bishop of Durham*, "before the Royal College of Surgeons of London, conveyed to me the impression not so much of a lecture as of a man *thinking aloud*"—a remark, previously made by Goldsmith, of himself.

Of the genius of Sir Charles Bell, as an artist merely, and independently of his literary, and scientific, and professional merits, it would not be too high praise, perhaps, to affirm, that few, if any, now living,—except, possibly, the *Landseers,* and some of his other pupils that have attained the highest eminence as painters—can be compared to him, in delicacy of touch, in force of expression, in accuracy of outline and drawing, in anatomical precision, in faithfulness of character, and in variety of delineation and effect. To establish this position, his splendid work, on the *"Anatomy of Expression in Painting,"* is alone sufficient; but any one examining, as I did, the *original sketches* accompanying that work—for they lost much in the hands of the engraver—and his numerous portfolios, containing real, or imaginary portraits of remarkable beggars, odd-looking people, paralytic men, dancing girls, Scotch lassies, tailors "clouting claes," quizzical-looking Frenchmen, landscapes of every variety of scene, in the Highlands, about Edinburgh and London, and many other parts of England, large and finished coloured drawings of the wounded at Waterloo, magnificent sketches of anatomical and surgical subjects for illustration of lectures; to say nothing of the exquisite *etchings* by his own hand, in his numerous publications; and of the immense number of engravings throughout all his works, copied from his original drawings, would declare, that if he had directed his attention and energies exclusively to the arts, he would have equalled, probably, *Pousin* or *Murillo,* or even *Raphael* himself. Indeed, I remember hearing Haydon, then his pupil, and now one of the greatest painters in England, declare that the *Lion's-Head,* I formerly spoke of, was in the style, and quite equal, in some respects, to the productions of *Rubens.*

The immense number of valuable publications by Sir Charles Bell—anatomical, surgical, physiological, pathological, practical, and literary, the work of a lifetime of indefatigable labour, all showing immense research, almost unexampled industry, profound learning, exquisite taste, unbounded practical skill—the result, in many instances, of information obtained on the fields of *Corunna* and *Waterloo;* for he was the first surgeon, after those great battles, to break all his engagements, and leave England, and enter the ranks, and dress, with his own hand, the wounded and comfort the dying—it would be impossible, in the present work, to notice, further, than present a simple outline of each.

1840 -1850

GEORGE CALVERT:

"THE ENGLISH ARISTOCRACY

DOES NOT FORM A CASTE"

1840

Criticism of the British class system, and of the privileges and pretensions of the upper classes, was perhaps the most stridently recurrent note in nineteenth-century American commentary. It is to the credit of Calvert that he does not indulge in sweeping criticisms but is both perspicacious and just in his judgments of the aristocracy. Calvert himself came from what would have been an American aristocracy had there been such a thing: he was a descendant of the Baltimore family of Maryland, and born to wealth and privilege. On graduation from Harvard College in 1823 he sailed for England under the care of no less than Stafford Canning, then British Minister to Washington. Like those other Harvard graduates Everett and Bancroft, he moved on to Göttingen for study, and then to Edinburgh, where he studied law. After his return to America he ventured briefly into journalism, then took up permanent residence in Newport, where he wrote gentlemanly books on Shakespeare, Goethe, and other literary figures, and dabbled in poetry and drama. His *Scenes and Thoughts in Europe* was largely a product of his second trip to Britain and the Continent, from 1840 to 1843.

From George H. Calvert, *Scenes and Thoughts in Europe. By an American* (New York, 1846), pp. 11–15.

Leamington, September 1840

The day after the date of my last, we left London for Leamington in Warwickshire, where we have been for a month. . . .

My reading at Leamington has been chiefly of newspapers. From them, however, something may be learnt by a stranger. They reflect the surface of society; and as surfaces mostly take their shape and hue from depths beneath them, one may read in newspapers somewhat more than they are paid for printing. Even the London "Satirist," the rankest sewer of licentiousness, has a social and political significance. It could only live in the shade of an Aristocracy. The stomach of omnivorous scandal were alone insufficient to digest its gross facts and fabrications. The Peer is dragged through a horsepond for the sport of the plebeian. The artisan chuckles to see Princes and Nobles wallowing in dirt, in print. The high are brought so low that the lowest can laugh at them: the proud, who live on contempt, are pulled down to where themselves can be scorned by the basest. The wit consists chiefly in the contrast between the elevation of the game and the filthiness of the ammunition wherewith it is assailed; between the brilliancy of the mark and the obscurity of the marksman. A register is kept of Bishops, Peeresses, Dukes, Ambassadors, charged with being swindlers, adulterers, buffoons, panders, sycophants; and this is one way of keeping Englishmen in mind that all men are brothers. It is a weekly sermon, suited to some of the circumstances of the times and people, on the text—"But many that are first shall be last."

England looks everywhere aristocratical. A dominant idea in English life is possession by inheritance. Property and privilege are nailed by law to names. A man, by force of mind, rises from lowliness to a Dukedom: the man dies, but the Dukedom lives, and lifts into eminence a dullard perhaps, or a reprobate. The soul has departed, and the body is unburied. Counter to the order of nature, the external confers instead of receiving life; and whereas at first a man made the Dukedom, afterwards 'tis the Dukedom that makes the man. Merit rises, but leaves behind it generations of the unmeritorious not only to feed on its gains, but to possess places that should never be filled but by the deserving. In an hereditary aristocracy the noble families form knots on the trunk of a nation, drawing to themselves sap which, for the public health, should be equally distributed. Law and custom attach power and influence to names and lands: whoso own these, govern, and so rigid and cherished are primogeniture and entail, that much of them is possessed without an effort or a natural claim. The possessor's whole right is arbitrary and artificial.

To ascribe the short-comings of England to the aristocratic principle, were as shallow as to claim for it her many glories. In her development it has played its part according to her constitutional temperament; but her development has been richer and healthier than that of her neighbors, because her aristocracy has had its roots in the people, or rather because (a false aristocracy having been hitherto in Europe unavoidable) her people have been manly and democratic enough not to suffer one distinct in blood to rear itself among them. Compare English with any other aristocracy, and this in it is notable and unique; it does not form a caste. It is not, like the German, or Russian, or Italian, a distinct breed from that of the rest of the nation; nay, its blood is ever renewed from the veins of the people. This is the spring of its life; this has kept it in vigor; this strengthens it against degeneracy. It sucks at the breast of the mighty multitude. Hence at bottom it is, that the English Peer is in any part of the world a higher personage than the German Count or Italian Prince. He cannot show pedigrees with them, and this, a cause of mortification to his pride, is the very source of his superiority.

From this cause, English Aristocracy is less far removed than any other in Europe from a genuine Aristocracy, or government of the Best, of which, however, it is still but a mockery. It is not true that all the talent in the realm gravitates towards the House of Lords, but some of it does; and as such talent is, of course, in alliance with worldly ambition, the *novi homines* in Parliament are apt not to be so eminent for principle as for intellect. Until men shall be much purer than they have yet been, no nation will, under any form of polity, throw up its best men into high places. The working of the representative system with us has revealed the fact, that with free choice a community chooses in the long run men who accurately represent itself. Should therefore Utopia lie embosomed in our future, instead of the present very mixed assemblage, our remote posterity may look for a Congress that will present a shining level of various excellence. Only, that should so blessed an era be in store, Congresses and all other cunning contrivances called governments will be superfluous. In England, in legislation and in social life, most of the best places are filled by men whose ancestors earned them, and not themselves. These block the way to those who, like their ancestors, are capable in a fair field of winning eminence. By inheritance are enjoyed posts demanding talent, liberality, refinement—qualities not transmissible. It is subjecting the spiritual to the corporeal. It is setting the work of man, Earls and Bishops, over the work of God, men. The world is ever prone to put itself in bondage to the external: laws should aim to counteract the tendency. Here this bondage is methodized and legalized. The body politic has got to be but feebly organic. Men are obliged in every direction to conform rigidly to old forms; to reach their end by mechanical routine. A man on entering life finds himself fenced in between ancient walls. Every Englishman is free relatively to every other living Englishman, but is a slave to his forefathers. He must put his neck under the yoke of prescription. The life of every child in England is too rigorously predestined. . . .

This is a rich theme, which I have merely touched. It is pregnant too with comfort to us with our unbridled democracy. May it ever remain unbridled.

CHARLES LESLIE RECALLS JOSEPH TURNER

1840

Like many other aspiring painters, young Charles Leslie turned instinctively to London for the training he could not hope to get in the young Republic. In 1811, at the age of seventeen, he settled down in London under the patronage of two other Americans, Benjamin West and Washington Allston. Like West—rather than Allston—he found England so much to his liking that he stayed there the rest of his life. A great success as a painter of historical and literary subjects and appointed, eventually, professor of painting at the Royal Academy, Leslie is remembered today not for his paintings but rather for his biographies of the painters Constable and Reynolds, and for the lively *Autobiographical Recollections* from which we take this picture of Turner.

Turner was very amusing on the varnishing, or rather the painting days, at the Academy. Singular as were his habits, for nobody knew where or how he lived, his nature was social, and at our lunch

From Charles Robert Leslie, *Autobiographical Recollections*, Tom Taylor, ed. (Boston, 1840), pp. 134–138.

on those anniversaries, he was the life of the table. The Academy has relinquished, very justly, a privilege for its own members which it could not extend to all exhibitors. But I believe, had the varnishing days been abolished while Turner lived, it would almost have broken his heart. When such a measure was hinted to him, he said, "Then you will do away with the only social meetings we have, the only occasions on which we all come together in an easy unrestrained manner. When we have no varnishing days we shall not know one another."

In 1832, when Constable exhibited his "Opening of Waterloo Bridge," it was placed in the school of painting—one of the small rooms at Somerset House. A sea-piece, by Turner, was next to it—a grey picture, beautiful and true, but with no positive colour in any part of it. Constable's "Waterloo" seemed as if painted with liquid gold and silver, and Turner came several times into the room while he was heightening with vermilion and lake the decorations and flags of the city barges. Turner stood behind him, looking from the "Waterloo" to his own picture, and at last brought his palette from the great room where he was touching another picture, and putting a round daub of red lead, somewhat bigger than a shilling, on his grey sea, went away without saying a word. The intensity of the red lead, made more vivid by the coolness of his picture, caused even the vermilion and lake of Constable to look weak. I came into the room just as Turner left it. "He has been here," said Constable, "and fired a gun." On the opposite wall was a picture, by Jones, of Shadrach, Meshach, and Abednego in the furnace. "A coal," said Cooper, "has bounced across the room from Jones's picture, and set fire to Turner's sea." The great man did not come again into the room for a day and a half; and then, in the last moments that were allowed for painting, he glazed the scarlet seal he had put on his picture, and shaped it into a buoy.

In finishing the "Waterloo Bridge" Constable used the palette knife more than the pencil. He found it the only instrument by which he could express, as he wished, the sparkle of the water.

Parsimonious as were Turner's habits, he was not a miser. It was often remarked, that he had never been known to give a dinner. But when dining with a large party at Blackwall, the bill, a heavy one, being handed to Chantrey (who headed the table), he threw it to Turner by way of joke, and Turner paid it, and would not allow the company to pay their share. I know, also, that he refused large offers for his "Téméraire," because he intended to leave it to the nation.

Like Sir Joshua Reynolds, he avoided expressing his opinions of living artists. I never heard him praise any living painter but

Stothard; neither did I ever hear him disparage any living painter, nor any living man.

Mr. Ruskin, in a lecture he delivered at Edinburgh, draws a touching picture of the neglect and loneliness in which Turner died.[1] This picture however, must lose much of its intended effect when it is known that such seclusion was Turner's own fault. No death-bed could be more surrounded by attentive friends than his might have been, had he chosen to let his friends know where he lived. He had constantly dinner invitations, which he seldom even answered, but appeared at the table of the inviter or not as it suited him. His letters were addressed to him at his house in Queen Ann Street; but the writers never knew where he really resided. It may well be supposed that a man so rich, advanced in life, and, as was thought, without near relations, should be much courted. He had for many years quoted in the Academy catalogues a MS. poem, "The Fallacies of Hope;" and I believe that among his papers such as MS., though not in poetic form, was found by some of his friends to be his will. . . .

It is greatly to be regretted that Turner never would sit for a portrait, excepting when he was a young man, and then only for a profile drawing by Dance. This is, therefore, the only satisfactory likeness of him extant.

It happened, of course, as with every eminent man, that as soon as he was dead the shop-windows exhibited wretched libels on his face and figure, the most execrable of which was from a sketch by Count D'Orsay.

Turner was short and stout, and he had a sturdy sailor-like walk. There was, in fact, nothing elegant in his appearance, full of elegance as he was in art; he might be taken for the captain of a river steamboat at a first glance; but a second would find far more in his face than belongs to any ordinary mind. There was that peculiar keenness of expression in his eye that is only seen in men of constant habits of observation. His voice was deep and musical, but he was the most confused and tedious speaker I ever heard. In careless conversation he often expressed himself happily, and he was very playful: at a dinner table nobody more joyous. He was, as I have said, a social man in his nature; and it is probable that his recluse manner of living arose very much from the strong wish, which every artist must feel, to have his time entirely at his own command.

---

1. "Cut off, in great part," says Mr. Ruskin, "from all society, first by labour, and last by sickness, hunted to his grave by the malignity of small critics and the jealousies of hopeless rivalry, he died in the house of a stranger."

It fell to my lot to select the first of his pictures that went to America. Mr. James Lenox, of New York, who knew his works only from engravings, wished very much to possess one, and wrote to me to that effect. I replied, that his rooms were full of unsold works, and I had no doubt he would part with one. Mr. Lenox expressed his willingness to give £ 500 for anything he would part with. His countenance brightened, and he said at once, "He may have that, or that, or that"—pointing to three not small pictures. I chose a sunset view of Staffa, which I had admired more than most of his works from the time when it was first exhibited. It was in an old frame, but Turner would have a handsome new one made for it. When it reached New York, Mr. Lenox was out of town; and we were in suspense some time about its reception. About a fortnight after its arrival he returned to New York, but only for an hour, and he wrote to me, after a first hasty glance, to express his great disappointment. He said he could almost fancy the picture had sustained some damage on the voyage, it appeared to him so indistinct throughout. Still he did not doubt its being very fine, and he hoped to see its merits on farther acquaintance; but for the present he could not write to Mr. Turner, as he could only state his present impression.

Unfortunately, I met Turner, at the Academy, a night or two after I received this letter, and he asked if I had heard from Mr. Lenox. I was obliged to say yes.

"Well, and how does he like the picture?"

"He thinks it indistinct."

"You should tell him," he replied, "that indistinctness is my fault."

In the meantime, I had answered Mr. Lenox's letter, pointing out, as well as I could, the merits of the picture, and concluded by saying, "If, on a second view, it gains in your estimation, it will assuredly gain more and more every time you look at it." Mr. Lenox, in reply said, "You have exactly described what has taken place, I now admire the picture greatly, and I have brought one or two of my friends to see it as I do, but it will never be a favourite with the multitude. I can now write to Mr. Turner, and tell him conscientiously how much I am delighted with it.

Mr. Lenox soon afterwards came to London, and bought another picture of Turner's, at a sale, and, I think, another of himself, and would have bought "The Téméraire," but Turner had then determined not to sell it.

It was reported that Turner had declared his intention of being buried in his "Carthage," the picture now in the National Gallery. I was told that he said to Chantrey, "I have appointed you one of my executors. Will you promise to see me rolled up in it?" "Yes," said Chantrey; "and I promise you also that as soon as you are buried I will see you taken up and unrolled."

This was very like Chantrey, and the story was so generally believed, that when Turner died, and Dean Milman heard he was to be buried in St. Paul's, he said, "I will not read the service over him if he is wrapped up in that picture."

I have said Turner often expressed himself happily. I remember that when it was proposed that the new Houses of Parliament were to be decorated with pictures, he said, "Painting can never show her nose in company with architecture but to have it snubbed."

CATHARINE SEDGWICK:

"ORDER IS ENGLAND'S . . . FIRST LAW"

1840

Catharine Sedgwick, member of one of the powerful Federalist families of Massachusetts—for a generation they dominated the Berkshires—was one of the first and certainly the most successful of American women novelists. Hawthorne called her, somewhat wildly, "our most truthful novelist"; in her time *Hope Leslie, Redwood, The Lintons,* and others were certainly more widely read than anything Hawthorne wrote. Her observations on Britain were made in a fifteen-month journey through Britain and Europe in 1839 and 1840.

Order is England's, as it is Heaven's, first law. Coming from our head-over-heels land, it is striking and beautiful to see the precise order that prevails here. In the public institutions, in private houses, in the streets and thoroughfares, you enjoy the security and comfort of this Heaven-born principle. It raises your ideas of the capacities of human nature to see such masses of beings as there are in London kept, without any violation of their liberty, within the bounds of

From Catharine Sedgwick, *Letters from Abroad* (New York, 1841), I, pp. 111–112.

order. I am told the police system of London has nearly attained perfection. I should think so from the results. It is said that women may go into the street at any hour of the night without fear or danger; and I know that Mrs. —— has often left us after ten o'clock, refusing the attendance of our servant as superfluous, to go alone through several streets to the omnibus that takes her to her own home.

The system of ranks here, as absolute as the Oriental *caste,* is the feature in English society most striking to an American. For the progress of the human race it was worth coming to the New World to get rid of it. Yes, it was worth all that our portion of the human family sacrificed, encountered, and suffered. This system of castes is the more galling, clogging, and unhealthy, from its perfect unfitness to the present state of freedom and progress in England.

Travellers laugh at our pretensions to equality, and Sir Walter Scott has said, as truly as wittily, that there is no perfect equality except among the Hottentots. But our inequalities are as changing as the surface of the ocean, and this makes all the difference. Each rank is set about here with a thorny, impervious, and almost impassable hedge. We have our walls of separation, certainly; but they are as easily knocked down or surmounted as our rail-fences.

BRONSON ALCOTT:
"EVERY ENGLISHMAN IS
A FORTIFICATION"

1842

Bronson Alcott, contributor of the famous "Orphic Sayings" to the *Dial,* was perhaps the most transcendental of all the transcendentalists. One of the earliest and most original educational reformers in America, he anticipated in his famous Temple School in Boston some of the teachings of Froebel. His English friends had already created an Alcott House in England; he went over in 1842 to spread the gospel of reform and to find recruits for the Utopian community which he was shortly to establish at Fruitlands. Before landing in England he noted in his diary that "troops of gentlest, purest, sublimest thoughts usurped my brain all night," but once in London, he found that "the din and huddle about me pain and confuse my senses."

Alcott did in fact recruit some English transcendentalists for his experiment, but Fruitlands was not a success. It is remembered today chiefly because his daughter Louisa wrote a fascinating account of it, just as Alcott himself is remembered chiefly as Father of *Little Women.* Yet while Alcott was to many—such as Carlyle—an object of fun, Thoreau, who saw deeper, called him "the sanest man I ever knew."

From *The Journals of Bronson Alcott,* Odel Shepard, ed. (Boston, 1938), pp. 160–165.

June 6 [1842]. We reached London Bridge, in the very heart of the city, at 5 P.M. . . . The cabman drove us at once to the London Coffee House, Ludgate Street, near St. Paul's. After taking some refreshment, I walked around St. Paul's and then down through Temple Bar, Charing Cross and the Strand, and back to my lodgings to bed. St. Paul's is a commanding structure, overwrought with ornament and built by Sir Christopher Wren. But I found myself transmuting the material into the spiritual architecture instantly, and St. Paul, with the other Apostles, seemed to me to emblem the fortunes which their doctrines have had in the world. There they stand above the din and smoke of the town, their voices spent ere they reach the multitude below, their sublime inspirations all hardened into dogma and ritual, their prophet a mystery even to the few who tread the aisles within. Effigies and echoes of the Everlasting Word—its Christ a ghost, and its priests ossified at the heart.

London seems a rare union of the costly, elegant, magnificent, with the useful, convenient and plain. Everything I see implies great resource and is executed in a finished style. All is solid, substantial, for comfort and use. But all is for the Body.

June 17. I am sure that I shall not remain longer than I can help in London. The din and huddle about me pain and confuse my senses. Everybody looks leonine. The voice, build, gait, manners of the men and women I meet, their opinions, sentiments, institutions, betray the race I am seeing. Every Englishman is a fortification. Organized of blood, he finds necessities for spilling it. Warlike in his temper, his dispositions reappear in the genius and cast of the British institutions. A peaceman he is not, whatever he may pretend to be. He lacks repose, tenderness, poise. Strife, unrest, antagonism, declares its presence everywhere.

This I say of the metropolis. The country may report better of itself and tenants when I visit it.

June 25. Ride to Chelsea and spend an hour with Carlyle. Ah, me! Saul amongst the prophets, 'Twas a dark hour with him, impatient as he was of any interruption, and faithless in all social reforms. His wit was sombre as it was pitiless; his merriment had madness in it; his humor tragical even to tears. There lay smouldering in him a French Revolution, a seething Cromwellian Rebellion; nor could the deep mellowness of his tones, resonant in his broad northern accent, hide the restless melancholy, the memory-fed genius, the lapse of prophecy into the graves of history whereinto, with his hero whom he was disinterring, himself was descending—the miming giant overmastered by the ghosts he evoked from their slumbers, the dead dealing with the dead dolefully enough.

I said: "The living breathe with the living, nor go prowling about the sepulchres by the sweet light of day—intent on the charities and humanities for dispelling the darkness and driving afar the spectres."

His conversation was cynical, trivial, and gave no pleasure. He needs rest; must get this book off his brain to find his better self and speak sanely to his contemporaries. I know his trouble; also his cure. Emerson will sadden when you tell him what I write, but 'tis another instance, and a sad one, of the suicide of pen, in which literature so abounds. But this of Carlyle is the most melancholy of these times, and 'tis doubtful if he come out of it soon, if ever.

I purpose calling again, wishing he may be in better mood.

July 4. Visited Westminster Abbey. Prayers were being chanted, with responses from the choir, as I entered. The service is imposing, but derives its interest from historical associations, altogether. It is a spectacle merely. There is no worship in it. A pantomimic ritual. A masked show. . . .

July 5. Saw George Thompson at a meeting of delegates from all parts of the realm to discuss the Corn Laws and devise measures for the relief of the people. Statements were made of the distresses of the working classes, most appalling to hear, and a petition was drawn for asking Parliament's instant attention and relief. But the delegates have little or no hope of finding favor, and have extreme measures, I believe, in reserve. Blood is to be spilled, and not on questions of policy but of life. The growling, hungering multitude will bear their wrongs no longer.

I passed the night at Carlyle's, but we sped no better than at first. "Work! Work!" is with him both motto and creed; but 'tis all toil of the brain, a draught on the memory, a sacrifice of the living to the dead, instead of devotion to living humanity and a taste of her ennobling hopes. Ah, woe is me! My brothers all are sold to the dark spirit of Time. No man hopes aught of himself or of another. The golden chain of love is snapped asunder, and each sits now sullenly apart, weaving a chaplet for his own brow, or else rushes madly into the embraces of another, a refugee from himself. . . .

July 12. I left Emerson's letter to Miss Martineau with a friend of hers in Regent's Park and then visited St. Paul's Cathedral. This is a grand structure—a monument to the artist, Sir Christopher Wren, and the age in which he lived. It is a triumph of human genius over the material elements. Here are statues of Howard and Dr. Johnson, with numerous effigies of sanguinary warriors in whose prowess and fame England so delights, desecrating her noblest cathedral by making it the receptacle of these blood-stained priests of Moloch. The view from the top of the great dome commands all London, its suburbs and the surrounding country for many miles. A huge den this, truly, wherein Beelzebub whelps, the roar of whose voice reverberates throughout the whole civilized world. But the reign of the Beast is near its end; and London with its gaudy glories, its cruelties and enormities, its thrones and hierarchies lording it over the souls and bodies of men, shall become the foot-stool of a nobler race of kings.

July 21. Called on J. M. Morgan and saw his painting of a Design for a Self-Supporting Institution, at his rooms in Holborn. He descanted long, and with great good will, on his plans for relieving the needy and distressed; but relies on the Church for support and seeks to redeem his own name from disgrace by denying his former intimacy with Mr. Owen. He is another sad instance of apostacy from the principles so livingly affirmed by Mr. Greaves. I recognized but little of the wise humanity that pervades his *Hampden in the Nineteenth Century*. Morgan, Biber, Heraud, Oldham, Smith, Marston—these are all fallen, and there remains but Lane and Wright in whom the divine fire still burns.

I saw George Thompson again, and heard O'Connell, Jos. Hume, M.P., Jos. Sturge, and Sidney Smith at the Anti-Corn-Law Conference at the King's Arms, Westminster. The meeting reminded me of our Abolition and Non-Resistance Conventions, and the speakers of Garrison and Wright and Phillips. Fierce denunciations, discontent, sedition, desperation, rang throughout the hall; but neither people, delegates, nor leaders seemed at all aware of the remedy for the social evils under which they are now writhing in sorrow, disappointment, hunger. It is not bread nor wages, and so I told Thompson, but property, gain, and the lust of gain—that these are the parents of the ills they suffer. But Thompson is too busy to hear, and the people too hungry to believe.

Had a short interview with Robert Owen at his rooms in Pall Mall. He read me a letter which he had just written, addressed to Sir Robert Peel, proposing his remedy for the distress of the nation; but he seemed little wiser than the Premier, Parliament, and reformers. Property, property still, and the people still enslaved to their lusts and passions.

THE REVEREND HENRY COLEMAN

SEES THE HORRORS

OF THE COPPER MINES

1843

Henry Coleman was trained for the ministry but early abandoned that career for farming. His success here was notable, and he was appointed to conduct a series of annual surveys of the agriculture of Massachusetts. In 1843 he went to England and the Continent to study farming and soil chemistry, and it was on one of his visits to Cornwall that he visited the copper mines whose horrors he here describes. Coleman returned to Britain in 1849 and died there the same year.

I came here to visit my friends, Mr. and Mrs. Pendarves. Mr. P. is a large proprietor. One of his mines within the last twenty years has yielded him £ 80,000. He has been a member of Parliament for many years. They were anxious that I should see the mining district; and since I have been in England they have treated me with such extraordinary kindness, that I felt it would be hardly right for me to quit England without visiting them, and I had likewise a great desire to do it. I came here about ten days since; and have found much to be

From Henry Coleman, *European Life and Manners* (Boston, 1849), I. pp. 294–299.

seen interesting in an agricultural view, as well as in other respects. After seeing the mining country generally, it was proposed a week ago, that I should explore one of the richest copper mines, and rather incautiously I agreed to the project, which was to be carried into execution on the coming Saturday. After engaging to do it, I had a dozen minds to abandon the project, and for two or three nights I got very little sleep, from the apprehension of what I was to go through; I felt, indeed, very much like a condemned criminal, who was looking forward to his execution. I dare say you will smile at this; and the idea that I should think *so much* of what hundreds of men do every day of their lives without thinking *at all* of it, may amuse you; but to a novice and a landsman, it was no small affair to descend by a ladder in utter darkness, into the bowels of the earth six or seven hundred feet below the surface. The morning however came, and after having said my prayers and eaten a very imperfect and hurried breakfast, I left for the mine, and reached there at half-past nine with my heart in my mouth, wishing that almost any thing could happen, that I should not be obliged to go down. But there was no alternative, and I proceeded to prepare myself. First, every article of clothing was to be taken off, and I must put on a flannel shirt, flannel drawers, canvas trousers, canvas jacket, cow-hide shoes without any stockings, a white, flat hat, which seemed to me to be made of board, and resembled a barber's wash-basin inverted, and above all, a white nightcap. The white nightcap, which came down to my eyes, with the exception of the black bows, seemed to me so much like the cap which was to be drawn over the eyes before the poor fellows were swung off, that I really felt very much like one being led to execution. A candle was then put into my hands stuck in a piece of clay, which we lighted at the mouth of the shaft, and with one man with a candle before, and another after, we proceeded to descend. "Hold on," was the cry; "take care of your candle;" "mind your steps;" "grasp the round of the ladder;" "put your foot on the round before you let go your hand," were the exhortations continually given, and sufficiently startling, when you felt that a single mis-step or the breaking of a single round, might send you down into unfathomable darkness, from whence there would be no ascent. There were occasional platforms on which the different ladders rested, where we took breath, but the greatest care was requisite in order to reach the next ladder in safety; and at repeated intervals, we saw immense caverns or drifts, off at the sides, and penetrating to unknown depths. At last, when we had descended between six and seven hundred feet, the guide said here we would quit the shaft, and commence our horizontal explorations. We left the ladders and then took a side cut by a passage which we traversed—so low that we were obliged to keep our heads as low as our hips—dark, damp, and dismal, sometimes crossing a pile of broken stones; at others, crossing on planks over holes of unknown depth, with many cautions to "look out," when there was nothing to look at but those deep pits and caverns; occasionally coming to open chambers, where we could stand erect; at other times, to crevices, where only a man of moderate dimensions could wriggle through plank-fashion; at other times, to holes where you could only pass upon your hands and knees, sometimes stumbling among rubbish, sometimes going over shoes in water. When at last, in a sort of lofty chamber, we sat ourselves down to rest, we soon heard at a distance, the rumbling of a carriage, like far off thunder, and a loaded rail-car was driven by us by men with torches in their hands, half-clad, and so black, with their eyes shining like cats' eyes in the dark, that they looked like children who had never known any other home than these infernal regions. So we pursued our way through one crevice and another, one dark chamber and another, over one frightful hole and another; sometimes ascending and descending wooden ladders; sometimes upon rope ladders which could not be held still, and which left you swinging over these frightful abysses, occasionally hearing at vast distances the pecking of the miners, occasionally seeing far off in the extended and dark galleries, sometimes fifty feet above you and sometimes as far below you, parties of miners with their candles stuck upon the walls, beating and breaking and drilling the hard stones, and looking I can hardly tell you like what; and sometimes in our long walks passing several parties of these inhabitants of the lower regions; sometimes meeting a single one, so black and looking so different from anything you see above, that you start back from him with a sort of instinctive shudder; when, after awhile, we were ordered to stand still. Then began a discharge of successive and terrific explosions (the charges for which, had been ordered to be kept until I was near enough to hear them, and at the same time secure from injury). At first the cry ran through the mines, "take care, take care," which, without seeing any person, you heard repeated from one to the other, until the sound seemed to die away at an almost immeasurable distance, and you heard the miners everywhere dropping their tools and preparing for the blast; then came a tremendous explosion, which seemed directly under our feet; then another and another in quick succession; then several at once, which you heard echoed and reechoed, as the reverberation passed along through the deep and distant galleries; and then the whole seemed to be answered by a general discharge so far off that the sound appeared scarcely audible. The mine now became full of smoke; the heat below was very great, certainly as high as eighty degrees, and it had grown hotter and hotter. My breathing now was very difficult, and I felt quite faint, but did not dare complain. After having traversed, for aught I know, miles under ground in this way, and seen the whole process of getting out the ore, it was determined to return to the shaft and commence the ascent. This we reached after awhile—how found by the guides heaven only knows, for I myself had no more idea in what direction we were going than if I had been utterly blind. The ascent was extremely laborious, and had it not been for the successive rests, I believe I should have given up in despair, and taken the fatal plunge. I cannot tell you how grateful I was when it was announced that day-light could now be seen; and still more so when I stepped from the top round of the ladder in broad day-light, and felt myself once more upon the surface of the earth. My first impulse was to thank God for my safety; never was any poor wretch who had been reprieved at the foot of the scaffold, more thankful; my second was to look at myself, and admire my own appearance; my third was to enjoy the shouts of laughter of the workmen, men and women above ground, who saw me emerge, looking like the very d——l himself, and of Mr. Pendarves, who had been waiting until he had almost given us up in despair to see me come out. A good warm bath, a thorough ablution in a warm room, and some clean clothes, soon made "Richard himself again." I would not have missed the enterprise upon any account . . . but I hardly know what would induce me to repeat it, and thus ends my mining experience. There are seven hundred people at work in this mine, and there is a population of eighty thousand miners in the neighborhood. The life which these poor fellows lead, is certainly hard enough; and yet they prefer it to "going to grass," as they term working upon the land. The time employed in actual mining is about eight hours in twenty-four; but including the time taken up in ascending and descending, in dressing and washing, and in taking care of their tools, they are occupied about twelve hours. Their regular wages are almost ten shillings per week; but as they often take jobs or work upon tribute, as it is called, having a certain percentage upon the sales of their ore, they sometimes make several pounds per week, if they happen to get a good 'pitch,' as they term it. This, however, is of course wholly uncertain. Their lives are shortened by their labor, and they seldom live beyond forty-five years.

Many of them are destroyed by various accidents. On coming out, they have always a warm bath and clean clothes to put on; but as they have families to provide for, on their small wages, they are compelled to live very meanly, seldom getting meat, and no tea or butter. Many of them are tee-totalers, but the state of morals here in some other respects is said to be most deplorable. England and Scotland in every part, among the lower classes (Ireland is an excption) must be said, in respect to dissoluteness, to be rotten to the core.

HENRY JAMES, SR.:
RECOLLECTIONS OF
THOMAS CARLYLE

c. 1844

Probably no English philosopher of the nineteenth century had a greater fascination for Americans than Carlyle; it is a fascination hard to explain. As we said earlier, the fact is that most of Carlyle's American admirers—Emerson most conspicuously—misunderstood him. They saw in him, or read in him, a fellow transcendentalist; they looked to him to translate German philosophy into English transcendentalism; they shared some of his admiration for the Nordic race and for Great Men. It took the shock of Carlyle's support to the South and slavery to disillusion most of his American followers.

Henry James, Sr., was one of the few Americans who took Carlyle's measure from the beginning. Remembered today chiefly as the father of William and Henry James, he was in his own right a man of substance and distinction. Born to wealth, he early abandoned a mercantile career and gave himself over to philosophy and literature, which he cultivated both directly and vicariously the rest of his life. It was on his visit to England in 1837 that he became converted to Swedenborgianism—a religion which (like Carlyle) had a curious fascination for the transcendentalists. His visit to Carlyle was made

From Henry James (Sr.), "Recollections of Carlyle," *Atlantic Monthly*, May 1881, pp., 423–458.

during his second visit to England, at the behest of his friend Emerson. His essay on Carlyle was originally a lecture, written about 1855. It remains probably the most perspicacious of all contemporary interpretations.

I intend no disparagement of Carlyle's moral qualities, in saying that he was almost sure finally to disappoint one's admiration. I merely mean to say that he was without that breadth of humanitary sympathy which one likes to find in distinguished men; that he was deficient in spiritual as opposed to moral force. He was a man of great simplicity and sincerity in his personal manners and habits, and exhibited even an engaging sensibility to the claims of one's physical fellowship. But he was wholly impenetrable to the solicitations both of your heart and your understanding. I think he felt a helpless dread and distrust of you instantly that he found you had any positive hope in God or practical love to man. His own intellectual life consisted so much in bemoaning the vices of his race, or drew such inspiration from despair, that he could not help regarding a man with contempt the instant he found him reconciled to the course of history. Pity is the highest style of intercourse he allowed himself with his kind. He compassionated all his friends in the measure of his affection for them. "Poor John Sterling," he used always to say; "poor John Mill, poor Frederic Maurice, poor Neuberg, poor Arthur Helps, poor little Browning, poor little Lewes," and so on; as if the temple of his friendship were a hospital, and all its inmates scrofulous or paralytic. You wondered how any mere mortal got legitimately endowed with a commiseration so divine for the inferior race of man; and the explanation that forced itself upon you was that he enjoyed an inward power and beatitude so redundant as naturally to seek relief in these copious outward showers of compassionate benediction. Especially did Carlyle conceive that no one could be actively interested in the progress of the species without being intellectually off his balance, and in need of tenderness from all his friends. His own sympathy went out freely to cases of individual suffering, and he believed that there was an immense amount of *specific* divine mercy practicable to us. That is to say, he felt keenly whatever appealed to his senses, and willingly patronized a fitful, because that is a picturesque, Providence in the earth. He sympathized with the starving Spitalfield weaver; and would have resented the inhumanity of the slave's condition as sharply as any one, if he had had visual contact with it, and were not incited, by the subtle freemasonry that unites aristocratic pretension in politics, to falsify his human instincts. I remember the pleasure he took in the promise that Indian corn might be found able to supplant the diseased potato in Ireland; and he would doubtless have admitted ether and chloroform to be exquisitely ordained ministers of the Divine love. But as to any sympathy with human nature itself and its inexorable wants, or any belief in a breadth of the Divine mercy commensurate with those wants, I could never discern a flavor of either in him. He scoffed with hearty scorn at the contented imbecility of Church and State with respect to social problems, but his own indifference to these things, save in so far as they were available to picturesque palaver, was infinitely more indolent and contented. He would have been the last man formally to deny the Divine existence and providence; but that these truths had any human virtue, any living efficacy to redeem us out of material and spiritual penury, I do not think he ever dreamt of such a thing. That our knowledge of God was essentially expansive; that revelation contemplated its own spiritual enlargement and fulfilment in the current facts of human history, in the growth and enlargement of the human mind itself,—so that Thomas Carlyle, if only he had not been quite so stubborn and conceited, might have proved himself far better and not far worse posted in the principles of the Divine administration than even Plato was, and so have freed himself from the dismal necessity he was all his life under to ransack the grave of the dead, in order to find some spangle, still untarnished, of God's reputed presence in our nature,—all this he took every opportunity to assure you was the saddest bosh. "Poor John Mill," he exclaimed one night,—"poor John Mill is writing away there in the Edinburgh Review about what he calls the Philosophy of History! As if any man could ever know the road he is going, when once he gets astride of such a distracted steed as that!"

But to my note-book.

"I happened to be in Carlyle's library, the other day, when a parcel was handed in which contained two books, a present from some American admirer. One of the books proved to be a work of singular intellectual interest, as I afterwards discovered, entitled *Lectures on the Natural History of Man,* by Alexander Kinmont, of Cincinnati; the other a book of Poems. Carlyle read Mr. Kinmont's titlepage, and exclaimed: 'The natural history of man, forsooth! And from Cincinnati too, of all places on this earth! We had a right, perhaps, to expect some light from that quarter in regard to the natural history of the hog; and I can't but think that if the well-disposed Mr. Kinmont would set himself to study the unperverted mystery he would employ his powers far more profitably to the world. I am sure he would employ them far less wearisomely to me. There!' he continued, handing me the book, 'I freely make over to you all my right of insight into the natural history of man as that history dwells in the portentous brain of Mr. Alexander Kinmont, of Cincinnati, being more than content to wait myself till he condescend to the more intelligible animal.' And then opening to the blank leaf of the volume of Poems, and without more ado, he said, 'Permit me to write my friend Mrs. So-and-So's name here, who perhaps may get some refreshment from the poems of her countryman; for, decidedly, I shall not.' When I suggested to him that he himself did nothing all his days but philosophize in his own way—that is, from the artist point of view, or ground of mere feeling—and that his prose habitually decked itself out in the most sensuous garniture of poetry, he affected the air of M. Jourdain, in Molière, and protested half fun, half earnest, that he was incapable of a philosophic purpose of poetic emotion."

Carlyle had very much of the narrowness, intellectual and moral, which one might expect to find in a descendant of the old Covenanting stock, bred to believe in God as essentially inhuman, and in man, accordingly, as exposed to a great deal of divine treachery and vindictiveness, which were liable to come rattling about his devoted ears the moment his back was turned. I have no idea, of course, that this grim ancestral faith dwelt in Carlyle in any acute, but only in chronic, form. He did not actively acknowledge it; but it was latent in all his intellectual and moral personality, and made itself felt in that cynical, mocking humor and those bursts of tragic pathos which set off all his abstract views of life and destiny. But a genuine pity for man as sinner and sufferer underlay all his concrete judgments; and no thought of unkindness ever entered his bosom except for people who believed in God's undiminished presence and power in human affairs, and were therefore full of hope in our social future. A moral reformer like Louis Blanc or Robert Dale Owen, a political reformer like Mr. Cobden or Mr. Bright, or a dietetic reformer like the late Mr. Greaves or our own Mr. Alcott, was sure to provoke his most acrid intellectual antipathy.

Moral force was the deity of Carlyle's unscrupulous worship —the force of unprincipled, irresponsible will; and he was ready to glorify every historic vagabond, such as Danton or Mirabeau, in whom that quality reigned supreme. He hated Robespierre because he was inferior in moral or personal force to his rivals, being himself a victim to ideas—or, as Carlyle phrased it, to formulas. Picturesqueness in man and Nature was the one key to his intellectual favor; and it made little difference to his artist eye whether the man were spiritually angel or demon. Besides, one never practically surmounts his own idea of the Divine name; and Carlyle, inheriting and cherishing for its picturesque capabilities this rude Covenanting conception, which makes God a being of the most aggravated moral dimensions, of a wholly superhuman egotism or sensibility to his own consequence, of course found Mahomet, William the Conqueror, John Knox, Frederic the Second of Prussia, Goethe, men after God's own heart, and coolly told you that no man in history was ever unsuccessful who deserved to be otherwise.

Too much cannot be said of Carlyle in personal respects. He was a man of even a genial practical morality, and unexceptionable good neighbor, friend, and citizen. But in all larger or human regards he was a literalist of the most unqualified pattern, incapable of uttering an inspiring or even a soothing word in behalf of any struggling manifestation of human hope. It is true, he abused every recognized guide of the political world with such hearty good-will that many persons claimed him at once as an intelligent herald of the new or spiritual divine advent in human nature. But the claim was absurdly unfounded. He was an amateur prophet exclusively—a prophet "on his own hook," or in the interest of his own irritable cuticle—without a glimmer of sympathy with the distinctively public want, or a gleam of insight into its approaching divine relief; a harlequin in the guise of Jeremiah, who fed you with laughter in place of tears, and put the old prophetic sincerity out of countenance by his broad, persistent winks at the by-standers over the foot-lights.

My note-book has this record:

"I heard Carlyle, last night, maintain his habitual thesis against Mr. Tennyson, in the presence of Mr. Moxon and one or two other persons. Carlyle rode a very high horse indeed, being inspired to mount and lavishly ply the spur by Mr. Tennyson, for whom he has the liveliest regard; and it was not long before William the Conqueror and Oliver Cromwell were trotted out of their mouldy cerements, to affront Sir Robert Peel and the Irish viceroy, whose name escapes me. 'Nothing,' Carlyle over and over again said and sung,—'nothing will ever pry England out of the slough she is in, but to stop looking at Manchester as heaven's gate, and free-trade as the everlasting God's law man is bound to keep holy. The human stomach, I admit, is a memorable necessity, which will not allow itself, moreover, to be long neglected; and political economy no doubt has its own right to be heard among all our multifarious jargons. But I tell you the stomach is not the supreme necessity our potato-evangelists make it, nor is political economy any tolerable substitute for the eternal veracities. . . .

Carlyle was, in truth, a hardened declaimer. He talked in a way vastly to tickle his auditors; and his enjoyment of their amusement was lively enough to sap his own intellectual integrity. Artist like, he precipitated himself upon the picturesque in character and manners wherever he found it, and he did not care a jot what incidental interest his precipitancy lacerated. He was used to harp so successfully on one string—the importance to men of *doing*—and the mere artistic effects he produced so infatuated him, that the whole thing tumbled off at last into a sheer insincerity, and he no longer saw any difference between *doing* well and *doing* ill. He who best denounced a canting age became himself its most signal illustration, since even his denunciation of the vice succumbed to the prevalent usage, and announced itself at length a shameless cant. . . .

I recur again to my note-book.

"I was diverted last evening by an account Carlyle gave of a conversation he had had with Lord John Manners and some other of the *dilettanti* aristocratic reformers, who had been led by his books to suppose that he had some practical notion, at all events some honest desire, of reform, and therefore called upon him to take counsel. Carlyle had evidently been well pleased by a visit so deferential from such distinguished swells; but so far was he from feeling the least reflective sympathy with the motive of it, that he regarded the whole affair as ministering properly to the broadest fun. 'They asked me,' he said, 'with countenances of much interrogation, what it was, just, that I would have them to do. I told them that I had no manner of counsel to bestow upon them; that I didn't know how they lived at all up there in their grand houses, nor what manner of tools they had to work with. All I knew was, I told them, that they must be doing something erelong, or they would find themselves on the broad road to the devil.' And he laughed as if he would rend the roof." . . .

Carlyle is not at all primarily the man of humanitary ideas and sympathies which many people fancy him to be. Of course he has a perfect right to be what he is, and no one has a keener appreciation of him in that real light than I have. I only insist that he has no manner of right to be reported to us in a false light, as we shall thereby lose the lesson which legitimately accrues to us from his immense personality. Lord John Manners is a sincere sentimentalist, who really believes that by reviving old English sports, and putting new vigor into existing Christmas, May-day, and other festivities, and inaugurating generally a sort of systematic, voluntary humility on the part of the aristocracy towards the dependent classes, revolution may be indefinitely staved off, and England saved from the terrors of a speedy "kingdom come." And Carlyle, if ideas were really uppermost with him, would have treated his visitors' weaknesses tenderly, and shown them, by reference to certain well-established principles of human nature—the indomitable instinct of freedom, for example—how very disproportionate their remedy was to the formidable disease in hand. As it was, he sent them away unblessed, and, so far as he could effect such a result, disheartened. ... He was not constitutionally arrogant; he was a man of real modesty; he was even, I think, constitutionally diffident. He was a man, in short, whom you could summer and winter with, without ever having your self-respect wantonly affronted as it habitually is by mere conventional men and women. He was, to be sure a very sturdy son of earth, and capable at times of exhibiting the most helpless natural infirmity. But he would never ignore nor slight your human fellowship because your life or opinions exposed you to the reproach of the vain, the frivolous, the self-seeking. He would of course curse your gods ever and anon in a manful way, and scoff without mercy at your tenderest intellectual hopes and aspirations; but upon yourself personally, all the while—especially if you should drink strong tea and pass sleepless nights, or suffer from tobacco, or be menaced with insanity, or have a gnawing cancer under your jacket—he would have bestowed the finest of his wheat. He might not easily have forgiven you if you used a vegetable diet, especially if you did so on principle; and he would surely have gnashed his teeth upon you if you should have claimed any scientific knowledge or philosophic insight into the social problem,—the problem of man's coming destiny upon the earth. But within these limits you would have felt how truly human was the tie that bound you to this roaring, riotous, most benighted, yet not unbenignant brother. Leave England, above all, alone; let her stumble on from one slough of despond to another, so that he might have the endless serene delight of walloping her chief "niggers"—Peel, Palmerston, Russell, Brougham, and the rest,—and he would dwell forever in friendly content with you. But only hint your belief that these imbecile statesmen were the true statesmen for the time, the only men capable, *in virtue of that very imbecility,* of truly coworking with the Providence that governs the world, and is guiding it full surely to a haven of final peace and blessedness, and he would fairly deluge you with the vitriol of his wrath. No; all that can be said for Carlyle on this score is, that, having an immense eye for color, an immense genius for scenic effect, be seized with avidity upon every crazy, time-stained, dishonored rag of personality that still fluttered in the breeze of history, and lent itself to his magical tissues; and he did not like that any one should attempt to dispute his finery with him. The habit was tyrannous, no doubt, but no harm, and only amusement, could have come of it; least of all would it have pushed him to his melancholy "latter-day" drivel, had it not been for the heartless people who hang, for their own private ends, upon the skirts of every pronounced man of genius, and do their best, by stimulating his vanity, to make him feel himself a god. . . .

Whatever be Carlyle's interest in any question of life or destiny, he talks so well and writes so well that it can hardly escape being all swallowed up in talk or writing; and he would regard you as a bore of the largest calibre if, talking in the same sense with him, you yet did not confine yourself to talk, but went on to organize your ideas in some appropriate action."

You would say, remembering certain passages in Carlyle's books—notably his *Past and Present* and his pamphlet on Chartism—that he had a very lively sympathy with reform and a profound sentiment of human fellowship. He did, indeed, dally with the divine ideas long enough to suck them dry of their rhetorical juices, but then dropped them, to lavish contempt on them ever after when anybody else should chance to pick them up and cherish them, not for their rhetorical uses, but their absolute truth. He had no belief in society as a living, organizing force in history, but only as an empirical necessity of the race. He had no conception of human brotherhood or equality as the profoundest truth of science, disclosing a hell in the bosom wherever is is not allowed to reveal a heaven, but only as an emotional or sentimental experience of happily endowed natures. . . .

Again to my note-book.

"I went to see Carlyle last night to get permission to bring a friend—J. McK.—to see him the next day, who had it much at heart to thank him for the aid and comfort his books had given him, years ago, away out on the shores of Lake Erie. Would he treat the friend kindly, in case I brought him; or would he altogether pulverize him, as he had erewhile pulverized a certain person we both wotted of? Nay, nay; he would be all that Chesterfield himself could desire of polite and affable! Well, then, what would be the most auspicious hour? When would the inward man be most unpuckered?—for I should really be sorry to see my friend go home with his ardent thirst of worship all unslaked. 'Ask Jane,' was the reply. 'What she appoints, I will give my diligence to conform to.' Mrs. Carlyle, who sat upon the sofa beside us, obligingly entered into my anxieties, and said, 'You shall bring your friend to-morrow, after dinner, or between two and three o'clock; for I often observe that is a very placid hour with the creature, and I think we may reckon upon a great success if we will just avail ourselves of it.' Accordingly, we did not fail to be in the little Chelsea parlor this afternoon, at the hour appointed, my friend and I—not without a certain prophetic tremor, I can assure you, on my part, for his raised expectations. As we entered the room Carlyle stood upon a chair, with his back to us, vainly trying, to all appearance, to close his inside window-shutters. He did not at all desist on our entrance, but cried out, 'Is that you, J., and have you brought your friend McK. with you? I don't know whether he is at all related to *my* friend, Sandy McK., of Glasgow. If he is, he can't be related to a worthier man.' By this time he had reduced his refractory window-shutter to order, and descended from his perch to take a first look at his guest. My friend of course made a neat little salutatory expressive of his intellectual obligations, and the need he felt to make some sort of avowal of them, before he again set his face westward. 'I don't believe a word of it!' said Carlyle, as my friend gracefully perorated. 'I don't believe a word of it! I don't believe that I ever helped any man. I don't believe that any man ever helped another. It is indeed unspeakably folly to conceive such a thing. The only man I ever found—and him I didn't find —who seemed to me sincere in such a thought was a ship captain, some time ago, who wrote to me to say, without giving me name or address, that he had called his vessel the Thomas Carlyle, because he had got some good, he fancied, from my books. I thought it behooved me to look the man up, so I traversed the London docks from end to end, asking of the sailors ever and anon if they knew any vessel in those parts bearin' the portentous name of Thomas Carlyle; but it was all in vain, and I returned home persuaded that, whatever else might betide me, I should probably never see under this sun the extraordinary individual who had named his vessel the Thomas Carlyle.' You may easily imagine the sudden pallor that came over my friend's ruddy devotion. It was not that Carlyle intended out of pure wantonness to mock the admiration he lives to conciliate. It was only that he chanced at that moment to feel the ghastly disproportion which existed between his real aims and those lent him by the generous faith of his disciples; and instead of doing penance by himself for the diversity, he preferred to make the devotee pay his share of the penalty." . . .

It always appeared to me that Carlyle valued truth and good as a painter does his pigments—not for what they are in themselves, but for the effects they lend themselves to in the sphere of production. Indeed, he always exhibited a contempt, so characteristic as to be comical, for every one whose zeal for truth or good led him to question existing institutions with a view to any practical reform. He himself was wont to question established institutions and dogmas with the utmost license of scepticism, but he obviously meant nothing beyond the production of a certain literary surprise, or the enjoyment of his own aesthetic power. Nothing maddened him so much as to be mistaken for a reformer, really intent upon the interests of God's righteousness upon the earth, which are the interests of universal justice. This is what made him hate Americans, and call us a nation of bores—that we took him at his word, and reckoned upon him as a sincere well-wisher to his species. He hated us, because a secret instinct told him that our exuberant faith in him would never be justified by closer knowledge; for no one loves the man who forces him upon a premature recognition of himself. I recall the uproarious mirth with which he and Mrs. Carlyle used to recount the incidents of a visit they had received from a young New England woman, and describe the earnest, devout homage her credulous soul had rendered him. It was her first visit abroad, and she supposed—poor thing!—that these famous European writers and talkers, who so dominated her fancy at a distance, really meant all they said, were as innocent and lovely in their lives as in their books; and she no sooner crossed Carlyle's threshold, accordingly, than her heart offered its fragrance to him as liberally as the flower opens to the sun. And Carlyle, the inveterate comedian, instead of being humbled to the dust by the revelation which such simplicity suddenly flashed upon his own eyes of his essentially dramatic genius and exploits, was irritated, vexed, and outraged by it as by a covert insult. His own undevout soul had never risen to the contemplation of himself as the priest of a really infinite sanctity; and when this clear-eyed barbarian, looking past him to the substance which informed him, made him feel himself for the moment the transparent mask or unconscious actor he was, his self-consciousness took the alarm. She sat, the breathless, silly little maid, between him and Mrs. Carlyle, holding a hand of each, and feeling the while her anticipations of Paradise on earth so met in this foolish encounter that she could not speak, but barely looked the pious rapture which filled her soul. . . .

The main intellectual disqualification, then, of Carlyle, in my opinion, was the absoluteness with which he asserted the moral principle in the human bosom, or the finality which his grim imagination lent to the conflict of good and evil in men's experience. He never had the least idea, that I could discover, of the true or intellectually educative nature of this conflict, as being purely ministerial to a new and final evolution of *human nature itself* into permanent harmony with God's spiritual perfection. He never expressed a suspicion, in intercourse with me—on the contrary, he always denounced my fervent conviction on the subject as so much fervent nonsense—that out of this conflict would one day emerge a positive or faultless life of man, which would otherwise have been impracticable; just as out of the conflict of alkali and acid emerges a neutral salt which would otherwise be invisible. On the contrary, he always expressed himself to the effect that the conflict was absolutely *valid in itself;* that it constituted its own end, having no other result than to insure to good men the final dominion of evil men, and so array heaven and hell in mere chronic or fossil antagonism. The truth is, he had no idea but of a carnal or literal rectitude in human nature—a rectitude secured by an unflinching inward submission to some commanding *outward* or *personal* authority. The law, not the gospel, was for him the true bond of intercourse between God and man, and between man and man as well. That is to say, he believed in our moral instincts, not as constituting the mere carnal body or rude husk of our spiritual manhood, but its inmost kernel or soul; and hence he habitually browsed upon "the tree of the knowledge of good and evil," as if it had been divinely commended to us for that purpose, or been always regarded as the undisputed tree of life, not of death. He was mother Eve's own darling cantankerous Thomas, in short, the child of her dreariest, most melancholy old age; and he used to bury his worn, dejected face in her penurious lap, in a way so determined as forever to shut out all sight of God's new and better creation.

MARGARET FULLER VISITS CARLYLE:
"IT WAS VERY TITANIC
AND ANTI-CELESTIAL"

1846

Here, for comparison, is another view of Carlyle by another of Emerson's emissaries. Margaret Fuller was the American Madame de Staël. An infant prodigy—she read Ovid at six—she grew up to be the leading bluestocking of Victorian New England, and the leading woman critic. She was one of the editors of the famous but short-lived *Dial;* she held a series of brilliant "Conversations" in Boston to which the ladies of that city flocked; she wrote for Horace Greeley's *Tribune;* she championed women's rights. Hawthorne, who disliked her, probably used her as a model for his Zenobia in *The Blithedale Romance.* In the summer of 1846 she threw up her American career, visited in England—where she met the Carlyles—went on to Italy to resume her friendship with Mazzini, fell in love with the impecunious "Count" Ossoli, and either did or did not marry him, but did have his child. Mixed up in the revolutions that were sweeping Italy in the late forties, she fled to Florence, wrote a history of the Roman Revolution, and took ship to America. The ship went down off the coast of Long Island with Margaret, her husband, her baby, and her manuscript.

From R. W. Emerson, W. H. Channing, and J. F. Clarke, *Memoirs of Margaret Fuller Ossoli* (Boston, 1860), II, pp. 184–188.

To Ralph Waldo Emerson

Paris November 16, 1846

Of the people I saw in London, you will wish me to speak first of the Carlyles. Mr. C. came to see me at once, and appointed an evening to be passed at their house. That first time, I was delighted with him. He was in a very sweet humor—full of wit and pathos, without being overbearing or oppressive. I was quite carried away with the rich flow of his discourse; and the heavy, noble earnestness of his personal being brought back the charm which once was upon his writing, before I wearied of it. I admired his Scotch, his way of singing his great full sentences, so that each one was like the stanza of a narrative ballad. He let me talk, now and then, enough to free my lungs and change my position, so that I did not get tired. That evening, he talked of the present state of things in England, giving light, witty sketches of the men of the day, fanatics and others, and some sweet, homely stories he told of things he had known of the Scotch peasantry. Of you he spoke with hearty kindness; and he told, with beautiful feeling, a story of some poor farmer, or artisan, in the country, who on Sunday lays aside the cark and care of that dirty English world, and sits reading the *Essays,* and looking upon the sea.

I left him that night, intending to go out very often to their house. I assure you there never was anything so witty as Carlyle's description of —— ——. It was enough to kill one with laughing. I, on my side, contributed a story to his fund of anecdote on this subject, and it was fully appreciated. Carlyle is worth a thousand of you for that—he is not ashamed to laugh, when he is amused, but goes on in a cordial human fashion.

The second time, Mr. C. had a dinner-party, at which was a witty, French, flippant sort of man, author of a History of Philosophy, and now writing a Life of Goethe, a task for which he must be as unfit as irreligion and sparkling shallowness can make him. But he told stories admirably, and was allowed sometimes to interrupt Carlyle a little, of which one was glad, for, that night, he was in his more acrid mood; and, though much more brilliant than on the former evening, grew wearisome to me, who disclaimed and rejected almost everything he said.

For a couple of hours, he was talking about poetry, and the whole harangue was one eloquent proclamation of the defects in his own mind. Tennyson wrote in verse because the schoolmasters had taught him that it was great to do so, and had thus, unfortunately, been turned from the true path for a man. Burns had, in like manner, been turned from his vocation. Shakespeare had not had the good sense to see that it would have been better to write straight on in prose—and such nonsense, which, though amusing enough at first, he ran to death after a while. The most amusing part is always when he comes back to some refrain, as in the French Revolution of the *sea-green*. In this instance, it was Petrarch and *Laura*, the last word pronounced with his ineffable sarcasm of drawl. Although he said this over fifty times, I could not ever help laughing when *Laura* would come—Carlyle running his chin out, when he spoke it, and his eyes glancing till they looked like the eyes and beak of a bird of prey. Poor Laura! Lucky for her that her poet had already got her safely canonized beyond the reach of this Teufelsdröckh vulture.

The worst of hearing Carlyle is that you cannot interrupt him. I understand the habit and power of haranguing have increased very much upon him, so that you are a perfect prisoner when he has once got hold of you. To interrupt him is a physical impossibility. If you get a chance to remonstrate for a moment, he raises his voice and bears you down. True, he does you no injustice, and, with his admirable penetration, sees the disclaimer in your mind, so that you are not morally delinquent; but it is not pleasant to be unable to utter it. The latter part of the evening, however, he paid us for this, by a series of sketches, in his finest style of railing and raillery, of modern French literature, not one of them, perhaps, perfectly just, but all drawn with the finest, boldest strokes, and, from his point of view, masterly. All were depreciating, except that of Béranger. Of him he spoke with perfect justice, because with hearty sympathy.

I had, afterward, some talk with Mrs. C., whom hitherto I had only *seen*, for who can speak while her husband is there? I like her very much; she is full of grace, sweetness, and talent. Her eyes are sad and charming.

After this, they went to stay at Lord Ashburton's, and I only saw them once more, when they came to pass an evening with us. Unluckily, Mazzini was with us, whose society, when he was there alone, I enjoyed more than any. He is a beauteous and pure music; also, he is a dear friend of Mrs. C.; but his being there gave the conversation a turn to "progress" and ideal subjects, and C. was fluent in invectives on all our "rose-water imbecilities." We all felt distant from him, and Mazzini, after some vain efforts to remonstrate, became very sad. Mrs. C. said to me, "These are but opinions to Carlyle; but Mazzini, who has given his all, and helped bring his friends to the scaffold, in pursuit of such subjects, it is a matter of life and death."

All Carlyle's talk, that evening, was a defence of mere force —success the test of right; if people would not behave well, put collars round their necks; find a hero, and let them be his slaves, &c. It was very Titanic, and anti-celestial. I wish the last evening had been more melodious. However, I bid Carlyle farewell with feelings of the warmest friendship and admiration. We cannot feel otherwise to a great and noble nature, whether it harmonize with our own or not. I never appreciated the work he has done for his age till I saw England. I could not. You must stand in the shadow of that mountain of shams, to know how hard it is to cast light across it.

RALPH WALDO EMERSON
ON ENGLISH TRAITS

1847–48

Emerson made his first visit to England in 1833, when he was still a young man, and unknown. His visit in 1848, in response to invitations to preach and lecture in various parts of Britain, was something in the nature of a triumphal tour, for he was by now famous on both sides of the water. Letters to his wife Lydia and to friends from England give interesting insight to his immediate and spontaneous reactions, and illuminate what he thought he was about. Thus to Margaret Fuller, April 25, '48, "Though the book is large & voluminous I am not now eager to go on with it. Indeed my interest already flags. But I leave England with an increased respect for the Englishman. His stuff or substance seems to be the best in the world. I forgive him all his pride. My respect is the more generous that I have no sympathy with him, only an admiration. . . ."

And of the great men—he was not easily imposed on, Emerson: "The great men Macaulay, Hallam, Sedgwick, and their distinguished peers at dinner tables, Austin, Thackeray, Milman, Croker, etc., I saw only as spectacles. Theirs is bread that ends in the using, and no seed." . . . "I am working away in

---

1. From *Letters of Ralph Waldo Emerson*, Ralph L. Rusk, ed. (Boston, 1939), IV, pp. 62, 63, 68–69.

these mornings on some papers, which, if I do not as I suppose I shall not, get ready for lectures here will serve me in a better capacity as a kind of Book of Metaphysics to print at home." And to Lydia, May 4, '48," I pray you never to imagine for a moment what would be most untrue, that I have any skill to sail in this sea of England. I am the most unqualified of all the Americans to live here. You know my incurable unfitness for what is called society. Bad as that infirmity is in America it is far worse misfortune here. I never call on the fine friends who have invited me but let them all go and of course they me".[1]

It is pointless to try to do justice to this masterpiece in a brief introduction. If William Dean Howells' observation that "it is a book about the English that makes all other comment seem idle and superfluous palaver" is something of an exaggeration, it is not an exaggeration to assert that *English Traits* is the most perspicacious, the most profound, and the most enduring of all books on the English character. Ideally it should be reprinted in full; we will have to content ourselves with three chapters.

From Ralph Waldo Emerson, *English Traits* (Boston, 1856—and many editions thereafter), Chapters VI, VIII, and XVIII.

Manners

I find the Englishman to be him of all men who stands firmest in his shoes. They have in themselves what they value in their horses—mettle and bottom. On the day of my arrival at Liverpool, a gentleman, in describing to me the Lord Lieutenant of Ireland, happened to say, "Lord Clarendon has pluck like a cock and will fight till he dies;" and what I heard first I heard last, and the one thing the English value is *pluck.* The word is not beautiful, but on the quality they signify by it the nation is unanimous. The cabmen have it; the merchants have it; the bishops have it; the women have it; the journals have it—the *Times* newspaper they say is the pluckiest thing in England, and Sydney Smith had made it a proverb that little Lord John Russell, the minister, would take the command of the Channel fleet to-morrow.

They require you to dare to be of your own opinion, and they hate the practical cowards who cannot in affairs answer directly yes or no. They dare to displease, nay, they will let you break all the commandments, if you do it natively and with spirit. You must be somebody; then you may do this or that, as you will.

Machinery has been applied to all work, and carried to such perfection that little is left for the men but to mind the engines and feed the furnaces. But the machines require punctual service, and as they never tire, they prove too much for their tenders. Mines, forges, mills, breweries, railroads, steam-pump, steam-plough, drill of regiments, drill of police, rule of court and shop-rule have operated to give a mechanical regularity to all the habit and action of men. A terrible machine has possessed itself of the ground, the air, the men and women, and hardly even thought is free.

The mechanical might and organization requires in the people constitution and answering spirits; and he who goes among them must have some weight of metal. At last, you take your hint from the fury of life you find, and say, one thing is plain, this is no country for fainthearted people: don't creep about diffidently; make up your mind; take your own course, and you shall find respect and furtherance.

It requires, men say, a good constitution to travel in Spain. I say as much of England, for other cause, simply on account of the vigor and brawn of the people. Nothing but the most serious business could give one any counterweight to these Baresarks, though they were only to order eggs and muffins for their breakfast. The Englishman speaks with all his body. His elocution is stomachic—as the American's is labial. The Englishman is very petulant and precise about his accommodation at inns and on the roads; a quiddle about his toast and his chop and every species of convenience, and loud and pungent in his expressions of impatience at any neglect. His vivacity betrays itself at all points, in his manners, in his respiration, and the inarticulate noises he makes in clearing the throat—all significant of burly strength. He has stamina; he can take the initiative in emergencies. He has that *aplomb* which results from a good adjustment of the moral and physical nature and the obedience of all the powers to the will; as if the axes of his eyes were united to his backbone, and only moved with the trunk.

This vigor appears in the incuriosity and stony neglect, each of every other. Each man walks, eats, drinks, shaves, dresses, gesticulates, and, in every manner acts and suffers without reference to the bystanders, in his own fashion, only careful not to interfere with them or annoy them; not that he is trained to neglect the eyes of his neighbors—he is really occupied with his own affair and does not think of them. Every man in this polished country consults only his convenience, as much as a solitary pioneer in Wisconsin. I know not where any personal eccentricity is so freely allowed, and no man gives himself any concern with it. An Englishman walks in a pouring rain, swinging his closed umbrella like a walking-stick; wears a wig, or a shawl, or a saddle, or stands on his head, and no remark is made. And as he has been doing this for several generations, it is now in the blood.

In short, every one of these islanders is an island himself, safe, tranquil, incommunicable. In a company of strangers you would think him deaf; his eyes never wander from his table and newspaper. He is never betrayed into any curiosity or unbecoming emotion. They have all been trained in one severe school of manners, and never put off the harness. He does not give his hand. He does not let you meet his eye. It is almost an affront to look a man in the face without being introduced. In mixed or in select companies they do not introduce persons; so that a presentation is a circumstance as valid as a contract. Introductions are sacraments. He withholds his name. At the hotel, he is hardly willing to whisper it to the clerk at the book-office. If he give you his private address on a card, it is like an avowal of friendship; and his bearing, on being introduced, is cold, even though he is seeking your acquaintance and is studying how he shall serve you.

It was an odd proof of this impressive energy, that in my lectures I hesitated to read and threw out for its impertinence many a disparaging phrase which I had been accustomed to spin, about poor, thin, unable mortals—so much had the fine physique and the personal vigor of this robust race worked on my imagination.

I happened to arrive in England at the moment of a commercial crisis. But it was evident that let who will fail, England will not. These people have sat here a thousand years, and here will continue to sit. They will not break up, or arrive at any desperate revolution, like their neighbors; for they have as much energy, as much continence of character as they ever had. The power and possession which surround them are their own creation, and they exert the same commanding industry at this moment.

They are positive, methodical, cleanly and formal, loving routine and conventional ways; loving truth and religion, to be sure, but inexorable on points of form. All the world praises the comfort and private appointments of an English inn, and of English households. You are sure of neatness and of personal decorum. A Frenchman may possibly be clean; an Englishman is conscientiously clean. A certain order and complete propriety is found in his dress and in his belongings.

Born in a harsh and wet climate, which keeps him in doors whenever he is at rest, and being of an affectionate and loyal temper, he dearly loves his house. If he is rich, he buys a demesne and builds a hall; if he is in middle condition, he spares no expense on his house. Without, it is all planted; within, it is wainscoted, carved, curtained, hung with pictures and filled with good furniture. 'Tis a passion which survives all others, to deck and improve it. Hither he brings all that is rare and costly, and with the national tendency to sit fast in the same spot for many generations, it comes to be, in the course of time, a museum of heirlooms, gifts and trophies of the adventures and exploits of the family. He is very fond of silver plate, and though he have no gallery of portraits of his ancestors, he has of their punch-bowls and porringers. Incredible amounts of plate are found in good houses, and the poorest have some spoon or sauce-pan, gift of a godmother, saved out of better times. . . .

They keep their old customs, costumes, and pomps, their wig and mace, sceptre and crown. The Middle Ages still lurk in the streets of London. The Knights of the Bath take oath to defend injured ladies; the gold-stick-in-waiting survives. They repeated the ceremonies of the eleventh century in the coronation of the present Queen. A hereditary tenure is natural to them. Offices, farms trades and traditions descend so. Their leases run for a hundred and a thousand years. Terms of service and partnership are life-long, or are inherited. "Holdship has been with me," said Lord Eldon, "eight-and-twenty years, knows all my business and books." Antiquity of usage is sanction enough. Wordsworth says of the small freeholders of Westmoreland, "Many of these humble sons of the hills had a consciousness that the land which they tilled had for more than five hundred years been possessed by men of the same name and blood." The ship-carpenter in the public yards, my lord's gardener and porter, have been there for more than a hundred years, grandfather, father, and son.

The English power resides also in their dislike of change. They have difficulty in bringing their reason to act, and on all occasions use their memory first. As soon as they have rid themselves of some grievance and settled the better practice, they make haste to fix it as a finality, and never wish to hear of alteration more.

Every Englishman is an embryonic chancellor: his instinct is to search for a precedent. The favorite phrase of their law is, "a custom whereof the memory of man runneth not back to the contrary." The barons say, *"Nolumus mutari;"* and the cockneys stifle the curiosity of the foreigner on the reason of any practice with "Lord, sir, it was always so." They hate innovation. Bacon told them, Time was the right reformer; Chatham, that "confidence was a plant of slow growth;" Canning, to "advance with the times;" and Wellington, that "habit was ten times nature." All their statesmen learn the irresistibility of the tide of custom, and have invented many fine phrases to cover this slowness of perception and prehensility of tail.

A sea-shell should be the crest of England, not only because it represents a power built on the waves, but also the hard finish of the men. The Englishman is finished like a cowry ⁻ a murex. After the spire and the spines are formed, or with the formation, a juice exudes and a hard enamel varnishes every part. The keeping of the proprieties is as indispensable as clean linen. No merit quite countervails the want of this, whilst this sometimes stands in lieu of all. "'Tis in bad taste," is the most formidable word an Englishman can pronounce. But this japan costs them dear. There is a prose in certain Englishmen which exceeds in wooden deadness all rivalry with other countrymen. There is a knell in the conceit and externality of their voice, which seems to say, *Leave all hope behind.* In this gibralter of propriety, mediocrity gets intrenched and consolidated and founded in adamant. An Englishman of fashion is like one of those souvenirs, bound in gold vellum, enriched with delicate engravings on thick hot-pressed paper, fit for the hands of ladies and princes, but with nothing in it worth reading or remembering.

A severe decorum rules the court and the cottage. When Thalberg the pianist was one evening performing before the Queen at Windsor, in a private party, the Queen accompanied him with her voice. The circumstance took air, and all England shuddered from sea to sea. The indecorum was never repeated. Cold, repressive manners prevail. No enthusiasm is permitted except at the opera. They avoid every thing marked. They require a tone of voice that excites no attention in the room. Sir Philip Sidney is one of the patron saints of England, of whom Wotton said, "His wit was the measure of congruity."

Pretension and vaporing are once for all distasteful. They keep to the other extreme of low tone in dress and manners. They avoid pretension and go right to the heart of the thing. They hate nonsense, sentimentalism and highflown expression; they use a studied plainness. Even Brummel, their fop, was marked by the severest simplicity in dress. They value themselves on the absence of every thing theatrical in the public business, and on conciseness and going to the point, in private affairs.

In an aristocratical country like England, not the Trial by Jury, but the dinner, is the capital institution. It is the mode of doing honor to a stranger, to invite him to eat—and has been for many hundred years. "And they think," says the Venetian traveller of

1500, "no greater honor can be conferred or received, than to invite others to eat with them, or to be invited themselves, and they would sooner give five or six ducats to provide an entertainment for a person, than a groat to assist him in any distress." It is reserved to the end of the day, the family-hour being generally six, in London, and if any company is expected, one or two hours later. Every one dresses for dinner, in his own house, or in another man's. The guests are expected to arrive within half an hour of the time fixed by card of invitation, and nothing but death or mutilation is permitted to detain them. The English dinner is precisely the model on which our own are constructed in the Atlantic cities. The company sit one or two hours before the ladies leave the table. The gentlemen remain over their wine an hour longer, and rejoin the ladies in the drawing-room and take coffee. The dress-dinner generates a talent of table-talk which reaches great perfection: the stories are so good that one is sure they must have been often told before, to have got such happy turns. Hither come all manner of clever projects, bits of popular science, of practical invention, of miscellaneous humor; political, literary and personal news; railroads, horses, diamonds, agriculture, horticulture, pisciculture and wine.

English stories, *bonmots* and the recorded table-talk of their wits, are as good as the best of the French. In America, we are apt scholars, but have not yet attained the same perfection: for the range of nations from which London draws, and the steep contrasts of condition, create the picturesque in society, as broken country makes picturesque landscape; whilst our prevailing equality makes a prairie tameness: and secondly, because the usage of a dress-dinner every day at dark has a tendency to hive and produce to advantage everything good. Much attrition has worn every sentence into a bullet. Also one meets now and then with polished men who know every thing, have tried every thing, and can do every thing, and are quite superior to letters and science. What could they not, if only they would?

Character

The English race are reputed morose. I do not know that they have sadder brows than their neighbors of northern climates. They are sad by comparison with the singing and dancing nations: not sadder, but slow and staid, as finding their joys at home. . . . The Englishman finds no relief from reflection, except in reflection. When he wishes for amusement, he goes to work. His hilarity is like an attack of fever. Religion, the theatre and the reading the books of his country all feed and increase his natural melancholy. The police does not interfere with public diversions. It thinks itself bound in duty to respect the pleasures and rare gayety of this inconsolable nation; and their well-known courage is entirely attributable to their disgust of life.

I suppose their gravity of demeanor and their few words have obtained this reputation. As compared with the Americans, I think them cheerful and contented. Young people in this country are much more prone to melancholy. The English have a mild aspect and a ringing cheerful voice. They are large-natured and not so easily amused as the southerners, and are among them as grown people among children, requiring war, or trade, or engineering, or science, instead of frivolous games. They are proud and private, and even if disposed to recreation, will avoid an open garden. They sported sadly; *ils s'amusaient tristement, selon la coutume de leur pays,* said Froissart; and I suppose never nation built their party-walls so thick, or their garden-fences so high. Meat and wine produce no effect on them. They are just as cold, quiet and composed, at the end, as at the beginning of dinner.

The reputation of taciturnity they have enjoyed for six or seven hundred years; and a kind of pride in bad public speaking is noted in the House of Commons, as if they were willing to show that they did not live by their tongues, or thought they spoke well enough if they had the tone of gentlemen. In mixed company they shut their mouths. A Yorkshire mill-owner told me he had ridden more than once all the way from London to Leeds, in the first-class carriage, with the same persons, and no word exchanged. The club-houses were established to cultivate social habits, and it is rare that more than two eat together, and oftenest one eats alone. Was it then a stroke of humor in the serious Swedenborg, or was it only his pitiless logic, that made him shut up the English souls in a heaven by themselves?

They are contradictorily described as sour, splenetic and stubborn—and as mild, sweet and sensible. The truth is they have great range and variety of character. Commerce sends abroad multitudes of different classes. The choleric Welshman, the fervid Scot, the bilious resident in the East or West Indies, are wide of the perfect behavior of the educated and dignified man of family. So is the burly farmer; so is the country squire, with his narrow and violent life. In every inn is the Commercial-Room, in which "travellers," or bagmen who carry patterns and solicit orders for the manufacturers, are wont to be entertained. It easily happens that this class should characterize England to the foreigner, who meets them on the road and at every public house, whilst the gentry avoid the taverns, or seclude themselves whilst in them.

But these classes are the right English stock, and may fairly show the national qualities, before yet art and education have dealt with them. They are good lovers, good haters, slow but obstinate admirers, and in all things very much steeped in their temperament, like men hardly awaked from deep sleep, which they enjoy. Their habits and instincts cleave to nature. They are of the earth, earthy; and of the sea, as the sea-kinds, attached to it for what it yields them, and not from any sentiment. They are full of coarse strength, rude exercise, butcher's meat and sound sleep; and suspect any poetic insinuation or any hint for the conduct of life which reflects on this animal existence, as if somebody were fumbling at the umbilical cord and might stop their supplies. They doubt a man's sound judgment if he does not eat with appetite, and shake their heads if he is particularly chaste. Take them as they come, you shall find in the common people a surly indifference, sometimes gruffness and ill temper; and in minds of more power, magazines of inexhaustible war, challenging

> The ruggedest hour that time and spite dare bring
> To frown upon the enraged Northumberland.

They are headstrong believers and defenders of their opinion, and not less resolute in maintaining their whim and perversity. Hezekiah Woodward wrote a book against the Lord's Prayer. And one can believe that Burton, the Anatomist of Melancholy, having predicted from the stars the hour of his death, slipped the knot himself round his own neck, not to falsify his horoscope.

Their looks bespeak an invincible stoutness: they have extreme difficulty to run away, and will die game. Wellington said of the young coxcombs of the Life-Guards, delicately brought up, "But the puppies fight well;" and Nelson said of his sailors, "They really mind shot no more than peas." Of absolute stoutness no nation has more or better examples. They are good at storming redoubts, at boarding frigates, at dying in the last ditch, or any desperate service which has daylight and honor in it; but not, I think, at enduring the rack, or any passive obedience, like jumping off a castle-roof at the word of a czar. Being both vascular and highly organized, so as to be very sensible of pain; and intellectual, so as to see reason and glory in a matter.

Of that constitutional force which yields the supplies of the day, they have the more than enough; the excess which creates courage on fortitude, genius in poetry, invention in mechanics, enterprise in trade, magnificence in wealth, splendor in ceremonies, petulance and projects in youth. The young men have a rude health which runs into peccant humors. They drink brandy like water, cannot expend their quantities of waste strength on riding, hunting, swimming and fencing, and run into absurd frolics with the gravity of the Eumenides. They stoutly carry into every nook and corner of the earth their turbulent sense; leaving no lie uncontradicted; no pretension unexamined. They chew hasheesh; cut themselves with poisoned creases; swing their hammock in the boughs of the Bohon Upas; taste every poison; buy every secret; at Naples they put St. Januarius's blood in an alembic; they saw a hole into the head of the "winking Virgin," to know why she winks; measure with an English footrule every cell of the Inquisition, every Turkish caaba, every Holy of holies; translate and send to Bentley the arcanum bribed and bullied away from shuddering Bramins; and measure their own strength by the terror they cause. These travellers are of every class, the best and the worst; and it may easily happen that those of rudest behavior are taken notice of and remembered. The Saxon melancholy in the vulgar rich and poor appears as gushes of ill-humor, which every check exasperates into sarcasm and vituperation. There are multitudes of rude young English who have the self sufficiency and bluntness of their nation, and who, with their disdain of the rest of mankind and with this indigestion and choler, have made the English traveller a proverb for uncomfortable and offensive manners. It was no bad description of the Briton generically, what was said two hundred years ago of one particular Oxford scholar: "He was a very bold man, uttered any thing that came into his mind, not only among his companions, but in public coffee-houses, and would often speak his mind of particular persons then accidentally present, without examining the company he was in; for which he was often reprimanded and several times threatened to be kicked and beatten." . . .

But it is in the deep traits of race that the fortunes of nations are written, and however derived—whether a happier tribe or mixture of tribes, the air, or what circumstance that mixed for them the golden mean of temperament—here exists the best stock in the world, broad-fronted, broad-bottomed, best for depth, range and equability; men of aplomb and reserves, great range and many moods, strong instincts, yet apt for culture; war-class as well as clerks; earls and tradesmen; wise minority, as well as foolish majority; abysmal temperament, hiding wells of wrath, and glooms on which no sunshine settles, alternated with a common sense and humanity which hold them fast to every piece of cheerful duty; making this temperament a sea to which all storms are superficial; a race to which their fortunes flow, as if they alone had the elastic organization at once fine and robust enough for dominion; as if the burly inexpressive, now mute and contumacious, now fierce and sharp-tongued dragon, which once made the island light with his fiery breath, had bequeathed his ferocity to his conqueror. They hide virtues under vices, or the semblance of them. It is the misshapen hairy Scandinavian troll again, who lifts the cart out of the mire, "threshes the corn that ten day-laborers could not end," but it is done in the dark and with muttered maledictions. He is a churl with a soft place in his heart, whose speech is a brash of bitter waters, but who loves to help you at a pinch. He says no, and serves you, and your thanks disgust him. Here was lately a cross-grained miser, odd and ugly, resembling in countenance the portrait of Punch with the laugh left out; rich by his own industry; sulking in a lonely house; who never gave a dinner to any man and disdained all courtesies; yet as true a worshipper of beauty in form and color as ever existed, and profusely pouring over the cold mind of his countrymen creations of grace and truth, removing the reproach of sterility from English art, catching from their savage climate every fine hint, and importing into their galleries every tint and trait of sunnier cities and skies; making an era in painting; and when he saw that the splendor of one of his pictures in the Exhibition dimmed his rival's that hung next it, secretly took a brush and blackened his own.[1]

They do not wear their heart in their sleeve for daws to peck at. They have that phlegm or staidness which it is a compliment to disturb. "Great men," said Aristotle, "are always of a nature originally melancholy." 'Tis the habit of a mind which attaches to abstractions with a passion which gives vast results. They dare to displease, they do not speak to expectation. They like the sayers of No, better than the sayers of Yes. Each of them has an opinion which he feels it becomes him to express all the more that it differs from yours. They are meditating opposition. This gravity is inseparable from minds of great resources. . . .

They have great range of scale, from ferocity to exquisite refinement. With larger scale, they have great retrieving power. After

---

[1]The painter was J. M. W. Turner, (ed.).

running each tendency to an extreme, they try another tack with equal heat. More intellectual than other races, when they live with other races they do not take their language, but bestow their own. They subsidize other nations, and are not subsidized. They proselyte, and are not proselyted. They assimilate other races to themselves, and are not assimilated. The English did not calculate the conquest of the Indies. It fell to their character. So they administer, in different parts of the world, the codes of every empire and race; in Canada, old French law; in the Mauritius, the Code Napoleon; in the West Indies, the edicts of the Spanish Cortes; in the East Indies, the Laws of Menu; in the Isle of Man, of the Scandinavian Thing; at the Cape of Good Hope, of the old Netherlands; and in the Ionian Islands, the Pandects of Justinian.

They are very conscious of their advantageous position in history. England is the lawgiver, the patron, the instructor, the ally. Compare the tone of the French and of the English press: the first querulous, captious, sensitive about English opinion; the English press never timorous about French opinion, but arrogant and contemptuous.

They are testy and headstrong through an excess of will and bias; churlish as men sometimes please to be who do not forget a debt, who ask no favors and who will do what they like with their own. With education and intercourse, these asperities wear off and leave the good-will pure. If anatomy is reformed according to national tendencies, I suppose the spleen will hereafter be found in the Englishman, not found in the American, and differencing the one from the other. I anticipate another anatomical discovery, that this organ will be found to be cortical and caducous; that they are superficially morose, but at last tender-hearted, herein differing from Rome and the Latin nations. Nothing savage, nothing mean resides in the English heart. They are subject to panics of credulity and of rage, but the temper of the nation, however disturbed, settles itself soon and easily, as, in this temperate zone, the sky after whatever storms clears again, and serenity is its normal condition.

A saving stupidity masks and protects their perception, as the curtain of the eagle's eye. Our swifter Americans, when they first deal with English, pronounce them stupid; but, later, do them justice as people who wear well, or hide their strength. To understand the power of performance that is in their finest wits, in the patient Newton, or in the versatile transcendent poets, or in the Dugdales, Gibbons, Hallams, Eldons and Peels, one should see how English day-laborers hold out. High and low, they are of an unctuous texture. There is an adipocere in their constitution, as if they had oil also for their mental wheels and could perform vast amounts of work without damaging themselves.

Even the scale of expense on which people live, and to which scholars and professional men conform, proves the tension of their muscle, when vast numbers are found who can each lift this enormous load. I might even add, their daily feasts argue a savage vigor of body.

No nation was ever so rich in able men; "Gentlemen," as Charles I said of Strafford, "whose abilities might make a prince rather afraid than ashamed in the greatest affairs of state;" men of such temper, that, like Baron Vere, "had one seen him returning from a victory, he would by his silence have suspected that he had lost the day; and, had be beheld him in a retreat, he would have collected him a conqueror by the cheerfulness of his spirit.

The national temper, in the civil history, is not flashy or whiffling. The slow, deep English mass smoulders with fire, which at last sets all its borders in flame. The wrath of London is not French wrath, but has a long memory, and, in its hottest heat, a register and rule.

Half their strength they put not forth. They are capable of a sublime resolution, and if hereafter the war of races, often predicted, and making itself a war of opinions also (a question of despotism and liberty coming from Eastern Europe), should menace the English civilization, these sea-kings may take once again to their floating castles and find a new home and a second millennium of power in their colonies.

The stability of England is the security of the modern world. If the English race were as mutable as the French, what reliance? But the English stand for liberty. The conservative, money-loving, lord-loving English are yet liberty-loving; and so freedom is safe: for they have more personal force than any other people. The nation always resist the immoral action of their government. They think humanely on the affairs of France, of Turkey, of Poland, of Hungary, of Schleswig Holstein, though overborne by the statecraft of the rulers at last.

Does the early history of each tribe show the permanent bias, which, though not less potent, is masked as the tribe spreads its activity into colonies, commerce, codes, arts, letters? The early history shows it, as the musician plays the air which he proceeds to conceal in a tempest of variations. In Alfred, in the Northmen, one may read the genius of the English society, namely that private life is the place of honor. Glory, a career, and ambition, words familiar to the longitude of Paris, are seldom heard in English speech. Nelson wrote from their hearts his homely telegraph, "England expects every man to do his duty."

For actual service, for the dignity of a profession, or to appease diseased or inflamed talent, the army and navy may be entered (the worst boys doing well in the navy); and the civil service in departments where serious official work is done; and they hold in esteem the barrister engaged in the severer studies of the law. But the calm, sound and most British Briton shrinks from public life as charlatanism, and respects an economy founded on agriculture, coalmines, manufactures or trade, which secures an independence through the creation of real values.

They wish neither to command nor obey, but to be kings in their own houses. They are intellectual and deeply enjoy literature; they like well to have the world served up to them in books, maps, models, and every mode of exact information, and, though not creators in art, they value its refinement. They are ready for leisure, can direct and fill their own day, nor need so much as others the constraint of a necessity. But the history of the nation discloses, at every turn, this original predilection for private independence, and however this inclination may have been disturbed by the bribes with which their vast colonial power has warped men out of orbit, the inclination endures, and forms and reforms the laws, letters, manners and occupations. They choose that welfare which is compatible with the commonwealth, knowing that such alone is stable; as wise merchants prefer investments in the three per cents.

Result

England is the best of actual nations. It is no ideal framework, it is an old pile built in different ages, with repairs, additions and makeshifts; but you see the poor best you have got. London is the epitome of our times, and the Rome of to-day. Broad-fronted, broad-bottomed Teutons, they stand in solid phalanx foursquare to the points of compass; they constitute the modern world, they have earned their vantage ground and held it through ages of adverse possession. They are well marked and differing from other leading races. England is tender-hearted. Rome was not. England is not so public in its bias; private life is its place of honor. Truth in private life, untruth in public, marks these home-loving men. Their political conduct is not decided by general views, but by internal intrigues and personal and family interest. They cannot readily see beyond England. The history of Rome and Greece, when written by their scholars, degenerates into English party pamphlets. They cannot see beyond England, nor in England can they transcend the interests of the governing classes. "English principles" mean a primary regard to the interests of property. England, Scotland and Ireland combine to check the colonies. England and Scotland combine to check Irish manufactures and trade. England rallies at home to check Scotland. In England, the strong classes check the weaker. In the home population of near thirty millions, there are but one million voters. The Church punishes dissent, punishes education. Down to a late day, marriages performed by dissenters were illegal. A bitter class-legislation gives power to those who are rich enough to buy a law. The game-laws are a proverb of oppression. Pauperism incrusts and clogs the state, and in hard times becomes hideous. In bad seasons, the porridge was diluted. Multitudes lived miserably by shell-fish and sea-ware. In cities, the children are trained to beg, until they shall be old enough to rob. Men and women were convicted of poisoning scores of children for burial-fees. In Irish districts, men deteriorated in size and shape, the nose sunk, the gums were exposed, with diminished brain and brutal form. During the Australian emigration, multitudes were rejected by the commissioners as being too emaciated for useful colonists. During the Russian war, few of those that offered as recruits were found up to the medical standard, though it had been reduced.

The foreign policy of England, though ambitious and lavish of money, has not often been generous or just. It has a principal regard to the interest of trade, checked however by the aristocratic bias of the ambassador, which usually puts him in sympathy with the continental Courts. It sanctioned the partition of Poland, it betrayed Genoa, Sicily, Parga, Greece, Turkey, Rome and Hungary.

Some public regards they have. They have abolished slavery in the West Indies and put an end to human sacrifices in the East. At home they have a certain statute hospitality. England keeps open doors, as a trading country must, to all nations. It is one of their fixed ideas, and wrathfully supported by their laws in unbroken sequence for a thousand years. In *Magna Charta* it was ordained that all "merchants shall have safe and secure conduct to go out and come into England, and to stay there, and to pass as well by land as by water, to buy and sell by the ancient allowed customs, without any evil toll, except in time of war, or when they shall be of any nation at war with us." It is a statute and obliged hospitality and peremptorily maintained. But this shop-rule had one magnificent effect. It extends its cold unalterable courtesy to political exiles of every opinion, and is a fact which might give additional light to that portion of the planet seen from the farthest star. But this perfunctory hospitality puts no sweetness into their unaccommodating manners, no check on that puissant nationality which makes their existence incompatible with all that is not English.

What we must say about a nation is a superficial dealing with symptoms. We cannot go deep enough into the biography of the spirit who never throws himself entire into one hero, but delegates his energy in parts or spasms to vicious and defective individuals. But the wealth of the source is seen in the plenitude of English nature. What variety of power and talent; what facility and plenteousness of knighthood, lordship, ladyship, royalty, loyalty; what a proud chivalry is indicated in "Collins's Peerage," through eight hundred years! What dignity resting on what reality and stoutness! What courage in war, what sinew in labor, what cunning workmen, what inventors and engineers, what seamen and pilots, what clerks and scholars! No one man and no few men can represent them. It is a people of myriad personalities. Their many-headedness is owing to the advantageous position of the middle class, who are always the source of letters and science. Hence the vast plenty of their aesthetic production. As they are many-headed, so they are many-nationed: their colonization annexes archipelagoes and continents, and their speech seems destined to be the universal language of men. I have noted the reserve of power in the English temperament. In the island; they never let out all the length of the reins, there is no Berserkir rage, no abandonment or ecstasy of will or intellect, like that of the Arabs in the time of Mahomet, or like that which intoxicated France in 1789. But who would see the uncoiling of that tremendous spring, the explosion of their well-husbanded forces, must follow the swarms which pouring now for two hundred years from the British islands, have sailed and rode and traded and planted through all climates, mainly following the belt of empire, the temperate zones, carrying the Saxon seed, with its instinct for liberty and law, for arts and for thought—acquiring under some skies a more electric energy than the native air allows—to the conquest of the globe. Their colonial policy, obeying the necessities of a vast empire, has become liberal. Canada and Australia have been contented with substantial independence. They are expiating the wrongs of India by benefits; first, in works for the irrigation of the peninsula, and roads, and telegraphs; and secondly, in the instruction of the people, to qualify them for self-government, when the British power shall be finally called home.

Their mind is in a state of arrested development,—a divine cripple like Vulcan; a blind *savant* like Huber and Sanderson. They do not occupy themselves on matters of general and lasting import, but on a corporeal civilization, on goods that perish in the using. But they read with good intent, and what they learn they incarnate. The English mind turns every abstraction it can receive into a portable utensil, or a working institution. Such is their tenacity and such their practical turn, that they hold all they gain. Hence we say that only the English race can be trusted with freedom—freedom which is double-edged and dangerous to any but the wise and robust. The English designate the kingdoms emulous of free institutions, as the sentimental nations. Their culture is not an outside varnish, but is thorough and secular in families and the race. They are oppressive with their temperament, and all the more that they are refined. I have sometimes seen them walk with my countrymen when I was forced to allow them every advantage, and their companions seemed bags of bones.

There is cramp limitation in their habit of thought, sleepy routine, and a tortoise's instinct to hold hard to the ground with his claws, lest he should be thrown on his back. There is a drag of inertia which resists reform in every shape—law-reform, army-reform, extension of suffrage, Jewish franchise, Catholic emancipation—the abolition of slavery, of impressment, penal code and entails. They praise this drag, under the formula that it is the excellence of the British constitution that no law can anticipate the public opinion. These poor tortoises must hold hard, for they feel no wings sprouting at their shoulders. Yet somewhat divine warms at their heart and waits a happier hour. It hides in their sturdy will. "Will," said the old philosophy, "is the measure of power," and personality is the token of this race. *Quid vult valde vult.* What they do they do with a will. You cannot account for their success by their Christianity, commerce, character, common law, Parliament, or letters, but by the contumacious sharptongued energy of English *naturel,* with a poise impossible to disturb, which makes all these its instruments. They are slow and reticent, and are like a dull good horse which lets every nag pass him, but with whip and spur will run down every racer in the field. They are right in their feeling, though wrong in their speculation.

The feudal system survives in the steep inequality of property and privilege, in the limited franchise, in the social barriers which confine patronage and promotion to a caste, and still more in the submissive ideas pervading these people. The fagging of the schools is repeated in the social classes. An Englishman shows no mercy to those below him in the social scale, as he looks for none from those above him; any forbearance from his superiors surprises him, and they suffer in his good opinion. But the feudal system can be seen with less pain on large historical grounds. It was pleaded in mitigation of the rotten borough, that it worked well, that substantial justice was done. Fox, Burke, Pitt, Erskine, Wilberforce, Sheridan, Romilly, or whatever national man, were by this means sent to Parliament, when their return by large constituencies would have been doubtful. So now we say that the right measures of England are the men it bred; that it has yielded more able men in five hundred years than any other nation; and, though we must not play Providence and balance the chances of producing ten great men against the comfort of ten thousand mean men, yet retrospectively, we may strike the balance and prefer one Alfred, one Shakspeare, one Milton, one Sidney, one Raleigh, one Wellington, to a million foolish democrats.

The American system is more democratic, more humane; yet the American people do not yield better or more able men, or more inventions or books or benefits than the English. Congress is not wiser or better than Parliament. France has abolished its suffocating old *régime*, but is not recently marked by any more wisdom or virtue.

The power of performance has not been exceeded—the creation of value. The English have given importance to individuals, a principal end and fruit of every society. Every man is allowed and encouraged to be what he is, and is guarded in the indulgence of his whim. "Magna Charta," said Rushworth, "is such a fellow that he will have no sovereign." By this general activity and by this sacredness of individuals, they have in seven hundred years evolved the principles of freedom. It is the land of patriots, martyrs, sages and bards, and if the ocean out of which it emerged should wash it away, it will be remembered as an island famous for immortal laws, for the announcements of original right which make the stone tables of liberty.

WILLIAM WARE:

THE MATERIALISM AND HYPOCRISY

OF THE ENGLISH

1850

William Ware was the son of the famous Henry Ware, Hollis Professor of Divinity at Harvard University. After his graduation from Harvard College, Ware followed his father into the church, becoming, in 1821, minister to the First Unitarian Church of New York. After fifteen years of the ministry, Ware abandoned it for journalism and acquired control of the *Christian Herald*; it was to this periodical that he contributed many of those essays later collected in *Julian, or Scenes in Judea*. In 1848 Ware went abroad for journalistic copy: and for health. He got his copy, *Sketches of European Capitals*, (1851) but his search for health was in vain and he died shortly after his return to the United States, before he could see his biography of his friend Washington Allston through the press.

To any American traveller through England, it must be quite observable how commerce and the love of money, stocks and trade, all throughout England, override letters, art, nobility—every thing, in a word, but law. England is still comparatively free and law-

From William Ware, *Sketches of European Capitals* (Boston, 1851), pp. 291–294, 296–303.

abiding. But once England was known abroad rather by her great names in literature and science—Bacon, Locke, Shakspeare, Milton, Newton, Davy, were the names first suggested. Now they are of quite another character; Manchester, Birmingham, Sheffield, are to-day words of a more powerful spell. . . . The London man of business is now the true earl, baron, duke of the empire. The lust of wealth has seized all hearts, and enslaved them and bound them in chains stronger even—though so different—than those which bound the old lords of the soil in the days of Charles the Second. This modern chivalry is an improvement upon the old in point of morals, but would not, I fear, be thought so genteel. The Lovelaces would probably be considered a more gentlemanly breed in the calendar where such things are graduated, than the brewer, the grocer, the cotton-spinner, the ironmonger, who now reign in the ascendant. But the world will generally agree to bestow honor and reverence where the power is, and in 1850 money is power.[1] Money is, in England, King, Lords, and Commons. Money is the real nobility. Bankers are the true ministry, and determine questions of peace and war, and make the treaties. The Rothschilds, though they cannot get into Parliament, rule with equal despotism on the outside. The England of the nineteenth century is but one vast counting-house. The slur of Napoleon is truer now than when first uttered, that England is a nation of shopkeepers. . . .

In England the very occupation of the people seems to be strain-ing at gnats and swallowing camels. They are filled with a very virtuous indignation at the continued existence of American slavery, although it was they who planted it here, and that, too, against our will and most earnest remonstrances, while at the same time they swallow without difficulty the slavery of one hundred and fifty millions of Hindoos. In what proportion out of the whole there is personal slavery, where there is buying and selling, and labor with-out remuneration, that basest, meanest form of tyranny, I know not, though the proportion is very great, but that there is political slavery there throughout that whole immense population all the world knows . . . natives doing all the work for what rice and rupees will keep them from starving. Notwithstanding the frequent display on the part of travelling Englishmen and the review-writing English-

---

1. The pride of money is the universal pride of the English; and the love of displaying it in the most ostentatious expenditures, is another trait quite observable. To throw about money with an expression of sovereign contempt for those to whom it is thrown, is al-together English. The Americans love money and love more to spend it—but almost never in that spirit. . . .

men, of the most generous sentiments and sympathies on behalf of the blacks, and their expression of wonder and regret that the American white should refuse to consort on equal terms with the free African, it is still true that color, even the light olive tint of the Hindoo, bears the same mark of degradation in Calcutta, and to many even in London as here, and the white Englishman will not sit at meat with the East Indian, though he be a prince or a philosopher. There were gentlemen, who, though invited, would not dine in company with Ram Mohun Roy, though a full-blooded Rajah, and a most learned and accomplished man—"indignantly refusing to sit at table with that black fellow." They lecture the world on the virtues and duties of peace, but without scruple will let loose the dogs of war whenever their flannels, their cottons, their woollens, iron, or opium, are interfered with. They give suppers and breakfasts, and have all their equipages in full liveried action on Sundays, whereby armies of servants of higher and lower degrees are detained in personal attendance on their masters throughout the day, and, for a pretence, stop the Sunday mail, that all the various operatives connected therewith may be at leisure to go to church as they ought to do, and say their prayers. They are sadly pained that the American should love the dollar so well, the only difference being that their love of the pound is the same, only five times as much. They have made a great ado, and with justice and sense, about the virtue of temperance in England—there is need of it, for the English, and still more the Scotch and Irish, are a nation of hard drinkers; but, at the same time, made cruel and cowardly war, but a few years since, upon the Chinese, to compel them to get drunk on the opium which they first forced them to buy at the point of the bayonet. They are really mortified that we, who they cannot, to their manifest chagrin, deny, sprung from English blood, are still so low in civilization that we produce little literature, and no art, as yet . . . not remembering that England, a thousand years older than we at that time, produced no artists before the middle of the eighteenth century, and to this day has produced not one of the highest class; . . . England riots in luxuries obtained at the expense of the comfort and subsistence of the lower classes, from which she wrings by taxes, direct and indirect, the last penny that will just leave the life in the body, over whom she at the same time utters the most touching lamentations for their hardships and miseries. The female sex is, in this case, the grand sacrifice, who, in this respect at least, are slaves—though living on the boasted soil of England, that they are compelled to *work without remuneration;* for that cannot be called remuneration which fails not only to support life in tolerable comfort, but to support it at all; and to save from starvation by cold and hunger, resort must be had to vices which, were God no more merciful than man, would destroy soul as well as body. They make long prayers and many of them, according to some travellers, especially among the higher classes; yet seamstresses, the Spitalfield weavers, the weavers and spinners in Manchester and Glasgow, and especially the innumerable slaves of the slopshop, live in misery and die in want, without any adequate effort being made to fix by law a tariff—as easy to be agreed upon, at least, as any other tariff—of prices for labor, by which it should no longer be in the power of the richer to defraud the poorer of their toil or their time.

1850-1860

FREDERICK LAW OLMSTED:
THE FARM LABORERS ARE
DEGRADED, BRUTAL AND LICENTIOUS

1850

One of the great figures in American cultural history, Olmsted made a reputation in three fields. Born in Connecticut in 1822, he was prevented by illness from going to Yale; instead he went on exploratory walking tours throughout the Eastern states and Canada and then, to satisfy his wanderlust—shipped on a cargo vessel to China. On his return he turned to farming and became one of the pioneers in scientific farming. It was this interest which took him to England in 1850, where with his friend Charles Brace (whom we shall meet later) he covered most of England on foot. On his return to America he was assigned the task of reporting on conditions in the South: the result was three famous works, *A Journey to the Seaboard States* (1856), *A Journey Through Texas* (1857), and *A Journey in the Back Country* (1860), all in all the best account of life in the South on the eve of war in our literature. Then, in the sixties, Olmsted found what was to be his real career: landscape architecture on a grand scale. With Calvert Vaux he laid out the famous Central Park in New York City; later he was in charge of the landscap-

From Frederick Law Olmsted, *Walks and Talks of an American Farmer in England*, (London, 1852), Chapters V and XL.

ing of the National Capitol, the University of California, the Boston Park system, and, most successful of all, the World's Columbian Exposition in Chicago in 1893.

After we had wandered for about an hour through the streets the first afternoon we were ashore [in Liverpool], I remarked that we had not yet seen a single well-dressed man, not one person that in America would have been described as "of respectable appearance." We were astonished to observe with what an unmingled stream of poverty the streets were swollen, and J. remarked that if what we had seen was a fair indication of the general condition of the masses here, he should hardly feel justified in dissuading them from using violent and anarchical means to bring down to themselves a share of the opportunities and comforts of those "higher classes" that seem to be so utterly separated from them. There are a great many Irish in Liverpool, but the most that we had thus far seen evidently were English, yet not English as we have known them. Instead of the stout, full-faced John Bulls, we had seen but few that were not thin, meagre, and pale. There was somewhat rarely an appearance of actual misery, but a stupid, hopeless, state-prison-for-life sort of expression. There were not unfrequently some exceptions to this, but these were men almost invariably in some uniform or livery, as railroad hands, servants, and soldiers.

The next morning, in the court-yard of the Exchange (the regular 'Change assemblage seemed to meet out of doors), we saw a large collection of the merchants. There was nothing to distinguish them from a company of a similar kind with us, beyond a general English-ness of features and an entire absence of all *oddities*—with astonishing beards and singularities of costume. One young man only wore small clothes and leggins, which would perhaps have disagreeably subjected him to be noticed with us. They were stouter than our merchants, and more chubby-faced, yet not looking in vigorous health. They were, on the whole, judging by a glance at their outsides, to be more respected than any lot of men of the same number that I ever saw together in Wall street. Many of them, and most the well-dressed men that we have seen in the streets, have had a green leaf and simple *posy* in a button-hole of their coats.

The shopkeepers of the better class, or retail merchants, are exactly the same men, to all appearance, that stand behind the counters with us. *Merchant,* means only a wholesale dealer in England; retailers are *shopkeepers*. The word *store* is never applied to a building; but the building in which goods are stored is a *warehouse*.

Women are more employed in trade than with us; I have no doubt with every way great advantage. The women in the streets are more noticeably different from ours than the men. In general, they are very cheaply and coarsely clad. Many of the lower class have their outer garments ordinarily drawn up behind, in the scrubbing-floor fashion. Caps are universally worn, and being generally nice and white, they have a pleasant effect upon the face. The very poorest women look very miserably. We see bruised eyes not unfrequently, and there is evidently a good deal of hard drinking among them. They are larger and stouter, and have coarser features. There are neither as many pretty nor as many ugly faces as with us; indeed, there are very few remarkably ill favoured in that respect, and almost none strikingly handsome. The best faces we have seen were among the fishstalls in market. With scarcely an exception, the fish-women were very large and tall, and though many of them were in the neighbourhood of fifty, they had invariably full, bright un-wrinkled faces, beautiful red cheeks, and cheerful expression. English women, generally, appear more bold and self-reliant, their *action* is more energetic, and their carriage less graceful and droop-ing than ours. Those well dressed that we have seen, while *shopping*, for instance, are no exceptions. Those we have met to converse with are as modest and complaisant as could be desired, yet speak with a marked promptness and confidence which is animating and attrac-tive. We met a small company last night at the residence of a gentleman to whom we had a letter, and spent the evening precisely as we should at a small tea-party at home; we might easily have imagined ourselves in New England. The gentlemen were no way different, that we noticed, from cultivated men with us, and the ladies only seemed rather more frank, hearty, and sincere-natured than we should expect ours to be to strangers.[1] There was nothing in their dresses that I can think of as peculiar, yet a general air, not American—a heavier look and more *crinkles*, and darker and more mixed-up colours. We see many rather nice-looking females, proba-bly coming in from the country, driving themselves about town as if they understood it, in jaunty-looking chaises and spring-carts. As J. and I were standing this noon by the window of a curiosity-shop, a

1. These ladies were Irish. The remark hardly applies to English ladies, certainly not unless you meet them domestically. The English in their *homes*, and the English *"in company,"* are singularly opposite characters.

lady addressed us: "This is very curious; have you noticed it?" (pointing at something within the window). "I wish you would help me to read what is written upon it." She spoke exactly as if she *belonged to our party*. She was not young or gayly-dressed, but had all the appearance and used the language of a well-bred and educated woman. We conversed with her for a minute or two about the article, which was some specimen of Australian natural history.

There are a good many soldiers moving about in fine undress uniforms; one regiment is in blue, which I did not suppose the British ever used. The men look well—more intelligent than you would suppose. Many are quite old, grey-headed, and all are very neat and orderly in the streets.

The children look really *punchy*. It strikes me the young ones are dressed much older, while the young men are clothed much more boyishly than in America. Quite large children, of both sexes, are dressed exactly alike, and whether girls or boys (they look between both), you cannot guess—girls with fur hats, such as full-grown men wear, and boys in short dresses and pantalettes. . . .

It would be more strange to you to see long, narrow streets, full from one end to the other, of the poorest-looking people you ever saw, women and children only, the men being off at work, I suppose, sitting, lounging, leaning on the door-steps and side-walks, smoking, knitting, and chatting; the boys playing ball in the street, or marbles on the flagging; no break in the line of tall, dreary houses, but strings of clothes hung across from opposite second-story windows to dry; all dwellings, except a few cellar, beer, or junk shops. You can see nothing like such a dead mass of pure poverty in the worst quarter of our worst city. In New York, such a street would be ten times as filthy and stinking, and ten times as lively; in the middle of it there would be a large fair building, set a little back (would that I could say with a few roods of green turf and shrubbery between it and the gutter in which the children are playing), with the inscription upon it, "Public Free School;" across from the windows would be a banner with the "Democratic Republican Nominations;" hand-organs would be playing, hogs squealing, perhaps a stampede of firemen; boys would be crying newspapers, and the walls would be posted with placards, appealing, with whatever motive, to patriotism and duty, showing that statesmen and demagogues could calculate on the people's reading and thinking there. There would be gay grog-shops too, with liberty poles before them, and churches and Sunday-school rooms (with lying faces of granite-painted pine) by their side. The countenances of the people here, too, exhibited much less, either of virtuous or vicious character, than you would discern among an equally poor multitude in America, yet among the most miserable of them (they were Irish), I was struck with some singularly intelligent, and even beautiful faces, so strangely out of place, that if they had been cleaned and put in frames, so the surroundings would not appear, you would have taken them for those of delicate, refined, and intellectual ladies.

Thursday morning, May 30th

We packed all our travelling matter, except a few necessaries, in two trunks and a carpet-bag, and I took them in a public carriage to the freight station, to be sent to London. The trunks were received, but the bag the clerks refused, and said it must be sent from the passenger station. I had engaged to meet my friends in a few minutes at the opposite side of the town from the passenger station, and the delay of going there would vexatiously disarrange our plans. I therefore urged them to take it, offering to pay the passenger luggage extra, freight, &c. They would be happy to accommodate me, but their rules did not admit of it. A *carpet-bag* could not be sent from the station at any price. I jumped on to the box, and drove quickly to the nearest street of shops, where, at a grocers's, I bought for twopence a coffee-sack, and enclosing the bag, brought it in a few minutes back to the station. There was a good laugh, and they gave me a receipt at once for a *sack*—to be kept in London until called for.

On the quay, I noticed a bareheaded man drawing with coloured crayons on a broad, smooth flagstone. He had represented, in a very skillful and beautiful manner, a salmon laid on a china platter, opposite a broken plate of coarse crockery; between these were some lines about a "rich man's dish" and a "poor man's dinner." He was making an ornamental border about it, and over all was written, *"Friends! I can get* NO WORK; *I must do this or starve."*

His hat, with a few pence in it, stood by the side of this. Was it not eloquent? . . .

We were bound for Monmouth that night, and soon after sunset, having one of the farm laborers for a guide, we struck across the fields into another lane. About a mile from the farmhouse, there was a short turn, and at the angle—the lane narrow and deep as usual—was a small, steep-roofed, stone building, with a few square and arched windows here and there in it, and a perfectly plain cube of stone for a tower, rising scarcely above the roof-tree, with an iron staff and vane on one of its corners—"Saint Some-one's parish church." There was a small graveyard, enclosed by a hedge, and in a corner of this, but with three doors opening in front upon the lane, was a long, crooked, dilapidated old cottage. On one of the stone thresholds, a dirty, peevish-looking woman was lounging, and before her, lying on the ground in the middle of the lane, were several boys and girls playing or quarreling. They stopped as we came near, and rolling out of the way, stared at us silently, and without the least expression of recognition, while we passed among them. As we went on, the woman said something in a sharp voice, and our guide shouted in reply, without, however, turning his head, "Stop thy maw—am going to Ameriky, aw tell thee." It was his "missis," he said.

"Those were not your children that lay in the road?"

"Yaas they be—foive of 'em."

So we fell into a talk with him about his condition and prospects. . .

We had been walking for some miles, late in a dusky evening, upon a hilly road, with an old peasant women, who was returning from market, carrying a heavy basket upon her head and two others in her hands. She had declined to let us assist her in carrying them, and though she had walked seven miles in the morning and now nearly that again at night, she had overtaken us, and was going on at a pace that for any great distance we should have found severe. At a turn of the road we saw the figure of a person standing still upon a little rising ground before us, indistinct in the dusk, but soon evidently a young woman. It is my child, said the woman, hastily setting down her baskets and running forward, so that they met and embraced each other half way up the hill. The young woman then came down to us, and, taking the great basket on her head, the two trudged on with rapid and animated conversation, in kind tones asking and telling of their experiences of the day, entirely absorbed with each other, and apparently forgetting that we were with them, until, a mile or two further on, we came near the village in which they lived.

Our guide was a man of about forty, having a wife and seven children; neither he nor any of his family (he thought) could read or write, and, except with regard to his occupation as agricultural laborer, I scarcely ever saw a man of so limited information. He could tell us, for instance, almost no more about the church which adjoined his residence than if he had never seen it—not half so much as we could discover for ourselves by a single glance at it. He had nothing to say about the clergyman who officiated in it, and could tell us nothing about the parish, except its name, and that it allowed him and five other laborers to occupy the "almhouse" we had seen, rent free. He couldn't say how old he was (he appeared about forty); but he could say, "like a book," that God was what made the world, and that "Jesus Christ came into the world to save sinners, of whom he was chief"—of the truth of which latter clause I much doubted, suspecting the arch fiend would rank higher, among his servants, the man whose idea of duty and impulse of love had been satisfied with cramming this poor soul with such shells of spiritual nourishment. He thought two of his children knew the catechism and the creed; did not think they could have learned it from a book; they might, but he never heard them read; when he came home and had gotten his supper, he had a smoke and then went to bed. His wages were seven shillings—sometimes had been eight—a week. None of his children earned any thing; his wife, it might be, did somewhat in harvest-time. But take the year through, *one dollar and sixty-eight cents* a-week was all they earned to support themselves and their large family. How could they live? "Why, indeed, it was hard," he said; "sometimes, if we'd believe him, it had been as much as he could do to keep himself in tobacco!" He mentioned this as if it was a vastly more memorable hardship than that, oft-times, he could get nothing more than dry bread for his family to eat. It was a common thing that they had nothing to eat but dry bread. He got the flour—*fine, white wheaten flour*—from the master. They kept a hog, and had so much bacon as it would make to provide them with meat for the year. They also had a little potato patch, and he got cheese sometimes from the master. He had tea, too, to his supper. The parish gave him his rent, and he never was called upon for tithes, taxes, or any such thing. In addition to his wages, the master gave him, as he did all the laborers, three quarts either of cider or beer a-day, sometimes one and sometimes the other. He liked cider best—thought there was "more strength to it." Harvest-time they got six quarts, and sometimes, when the work was very hard, he had had ten quarts.

He had heard of America and Australia as countries that poor folks went to—he did not well know why, but supposed wages were higher, and they could live cheaper. His master and other gentlemen had told him about those places, and the laboring people talked about them among themselves. They had talked to him about going there. (America and Australia were all one—two names for the same place, for all that he knew.) He thought his master or the parish would provide him the means of going, if he wanted. We advised him to emigrate then, by all means, not so much for himself as for his children; the idea of his bringing seven, or it might yet be a dozen, more beings into the world to live such dumb-beast lives, was horrible to us. I told him that in America his children could go to school, and learn to read and write and to enjoy the revelation of God; and as they grew up they would improve their position, and might be land-owners and farmers themselves, as well off as his master; and he would have nothing to pay, or at least but a trifle that he could gratefully spare, to have them as well educated as the masters' son was being here; that where I came from the farmers would be glad to give a man like him, who could "plow and sow and reap and mow as well as any other in the parish," eighteen shillings a-week—

"And how much beer?"

"None at all!"

"None at all? ha, ha! he'd not go then—you'd not catch him workin' withouten his drink. No, no! a man 'ould die off soon that gait."

It was in vain that we offered fresh meat as an offset to the beer. There was "strength," he admitted, in beef, but it was wholly incredible that a man could work on it. A working-man must have zider or beer—there was no use to argue against that. That "Jesus Christ came into the world to save sinners," and that "work without beer is death," was the alpha and omega of his faith.

The laborers in this part of England (Hereford, Monmouth, Gloucester, and Wiltshire) were the most degraded, poor, stupid, brutal, and licentious that we saw in the kingdom. We were told that they were of the purest Saxon blood, as was indeed indicated by the frequency of blue eyes and light hair among them. But I did not see in Ireland, or in Germany or in France, nor did I ever see among our negroes or Indians, or among the Chinese or Malays, men whose tastes were such mere instincts, or whose purpose of life and whose mode of life was so low, so like that of domestic animals altogether, as these farm-laborers.

I was greatly pained, mortified, ashamed of old mother England, in acknowledging this; and the more so that I found so few Englishmen who realized it, or who, realizing it, seemed to feel that any one but God, with His laws of population and trade, was at all accountable for it. Even a most intelligent and distinguished Radical, when I alluded to this element as a part of the character of the country, in replying to certain very favorable comparisons he had been making of England with other countries, said—"We are not used to regard that class in forming a judgment of national character." And yet I suppose that class is larger in numbers than any other in the community of England. Many have even dared to think that, in the mysterious decrees of Providence, this balance of degradation and supine misery is essential to the continuance of the greatness; prosperity, and elevated character of the country—as if it were not indeed a part of the country.

A minister of the Gospel, of high repute in London, and whose sermons are reprinted and often repeated in America, from the words of Christ, "the poor ye have always among you," argued lately that all legislation or cooperative benevolence that had the tendency and hope of bringing about such a state of things that a large part of every nation should be independent of the charity of the other part, was heretical and blasphemous. Closely allied to such ideas are the too common notions of rulers and subjects.

HORACE GREELEY
VIEWS THE ENGLISH SCENE
AND INTERPRETS
THE ENGLISH CHARACTER

1851

Horace Greeley, generally acknowledged to be the greatest of American newspaper editors, came down from Vermont to New York City as a mere boy and at the age of thirty founded the *New-York Daily Tribune*, which he promptly made the most nearly national paper in the United States. His innate radicalism and his journalistic flair for innovation led him to open his paper to every new idea and every prominent liberal or radical writer on both sides of the water. In 1851 Greeley made his first trip to England, to serve as judge at the famous Crystal Palace Exhibition, and while there made a hasty trip through the countryside and onto the Continent which he described in a series of letters to his newspaper. Greeley's influence and power grew with the years; to large segments of the population north of the Mason-Dixon line his voice—or that of the *Tribune*—had an almost scriptural authority, and he did as much to rally support to the cause of antislavery as any man in the country. After the war he allowed himself to be seduced into politics, accepted the

From Horace Greeley, *Glances at Europe, in a Series of Letters from Great Britain, France, Italy, Switzerland etc., during the Summer of 1851* (New York, 1851), pp. 53–56, 79–83.

nomination for the presidency in 1872, and went down to defeat. A lifelong advocate of public-school education, he was, not surprisingly, shocked by the backwardness of public education in Britain at mid-century.

London, Thursday, May 15, 1851

Apart from the Great Exhibition, this is a season of intellectual activity in London. Parliament is (languidly) in session; the Aristocracy are in town; the Queen is lavishly dispensing the magnificent hospitalities of Royalty to those of the privileged caste who are invited to share them; and the several Religious and Philanthropic Societies, whether of the City or the Kingdom, are generally holding their Anniversaries, keeping Exeter Hall in blast almost night and day. I propose to give a first hasty glance at intellectual and general progress in Great Britain, leaving the subject to be more fully and thoroughly treated after I shall have made myself more conversant with the facts in the case.

A spirit of active and generous philanthropy is widely prevalent in this country. While the British pay more in taxes for the support of Priests and Paupers than any other people on earth, they at the same time give more for Religious and Philanthropic purposes. Their munificence is not always well guided; but on the whole very much is accomplished by it in the way of diffusing Christianity and diminishing Human Misery. . . .

For POPULAR EDUCATION, there is much doing in this Country, but in a disjointed, expensive, inefficient manner. Instead of one all-pervading, straight-forward, State-directed system, there are three or four in operation, necessarily conflicting with and damaging each other. And yet a vast majority really desire the Education of All, and are willing to pay for it. John Bull is good at paying taxes wherein he has had large experience; and if he grumbles a little now and then at their amount as oppressive, it is only because he takes pleasure in grumbling, and this seems to afford him a good excuse for it. He would not be deprived of it if he could: witness the discussions of the Income Tax, which every body denounces while no one justifies it abstractly; and yet it is always upheld, and I presume always will be. If the question could now be put to a direct vote, even of the tax-payers alone—"Shall or shall not a system of Common School Education for the United Kingdoms be maintained by a National Tax?"—I believe Free Schools would be triumphant. Even if such a

system were matured, put in operation, and to be sustained by
Voluntary Contributions alone or left to perish, I should not despair
of the result.

But there is a lion in the path, in the shape of the Priesthood of
the Established Church, who insist that the children shall be indoctrinated in the dogmas of their creed, or there shall be no State
system of Common Schools; and, behind these, stand the Roman
Catholic Clergy, who virtually make a similar demand with regard to
the children of Catholics. The unreasonableness, as well as the
ruinous effects of these demands, is already palpable on our side of
the Atlantic. If, when our City was meditating the Croton Water
Works, the Episcopal and Catholic Priesthood had each insisted that
those works should be consecrated by their own Hierarchy and by
none other, or, in default of this, we should have no water-works at
all, the case would be substantially parallel to this. Or if there were in
some city a hundred children, whose parents were of diverse creeds,
all blind with cataract, whom it was practicable to cure altogether,
but not separately, and these rival Priesthoods were respectively to
insist—"They shall be taught our Creed and Catechism, and no
other, while the operation is going on, or there shall be no operation
and no cure," that case would not be materially diverse from this. In
vain does the advocate of Light say to them, "Pray, let us give the
children the inestimable blessing of sight, and then YOU may teach
your creed and catechism to all whom you can persuade to learn
them," they will have the closed eyes opened according to Loyola or
to Laud, or not opened at all! Do they not provoke us to say that their
insisting on an impossible, a suicidal condition, is but a cloak, a blind,
a fetch, and that their real object is to keep the multitude in darkness? I am thankful that we have few clergymen in America who
manifest a spirit akin to that which to this day deprives half the
children of these Kingdoms of any considerable school education
whatever.

I think nothing unsusceptible of mathematical demonstration
can be clearer than the imperative necessity of Universal Education,
as a matter simply of Public Economy. In these densely peopled
islands, where service is cheap, and where many persons qualified to
teach are maintaining a precarious struggle for subsistence, a system
of General Education need not cost half so much as in the United
States, while wealth is so concentrated that taxes bear less hardly
here, in proportion to their amount, than with us. Every dollar
judiciously spent on the education of poor children, would be more
than saved in the diminution of the annual cost of pauperism and

crime, while the intellectual and industrial capacity of the people would be vastly increased by it. I do not see how even Clerical bigotry, formidable as it deplorably is, can long resist this consideration among a people so thrifty and saving, as are in the main the wielders of political power in this country. . . .

Ragged Schools

In the evening I attended the Ragged School situated in Carter's-field Lane, near the Cattle-Market in Smithfield [where John Rogers was burned at the stake by Catholics, as Catholics had been burned by Protestants before him. The honest, candid history of Persecution for Faith's sake, has never yet been written; whenever it shall be, it must cause many ears to tingle].

It was something past 7 o'clock when we reached the rough old building, in a filthy, poverty-stricken quarter, which has been rudely fitted up for the Ragged School—one of the first, I believe, that was attempted. I should say there were about four hundred pupils on its benches, with about forty teachers; the pupils were at least two-thirds males from five to twenty years old, with a dozen or more adults. The girls were a hundred or so, mainly from three to ten years of age; but in a separate and upper apartment ascending out of the main room, there were some forty adult women, with teachers exclusively of their own sex. The teachers were of various grades of capacity; but, as all teach without pay and under circumstances which forbid the idea of any other than philanthropic or religious attractiveness in the duty, they are all deserving of praise. The teaching is confined, I believe, to rudimental instruction in reading and spelling, and to historic, theologic and moral lessons from the Bible. As the doors are open, and every one who sees fit comes in, stays so long as he or she pleases, and then goes out, there is much confusion and bustle at times, but on the whole a satisfactory degree of order is preserved, and considerable, though very unequal, progress made by the pupils.

But such faces! such garments! such daguerreotypes of the superlative of human wretchedness and degradation! These pupils were gathered from among the outcasts of London—those who have no family ties, no homes, no education, no religious training, but were born to wander about the docks, picking up a chance job now and then, but acquiring no skill, no settled vocation, often compelled to steal or starve, and finally trained to regard the sheltered, well fed, and respected majority as their natural oppressors and their natural prey. Of this large class of vagrants, amounting in this city to thousands, Theft and (for the females) Harlotry, whenever the cost of a loaf of bread or a night's lodging could be procured by either, were as matter-of-course resorts for a livelihood as privateering, campaigning, distilling or (till recently) slave-trading was to many respected and well-to-do champions of Order and Conservatism throughout Christendom. And the outcasts have ten times the excuse for their moral blindness and their social misdeeds that their well-fed competitors in iniquity ever had. They have simply regarded the world as their oyster and tried to open its hard shells as they best could, not indicating thereby a special love of oysters but a craving appetite for food of some kind. It was oyster or nothing with them. And in the course of life thus forced upon them, the males who survived the period of infancy may have averaged twenty-five years of wretched, debased, brutal existence, while the females, of more delicate frame and subjected to additional evils, have usually died much younger. But the gallows, the charity hospitals, the prisons, the work-houses (refuges denied to the healthy and the unconvicted), with the unfenced kennels and hiding-places of the destitute during inclement weather, generally saw the earthly end of them all by the time that men in better circumstances have usually attained their prime. And all this has been going on unresisted and almost unnoticed for countless generations, in the very shadows of hundreds of church steeples, and in a city which pays millions of dollars annually for the support of Gospel ministrations. . . .

The School was dismissed, and every one requested to leave who did not choose to attend the prayer-meeting. No effort was made to induce any to stay—the contrary rather. I was surprised to see that three-fourths (I think) staid; though this was partly explained afterwards by the fact that by staying they had hopes of a night's lodging here and none elsewhere. That prayer-meeting was the most impressive and salutary religious service I have attended for many years. Four or five prayers were made by different teachers in succession—all chaste, appropriate, excellent, fervent, affecting. A Hymn was sung before and after each by the congregation—and well sung. Brief and cogent addresses were made by the superintendent and (I believe) an American visitor. Then the School was dismissed, and the pupils who had tickets permitting them to sleep in the dormitory below filed off in regular order to their several berths. The residue left the premises. We visiters were next permit-

ted to go down and see those who staid—of course only the ladies
being allowed to look into the apartment of the women. O the
sadness of that sight! There in the men's room were perhaps a
hundred men and boys, sitting up in their rags in little compartments of naked boards, each about half-way between a bread-tray
and a hog-trough, which, planted close to each other, were to be
their resting-places for the night, as they had been for several
previous nights. And this is a very recent and very blessed addition
to the School, made by the munificence of some noble woman, who
gave $500 expressly to fit up some kind of a sleeping-room, so that
those who had attended the School should not *all* be turned out (as a
part still necessarily are) to wander or lie all night in the always cold,
damp streets. There are not many hogs in America who are not
better lodged than these poor human brethren and sisters, who now
united, at the suggestion of the superintendent, in a hymn of praise
to God for all His mercies. Doubtless, many did so with an eye to the
shelter and hope of food (for each one who is permitted to stay here
has a bath and six ounces of bread allowed him in the morning); yet
when I contrasted this with the more formal and stately worship I
had attended at Westminster Abbey in the morning, the preponder-
ance was decidedly not in favor of the latter. . . .

Justice, Manly Dealing and Fair Play

Liverpool, Wednesday, August 6, 1851

I do not wholly like these cold and stately English, yet I think I am
not blind to their many sterling qualities. The greatness of England,
it is quite confidently asserted, is based upon her conquests and
plunderings—on her immense Commerce and unlimited Foreign
Possessions. I think otherwise. The English have qualities which
would have rendered them wealthy and powerful though they had
been located in the center of Asia instead of on the western coast of
Europe. I do not say that these qualities could have been developed
in Central Asia, but if they *had* been, they would have insured to
their possessors a commanding position. Personally, the English do
not attract nor shine; but collectively they are a race to make their
mark on the destinies of mankind.

In the first place, they are eminently *industrious*. I have seen no
country in which the proportion of idlers is smaller. I think American labor is more efficient, day to day or hour to hour, than British;
but we have the larger proportion of non-producers—petty clerks in

the small towns, men who live by their wits, loungers about bar-rooms, &c. There is here a small class of wealthy idlers not embrac-ing nearly *all* the wealthy, nor of the Aristocracy, by any means), and a more numerous class of idle paupers or criminals; but Work is the general rule, and the idlers constitute but a small proportion of the whole population. Great Britain is full of wealth, not entirely but mainly because her people are constantly producing. All that she has plundered in a century does not equal the new wealth produced by her people every year.

The English are eminently devotees of *Method* and *Economy*. I never saw the rule, "A place for everything, and everything in its place," so well observed as here. The reckless and the prodigal are found here as every where else, but they are marked exceptions. Nine-tenths of those who have a competence know what income they have, and are careful not to spend more. A Duchess will say to a mere acquaintance, "I cannot afford" a proposed outlay—an avowal rarely and reluctantly made by an American, even in moderate circumstances. She means simply that other demands upon her income are such as to forbid the contemplated expenditure, though she could of course afford this if she did not deem those of prior consequence. No Englishman is ashamed to be economical, nor to have it known that he is so. Whether his annual expenditure be fifty pounds or fifty thousand, he tries to get his money's worth. I have been admonished and instructed by the systematic economy which is practiced even in great houses. You never see a lighted candle set down carelessly and left to burn an hour or two to no purpose, as is so common with us; if you leave one burning, some one speedily comes and quietly extinguishes the flame. Said a friend: "You never see any paper in the streets here as you do in New-York (swept out of the stores, &c.) the English throw nothing away." We speak of the vast parks and lawns of the Aristocracy as so much land taken out of use and devoted to mere ostentation; but all that land is growing timber or furnishing pasturage—often both. The owner gratifies his taste or his pride by reserving it from cultivation, but he does not forget the main chance. So of his Fisheries and even Game-Preserves. Of course, there *are* noblemen who would scorn to sell their Venison or Partridges; but Game is abundant in the hotels and refectories—too much so for half of it to have been obtained by poaching. Few whose estates might yield them ten thousand a year are content with nine thousand.

The English are eminently a *practical* people. They have a living faith in the potency of the Horse-Guards, and in the maxim that

"Safe bind is sure find." They have a sincere affection for roast beef. They are quite sure "the mob" will do no harm if it is vigilantly watched and thoroughly overawed. Their obstreperous loyalty might seem inconsistent with this unideal character, but it is only seeming. When the portly and well-to-do Briton vociferates "God save the Queen!" with intense enthusiasm, he means "God save my estates, my rents, my shares, my consols, my expectations." The fervor of an Englishman's loyalty is usually in a direct ratio with the extent of his material possessions. The poor like the Queen personally, and like to gaze at royal pageantry; but they are not fanatically loyal. One who has seen Gen. Jackson or Harry Clay publicly enter New-York or any other city finds it hard to realize that the acclamations accorded on like occasions to Queen Victoria can really be deemed enthusiastic.

Gravity is a prominent feature of the English character. A hundred Englishmen of any class, forgathered for any purpose of conference or recreation, will have less merriment in the course of their sitting than a score of Frenchmen or Americans would have in a similar time. Hence it is generally remarked that the English of almost any class show to least advantage when attempting to enjoy themselves. They are as awkward at a frolic as a bear at a dance. Their manner of expressing themselves is literal and prosaic; the American tendency to hyperbole and exaggeration grates harshly on their ears. They can only account for it by a presumption of ill breeding on the part of the utterer. Forward lads and "fast" people are scarce and uncurrent here. A Western "screamer," eager to fight or drink, to run horses or shoot for a wager, and boasting that he had "the prettiest sister, the likeliest wife and the ugliest dog in all Kentuck," would be no where else so out of place and incomprehensible as in this country, no matter in what circle of society.

The *Women* of England, of whatever rank, studiously avoid peculiarities of dress or manner and repress idiosyncrasies of character. No where else that I have ever been could so keen an observer as Pope have written:

> Nothing so true as what you once let fall;
> Most women have no character at all.

Each essays to think, appear and speak as nearly according to the orthodox standard of Womanhood as possible. Hardly one who has any reputation to save could tolerate the idea of attending a Woman's Rights Convention or appearing in a Bloomer any more than that of standing on her head in the Haymarket or walking a tight-rope across the pit of Drury Lane. So far as I can judge, the ideas which underlie the Woman's Rights movement are not merely repugnant but utterly inconceivable to the great mass of English women, the last Westminster Review to the contrary notwithstanding.

I do not judge whether they are better or worse for this. Their conversation is certainly tamer and less piquant than that of the American or the French ladies. I think it evinces a less profound and varied culture than that of their German sisters; but none will deny them the possession of sterling and amiable qualities. Their physical development is unsurpassed, and for good reasons—their climate is mild and they take more exercise than our women do. Their fullness of bust is a topic of general admiration among the foreigners now so plentiful in England, and their complexions are marvelously fair and delicate. Except by a very few in Ireland, I have not seen them equaled. And, on the whole, I do not know that they are better mothers than the English, especially of the middle classes. . . .

I have said that the British are not in manner a winning people. Their self-conceit is the principal reason. They have solid and excellent qualities, but their self-complacency is exorbitant and unparalleled. The majority are not content with esteeming Marlborough and Wellington the greatest Generals and Nelson the first Admiral the world ever saw, but claim alike supremacy for their countrymen in every field of human effort. They deem Machinery and Manufactures, Railroads and Steamboats, essentially British products. They regard Morality and Philanthropy as in effect peculiar to "the fast anchored isle," and Liberty as an idea uncomprehended, certainly unrealized, any where else. They are horror-stricken at the toleration of Slavery in the United States, in seeming ignorance that our Congress has no power to abolish it and that their Parliament, which *had* ample power, refused to exercise it through generations down to the last quarter of a century. They cannot even consent to go to Heaven on a road common to other nations, but must seek admission through a private gate of their own, stoutly maintaining that their local Church is the very one founded by the Apostles, and that all others are more or less apostate and schismatic. Other Nations have their weak points—the French, Glory; the Spaniards, Orthodoxy; the Yankees, Rapacity; but Bull plunders India and murders Ireland, yet deems himself the mirror of Beneficence and feeds his self-righteousness by resolving not to fellowship slaveholders of a different fashion from himself; he is perpetually fighting and extending his possessions all over the globe, yet wondering that French and Russian ambition *will* keep the world always in hot water. Our Yankee self-conceit and self-laudation are immoderate; but nobody else is so perfect on all points—himself being the judge—as Bull.

There is one other aspect of the British character which impressed me unfavorably. Everything is conducted here with a sharp eye to business. For example, the manufacturing and trafficking classes are just now enamored of Free Trade—that is, freedom to buy raw staples and sell their fabrics all over the world—from which they expect all manner of National and individual benefits. In consequence, these classes seize every opportunity, however unsuitable, to commend that policy to the strangers now among them as dictated by wisdom, philanthropy and beneficence, and to stigmatize its opposite as impelled by narrow-minded selfishness and only upheld by prejudice and ignorance. The French widow who appended to the high-wrought eulogium engraved on her husband's tombstone that "His disconsolate widow still keeps the shop No. 16 Rue St. Denis," had not a keener eye to business than these apostles of the Economic faith. No consideration of time or place is regarded; in festive meetings, peace conventions, or gatherings of any kind, where men of various lands and views are notoriously congregated, and where no reply could be made without disturbing the harmony and distracting the attention of the assemblage, the disciples of Cobden are sure to interlard their harangues with advice to foreigners substantially thus—"N.B. Protection is a great humbug and great waste. Better abolish your tariffs, stop your factories and buy at our shops. We're the boys to give you thirteen pence for every shilling." I cannot say how this affected others, but to me it seemed hardly more ill-mannered than impolitic.

Yet the better qualities in the English character decidedly preponderate. Naturally, this people love justice, manly dealing, fair play; and though I think the shop-keeping attitude is unfavorable to this tendency, it has not effaced it. The English have too much pride to be tricky or shabby, even in the essentially corrupting relation of buyer and seller. And the Englishman who may be repulsive in his out-of-door intercourse or spirally inclined in his dealings, is generally tender and truthful in his home. There only is he seen to the best advantage. When the day's work is over and the welcome shelter of his domestic roof is attained, he husks off his formality with his great-coat and appears to his family and his friends in a character unknown to the outer world. The quiet comfort and heartfelt warmth of an English fireside must be felt to be appreciated. These

Britons, like our own people, are by nature not demonstrative; they do not greet their wives before strangers with a kiss, on returning from the day's business, as a Frenchman may do; and if very glad to see you on meeting, they are not likely to say so in words; but they cherish warm emotions under a hard crust of reserve and shyness, and lavish all their wealth of affection on the little band collected within the magic circle of Home.

HENRY TUCKERMAN:

ART IS

"AN EXOTIC PLANT IN ENGLAND"

1852

Henry Tuckerman is best remembered—if indeed he is remembered at all—for his pioneer book, *America and her Critics.* He was by profession a journalist and a man of letters, by avocation a traveler and a student of travel. After graduation from Harvard College he made the first of many trips abroad, this time to Italy, which was for long his favorite country. There in 1835 he wrote *The Italian Sketch Book*—somewhat in the style of Irving's *Sketch Book,* and there too, on a subsequent visit, a novel, *Isabel, or Sicily, a Pilgrimage.* Thereafter he settled down for some time as editor of the *Boston Miscellany of Literature and Fashion.* His *Month in England* came in 1852 and had the benefit of familiarity with Continental habits and institutions.

There is a culminating point in national life which is distinctive—an element of the social economy which is ideal, and forms the characteristic interest to a stranger. In Greece, it is especially architecture and statuary; in Italy, it is painting; in Germany, music; in France, military glory; in America, scenery; and, in Lon-

From Henry Tuckerman, *A Month in England* (New York, 1853), pp. 65–66, 159–163.

don, literature. Climate and necessity have much to do with this form of human development there. The sensitive and thoughtful are conscious of an unwonted pleasure from indoor life, where there is so little sunshine; and the sense of retirement is quickened in the midst of so great material activity. The feel of a carpet, the support of an arm-chair, and the sight of curtains and a fire, possess charms unknown where a gay street population, and gardens under a bright sky, make it a sacrifice to remain in the house. Within, there must be resources; where there is isolation, comfort is studied; domesticity engenders mental occupation; and hence the prolific authorship of the British metropolis. I realize, when housed in London, why it is a city so favorable to brain-work. The exciting transitions of temperature which keep transatlantic nerves on the stretch, are seldom experienced in that humid atmosphere. The prevalence of clouds is favorable to abstraction. The reserve and individuality of English life, surrounded but never invaded by the multitude, gives singular intensity to reflection; baffled without, we naturally seek excitement within; the electric current of thought and emotion flashes more readily because it is thus compressed; the spectacle of concentrated human life, and its daily panorama, incites the creative powers; we are not often won to vagrant moods by those alluring breezes that steal in at our casement at Rome, or tempted to stroll away from book and pen by the cheerful groups that enliven the sunny Boulevards; and therefore, according to the inevitable law of compensation, we build castles in the air in self-defence, and work veins of argument or seek pearls of expression, with rare patience, beneath the smoky canopy and amid the ceaseless hubbub of London. . . .

Comfort and utility are too exclusively the national ideal, for art to be other than an exotic plant in England; where it is an indigenous product, the result, though often exquisite, is limited. A few deservedly celebrated native artists illustrate this department of human culture; but they are comparatively isolated. In no broad sense can art be said to have attained the dignity of a national language, an expression and representation of the universal mind, as in ancient Greece, modern Italy, and Germany. The sense of beauty and devotion to the ideal, are rare exceptions, not normal phases of English character. As a general truth, it may be declared, that art flourishes in Great Britain socially as an aristocratic element; popularly, under a humorous guise; and professionally, in the lives of a small number of men of decided genius. The absence of taste is manifest, at once, in the dwellings, the costume, and the ordinary arrangements of life; and when a shape or a scene arrests the eye by its artistic merit, they are usually related to convenience and economy. In the landscape gardening, railway dépôts, cutlery, fire-places, bridges, pottery, and hay-ricks, we often see the most striking grace, appropriateness, and skill; but seldom do the same characteristics assert themselves in domestic architecture or statuary. A tunnel, brewery, or chintz pattern, are more significant of the national mind than exclusive forms of art. Beauty is chiefly allied to the service of trade and wealth. In vehicles and ship-building the Americans excel their brother utilitarians. As a use art is prolific in England, as an aspiration sterile. The superb private collections are made up almost entirely of foreign pictures; and these, from the fact of their being an individual luxury, instead of a popular blessing, as on the continent, testify, like the conservatories filled with tropical flowers, to a rare and costly gratification. Look at the history of national development in literature, and on the stage, and how exuberant is the product, and general the appreciation, compared with that which attends the fine arts.

We have been reproached with our absurd imitation of classic models in public buildings, designed for purposes of mere convenience or traffic; but there are more anomalies in stone in London than of wood in the cities of America; no specimens of incongruous architecture can outvie many of the churches of the British metropolis. Club-houses boast there the most expensive embellishment; Cruikshank is the most popular limner; the engraver often grows rich, while the historical painter is driven to suicidal despair. And, in the case of successful men of genius, in the higher branches of art, what is the process of their triumph over financial difficulties? that of noble patronage or academic favor. The most lucrative sphere of painting in England is portraiture; and to render it such, great ability must coincide with the endorsement of a clique, and the prestige of fashion. Reynolds and Lawrence were the oracles of the Royal Academy, and the pets of the aristocracy. Flaxman, Barry, and Gainsborough, were unappreciated while they lived. St. Paul's and Westminster Abbey are grand and memorable exceptions to the general dearth of architectural grandeur in a city of unequalled magnitude.

There are, too, special causes which limit the enjoyment of such art as does exist. To view pictures is a contemplative act, one which demands time and self-possession; and he who has once acquired the habit of musing, by the hour, in the tribune of the Florence gallery, or passing days in the halls of the Vatican, will scarcely endure twice the martyrdom of being led around by a gabbling *cicerone*, with a flock of other victims, to catch glimpses of the pictures in an English mansion. The very aspect of resorts intended to gratify taste, shows, to the practised eye, that art is not native here, nor "to the manner born." Compare a London arcade with the Palais Royal, the arrangement of goods in a shop in Regent street, and the manners of the attendant, with those encountered in the Rue Vivienne, or the Piazza San Marco; or a visit to the National Academy and the Louvre; how mean the surroundings, and commonplace the rooms of the one, and what magnificent saloons, and admirable order enchant you in the other. In Paris and Rome we seem to inhale an atmosphere of art; it is a portion of existence, a familiar necessity; in London it must be painfully sought, and when found, often affects us like the sight of an eastern prince, with silken robe and pearly coronet, dragged along in a triumphal procession of northern invaders.

The acquisition of the Cartoons of Raphael, and the Elgin marbles, is no more an evidence of national art, than the temporary deposite of the spoils of the Vatican in the Louvre. The best decorative art in the kingdom is of foreign origin; Verrio was born in Naples, Gibbons in Holland. It is to the achievements and dominant taste of a country that we must look for proofs of her artistic genius; and it is remarkable what a large number of painters in England have excelled in special qualities, and risen to a certain point, without ever attaining the completeness of power, and fertility of result, which distinguish the Italian, Spanish, and Flemish masters. In the portraits of Jackson, Ramsey, Hoppner, Owen, Copley, Harlow, Opie, and others, there are distinctive excellences, but, in few instances are they unaccompanied by serious defects; and all these painters are so inferior to Vandyke and Titian, as to have failed in establishing a world-renowned school of portraiture. In Allan, Romney, Northcote, Mortimer, Burnet, Raeburn, and others, who tried their skill in a broader sphere, is it not acknowledged that the executive faculty was too limited and unreliable, to do justice to their respective genius? The vague and sublime effects of Martin are among the few specimens of modern English art, that seem born of original inspiration. Haydon succeeded only in two or three instances, after countless experiments, as a disciple of high art. Indeed, it would seem, that the less ambitious the more successful, is the rule of art in England, as evinced in the depth of tone and aerial distances of the water-color painters, in such humble subjects as the "Corn-Field," and "Old Mill," of Constable, and the sweet pastoral views of Wilson and Collins.

WARREN ISHAM:
THE ABOMINATIONS OF
THE ENGLISH LEGAL SYSTEM

1853

Law and Justice in England Illustrated

That the civil code of English law, is, in its main features, in accordance with the principles of justice, is not to be denied, crooked and labyrynthine as are the highways which lead to the true result, and numerous as are the by-ways which lead off at every point, into the vast fields of error in which the great interests of justice are too often swamped.

This just and righteous code of English civil law, with certain rather uncomely *appendices,* has answered its purpose very well in this kingdom, which is to give the *color* of right to the most abominable system of oppression the world ever saw, the sturdy pillars of justice every where rising upon the view, to garnish the fabric.

But it is like *stealing the livery of heaven*—to cover an ulcerous carcass, the shame of whose nakedness would otherwise excite loathing and disgust. Under the broad shield of the law, every man, as "a free-born Englishman," is secure against the invasion of his rights. The tenant of the lowly hovel can eat his crust with as much security

From Warren Isham, *The Mud Cabin* (New York, 1853), pp. 262–271.

as the proudest peer can revel in his banqueting halls, Justice standing over them both alike with uplifted shield to protect.

It is not for Justice to trouble herself about matters of state—not for her to pry into the secrets of an organic structure of society, which has operated to throw the different classes of society heaven-wide asunder, and to subject the lower to the necessity of a standing destitution—all this is supposed to be far without the range of her optics, and to be separated from her jurisdiction by an impassable gulf.

The limits of her jurisdiction are all mapped out before her, and she is forbidden, under pain of expulsion from the kingdom, to overstep them. She is to take things as William the Conqueror left them in a semi-barbarous age, and keep them so. To this end she has been empowered to extend just protection enough to the humble poor, to keep them from being starved out and becoming extinct, which would be as great a calamity as to have them rise to circumstances of comfort and respectability; for, in either case, the foundations of society and of the government would be equally taken away, and the entire fabric come down with a crash.

And, after all, what benefit does the working man derive from the protection of law? In all the annals of British oppression, when and *where* was such a thing ever heard of as that a poor farm laborer availed himself of the law to recover his rights or avenge his wrongs? Never, and nowhere. Generally the paltry pittance allowed for his labor is promptly paid; but I have heard of cases where it was withheld, and the poor suffering wretches, instead of turning their eyes to the law for protection, only turned them to the work-house for refuge.

The reason is two-fold; in the first place, they are entirely destitute of the means to prosecute their rights, and they are thus met at the threshold with a physical impossibility. In the next place, they have not the *spirit* to do it, if they had the means, which amounts to a moral impossibility. *What!* a farm-laborer standing up in a court of law to vindicate his rights against his oppressor! Why, it would be a spectacle, I had almost said, which would fill all England with alarm for the safety of the institutions of the country.

And these are the "free-born Englishmen" who tread the *soil* of England, under the broad shield of *Magna Charta*—who cannot be hung or transported without a trial by jury, nor be cast into jail (where they would grow fat) without being entitled to the privilege of *habeas corpus*.

But I spoke of certain uncomely *appendices* to the common law of

England, in a way which conveyed a hint, that we need not even penetrate beneath the surface to discover very hideous things. Nor need we. It was not enough that the law was powerless for good to the poor starving laborer, and only efficient in protection to his oppressor; *special provisions* must be appended to it, to place the former still more at the mercy of the latter—*provisions* which would disgrace a barbarous age.

Take the game-laws for one example. By the provisions of these laws the landlord's game may overrun and destroy the crops of his tenant, and he not only has no remedy at law, but if he attempts to protect himself by destroying the game, he is liable to imprisonment, and, under certain circumstances, to transportation. Nor have these laws remained a dead letter upon the statute-book; they have been rigorously enforced, and as the penalty, many an industrious farmer has been sent to Botany Bay, and his family consigned to the workhouse. . . .

The following tragical case, which is only an illustration and confirmation of the above, was related to me on the most undoubted authority. In the near neighborhood of one of those magnificent parks, through which I have rambled with so much delight, a small farmer, who was entirely dependent upon the avails of his crops for the payment of his rent, and the support of his family, established himself. No sooner had his first crop made its appearance above the surface, than it was eaten down and totally destroyed by hundreds of rabbits from the park. He complained and entreated, but in vain. He planted his ground the second time, determined, if possible, to protect himself. He set snares, and thus caught many of the rabbits, but not enough to save his crop. In the mean time, the gamekeeper "got wind" of what was going on, prosecuted the humble tenant farmer, convicted and cast him into prison. And when the poor man had thus paid the penalty for his offence, and was set at liberty, he was prosecuted again by the inhuman landlord, for the rent of the very land on which his own rabbits had destroyed the crops, and again he was cast into prison, and his family sent to the workhouse. Where, in all the oppressions of earth, can be found greater atrocities than that?

You may call it an extreme case, or call it what you will, it is an example of the atrocities to which every tenant farmer in England is liable, and to which, according to the above authority, *thousands* of them fall victims.

But the other day, it was stated in the papers, that two fine boys, aged twelve and thirteen, were innocently diverting themselves, by putting their hands under the stones in the tail of a mill race, to feel after fish, and enjoying the sport of following them from one retreat to another; and while they were thus engaged in their merry pastime in "merrie England," they were pounced upon by the gamekeeper, hurried before the magistrate, and condemned to a month's imprisonment for an infraction of the game laws.

All over the kingdom there is constant trouble from this source. And then, think of the ship loads who are transported to a convict shore, (after the second or third offence,) for no higher crime than shooting a rabbit, to save themselves and families from starvation; or, it may be, to have a little sport, as well as "their superiors."

If it were not for these things—if, in traversing the country, you could only see stately palaces, and extended pleasure-grounds, variegated and beautified with gardens and parks, running streams and verdant groves, while the wild game were starting up and flitting away from before you at every step, the whole being rendered doubly attractive by hospitality and good cheer; and if, under the influence of some mysterious spell, the conviction could be wrought, that all these lovely and beautiful things were productive only of comfort and enjoyment, how changed would be the aspect of things upon this island, and what a charm would rest down upon it! But, alas! there breaks unbidden upon the pleasant reverie, the saddening thought, that it is the price of tears and blood; that to support one man in a style of princely ease, hundreds must suffer privation and want, and be liable to be cast into prison, and transported, with the brand of infamy upon them, to the other side of the globe, if they attempt to defend themselves against oppressions that would destroy them. . . .

What seem to us the stupidity of this people in submitting to such things, strikes us with wonder; but the secret of it is, that all their ideas of order, from their infancy up, have been associated with such a state of things. The first idea of order which breaks upon the opening mind of childhood and youth, as it comes echoing down from the powers above, is that the nobility and gentry are the corner-stone on which it rests, and that there could be no such thing as order, if there were no such corner-stone to uphold it. That is the plain English of the matter. This great first idea "grows with their growth and strengthens with their strength," until they come to look upon the poverty, wretchedness and woe, which follow in the train, as a necessary component part of the most perfect system of order the world ever saw. And if one gets his eyes a little open to the absurdity and folly of this idea, it is as much as his reputation and his peace are worth to avow it, for he is branded at once as an enemy to all order, and a promoter of discord, anarchy, and ruin.

But let us turn our eyes for a moment to the poor victim of the press-gang. See him as he is taking a careless stroll with a lover or sister, pounced upon by the merciless gang, ironed, and forced away, amid screams of agony which should move a heart of stone to sympathy. I have been told of instances of distress thus occasioned of the most heart-rending character—of the terrified victim being torn away, with a sister, lover, brother, father, or mother hanging in frenzy to his arm, screaming in vain for pity, and then sinking senseless to the earth. . . .

They say the impressment laws have been modified; but have they been repealed? who will say that? And how can they be modified so as essentially to change their character, without an absolute repeal? Let common sense answer that question. Let the next war answer it.

Take the laws of seizure, as another instance, or rather the setting aside of all law by a special dispensation in favor of the landlord, to enable him to seize the effects of the tenant, and sacrifice them to the highest bidder, to get his rent, without going through the ordinary process of law. That is taking the pound of flesh in good earnest. The more unfortunate the poor tenant is, the more liable of course he is to be pounced on; and the very implements, or stock, which he has purchased on credit, and not paid for, may be taken, and are often taken, to pay the landlord's rent, which is almost the same thing as taking them from an innocent third party. The enforcement of this landlord's law has contributed not a little to aggravate the distress, and stir up disturbance in Ireland. . . .

I have only given an inkling of the iniquity of this system; its abominations cry to heaven against the oppressor, and fearful is the account which stands over against him for final adjustment.

And now, in view of all these things, in the name of humanity, I ask, what has justice to do in England? what has her (so called) matchless civil code to do, so far as the working classes are concerned, but to uphold, as I said before, one of the most odious systems of oppression the world ever saw? Elude the real point at issue as we will, it comes to this, that the common law of England is not only powerless of protection to the poor man, but is absolutely armed against him, for the special benefit of his oppressors.

NATHANIEL HAWTHORNE
VIEWS OUR OLD HOME

1853–57

More fully than any other American except Henry James, Hawthorne confesses the ambivalence of the nineteenth-century American intellectual when he confronted the Mother Country. At times, especially in the published version of his English notebooks, which he called *Our Old Home*, Hawthorne is as romantic as Washington Irving himself; at times he is as acidulous as a John or Henry Adams. He was, as Henry James put it in his masterly essay on *Hawthorne*, "exquisitely provincial," and he carried his provincialism with him wherever he went, judging the English and later the Italian character by the standards of New England Puritanism, though with charity not characteristic of the Puritans. Lowell caught the essence of his character in one of the happiest of his portraits in *A Fable for Critics:*

> A frame so robust, with a nature so sweet,
> So earnest, so graceful, so lithe and so fleet,
> Is worth a descent from Olympus to meet.
> 'T is as if a rough oak that for ages had stood,
> With his gnarled bony branches like ribs of the wood,
> Should bloom, after cycles of struggle and scathe,
> With a single anemone trembly and rathe . . .

Hawthorne's visit to England, from 1853 to 1857, was in a sense fortuitous. He had been content, for the first half-century of his life, to put down his

From Nathaniel Hawthorne, *Our Old Home* (Boston, 1863), pp. 64–84, 327–361.

322

roots ever deeper in his native Salem, in Concord and Boston, and showed little desire to extend his horizons beyond that corner of the Bay Colony and State whose history and legends he had recreated by his rich imagination. But in 1852 Hawthorne's classmate from Bowdoin College, Franklin Pierce, was nominated for the presidency, and asked his old friend to write a campaign biography of him. Hawthorne did—good enough as such things go—and was rewarded for his contribution by appointment to the post of American consul at Liverpool, probably the most lucrative post in the American foreign service. During his four years as consul Hawthorne filled his note books with observations and commentary; from these he later quarried the articles which he published in the *Atlantic Monthly* and, eventually, in book form.

Hawthorne's revelation of English manners and character is, like most of his writing, at once penetrating and delicate; he sees everything, but much that he sees is presented obliquely. The prevalent note is one of affection, but there is sharpness, too, and resentment. Hawthorne's affection for the Mother Country was in large part a product of his own imagination rather than of his experiences in the harsh and ugly city of Liverpool. He was never quite at home in England, notwithstanding the title he gave his book, and he certainly did not embrace it uncritically, yet he could write that "almost always, in visiting such scenes as I have been attempting to describe, I had a singular sense of having been there before . . . This was . . . a delightful emotion, fluttering about me like a faint summer wind and filling my imagination with a thousand half-remembrances which looked as vivid as sunshine at a side glance, but faded quite away whenever I attempted to define and grasp them."

Hawthorne never quite came to terms with England; in a sense he knew it too well when he came to submit himself to the pleasures and excitements which a stranger might find, and which he himself found in Italy. It is revealing that though he was able to transcribe something of his Italian experience into one of the best of his novels, *The Marble Faun,* he was never able to use his English experiences in the same way, and left all three of his fictional interpretations of Americans in England unfinished at his death. As with other major commentators—Cooper, the Adamses, Henry James and Howells, his relationship with England was difficult and complex. He thought the English the most admirable of people, but deeply resented, on behalf of his countrymen, the Englishman's calm assurance of his superiority to all other peoples and his superciliousness towards America and Americans. "Not an Englishman of them all" he wrote in an oft-quoted sentence," ever spared America for courtesy's sake, or kindness," but he hastened to add, "nor in my opinion would it contribute in the least to any mutual advantage and comfort if we were to besmear each other all over with butter and honey." Like Emerson he was confident that the future belonged to the American branch of the English race (he never did take in that there were other Americans than British), and when he left England he entrusted his notebooks to an English friend with instructions that if not reclaimed the seals might be broken in the year 1900, "by which time England will probably be a minor republic under the protection of the United States. If my countrymen of that day partake in the least of my feelings, they will treat you generously."

Our Old Home appeared originally in a series of essays in the *Atlantic Monthly* in 1862 and in 1863. It was published in book form in 1863 with a dedication to Franklin Pierce, a bold and defiant gesture at a time when the ex-President was regarded as a Doughface—a Northern man with Southern sympathies. In this, as in all things, Hawthorne went his own way.

Leamington Spa: "A Singular Tenderness for Stone-incrusted Institutions"

Whether in street or suburb, Leamington may fairly be called beautiful, and, at some points, magnificent; but by and by you become doubtfully suspicious of a somewhat unreal finery: it is pretentious, though not glaringly so; it has been built with malice aforethought, as a place of gentility and enjoyment. Moreover, splendid as the houses look, and comfortable as they often are, there is a nameless something about them, betokening that they have not grown out of human hearts, but are the creations of a skilfully applied human intellect: no man has reared any one of them, whether stately or humble, to be his life-long residence, wherein to bring up his children, who are to inherit it as a home. They are nicely contrived lodging-houses, one and all—the best as well as the shabbiest of them—and therefore inevitably lack some nameless property that a home should have. This was the case with our own little snuggery in Lansdowne Circus, as with all the rest; it had not grown out of anybody's individual need, but was built to let or sell, and was therefore like a ready-made garment—a tolerable fit, but only tolerable.

All these blocks, ranges, and detached villas are adorned with the finest and most aristocratic names that I have found anywhere in England, except perhaps, in Bath, which is the great metropolis of that second-class gentility with which watering-places are chiefly populated. Lansdowne Crescent, Lansdowne Circus, Lansdowne Terrace, Regent Street, Warwick Street, Clarendon Street, the Upper and Lower Parade: such are a few of the designations. Parade, indeed, is a well-chosen name for the principal street, along which the population of the idle town draws itself out for daily review and display. I only wish that my descriptive powers would enable me to throw off a picture of the scene at a sunny noontide, individualizing each character with a touch; the great people alighting from their carriages at the principal shop-doors; the elderly ladies and infirm Indian officers drawn along in Bath-chairs; the comely, rather than pretty, English girls, with their deep, healthy bloom, which an American taste is apt to deem fitter for a milkmaid than for a lady; the mustached gentlemen with frogged surtouts and a military air; the nursemaids and chubby children, but no chubbier than our own, and scampering on slenderer legs; the sturdy figure of John Bull in all varieties and of all ages, but ever with the stamp of authenticity somewhere about him.

To say the truth, I have been holding the pen over my paper, purposing to write a descriptive paragraph or two about the throng on the principal Parade of Leamington, so arranging it as to present a sketch of the British out-of-door aspect on a morning walk of gentility; but I find no personages quite sufficiently distinct and individual in my memory to supply the materials of such a panorama. Oddly enough, the only figure that comes fairly forth to my mind's eye is that of a dowager, one of hundreds whom I used to marvel at, all over England, but who have scarcely a representative among our own ladies of autumnal life, so thin, careworn, and frail, as age usually makes the latter.

I have heard a good deal of the tenacity with which English ladies retain their personal beauty to a late period of life; but (not to suggest that an American eye needs use and cultivation before it can quite appreciate the charm of English beauty at any age) it strikes me that an English lady of fifty is apt to become a creature less refined and delicate, so far as her physique goes, than anything that we Western people class under the name of woman. She has an awful ponderosity of frame, not pulpy, like the looser development of our own few fat women, but massive with solid beef and streaky tallow; so that (though struggling manfully against the idea) you inevitably think of her as made up of steaks and sirloins. When she walks, her advance is elephantine. When she sits down, it is on a great round space of her Maker's footstool, where she looks as if nothing could ever move her. She imposes awe and respect by the muchness of her personality, to such a degree that you probably credit her with far greater moral and intellectual force than she can fairly claim. Her visage is usually grim and stern, seldom positively forbidding, yet calmly terrible, not merely by its breadth and weight of feature, but because it seems to express so much well-founded self-reliance, such acquaintance with the world, its toils, troubles, and dangers, and such sturdy capacity for trampling down a foe. Without anything positively salient, or actively offensive, or, indeed, unjustly formidable to her neighbors, she has the effect of a seventy-four gun-ship in time of peace; for, while you assure yourself that there is no real danger, you cannot help thinking how tremendous would be her onset if pugnaciously inclined, and how futile the effort to inflict any counter-injury. She certainly looks tenfold—nay, a hundred-fold—better able to take care of herself than our slender-framed and haggard womankind; but I have not found reason to suppose that the English dowager of fifty has actually greater courage, fortitude, and strength of character than our women of similar age, or even a tougher physical endurance than they. Morally, she is strong, I suspect, only in society, and in the common routine of social affairs, and would be found powerless and timid in any exceptional strait that might call for energy outside of the conventionalities amid which she has grown up.

You can meet this figure in the street, and live, and even smile at the recollection. But conceive of her in a ball-room, with the bare, brawny arms that she invariably displays there, and all the other corresponding development, such as is beautiful in the maiden blossom, but a spectacle to howl at in such an over-blown cabbage-rose as this.

Yet, somewhere in this enormous bulk there must be hidden the modest, slender, violet-nature of a girl whom an alien mass of earthliness has unkindly overgrown; for an English maiden in her teens, though seldom so pretty as our own damsels, possesses, to say the truth, a certain charm of half-blossom, and delicately folded leaves, and tender womanhood shielded by maidenly reserves, with which, somehow or other, our American girls often fail to adorn themselves during an appreciable moment. It is a pity that the English violet should grow into such an outrageously developed peony as I have attempted to describe. I wonder whether a middle-aged husband ought to be considered as legally married to all the

accretions that have overgrown the slenderness of his bride, since he
led her to the altar, and which make her so much more than he ever
bargained for! Is it not a sounder view of the case, that the matrimonial bond cannot be held to include the three fourths of the wife that
had no existence when the ceremony was performed? And as a
matter of conscience and good morals, ought not an English married pair to insist upon the celebration of a silver-wedding at the end
of twenty-five years, in order to legalize and mutually appropriate
that corporeal growth of which both parties have individually come
into possession since they were pronounced one flesh? . . .

You find old churches and villages in all the neighboring country, at the distance of every two or three miles; and I describe them,
not as being rare, but because they are so common and characteristic. The village of Whitnash, within twenty minutes' walk of
Leamington, looks as secluded, as rural, and as little disturbed by the
fashions of to-day, as if Dr. Jephson had never developed all those
Parades and Crescents out of his magic well. I used to wonder
whether the inhabitants had ever yet heard of railways, or, at their
slow rate of progress, had even reached the epoch of stage coaches.
As you approach the village, while it is yet unseen, you observe a tall,
overshadowing canopy of elm-tree tops, beneath which you almost
hesitate to follow the public road, on account of the remoteness that
seems to exist between the precincts of this old-world community
and the thronged modern street out of which you have so recently
emerged. Venturing onward, however, you soon find yourself in the
heart of Whitnash, and see an irregular ring of ancient rustic dwellings surrounding the village-green, on one side of which stands the
church, with its square Norman tower and battlements, while close
adjoining is the vicarage, made picturesque by peaks and gables. At
first glimpse, none of the houses appear to be less than two or three
centuries old, and they are of the ancient, wooden-framed fashion,
with thatched roofs, which give them the air of birds' nests, thereby
assimilating them closely to the simplicity of nature.

The church-tower is mossy and much gnawed by time; it has
narrow loopholes up and down its front and sides, and an arched
window over the low portal, set with small panes of glass, cracked,
dim, and irregular, through which a by-gone age is peeping out into
the day-light. Some of those old, grotesque faces, called gargoyles,
are seen on the projections of the architecture. The churchyard is
very small, and is encompassed by a gray stone fence that looks as
ancient as the church itself. In front of the tower, on the village-
green, is a yew-tree of incalculable age, with a vast circumference of

trunk, but a very scanty head of foliage; though its boughs still keep some of the vitality which, perhaps, was in its prime when the Saxon invaders founded Whitnash. A thousand years is no extraordinary antiquity in the lifetime of a yew. We were pleasantly startled, however, by discovering an exuberance of more youthful life than we had thought possible in so old a tree; for the faces of two children laughed at us out of an opening in the trunk, which had become hollow with long decay. On one side of the yew stood a framework of worm-eaten timber, the use and meaning of which puzzled me exceedingly, till I made it out to be the village-stocks; a public institution that, in its day, had doubtless hampered many a pair of shank-bones, now crumbling in the adjacent churchyard. It is not to be supposed, however, that this old-fashioned mode of punishment is still in vogue among the good people of Whitnash. The vicar of the parish has antiquarian propensities, and had probably dragged the stocks out of some dusty hiding-place and set them up on the former site as curiosity.

I disquiet myself in vain with the effort to hit upon some characteristic feature, or assemblage of features, that shall convey to the reader the influence of hoar antiquity lingering into the present daylight, as I so often felt it in these old English scenes. It is only an American who can feel it; and even he begins to find himself growing insensible to its effect, after a long residence in England. But while you are still new in the old country, it thrills you with strange emotion to think that this little church of Whitnash, humble as it seems, stood for ages under the Catholic faith, and has not materially changed since Wickliffe's days, and that it looked as gray as now in Bloody Mary's time, and that Cromwell's troopers broke off the stone noses of those same gargoyles that are now grinning in your face. So, too, with the immemorial yew-tree; you see its great roots grasping hold of the earth like gigantic claws, clinging so sturdily that no effort of time can wrench them away; and there being life in the old tree, you feel all the more as if a contemporary witness were telling you of the things that have been. It has lived among men, and been a familiar object to them, and seen them brought to be christened and married and buried in the neighboring church and churchyard, through so many centuries, that it knows all about our race, so far as fifty generations of the Whitnash people can supply such knowledge.

And, after all, what a weary life it must have been for the old tree! Tedious beyond imagination! Such, I think, is the final impression on the mind of an American visitor, when his delight at finding something permanent begins to yield to his Western love of change, and he becomes sensible of the heavy air of a spot where the forefathers and foremothers have grown up together, intermarried, and died, through a long succession of lives, without any intermixture of new elements, till family features and character are all run in the same inevitable mould. Life is there fossilized in its greenest leaf. The man who died yesterday or ever so long ago walks the village-street to-day, and chooses the same wife that he married a hundred years since, and must be buried again to-morrow under the same kindred dust that has already covered him half a score of times. The stone threshold of his cottage is worn away with his hobnailed footsteps, shuffling over it from the reign of the first Plantagenet to that of Victoria. Better than this is the lot of our restless countrymen, whose modern instinct bids them tend always towards "fresh woods and pastures new." Rather than such monotony of sluggish ages, loitering on a village-green, toiling in hereditary fields, listening to the parson's drone lengthened through centuries in the gray Norman church, let us welcome whatever change may come,—change of place, social customs, political institutions, modes of worship,—trusting that, if all present things shall vanish, they will but make room for better systems, and for a higher type of man to clothe his life in them, and to fling them off in turn.

Nevertheless, while an American willingly accepts growth and change as the law of his own national and private existence, he has a singular tenderness for the stone-incrusted institutions of the mother-country. The reason may be (though I should prefer a more generous explanation) that he recognizes the tendency of these hardened forms to stiffen her joints and fetter her ankles, in the race and rivalry of improvement. I hated to see so much as a twig of ivy wrenched away from an old wall in England. . . .

Almost always, in visiting such scenes as I have been attempting to describe, I had a singular sense of having been there before. The ivy-grown English churches (even that of Bebbington, the first that I beheld) were quite as familiar to me, when fresh from home, as the old wooden meeting-house in Salem, which used, on wintry Sabbaths, to be the frozen purgatory of my childhood. This was a bewildering, yet very delightful emotion fluttering about me like a faint summer wind, and filling my imagination with a thousand half-remembrances, which looked as vivid as sunshine at a side-glance, but faded quite away whenever I attempted to grasp and define them. Of course, the explanation of the mystery was, that history, poetry, and fiction, books of travel, and the talk of tourists, had given me pretty accurate preconceptions of the common objects of English scenery, and these, being long ago vivified by a youthful fancy, had insensibly taken their places among the images of things actually seen. Yet the illusion was often so powerful, that I almost doubted whether such airy remembrances might not be a sort of innate idea, the print of a recollection in some ancestral mind, transmitted, with fainter and fainter impress through several descents, to my own. I felt, indeed, like the stalwart progenitor in person, returning to the hereditary haunts after more than two hundred years, and finding the church, the hall, the farm-house, the cottage, hardly changed during his long absence—the same shady by-paths and hedge-lanes, the same veiled sky, and green lustre of the lawns and fields—while his own affinities for these things, a little obscured by disuse, were reviving at every step.

An American is not very apt to love the English people, as a whole, on whatever length of acquaintance. I fancy that they would value our regard, and even reciprocate it in their ungracious way, if we could give it to them in spite of all rebuffs; but they are beset by a curious and inevitable infelicity, which compels them, as it were, to keep up what they seem to consider a wholesome bitterness of feeling between themselves and all other nationalities, especially that of America. They will never confess it; nevertheless, it is as essential a tonic to them as their bitter ale. Therefore—and possibly, too, from a similar narrowness in his own character—an American seldom feels quite as if he were at home among the English people. If he do so, he has ceased to be an American. But it requires no long residence to make him love their island, and appreciate it as thoroughly as they themselves do. For my part, I used to wish that we could annex it, transferring their thirty millions of inhabitants to some convenient wilderness in the great West, and putting half or a quarter as many of ourselves in their places. The change would be beneficial to both parties. We, in our dry atmosphere, are getting too nervous, haggard, dyspeptic, extenuated, unsubstantial, theoretic, and need to be made grosser. John Bull, on the other hand, has grown bulbous, long-bodied, short-legged, heavy-witted, material, and, in a word, too intensely English. In a few more centuries he will be the earthliest creature that ever the earth saw. Heretofore Providence has obviated such a result by timely intermixtures of alien races with the old English stock; so that each successive conquest of England has proved a victory by the revivification and improvement of its native manhood. Cannot America and England hit upon some scheme to secure even greater advantages to both nations?

Glimpse of English Poverty:
"They Starve Patiently, Sicken Patiently, and Die Patiently"

Becoming an inhabitant of a great English town, I often turned aside from the prosperous thoroughfares (where the edifices, the shops, and the bustling crowd differed not so much from scenes with which I was familiar in my own country), and went designedly astray among precincts that reminded me of some of Dicken's grimiest pages. There I caught glimpses of a people and a mode of life that were comparatively new to my observation, a sort of sombre phantasmagoric spectacle, exceedingly undelightful to behold, yet involving a singular interest and even fascination in its ugliness.

Dirt, one would fancy, is plenty enough all over the world, being the symbolic accompaniment of the foul incrustation which began to settle over and bedim all earthly things as soon as Eve had bitten the apple; ever since which hapless epoch, her daughters have chiefly been engaged in a desperate and unavailing struggle to get rid of it. But the dirt of a poverty-stricken English street is a monstrosity unknown on our side of the Atlantic. It reigns supreme within its own limits, and is inconceivable everywhere beyond them. We enjoy the great advantage, that the brightness and dryness of our atmosphere keep everything clean that the sun shines upon, converting the larger portion of our impurities into transitory dust which the next wind can sweep away, in contrast with the damp, adhesive grime that incorporates itself with all surfaces (unless continually and painfully cleansed) in the chill moisture of the English air. Then the all-pervading smoke of the city, abundantly intermingled with the sable snow-flakes of bituminous coal, hovering overhead, descending, and alighting on pavements and rich architectural fronts, on the snowy muslin of the ladies, and the gentlemen's starched collars and shirt-bosoms, invests even the better streets in a half-mourning garb. It is beyond the resources of Wealth to keep the smut away from its premises or its own fingers' ends; and as for Poverty, it surrenders itself to the dark influence without a struggle. Along with disastrous circumstances, pinching need, adversity so lengthened out as to constitute the rule of life, there comes a certain chill depression of the spirits which seems especially to shudder at cold water. In view of so wretched a state of things, we accept the ancient Deluge not merely as an insulated phenomenon, but as a periodical necessity, and acknowledge that nothing less than such a general washing-day could suffice to cleanse the slovenly old world of its moral and material dirt.

Gin-shops, or what the English call spirit-vaults, are numerous in the vicinity of these poor streets, and are set off with the magnificence of gilded door-posts, tarnished by contact with the unclean customers who haunt there. Ragged children come thither with old shaving-mugs, or broken-nosed teapots, or any such makeshift receptacle, to get a little poison or madness for their parents, who deserve no better requital at their hands for having engendered them. Inconceivably sluttish women enter at noonday and stand at the counter among boon-companions of both sexes, stirring up misery and jollity in a bumper together, and quaffing off the mixture with a relish. As for the men, they lounge there continually, drinking till they are drunken,—drinking as long as they have a half-penny left, and then, as it seemed to me, waiting for a sixpenny miracle to be wrought in their pockets so as to enable them to be drunken again. Most of these establishments have a significant advertisement of "Beds," doubtless for the accommodation of their customers in the interval between one intoxication and the next. I never could find it in my heart, however, utterly to condemn these sad revellers, and should certainly wait till I had some better consolation to offer before depriving them of their dram of gin, though death itself were in the glass; for methought their poor souls needed such fiery stimulant to lift them a little way out of the smothering squalor of both their outward and interior life, giving them glimpses and suggestions, even if bewildering ones, of a spiritual existence that limited their present misery. The temperance-reformers unquestionably derive their commission from the Divine Beneficence, but have never been taken fully into its counsels. All may not be lost, though those good men fail. . . .

The population of these dismal abodes appeared to consider the sidewalks and middle of the street as their common hall. In a drama of low life, the unity of place might be arranged rigidly according to the classic rule, and the street be the one locality in which every scene and incident should occur. Courtship, quarrels, plot and counterplot, conspiracies for robbery and murder, family difficulties or agreements,—all such matters, I doubt not, are constantly discussed or transacted in this sky-roofed saloon, so regally hung with its sombre canopy of coal-smoke. Whatever the disadvantages of the English climate, the only comfortable or wholesome part of life, for the city poor, must be spent in the open air. The stifled and squalid rooms where they lie down at night, whole families and neighborhoods together, or sulkily elbow one another in the daytime, when a settled rain drives them within doors, are worse horrors than it is worth while (without a practical object in view) to admit into one's imagination. No wonder that they creep forth from the foul mystery of their interiors, stumble down from their garrets, or scramble up out of their cellars, on the upper step of which you may see the grimy housewife, before the shower is ended, letting the raindrops gutter down her visage; while her children (an impish progeny of cavernous recesses below the common sphere of humanity) swarm into the daylight and attain all that they know of personal purification in the nearest mud-puddle. It might almost make a man doubt the existence of his own soul, to observe how Nature has flung these little wretches into the street and left them there, so evidently regarding them as nothing worth, and how all mankind acquiesce in the great mother's estimate of her offspring. For, if they are to have no immortality, what superior claim can I assert for mine? And how difficult to believe that anything so precious as a germ of immortal growth can have been buried under this dirt-heap, plunged into this cesspool of misery and vice! As often as I beheld the scene, it affected me with surprise and loathsome interest, much resembling, though in a far intenser degree, the feeling with which, when a boy, I used to turn over a plank or an old log that had long lain on the damp ground, and found a vivacious multitude of unclean and devilish-looking insects scampering to and fro beneath it. Without an infinite faith, there seemed as much prospect of a blessed futurity for those hideous bugs and many-footed worms as for these brethren of our humanity and co-heirs of all our heavenly inheritance. Ah, what a mystery! Slowly, slowly, as after groping at the bottom of a deep, noisome, stagnant pool, my hope struggles upward to the surface, bearing the half-drowned body of a child along with it, and heaving it aloft for its life, and my own life, and all our lives. Unless these slime-clogged nostrils can be made capable of inhaling celestial air, I know not how the purest and most intellectual of us can reasonably expect ever to taste a breath of it. The whole question of eternity is staked there. If a single one of those helpless little ones be lost, the world is lost!

The women and children greatly preponderate in such places; the men probably wandering abroad in quest of that daily miracle, a dinner and a drink, or perhaps slumbering in the daylight that they may the better follow out their cat-like rambles through the dark. Here are women with young figures, but old, wrinkled, yellow faces, tanned and blear-eyed with the smoke which they cannot spare from their scanty fires,—it being too precious for its warmth to be swallowed by the chimney. Some of them sit on the doorsteps, nursing their unwashed babies at bosoms which we will glance aside from, for the sake of our mothers and all womanhood, because the fairest spectacle is here the foulest. Yet motherhood, in these dark abodes, is strangely identical with what we have all known it to be in the happiest homes. Nothing, as I remember, smote me with more grief and pity (all the more poignant because perplexingly entangled with an inclination to smile) than to hear a gaunt and ragged mother priding herself on the pretty ways of her ragged and skinny infant, just as a young matron might, when she invites her lady friends to admire her plump, whiterobed darling in the nursery. Indeed, no womanly characteristic seemed to have altogether perished out of these poor souls. It was the very same creature whose tender torments make the rapture of our young days, whom we love, cherish, and protect, and rely upon in life and death, and whom we delight to see beautify her beauty with rich robes and set it off with jewels, though now fantastically masquerading in a garb of tatters, wholly unfit for her to handle. I recognized her, over and over again, in the groups round a doorstep or in the descent of a cellar, chatting with prodigious earnestness about intangible trifles, laughing for a little jest, sympathizing at almost the same instant with one neighbor's sunshine and another's shadow; wise, simple, sly, and patient, yet easily perturbed, and breaking into small feminine ebullitions of spite, wrath, and jealousy, tornadoes of a moment, such as vary the social atmosphere of her silken-skirted sisters, though smothered into propriety by dint of a well-bred habit. Not that there was an absolute deficiency of good-breeding, even here. It often surprised me to witness a courtesy and deference among these ragged folks, which, having seen it, I did not thoroughly believe in, wondering whence it should have come. I am persuaded, however, that there were laws of intercourse which they never violated—a code of the cellar, the garret, the common staircase, the doorstep, and the pavement, which perhaps had as deep a foundation in natural fitness as the code of the drawing-room.

Yet again I doubt whether I may not have been uttering folly in the last two sentences, when I reflect how rude and rough these specimens of feminine character generally were. They had a readiness with their hands that reminded me of Molly Seagrim and other heroines in Fielding's novels. For example, I have seen a woman meet a man in the street, and, for no reason perceptible to me, suddenly clutch him by the hair and cuff his ears—an infliction which he bore with exemplary patience, only snatching the very earliest opportunity to take to his heels. Where a sharp tongue will not serve the purpose, they trust to the sharpness of their finger-nails, or incarnate a whole vocabulary of vituperative words in a resounding slap, or the downright blow of a doubled fist. All English people, I imagine, are influenced in a far greater degree than ourselves by this simple and honest tendency, in cases of disagreement, to batter one another's persons. . . .

In such disastrous circumstances as I have been attempting to describe, it was beautiful to observe what a mysterious efficacy still asserted itself in character. A woman, evidently poor as the poorest of her neighbors, would be knitting or sewing on the doorstep, just as fifty other women were; but round about her skirts (though wofully patched) you would be sensible of a certain sphere of decency, which, it seemed to me, could not have been kept more impregnable in the cosiest little sitting-room, where the teakettle on the hob was humming its good old song of domestic peace. Maidenhood had a similar power. The evil habit that grows upon us in this harsh world makes me faithless to my own better perceptions; and yet I have seen girls in these wretched streets, on whose virgin purity, judging merely from their impression on my instincts as they passed by, I should have deemed it safe, at the moment, to stake my life. The next moment, however, as the surrounding flood of moral uncleanness surged over their footsteps, I would not have staked a spike of thistle-down on the same wager. Yet the miracle was within the scope of Providence, which is equally wise and equally beneficent (even to those poor girls, though I acknowledge the fact without the remotest comprehension of the mode of it), whether they were pure or what we fellow-sinners call vile. Unless your faith be deep-rooted and of most vigorous growth, it is the safer way not to turn aside into this region so suggestive of miserable doubt. It was a place "with dreadful faces thronged," wrinkled and grim with vice and wretchedness; and, thinking over the line of Milton here quoted, I come to the conclusion that those ugly lineaments which startled Adam and Eve, as they looked backward to the closed gate of Paradise, were no fiends from the pit, but the more terrible foreshadowings of what so many of their descendants were to be. God help them, and us likewise, their brethren and sisters! Let me add, that, forlorn, ragged, careworn, hopeless, dirty, haggard, hungry, as they were, the most pitiful thing of all was to see the sort of patience with which they accented their lot, as if they had been born into the world for that and nothing else. Even the little children had this characteristic in as perfect development as their grandmothers. . . .

In these streets the belted and blue-coated policeman appears seldom in comparison with the frequency of his occurrence in more reputable thoroughfares. I used to think that the inhabitants would have ample time to murder one another, or any stranger, like myself, who might violate the filthy sanctities of the place, before the law could bring up its lumbering assistance. Nevertheless, there is a supervision; nor does the watchfulness of authority permit the populace to be tempted to any outbreak. Once, in a time of dearth, I noticed a ballad-singer going through the street hoarsely chanting some discordant strain in a provincial dialect, of which I could only make out that it addressed the sensibilities of the auditors on the score of starvation; but by his side stalked the policeman, offering no interference, but watchful to hear what this rough minstrel said or sang, and silence him, if his effusion threatened to prove too soul-stirring. In my judgment, however, there is little or no danger of that kind: they starve patiently, sicken patiently, die patiently, not through resignation, but a diseased flaccidity of hope. If ever they should do mischief to those above them, it will probably be by the communication of some destructive pestilence; for, so the medical men affirm, they suffer all the ordinary diseases with a degree of virulence elsewhere unknown, and keep among themselves traditionary plagues that have long ceased to afflict more fortunate societies. Charity herself gathers her robe about her to avoid their contact. It would be a dire revenge, indeed, if they were to prove their claims to be reckoned of one blood and nature with the noblest and wealthiest by compelling them to inhale death through the diffusion of their own poverty-poisoned atmosphere. . . .

I was once present at the wedding of some poor English people, and was deeply impressed by the spectacle, though by no means with such proud and delightful emotions as seem to have affected all England on the recent occasion of the marriage of its Prince. It was in the Cathedral at Manchester, a particularly black and grim old structure, into which I had stepped to examine some ancient and curious wood-carvings within the choir. The woman in attendance greeted me with a smile (which always glimmers forth on the feminine visage, I know not why, when a wedding is in question), and asked me to take a seat in the nave till some poor parties were married, it being the Easter holidays, and a good time for them to marry, because no fees would be demanded by the clergyman. I sat down accordingly, and soon the parson and his clerk appeared at the altar, and a considerable crowd of people made their entrance at a side-door, and ranged themselves in a long, huddled line across the chancel. They were my acquaintances of the poor streets, or persons in a precisely similar condition of life, and were now come to their marriage-ceremony in just such garbs as I had always seen them wear: the men in their loafer's coats, out at elbows, or their laborers' jackets, defaced with grimy toil; the women drawing their shabby shawls tighter about their shoulders, to hide the raggedness beneath; all of them unbrushed, unshaven, unwashed, uncombed, and wrinkled with penury and care; nothing virginlike in the brides, nor hopeful or energetic in the bridegrooms; they were, in short, the mere rags and tatters of the human race, whom some east-wind of evil omen, howling along the streets, had chanced to sweep together into an unfragrant heap. Each and all of them, conscious of his or her individual misery, had blundered into the strange miscalculation of supposing that they could lessen the sum of it by multiplying it into the misery of another person. All the couples (and it was difficult, in such a confused crowd, to compute exactly their number) stood up at once, and had execution done upon them in the lump, the clergyman addressing only small parts of the service to each individual pair, but so managing the larger portion as to include the whole company without the trouble of repetition. By this compendious contrivance, one would apprehend, he came dangerously near making every man and woman the husband or wife of every other; nor, perhaps, would he have perpetrated much additional mischief by the mistake; but, after receiving a benediction in common, they assorted themselves in their own fashion, as they only knew how, and departed to the garrets, or the cellars, or the unsheltered street-corners, where their honeymoon and subsequent lives were to be spent. The parson smiled decorously, the clerk and the sexton grinned broadly, the female attendant tittered almost aloud, and even the married parties seemed to see something exceedingly funny in the affair; but for my part, though generally apt enough to be tickled by a joke, I laid it away in my memory as one of the saddest sights I ever looked upon.

JOHN LOTHROP MOTLEY:

"MACAULAY'S CONVERSATION
IS THE PERFECTION OF
THE COMMONPLACE"

1858

Motley—Whose mother, Anna Lothrop, we have already met—is with Prescott and Parkman the most distinguished of American romantic historians; his *Rise of the Dutch Republic* won him an international reputation, one which has held up well with the passing years. As a young man Motley (like Bancroft) studied at Göttingen University, where he made the acquaintance of Otto von Bismarck, and he put something of that experience into his novel *Morton's Hope*. Motley's friendship with the powerful Senator Sumner won him appointment to the Court of Vienna; after five difficult years there Motley was promoted, as it were, to the Court of St. James's. He found himself in difficulties with President Grant, and was peremptorily recalled in 1870. This curious view of Macaulay is a product of an earlier visit to London.

From *The Correspondence of John Lothrop Motley*, George William Curtis, ed. (New York, 1889), I, pp. 236–237.

TO HIS WIFE

London, May 30th, 1858

My Dearest Mary:

On Monday I dined with the Mackintoshes. Macaulay, Dean Milman, and Mr. and Mrs. Farrar composed the party. Of course you would like a photograph of Macaulay, as faithfully as I can give it. He impressed me on the whole agreeably. To me, personally, he spoke courteously, respectfully, showed by allusion to the subject in various ways that he was quite aware of my book and its subject, although I doubt whether he had read it. He may have done so, but he manifested no special interest in me. I believe that he is troubled about his health (having a kind of bronchial or asthmatic cough), and that he rarely dines out now-a-days, so that it is perhaps a good deal of a compliment that he came on this occasion on purpose to meet me. His general appearance is singularly commonplace. I cannot describe him better than by saying he has exactly that kind of face and figure which by no possibility would be selected, out of even a very small number of persons, as those of a remarkable personage. He is of the middle height, neither above nor below it. The outline of his face in profile is rather good. The nose, very slightly aquiline, is well cut, and the expression of the mouth and chin agreeable. His hair is thin and silvery, and he looks a good deal older than many men of his years—for, if I am not mistaken, he is just as old as his century, like Cromwell, Balzac, Charles V., and other notorious individuals. Now those two impostors, so far as appearances go, Prescott and Mignet, who are sixty-two, look young enough, in comparison, to be Macaulay's sons. The face, to resume my description, seen in front, is blank, and as it were badly lighted. There is nothing luminous in the eye, nothing impressive in the brow. The forehead is spacious, but it is scooped entirely away in the region where benevolence ought to be, while beyond rise reverence, firmness and self-esteem, like Alps on Alps. The under eyelids are so swollen as almost to close the eyes, and it would be quite impossible to tell the colour of those orbs, and equally so, from the neutral tint of his hair and face, to say of what complexion he had originally been. His voice is agreeable, and its intonations delightful, although that is so common a gift with Englishmen as to be almost a national characteristic.

As usual, he took up the ribands of the conversation, and kept them in his own hand, driving wherever it suited him. I believe he is thought by many people a bore, and you remember that Sydney

Smith spoke of him as "our Tom, the greatest engine of social oppression in England." I should think he might be to those who wanted to talk also. I can imagine no better fun than to have Carlyle and himself meet accidentally at the same dinner-table with a small company. It would be like two locomotives, each with a long train, coming against each other at express speed. Both, I have no doubt, could be smashed into silence at the first collision. Macaulay, however, is not so dogmatic, or so outrageously absurd as Carlyle often is, neither is he half so grotesque or amusing. His whole manner has the smoothness and polished surface of the man of the world, the politician, and the new peer, spread over the man of letters within. I do not know that I can repeat any of his conversation, for there was nothing to excite very particular attention in its even flow. There was not a touch of Holmes's ever bubbling wit, imagination, enthusiasm, and arabesqueness. It is the perfection of the commonplace, without sparkle or flash, but at the same time always interesting and agreeable. I could listen to him with pleasure for an hour or two every day, and I have no doubt I should thence grow wiser every day, for his brain is full, as hardly any man's ever was, and his way of delivering himself is easy and fluent.

JAMES HOPPIN:

THE INERADICABLE SUSPICIOUSNESS

OF THE BRITISH CHARACTER

1859

The Reverend James Hoppin was a man of many talents, or at least of many interests. A graduate of Yale College in 1840, he took a law degree from Harvard then turned to the Ministry. He studied theology at home and in Germany for four years and in 1850 became minister of the Crombie State Congregational Church in Salem, Massachusetts. A long visit abroad in 1859 and 1860 produced (some years later) the immensely popular *Old England, Its Art and Scenery,* which by 1893 had gone through twelve editions. On his return to the United States Hoppin became professor at the Yale Divinity School and the Union Theological Seminary in New York. Tiring of theology he turned, in 1879 to art, becoming professor of art history at the Yale School of Fine Arts. When Hoppin published his book on Old England, England was in some disrepute with Americans because of her alleged support of the Confederacy. In his preface to *Old England* Hoppin says that he has published the book in the hope of "inducing our countrymen who go abroad to spend more time in England than they are commonly inclined to do and to see that country more thoroughly instead of making it a stepping stone to the Continent." It is not certain that his own report on the English character furthered this objective.

From James M. Hoppin, *Old England, Its Art and Scenery* (New York, 1867), pp. 100–110.

That genial though thorough Englishman, "Arthur Helps," has made the remark that temperament is but the atmosphere of character, while its groundwork in nature may be fixed and unchangeable. This remark might explain the difference between the Englishman and the American, looking at both in their broad national traits. It has been pleasant to me to think that deep down under all the changes of history and circumstance, there was a common root to the two nations, and that this still is to be found. The temperament of the American, since his ancestors landed in New England and Virginia, has been affected by a thousand new influences. More oxygen has flowed into his soul as well as his lungs. His nature has been intensified. His sympathies have found another range of objects. But, after all, it is hard to wash away the original basis of nature. Its force and integrity remain. What can be more different than a genuine Yankee and a true John Bull? Yes, we can say they are no longer the same; but still they do not differ as an Englishman differs from a Frenchman, or a German, or an Italian. Many unchangeable qualities belong to each, though transformed. . . .

There is one quality in the English character patent to all observers, which is one of its least worthy features—suspicion. Whether it be so or not, there is almost always an apparent suspicion of every thing, and of everybody, in his looks and conduct. He seems to be suspicious lest his right-hand neighbor is a thief, his left-hand neighbor an artful imposter, and the man who sits opposite him a humbug. Sometimes when one really supposes he is on terms of easy confidence with an Englishman, some trivial thing happens to rouse the old John Bull suspicion, and your pleasant and intelligent companion is instantly transformed into a lump of ice and formality. Perhaps the next time you meet him, he will either not know you, or you are so disgusted as not to know him. This suspicion has seemed to me sometimes to poison an Englishman's own happiness. I remember a little incident in riding from Mansfield to Chesterfield through the Robin Hood forest region. The weather was good, the roads smooth, and all the company seemed to be in excellent spirits. Two burly gentlemen in front of me took an especial liking to each other, and chatted, and joked, and laughed, till the groves and orchards rang again. Something, however, jarred suddenly in their conversation, the English suspicion seemed to creep up into their faces, they looked at each other askance, the conversation dropped, each buttoned up his top-coat, settled himself in his seat, and one felt that if any thing more occurred between the two, it would be to pitch each other off the coach. This little circumstance had an evident effect upon the whole company. Each one seemed to be reminded that *he,* too, had been too free with his neighbor with whom he had no previous acquaintance. It was in vain after this to attempt to raise a conversation, and rain coming on, the discomfort and wetting confirmed this unsociability for the rest of the ride, into downright savage taciturnity.

On arriving at an English inn, apparently the same chill suspicion meets one. A prim landlady receives the traveler and consigns him immediately to the laconic offices of "Boots." He is shut up alone in a sombre-looking parlor; is obliged to ring, and ring, and ring, for the most common and indispensable services; eats his dinner alone and in silence; and when he leaves is besieged by the insolent demands of three or four understrappers, to whom he is not aware of having been indebted for any assistance. But the trim and pleasant-looking landlady appears again at this moment of departure, with the invariable courteous commonplace, "I hope you have passed an agreeable time, sir!"

I have indeed sometimes amused myself with the idea, that a traveler entering an English inn is looked upon in the light of an intruder upon a private family circle. He can get little information by asking questions; is expected to keep his own room, to make as little noise as possible, and give as little trouble. In traveling in England, one meets with few pleasant personal adventures, because it is rare that an Englishman suffers you to assist him, or suffers himself to be interested in you. I asked an educated Englishman once what was the reason of this. He said it was English phlegm. John Bull wouldn't absolutely take the trouble to ask questions or answer them, to sympathize with others, or to strive to win others' sympathies. He prefers to sit still and tranquilly digest his plumpudding. It is hard for a genuine Englishman to meet a stranger, as a Frenchman does, on the neutral platform of well-bred indifference. He must either be cool or hearty, suspicious or all-confiding. I have found in traveling in England that if I could chastise my own intemperate nationality, and not let it stick out offensively, that I soon made friends with Englishmen, who, in the end, would volunteer more in reference to their own failings than I should ever have thought of producing to them. Mutual pride prevents Englishmen and Americans from seeing each others' good traits and positive resemblances. And all Englishmen are not disagreeable, neither are all Americans insufferable. There are the pleasantest and sweetest people in the world in both nations; so there are undoubtedly the most insolent and contemptible. . . . For myself, whenever I have had the good fortune and skill to open the English oyster, I have rarely failed of finding a pearl. Dr. Bushnell was about right when he said, that you must break an Englishman's head and walk in, and you would find most excellent accommodations.

WILLIAM EVERETT:

THE DRAWBACKS AND ADVANTAGES

OF LIFE ON THE CAM

1859–63

William Everett had the misfortune to be the son of a very great man; he was no more able to live up to his father's reputation than was his father, Edward Everett. On his graduation from Harvard College in 1859 Everett betook himself to Trinity College, Cambridge, where he read classics for four years; he returned to Harvard to take one of the first Ph.D.'s in classics granted in America, to teach briefly at that institution, and then to spend the rest of his life as headmaster of the Adams Academy in Quincy, Massachusetts. On the *Cam* was first presented as a series of lectures at the Lowell Institute. It remains, all in all, the best account by an American of life at Cambridge —more perspicacious, on the whole, than the somewhat better known *Five Years at an English University* by his fellow Trinity classicist, Charles Astor Bristed. Though much of what Everett recounts dates from the early sixties, it is curiously innocent of any impact of the war, and it seems preferable to ascribe it to the more peaceful decade of the fifties.

From William Everett, *On the Cam* (London, 1866), pp. 264–273.

The relations of the Universities to the nation are not in England exactly the same as they are in this country. Oxford and Cambridge do not stand quite on the same footing, as regards the professions, with Yale and Harvard. The chief aspect in which colleges are regarded throughout this country is as the training for certain professions called liberal. As far as the Church is concerned, Cambridge and Oxford are even more important to England than our colleges to us. In the profession of the Law, also, there is about the same proportion there as here of young men who first go through the University, and of those who begin their law studies directly with nothing but a school education. In the profession of medicine there is a vast difference. Here, the majority of regular practitioners have a University education; there, it is, I think, decidedly the reverse. The reason of this is, that the medical profession does not stand on a level with the bar, the pulpit, the senate, or the army, as a calling for young gentlemen, and this it is which sends the prospective physicians to be educated elsewhere. The University in England is essentially an aristocratic institution, more so even than here. The majority of persons who go there, go to obtain the education of a gentleman. I do not mean to say that there are not many, and many of the most distinguished of the University, who belong to the lower classes. But they go to the University because it at once puts them on a higher platform, because it gives them an entrance into the Church, much more honourable than any they can get elsewhere. The University or the military service of the country is the natural destination of all young gentlemen, and you know how much that name means in England, including the whole landed aristocracy, titled or untitled. Neither the medical nor the commercial professions, what we call generally "business," are considered proper for a young gentleman to engage in. The son of a nobleman, a baronet, a large landed proprietor, a clergyman, must if possible go into the University or the army or navy; any other destination after his school life is closed is derogatory. A few sons of bankers may be taken into their fathers' counting-houses; a few persons interested in government, who are in a very great hurry to make officials of their sons, will give them a place in a government office at once; but as a rule, the civil life of all gentlemen is begun at the University of Oxford or Cambridge. In particular, those who are to make Parliament, government business, or diplomacy, the occupation of their life—and you will remember that in England men select these as the occupation of their lives, without being dependent either on popular election or oratorical ability, and without studying any other profession—always begin by acquiring that knowledge of men, that practice in the ways of society, that habit of getting information from voluminous works, that practice in putting their knowledge on paper, which nothing but a University can give. And hence you will get an idea of the position that the Universities occupy in England; they are not places of popular education, they are not means for diffusing education among the people, but they are the head-quarters of polite literature and exact science, and the great training schools for the governing classes. And this is so felt throughout England, that a farmer, or a country attorney, or a doctor in a small town, feels that by sending his son to college he will give him a rank among his fellow-citizens he never could have had without, and give the name a new lustre that will go far in accomplishing an Englishman's dearest wish, the founding of a family.

The University, then, is rather an aristocratic than a popular institution, as far as its direct education is concerned. England, as is well known, is becoming a government of the people more and more every day; the popular influences are constantly pressing harder on the old aristocratic and royal establishments; and one would naturally suppose that this would diminish the credit in which the Universities are held. And, to a certain extent, this is true. Already the Church is thrown open to candidates not from the Universities; already the retaining attorneys have ceased to value a barrister on his having taken a high degree; already commerce, engineering, mechanical science, are arrogating to themselves places on the list of liberal occupations that the old professions are reluctantly obliged to concede to them. Just at this crisis, just as one would think that the old, abuse-eaten, expensive, exclusive Universities must give up the hold they have so long had on the people of England—just as some new instructors for the people are loudly called for, they—the old, the wornout, the antediluvian—have stepped into the breach, and declared, like King Richard to the mob, when their champion was slain, "We will be your instructors, we, your Universities." It had long been conceded that the plan of written examinations, at stated times, followed by published lists of the success of the respective candidates, was an excellent stimulus to study. Accordingly, the two Universities appoint examinations all over the country, in all the principal towns and cities. They choose, out of their most eminent members, a large body of examiners. Each draws up examination papers in his favourite subject: not only in the chosen subjects of college instruction, the Ancient Languages and Mathematics, but in the Modern Languages, French, German, and Italian; in the Sciences, Botany, and Zoology, and Geology, and Chemistry, and Natural Philosophy; in English Literature, and the development of our language; in Ancient and Modern History; and in Music. To these examinations all persons, producing proper certificates of age, &c, are cordially invited; they are examined in various classes, according to the degree of proficiency they profess; the results of the examinations are published; those who pass, with a certain degree of credit, examinations of certain difficulty, receive from the Universities the eminently pleasing and honourable title of Associate in Arts, and are at once marked out to the whole nation as young men who will do credit to their teachers and employers. In this way, just at the time when the credit and authority of Oxford and Cambridge might be supposed to be diminishing, they have leapt to their feet, clothed in all their ancient might, and, like the combatants in the arena of old, cast a net of affection and influence over all England, fine as silk, but strong as steel. I know of no more noble effort; whether we consider the difficulty of assimilating old forms to new ·men, or the prejudice against adapting essentially aristocratic and exclusive institutions to all classes, or the reluctance that men of letters, used to their dear old conventual life, would naturally have to expend their treasures among the people, and themselves go from town to town to assist in their diffusion—all these things being remembered, I know, I say, of no more noble effort in the annals of education, than the establishment, by Cambridge and Oxford, of these Middle-Class Examinations.

You see in this system the old character of the University religiously preserved. It does not afford these candidates instruction, but a stimulus to receive instruction; not teaching, but a test of teaching. It stretches its influence over them, not so much coming down to them, as drawing them to it. And it still preserves its old aristocratic character—it does not make itself any more an institution of the people, it makes, even in the degree it gives them, a distinction between them and its own proper children, who live in its walls; and several, who in their youth have passed these examinations, and been received Associates of Arts, afterwards enter the University and take the regular degree, as if dissatisfied with their partial reception into the ranks of the learned.

Hence you see precisely the position held by the Universities —offering their own instruction, in a course expensive, arduous, and in some respects exclusive, to all who are able to avail themselves, they extend their authority as autocrats of education over the whole body of the English people. This is essentially an aristocratic theory, however popularized it may be. It tends, in fact, to create and to ratify formally an aristocracy of learning; an aristocracy to which any one is eligible, but to which when once elected, he is separated from those who have not entered. There is no law to prevent all the worshippers from forcing their way to any part of the Temple, from the Court of the Gentiles to the Holy of Holies—but be his place at the moment where he will, he is walled off for the time being —walled out from the select ones who have gone yet farther, while the crowd beyond are walled out from him.

And while thus creating a class distinct from others, the University goes yet farther, and keeps up its connection with them through life. By its preference in all appointments to Church offices, or posts as school teachers; by the prior claim it gives for all government posts; by the lucrative and honourable offices in its own immediate gift, or that of its colleges; by the facility and pleasure of returning to its walls, and the security of finding old friends still living there at whatever age you return; by its immediate concern in Parliament and elections—by all these the children of the University are bound to their mother all over England. When the clergyman in your parish begins the service, you can tell at once from which University he comes by the colour of his silk hood, white and black for Cambridge, red and black for Oxford. Yes, the University spreads out her arms all over England, and drops the seed of power and strength in its remotest corners, springing up into the stateliest of trees, overtopping the lowlier plants. In the halls of the legislature, the offices of state, the very King's palace—in the parish church and the school-room, in the hearts of India, the snows of Canada, the wilds of Australia, still we find her children, "wherever the chosen race and sons of England worship" learning "they turn their faces towards her":

> If she but stretch her hand
> She heaves the gods, the ocean, and the land.

But though both the Universities are essentially aristocratic, essentially institutions for the governing classes, they are of very different characters. The governing classes in England may be divided into two very distinct parts, which for want of a better name, I may call the old and the new aristocracy, though these names, like all such general appellations, will not hold in all cases. The old aristocracy consists of the old families, whether bearing noble titles or not, that have been accustomed for centuries to hold rank as the governing class, and are slow to admit innovations in their habits, or additions to their number. It comprehends nearly that whole body of landed proprietors, who own the greater part of the soil of England, and to some extent still cling to the theory that England, the whole country, belongs to them; that a man who owns ten acres of land has actually more right to enjoy the institutions of the country than a man who owns two, no matter what the comparison may be in other respects.

The new aristocracy consists of those who are forcing themselves every year into the ranks of the old, by wealth acquired in trade or commerce, by distinction at the bar, or, by sheer force of character and strength of mind, ousting from their seats the old effete houses that have run their race, and ceased to be of use. You might not be able to tell the difference between the two classes on a mere sight of their houses and estates; but the least intercourse with them, the least practice in their ways of talking, would show you that the power of the English government, the authority which for eight centuries has been connected with wealth and hereditary rank, is no longer in the hands of a single, united body, but that the old nobility —including quite as much the squirearchy, the country gentlemen without title, as the peerage—has yielded very much ground to a new set of men who have risen to their places, some by one means, some by another, but all in virtue of the new English civilization, as different from the old as the royal family now on the throne is different from the Stuarts. It is this that has preserved the aristocracy, the nobility, the landed gentry so long, and is likely to preserve it so much longer—that as one by one the old families become effete, a new set of men, born of the people, come in to take their places. In some cases, the new men insensibly fill exactly the places of the old; like the Norman nobles who went to Ireland, and became more Celtic than the Celts themselves; they become more noble than the nobility, more conservative than the conservatives. This is eminently true of pure *parvenus,* men who suddenly acquire large fortunes by doubtful means, who are enabled by one bound from obscurity to step into large estates; they ape not only the style of living, but the style of thinking and talking of the old aristocracy, change a good plain Saxon name for a Norman one, to which everybody knows they have no right, and talk about the Conqueror, as if they were the king-making Neville himself. But those who, without such freaks of fortune, have risen by steady industry and force of character to take their place among the magnates of the land, generally show that they are of another breed than the haughty peers that sought to hold both houses of Parliament as their own appanage in 1832.

We may then fairly draw this somewhat rough line of distinction in the whole English aristocracy,—the whole class from whom the Universities are recruited; and there can be no doubt that in general the first, the old aristocracy, chiefly patronize Oxford; the second, the new aristocracy, hold by Cambridge. Not, of course, invariably; many of the great baronial houses have been for centuries devoted to Cambridge—Howards and Cavendishes and Spencers and Fitzwilliams; and much of the new blood, that has only been allowed to flow in legislative veins for a few years, gets its last touch of refinement and spiritualization in the foundations of Cardinal Wolsey and William of Wykeham. But take all England through, count the whole body of that wondrous upper class which has for so long maintained an undaunted front against despotism, against democracy, against invasion—that class to which the middle rank look with admiration and awe, the proletarians with dread and hatred, extending as it does from the fox-hunting baron or earl, whose remote ancestor stripped the crown from some imbecile Plantagenet, up or down as you please, to the renowned lawyer whose father was a barber or a blacksmith—of all this great class the wing attached to conservatism and the world that is past finds its congenial atmosphere in Oxford; the wing devoted to progress and the new world of thought is faithful to Cambridge. This is the allowed, the universal reputation of the two Universities—Oxford the conservative, Cambridge the progressive; Oxford the tory, Cambridge the whig; Oxford the loyal or the Jacobite, Cambridge the revolutionary or the Hanoverian. If Oxford has sometimes stood, as in 1688, on the side of progress and emancipation, it is because the hand of tyranny was laid on her vested rights that she sought to preserve. If Cambridge, as in the rebellion of 1715, sided with the court, the high nobility, the established order of things, it was because the established order of things was on the side of liberty, and the revolutionists aimed at the revival of tyranny. We can well conceive of such an inversion—we know that a loud cry of chivalry and aristocracy may well be the watchword of rebellion, and that the devoted friend of progress and republicanism may give his life to uphold order and law. At the time of the Pretender's rebellion, the king quartered some troops at Oxford, at the same that he made a present of books to Cambridge. An Oxford muse, smarting under the imputation of disloyalty to the upstart German house, perpetrated this epigram on the two royal acts.

> Our royal master saw, with equal eyes,
> The wants of both his Universities;
> Troops he to Oxford sent, and reason why,—
> That learned body wanted loyalty;
> But sent his books to Cambridge, as discerning
> That that right loyal body wanted learning.

Sir William Browne, a distinguished Cambridge scholar, seeing deeper into the real feeling of the two institutions, and knowing full well what the habits and minds of Oxford men were, answered it by this still more condensed and pithy verse.

> The king to Oxford sent his troop of horse,
> For Tories own no argument but force;
> With equal care to Cambridge books he sent,
> For Whigs allow no force but argument.

Yes! It is not always safe to take the opinion of a corporate body about itself; but if there is one thing certain in the history of England, if there is one thing conceded by all parties, it is that Cambridge is the Whig University, the Liberal University, the home of advanced principles of government in all ages. I know that at Oxford there are abundance, particularly at this very moment, of noble and liberal-minded men. Perhaps at this instant, the views of her leaders are somewhat in advance of those of Cambridge. I know, too, that at Cambridge is many an old Tory, and bigoted divine. But on the whole, in the aggregate, the spirit of progress, the spirit of liberty, the spirit of free thought, that bids defiance to musty enactments, and antiquated ideas, and effete principles and abuses—this spirit, which, with all her prejudices, with all her obstinacy, with all her arrogance, is still the glory of England—this heavenly spirit still breathes strong and clear from the airy courts of Trinity, it sounds like a rushing mighty wind across the valley of the Cam, it peals in celestial tones from the organ of King's.

I need no better proof of this than the consideration of the present ministry and opposition in England. Lord Derby, the only leader under whom the Tories have a chance of power, is Chancellor of the University of Oxford. Lord Palmerston, the only man who can hold together all sections of the Liberal party, was formerly in Parliament from the University of Cambridge. I know I shall be told that Mr. Gladstone, the liberal Chancellor of the Exchequer, is member for the University of Oxford, and that Spencer Walpole, the Secretary for the Home Department under Lord Derby, is a member for the University of Cambridge. But I also know that when Mr. Gladstone left Oxford, he left it an arrant Tory, and that his views have undergone a steady modification in the liberal direction, and I know that Spencer Walpole is the most liberal and advanced of the conservative party, and sadly out of place with such antediluvians as his coadjutors.

Yes, let me repeat again, till the halls ring with the delightful sound, Cambridge is the liberal University, Cambridge is the camp from which the blast of progress has pealed through the ages.

1860-1870

HENRY ADAMS
DISCUSSES THE BLOCKADE
WITH MANCHESTER BUSINESSMEN

1861

The shadow of the American Civil War stretches across the whole of the sixties and, indeed, well beyond. To most Americans the issues of that war seemed as clear as the issues of World War II seemed to the British in 1939: the perpetuation of the Union, the destruction of Negro slavery, and the vindication of democratic government. Northerners—and it was generally they who visited Britain—could no more understand why Britain failed to see the nature of the war and to support the cause of the Union than British could have understood an American failure to see the nature of the crisis of 1939 and rally to the support of Britain. The British working classes did, and a good many middle-class intellectuals and liberals—John Bright, for example, and Leslie Stephen and John Stuart Mill—but the attitude of the government was one of frigidly correct neutrality but open sympathy with the Confederacy, and that of most of the aristocracy—and of the powerful London *Times*—one of sullen hostility to the North and admiration and enthusiasm for the South.

From "Henry Adams' 'Diary of a Visit to Manchester,'" Arthur Silver, ed. *American Historical Review*, October, 1945, pp. 79–89.

Two problems threatened to plunge the two great English-speaking nations into war. The first was the forcible removal of the Confederate emissaries Mason and Slidell from the *Trent* by Captain Wilkes—just the sort of thing the British had done with impunity during the Napoleonic Wars, but something they were quite unprepared to permit the United States to do. The second was the issue of the blockade—for the first year or two pretty much a paper blockade—which Lincoln had proclaimed for the whole of the Confederacy and which powerful interests in Britain proposed to break.

Young Henry Adams—he was still in his early twenties—was secretary to his father, Minister to the Court of St. James's, during the whole of the Civil War. An admirer of France and Italy, he had inherited some of the traditional Adams suspicion of Britain; passionately devoted to the cause of the Union, he was inclined to exaggerate British sympathy with the South; envious of his brother, Charles Francis, Jr., an officer in the Union ranks and fighting in Virginia, he was eager to make a contribution to the Union cause. For some time he had been contributing letters on the British scene, anonymously of course, to the *New York Times,* and some to London papers too. In November of '61 he embraced an opportunity to visit Manchester, whose textile industries depended heavily on southern cotton; he wished to ascertain for himself what were the chances of pressure from Manchester for breaking the Union blockade. By luck he arrived in Manchester the day Captain Wilkes boarded the *Trent.* He sent off his letter on Manchester to the *Atlantic Monthly,* but it came too late for publication; they turned it over to the *Boston Courier,* which published it December 16 under his name—a capital error. Soon the London *Times* picked it up and did not fail to criticize what appeared to be a breach of diplomatic manners. That put an end to young Adams's journalistic contributions from London, though later, in his famous *Education of Henry Adams,* he had a great deal to say about the role of England and the English during the War. In time Adams overcame his original dislike of England and became something of an Anglophile. As he says in the *Education:*

> London had become his vice. He loved his houses, his haunts, his habits, and even his hansom cabs. He loved growling like an Englishman, and going into society where he knew not a face, and cared not a straw . . . He had become English to the point of sharing their petty social divisions, their dislikes and prejudices against each other; he took England no longer with the awe of an American youth, but with the habit of an old and worn suit of clothes. As far as he knew this was all that England meant by special education.

Manchester, 8th Nov., 1861. Left London . . . in the five o'clock train by the Great Northern, from the station at King's Cross. With two fellow passengers, who were busily engaged in talking all the way to each other, I passed the tedious five hours and a half which lie between London and this city. We were true to our time, however, and before eleven I was on the doorstep of Mr. Stcll, who has so kindly offered to take charge of me for a few days; and a good fire, some supper and a cup of tea soon set me up again. We discussed politics a little while over a cigar, and I began at once on one part of my errand, by asking what was the feeling among the solid people of Manchester towards the North. My host evidently thought it not at all what it should be. He thought it was generally unfriendly and even hostile, but did not deny that the radical party, the Brights and Cobdens of Manchester, who have large influence are with us. The factories are running short time, or are wholly closed, and the operatives will, as a rule, have to be supported. We had a half hour of this talk, and then retired to bed.

Saturday, 9th Nov. . . . My host now came to start me on my labors, and we went together to the office of Mr. ———, a large commission merchant on whom I had a letter. I was received very kindly, and we had a talk of some length on the two subjects about which I was curious.

"My informants," I was assured, "were wrong in telling me that the people of Manchester wished the government to break the blockade. There was not a man of position in Manchester who would venture to say to Lord Palmerston, 'interfere for the cotton;' not a man; of that I might feel assured. Nor would Manchester give any encouragement now to any party which made the infraction of the blockade its war cry. If such a party existed, it was in Liverpool alone, and among the cotton-factors and persons connected immediately with the South.

"The present pressure on the spinners is an excellent thing, provided it does not last too long. They have forced such a quantity of goods on the market that in India certain classes of their fabrics are selling at a quarter below cost; the markets are supplied there for three months, and if the American trouble had not occured so as to check the rate of production, a disastrous financial panic must have taken place very soon. This, and not the want of cotton, is, in fact, the real difficulty now; for, though the spinners have reduced their rate of consumption one-third, they do not, even at that, sell more than a half of what they spin, and are forced to store the rest. He himself, though he had general orders to buy goods at discretion, was not buying at all. This, he considered, was proof that as yet the real difficulty lay not in want of raw cotton, but in the enormous quantity of unsalable goods.

"Still further, the stock of raw cotton in the market is held almost entirely by speculators. Except by special orders, spinners have not bought at the high prices, and even the speculators show their belief that cotton will come, by the cautiousness of their operations. All that is wanted to bring cotton in abundance into the market, was certainty that the blockade would last, and that American cotton would not come this winter. The instant this became certain, the trouble would end." I suggested that it lay in their own hands to produce the certainty; that a duty laid on slave-grown cotton would answer the purpose. He assented to this. "A duty of a half-penny a pound on American cotton would bring supplies from all parts of the world. But the measure was impossible, because neither the government nor the country would consent to such a violation of free-trade principles, merely for the benefit of Manchester. The whole nation at large dislikes Manchester, and is jealous of its growing influence. It would never permit such an infraction of principle on the mere pressure of the cotton interests."

Mr. ——'s partner happened to enter the room while we were talking, and was appealed to as authority on the question whether there were really any feeling in Manchester in favor of obtaining cotton at any risk. He hesitated, and was not so positive in denying it. He stated that he had no doubt if such a feeling existed now, it was among few people, and to no great extent. But he expressed a doubt as to what might be the turn of feeling, when the pressure was more directly felt. In other words, when the present stock of goods is used up, which will be in about two or three months, and the price of the manufactured articles rises to a point corresponding to the price of raw cotton, so that the spinner feels that vast amounts of money are to be made, then, and not till then, a party may be expected to appear in Manchester, which will demand the opening of the cotton ports. "But I might be certain that such a party would meet very warm opposition; at all events, there would be a hot contest."

This I believe to be the truth of the matter, and the real answer to one of the questions that I came here to ask about. So far as the cotton interests of Manchester are concerned, our Government will have two months more full swing over the South. At the end of that time, a party will arise in favor of ending the war by recognizing the insurgents, and, if necessary, breaking the blockade or declaring it ineffective. The radicals, the Indian and Colonial interests, and some others, will oppose the step, and there will be a severe contest; all supposing that affairs on our side remain in about their present position.

Some further discussion then took place on the probable results of the war, and its effects on trade. Mr. —— remarked that it was curious that the English had not yet really begun to appreciate the fact that there was a war. Very few of them saw that a great revolution in trade and commerce was already beginning to take place. In the final contest between free and slave labor, which has now broken out, few men are provident enough to be aware that the whole arrangement of the world's relations will have to find a readjustment, which will carry civilization and wealth to barbarous lands, and reduce civilized countries to barbarism. The whole balance is shifting. *Gare la dessous!* There can be no settled peace between freedom and slavery, till slavery has gone to the wall. . . .

Saturday is a half-holiday in Manchester, and I was not able to visit any of the mills or to see any more of the gentlemen I had letters for. So I hunted up my host again, and he took me up to the —— Club. Here I was introduced to several persons; one of them a very intelligent man, in the firm of —— & Company, large spinners, who have mills not far from the city. We had a good deal of talk together. I brought up the question of the blockade again, mentioning the fact that the belief in America was very general that England meant to break it, and that this belief had caused most of the irritation that existed there against England. It was the lowness of the motives that had disgusted us. He declared that the idea was ridiculous, and that *no one* contemplated it in the present position of affairs. But, then, if the war drags itself out indefinitely, to the loss and suffering of the rest of the world, and it becomes evident that neither party will yield and that a settlement is hopeless, then an intervention may take place for the benefit of foreign nations and mankind. I remarked that this was a dangerous latitude to allow, when the same party who judged the cause was to profit by the decision. He went on: "But such a latitude is a necessity. The world must, of course, have a right to decide where it considers its interests to overbalance those of a single nation. Suppose that the Southerners instead of a partial monopoly of cotton had a complete monopoly of grain of all kinds, and the world was to be famished by the blockade, would not intervention be justifiable? Suppose it were England instead of the North, who maintained the blockade, would not France interfere, and could England soberly blame her for doing so? There is no disposition in England to refuse to the Union a full and fair trial; but if, after what is evident to be such a trial, no step has been gained towards a settlement, foreign nations have a right to interfere, at least by a recognition of the South." This is not to be denied, I believe, in law, and yet it leaves the whole question as unsettled as ever. "Most

Englishmen," he stated, "would, no doubt, prefer to see a separation accomplished, yet this neither implies sympathy with the South nor hostile measures towards the North. It is a mere matter of private opinion." I assured him that on that point England was perfectly welcome to think what she liked. Her opinions were of no consequence to us, except as they indicated her actions. She had thought it her interest to weaken France and strengthen Austria, but instead of that it was Austria that was falling to pieces, and France that was stronger than ever, and I saw no reason why her policy should be more successful in America than in Europe.

After luncheon, we smoked a cigar, and discussed cotton. He talked of the Surat cotton, and stated that since the cotton pressure had begun, much more [Indian] attention had been paid to it, and the spinners had been surprised to find how well it answered their purposes. He was confident that already, whatever might be the fate of the American crop, Indian cotton had obtained a position and a hold upon the market that it would not lose. Whatever might happen, the cotton-trade never would go back to the old channels.

Sunday, 11th Nov. Manchester society seems to be much more like what one finds in American cities than like that of London. In Manchester as in America it seems to have fallen, or be falling, wholly into the hands of the young, unmarried people. In London the Court gives it dignity and tone, and the houses into which an admission is thought of most value, are generally apt to slight dancing. In Manchester, I am told, it is still the fashion for the hosts to see that their guests enjoy themselves. In London the guests shift for themselves, and a stranger had better depart at once as soon as he has looked at the family pictures. In Manchester one is usually allowed a dressing room at an evening party. In London a gentleman has to take his chance of going into the little ball room with his hair on end or his cravat untied. In Manchester it is still the fashion to finish balls with showy suppers, which form the great test of the evening period. In London one is regaled with thimbles full of ice-cream and hard seed cakes. I presume the same or similar differences run through all the great provincial towns. London society is a distinct thing, which the provinces are sensible not to try to imitate.

Monday, 12th November. To town about eleven. Delivered another of my letters, and the gentleman, hearing that I was anxious to see the great cotton show, sent me under the direction of a clerk to a mill in the city where they were spinning it entirely. . . . I was shown the whole process, as [is] usual in visiting mills, but there was nothing new to remark. The operatives were dirty, very coarsely dressed, and very stupid in looks; altogether much inferior to the American standard. About a quarter of the spindles were silent and as they told me, a corresponding number of the operatives discharged, to starve as they best might. . . .

The next visit was on the other tack. My host took me on Change and introduced me to Mr. ——, one of the M. P.'s for ——, an elderly man, with a very pleasing and dignified manner, who received me with much courtesy, and to whom I put at once the question which seems so difficult to obtain a thoroughly definite answer to. I stated that a great deal of doubt and contradiction existed as to the real attitude of Manchester towards our struggle in America, and I was anxious to learn from a really reliable source, what it was, and whether it were true that a party was forming there which intended to press the breaking of our blockade. The answer was certainly as frank and clear as anyone could wish. He assured me that he believed the feeling in Manchester to be one of sympathy with the Union, and of regret that the effort at this solution had ever been made. He knew of no party in Manchester forming to bring about the infraction of the blockade by Great Britain, nor did he believe that such a party could be created here or elsewhere. On the contrary, he believed he might tell me, that within a short time it had been proposed among some of the men of position in the city to make a public demonstration of sympathy with the North. The disposition was of good will towards us. I replied that it was very agreeable to hear this statement, on such good authority, and I was sure that any public declaration of good will would have a great effect in America where precisely the contrary belief had been preached, until it was looked upon as a matter of fact, beyond a shadow of doubt, that Manchester was bitterly hostile to us. The conversation lasted about fifteen minutes, and nothing could be more distinct than the statement which he made; nor do I know where to go for better authority on such a question.

Determined, however, to obtain all the information possible, I asked my host to introduce me to the Editor of the Manchester——. He took me accordingly, to the office of this journal, and to him I addressed the same question and received precisely the same reply. Yet he did not deny that it was not impossible, if the blockade lasted sufficiently long, that there might, in the course of the winter be an effort made to force the government to declare the blockade of one or two ports to be ineffectual. If the people grew restless and cotton failed to come, such a result might occur. He did not believe it would be possible to induce Parliament to lay a duty on slave-grown cotton; it would be in the teeth of all their principles. I remarked that it seemed to be a question between breaking the law of free trade and breaking the law of nations. But he said that the process was not likely to be contrary to the law of nations. It was clear that no blockade on a large scale could be perfect, and there must always be a loophole to crawl through if it were needed. As yet, however, this was mere speculation, and all would depend on the course things took. The ministry were well disposed towards us, he believed, and so was the majority of the nation; but the ministry were hard pressed at home, and any accident on our side might complicate matters exceedingly.

All these statements tend only the more to show that the conclusion I came to on Saturday, was the correct one. As yet, we need fear no active hostility from Manchester, but so soon as the mills can again be worked at a profit, difficulty and a hot contest may be expected, which will grow intense in proportion as the prospect of money-making increases. But in spite of their present assertions I think that in such a case the radicals, the anti-slavery interests, and the colonies, would unite in prefering a prohibitive duty, if necessary, to a war.

Wednesday, 13th November.... Such is the present position of this cotton question in Manchester. It cannot be doubted that if the blockade continues, Spring will find England nearly independent of America for this article, and we shall see the steady advances of a great revolution in the world's condition. Matters can never go back to where they were a year ago. Yet America can always compete with any country in the production of this staple, and no one wishes to see her unable to do so. All that is wanted is to open competition, and then the slave power may again be curbed to its due position in politics, while the shores of Africa may be made the scene of a new civilization, and India may rise again to her old wealth and glory. Some persons complain that such an event would be the ruin of the United States: that it would destroy the balance of trade and make America hopelessly the debtor of Europe. Why this should be so does not appear. A nation, like a private person, is wealthy and prosperous, not in proportion to what it receives but to what it spends. If our Civil War has taught us one fact with certainty, it is this: that our imports may be cut down with safety and even advantage, one hundred millions of dollars. If our receipts from cotton were lowered fifty millions we might still be rich; but though we exported cotton enough to pave our streets with gold, we should still be poor if we went on in that reckless extravagance which has already three times thrown the nation into bankrupcy.

Returned to London by the North Western in the evening, arriving safely before ten o'clock.

CHARLES FRANCIS AND HENRY ADAMS
TRACE THE PATTERN OF ENGLISH OPINION
ON THE AMERICAN CIVIL WAR

1862–65

Early in 1861 President Lincoln appointed Charles Francis Adams—son and grandson of former Presidents and himself a candidate for the presidency on two occasions—to the post of Minister to Britain, a position both his father and his grandfather had held. It was an appointment of historic significance, for as it turned out, the outcome of the Civil War depended in large part on the attitude and conduct of Great Britain, and it was Adams, rather than Secretary of State William Seward, who interpreted, moderated, and guided that attitude.

The South's gamble for independence was by no means a desperate one. It was based, rather, on wholly reasonable assumptions which, had they been sound, would almost have assured victory to the Confederacy: that Cotton was King; that to obtain cotton for her factories Britain would be forced to break the blockade and intervene on behalf of the Confederacy just as France had intervened on behalf of the Americans in 1778; that such intervention would involve the United States in war with Britain, and perhaps with France as well; and that out of this would emerge an independent South. President

From *A Cycle of Adams Letters, 1861–65*, Worthington C. Ford, ed. (Boston, 1920), I, pp. 190–193, 221, 243, 245–246, 251–252; II, pp. 58–61, 63–66, 96–97, 258–259.

Lincoln recognized the danger from the beginning—unlike his Secretary of State, who at one time blithely proposed a declaration of war on both Britain and France as a method of reuniting the country!—and so did his Minister Adams. Danger of "recognition" of the Confederacy darkened the diplomatic horizons for two years, and in the end it was Gettysburg and Vicksburg, rather than any considerations of principle, that averted the danger. Meantime Adams had won the grudging respect of the British government and had been successful in restraining the worst violations of neutrality. The Confederates' *Alabama* and other vessels, to be sure, were built and outfitted and allowed to escape from British waters—Britain paid dearly for that in the final arbitration of the Alabama Claims in 1873—but Adams was successful in preventing the Liverpool-built Laird rams ordered by the Confederates from putting out to sea. The dramatic confrontation of Minister Adams and Lord Russell on this crisis is part of history and almost of legend: "It is superfluous to tell your Lordship that this means war."

No other family in American history has been so addicted to diaries and letter writing as the Adamses; there is probably some truth in the popular belief that all Adams babies are born not with silver spoons in their mouths but with pens in their fists. The *Adams Papers,* now under way, promise to run to well over a hundred volumes. All during the war Minister Adams and his son Henry carried on a lively correspondence with the eldest son, Charles Francis, Jr., then in the Union army. Adams had enlisted in '61 and received appointment as lieutenant of the first Massachusetts Cavalry; he fought at Antietam and Gettysburg and in the Wilderness; by the close of the war he was colonel of the Fifth Massachusetts Cavalry, a Negro Regiment. After the war he had a long and distinguished career as railroad president, railroad commissioner, and amateur historian. We have here a fever chart of Anglo-American relations during these critical years.

CHARLES FRANCIS ADAMS TO HIS SON

London, September 26, 1862

Latterly indeed we have felt a painful anxiety for the safety of Washington itself. For it is very plain that the expedition of the rebels must have been long meditated, and that it embraced a plan of raising the standard of revolt in Maryland as well as Pennsylvania. It has been intimated to me that their emissaries here have given out significant hints of a design to bring in both those states to their combination, which was to be executed about the month of September. That such a scheme was imaginable I should have supposed, until the occurrence of General Pope's campaign and the effects of it as described in your letter of the 29th ulto. . . .

Thus far it has happened a little fortunately for our comfort here that most of our reverses have been reported during the most dead season of the year, when Parliament was not in session, the Queen and Court and ministry are all away indulging in their customary interval of vacation, and London is said to be wholly empty—the two millions and a half of souls who show themselves counting for nothing in comparison with the hundred thousand magnates that disappear. It is however a fact that the latter make opinion which emanates mainly from the clubhouses. Here the London *Times* is the great oracle, and through this channel its unworthy and degrading counsels towards America gain their general currency. I am sorry for the manliness of Great Britain when I observe the influence to which it has submitted itself. But there is no help for it now. The die is cast, and whether we gain or we lose our point, alienation for half a century is the inevitable effect between the two countries. The pressure of this conviction always becomes greatest in our moments of adversity. It is therefore lucky that it does not come when the force of the social combination is commonly the greatest also. We have thus been in a great degree free from the necessity of witnessing it in society in any perceptible form. Events are travelling at such a pace that it is scarcely conceivable to suppose some termination or other of this suspense is not approaching. The South cannot uphold its slave system much longer against the gradual and certain undermining of its slaveholding population. Its power of endurance thus far has been beyond all expectation, but there is a term for all things finite, and the evidences of suffering and of exhaustion thicken. The war now swallows up the children and the elders. And when they are drawn away, what becomes of the authority over the servants? It may last a little while from the force of habit, but in the end it cannot fail to be obliterated. . . .

CHARLES FRANCIS ADAMS TO HIS SON

London, October 17, 1862
General McClellan's work during the week ending the 18th has done a good deal to restore our drooping credit here. Most of the knowing ones had already discounted the capture of Washington

and the capitulation of the Free States. Some had gone so far as to presume the establishment of Jefferson Davis as the President instead of Lincoln. The last number of the *Edinburgh Review* has a wise prediction that this is to be effected by the joint labors of the *"mob"* and of *"the merchants"* of the city of New York. This is the guide of English intelligence of the nature of our struggle. Of course it follows that no sensible effect is produced excepting from hard blows. If General McClellan will only go on and plant a few more of the same kind in his opponent's eyes, I shall be his humble servant, for it will raise us much in the estimation of all our friends. Mr. Gladstone will cease to express so much admiration of Jefferson Davis, and all other things will begin to flow smoothly again.

We are all very quietly at home. Last week I made a flying trip into the north to pay a visit to a good friend of America in Yorkshire. It gave me an opportunity to see a very pretty region of country, and the ruins of Bolton Abbey and Barden Towers in the picturesque valley of the river Wharfe. If they only had a little more sunlight, it would be very exquisite. But the excessive profusion of verdure unrelieved by golden rays, and only covered with a leaden sky, gives an aspect of sadness to quiet scenery which I scarcely relish. On the whole I prefer the brilliancy of America, even though it be at the cost of a browner surface.

My friend is a Colonel of a volunteer regiment, after the fashion of almost everybody here. For the fear of Napoleon has made the whole world turn soldier. Whilst I was with him he had some exercise at target practice with two sections of his riflemen. I went up to witness it, and thought it on the whole very good. The distances were three, four and five hundred yards. The best hits were nineteen in twenty. Three tied at eighteen, and then all the way down to eleven, which was the poorest. It seemed to me excellent practice, but I do not profess to be a judge. I suppose our people in the army by this time are able to do full as well if not better. . . .

CHARLES FRANCIS ADAMS TO HIS SON

Mount Felix, Walton on Thames
December 25, 1862

Public matters remain yet in a profound state of repose, and probably will continue so for another month. The publication made by the Secretary of State of large portions of my Despatches for the past year has rather stirred a hornet's nest in the press, but I fancy it will prove only a nine days' wonder. I have said merely what everybody knows. The great body of the aristocracy and the wealthy commercial classes are anxious to see the United States go to pieces. On the other hand the middle and lower class sympathise with us, more and more as they better comprehend the true nature of the struggle. A good deal of dust was thrown into their eyes at first by the impudent pretense that the tariff was the cause of the war. All that is now over. Even the *Times* has no longer the assurance to repeat the fable. The true division now begins to make itself perceptible here as elsewhere in Europe—the party of the old and of the new, of vested rights and of well regulated freedom. All equally see in the convulsion in America an era in the history of the world, out of which must come in the end a general recognition of the right of mankind to the produce of their labor and the pursuit of happiness. Across all these considerations come occasionally individual and national interests which pervert the judgment for a time, but the world moves onward taking little note of temporary perturbations, and whatever may betide to us of this generation, the end is sure. . . .

HENRY ADAMS TO CHARLES FRANCIS ADAMS, JR.

London, January 23, 1863

The Emancipation Proclamation has done more for us here than all our former victories and all our diplomacy. It is creating an almost convulsive reaction in our favor all over this country. The London *Times* furious and scolds like a drunken drab. Certain it is, however, that public opinion is very deeply stirred here and finds expression in meetings, addresses to President Lincoln, deputations to us, standing committees to agitate the subject and to affect opinion, and all the other symptoms of a great popular movement peculiarly unpleasant to the upper classes here because it rests altogether on the spontaneous action of the laboring classes and has a pestilent squint at sympathy with republicanism. But the *Times* is on its last legs and has lost its temper. They say it always does lose its temper when it finds such a feeling too strong for it, and its next step will be to come round and try to guide it. We are much encouraged and in high spirits. If only you at home don't have disasters, we will give such a checkmate to the foreign hopes of the rebels as they never yet have had. . . .

Henry Adams to Charles Francis Adams, Jr.

London, January 27, 1863

Spring has come again and the leaves are appearing for the third time and we are still here, nor does there seem any immediate probability of our moving. In fact we are now one of the known and acknowledged units of the London and English world, and though politics still place more or less barriers in our path, the majority of people receive us much as they would Englishmen, and seem to consider us as such. I have been much struck by the way in which they affect to distinguish here between us and "foreigners"; that is, persons who don't speak English. The great difficulty is in the making acquaintances, for London acquaintances are nothing.

After a fortnight's violent pulling, pushing, threatening, shaking, cursing and coaxing, almost entirely done through private channels, we have at least succeeded in screwing the Government up to what promises to be a respectable position. How steady it will be, I don't know, nor how far they will declare themselves, do I know. But between our Government at home and our active and energetic allies here, we seem to have made progress. I went last night to a meeting of which I shall send you a report; a democratic and socialist meeting, most threatening and dangerous to the established state of things; and assuming a tone and proportions that are quite novel and alarming in this capital. And they met to notify Government that "they would not tolerate" interference against us. I can assure you this sort of movement is as alarming here as a slave insurrection would be in the South, and we have our hands on the springs that can raise or pacify such agitators, at least as regards our own affairs, they making common cause with us. I never quite appreciated the "moral influence" of American democracy, nor the cause that the privileged classes in Europe have to fear us, until I saw how directly it works. At this moment the American question is organizing a vast mass of the lower orders in direct contact with the wealthy. They go our whole platform and are full of the "rights of man." The old revolutionary leaven is working steadily in England. You can find millions of people who look up to our institutions as their model and who talk with utter contempt of their own system of Government. Within three months this movement has taken a development that has placed all our enemies on the defensive; has driven Palmerston to sue for peace and Lord Russell to proclaim a limited sympathy. I will not undertake to say where it will stop, but were I an Englishman

I should feel nervous. We have strength enough already to shake the very crown on the Queen's head if we are compelled to employ it all. You are not to suppose that we are intriguing to create trouble. I do not believe that all the intrigue in the world could create one of these great demonstrations of sympathy. But where we have friends, there we shall have support, and those who help us will do it of their own free will. There are few of the thickly populated districts of England where we have not the germs of an organisation that may easily become democratic as it is already antislavery. With such a curb on the upper classes, I think they will do little more harm to us.

The conduct of the affairs of that great republic which though wounded itself almost desperately, can yet threaten to tear down the rulers of the civilised world, by merely assuming her place at the head of the march of democracy, is something to look upon. I wonder whether we shall be forced to call upon the brothers of the great fraternity to come in all lands to the assistance and protection of its head. These are lively times, oh, Hannibal.

HENRY ADAMS TO CHARLES FRANCIS ADAMS, JR.

London, January 30, 1863
Politically things go on swimmingly here. The antislavery feeling of the country is coming out stronger than we ever expected, and all the English politicians have fairly been thrown over by their people. There was a meeting last night at Exeter Hall which is likely to create a revolution in public opinion which was begun by the great Manchester Meeting on the 31st December. Last night's meeting was something tremendous, unheard of since the days of reform. The cry was "Emancipation and reunion" and the spirit was dangerously in sympathy with republicanism. The Strand was blocked up in front of Exeter Hall by those who couldn't get in, and speeches were made in the street as well as in another hall opened to accommodate a part of the surplus. As for enthusiasm, my friend Tom Brown of Rugby school-days, who was one of the speakers, had to stop repeatedly and beg the people not to cheer so much. Every allusion to the South was followed by groaning, hisses and howls, and the enthusiasm for Lincoln and for everything connected with the North was immense. The effect of such a display will be very great, and I think we may expect from Lancashire on the arrival of the *George Griswold*, a response that will make some noise.

Next week Parliament will meet. Of course it will bring hot water, but the sentiment of the country will not tolerate any interference with us. I breath more easily about this than ever. My main anxiety is about the *Alabama* case, which has been the subject of the sharpest kind of notes between the Chief and Lord Russell. As these notes will probably now be published, I can say that in my opinion my Lord has been dreadfully used up, and if you don't howl with delight when you read the Chief's note to him of 30th December, you won't do what I did. But our cue is still friendship, and we don't want to irritate. The strong outside pressure that is now aroused to act on this Government will, I hope, help us to carry through all we want in time and with patience.

HENRY ADAMS TO CHARLES FRANCIS ADAMS, JR.

London, February 13, 1863

The last week here has been politically very quiet. I am surprised at it, for I thought that the meeting of Parliament would set the flood going. Lord Derby, however, put his foot on any interference with us, on the first night of the session, and so we have obtained a temporary quiet. But the feeling among the upper classes is more bitter and angry than ever, and the strong popular feeling of sympathy with us is gradually dividing the nation into aristocrats and democrats, and may produce pretty serious results for England. . . .

HENRY ADAMS TO CHARLES FRANCIS ADAMS, Jr.

London, 20 March, 1863

We are in a shocking bad way here. I don't know what we are ever going to do with this damned old country. Some day it will wake up and find itself at war with us, and then what a squealing there'll be. By the Lord, I would almost be willing to submit to our sufferings, just to have the pleasure of seeing our privateers make ducks and drakes of their commerce. I'll tell you what I mean to do. . . .

But meanwhile, as I say, we are in a worse mess here than we have known since the *Trent* affair, and the devil of it is that I am in despair of our getting any military success that would at all counterbalance our weight. Where our armies try to do anything they are invariably beaten, and now they seem to be tired of trying. I'll bet a sovereign to a southern shin-plaster that we don't take Charleston; either that we don't try or are beaten. I'll bet five golden pounds to a diminutive greenback that we don't clear the Mississippi, and that we don't hurt Richmond. My only consolation is that the Southerners are suffering dreadfully under the tension we keep them at, and as I prefer this to having fresh disasters of our own, I am in no hurry to see anyone move. But meanwhile we are in a tangle with England that can only be cleared with our excellent good navy cannon. If I weren't so brutally seasick, I would go into the navy and have a lick at these fat English turkey-buzzards.

At the same time, individually, I haven't at all the same dislike to the English. They are very like ourselves and are very pleasant people. And then they are quite as ready to blackguard themselves as anyone could wish, if they're only let alone. There are all the elements of a great, reforming, liberal party at work here, and a few years will lay in peace that old vindictive rogue [Palmerston] who now rules England and weighs like an incubus on all advance. Then you will see the new generation, with which it is my only satisfaction here to have some acquaintance, take up the march again and press the country into shape.

Thanks to Monckton Milnes, Tom Hughes and a few other good friends, I am tolerably well known now in the literary and progressive set. I was amused the other day to hear that I was put up for a Club in St. James's Street, by Mr. Milnes, and seconded by Lawrence Olifaunt, a thorough anti-American; and better commonly called here; the brother of Lord Hartington; the son of the Duke of Devonshire. Several other names are on the paper, I believe, but I don't know what they are. I'm thinking my character would not be raised in America if I were known to keep such malignant company. Certainly, however, aristocracy is not my strong point. My most sought acquaintances are men like Hughes, and his associates, the cultivated radicals of England.

How long I shall remain in contact with this sort of thing, who can say? Verily, the future is black and the ocean looks as though it were yawning for us on our approaching passage.

HENRY ADAMS TO CHARLES FRANCIS ADAMS, Jr.

July 23, 1863

I positively tremble to think of receiving any more news from America since the batch that we received last Sunday. Why can't we sink the steamers till some more good news comes? It is like an easterly storm after a glorious June day, this returning to the gloomy chronicle of varying successes and disasters, after exulting in the grand excitement of such triumphs as you sent us on the 4th. For once there was *no* drawback, unless I except anxiety about you. I wanted to hug the army of the Potomac. I wanted to get the whole of the army of Vicksburg drunk at my own expense. I wanted to fight some small man and lick him. Had I had a single friend in London capable of rising to the dignity of the occasion, I don't know what might n't have happened. But mediocrity prevailed and I passed the day in base repose.

It was on Sunday morning as I came down to breakfast that I saw a telegram from the Department announcing the fall of Vicksburg. Now, to appreciate the value of this, you must know that the one thing upon which the London press and the English people have been so positive as not to tolerate contradiction, was the impossibility of capturing Vicksburg. Nothing could induce them to believe that Grant's army was not in extreme danger of having itself to capitulate. The *Times* of Saturday, down to the last moment, declared that the siege of Vicksburg grew more and more hopeless every day. Even now, it refuses, after receiving all the details, to admit the fact, and only says that Northern advices report it, but it is not yet confirmed. Nothing could exceed the energy with which everybody in England has reprobated the wicked waste of life that must be caused by the siege of this place during the sickly season, and ridiculed the idea of its capture. And now the announcement was just as though a bucket of iced-water were thrown into their faces. They could n't and would n't believe it. All their settled opinions were overthrown, and they were left dangling in the air. You never heard such cackling as was kept up here on Sunday and Monday, and you can't imagine how spiteful and vicious they all were. Sunday evening I was asked round to Monckton Milnes' to meet a few people. Milnes himself is one of the warmest Americans in the world, and received me with a hug before the astonished company, crowing like a fighting cock. But the rest of the company were very cold. W. H. Russell was there, and I had a good deal of talk with him. He at least did not attempt to disguise the gravity of the occasion, nor to turn Lee's defeat into a victory. I went with Mr. Milnes to the Cosmopolitan Club afterwards, where the people all looked at me as though I were objectionable. Of course I avoided the subject in conversation, but I saw very clearly how unpleasant the news was which I brought. So it has been everywhere. This is a sort of thing that can be neither denied, palliated, nor evaded; the disasters of the rebels are unredeemed by even any hope of success. Accordingly the emergency has produced here a mere access of spite, preparatory (if we suffer no reverse) to a revolution in tone.

It is now conceded at once that all idea of intervention is at an end. The war is to continue indefinitely, so far as Europe is concerned, and the only remaining chance of collision is in the case of the ironclads. We are looking after them with considerable energy, and I think we shall settle them.

It is utterly impossible to describe to you the delight that we all felt here and that has not diminished even now. I can imagine the temporary insanity that must have prevailed over the North on the night of the 7th. Here our demonstrations were quiet, but, ye Gods, how we felt! Whether to laugh or to cry, one hardly knew. Some men preferred the one, some the other. The Chief was the picture of placid delight. As for me, as my effort has always been here to suppress all expression of feeling, I preserved sobriety in public, but for four days I've been internally singing Hosannahs and running riot in exultation. The future being doubtful, we are all the more determined to drink this one cup of success out. Our friends at home, Dana, John, and so on, are always so devilish afraid that we may see things in too rosy colors. They think it necessary to be correspondingly sombre in their advices. This time, luckily, we had no one to be so cruel as to knock us down from behind, when we were having all we could do to fight our English upas influence in front. We sat on the top of the ladder and did n't care a copper who passed underneath. Your old friend Judge Goodrich was here on Monday, and you never saw a man in such a state. Even for him it was wonderful. He lunched with us and kept us in a perfect riot all the time, telling stories without limit and laughing till he almost screamed.

I am sorry to say, however, that all this is not likely to make our position here any pleasanter socially. All our experience has shown that as our success was great, so rose equally the spirit of hatred on this side. Never before since the *Trent* affair has it shown itself so universal and spiteful as now. I am myself more surprised at it than I have any right to be, and philosopher though I aspire to be, I do feel strongly impressed with a desire to see the time come when our success will compel silence and our prosperity will complete the revolution. As for war, it would be folly in us to go to war with this country. We have the means of destroying her without hurting ourselves.

CHARLES FRANCIS ADAMS TO HIS SON

London, July 24, 1863
The last steamers brought us startling intelligence. Vicksburg fallen! There has been nothing like it since New Orleans. One was

the complement of the other. It sounds the knell of the confederation scheme. Great has been the disappointment and consternation here! Just at the moment, too, when they were hoping and believing its complete establishment and recognition at hand. Could anything be more provoking. The Salons of this great metropolis are in tears; tears of anger mixed with grief. They moreover refuse to be comforted. They madly struggled with the event, denying that it was possible. Fate cannot be so cruel!

Mr. Seward was kind enough to send me a special telegram announcing the event, which reached me at breakfast on Sunday morning. I tried to bear up under the intelligence with a suitable degree of moderation. Not having any idea how deeply our English friends would take it to heart, I ventured to indulge a slight sense of satisfaction. Fortunately I went to church in the city, where nobody knew me, and therefore nobody could be scandalised. It would have been hard on them, you know, to be joyful in the midst of their sorrow. Doubtless they would have been as much offended as they showed themselves on reading my famous letter exposing their secret practises. I took care to look resigned. The only persons whom I met were Americans, excepting perhaps Mr. Browning, and to him as to them I disclosed my secret. He, like them, appeared not to be depressed, but rather elated. Luckily, there was nobody at hand to mark the impropriety.

Five days have passed away. Another steamer has brought intelligence quite confirmatory, but not sufficient to overcome the determined incredulity that has succeeded the first shock. I recollect it was very much so with New Orleans. The only difference was that the passions had not then become so deeply enlisted in the struggle. . . .

Parliament is just now coming to an end. This is the third session since the breaking out of our troubles, and its position has not yet been essentially varied towards America. On looking back and remembering how I felt on each return of the body, it seems to me as if we had reason for gratulation that we are yet in peace with this country. The great causes of apprehension have died away. The cotton famine and Lancashire distress have not proved such serious troubles as we had feared. Great Britain has not in her domestic condition any cause to seek for violent or extraordinary remedial measures. The country is highly prosperous. I am well pleased that it should remain so, if it will only consent to indulge its predilections and its lamentations in words addressed to the empty air. Vox, et praeterea nihil!

CHARLES FRANCIS ADAMS TO HIS SON

London, July 31, 1863

It is intensely painful in the midst of such great prosperity here to read the shocking details of slaughter and destruction in our newspapers. Still more annoying is it to think how by the folly of these rogues we are playing into the hands of the malevolent in Europe. The privileged classes all over Europe rejoice in the thoughts of the ruin of the great experiment of popular government. I yet trust they count without their host. No thanks, however, to the madmen who try to work this mischief. The penalty we are paying for the great error of our ancestors is a most tremendous one. All I can pray for is that we do so once for all. To permit our posterity to run the risk of repeating it for the same fault on our part would be criminal indeed.

The London *Times* last Monday graciously allowed the people of England to believe that Vicksburg had actually fallen. The notion that General Lee was in possession of Washington and Baltimore is not quite so strong as it was, but I am not sure that it has been dissipated yet by any positive denial in that press. There was a general sense of the happening of some lamentable disaster here, the nature and extent of which had not been fully defined. The clearest evidence of this was found in the stock market, where a panic took place among the holders of the rebel loan. It fell from three per cent discount to seventeen, and has not stopped yet. I should not be surprised if some bankruptcies were to follow. People here must pay something for their pro-slavery sympathies. What a pity that the sum of their losses could not have been applied to the emancipation of the slaves! In that case England would have maintained her character for philanthropy, which has gone down, as it is, quite as far and as fast as the rebel loan. . . .

CHARLES FRANCIS ADAMS TO HIS SON

London, March 24, 1865

On this side my situation seems at last to be getting easy and comfortable, so far as freedom from anxiety is concerned. A great change of opinion has been going on in the last few months, in regard to the chances of the issue. People feel the power of our position and the weakness of that of the rebels. They are also not without some embarrassment respecting the possible consequence to themselves of their indiscreet betrayal of their true sentiments towards us. This has led to a singular panic in regard to what will be done by us, after a restoration. A week or two since you could not drive the notion out of their heads that we were not about to pounce at once upon Canada. This was corrected by the first debate that took place in Parliament on that subject. Last night there was another, the burden of which was absolute faith in our desire to remain on the most friendly relations. At the same time £ 50,000 was voted for the purpose of fortifying Quebec in case of accidents. The case then stands logically thus. If they *do* believe what they say, the money is thrown away, as no fortification can be necessary. If on the other hand they do not believe it, and that opinion is a just one, £ 50,000 will not go very far to putting Canada out of our reach. The fear that is implied is far more of a provocative than a resource in the dilemma.

Be this as it may, one thing seems for the present to be settled. That is, that no hope is left for any aid to the rebel cause. England will initiate nothing to help them in their critical moment. So far as any risk of an aggressive policy is concerned, it is over. Mr. Seward may now rely upon it, that if troubles supervene, it must happen very much by his own act. He has a right to exult in the success of his policy in carrying the country in its hour of peril clear of the hazards of foreign complications. The voluminous intrigues of the rebel emissaries have been completely baffled, their sanguine anticipations utterly disappointed. They have spent floods of money in directing the press, in securing aid from adventurers of all sorts, and in enlisting the services of ship and cannon builders with all their immense and powerful following, and it has been all in vain. So far as any efforts of theirs are concerned, we might enter Richmond tomorrow. This act of the drama is over. . . .

MOSES COIT TYLER ON
ENGLISH IMPRESSIONS OF AMERICA:
"AN AMPLITUDE, AND A SPLENDOR OF
NON-INFORMATION"

1862

In youth Moses Coit Tyler studied for the ministry, and for a brief time he held a pastorate in upstate New York. His interest in religion, however, became purely intellectual; for professional purposes it was metamorphosed, rather improbably, into a passion for gymnastics. In 1862 Tyler abandoned the ministry and went off to England to lecture on physical education. There is no evidence that his lectures made the faintest impression on England but it is clear that England made a strong impression on him. Already an ardent reformer, champion of temperance, women's rights, and Abolition, he reacted sharply against English attitudes and institutions. The only produce of this English visit was a series of newspaper articles later collected into book form as *Glimpses of England*. After his return to the United States, Tyler took up an academic career. He held a chair of literature at the University of Michigan, in Ann Arbor, and in 1881 moved to the new Cornell University, which, under the leadership first of Andrew D. White and then of Charles Kendall Adams, was pioneering in so many fields of education. Tyler held one of the first professorships of American history established in the country, and

From Moses Coit Tyler, *Glimpses of England* (New York, 1898), pp. 277–290.

wrote, during his Cornell years, the classical histories of American literature during the Colonial and Revolutionary eras, volumes which after more than seventy-five years are still the best in their field.

On Certain English Hallucinations Touching America

The longer I remain in England, the more perfectly do I seem to enter into the experience of a certain veracious countryman of mine—a New Englander and a son of Harvard—who, being in London so long ago as in the reign of Queen Anne, was much refreshed by the following bit of international talk held by him with a charming Englishwoman whom he met here in very excellent company:

"She asked me if all the people of my country were white, as she saw I was. She thought we were all black, as she supposed the Indians to be. She asked me how long I had been in the kingdom. When I told her 'a few months,' she said she was surprised to think how I could learn their language in so short a time. 'Methinks,' said she, 'you speak as plain English as I do.'"

Unfortunately, this traveller does not go on to mention any observations that fell from his fair English friend on the vast and bewildering theme of American geography; but had he done so, that single conversation, I doubt not, would have illustrated the three principal eccentricities of opinion which I refer to in the title of this paper, and which are still to be met with, not so infrequently, among our dear cousins over here: First, that we Americans are black, certainly not white; secondly, that our ordinary speech is not English—as, indeed, sometimes, perhaps it is not; and thirdly, that the topography of our country is one of those branches of knowledge which English people may sufficiently acquire by a process of evolution from their inward consciousness, and without the vulgar routine of studying mere maps or descriptive accounts of America. . . .

As I have begun these remarks by referring to the state of things in the last century, it may be worth considering whether herein is not to be found the deeper clue to the origin of that unlucky quarrel which broke out between the English and the Americans about a hundred years ago—a quarrel which already has had several notable consequences on both sides of the Atlantic, and is quite likely to have several more before the play is out. Can it be supposed, for instance,

that if King George the Third has taken the trouble to become even
tolerably well informed concerning his American subjects and their
country, he would ever have blundered into the preposterous and
disastrous policy he tried to enforce upon them? As to our side of
the quarrel, also, is it not possible that, even back of our political
suspicion and alarm over that policy, there lay a quite appreciable
amount of offended pride—of American sensitiveness wounded, of
provincial self-importance ruffled—merely through this persistent
indifference of the mother country to even the most rudimental
facts about us? Were we, then, such insignificant atoms in the great
British Empire? Perhaps we could have managed to put up with the
stamp act and the tea tax; but how were we ever to endure it that our
English masters should deem us of so little account, that the knowledge neither of ourselves, nor of our history, nor of our geography,
was worth the trouble of being correctly arrived at by them? . . .
In 1755, just after the direful fiasco of General Braddock in the woods
of Western Pennsylvania—a fiasco due almost wholly to the fact that
this brave Briton had not thought it worth his while to become even
moderately well acquainted with the country through which he was to
march his army, or with the ways of the people against whom he was
going to fight—a sarcastic comment on that British mode of doing
business in America was made by a very able man in Maryland, a
barrister who had received his education at Eton, at Cambridge, and
at the Temple.

> "Perhaps," said he jocosely, "in less than a century the Ministers of
> our gracious King may know that we inhabit a vast continent; and
> even the rural gentry over there will hear that we are not all black
> —that we live in houses, speak English, wear clothes, and have some
> faint notions of Christianity. 'Have you any cows or horses in
> Maryland, sir?' is a question I have been often asked, and when I
> answered in the affirmative, the reply has been, 'Oh, oh, you do not
> get them from old England, then?' But it is no wonder that such a
> question should be asked twenty miles from London, when a cer-
> tain parliamentary committee, during the application for the salt
> bill, were wise enough to ask an American witness, 'Have you any
> rivers in America?' 'Ah, pray, how many?' 'Well, pray tell us, did
> you ever kill any fish in passing any of your rivers, as you call
> them?'"

No reader of *The Virginians*—a carefully studied historic picture
of this very period of the Braddock fiasco—will fail to recall, as

bearing upon our present discussion, the remark of Sir Miles Harrington to his young nephew, just arrived from Virginia:

> "Thou hast a great look of thy father," said the jolly baronet. "Lord bless us, how we used to beat each other! Take it he was henpecked when he married, and Madam Esmond took the spirit out of him when she got him in her island. Virginia is an island. Ain't it an island?"

So, too, the official correspondence of certain Anglican prelates with their missionaries in America during those good old days, reveals in the ecclesiastical mind a similar state of unconcern as to all such pedantries as mere facts concerning those regions remote and infidel. Even in the early years of the reign of George the Third, the Archbishop of Canterbury, in writing to an eminent clergyman at New York, was accustomed to ask questions or to send directions touching missionaries in Newfoundland or in Georgia, His Grace supposing that those provinces were so near to New York that his correspondent would be in constant neighborly communication with the persons referred to. Amidst the earliest growls of discontent on the part of James Otis, over the new taxing policy of the government, one can even now detect the undertone of colonial annoyance on account of the very small place which we and our country then held in the British scheme of useful knowledge. "Divers of these colonies," exclaims that fiery agitator, "are well settled, not as the common people of England imagine, with a mongrel mixture of English, Indian, and negro, but with free-born British white subjects"; and he adds the facetious tale of a great minister of state, in the previous reign, who, "without knowing whether Jamaica lay in the Mediterranean, the Baltic, or the Moon," used to send thither official letters addressed "To the Governor of the Island of New England." . . .

Such was the state of the British mind concerning us a hundred years ago. Very naturally, an American coming to England in these latter days, and remembering, perhaps, some such tales as these, is apt to suppose that, by the present time at least, a great change must have taken place, and that there can no longer exist here, to any extent, the mental condition out of which could be born such eccentric notions concerning us and our country. Nevertheless, before a very long stay here, he will be likely to find himself now and then rubbing his eyes in much bewilderment, and trying to make out whether he be really awake, or only dreaming that he hears some of the marvellous things that seem to be spoken to him. Only a few weeks ago, in the south of England, on my stating, in reply to a common inquiry, that I was from New England, my interrogator, a well-dressed and well-spoken person, immediately asked me whether New England was one of the Northern or one of the Southern States. On another occasion, when, in reply to the same question, I mentioned that immediately before coming over I had lived in Boston, the lady with whom I talked expressed her gratification at hearing this, since she hoped that, on my return, I would convey a message to her cousin who "lived near there, in New Orleans." When I gently explained to her that it might be a good while before I should be able to visit New Orleans, which was "a long way from Boston—nearly so far as Constantinople from London," she confessed that she had not imagined such a distance between the two towns, and "in fact, had supposed that they were near enough to be connected by omnibus."

I cannot tell how many times I have had the experience in railway carriages, hotels, and other public places, of arguing with intelligent men and women about the war then in progress in America, and of finding them display an altogether charming uncertainty as to whether the State of Ohio might border upon the Gulf of Mexico or the Gulf of St. Lawrence, whether the Potomac do not take its rise in the Rocky Mountains, and whether those same Rocky Mountains be not a series of ambitious protuberances somewhere in the vicinity of Vermont. While the war was going on, many a time have I amused myself by mildly requesting people who had their minds quite firmly made up that separation between the North and the South was the easiest and most natural thing in the world, to be so good as to indicate just where the line of separation should be drawn. I once made this request of a very agreeable gentleman who held a clerkship in a government office; and he instantly replied, with the sweet composure of one whose wisdom could be expected to receive no further illumination on this side of the grave, that, "for the purpose of a dividing line between the Northern and the Southern States, the most obvious geographical object would be the Mississippi River." In 1863, an eminent American clergyman just then in London told me of his dining with a distinguished company but an evening or two before, and of there getting into the usual discussion with his next neighbor at the table, who happened to be a member of Parliament. From this British statesman the American traveller then received a perfect flood of illumination as to the naturalness, and, indeed, the necessity, of a dismemberment of the Union.

"Why, there are you Northerners," said he, "placed in North America all by yourselves! Then, there comes the isthmus—see, Panama, or whatever it is. Then, separated from you by this narrow bit of land, are the Southerners down there in South America. Now, my dear sir, I think you must admit, it is perfectly obvious that nature never meant you to be a Union!"

The reverend gentleman was forced to admit that something was, indeed, very obvious, and, in short, that he had never before been accustomed to view the problem in just that light.

Some time before the close of the war, I knew an English clergyman to maintain, in the presence of a full drawing-room, that "in this American war they ought to give their sympathy to the Virginians, because Virginia was originally settled by the Pilgrim Fathers, the most heroic stock that went out of England." Not long since, at a hotel in Wales, I met an affable gentleman who, not having then discovered that I was from America, very kindly gave me a vast amount of choice information about that country. Among other recondite things of his which I have stored away in my memory, was this,—that "the whole trouble in America is due to the fact that the country was originally settled, about the middle of the last century, by a great pack of spirit-rappers who ran away from England to avoid being roasted at the stake, as they should have been." I have found educated people here who have the idea that the civilized portion of the United States is a narrow strip of semi-luminous culture somewhere along the Atlantic coast; and that you have but to penetrate a few miles inland in order to reach the realms of primeval nature, and to encounter all the wild beasts of the forest. An English university man, much given to hunting in wild regions, once consulted me about an intended visit of his for such a purpose to New York, and he asked me "how far out of the town he would need to go in order to find good kangaroo shooting." From that moment, I have not wondered at the famous passage in Cobden's last speech, in which he expressed the wish to endow at Oxford and Cambridge a professorship of American history and geography: "I will undertake to say, and I speak advisedly, that I will take any undergraduate now at Oxford and Cambridge and ask him to put his finger on Chicago, and that he does not go within a thousand miles of it." . . .

After all, the truth seems to be, that knowledge of those portions of this planet which lie outside the boundaries of the United Kingdom have never yet been a matter to engage the very determined attention of the British Islanders; and it should not too much surprise us when, in our rambles through their country, we observe in them, concerning all matters of remote geography and ethnology, a depth, an amplitude, and a splendor of non-information, in the presence of which the alien observer is liable, unless carefully on his guard, to stand amazed and indeed convulsed.

JOHN LEWIS PEYTON:

THE WILKES AFFAIR—"IT
WAS NOT BECAUSE THEY LOVED"
THE CONFEDERACY "BUT BECAUSE
THEY DISLIKED THE YANKEES"

1862

John Peyton took a law degree from the University of Virginia in 1844 and practiced law in that state for eight years before embarking on a "secret mission" to Britain, France, and Austria on behalf of President Fillmore. On his return he moved to Illinois, where he was active in local politics. On the eve of the Civil War Peyton moved back to North Carolina; Like many Southerners, he opposed secession but enlisted in the state forces on the outbreak of the war. In 1861 North Carolina appointed him state agent to Britain; it was characteristic of the persistence of the principles of state sovereignty that the states should compete with the Confederacy itself in such diplomatic and economic missions. Once in England, Peyton worked closely with the Confederate agents Yancey and Mann to obtain diplomatic recognition and economic and financial aid. After the war Peyton stayed on in Britain, retiring to the island of Guernsey, where he died in 1896.

When the intelligence reached England it produced intense excitement, particularly in Liverpool, the principal seat of the ship-

From John Lewis Peyton, *The American Crisis, or Pages from the Notebook of a State Agent during the Civil War* (London, 1867), II, pp. 70–75, 85–86, 100–102.

ping interest of the country. On 'Change the utmost indignation was expressed; and immediately a notice was posted, calling a public meeting at the Cotton Salesroom, at three o'clock P.M. of the same day. In accordance with this announcement a meeting was held at the appointed time and place, which was crowded to excess. The meeting was quite as remarkable for its enthusiasm as for its numbers. Mr. Spence, author of "The American Union," an able dissertation upon the American Government, presided, and, on taking the chair, read the following resolution: "That this meeting . . . do earnestly call upon the Government to assert the dignity of the British flag by requiring prompt reparation for the outrage."

On hearing this resolution read, the meeting expressed in a most unmistakable manner the feeling by which it was pervaded. When silence had been in some measure restored, the chairman remarked, that when the news of the outrage had reached the town, the feeling created was one of surprise, mingled with indignation. He remarked that they had all heard of the sacred dignity of the American flag. That dignity, he proceeded to say, was a means by which the persons engaged in the nefarious slave trade could at once protect themselves, while fully enabling them to resist any attempt at search. He trusted it would not be tolerated that men prosecuting so nefarious a trade should be protected, and that men peacefully proceeding on their own affairs, under the protection of our flag, should be forcibly taken out of our ships. (Cheers.) . . . He said it was the duty of the people to press on the Government the imperative necessity of vindicating the honour and dignity of the British name and flag. (Loud and continued cheering.)

The resolution was then put to the meeting, and carried by a tremendous majority, amid the most deafening and enthusiastic cheers.

The excitement spread with electric rapidity. There was a spontaneous uprising of the whole people, as if a cord of indignation had vibrated in every heart. The honour and glory of the country seemed the first thought of all; the national pride and spirit were fully aroused, and were everywhere displayed in the most unmistakable manner, in the newspapers, at public meetings—for many others followed that in Liverpool—at the hustings, at the theatres, in the haunts of business, and on the public promenades. It was a grand sight thus to witness the agitation of a whole people at an indignity offered to their flag—a people naturally averse to war, and more largely engaged in commerce than any other people. Though they had so much to jeopardise, so much to lose in the contingency of war, there was now no hesitancy, no mean thought of self. It was palpable that all was working admirably for the cause of the Confederate States. Our agents, said the *Times,* spoke more eloquently from their distant prison than a hundred tongues could have done at London or Paris. They were invested with more hortatory power than Peter the Hermit, and more diplomatic persuasiveness than Talleyrand. Though the Commissioners had spoken with the tongues of angels they could never have stirred the British people to a tithe of the depth of feeling by which they were moved at the idea that the Government of the United States was ready at any moment to offer them insult.

. . . The Government acted with unexpected spirit and vigour. The intelligence of the affair reached London on Wednesday (November the 27th [1862]). A Cabinet Council was immediately held, and on Friday the 29th, Earl Russell was directed to prepare a despatch, and on the next day a Queen's messenger was on his way, . . .

In the interim between the 30th of November, when the Queen's messenger left for Washington, and the period of the return of the answer of the Government of the United States, January 3rd, 1862, there was comparative quiet in England, but only the restless slumber of the volcano, whose smouldering fires were ready to burst forth. The people waited with breathless impatience and anxiety the reply of the American Government. They felt that the issue of peace or war hung upon it. What that answer would be, no one could possibly divine. Men differed according to their hopes and fears, their feelings and interests. The war party were anxious that the British demand should be refused, as also those friendly to the South, while the peace party, and those who sympathised with the Federal Government, hoped that the demand would be complied with, and filled the mail bags with letters to their friends in America, and to the Government in Washington, urging upon them a pacific course; yet, for some weeks the matter would be in doubt, and left to painful conjecture. . . .

The events which transpired during this period, and the few weeks which followed the surrender of Mason and Slidell, taught me a useful lesson of worldly wisdom. I found that the English admiration of the South was a thing altogether separate and apart from anything like kindred love. They admired her endurance, her stubborn resolution, her indomitable pluck and gallantry, just as they would have admired the like qualities in a gladiator. They patted her upon the back, as the weaker of the two combatants, as they held up little Tom Sayers against Heenan. It was not because they loved her, but because they disliked the Yankees. They had no idea of drawing the sword in the contest, but warmly supported the Government in its neutral policy, except in so far as they were represented by the *Morning Herald,* the *Standard,* and a few other Conservative journals.

Whilst the prospect of a war was imminent, nothing could exceed the cordiality of the press towards the South. Where Mason and Slidell, and the Confederates generally, expected streams to flow, torrents rushed headlong. The papers never descanted so glowingly upon the immense resources of the Confederacy, the justice of her cause, the bravery of her people, and brilliancy of her future; the wisdom of her statesmanship, the skill of her generals, the heroism of her troops. For all time, they said, she will be England's ally. England will pay her the highest price for her cotton, and sell her the best and cheapest goods. She has no navy; but she should float on English bottoms in time of peace, and stand behind England's wooden walls in time of war. *Per contra,* the Yankees were denounced—described as mean and dishonest. Their country was, they asserted, ruined by the war, their government a miserable failure, their institutions rotten to the core, the people a turbulent mob.

THE REVEREND MONCURE CONWAY
SEES SHEFFIELD
AS A BATTLEFIELD WITH
CASUALTIES

1863

Born in Virginia of a slaveholding family, Conway attended Dickinson College in Pennsylvania, where he may have imbibed some doubts about the cosmic validity of slavery. He entered the Methodist ministry but he was never a very good Methodist, much preferring the writings of Coleridge and Emerson to those of Wesley. At the age of twenty-one he went to Harvard Divinity School and emerged a Unitarian and a Theodore Parker Unitarian at that, which was about as far as one could go and still remain in the church. He preached in Washington but was dismissed for his antislavery sentiments; he preached in Cincinnati—this was not long after Calvin and Harriet Beecher Stowe were there—and founded the western *Dial* magazine. In 1863 he went to England to spread the gospel of Unionism and made that country his home for most of the rest of his life. He became pastor at the South Place Chapel, in Finsbury, and from that vantage point wrote voluminously on literary and historical subjects—altogether some seventy volumes. On a return to the United States in the mid-eighties he devoted himself to rescuing the reputation of Thomas Paine from the vilification that had overwhelmed it; he edited

From Moncure D. Conway, "Sheffield—a Battle-Field of English Labor," *Harper's New Monthly Magazine*, March, 1863, pp. 483–484.

what is still the best collection of Paine's works and wrote what is still the best biography of that much misunderstood statesman. Conway died in Paris in 1907.

At length the sun was obscured; we entered into a yellow-brown fog; the engine uttered that horrible shriek which some one has compared to that of a dying pig with a bad conscience. I looked out and saw rising through the smoke a grove of tall chimneys. When I first looked upon Sheffield—now recognized as the field where the battle between capital and labor waxes hottest—with its dark pall overhanging it, penetrated by lurid tongues of flame, there seemed written over all, "The smoke of their torment ascendeth up for ever and ever."

Was it the effect of the yellow fog, or of the accumulated ignorance in human faces, that along these fearfully crowded streets I could think of nothing but the burdens of ancient woe and despair? They seemed to me a hard, unsmiling procession of those who have no rest, day nor night—who in the morning say, Would God it were evening! and in the evening, Would God it were morning!

The cabman drives rapidly. Beyond the crowd and the smoke we come to a fine hill; in the distance stretch other hills, and beneath them beautiful, well-tilled valleys, with grand old mansions; the sun shines out again on the superb prospect; the gates of a beautiful English home fly open; and soon by the hospitable fireside and the loaded table all wretchedness becomes phantasmal, and Sheffield the happiest of cities.

"What splendid residences there are around here! There must be a vast deal of wealth in Sheffield. About no city in England have I seen such charming environs."

"Yes," whispers a friend at my elbow, "there are fine houses, much luxury and wealth; but these things do not grow without roots. To-day you are with the foliage and fruit; to-morrow, no doubt, you will be exploring the roots beneath them."

To-morrow came, and down among the roots I went.

"Air! a glass of water! a gentleman has fainted!" There is a gathering round of pale women's faces, and now they are confused in one great, death-like face; there is an outer circle of the unmoved faces of men, half turned from their work. Casual remarks coming as from an infinite distance: "He's not used to the smell;" "the factory isn't good for delicate folk;" "cyanid tells on the heart." A slow pressing downward of the low ceiling; a quivering of discolored window-panes back to their places; the circle of women and children returned to their work; the visitor supported by arms into the court-yard. 'Tis a scene that came before my mind's eye several times; it was several times probable, but it did not occur. It took, however, a considerable reinforcement of nerve by resolution to keep it from occurring. And these are the atmospheres in which human beings—women—young girls—toil for ten or twelve in every twenty-four hours of their mortal lives, saving only the blessed day set apart for rest by the first of sanitary reformers!

It was through the magnificent establishment of Messrs. Dixon I went first—an old house, long celebrated for its fine Britannia wares, plating, and the like—in which I found Mr. Dixon, Jun., a most intelligent guide. I followed a dark piece of copper, saw it twisted like paper through twenty transformations, until it stood in silvery radiance ready to sit on any breakfast-table, reflecting in its bright cheeks the "shining morning faces" of the happiest household. There rose under the touch of swart fingers silver trees from whose branches shall depend fruits flushed with the pure skies of many climes over rich men's tables. Here are the bronze powder-flasks that shall hang idly by the sides of lords and squires sallying forth to while away the morning in their game-preserves. I fancy that some of them would never feel so serene again with their centre-pieces and ingeniously-pictured powder and wine flasks if they could get a clear look along the path by which each came, and see the faces and eyes that at each step gave some of their life and light to make its brightness. It takes a vast deal of sugar to sweeten one's tea after he has traced the making of his tea-pot. I find it difficult now to take up a plated fork without remembering the people I saw suspending it in the cyanid, whose poison they inhaled to the certain curtailment of their lives. This, however, is one of the healthiest of the establishments; and though the necessities of the work could not consist with complete health, no pains for that end are spared by the proprietors.

In the various plating and cutlery establishments that I went through I saw three kinds of work that are sure to shorten the lives of those who are employed in them. One of these I have mentioned, but this is less harmful than the rooms where filing is done, and where polishing by means of various oils, earths, and powders is carried on. The air in these rooms is entirely filled with the dust of metals or that of the dark earths and pulverized stones, and these are inevitably depositing a hard and poisonous incrustation upon the lungs. The estimated average reduction of life in these rooms is about ten years: it varies from five to fifteen years, according to the constitution of the person employed. The filers have, perhaps, the most deadly work, and those that I saw were all men. Those who were polishing with the earths and powders were chiefly girls. Their room was kept excessively warm, and they wore only close-fitting cotton gowns. Some of them were quite young, and some may have been once handsome, but now the eyes' brightness was a glitter, the only bloom was a flame. Standing at their silent work they seemed to me, in their mist-shrouds, so many doomed spirits toiling through some dreary purgatory. But if this was sad, that of which I was presently informed was more than sad—it is terrible! In answer to my question whether it was not possible to escape, or at least mitigate, the deleterious effects of these occupations, I was informed that a respirator had been invented which would to a great extent annul such effects; that the masters had every where endeavored to introduce it; but that the workers had steadily refused to wear it or permit it to be worn! Were any worker to enter the room with one of these on, he or she would be immediately commanded to remove it, and none would do a stroke of work until it was removed. The reason for this almost incredible fact is that those employed in these deleterious rooms receive comparatively high wages—from two to three pounds per week, perhaps—and they know that the wage is kept up by the danger. Remove the danger, and these departments of work become crowded, and wages, of course, lowered. There are only a few hundred "buffers" and "saw-grinders," for instance, in all Sheffield; the work requires little ingenuity, and if its fatal effects could be escaped by respirators there would be a rush of applicants. But by the help of the deadliness of their work the saw-grinders and buffers are enabled to demand almost their own price. They sell their lives, but sell them dear. They sell five, ten, or fifteen years of their lives at about the rate (as nearly as I could estimate) of one hundred pounds per year. I am glad to say Parliament has at length interfered to put a stop to this traffic in suicide, and by an act soon to come in force masters are required to exact the wearing of respirators. But what an idea does it give us of the struggle for existence in these over-crowded islands that there should be entire classes of laborers glad to convert and coin their very heart and lungs into money—to become employés of Death himself, if he but pay a guinea more in wages than Life! It may be they are martyrs, those grim investors in the grave, and that the few more pounds are sending children to school, and shall raise over their dead hearts happier homes. But, for that matter, all drudgery is self-murder of one kind or another. No man can toil through life twelve, or even ten, hours a day without atrophy to the intellect or starvation to the affections. Poor John Grahame there, with the iron entering his soul and body, knows very well that real living is not for him: he sees, however, in some little face one window amidst Sheffield smoke opening into the azure of hope; and his last will and testament (as on file in the highest Tribunal) runs thus: "I, John Grahame, give and bequeath to my son William Grahame all my earthly estate—to wit, twenty years of my life on earth." So John adjourns his soul's birth to his child.

JOHN FORNEY:

"THE COMMON TONGUE IS
MUCH BETTER SPOKEN
IN AMERICA"

1867

The remarkable thing about the English language in America is how much it has been and is like the English language in England. For the past two centuries, it can be said, an educated Englishman would have less difficulty understanding an American from New York than a Yorkshireman from old. Americans themselves have always been sensitive—and justly so—to English slurs on the American language. ("No curiosities, no ruins," said the Canterville Ghost to the American girl. "You have your language and your Navy.") Noah Webster asserted, back in the 1780s, that the best English was spoken in America and predicted what came to be true—that the speech of the common man in America would reveal fewer class or regional differences than that of the common man in the Mother Country.

John Forney was a politician and journalist who, when confronted by the slavery issue, changed from a Buchanan Democrat to a Lincoln Republican. Editor of newspapers in Washington and Philadelphia, he was at different times Clerk of the House of Representatives and Secretary of the United States Senate; in 1871 he was rewarded for his devotion to the Republican cause by

From John Forney, *Letters from Europe* (Philadelphia, 1867), pp. 339–343.

an appointment as collector of the Port of Philadelphia. This letter on the English and American language is one of many which he sent back to his newspaper from England in 1867.

Liverpool, August 20, 1867

The very worst side appears first in the United States. In Europe all the outer surface is polished and fascinating; and he who travels quickly has little time, and often less inclination, to break through the glittering shell. When he does he is filled with consternation at the sufferings of so many millions of his fellow-creatures. Everybody travels in our portion of America; and the intelligent foreigner, especially one who journeys for the purpose of using his eyes and his ears, and who examines nothing without some ulterior object of criticism, is perhaps not to be blamed when he gives way to his prejudices at the odd habits which in this way astonish him on every side. Had Mr. Dickens remained among us long enough, or had he allowed his really fearless nature to understand that the people he satirized some twenty-five years ago were not yet in the gristle of first manhood, and were bound upon confessedly the greatest mission ever started for the relief and the rescue of mankind, he would doubtless have revised many of his earlier impressions, and have evolved a more practical philosophy from that more careful observation. Coming over here, fully accustomed to all the things which excited the risibilities of Mr. Dickens, I have not attempted to restrain my own surprise at much that I see, and if I were to undertake to make an elaborate record of this experience you would generally sympathize with me. . . .

Our English critics speak most disparagingly of the nasal tones of the American dialect, but they never admit the fact that the large majority of their own people constantly spoil and drown their own language in the most savage jargon. Nothing is more agreeable to me than to hear our language spoken by an accomplished English gentleman or lady. Their cultivated voices, their delicate and exact pronunciation, and the charming avoidance of all clamor in conversation, are inexpressibly agreeable, yet the same may be said of the cultivated classes in our own country; but when the masses of the people of England and America are compared, no fair judge will deny that our common tongue is much better spoken by the latter. In fact, the lingual intercourse between the working people of England is so uncouth and barbaric as to sound more like the vernacular of Indian tribes. No Englishman, however censorious, can fail to understand an American, however ignorant; but my ingenuity has been frequently taxed to understand a single word of the incoherencies of men and women who were talking to each other in some of the rural districts I visited in Great Britain. There are at least a dozen different dialects, formed by variations in pronunciation, in England alone, while the distinction even of counties is so strongly marked in Scotland and Ireland that an accustomed ear will soon distinguish between the barbarous sounds, in conversation, by the natives of Aberdeen and Fife, of the shores of Lanark and Berwick, and a native of Ulster is as equally to be distinguished from his neighbor in Connaught as the semi-Anglican pronunciation of Dublin instantly strikes the ear as different from the peculiar tightness of utterance in Cork. I was informed on the authority of an eminent philologist, who had made the subject of dialects one of his particular studies, that a thorough Lancashireman, indulging in his country's habit of nipping some words and extending the sound of others, would scarcely be understood by an ordinary Londoner or Cockney, who, in turn, by changing his v into w, and removing the h from where it should and placing it where it should not be sounded, would almost speak an unknown tongue in the north of England, where there are curious varieties of intonation. There is what is called "a burr" in the pronunciation of Northumberland, in the northeast, and also in Cumberland, in the northwest of the Island. The two counties actually join, yet the natives pronounce so differently that the Cumbrian is not readily understood by the Northumbrian, and *vice versa.* Lancashire has not only a dialect of its own, but, as I hear, even a literature of its own, many books (badly spelled, to show the peculiar pronunciation), emanating from the local press every year, to the great delight of the native population. In the southern county of Dorset, there also is a particular literature, composed in the local tongue, as difficult to understand, without previous knowledge or close study, as that of Lancashire. The peculiar habit of the west of England, and particularly of Somersetshire, of giving the sound of z to the letter s, is balanced by the habit, in the eastern counties, of sounding i as if it were a. I was informed that it would be practicable to get a dozen Englishmen together, from various localities, who, for some little time at least, would understand each other as little as if they had never belonged to those

Who speak the tongue that Shakespeare spake.

PERCY ROBERTS:

"THE SPIRIT OF CONSERVATISM

DEEPLY IMBUES

THE NATIONAL CHARACTER"

1867

Percy Roberts ("Carte Blanche") was the European correspondent of the once famous *De Bow's Review,* for long the leading southern quarterly—a kind of rival to the *North American Review,* but with far more emphasis on commercial and economic matters.

The English are the genius of the practical. Metaphysical relations do not enlist them, unless they grapple some concrete effect. Transcendentalism they surrender to Germany and the clouds. Carlyle, De Quincey, Coleridge, and a few other of their best minds, have endeavored to turn them towards abstract and speculative philosophy, but only with indifferent and partial success. Bacon was, in many respects, the truest historical representative of the ideal Englishman. The promotion of earthly knowledge, the satisfaction of earthly wants, the amelioration of human conditions, the gratification of taste, and the general progress of a splendid material civilization, made up a code of philosophy which spoke in congenial

From Carte Blanche, "England and the English," *De Bow's Review, After the War Series,* III (1867) pp. 235–243.

provisions to the great mass of the British nation. The zenith above, and the horizon which circumscribes the visible world, are the metes of the empire they court. Out of the dominion which embraces the temporal man—his interests and relations—the English mind does not usually wander. It deals mainly with facts, and it must be acknowledged, with an ability which has never been surpassed. Deficient, upon the whole, perhaps, in invention, they possess in a supreme degree, the capacity to incarnate suggestions, and thereby minister to the wants, the comforts, and the happiness of mankind. The national intellect is built upon a solid adamant of common sense, and this it is which has enabled this small island to furnish us with so many wise financiers, so many sagacious statesmen, so many pithy books, so many healthy women, so much reasonable fashion in dress. The absence of the imaginative as a dominant element, qualified them all the better probably for the business of life. The faculty of seeing things as they are, without distortion or glamour, a hard, clear adaptation of means to ends, and bull-dog resolution and grip, make failure in individual enterprise or practical statesmanship a phenomenon.

The spirit of conservatism deeply imbues the national character. It evinces itself in the attachment to old laws, old customs, the love of homesteads, the cherishing of family souvenirs, the toughness of family ties, and the worship of household gods. They prefer, on the whole, to bear an ascertained evil rather than imperil their peace in quest of a speculative good. *Quieta non movere* is a cardinal maxim with them, in their laws, their social usage and their public polity. Innovation appeals to them, decked in the *bonnet rouge* of the faubourg St. Antoine, and their instinctive impulse is to recoil from it as from a torch of revolution.

A trade or profession is bequeathed as a hereditament from father to son, and with it the office or shop in which it was practised. The shop itself grows into the dignity of an heir-loom, and is stuck to with dogged reverence, long after an increase of wealth and wider relations entreat the hospitality of more commodious quarters. I was shown lately in London, a tailoring establishment, in which the goose had been wielded by father, son and grandsons for two centuries and a half; and in the ancient town of Chester I dined in a public-house which had been a hotel for one thousand years.

The lawyers and judges still bear their droll head-gear of wigs; the pomp and ancient circumstance of coronations are laboriously preserved; plum puddings are an article in the established religion; the humanities are still flogged into reluctant youth, and impressment remains a part of their naval code. A faint aroma of the long-ago hallows the whole body of their customs. No other nation ever combined in such apposite and indestructible marriage the Past and the Present. What we see now is young England truly, but young England with old England always peeping benignly over its shoulder. This curious interfusion is as pregnant of moral value as it is touching to the imagination, for it knits the nation into a solid and homogeneous unity.

The national love of the bygone is nurtured and organized as it were by the durable forms in which their current performance is cast. They foster the instinct by providing the material receptacles in which it may congenially lodge. Their houses challenge the action of time; their bridges are made of stone; their docks bid defiance to the sea; their railroads will endure with the hills; their terms of lease stretch from 99 to 999 years; their whole scheme of internal improvement has an eye fixed upon doomsday; and their very caprices are moulded in iron and wrought in marble.

Put up a new man against one of ancient birth, and other things being equal, the popular heart will turn to the candidate whose genealogy reaches to the Conqueror. Notwithstanding the constant movement towards reform, and the angry clamor of radicals, nobility in England is rooted deep in the affections of the people. It rests upon three enduring mud-sills of popularity; its antiquity, its wealth and its accessibility. The old families of the country, which stretch back until their origin is lost in moss-grown tradition, and whose names are associated with the great historical events which gave fame and state to England, appeal to the most universal element in the English nature. They are a living and visible link, connecting the present with the past; a link encrusted with memorials, which speak pleasingly to English pride.

The law of primogeniture has built up and retained in this nobility that essential foundation of all aristocracy, wealth. Many of them enjoy revenues large enough to sustain a regal establishment. This qualifies them to be munificent patrons, to perform noble charities and to comply with the most extravagant exactions of a cultivated taste. In the indulgence of this taste, they have contributed largely to embellish England, and, through the national vanity, to bewitch the popular imagination. Actuated by English enterprise and backed by English gold, they have assessed the world of its beautiful in art, its valuable in science, its curious in nature, and brought them back as spoils to enrich their English homes. The private caskets which contain these national jewels are themselves marvels of human achievement. The genius of architecture has wrought out its loftiest inspirations in the English castles and palaces, and their ornamental grounds incarnate the poet's dream of Paradise. Nor are these kept as sealed fountains from the multitude. They are unlocked to the free inspection and enjoyment of the commonalty, and are among their favorite resorts for recreation. Thither the people flock when they doff the harness of labor, and stretch their limbs for a bit of Sunday holiday. As Englishmen, they are proud of these splendid residences and these fairy lands of art, while a perfect liberty to enjoy them infuses a faint sense of proprietorship which imparts to the English pride a zest and potency.

Finally, nobility in England is susceptible of acquisition. Every actual Englishman is a possible lord. The diffusion of democratic ideas in the world for the past two centuries has assailed, with success, the principle of monopoly. In England it has breached the wall of exclusion in which rank was hedged, and opened it to the competition of energy, pluck and skill. A representative of the meanest rank in the social organization may aspire to its dignities. It is the final goal to which all the professions lift their aspirations. It is the fruition of English fame. It hangs above the lawyer, the physician, the artist, the writer, the soldier, the sailor, the scholar, the traveler, the student of science, a dazzling bribe for excellence. Even the mechanic looks hopefully through his mask of soot, admonished that the prize belongs to him, in whatever walk of life, who may strike a successful blow for the good of England. Hence, nobility is made the supreme object of popular ambition; and many a stout commoner . . . while he declaims with irascible eloquence against the abuse of class, is expending his substance and taxing his last energy to swell in his own person the list of the objurgated. Thus consecrated by antiquity, thus formidable by wealth, thus held up to contemplation as an attainable guerdon, great revolutions must occur before nobility can be extirpated as an estate of the British Constitution.

Had I the choice of a role in life, my preferences would unhesitatingly fix upon an English noble of unencumbered property. He enjoys much of the consideration which enures to a sovereign, divested of the latter's responsibilities, his social isolation and his limitations of personal freedom. He inherits a life estate of political influence, which he can wield personally or by proxy, just as his inclinations suggest. He can be Sir Oracle at home or an honored guest abroad; the prestige of nationality protects him wherever a vagrant fancy may carry him; his title is a *visé* to the best society in all lands, and his wealth enables him to make his own theory of happiness his only chart of action. . . .

There is a directness, an absolute point-blankness about the English which is partly a natural efflorescence and partly the result of a long and drastic commercial training. The superflous is disgusting to them, circuity they abhor, and parade is intolerable, save in certain pet ceremonials which are franchised by immemorial precedent. The Englishman shrinks from the dramatic as he would from a galvanic battery. He will do a heroic thing if you please, but would do it sedately and utterly purged of bluster. He is fond of rich fabrics, but economical of colors. He deals only in subdued tints. This rejection of the meretricious, this passion for the simple and the substantive, rises to the consistency and empire of a trait. It is reflected from the legislature, the bar, the pulpit; from manners, costume and even from the stage. A member of Parliament talks, but does not speak. If he aspired to declamation, he would probably have an audience of empty benches, unless his fellow-members remained to cry "hear, hear" injuriously. Charles Sumner would depopulate the House of Commons with a single oration. They value long wind, you see, mainly in horses. Barristers rarely venture into eloquence. They state their cases in unambitious periods, and argue colloquially. Clergymen dissertate admirably, but as a general thing do not preach—at least, not as we understand it. Acting conforms to the same unpronounced standards. Tragedy is compelled to dismount from stilts, and rest its buskin upon solid earth. Passion is too serious a thing in the English mind to have a fellow tear it to tatters. Rant, therefore, gets more cuffs than claps. Comedy is served likewise. Humor must not rollick over-much. Pungent as you like, but mannerly, please God. An Englishman enjoys his laugh as he says his prayers, soberly and like a gentleman.

In a nation italicized by such moral characteristics, a certain tone of manners logically results. We have a right to expect in them what we actually find, a sobriety of address and a general freedom from foppery in language, costume and demeanor. A degree of phlegm is constitutional, and polite usage has adopted and fostered it as its crowning virtue. Emotions are ostracized as being at once pastoral and dramatic. A display of feelings is presumptive evidence of bucolicism. Sensibilities, like curs, they accept as necessary evils, but exact, for the protection of society, that they shall be kept by their owners securely muzzled. . . .

The laws which govern this society are more critically observed than any enactment of Parliament. Referring for their sanctions to that most despotic of all powers, a severely-drilled public opinion, they reign with a dominion little short of omnipotent. English etiquette may excuse a breach of morals, but a solecism in breeding is to blaspheme the Holy Ghost. Such sharp social discipline has sensibly contributed to produce a type of gentleman unsurpassed in the *salons* of civilized society. It takes leisure and a good school of manners to form a race of gentlemen. A gentleman is, to a large extent, conventional, and requires as much education as the member of any other guild. The essential elements may be, and are, perhaps, native; but, like other natural endowments, they demand sedulous schooling to perform all of their functions acceptably. The English have the leisure and possess the nursery, and do not lack in that moral substratum upon which all true gentility must found. . . .

Whatever they undertake to do they perform conscientiously and thoroughly. Their hides lie in vats three years before they christen them leather. Their woollen cloth is made of wool and their linen of flax. Their guns shoot to the mark; their watches keep time, and their knives hold their edge. Their magazines graduate the fees they pay their contributors on the basis of a minimum, and not a maximum, as in America. Here an article is accepted if it falls *below* a certain price; there it is refused unless it rises in value *above* a certain price. This sways the best writing talents of the kingdom. Thus their periodical literature is a success, because in that, as in other enterprises, they organize victory. A long experience has demonstrated to this grave and sagacious people that there is no permanent escape from the law of *quid pro quo;* that cheap investments can only germinate into cheap returns. They estimate cautiously, decide upon the maturest deliberation, and then economize no expenditure necessary to fructify their schemes.

CONGRESSMAN GARFIELD
WATCHES THE DEBATE ON
THE REFORM BILL OF 1867

1867

"Dizzy has produced a Reform Bill" wrote John Lothrop Motley, who was in London at the time, "and jockeyed his party into supporting it, which is more liberal than anything [John] Bright would have ventured to propose." It was indeed, and while there had been earlier examples of the operation of Tory democracy, it was Disraeli who anticipated it in his novel, *Coningsby*, and who put it in practice when he came to political power. The debate which Garfield here describes, on August 8, had to do with a minor but important amendment to the bill, which provided that in constituencies that chose three members of Parliament no elector could vote for more than two—an amendment designed to secure minority representation. Bright found himself in the awkward position of opposing the amendment.

James A. Garfield had had a distinguished career, first in Ohio politics, then as a Civil War general. As a congressman from Ohio he rose to be, after the death of Thaddeus Stevens, the most powerful figure in the House. In 1880 he was elected to the Senate; instead of taking his seat in that body he allowed himself to be nominated (the first "dark horse" nominee) for the presidency.

From "Garfield in Europe, Extracts from the Journal of a Trip to Europe in 1867," *Century Magazine*, new series, V (1883–84), pp. 416–418.

Narrowly elected, he was on the way to a distinguished presidential career when on July 2, 1881, he was shot by an insane office seeker, Charles Guiteau.

Thursday, August 8, 1867

. . . At 4, we went to Westminster Hall. I sent Mr. Chase's letter to John Bright, who came out and got me in back of the Peers' seat, under the Speaker's gallery, where I had a fine view, and where I staid—except when divisions were being taken—till near midnight.

When I went in at half-past 4, petitions were being presented in open house; each member reading his petition, and carrying it to the Speaker's table. There are no pages, and, besides the doorkeepers, there appear to be no officers in the House, except the Speaker, who wears a full-bottomed wig, and three clerks, who sit directly before him, in half, or short wigs.

When a member read a petition of four thousand citizens of Birmingham in favor of Lord Cairns's amendment for a third vote in tripartite constituencies, Bright followed with a monster petition on the other side. Then followed a volley of questions fired at the Administration from all sides, and their responses. Disraeli sat passionless and motionless, except a trotting of the foot, indicative of a high pitch of intellectual activity and expectancy. His face reveals nothing. The most pointed allusions, either of logic, fact, or wit, fail to move a muscle or change a line of the expression.

At 5, the Reform Bill is announced, and all sounds subside in the crowded hall—so full that several members sit in the gallery. Disraeli, in a very calm, somewhat halting way, goes over the chief points of the Lords' amendments, puts them very adroitly, and in a very conciliatory tone speaks about twenty minutes. Meanwhile, Bright has been sitting on the second row, and next the gangway, taking a note now and then, manifesting a little nervousness in the hands and fingers, and occasionally passing his hand over his ample forehead. Mill is settled down in his seat, with his chin resting in the palm of his hand, and giving close attention, as he does to everything that passes. By the way, his face greatly disappoints me in one respect: there is nothing of the Jovine breadth and fullness of brow I expected; but there is great depth from brow to cerebellum, and strong, well-defined features. There is a nervous twitching of the muscles of his head and face, which probably results from hard work. Gladstone rises and opens the debate on the Opposition side, in an adroit speech of eight minutes, evidently reserving himself for a fuller assault later in the evening. He is the most un-English speaker I have yet heard, and the best. Disraeli shows great tact in determining how far to persist and when to yield. In that essential point of leadership, Palmerston has probably never been excelled. Disraeli is no mean disciple of his. Gladstone, with more ability than either, is said to be especially lacking in that respect.

After several more amendments have been given up with apparent reluctance, but for the sake of harmony, the amendment of Lord Cairns is reached, on which the ministry intend to make a stubborn fight. Bright opens the attack in a speech of half an hour or more. Though cordially disliked by the Tories, he compels attention at once. With a form like that of Senator Wilson, of Massachusetts, he has a large, round, full, fine, massive head, and straight, almost delicate nose. He has a full, rotund voice, and, like Gladstone, is un-English in his style—that is, he speaks right on, with but little of that distressful hobbling which marks the mass of Parliamentary speakers. With all my sympathy with Bright and the Liberals, I am inclined to favor the amendment. I remember Mill's discussion of it in his *Representative Government,* and his approving reference to the work of Hare on the same subject. Bright put the case very strongly on his side, and pointed out the anomalies it would produce; but I thought they would result from the limited application of the principle, rather than from the principle itself. I also thought it a little inconsistent in him, who has been so bold an advocate for change, to object to this as an innovation. But he put his case very strongly, and made us sympathize with his earnestness. Many speeches were leveled at him; but, like all politicians, he seems to have become a pachyderm, and paid no attention to it. Howmuchsoever they may affect to despise him, they cannot blink the fact, which even the *Times* admitted this morning in a mean attack on him, that "John Bright was the most skillful speaker in England, and, in some kinds of oratory, the first orator."

I notice that many of the leaders were high honor men at the universities. Gladstone took a "double-first"; Roundell Palmer took a "first" in classics, and many other classic honors and prizes. Mill is not a University man, but his *Logic* has been a text-book at Oxford for twenty years. Tom Hughes, who made Rugby and himself immortal, was not a first-class scholar. Forster is a good speaker and a Radical, but I do not know what his scholarship was.

At 10, Gladstone rose and spoke for nearly an hour, going into the whole question with great clearness and incisive force. He spoke with much more feeling than any other except Bright. Gladstone was followed by Lowe, who is considered the strongest man of his school in the House. He sits on the Opposition side; but on this question of suffrage is Conservative. He is nearly blind, and spoke without notes and with his eyes apparently shut. He combines sharpness with a remarkable toughness of intellectual fiber, which makes a powerfull assailant. It was exceedingly fine the way he sought out and javelined the exposed joints of his antagonist's harness. Gladstone winced manifestly. About half past 11 a division was had, which resulted: 206 against and 258 in favor (ed: actually 204 to 253). This is a strong example of the influence of the Ministry. When the same principle was discussed in the Commons a few weeks ago, Disraeli made a strong speech against it, and it was negatived by 140 majority. It had been very curious to see what different and opposite motives have moved men to favor this new feature in representative government. Mill votes for this only as an installment of what he has long advocated as a *doctrinaire;* that minorities should be represented, and he hopes to see it prevail in all elections. He thinks it will vitalize voters, and virtually extend the suffrage. He votes for it as a higher step toward democracy. Gladstone opposes it for this very reason, and several others because it will give them a Tory member. The *Times* favors it for this reason, and because it thinks it will control the democratic tendencies of the bill.

The measure seems to me to be vulnerable; first, because of the practical difficulties in carrying it into operation; secondly, because of its partial application.

The voting-paper clause was taken up, and the House of Commons refused to concur with the Lords.

I left the Commons a little before midnight, having witnessed the practical consummation of the greatest advance toward political liberty made in England in a century.

THE REVEREND ANDREW PEABODY
OBSERVES A SPECIMEN
OF ENGLISH PULPIT ELOQUENCE

1867

Andrew Peabody was one of the most distinguished of American Unitarians. Something of a prodigy, he was admitted to Harvard College as a sophomore at the age of thirteen and received his degree at the age of fifteen, and at seventeen he was principal of a New Hampshire Academy. He then took a divinity degree and was pastor of the Portsmouth, New Hampshire, Unitarian Church when he was called to the Chair of Christian Morals at Harvard University. Probably the most beloved of Harvard professors, he served, at times, as acting president of the university. In between teaching, preaching, and traveling he found time to write some hundred and twenty books and pamphlets.

Charles Spurgeon, the subject of this commentary, was in his way quite as precocious and quite as brilliant as Peabody. Converted as a mere boy to the Baptist faith, he was at twenty-two pastor of one of the largest churches in London, a church which his eloquence and address speedily made by far the largest. His rapt parishioners built him a Tabernacle seating four thousand, and the thousands who were unable to hear him could buy his printed

From Andrew P. Peabody, *Reminiscences of Travel* (Cambridge, Mass., 1868), pp. 19–24.

sermons—altogether twenty-five hundred of them. Spurgeon carried on his parish duties, set up a training college for ministers, established an orphanage, and engaged in social work and social reform with great effectiveness.

English pulpit eloquence, in general, seemed to me utterly unworthy of its office, and entirely below the demand of the times; and I always found the most meagre preaching where the apparatus for the highly artistical performance of religious services was the most ample and elaborate. I attended, one Sunday evening, one of the meetings for the people of which we have heard so much, under the dome of St. Paul's. There could not have been less than three or four thousand persons present. The preachers had come from Edinburgh, and was announced by placards all over the city for eight or ten days beforehand. His sermon was just fifteen minutes long, consisted only of desultory remarks by which I thought he was groping his way toward a subject, and while I was listening with some solicitude for the announcement of his theme he broke off with the closing doxology. The sermons that I heard at the Temple Church, Westminster Abbey, and sundry cathedrals, were, in general, admirably written, but jejune or trite in thought, and cold as an iceberg. The ministers of the parish churches, especially those of the evangelical party, impressed me much more favorably. They preach like men thoroughly in earnest; but they have not yet found the most efficient way of doing their work. They are very much in the habit of preaching from partially written sermons, extemporizing at frequent intervals, with a small Bible in the hand from which they read illustrative texts, often naming the chapter and verse. Their evident sincerity and earnestness greatly interested me; yet it seemed to me—I know not if it were so—as if they were in a transition state, as if this method had but lately come into use; they had not yet become accustomed to it, and were forfeiting the advantages of the fully written sermon, without having acquired due freedom and power in extempore utterance.

Of course I heard Spurgeon, and I regard it as a great privilege to have heard him. His Tabernacle is on the Surrey side of the Thames, about a mile and a half from Temple Bar, an immense building, severely simple in style, with a row of Doric pillars and a Grecian pediment in front. Within, two deep galleries extend along all four sides of the edifice. There is no pulpit. The preacher stands surrounded by hearers, on a semicircular platform which projects from the lower gallery, opposite the entrance-doors. The church, when I was there, was entirely full, and it is said to contain not less than four thousand persons. The audience were breathlessly still, except at the close of the prayers and the exposition, and at pauses between the heads of the sermon, when there was a tumultuous explosion of suppressed breathing, coughing, and analogous processes. The service was two hours and a half in length; yet no one seemed to be fatigued. There were three hymns sung by the congregation without any instrumental accompaniment, and the sound was "as the voice of many waters." There were two prayers, and a reading of Scripture with an able and copious exposition. The sermon was strongly Calvinistic, and I could not entirely sympathize with its doctrinal statements; but it was real preaching, and the preaching of the church dignitaries seemed child's play as compared with it.

Spurgeon has a physiognomy full of strength and beauty. The ordinary engravings of him are like him, yet unlike. They give him a somewhat coarse, sensuous look, which he may perhaps have, when his features are in repose; but in preaching his countenance is radiant, spiritual, and wonderfully vivid in its play and in its prompt adaptation to the thought he utters. His voice is the finest I ever heard. Every syllable could be clearly distinguished by every ear in his vast audience, and his tones were all those of easy, colloquial discourse, with no rant, and no striving for effect. There are in his early printed sermons passages revolting for their coarseness and irreverence, poor jokes, stale anecdotes, illustrations drawn from low life; but I am inclined to think that these were due to his then imperfect culture. He has evidently been a rapidly improving man, and he must have made himself familiar with the best models of style. When I heard him, there was not a word which could offend the most fastidious taste. His language was pure English, with a predominance of the Saxon element. His words were singularly well chosen. There is a rare intensity and lifelikeness in his mode of stating religious truth, which arrests and enchains the attention. Without degrading spiritual themes, he makes them seem almost visible and tangible. His imagery is sensuous, as appealing to the perceptive faculties, yet pure and elevating to the thought. He translates, as it were, the language and the narratives of Scripture, the parables and similes of the Gospels, into the things that most nearly correspond to them in our own time, and says just what it may be supposed the apostles would have written in England in the nineteenth century, in lieu of what they wrote in the first century in Palestine. Such preaching teaches the common people as they can be taught in no other way; interprets to them what would else be unintelligible. One cannot hear Spurgeon without being not only convinced of his sincerity, but impressed with the entire absence of self-reference, his complete identification with his work, and his burning zeal in the cause of his Divine Master. There can be no doubt that he is now exerting a more extended influence than any other preacher in the kingdom, and is second to none among the moral forces in the great metropolis.

Next to him in his power as a popular preacher, his superior by far in culture, his equal in self-devoted zeal, is Newman Hall, whom many of my readers have recently heard. I heard him preach at St. James's Hall, to an immense audience, composed almost wholly of the poorest classes—of persons who are never seen in any church. His sermon was remarkable for its entire freedom from dogmatic subtleties, its directness, simplicity, and intense earnestness. Spurgeon speaks as though he were wholly absorbed in his subject; Hall, as if he took up into his own strong emotional nature the needs, wants, trials, infirmities, and sorrows of his entire audience. With his hale and bluff manhood there is a wonderful closeness and tenderness of sympathy, and the coarse, rude people hang upon his words, as if a brother, who felt all that they feel, were pleading with them for their highest good.

At the widest possible distance from these men is another great preacher, well known by his writings on this side of the Atlantic —Martineau. I heard but one sermon from him, and that was a discourse of very extraordinary power and merit. It was undoubtedly occasioned by his then recent rejection as a candidate for the Professorship of Intellectual Science in the London University, in effecting which the decisive weight was thrown into the adverse scale by well known positivists. The sermon was a profoundly philosophical vindication of the Divine Providence against the postulates of the positive philosophy. So much, so deep, and so fructifying thought can seldom have been condensed into the same space; and though his hearers listened intently, as if accustomed to highly concentrated spiritual nutriment, there are few congregations in Christendom which such a discussion would not have overtaxed. With the philosophy there ran along a rich vein of devout sentiment, so that to recipient minds there was edification no less than instruction. But the preacher's manner was chilling. His voice is clear and strong; but his delivery is almost monotonous—not the monotony of indifference or dullness, but of suppressed feeling—still less the monotony of feebleness, but of reserved and smothered power. His oratory is eminently that of a commanding mind, weighty and impressive; but at the same time it is heavy and unexciting.

I have spaced only to add, that Martineau approaches the normal type of English oratory much more nearly than Spurgeon or Hall. Old England prefers in her orators, with the gravity and wisdom, the subdued and quiet tone and style of mature, if not of senile age.

S. R. FISKE:

THE TRAGIC LOT OF

WOMEN IN ENGLAND

1868

Americans have habitually been confused about the position of women in English society, and perhaps never more than in the Victorian era. On the one hand England had a Queen—something the United States could never achieve—and every English Lady was a great lady by definition. On the other hand the English did not really take women seriously; their greatest novelist wrote under a man's name—George Eliot—and even their brightest girls were not admitted to Oxford or Cambridge—and where else could they go? As for the lower classes, the lot of women there was indeed hard, and frequently tragic.

Stephen Ryder Fiske, a drama critic and theater manager, knew England well and lived there for several years during the 1870s, managing the St. James's Theatre and the Royal English Opera Company. Earlier a drama critic on the *New York Herald,* he founded the *New York Dramatic Mirror;* wrote plays himself, in addition to his *English Photographs;* and introduced Mary Anderson and Madame Modjeska to the New York stage.

From S. R. Fiske, "English Photographs by an American, No. VI, Women in England and America," *Harper's New Monthly Magazine,* XXXVIII (1868–69), pp. 93–97.

Women are worse treated in Great Britain than in any other civilized country. High or low, rich or poor, married or single, none of them escape from some of the disabilities, prejudices, and injustices from which their sex suffers. They are obliged to endure not only all the pains and penalties inflicted upon the women of other nations, but also certain special injuries and annoyances invented and practiced by Englishmen alone. Perhaps an American notices this state of affairs more quickly than other observers, because he comes from a country in which, according to the judgment of foreign critics, the women are treated too well. But the Americans do not believe that it is possible to be too kind to women. They hold that, while men may have been created "a little lower than the angels," women were formed upon a perfect equality with the celestial personages. Nor is this a mere sentimental belief, as immaterial as French politeness; it is carried into practical effect in a thousand ways, and to a great extent it modifies and mollifies the habits, customs, and manners of the people. The result is, as our critics tell us, that the American women are spoiled. But in England the case is even worse; for here the men are spoiled. . . .

The inferior position of Englishwomen is first apparent to a foreigner in a variety of little details. Returning from an early-morning ride, he notices the cottages of the working-people by the road-side. The women are up and about, making the fires, carrying the coals, opening the house, while the men are still snoring soundly. I should like to see an American husband wait for his wife, or an American son for his mother, to perform these matutinal functions. If he were not speedily bewigged by his own better-half, a more serious punishment would be adjudged him by a vigilance committee of neighboring housewives. Or breakfast is being prepared, and you notice the women buttering the bread so as to save their lords and masters the slightest unnecessary exertion. An American husband might eat dry bread forever if he were unwilling to butter it himself. Then you catch sight of a woman on her knees lacing or unlacing a man's boots. So menial a service would scandalize the best American wives. If an Englishman want a pipe, it is the woman who fills it and hands him the light; if his pot need replenishing, it is the woman who procures and pours out the ale; if there be an errand to be done, it is the woman who trots off while the man loafs or rests at home. In short, Englishwomen belonging to what are called the lower classes are evidently the servants of the men, while in America the men are as evidently the servants of the women, only that this latter service being that of the stronger to the weaker, never seems like servitude, even in the humblest families, but takes the nobler forms of politeness, solicitude, and duty.

But this sketch has darker tints. These lower-class women not only perform menial services, but they are treated far worse than any other servants in the world. Many of them are married only in name. From various causes, but mainly from lack of education, the marriage-rites are lightly esteemed by these poor women—or rather not by the women, who would give almost their lives for honest marriage-lines, but by their fathers and the fathers of their children. As among the negroes of the South before emancipation, a man and woman agree to live together; their relatives, friends, and neighbors acknowledge the implied relationship by calling the woman "Mrs.," and the upper classes care nothing about it, since it does not immediately concern them, and is pretty sure to provide another generation of laborers for the work of the future. In the South emancipation had to be attended by the solemnization of thousands of marriages, which might have been made in heaven years before, but had not been legally ratified on earth; and so in England, any genuine reform among the lower orders will have to be commenced by a joint crusade of clergymen and teachers—the former for the parents, the latter for the children. At present, all concerned accept the situation; the unmarried couples congratulate themselves upon having saved the parson's fees, and spend more than the fees in drink to celebrate their economy; and the women, having lost their virtue, often find themselves linked with brutes who had no virtue of their own to lose, and who soon deprive them of every comfort in life.

Even when things turn out better than this, the man never treats his mistress quite so well as he would his wife. He feels that she has no hold upon him, while he has every hold upon her. The language he uses to her is colored with this conscious superiority. If she offend him he knocks her down or beats her, and she has no redress, fearing to go to the magistrate lest she should thereby lose a home. If she be his wife her tongue is tied quite as tightly; for then she is obliged to go home to him to suffer fresh brutalities. I do not say that all the laboring class of Englishmen are drunkards, but the most of them drink too much, and they drink a poison of which the women feel the dire effects. The women drink also, and society countenances them in this vice. To see an English ale-house or gin-palace, with the women standing up at the counter and behind the counter, is a positive shock to a stranger. Nowhere else can you meet so disgusting a sight, so brutalizing a custom. On the Continent women are to be seen sitting in *cafés* or *bier-gartens,* and sharing their light wine, coffee, or chocolate with male friends; but nowhere on the Continent is there such a licensed Pandemonium as an English bar. . . .

Custom may blind the eyes and deafen the ears of Englishmen to the sights and sounds of vice among women that startle the foreigner at every turn; but this monster, Custom, is a part of the ill-treatment of Englishwomen. . . . Custom permits prostitutes to take entire possession of the Haymarket and its vicinity after ten o'clock at night. Custom opens dance-houses and promenade concerts for the express accommodation of prostitutes, although the authorities who license them know that they are simply places of assignation. Custom sets apart certain districts of London for the residences of lewd women. Custom keeps open night-houses, in order that prostitutes may be able to get drunk after the regular taverns have closed at midnight. Custom is responsible for all this; but Englishmen are responsible for the custom. . . .

Of grosser kinds of cruelty, such as wife-beating, wife-kicking, and wife-murder, Englishmen appear to have almost the monopoly. It is sickening to read in the police reports of the daily papers the records of those crimes against the persons of women which disfigure the current annals of England. Taking a paper at random from the file before me, I find that the reports open with three attempts at picking pockets; then comes a rape case; then a woman robbed with violence; then a woman thrown out of a window; then a woman beaten to death; then a woman poisoned. Better all the stabbing and shooting affrays between men in the United States than these continual assaults upon women in a country where every common man professes to know how to use his fists—but prefers his teeth or his boots—and every ruffian displays his knowledge of "the manly art" by hitting some defenseless woman with a club or an axe. Englishmen are conscious of their superiority over "the fiery Frenchmen, the stupid Germans, the assassinating Italians, the dumfounded Spaniards, and the rowdy Americans," to use Mr. Roebuck's elegant adjectives; but if any of these barbarians heard a woman's voice exclaiming, "Don't kick me any more, please, Bill! I'll do all you want if you won't kick me any more!" I would not insure Bill's life for a farthing. But in civilized England a crowd recently heard these cries, and waited patiently outside till Bill had kicked his woman into eternity. Still, as I have before hinted, there are injuries which torture women more crucially than black eyes or slit throats. Like the old Christians, they care less for wounds which kill the body than for those which kill the soul. I am often surprised, however, that they bear physical wrongs so patiently. Elsewhere women sometimes kill or horsewhip their seducers; in England they quietly go upon the town, and send their children to "baby-farmers" to be starved. At Milwaukie recently an English laborer attempted to beat his sick wife one Sunday afternoon. He had an easy antagonist by his own fireside; but suddenly the door was burst open, and in walked a dozen Irish viragos, who thumped him with mops and pokers until he cried for mercy and swore that he would never molest his wife again. In America, too, women have coolly sacked the grog-shop that was ruining their husbands, pouring the liquors into the streets and threatening the landlord with tar and feathers if he complained. Are Englishwomen less brave at home than across the seas? Is there no heroism in the breasts that have suckled so many heroes? One good example of extempore justice, with only Judge Lynch on the bench, would be worth a dozen tardy convictions and merciful sentences before the stipendiary magistrates.

HELEN HUNT JACKSON:
THE FACES OF THE
NEWHAVEN FISHWIVES ARE
"FULL OF BEAUTY"

1869

Daughter of an Amherst College professor and schoolmate of Emily Dickinson, Helen Fiske first married Edward Hunt. In her mid-thirties widowhood forced her to earn a living, and she then produced three pieces of writing any one of which would have insured her a permanent place in American literature: the "Saxe Holm" stories, in their day immensely popular; *A Century of Dishonor,* which did more to rally public support to the mistreated and exploited Indian than any other writing of the century; and *Ramona,* a romantic novel about life in Spanish California which won instant popularity and literary acclaim. Mrs. Jackson, as she became, also contributed several hundred articles and essays to contemporary magazines, chiefly the *Independent* and *Hearth and Home.*

Whoever would see the Newhaven fishwives at their best must be on the Newhaven wharf by seven o'clock in the morning, on a day when the trawlers come in and the fish is sold. The scene is a study for a painter.

From Helen Hunt Jackson, *Glimpses of Three Coasts* (Boston, 1886), pp. 189–195.

The fish are in long, narrow boxes, on the wharf, ranged at the base of the sea wall; some sorted out, in piles, each kind by itself: skates, with their long tails, which look vicious, as if they could kick; hake, witches, brill, sole, flounders, hugh catfish, crayfish, and herrings, by the ton. The wall is crowded with men, Edinburgh fishmongers, come to buy cheap on the spot. The wall is not over two feet wide; and here they stand, lean over, jostle, slip by to right and left of each other, and run up and down in their eager haste to catch the eye of one auctioneer, or to get first speech with another. The wharf is crowded with women,—an army in blue, two hundred, three hundred, at a time; white caps bobbing, is a sight worth going to Scotland for. . . .

On the morning when I drove out from Edinburgh to see this scene, a Scotch mist was simmering down,—so warm that at first it seemed of no consequence whatever, so cold that all of a sudden one found himself pierced through and through with icy shivers. This is the universal quality of a Scotch mist or drizzle.

The Newhaven wharf is a narrow pier running out to sea. On one side lay the steam trawlers, which had just unloaded their freight; on the other side, on the narrow, rampart-like wall of stone, swarmed the fishmonger men. In this line I took my place, and the chances of the scramble. Immediately the jolly fishwives caught sight of me, and began to nod and smile. They knew very well I was there to "speir" at them.

"Ye'll tak cauld!" cried one motherly old soul, with her white hair blowing wildly about almost enough to lift the cap off her head. "Com doon! Ye'll tak cauld."

I smiled, and pointed to my water-proof cloak, down which, it must be admitted, the "mist" was trickling in streams, while the cloak itself flapped in the wind like a loose sail. She shook her head scornfully.

"It's a grat plass to tak cauld!" she cried. "Ye'll doo wull to com doon."

There were three auctioneers: one, a handsome, fair-haired, blue-eyed young fellow, was plainly a favorite with the women. They flocked after him as he passed from one to another of the different lots of fish. They crowded in close circles around him, three and four deep; pushing, struggling, rising on tiptoes to look over each other's shoulders and get sight of the fish.

"What's offered for this lot o'fine herrings? One! One and sax! Thrippence ha'! Going, going, gone!" rang above all the clatter and chatter of the women's tongues. It was so swift that it seemed over before it was fairly begun; and the surging circles had moved along to a new spot and a new trade. The eyes of the women were fixed on the auctioneer's eyes; they beckoned; they shook forefingers at him; now and then a tall, stalwart one, reaching over less able-bodied comrades, took him by the shoulder, and compelled him to turn her way; one, most fearless of all, literally gripped him by the ear and pulled his head around, shrieking out her bid. When the pressure got unbearable, the young fellow would shake himself like a Newfoundland dog, and, laughing good-naturedly, whirl his arms wide round to clear a breathing space; the women would fall back a pace or two, but in a moment the rings would close up again, tighter than ever.

The efforts of those in the outer ring to break through or see over the inner ones were droll. Arms and hands and heads seemed fairly interlinked and interwoven. Sometimes a pair of hands would come into sight, pushing their way between two bodies, low down —just the two hands, nothing more, breaking way for themselves, as if in a thicket of underbrush; presently the arms followed; and then, with a quick thrust of the arms to right and left, the space would be widened enough to let in the head, and when that was fairly through the victory was won. Straightening herself with a big leap, the woman bounded in front of the couple she had so skilfully separated, and a buzzing "bicker" of angry words would rise for a moment; but there was no time to waste in bad temper where bargains were to be made or lost in the twinkling of an eye.

An old sailor, who stood near me on the wall, twice saved me from going backwards into the sea, in my hasty efforts to better my standpoint. He also seemed to be there simply as a spectator, and I asked him how the women knew what they were buying; buying, as they did, by the pile or the box.

"Oh, they'll giss, verra near," he said; "they've an eye on the fish sense they're bawn. God knows it's verra little they mak," he added, "an' they'll carry's much's two men o'us can lift. They're extrawnery strang."

As a lot of catfish were thrown down at our feet, he looked at them with a shudder and exclaimed—

"I'd no eat that."

"Why not?" said I. "Are they not good?"

"Ah, I'd no eat," he replied, with a look of superstitious terror spreading over his face. "It doesna look richt."

A fresh trawler came in just as the auction had nearly ended. The excitement renewed itself fiercely. The crowd surged over to the opposite side of the pier, and a Babel of voices arose. The skinner was short and fat, and in his dripping oilskin suit looked like a cross between a catfish and a frog.

"Here, you Rob," shouted the auctioneer, "what do you add to this fine lot o'herrin'?"

"Herring be d——d!" growled the skipper, out of temper, for some reason of his own; at which a whirring sound of ejaculated disapprobation burst from the women's lips.

The fish were in great tanks on the deck. Quickly the sailors dipped up pails of the sea-water, dashed it over them, and piled them into baskets, in shining, slippery masses: the whole load was on the pier, sorted, and sold in a few minutes.

Then the women settled down to the work of assorting and packing up their fish. One after another they shouldered their creels and set off for Edinburgh. They seemed to have much paying back and forth of silver among themselves, one small piece of silver that I noticed actually travelling through four different hands in the five minutes during which I watched it. Each woman wore under her apron, in front, a sort of apron-like bag, in which she carried her money. There was evidently rivalry among them. They spied closely on each other's loads, and did some trafficking and exchange before they set off. One poor old creature had bought only a few crayfish, and as she lifted her creel to her back, and crawled away, the women standing by looked over into her basket, and laughed and jeered at her; but she gave no sign of hearing a word they said.

Some of them were greatly discontented with their purchases when they came to examine them closely, especially one woman who had bought a box of flounders. She emptied them on the ground, and sorted the few big ones, which had been artfully laid on the top; then, putting the rest, which were all small, in a pile by themselves, she pointed contemptuously to the contrast, and, with a toss of her head, ran after the auctioneer, and led him by the sleeve back to the spot where her fish lay. She was as fierce as Christie herself could have been at the imposition. She had paid the price for big flounders, and had got small ones. The auctioneer opened his book and took out his pencil to correct the entry which had been made against her.

"Wull, tak aff saxpence," he said.

"Na! na!" cried she. "They're too dear at seven saxpence."

"Wull, tak aff a saxpence; it is written noo—seven shillin'."

She nodded, and began packing up the flounders.

"Will you make something on them at that price?" I asked her.

"Wull, I'll mak me money back," she replied; but her eyes twinkled, and I fancy she had got a very good bargain, as bargains go in Newhaven; it being thought there a good day's work to clear three shillings—a pitiful sum, when a woman, to earn it, must trudge from Newhaven to Edinburgh (two miles) with a hundred pounds of fish on her back, and then toil up and down Edinburgh hills selling it from door to door. One shilling on every pound is the auctioneer's fee. He has all the women's names in his book, and it is safe to trust them; they never seek to cheat, or even to put off paying. "They'd rather pay than not," the blue-eyed auctioneer said to me. "They're the honestest folks i' the warld."

As the last group was dispersing, one old woman, evidently in a state of fierce anger, approached and poured out a torrent of Scotch as bewildering and as unintelligible to me as if it had been Chinese. Her companions gazed at her in astonishment; presently they began to reply, and in a few seconds there was as fine a "rippet" going on as could have been heard in Cowgate in Tam's day. At last a woman of near her own age sprang forward, and approaching her with a determined face, lifted her right hand with an authoritative gesture, and said in vehement indignation, which reminded me of Christie again—

"Keep yersil, an' haud yer Tongue, noo!"

"What is she saying?" I asked. "What is the matter?"

"Eh, it is jist nathin' at a'," she replied. "She's thet angry, she doesna knaw hersil."

The faces of the Newhaven women are full of beauty, even those of the old women: their blue eyes are bright and laughing, long after the sea wind and sun have tanned and shrivelled their skins and bleached their hair. Blue eyes and yellow hair are the predominant type; but there are some faces with dark hazel eyes of rare beauty and very dark hair—still more beautiful—which, spite of its darkness, shows glints of red in the sun. The dark blue of their gowns and cloaks is the best color-frame and setting their faces could have; the bunched fulness of the petticoat is saved from looking clumsy by being so short, and the cloaks are in themselves graceful garments. The walking in a bent posture, with such heavy loads on the back, has given to all the women an abnormal breadth of hip, which would be hideous in any other dress than their own. This is so noticeable that I thought perhaps they wore under their skirts, to set them out, a roll, such as is worn by some of the Bavarian peasants. But when I asked one of the women, she replied—

"Na, na, jist the flannel; a' tuckit."

"Tucked all the way up to the belt?" said I.

"Na, na," laughing as if that were a folly never conceived of, "na, na." And in a twinkling she whipped her petticoat high up, to show me the under petticoat, of the same heavy blue cloth, tucked only a few inches deep. Her massive hips alone were responsible for the strange contour of her figure.

The last person to leave the wharf was a young man with a creel of fish on his back. My friend the sailor glanced at him with contempt.

"There's the only man in all Scotland that 'ud be seen carryin' a creel o' fish on his back like a woman," said he. "He's na pride aboot him."

"But why should n't men carry creels?" I asked. "I'm sure it is very hard work for women."

The sailor eyed me for a moment perplexedly, and then as if it were waste of words to undertake to explain self-evident propositions, resumed—

"He worked at it when he was a boy, with his mother; an' now he's no pride left. There's the whole village been at him to get a barrow; but he'll not do 't. He's na pride aboot him."

What an interesting addition it would be to the statistics of foods eaten by different peoples to collect the statistics of the different foods with which pride's hunger is satisfied in different countries! Its stomach has as many and opposite standards as the human digestive apparatus. It is, like everything else, all and only a question of climate. Not a nabob anywhere who gets more daily satisfaction out of despising his neighbors than the Newhaven fishermen do out of their conscious superiority to this poor soul, who lugs his fish in a basket on his back like a woman, and has "na pride aboot him." . . .

As I drove out of the village I found a knot of the women gossiping at a corner. They had gathered around a young wife, who had evidently brought out her baby for the village to admire. It was dressed in very "braw attire" for Newhaven—snowy white, and embroidery, and blue ribbons. It was but four weeks old, and its tiny red face was nearly covered up by the fine clothes. I said to a white-haired women in the group—

"Do you recollect when it was all open down to the sea here —before this second line of newer cottages was built?"

She shook her head and replied, "I'm na so auld's I luik; my hair it wentit white—" After a second's pause, and turning her eyes out to sea as she spoke, she added, "A' 't once it wentit white."

A silence fell on the group, and looks were exchanged between the women. I drove away hastily, feeling as one does who has unawares stepped irreverently on a grave. Many grief-stricken queens have trod the Scottish shores; the centuries still keep their memory green, and their names haunt one's thoughts in every spot they knew. But more vivid to my memory than all these returns and returns the thought of the obscure fisherwoman whose hair, from a grief of which the world never heard, "a' 't once wentit white."

JAMES RUSSELL LOWELL ON
A CERTAIN CONDESCENSION
IN FOREIGNERS

1869

Nothing, over the years, had so exasperated Americans as precisely this condescension of which Lowell speaks, much of it unintentional, but much of it intentional, too. Lowell's gentle objections are directed to "foreigners" to be sure, but chiefly to the English. After all, it had always been easy for both Americans and English to ignore foreign condescension because it was usually expressed in a foreign tongue, or because—as with the English—foreign opinion didn't count anyway. Lowell had always been something of an Anglophile, and his Anglophilia, largely a product of his immersion in English literature, was to grow on him with the years and to achieve a kind of apocalypse in his appointment as Minister to the Court of St. James's. The resentment against English condescension and superciliousness which he expresses in this famous essay was doubtless greatly exacerbated by his resentment against British conduct toward the United States during the American Civil War, a resentment which achieved classic expression in the moving "Jonathan to John" of the *Biglow Papers;* a poem quoted in the Introduction to this collection which might have been used with equal appropriateness in our extracts from the Adams papers.

From James Russell Lowell, "On a Certain Condescension in Foreigners,"*Atlantic Monthly,* January, 1869. Reprinted in Lowell's *Fireside Travels* and many times thereafter.

In the natural course of things we succeeded to [the] unenviable position of general butt. The Dutch had thriven under it pretty well, and there was hope that we could at least contrive to worry along. And we certainly did in a very redoubtable fashion. Perhaps we deserved some of the sarcasm more than our Dutch predecessors in office. We had nothing to boast of in arts or letters, and were given to bragging overmuch of our merely material prosperity, due quite as much to the virtue of our continent as to our own. There was some truth in Carlyle's sneer, after all. Till we had succeeded in some higher way than this, we had only the success of physical growth. Our greatness, like that of enormous Russia, was greatness on the map—barbarian mass only; but had we gone down, like that other Atlantis, in some vast cataclysm, we should have covered but a pin's point on the chart of memory, compared with those ideal spaces occupied by tiny Attica and cramped England. At the same time, our critics somewhat too easily forgot that material must make ready the foundation for ideal triumphs, that the arts have no chance in poor countries. But it must be allowed that democracy stood for a great deal in our shortcoming. The *Edinburgh Review* never could have thought of asking, "Who reads a Russian book?" and England was satisfied with iron from Sweden without being impertinently inquisitive after her painters and statuaries. Was it that they expected too much from the mere miracle of Freedom? Is it not the highest art of a Republic to make men of flesh and blood, and not the marble ideals of such? It may be fairly doubted whether we have produced this higher type of man yet. Perhaps it is the collective, not the individual, humanity that is to have a chance of nobler development among us. We shall see. We have a vast amount of imported ignorance, and, still worse, of native ready-made knowledge, to digest before even the preliminaries of such a consummation can be arranged. We have got to learn that statesmanship is the most complicated of all arts, and to come back to the apprenticeship system too hastily abandoned. At present, we trust a man with making constitutions on less proof of competence than we should demand before we gave him our shoe to patch. We have nearly reached the limit of the reaction from the old notion, which paid too much regard to birth and station as qualifications for office, and have touched the extreme point in the opposite direction, putting the highest of human functions up at auction to be bid for by any creature capable of going upright on two legs. In some places, we have arrived at a point at which civil society is no longer possible, and already another reaction has begun, not backwards to the old system, but towards fitness either from natural aptitude or special training. But will it always be safe to let evils work their own cure by becoming unendurable? Every one of them leaves its taint in the constitution of the body politic, each in itself, perhaps, trifling, yet altogether powerful for evil.

But whatever we might do or leave undone, we were not genteel, and it was uncomfortable to be continually reminded that, though we should boast that we were the Great West till we were black in the face, it did not bring us an inch nearer to the world's West-End. That sacred enclosure of respectability was tabooed to us. The Holy Alliance did not inscribe us on its visiting-list. The Old World of wigs and orders and liveries would shop with us, but we must ring at the area-bell, and not venture to awaken the more august clamors of the knocker. Our manners, it must be granted, had none of those graces that stamp the caste of Vere de Vere, in whatever museum of British antiquities they may be hidden. In short, we were vulgar.

This was one of those horribly vague accusations, the victim of which has no defence. An umbrella is of no avail against a Scotch mist. It envelops you, it penetrates at every pore, it wets you through without seeming to wet you at all. Vulgarity is an eighth deadly sin, added to the list in these latter days, and worse than *this* world—far the more important of the two in the minds of most men. It profits nothing to draw nice distinctions between essential and conventional, for the convention in this case *is* the essence, and you may break every command of the decalogue with perfect good breeding, nay, if you are adroit, without losing caste. We, indeed, had it not to lose, for we had never gained it. "*How* am I vulgar?" asks the culprit, shudderingly. "Because thou are not like unto Us," answers Lucifer, Son of the Morning, and there is no more to be said. The god of this world may be a fallen angel, but he has us *there!* We were as clean—so far as my observation goes, I think we were cleaner, morally and physically, than the English, and therefore, of course, than everybody else. But we did not pronounce the diphthong *ou* as they did, and we said *eether* and not *eyther,* following therein the fashion of our ancestors, who unhappily could bring over no English better than Shakespeare's; and we did not stammer as they had learned to do from the courtiers, who in this way flattered the Hanoverian king, a foreigner among the people he had come to reign over. Worse than all, we might have the noblest ideas and the finest sentiments in the world, but we vented them through that organ by which men are led rather than leaders, though some physiologists would persuade us that Nature furnishes her captains with a fine handle to their faces, that Opportunity may get a good purchase on them for dragging them to the front.

This state of things was so painful that excellent people were not wanting who gave their whole genius to reproducing here the original Bull, whether by gaiters, the cut of their whiskers, by a factitious brutality in their tone, or by an accent that was forever tripping and falling flat over the tangled roots of our common tongue. Martyrs to a false ideal, it never occurred to them that nothing is more hateful to gods and men than a second-rate Englishman, and for the very reason that this planet never produced a more splendid creature than the first-rate one, witness Shakespeare and the Indian Mutiny. Witness that truly sublime self-abnegation of those prisoners lately among the bandits of Greece, where average men gave an example of quiet fortitude for which all the stoicism of antiquity can show no match. Witness the wreck of the Birkenhead, an example of disciplined heroism, perhaps the most precious, as the rarest, of all. If we could contrive to be not too unobtrusively our simple selves, we should be the most delightful of human beings, and the most original; whereas, when the plating of Anglicism rubs off, as it always will in points that come to much wear, we are liable to very unpleasing conjectures about the quality of the metal underneath. Perhaps one reason why the average Briton spreads himself here with such an easy air of superiority may be owing to the fact that he meets with so many bad imitations as to conclude himself the only real thing in a wilderness of shams. He fancies himself moving through an endless Bloomsbury, where his mere apparition confers honor as an avatar of the court-end of the universe. Not a Bull of them all but is persuaded he bears Europa upon his back. This is the sort of fellow whose patronage is so divertingly insufferable. Thank Heaven he is not the only specimen of cater-cousinship from the dear old Mother Island that is shown to us! Among genuine things, I know nothing more genuine than the better men whose limbs were made in England. So manly-tender, so brave, so true, so warranted to wear, they make us proud to feel that blood is thicker than water.

But it is not merely the Englishman; every European candidly admits in himself some right of primogeniture in respect of us, and pats this shaggy continent on the back with a lively sense of generous unbending. The German who plays the bass-viol has a well founded contempt, which he is not always nice in concealing, for a country so few of whose children ever take that noble instrument between their knees. His cousin, the Ph. D. from Göttingen, cannot help despising a people who do not grow loud and red over Aryans and Turanians,

and are indifferent about their descent from either. The Frenchman feels an easy mastery in speaking his mother tongue, and
attributes it to some native superiority of parts that lifts him high
above us barbarians of the West. The Italian *prima donna* sweeps a
curtsy of careless pity to the over-facile pit which unsexes her with
the *bravo!* innocently meant to show a familiarity with foreign usage.
But all without exception make no secret of regarding us as the
goose bound to deliver them a golden egg in return for *their* cackle.
Such men as Agassiz, Guyot, and Goldwin Smith come with gifts in
their hands; but since it is commonly European failures who bring
hither their remarkable gifts and acquirements, this view of the case
is sometimes just the least bit in the world provoking. To think what
a delicious seclusion of contempt we enjoyed till California and our
own ostentatious *parvenus,* flinging gold away in Europe that might
have endowed libraries at home, gave us the ill repute of riches!
What a shabby downfall from the Arcadia which the French officers
of our Revolutionary War fancied they saw here through Rousseau-
tinted spectacles! Something of Arcadia there really was, something
of the Old Age; and that divine provincialism were cheaply re-
purchased could we have it back again in exchange for the tawdry
upholstery that has taken its place. . . .

   During our civil war an English gentleman of the highest description was kind enough to call upon me, mainly, as it seemed, to
inform me how entirely he sympathized with the Confederates, and
how sure he felt that we could never subdue them—"they were the
gentlemen of the country, you know." Another, the first greetings
hardly over, asked me how I accounted for the universal meagreness
of my countrymen. To a thinner man than I, or from a stouter man
than he, the question *might* have been offensive. The Marquis of
Hartington[1] wore a secession badge at a public ball in New York. In a
civilized country he might have been roughly handled; but here,
where the *bienséances* are not so well understood, of course nobody
minded it. A French traveller told me he had been a good deal in the
British colonies, and had been astonished to see how soon the people
became Americanized. He added, with delightful *bonhomie,* and as if
he were sure it would charm me, that "they even began to talk

---

1. One of Mr. Lincoln's neatest strokes of humor was his treatment of this gentleman
when a laudable curiosity induced him to be presented to the President of the Broken
Bubble. Mr. Lincoln persisted in calling him Mr. Partington. Surely the refinement of good
breeding could go no further. Giving the young man his real name (already notorious in the
newspapers) would have made his visit an insult. Had Henri IV done this, it would have been
famous.

through their noses, just like you!" I was naturally ravished with this testimony to the assimilating power of democracy, and could only reply that I hoped they would never adopt our democratic patent method of seeming to settle one's honest debts, for they would find it paying through the nose in the long run. I am a man of the New World, and do not know precisely the present fashion of May-Fair, but I have a kind of feeling that if an American (*mutato nomine, de te* is always frightfully possible) were to do this kind of thing under a European roof, it would induce some disagreeable reflections as to the ethical results of democracy. I read the other day in print the remark of a British tourist who had eaten large quantities of our salt, such as it is (I grant it has not the European savor), that the Americans were hospitable, no doubt, but that it was partly because they longed for foreign visitors to relieve the tedium of their dead-level existence, and partly from ostentation. What shall we do? Shall we close our doors? Not I, for one, if I should so have forfeited the friendship of L[eslie] S[tephen], most lovable of men. He somehow seems to find us human, at least, and so did Clough, whose poetry will one of these days, perhaps, be found to have been the best utterance in verse of this generation. And T. H., the mere grasp of whose manly hand carries with it the pledge of frankness and friendship, of an abiding simplicity of nature as affecting as it is rare!

The fine old Tory aversion of former times was not hard to bear. There was something even refreshing in it, as in a northeaster to a hardy temperament. When a British parson, travelling in New-foundland while the slash of our separation was still raw, after prophesying a glorious future for an island that continued to dry its fish under the aegis of Saint George, glances disdainfully over his spectacles in parting at the U. S. A., and forebodes for them a "speedy relapse into barbarism," now that they have madly cut themselves off from the humanizing influences of Britain, I smile with barbarian self-conceit. But this kind of thing became by degrees an unpleasant anachronism. For meanwhile the young giant was growing, was beginning indeed to feel tight in his clothes, was obliged to let in a gore here and there in Texas, in California, in New Mexico, in Alaska, and had the scissors and needle and thread ready for Canada when the time came. His shadow loomed like a Brocken-spectre over against Europe—the shadow of what they were coming to, that was the unpleasant part of it. Even in such misty image as they had of him, it was painfully evident that his clothes were not of any cut hitherto fashionable, nor conceivable by a Bond Street tailor—and this in an age, too, when everything depends upon clothes, when, if we do not keep up appearances, the seeming-solid frame of this universe, nay, your very God, would slump into himself, like a mockery king of snow, being nothing, after all, but a prevailing mode, a make-believe of believing. From this moment the young giant assumed the respectable aspect of a phenomenon, to be got rid of if possible, but at any rate as legitimate a subject of human study as the glacial period or the silurian what-d'ye-call-ems. If the man of the primeval drift-heaps be so absorbingly interesting, why not the man of the drift that is just beginning, of the drift into whose irresistible current we are just being sucked whether we will or no? If I were in their place, I confess I should not be frightened. Man has survived so much, and contrived to be comfortable on this planet after surviving so much! I am something of a protestant in matters of government also, and am willing to get rid of vestments and ceremonies and to come down to bare benches, if only faith in God take the place of a general agreement to profess confidence in ritual and sham. Every mortal man of us holds stock in the only public debt that is absolutely sure of payment, and that is the debt of the Maker of this Universe to the Universe he has made.

It will take England a great while to get over her airs of patronage toward us, or even passably to conceal them. She cannot help confounding the people with the country, and regarding us as lusty juveniles. She has a conviction that whatever good there is in us is wholly English, when the truth is that we are worth nothing except so far as we have disinfected ourselves of Anglicism. She is especially condescending just now, and lavishes sugar-plums on us as if we had not outgrown them. I am no believer in sudden conversions, especially in sudden conversions to a favorable opinion of people who have just proved you to be mistaken in judgment and therefore unwise in policy. I never blamed her for not wishing well to democracy—how should she?—but Alabamas are not wishes. Let her not be too hasty in believing Mr. Reverdy Johnson's pleasant words. Though there is no thoughtful man in America who would not consider a war with England the greatest of calamities, yet the feeling toward her here is very far from cordial, whatever our Minister may say in the effusion that comes after ample dining. Mr. Adams, with his famous "My Lord, this means war," perfectly represented his country. Justly or not, we have a feeling that we have been wronged, not merely insulted. The only sure way of bringing about a healthy relation between the two countries is for Englishmen to clear their minds of the notion that we are always to be treated as a kind of inferior and deported Englishman whose nature they perfectly understand, and whose back they accordingly stroke the wrong way of the fur with amazing perseverance. Let them learn to treat us naturally on our merits as human beings, as they would a German or a Frenchman, and not as if we were a kind of counterfeit Briton whose crime appeared in every shade of difference, and before long there would come that right feeling which we naturally call a good understanding. The common blood, and still more the common language, are fatal instruments of misapprehension. Let them give up *trying* to understand us, still more thinking that they do, and acting in various absurd ways as the necessary consequence, for they will never arrive at that devoutly-to-be-wished consummation till they learn to look at us as we are and not as they suppose us to be. Dear old long-estranged mother-in-law, it is a great many years since we parted. Since 1660, when you married again, you have been a step-mother to us. Put on your spectacles, dear madam. Yes, we *have* grown, and changed likewise. You would not let us darken your doors, if you could help it.

1870-1880

CHARLES GODFREY LELAND

BECOMES A ROMANY *RYE*

1870s

Charles Godfrey Leland is one of the most bizarre, and most interesting, characters in American cultural history. Born to wealth, he attended the College of Princeton and after graduation traveled for years on the Continent, studying at Heidelberg and Munich, learning Italian, and laying a foundation for his later studies of Etruscan and Roman culture. He returned to Philadelphia to edit *Graham's Magazine*, one of the best of the era; he had a fling at the law; then turned to literature. He invented, or created, Hans Breitmann, a "Pennsylvania Dutchman" who became in time one of the most popular of all American folk characters, as *The Breitmann Ballads* were some of the most popular of folk literature. In 1863 Leland enlisted in the Union army, just in time for Gettysburg. After the war he edited Forney's *Philadelphia Press*. Then in 1869 Leland moved—permanently, as it turned out (or as permanently as anything ever was with him)—to London. There he cultivated all the interesting men of letters, learned Romany, founded the Rabelais Club, which was just right for him, got deeply involved in the development of industrial arts for the schools, wrote books and essays on gypsies, and on language and slang. He later moved to Italy, where he studied and wrote on Etruscan remains and on the occult, and died in Florence in 1903.

From Charles Godfrey Leland, *Memoirs* (London, 1894), pp. 416–421.

When I returned to Brighton, after getting into lodgings, I began to employ or amuse myself in novel fashion. Old Gentilla Cooper, the gypsy, had an old brother named Matthias, a full-blood Romany, of whom all his people spoke as being very eccentric and wild, but who had all his life a fancy for picking up the old "Egyptian" tongue. I engaged him to come to me two or three times a week, at half-a-crown a visit, to give me lessons in it. As he had never lived in houses, and, like Regnar Lodbrog, had never slept under a fixed roof, unless when he had taken a nap in a tavern or stable, and finally, as his whole life had been utterly that of a gypsy in the roads, at fairs, or "by wood and wold as outlaws wont to do," I found him abundantly original and interesting. And as on account of his eccentricity and amusing gifts he had always been welcome in every camp or tent, and was watchful withal and crafty, there was not a phase, hole, or corner of gypsy life or a member of the fraternity with which or whom he was not familiar. I soon learned his jargon, with every kind of gypsy device, dodge, or peculiar custom, and, with the aid of several works, succeeded in drawing from the recesses of his memory an astonishing number of forgotten words. Thus, to begin with, I read to him aloud the Turkish Gypsy Dictionary of Paspati. When he remembered or recognised a word, or it recalled another, I wrote it down. Then I went through the vocabularies of Liebrich, Pott, Simson, etc., and finally through Brice's Hindustani Dictionary and the great part of a much larger work, and one in Persian. The reader may find most of the results of Matty's teaching in my work entitled *The English Gypsies and their Language.* Very often I went with my professor to visit the gypsies camped about Brighton, far or near, and certainly never failed to amuse myself and pick up many quaint observations. In due time I passed to that singular state when I could never walk a mile or two in the country anywhere without meeting or making acquaintance with some wanderer on the highways, by use of my newly-acquired knowledge. Thus, I needed only say, "Seen any of the Coopers or Bosvilles lately on the drum?" (road), or "Do you know Sam Smith?" etc., to be recognised as one of the grand army in some fashion. Then it was widely rumoured that the Coopers had got a *rye*, or master, who spoke Romany, and was withal not ungenerous, so that in due time there was hardly a wanderer of gypsy kind in Southern England who had not heard of me. And though there are thousands of people who are more thoroughly versed in Society than I am, I do not think there are many so much at home in such extremely *varied* phases of it as I have been. I have sat in a gypsy camp, like one of them, hearing all their little secrets and

talking familiarly in Romany, and an hour after dined with distinguished people; and this life had many other variations, and they
came daily for many years. My gypsy experiences have not been so
great as those of Francis H. Groome (once a pupil and *protégé* of
Benfey), or the Grand Duke Josef of Hungary, or of Dr. Wlislocki,
but next after these great masters, and as an all-round gypsy rye in
many lands, I believe that I am not far behind any *aficionado* who has
as yet manifested himself.

To become intimate, as I did in time, during years in Brighton,
off and on, with all the gypsies who roamed the south of England, to
be beloved of the old fortune-tellers and the children and mothers as
I was, and to be much in tents, involves a great deal of strangely
picturesque rural life, night-scenes by firelight, in forests and by
river-banks, and marvellously odd reminiscences of other days.
There was a gypsy child who knew me so well that the very first
words she could speak were "O 'omany 'i" (O Romany rye), to the
great delight of her parents.

After a little while I found that the Romany element was spread
strangely and mysteriously round about among the rural population
in many ways. I went one day with Francis H. Groome to Cobham
Fair. As I was about to enter a tavern, there stood near by three men
whose faces and general appearance had nothing of the gypsy, but
as I passed one said to the other so that I could hear—

"Dikk adovo rye, se o Romany rye, yuv, tàcho!" (Look at that gentleman; he is a gypsy gentleman, sure!)

I naturally turned my head hearing this, when he burst out
laughing, and said—

"I told you I'd make him look round."

Once I was startled at hearing a well-dressed, I may say a
gentlemanly-looking man, seated in a gig with a fine horse, stopping
by the road, say, as I passed with my wife—

"Dikk adovo gorgio adoi!" (Look at that Gentile, or no-gypsy!)

Not being accustomed to hear myself called a *gorgio,* I glanced up
at him angrily, when he, perceiving that I understood him and was
of the mysterious brotherhood, smiled, and touched his hat to me.
One touch of nature makes the whole world grin.

But the drollest proposal ever made to me in serious earnest
came from that indomitable incarnate old *gypssissimus Tsingarorum,*
Matthew Cooper, who proposed that I should buy a donkey. He
knew where to get one for a pound, but £ 2 10s. would buy a
"stunner." He would borrow a small cart and a tent, and brown my
face and hands so that I would be dark enough, and then on the

drum—"over the hills." As for all the expenses of the journey, I need not spend anything, for he could provide a neat nut-brown maid, who would not only do all our cooking, but earn money enough by fortune-telling to support us all. I would be expected, however, to greatly aid by my superior knowledge of ladies and gentlemen; and so all would go merrily on, with unlimited bread and cheese, bacon and ale, and tobacco—into the blue away!

I regret to say that Matthew expected to inherit the donkey.

I remember that one very cold morning I was riding alone to the meet on a monstrous high black horse which Goodchild had bought specially for me, when I met two gypsy women, full blood, selling wares, among them woollen mittens—just what I wanted, for my hands were almost frozen in Paris kids. The women did not know me, but I knew them by description, and great was the amazement of one when I addressed her by name and in Romany.

"Pen a mandy, Priscilla Cooper, so buti me sosti del tute for adovo pustini vashtini?" (Tell me, Priscilla Cooper, how much should I give you for those woollen gloves?)

"Eighteen pence, master." The common price was nine pence.

"I will *not* give you eighteen pence," I replied.

"Then how much *will* you give, master?" asked Priscilla.

"Four shillings will I give, and not a penny less—*miri pen*—you may take it or leave it."

I went off with the gloves, while the women roared out blessings in Romany. There was something in the whole style of the gift, or the *manner* of giving it, which was specially gratifying to gypsies, and the account thereof soon spread far and wide over the roads as a beautiful deed.

The fraternity of the roads is a strange thing. Once when I lived at Walton there was an old gypsy woman named Lizzie Buckland who often camped near us. A good and winsome young lady named Lillie Doering had taken a liking to the old lady, and sent her a nice Christmas present of clothing, tea, etc., which was sent to me to give to the Egyptian mother. But when I went to seek her, she had flown over the hills and far away. It made no difference. I walked on till I met a perfect stranger to me, a woman, but "evidently a traveller." "Where is old Liz?" I asked. "Somewhere about four miles beyond Moulsey." "I've got a present for her; are you going that way?" "Not exactly, but I'll take it to her; a few miles don't signify." I learned that it had gone from hand to hand and been safely delivered. It seems a strange way to deliver valuables, to walk forth and give them to the first tramp whom you meet; but I knew my people.

MONCURE CONWAY:
JOSEPH ARCH LAUNCHES
AN AGRARIAN REVOLUTION

1872

Joseph Arch was a plain farm laborer, self-taught and self-made. He became a lay preacher for the Methodists and, in his thirties, an assiduous student. In 1872, at the age of forty-six, he inaugurated a campaign to organize the hitherto unorganized and exploited farm laborers of England. Thereafter he had a spectacular rise and a somewhat languishing decline. He was elected to Parliament, but failed of reelection—probably because he was "counted out." The Farmers' Union declined almost as rapidly as it had grown and Arch retired, a frustrated man. It was, of course, inevitable that the Reverend Moncure Conway should sympathize with Arch, as he sympathized with all liberal causes. As we have met Mr. Conway before we need not introduce him again.

England is at this moment passing through a revolution, as important as that of the sixteenth century. The general of the earlier agitation was a great soldier, and his victory was, in smiting one neck, to behead every English tyrant for all time to come. The purpose of

From Moncure Conway, "Agricultural Laborers in England," *Harper's New Monthly*, XLVI (1872–73), pp. 689–694.

the present revolution is to behead the lordly oppressors of agricultural labor, and its general is a humble son of the soil. To-day the wealthiest peer of the realm grows pale at the name of Joseph Arch. And any one who has looked into his eye or heard his voice will not wonder that it should be so. The weary voices of millions who are hopeless are heard through his simple eloquence. Ages of patient suffering, and generations that have long groaned in the prison of Giant Despair, find their first morning ray in the fire of his eye. Amidst scowling noblemen and angry landlords this man has for some time journeyed through the length and breadth of England, seeking to form "unions" of farm laborers, and to combine these unions into a vast national organization. His journeys, even in this limited area, have been such as to recall the labors of Catholic missionaries in earlier times. During each day he visits the homes of the laborers, and learns their exact condition; he takes care to visit all who have suffered wrongs by eviction; and every evening he speaks to the assembled laborers with a force which never fails, and a perseverance which never grows weary. He has been the means of organizing England into some twenty-five districts, each of which includes many different unions—all together representing a kind of United States of Labor. Already in these regions wages have risen; and it is a saying that where Arch goes starvation flies. The poor women cry out as he passes, "God bless you! Our children never had meat until you came." But Joseph Arch is not the man to be contented because the lord's fears lead him to gild his serf's chain; he has a settled purpose and plan, with which he is steadily carrying not the farm laborers only, but the sympathy of the disinterested intelligence of the country, though that plan surely contains a revolution of the land laws of Great Britain.

I have just had the opportunity of conversing with this very remarkable man, and it was not a very easy one to secure. I had already driven ten miles out from Stratford-on-Avon to the village of Barford, in Warwick, where his cottage stands, only to learn that it was a very rare thing indeed for one to find him there. And when he visits any large city, the need of distinguished politicians and landowners—friends or foes—to consult him renders him as busy as the Premier himself. At length, however, I have had the good fortune to obtain from him personally a full statement of the situation and prospects of the great movement he represents. I found him, so far as personal appearance and bearing are concerned, a representative country laborer. He is a sturdy Saxon man, with blonde complexion and light blue eyes, a straight, frank look, and strong features. His face is weather-beaten, and bears traces of small-pox; the underface is squarish, the cheek-bones prominent, the forehead high and broad. But he is gifted with that which Saad regarded as his greatest earthly treasure—a sweet voice; and this voice has its own physiognomy in a most innocent and winning smile. With perfect independence and simplicity in his manner he takes his seat before the noble lord or the humble laborer, and with equal courtesy; he converses with the utmost frankness, as one who has nothing to conceal; and he has the highest charm of a reformer—the faculty of completely forgetting himself in his cause.

In the pretty village of Barford, near Warwick, where he now owns a pleasant little cottage and garden, Joseph Arch was born about forty-five years ago. He was born to the life that in England most nearly recalls the inscription over the Inferno—"All hope abandon, ye who enter here." It is very little, comparatively, when an English artisan rises in the social scale and attains education and wealth; but any similar ascent from the ranks of the farm laborers is so nearly impossible that the English agricultural laborer finds not even a myth, such as other working classes have in Whittington, to tell his children of a farm hand transformed. In this valley without a horizon Joseph Arch was born, and he has at least been able to show his comrades that if their case does not admit of culture, wealth, or social advancement, it may admit that light which the mansions can not monopolize—the light which comes of the glow of human sympathy. While laboring in the field Arch taught himself to read, and the companions of his toil ever after were the Bible and the newspaper. He was married at the age of twenty-five, and had two children at the time when he first felt the terrible pressure of want. He was getting 1s. 6d. per day, and he struck. From that time he never took regular employment, but worked by the job. He was an excellent hand, especially in hedge-planting. This caused him to live a somewhat nomadic life, which enabled him also to see the many varieties of condition among those suffering under a common oppression. For years he wandered about doing piece-work from farm to farm, and from county to county, often finding his night's lodging in some old barn or under the hedge-row. His supper might be a dry crust, but he had his bit of tallow candle by which to study his Bible and to read his newspaper. Almost insensibly he began preaching. He had been from early life connected with the Primitive Methodist connection (which then differed from the Wesleyan body in having the largest power in its government in the hands of the laity), and he was ordained as a local preacher. He preached with great acceptance to the poor, among whom he associated, and by his high conduct and his abstinence from drink did much to elevate their moral as well as physical condition in many places.

For twenty years, as he told me, he brooded over the heavy wrongs of the laboring classes in the rural districts. He made tremendous efforts to raise his fine children out of the slough of county serfdom, and has to-day the pleasure of seeing his eldest son, at the age of twenty, a sergeant in the army, with a fair prospect of promotion. His industrious wife and an intelligent daughter do much to assist him in the great work to which his life is now devoted.

Early in February, 1872, two farm laborers came from Wellesbourne to Barford to see him. The three consulted concerning the sad condition of their class, and it was then and there that the idea was born of an agricultural laborers' union, similar to the unions which had done so much for the artisans in cities. It may seem to an American reader strange that the farm laborers should have been so slow in coming to this idea and purpose. But it must be remembered that these are an exceptional class of laborers, in position, ignorance, and opportunities very much resembling those who were lately slaves in the Southern States of America. The artisans of cities know how to read, and they have many opportunities for consultation. The rural laborers living on great estates are unable to get any education, can rarely read or write, and are fast chained to their heavy task by the wolf that stands ready to spring on any who attempt to leave it for an instant.

The visit of the two laborers was followed by Arch at once going to Wellesbourne. It was only a day or two afterward, but he found gathered a meeting of a thousand farm laborers. The great chestnut-tree in the village, under which he stood while he addressed this crowd, already, in many eyes, has taken its place in the rank of sacred trees, like the Charter Oak, or the Liberty Tree in Boston. Under it was born the movement which is now revolutionizing England, and is fraught with social and political consequences which never appeared in the vision of those who began it.

This poor Methodist preacher and farm laborer has proved himself a born general. When the late agricultural strikes occurred the men had almost nothing to fall back upon. The sight of their hungry wives and children almost maddened them, and it seemed inevitable that in certain places there would be outbreaks of physical violence. Nay, there is, I fear, good reason to believe that the great land-owners ardently desired that there should be some acts of violence. They knew exactly how to deal with that kind of proceeding. But they were totally unprepared for what actually occurred. Joseph Arch, chosen by the universal suffrage of the sufferers to be their general, posted, night and day, to every village where the strikers were gathered, and curbed them with the hand of a Wellington. At one meeting he was interrupted by shouts of "Burn down their big houses!" when, with flashing eye, he thundered, "In that case, count Joseph Arch against you!" Scores of times he had to gather up this wild energy and wrath, and inclose it like a potent steam in the engine which he meant to build, by whose orderly working millions were to be uplifted. "I have lived forty-five years," he would say, "without breaking the law, and I don't mean to begin now." He spoke to the people with a voice and manner in which calm self-restraint was singularly blended with fervor and enthusiasm. He showed, too, that he was a philosopher by the art with which, having called the lightning to the eye of the crowd before him, he drew it aside from spending its force upon this or that oppressive nobleman or evicting farmer. "Do not aim at them," he would say; "they, like ourselves, are the victims of a hereditary evil system; it has come down to them and us from past centuries. Their deeds only illustrate the bad system they did not make. Strike that."

"How shall we strike that?"

"How? Why, form a union. Join hand to hand, heart to heart, penny to penny, and you will be able to command your own future."

Often, when such hot words had come leaping from the heart of the speaker, it would be like a warm day rising over a frosty field; hearts would be thawed, eyes would glisten, and most likely the crowd would break out in chorus with one of those union hymns to whose music the laborers' cause goes "marching on." And their hymns are sometimes excellent. Here are some lines which remind one of the pretty theme of the ancient Hindoo fable where the pigeons, caught in the fowler's net, all resolve to try their wings together at the same moment, and sail away with the net far beyond their enemy's reach:

> Arouse, arouse, ye sons of toil,
>   In one united band;
> Ye tillers of the soil,
>   Together firmly stand!
> United all in heart and hand,
> No longer you'll be ropes of sand,
> But formed in one strong cable:
> Single you're an easy prey,
> Be not misled by those who say,

> Your hours of labor and your pay
> Will better if at home you stay;
> But one and all determined say,
> "We'll join the Laborers' Union!"

Their latest rhyme is one called *"The Joseph Arch Song,"* which, it may be seen, has in it the ring and beat of the anthem to which the heroes of another free-labor battle marched to save another "Union:"

> Under the spreading branches of the far-famed
>   Wellesbourne oak,
> Joseph Arch, the laborers' chief, the welcome
>   scheme first spoke:
> More rest, more wages, and more food, and a bit
>   of land to rent;
> And a union strong we'll form ere long: the news
>   like wild-fire went,
>   The news like wild-fire went,
>   The news like wild-fire went:
> And a union strong we'll form ere long: the news
>   like wild-fire went. . . .
> So here's success to Joseph Arch, that truthful,
>   fearless man!
> May he carry on the noble work at Wellesbourne
>   oak began!
> He's honest, manly, in the Right, and hard he hits
>   the nail—
> Has the cause in hand of the Union Band, and we
>   know he will prevail!
>   And we know, etc.

This ballad very well states the child-like faith with which the unionists look up to their leader. He is so dear to them that if he be by, even the most friendly Parliamentary orator can scarcely get a full hearing for the cries of "Arch!" "Arch!" And while he is speaking the crow is still as the slumbering infant, save when a sob at some sad narrative, or a burst of laughter at some droll story, breaks in on the spell of his homely eloquence. . . .

The cause of the agricultural laborer has gradually taken a deep hold upon the people of London. There has long been a conventional feeling on the subject, and it has been, any time these twenty years, common to hear gentlemen speak of the farm hands' condition as a "blot on the 'scutcheon" of England. The unequal struggle between the squires and the laborers finally aroused sufficient interest in the great metropolis for a number of gentlemen to get together, and call a meeting on the subject at Exeter Hall. It was announced that the Lord Mayor would preside, and a large crowd assembled. When, however, the Lord Mayor came to the door, and found that the republican Sir Charles Dilke was upon the list of speakers, and when he beheld the formidable radical Charles Bradlaugh on the platform—heavily loaded, no doubt, with a political fulmination—his honor withdrew, and left the chair to be taken by Mr. Samuel Morley, M.P. The Lord Mayor, it was generally thought, was rather naïve to imagine that politics could be kept out of such a matter at a public meeting in London. . . . The most striking feature of the evening was the impression which was made by Joseph Arch. He and a laborer from Somersetshire were the only uneducated speakers. No one who looked upon the plain, middle-sized man, with his weather-beaten look, could have formed any high anticipation as to the effect he would produce. Yet his was the speech of the evening. Hardly had he spoken one minute before the meeting was filled with wild excitement. Every sentence was as a blow driving a nail to the head. Yet he spoke with quiet, solid deliberation. "Gentlemen," he said, at one point, with the air of a man making a serious, however surprising, statement—"gentlemen, the laborers desire to be treated like men, not to be housed like pigs, and left to the tyranny of a farmer or a squire; and if they can not be treated like men in England, I appeal to the country to send them to America. This country paid twenty millions to liberate the negroes of the West Indies. What has it done for its slaves at home?" These words were followed by such wild, ringing cheers as only they could remember in Exeter Hall who attended the mass-meetings of sympathy for the Union cause in America. (How every great cause calls up the same elements, shows the same physiognomy, and utters the same voice!) . . .

Mr. Mitchell, the other laboring man who spoke, told a doleful story of how often he had suffered the pangs of hunger when, at eighteen years of age, he had followed the plow, working from six in the morning until ten at night without having two-pennyworth of food in him. The wages were seven shillings a week. "The living was tea-kettle broth for breakfast. Two or three little pieces of bread were put in the breakfast pot, which held three quarts, and then the bread was soaked with hot water. For dinner they got a few potatoes and a square inch of bacon fried in the pan for a family of seven, the fat going on the potatoes, and the meat being the father's dinner. For tea they soaked burned bread, and put a little treacle on it, that being carried to the husband in the field by the woman. For supper they got little pieces of bread and skim-milk cheese. As for dwellings, I have known thirteen huddling together in one room on what they called a 'shakedown,' like hounds in a kennel. Last week I spoke to an old man at Yeovil, whose master told him he could not give him more than five shillings a week, and who said he was then literally starving. I will do my best to elevate my countrymen, and run the risk of the horse-pond."

This Parthian arrow which Mitchell let fly referred to the speech which the Bishop of Gloucester and Bristol recently made, in which he advised the farmers to "duck in the horse-pond" any agitator that came into their neighborhood to make their laborers dissatisfied. It is now called "the bishop's baptism."

It is a consoling fact that the statements of Mitchell have caused a furious excitement among squires and farmers in various parts of the country, causing them to besiege the press with denials of their truth. These denials showed plainly that such scandals were unknown, in some counties at least, and especially it appeared that in the North labor is better compensated, though still the families suffer much, even in the most favorable regions. But at the very time that these country gentlemen were thus furiously denouncing Mitchell's statement, an investigation was going on in Somersetshire which presents a gloomier picture even than that which the farm hand drew at Exeter Hall. At one of the meetings held in that county Charles Wright, described as an elderly man, was examined and cross-examined, as follows:

Question. "Have you been a farm laborer all your life?" *Answer.* "Yes."

Q. "Do you remember when the standing wages for the best men were seven shillings a week?" *A.* "Yes." (A voice: "I do; six shillings.")

Q. "The laborer twenty years of age had only seven shillings?" *A.* "Yes."

Q. "Did you ever have parish relief?" *A.* "When my wife died I had a little. She left me with seven children."

Q. "Your wages some ten or eleven years ago were raised to eight shillings a week?" *A.* "Yes; and last summer they were ten shillings."

Q. "After harvest did your master say to you, 'There's five shillings a week for you if you continue to live with me; if not, go home?' Is that true?" *A.* "Yes, it is."

Q. "How much house rent did you have to pay out of that?" *A.* "One shilling and sevenpence half-penny a week."

Q. "On wet days were your wages paid?" *A.* "No; I lost the time."

Q. "When you were at harvest till ten or eleven o'clock did you get anything extra?" *A.* "No." (A voice: "A quart of sour cider!")

Here the chairman asked if any one wished to put any further questions. A gentleman called out that his father had once worked for nine shillings a week, and was now worth £2000. Abraham Burt was next examined. His experience repeated that of the above as to wages. He was then asked how many children he had.

A. "Six."

Q. "How many bedrooms have you?" *A.* "One."

Q. "How many bedsteads?" *A.* "Two."

Q. "Do you all sleep in one room?" *A.* "Yes."

Henry Montague, carter, testified to receiving twelve shillings a week, working from 5 A.M. to 7 P.M. usually; but in harvest till 10 or 11 P.M.,and half a day Sunday, without extra pay. Walter Montagne, shepherd, received ten shillings per week; for joining the union he was dismissed from employment; no other farmer would employ him, and he was at that moment on the brink of starvation.

These facts might have slept in the little local paper of Yeovil, had not the furious squires elicited them, and brought them to the columns of the *Times.* They reveal a state of things which most assuredly will not be permitted to continue. When Hallam showed that the laboring classes engaged in agricultural labor in England were better provided with the means of subsistence in the reign of Edward III, or of Henry VI, than now, the country was scandalized, but came to the conclusion that it was a temporary phase of the national condition; but since then the progress has been steadily from bad to worse, and it never was worse than now. There is a strong determination to do something, but a great difference as to what is to be done. Canon Girdlestone demands moral effort. Some of the political economists, reluctant to give up the idea that the law of supply and demand is the universal panacea, declare that the laborer only needs education, and to cease bringing so many children into the world. But at the great meeting at Exeter Hall, Charles Bradlaugh, the most hated man in England by all religious or political conservatives, rose, and, though met by a storm of confusion, which prevented him from speaking, managed to offer, as an addendum to a resolution, the following: "And that there can be no permanent improvement in the condition of the agricultural laborers until there is a vital change in the land laws, so as to give to the people their rightful part in the land." Having sat down quietly, Mr. Morley, the chairman, awaited the cessation of the angry noises with which the "Iconoclast," as he is popularly termed, had been assailed. The chairman then put the Bradlaugh amendment to the meeting, and to the surprise of those who had made the confusion, it was —overwhelmingly carried! The fact was, the noisy ones were those who had come with the hope that the meeting would end with sentimentality, and perhaps a charitable collection for the "poor laborer." But the majority had a deeper purpose; and whatever it may have thought of Bradlaugh, it was not prepared to vote against his resolution. On the following day the London *Times* said that Bradlaugh was the one person in the meeting who had touched upon the real issue.

It can, therefore, be no longer doubted that these humble unionists have brought us to the door of a revolution. There were 750,000 agricultural laborers in England and Wales at the last census. It is estimated that to give to all the able-bodied farm laborers an increase of five shillings per week would amount to little over five millions of pounds. We are now paying the farmers, under whom and under whose lords these people are starving, eighty millions for meat which was bought for forty millions a few years ago. Yet no penny of this mighty increase in the value of butcher's-meat ever reaches the farm hand.

CHARLES LORING BRACE:
"DARWIN WAS AS SIMPLE
AND JOVIAL AS A BOY"

1872

We have already met the interesting young Charles Brace walking through England with Olmsted in 1850. A graduate of Yale College in 1846, Brace had planned to study theology but was distracted into a career of good works instead. After his visit to England he moved on to Hungary, where his open sympathies for Kossuth and for revolution secured him arrest and imprisonment; he took his revenge with a book on Hungary in 1852. By then he had already found his life work: the care of homeless boys and girls in the great cities. In 1853 he founded the Children's Aid Society of New York, which eventually found homes for over a hundred thousand city waifs. A friend to most of the Boston and New York reformers, Brace was inevitably caught up in numerous interlocking reforms, such as penal reform, the prevention of cruelty to animals, and the war on the slums. This visit to Darwin at Down was a product of the first of many trips abroad.

Down, Bromley, Kent, July 12, 1872

My dear J———:
I am at Mr. Darwin's with Mrs. Brace for the night. It is a country to delight R.'s heart. Green, thick hedges, narrow, shaded lanes,

From *The Life of Charles Loring Brace,* Emma Brace, ed. (New York, 1894), pp. 319–321.

glimpses of parks and oak-openings, old mossy villages, quaint churches, pretty spires rising over the tree-tops, birds singing (the lark rose just now, singing), the air full of fragrance, all quiet and repose. The house an old one, added to and covered with lime, green all around, a trim garden with bright flowers, a lawn, and a long green meadow with trees, and kitchen-garden full of fruit and vegetables, and the flower houses where Mr. D. has made his experiments. In driving here this afternoon, we passed through a lane over a mile long, with hedges higher than a man, and the banks covered with scarlet poppy, and so narrow that two wagons could hardly pass one another, and all arched with trees. It passed through the estate of Sir John Lubbock, who is a neighbor of Darwin's. As we came in, Darwin himself was standing in his drawing-room and met us most cordially, taking both my hands. Mrs. D., too, most kind and hearty. I had a little stroll in the garden before we dressed for dinner. He has there a (Cal.) *Sequoia* thirty feet high, I think some twenty years old, though none remembers exactly the date of its planting. (Figs grow nicely in his garden.) We calculated that this tree will get its growth when England is a republic!

Darwin was as simple and jovial as a boy, at dinner, sitting up on a cushion in a high chair, very erect, to guard his weakness. Among other things, he said "his rule in governing his children was to give them lump-sugar"! He rallied us on our vigorous movements, and professed to be dazzled at the rapidity of our operations. He says he never moves, and though he can only work an hour or two every day, by always doing that, and having no break, he accomplishes what he does. He left us for half an hour after dinner for rest, and then returned to his throne in the parlor.

We had a lively talk on the instincts of dogs (several persons being there) and on "cross-breeding," and he became animated explaining his experiments in regard to it. . . . I was telling him that the California primitive skulls were of a remarkably good type. He gave one of his lighting-up smiles, which seemed to come way out from under his shaggy eyebrows. "Yes." he said; "it is very unpleasant of these facts; they won't fit in as they ought to!". . . . He told us, with such glee, of a letter he had just got from a clergyman, saying that "he was delighted to see, from a recent photograph, that no man in England was more like the monkey he came from!" and of another from an American clergyman (?) beginning with, "You d——d scoundrel!" and sprinkled with oaths and texts. . . . These things amuse him; but not a word did he say of his own success or fame. He breakfasts at half past seven, but sat by us later, as we ate, and joked and cut for us, and was as kind as could be. I never met a more simple, happy man—as merry and keen as Dr. Gray, whom he loves much. Both he and Lyell think Dr. Gray the soundest scientific brain in America. . . . "How unequally is vitality distributed," he said, as he heard what we did every day. . . . His parting was as of an old and dear friend. I hope this picture of the best brain in Europe will not weary you.

JOHN BURROUGHS:
ENGLISH AND AMERICAN
CHARACTERISTICS COMPARED

1873

John Burroughs, who lived until the 1920s, came to be a kind of combination of Thoreau and Audubon—Thoreauvian in his sharp eye for natural science and his ability to root his philosophy in nature, audubonian in his wanderlust and his devotion to the study of birds. Born near the foothills of the Catskills, Burroughs spent most of his life there, or on the banks of the Hudson, observing nature in all her manifestations, and writing about it with insight and grace. He early came under the influence of Emerson, but eventually it was Whitman who affected him most deeply. "I owe more to him than to any man in the world," he confessed, and his first book was on Whitman. As early as 1865 he contributed the first of his nature essays to the *Atlantic Monthly*—an essay so Emersonian in character that it was assigned, in the *Atlantic* index, to Emerson; his first book, *Wake-Robin*, followed in a few years. *Winter Sunshine* is the result of a visit to England in 1881. In time Burroughs became a Sage, in time he became a national legend. He helped John Muir save the Yosemite as a state park; he went camping with President Theodore Roosevelt; he was regularly photographed in his Catskill dwelling

From John Burroughs, *Winter Sunshine* (Boston, 1881), pp. 190–204.

with his ancient friends, Thomas Edison and Henry Ford. His nature writings, suffused as they are with Emersonian mysticism and Bergsonian vitalism, have a very Victorian flavor.

English and American Characteristics Compared

England is a mellow country, and the English people are a mellow people. They have hung on the tree of nations a long time, and will, no doubt, hang as much longer; for windfalls, I reckon, are not the order in this island. We are pitched several degrees higher in this country. By contrast, things here are loud, sharp, and garish. Our geography is loud; the manners of the people are loud; our climate is loud, very loud, so dry and sharp, and full of violent changes and contrasts; and our goings-out and comings-in as a nation are anything but silent. Do we not occasionally give the door an extra slam, just for effect?

In England, everything is on a lower key, slower, steadier, gentler. Life is, no doubt, as full, or fuller, in its material forms and measures, but less violent and aggressive. The buffers the English have between their cars to break the shock, are typical of much one sees there.

All sounds are softer in England; the surface of things is less hard. The eye of day and the face of Nature are less bright. Everything has a mellow, subdued cast. There is no abruptness in the landscape, no sharp and violent contrasts, no brilliant and striking tints in the foliage. A soft, pale yellow is all one sees in the way of tints along the borders of the autumn woods. English apples (very small and inferior, by the way) are not so highly colored as ours. The blackberries, just ripening in October, are less pungent and acid; and the garden vegetables, such as cabbage, celery, cauliflower, beet, and other root crops, are less rank and fibrous; and I am very sure that the meats also are tenderer and sweeter. There can be no doubt about the superiority of mutton; and the tender and succulent grass, and the moist and agreeable climate, must tell upon the beef also.

English coal is all soft coal, and the stone is soft stone. The foundations of the hills are chalk instead of granite. The stone with which most of the old churches and cathedrals are built would not endure in our climate half a century; but in Britain the tooth of Time is much blunter, and the hunger of the old man less ravenous, and the ancient architecture stands half a millennium, or until it is slowly worn away by the gentle attrition of the wind and rain. . . .

In keeping with this elemental control and moderation, I found the character and manners of the people gentler and sweeter than I had been led to believe they were. No loudness, brazenness, impertinence; no oaths, no swaggering, no leering at women, no irreverence, no flippancy, no bullying, no insolence of porters, or clerks, or conductors, no importunity of boot-blacks or newsboys, no omnivorousness of hackmen—at least, comparatively none—all of which an American is apt to notice and I hope appreciate. In London, the boot-black salutes you with a respectful bow, and touches his cap, and would no more think of pursuing you or answering your refusal than he would of jumping into the Thames. The same is true of the newsboys. If they were to scream and bellow in London, as they do in New York or Washington, they would be suppressed by the police, as they ought to be. The vender of papers stands at the corner of the street, with his goods in his arms, and a large placard spread out at his feet, giving in big letters the principal news-headings. . . .

There is, indeed, a charm about these ancestral races that goes to the heart. And herein was one of the profoundest surprises of my visit, namely, that, in coming from the New World to the Old, from a people the most recently out of the woods of any, to one of the ripest and venerablest of the European nationalities, I should find a race more simple, youthful, and less sophisticated than the one I had left behind me. Yet this was my impression. We have lost immensely in some things, and what we have gained is not yet so obvious or so definable. We have lost in reverence, in homeliness, in heart and conscience—in virtue, using the word in its proper sense. To some the difference which I note may appear a difference in favor of the greater 'cuteness, wideawakeness, and enterprise of the American, but is simply a difference expressive of our greater forwardness. . . . We are a more alert and curious people, but not so simple—not so easily angered, nor so easily amused. We have partaken more largely of the fruit of the forbidden tree. The English have more of the stay-to-home virtues, which, on the other hand, they no doubt pay pretty well for by their more insular tendencies.

The youths and maidens seemed more simple, with their softer and less intellectual faces. When I returned from Paris the only person in the second class compartments of the car with me, for a long distance, was an English youth eighteen or twenty years old, returning home to London after an absence of nearly a year, which he had spent as waiter in a Parisian hotel. He was born in London and had spent nearly his whole life there, where his mother, a widow, then lived. He talked very freely with me, and told me his troubles, and plans, and hopes, as if we had long known each other. What especially struck me in the youth was a kind of sweetness and innocence—perhaps what some would call "greenness"—that at home I had associated only with country boys and not even with them latterly. The smartness and knowingness and a certain hardness or keenness of our city youths—there was no trace of it at all in this young Cockney. But he liked America travelers better than those from his own country. They were more friendly and communicative—were not so afraid to speak to "a fellow," and at the hotel were more easily pleased.

The American is certainly not the grumbler the Englishman is; he is more cosmopolitan and conciliatory. The Englishman will not adapt himself to his surroundings; he is not the least bit an imitative animal; he will be nothing but an Englishman, and is out of place —an anomaly—in any country but his own. To understand him, you must see him at home in the British island, where he grew, where he belongs, where he has expressed himself and justified himself, and his interior, unconscious characteristics are revealed. There he is quite a different creature from what he is abroad. There he is "sweet," but he sours the moment he steps off the island. In this country he is too generally arrogant, fault-finding, and supercilious. The very traits of loudness, sharpness, and unleavenedness which I complain of in our national manners, he very frequently exemplifies in an exaggerated form.

The Scotch or German element no doubt fuses and mixes with ours much more readily than the purely British. . . .

As for the charge of brutality that is often brought against the English . . . there is, doubtless, good ground for it, . . . I am persuaded there is a kind of brutality among the lower orders in England that does not exist in the same measure in this country—an ignorant animal coarseness, an insensibility, which gives rise to wife-beating and kindred offenses. But the brutality of ignorance and stolidity is not the worst form of the evil. It is good material to make something better *of*. It is an excess and not a perversion. It is not man fallen, but man underdeveloped. Beware, rather, that refined, subsidized brutality; that thin, depleted, moral consciousness; or that contemptuous, cankerous, euphemistic brutality, of which, I believe, we can show vastly more samples than Great Britain. Indeed, I believe, for the most part, that the brutality of the

English people is only the excess and plethora of that healthful, muscular robustness and full-bloodedness for which the nation has always been famous, and which it should prize beyond almost anything else. But for our brutality, our recklessness of life and property, the brazen ruffianism in our great cities, the hellish greed and robbery and plunder in high places, I should have to look for a long time to find so plausible an excuse.

A London crowd I thought the most normal and unsophisticated I had ever seen ... There was to me something notably fresh and canny about them, as if they had only yesterday ceased to be shepherds and shepherdesses. They certainly were less developed, in certain directions, or shall I say depraved, than similar crowds in our great cities. They are easily pleased, and laugh at the simple and childlike, but there is little that hints of an impure taste, or of abnormal appetites. I often smiled at the tameness and simplicity of the amusements, but my sense of fitness, or proportion, or decency, was never once outraged. They always stop short of a certain point—the point where wit degenerates into mockery, and liberty into license: nature is never put to shame, and will commonly bear much more. Especially to the American sense did their humorous and comic strokes, their negrominstrelsy, and attempts at Yankee comedy, seem in a minor key. . . . The characteristic flavor of the humor and fun-making of the average English people, as it impressed my sense, is what one gets in Sterne—very human and stomachic, and entirely free from the contempt and superciliousness of most current writers. I did not get one whiff of Dickens anywhere. No doubt, it is there in some form or other, but it is not patent, or even appreciable, to the sense of such an observer as I am. . . .

The English regard us as a wonderfully patient people, and there can be no doubt but we put up with abuses unknown elsewhere. If we have no big tyrant, we have ten thousand little ones, who tread upon our toes at every turn. The tyranny of corporations and of public servants of one kind and another, as the ticket-man, the railroad-conductor, or even of the country stage-driver, seem to be features peculiar to American democracy. In England, the traveler is never snubbed, or made to feel that it is by somebody's sufferance that he is allowed aboard or to pass on his way.

If you get into an omnibus or a railroad or tramway carriage in London, you are sure of a seat. Not another person can get aboard after the seats are all full. Or, if you enter a public hall, you know you will not be required to stand up unless you pay the standing-up price. There is everywhere that system, and order, and fair dealing, which all men love. The science of living has been reduced to a fine point. You pay a sixpence and get a sixpence worth of whatever you buy. There are all grades and prices, and the robbery and extortion so current at home appear to be unknown.

I am not contending for the superiority of everything English, but would not disguise from myself or my readers the fact of the greater humanity and consideration that prevail in the mother country. Things here are yet in the green, but I trust there is no good reason to doubt that our fruit will mellow and ripen in time like the rest.

EHRMAN SYME NADAL:
THE DULLNESS AND
THE COMFORT
OF ENGLISH SOCIETY

1870s

Ehrman Nadal's father was a Methodist clergyman who eventually became president of the newly founded Drew University, in New Jersey; Nadal himself, after a career in the civil and the foreign service , and a foray into academic life, ended up as a horse breeder. A graduate of Yale College, he worked for some years in the Philadelphia mint; in the early seventies he was appointed one of the secretaries to the London legation and spent roughly a decade in London: *Impressions of London Social Life* is the product of that experience—an experience which he greatly enjoyed. Returning to America, he became secretary to the New York Board of Civil Service Examiners, and, in 1892, lecturer on literature at Columbia University. In old age—and he lived to be almost ninety—he turned to raising horses.

I found everywhere an excessive respect of the individual for the sentiment of the mass—I mean in regard to behaviour. In matters of opinion there is greater latitude than with us. Nowadays a man in England may believe anything he chooses; the reason being, I suppose, that beliefs have not much root or practical importance. Au-

From E. S. Nadal, *Impressions of London Social Life* (New York, 1875), pp. 10–32.

thority seems to have left the domain of thought and literature, and to have invaded that of manners. Of the two sorts of tyranny, I think I should prefer the first. I should rather be compelled to write my poetry in pentameters, and to speak with respect of the Church and the Government, than to be forever made to behave as other people dictate. I know Englishmen do not accept this as true of themselves. One of them, to whom I had hinted something of the sort, said, "Oh, I don't know; we do about as we please." Precisely; but they have lived so constantly in the eyes of other people, have got so used to conforming, that they never think of wanting to do what society would disapprove of. They have been so in the habit of subduing whatever native individuality they possess, that they have at last got rid of it. Of course, it would be impossible to make them believe this. They mistake their inattention, the hostile front they present to the world, and their indifference to the strictures of foreigners when they are abroad, for real independence and a self-reliant adherence to nature. But there seems to me to be something conventional even about the rude and lounging manners of which they are so proud. It is like the "stand-at-ease" of soldiers. It would be highly improper and contrary to orders to do anything else. . . .

In this very great self-consciousness and doubt as to what to say and do, it was an advantage to have some particular tone set and the range of conversation narrowed within some well-understood limits. By this, language, as a medium of expression, is abolished, and becomes a means of getting along comfortably with friends. Certain things are set apart as good for men to converse upon—the races, horseflesh, politics, anything in short, providing it is not discussed in a definite or original manner. No man should say anything which might not be very well said by any one else. Each man has an infallible guide in the rest. He must set his clock by them, and regulate it carefully when it inclines to go faster. . . .

The young men have deteriorated from the energy of their fathers of forty years ago, who must have been a very amusing class of men. The strong pressure of public sentiment prevents these young men from acquiring the old physical vigour and freedom of the British upper class; and as they have no task set them they are driven unavoidably into dullness. They never swear, or rarely. The "demmes" and "egads" of their ancestors are quite out of employ-ment. They even sin with a certain decorum. For instance, it is very "bad form" to dance with the ladies at the casinos, though there is no impropriety in leaving those places in their company. The few men who are literary and intellectual make, perhaps, the weakest impression. The thin wash of opinion which forms their conversation evaporates, and leaves a very slight sediment. They have the contagious weariness I have noticed in the agricultural population along the water-courses of Illinois and Missouri. In the latter it is the result of fever and ague, and the long eating of half-baked bread. The voices of those people seemed to struggle up from a region below their lungs, and in them the peculiarity, besides wearying, intensely repelled and disgusted. In men as charmingly dressed and beautifully clean as these Englishmen, the offensive quality was missed, but there was the same weariness and a vapidity that inoculated and subdued you. There often seemed to me an effeminate sound in the talk, not only of the intellectual sort, but even of the faster men. . . .

I have said that English-society people make but little effort to impress or astonish; and I explained that they have no wish to be thought individually remarkable, because that sort of ambition among them is a very exceptional thing. What they do value is the "getting on;" and the inevitable effect of living among them is to make one think that that is the best thing one can do. Certainly those old familiar ideas of the poets and moralists, "truth, innocence, fidelity, affection, &c.," which one always felt at home with in the snug corners of the parlours at the village sewing-circles, suddenly became strange to me and very unreal and whimsical. They danced off at a distance in the oddest and most fantastical manner. If anybody sneered at "upholstery," or spoke contemptuously of rank and fashion, you at once fancied some one had snubbed him; if he praised virtue, you suspected him of wanting a dinner. But while the lust of the eyes and the pride of life are everything to upper-class Englishmen, you hear wonderfully little said about these things. Carlyle and Thackeray, the poets and satirists and the goody old maids who write the novels, though they have quite shut the mouths of these brave gentlemen, have by no means driven such thoughts out of their hearts. To give you to understand that they are persons of consequence, they would think the last degree of vulgarity. Yet, if they do not claim consequence, it is not because they do not value consequence. They know that to assert openly their demand is not the best way to have it accorded them. The avidity of Mrs. Governor Brown and Mrs. Judge Jones for the best rooms at the hotels, and the recognition and sympathy of all the railway conductors, is unknown in England. But the two manners, so different apparently, are not so different essentially. Both demand consideration and consequence—the one only more successfully than the other. The quiet demeanour, the sedulous avoidance of self-assertion, the critical look, the slightly reserved bearing, say very plainly, "See, I am a person of consequence." Both make the same inferior claim. The one makes it in a wise, refined, and successful way the other in a foolish, vulgar, and unsuccessful way. . . .

Of the external advantage of London society I have already spoken. Its machinery is nearly perfect. One meets numbers of persons who not only bear themselves perfectly, but seem to think and feel almost with perfection; women sensible and gracious, men from whom reflection and high purpose have removed every trace of triviality. Parties and receptions have this advantage; we have the perfection of social ease with those to whom we are under no obligation to be agreeable. The guests cannot be unconscious and oblivious of the host, nor the host of the guests. But between those who meet on common ground there may be silence or conversation, just as is most comfortable. Hence the benefit of such an organised social establishment as London possesses. The great distinction which rank and money obtain in England may perhaps be irksome to those who spend their lives in the midst of its society. To a stranger or sojourner, it is a novel and interesting feature. One felt that here was company which, however it might be in Saturn and Jupiter, no set of tellurians at least could affect to despise. You enjoyed this sensation. All round this wide planet, through the continents and the islands of the sea, among the Franks and the Arabs, the Scandinavians, the Patagonians, and the Polynesians, there were none who could give themselves airs over this. The descendants of Adam, the world over, could show nothing better.

JOHN FISKE:

"WHAT COULD BE MORE GRAND THAN THE LIFE I HAVE LED HERE?"

1873

John Fiske was a Victorian polymath. In 1863, when he graduated from Harvard at the age of twenty-one, he already knew twenty languages and was not unlearned in history, philosophy, ethnology, and science. He was one of the first to accept in full the implications of the new Darwinian theory of evolution, and was enraptured by Herbert Spencer, whose "mocking-bird" he became. After a brief foray into law, he abandoned that for scholarship; he lectured on philosophy at Harvard and became assistant librarian of the university (he is reputed to have read all the books in the library). In 1872 he published his first book, *Myths and Myth-Makers,* and launched himself on the ambitious *Outlines of Cosmic Philosophy.* In 1873 friends and family financed this first trip to England and the Continent. There he met all of his gods—philosophical gods like Spencer and Darwin and Mill, literary gods like George Eliot and Ruskin and Tennyson. He was admitted to the Athenaeum Club and to the High Table of Oxford and Cambridge colleges; he heard a dozen concerts—he was himself something of a pianist—and somehow he found time to complete two volumes of his *Cosmic Philosophy.*

From *The Letters of John Fiske,* Ethel F. Fiske, ed. (New York, 1940), pp. 255–256, 265–266, 269–276, 286–288.

For the rest of his life Fiske devoted himself to the popularization of Spencerian evolution, and to writing and expounding American history. He lectured everywhere—even to President Hayes and his cabinet; he wrote a dozen volumes of history, some of them, like *The Critical Period,* still widely read. Fiske represented better than most the emergence of a new colonialism—the kind of colonialism so ostentatious in the shift to Romanesque and Renaissance architecture, and the arrangement of international marriages. As he thought Spencer the greatest philosopher of all time, so he thought Oxford the perfection of universities and the Athenaeum the perfection of clubs.

> *11 Craven Street, Strand, London, England*
> *October 6, 1873*

Dear Abby:

You don't know how odd the sense of the lapse of time is with me, already it seems ages since I left Ipswich October 2. I reached Cambridge at 5 o'clock that afternoon and put up at the *Red Lion.* Friday morning I went first to the University Library—300,000 volumes—and introduced myself to Mr. Bradshaw, the chief librarian, a man about forty years old. He treated me with great cordiality, showed me all over the grand library from cellar to attic, showed me all the curiosities, and explained very fully their system of cataloguing—wherein I again maintain that Ezra Abbot has beat them out of sight. After a delightful forenoon together we went to Bradshaw's rooms in King's College to lunch. Such luxurious college rooms I never saw; ours at Harvard are very inferior in comparison. The librarian is a senior Fellow of the college, has a man servant of his own, and lives like a nabob. There was a piano, also *fine* pictures, bustuettes, and everything jolly. Bradshaw is rather a swell chap; quite a Don, you know; and perhaps more swell than profound, but very satisfactory in his good-breeding and kindliness of manner. Nobody else was in town as the term was only just beginning. Bradshaw had seen "Stubby" Child quite recently.

Later I explored the buildings and grounds of King's Trinity, St. John's, Caius, Corpus Christi, Pembroke, and St. Peter's. The buildings and grounds at Cambridge so far surpass what we have at Harvard, that there is no use in talking of them the same day. Anything more perfectly enchanting I have never seen; and they all acknowledge—even the Cambridge men themselves—that Oxford is still finer. So you see there's a treat yet in store for me. I don't wonder the people here are proud of the universities.

After a long ramble about the premises, I attended vesper service in King's Chapel, of which I enclose a picture, that you may see how strongly it suggests our College Library. I think the architect of Gore Hall had the King's Chapel in his mind.

Saturday, I wandered into the rear of King's, and spied two young ladies at a distance, who looked too trim and pretty to be anything but Americans, and an elderly gentleman with them. Coming nearer, I thought I had seen their faces in Cambridge, U.S., but couldn't say when or where. Presently their father stepped up, and called me by name, and introduced himself as Mr. Dixwell, of Cambridge, with two daughters. His son was in the class of '70 at Harvard, and consequently a student of mine. We all got very well acquainted immediately and took a long walk together about the grounds.

Having visited Trinity Library the day before, in virture of my position at Harvard, I was now able to help the Dixwells to get in there and see the curiosities. And I should have observed that we saw the very telescope which Newton invented and used for his own researches. It looks as much like our Harvard telescope as a bark canoe looks like the steamer *Olympus*. The greater the wonder at what he accomplished. I never felt more like echoing the sentiment engraved on the pedestal of his statue in Trinity Chapel

"Isaacus Newton
Qui humanum genus ingenio superavit"

After we got back to the *Red Lion*, where the Dixwells were also stopping, I was introduced to Mrs. Dixwell, and dined with them, and had a delightful time. Mrs. Dixwell will call upon you and give you this letter. I hope you will do your half toward keeping up the acquaintance, for I'm sure you will find it pleasant. I am glad to hear the Dixwells say, after travelling all over Europe, that they have seen *nothing* more exquisite than the Lakes of Killarney and no city more grandly picturesque than Edinburgh.

London, October 31, 1873

Dear Abby:

. . . Tuesday morning I went to Oxford from Paddington Station. Put up at the Clarendon. I looked about the colleges. Spent the evening with Max Müller at his lovely house, and played with his little daughter who reminded me of Maud. Next day Max took me all over the Bodleian Library, and I lunched with him in the buttery at All Souls' College. He had to give a lecture, and I tramped steadily about town till 6 P.M., and explored Queen's, University, Magdalen,

St. Marys, Merton, Christ Church, Oriel, Brasenose, Balliol, Trinity and St. John's Colleges. At 8 o'clock I made for London. The distance being 50 miles, we made it in just 3 hours!

This was a brief trip to Oxford; but I shall remember it as long as I live, even if I never make another visit there. The city is exquisitely beautiful—too beautiful to be thoroughly appreciated except by living there a while and drinking it in slowly. But as for the colleges, I do really think that they are not equal to the colleges at Cambridge. The effect of the sweet river Cam winding through the college grounds at Cambridge is an effect which Oxford has nothing to equal. I think, on the whole, that I have never seen anything so lovely, so peaceful, so sequestered, so resting to the soul, as the groves in the rear of Trinity and St. John's at Cambridge. In point of architecture, on the other hand, I think Oxford is somewhat superior. But when one thinks of Harvard in comparison with either of them, one laughs. I wonder sometimes—since we plainly don't know how to design a decent building ourselves—that we don't honestly confess our stupidity, and show some grains of sense by *copying* the Oxford or Cambridge buildings literally! Since I have been over here I have seen enough good architecture to realize what a wonderful hold it can take upon one's soul. But we lose all that in America. Architecture seems to be our weakest point. What a monstrosity is the Memorial Hall compared to the buildings of Christ Church in Oxford! I understand it now as I couldn't when at home.

As for Max Müller, he is one of the handsomest men I ever saw, straight as an arrow, fair smooth complexion, dark eyes, and grey hair, though not fifty years old I should say. But his face is not half so interesting as the homely face of Lewes; and generally I thought him a very tame and uninteresting person. Not only that, but he didn't impress me as a profound or original man, but rather as a shallow and loose-thinking sort of person. He is fearfully swell in his get-up, and in his manners, but he lacks sincerity and frankness. Spencer has a sort of scientific straightforwardness in his manner, which has no nonsense about it, and is very attractive. Lewes has a smile like that of an angel, which seems to express absolute purity, sweetness, and frankness. Max Müller, in comparison, appears like a self-conscious popinjay. In talking with Spencer and Lewes, I feel my own insignificance strongly. In talking with Max Müller, I was more inclined to be impressed with *his* insignificance—at least, as compared with his reputation. Moreover, you would confide in Spencer or Lewes in a moment, or in Dr. Muir, or in Ralston—but decidedly not in Max Müller. However, the good man treated me very cordially, and perhaps I ought not to go to criticising him so ruthlessly. Only a fellow can't help getting his impressions, you know.

67 Great Russell St.
London, W.C., England
November 13, 1873

Dear Abby:

... Sunday Jeremiah Curtin and I went out to Macmillan's, without Mrs. Jeremiah. You see Mac didn't know that Jeremiah had a wife and so invited him to come with me, and Mrs. Jeremiah was only too glad to be out of the scrape, for she is terribly afraid of "big folks." I never shall forget that day, one of the sweetest of my life. The ground was damp after a lovely shower, and the grass, still as green as in August, strewn with yellow leaves, while plenty of bright roses were still blooming. What do you think of roses out of doors in November? It was so lovely in the country, I say country although "Upper Tooting, S.W." is within the limits of London. It was one of those days when I feel that I don't want to go to Heaven, for this earth is quite enough. For the first time I believe I fairly drank in the incomparable sweetness of English landscape.

There were all the Macmillans and Mrs. Macmillan's sister, Miss Pignatel, pronounce it Frenchwise—and Miss Florence Freeman. We had a delicious dinner in the library, heaps of Beethoven and Schubert, and Miss Margaret Macmillan played, and I played. Miss Pignatel puts her whole soul into her music, and she has wonderful execution and is such a fine pianist that I have dreamed of Miss Mehlig's playing for two nights since. Miss Pignatel is a favorite pupil of Clara Schumann. Besides her playing, she is one of the most charmingly refined ladies I ever saw—she would captivate you —something like Miss Catherine Ireland and Mrs. Lambard mixed together, do you catch the idea? We got mighty fond of each other all around and I am invited to go there for Christmas Day, to join in a good old Christmas powwow. I can't tell you how dear MacMillan's place seems to me after my two visits.

The next day Monday Nov. 10 came the grand dinner given for me by Spencer, with Lewes, Tyndall, Huxley and Dr. Jackson who made our number even. The dinner was served in Spencer's private parlour, with choice wines. If you had been there, my dear, you would have heard some brilliant conversation, I can tell you. As for Lewes, he was full of the old cat, and kept us in a roar most of the time. What a flow of spirits! And how *spirituelle* he is! I was saying that very soon we should see Evolution taken up by the orthodox.

"To be sure," said Lewes, "for don't you see that Evolution requires an Evolver?" Huxley was telling about something I said in my Agassiz article, when Spencer blandly interrupted with "What will Agassiz say to all that?" "O," said Lewes, "he will say what Louis XIV said after the battle of Ramillies—*Dieu m'a abandonné; et après tout ce que j'ai fait pour Lui!!!*" What a comical fellow Lewes is! Tyndall didn't say so much but smiled on us benignly and said we were such fearful reprobates he should have to cut our society. I believe we discussed pretty much the whole universe from cellar to attic, and I didn't sit and eat and say nothing, either. Spencer was gentle and admirable as always; and the reverence which all these men feel for him was thoroughly apparent in the way in which they listened to every word that came out of his mouth.

I am quite wild over Huxley. He is as handsome as an Apollo: his photograph doesn't begin to do him justice. I never saw such magnificent eyes, they are black and his face expresses an eager burning intensity, there is none of that self-satisfied smirk which has crept into the picture. He seems earnest—immensely in earnest—and thoroughly frank and cordial and modest. And, by Jove, what a pleasure it is to meet such a clean-cut mind! It is like Saladin's sword which cut through the cushion. When we parted it was a heart-felt grip that I gave his hand, I can tell you. There is no doubt at all that he is a grand man, too. Of course I had formed opinions of all these men but it is interesting to see how they seem in the flesh after one has known them in a shadowy way so long. Reading their books doesn't give you the flesh-and-blood idea of them. But once to see such as man as Huxley is never to forget him.

Well what do you and Martha think of that for an evening?

Today came my lunch with Darwin as planned, at his daughter's, Mrs. Litchfield's house on Portman Square, not far from "Mrs. Jarley's Waxworks." Darwin and his wife, Frank Darwin, whom I saw in Boston two years ago, Miss Bessie Darwin, Mrs. Litchfield, and Dr. Hooker, the greatest living botanist, and Mrs. Hooker made up the party. Darwin is the dearest, sweetest, loveliest old Grandpa that ever was. There is no doubt that Spencer is the profoundest thinker of all these men but Darwin impresses me with his strength more than any man I have ever seen. There is a charming kind of quiet strength about everything he does. He is not burning and eager like Huxley. He has a mild blue eye and his manner is full of repose. He is the gentlest of gentle old fellows. None of these men seem to know how great they are; but Darwin is one of the most truly modest men I ever saw, the combination of power and quiet modesty in him is more impressive than I can describe. I think he would make a noble picture after the style of the picture mother painted which I call "Galileo." His long white hair and enormous white beard make him very picturesque. And what is so delightful to see as that perfect frankness and guileless simplicity of manner which comes from a man having devoted his whole life to some great idea, without a thought of self and without ever having become a "man of the world"?

I had a warm greeting from the dear old man, and I am afraid I shall never see him again for his health is very bad and he had to make a special effort to see me today. Of all my days in England, I prize today the most; and what I pity *you* most of all for, my dear, is that you haven't seen our grand old Darwin! My lunch with him was the climax of everything thus far. I think we both felt it might be the last time. He came to the door with me and gave me a warm grip of the hand and best wishes, and watched me down the road till I turned the corner, when I took off my hat and bowed good-bye.

London, England
November 18, 1873

Dear Abby:
I was somewhat tickled at George Roberts's idea, that perhaps I wasn't well enough known here to get my book published. To be sure I had the same misgivings myself when I first arrived and found that Youmans wasn't going to be here. It didn't take long however to dispel them, for you see there were three firms that wanted the book the instant they heard of it, as I told you; Macmillan, Trübner, Williams & Norgate. I am not so well known here as in Boston, but I am almost as well known as in New York, my Myth-book has had a thundering run here; *everybody* seems to have read it, and my name introduces me everywhere because it at once suggests "Myths and Myth-Makers." Trübner, who sells it, calls it "one of the successes of the day." À propos of the above, Youmans writes that he is delighted at my arrangement with Macmillan, that he couldn't have got better terms for me, and that I seem to "know how to take care of myself." He thinks Macmillan the best publisher I could have here.

Speaking of successes, Vol. I of Lewes's book *Problems of Life and Mind* appeared Saturday, November 15, and Trübner sold 300 copies that day—very good for the first volume of a heavy work. I hope Macmillan will do one-sixth as well with mine and sell 50 the first day! Ralston is going to blow my trumpet in advance in the "Athenaeum." I read Lewes's book in the sheets, he gave me a copy, which I finished Friday night the 14th before the book appeared Saturday. I consider his treatment of Kant one of the most masterly pieces of philosophical criticism I ever read. I told Darwin about it and found that he has a great admiration for Lewes's straightforward and clean-cut mind. I have made up my mind that Lewes will have a permanent place in history as the critic of Kant, to say nothing of the other things he has done.

Friday evening I heard a concert at St. James's Hall; Wagner's *Meistersinger von Nürnberg,* Beethoven's Fifth Symphony, and a piano concerto of Raff's played by Von Bülow, for 1 shilling! I think Von Bülow a great pianist, but not so great as Rubinstein; and I don't think I enjoy his playing so much as Miss Mehlig's. The orchestra was good, but I have heard nothing yet equal to Theodore Thomas's. There are oceans of concerts—concerts every day somewhere—but I go to very few. And I have given up my piano, too busy to use it.

At Trubner's store yesterday I saw Dr. Reinhold Rost, and I also saw some little Oppenheim girls, perfect litle angels; and I stopped to tell them stories. Last Sunday I dined at Trübner's with a lot of people—Miss Annie Thomas who writes novels, and Florence Marryatt, and a lot of German *savants* whose names are not specially noted, and Mr. Henry Barnard. This is a sort of golden age 'ere in h'old h'England.

Where do you suppose I spent last evening? At my old place, 11 Craven Street, Strand, with the beautiful Miss Janet Hathaway, of Milwaukee! Who next? She is on her way to Rome to study drawing and painting.

I don't know where I shall go from here: Paris looks a little squally, and I doubt if my book will let me get to Italy before spring. Macmillan would rather have me nearer. I don't care so much for Paris anyway as some people do. You don't catch me coming to Europe *alone* again.

67 Great Russell St.
Bloomsbury, London, S.C.
November 22, 1873

Dear Abby:
I enclose my invitation to dine with the "Citizens of Noviomagus," a club composed entirely of members of the Royal Society of Antiquaries, who have paid this compliment to the author of "Myths and Mythmakers." . . .

I put on my swallow-tail and presented myself at the tavern in Lincoln's Inn Fields—very near where old *Mr. Tulkinghorn* was shot. I was seated at the *left* hand of the Lord High President of the Society of Antiquaries, which is the place of honour—for they do everything by contraries at "Noviomagus." The Lord High is a gay old cove of seventy-five, with a fat paunch and enormous snow-white beard. We had a *stupendous* dinner—quite beyond anything you ever saw. I wish you could have seen the table. Such lovely flowers! And our finger-bowls held richly perfumed water instead of the ordinary H_2O. The Lord High toasted "our brilliant American guest," but pitched into me, according to the rules of "Noviomagus," and said that he never did see a decent American, but that I was the meanest American he had ever set eyes on, and had written altogether the most insuffera-bly tedious and worthless book. Whereupon I rose and replied to the toast, saying that it would have to be a cussed mean American who wasn't equal to any ten Englishmen, high or low, and I must say that of all the unmannerly snobs I had ever come across the Lord High was the worst; as for his dinner, an American wouldn't set it before his dog, and *I didn't believe his old champagne cost half a crown a bottle!!!* Whereat there ensued *tremendous* applause and ringing of glasses, and cheers for the "Mythmaker," who was declared to have won "Noviomagian" honour. Apart from all this nonsense, they were very nice old fellows, and I had a most delightful evening. The Lord High, especially, was a charming and most cultivated old gentleman.

Spencer called that same day, before the dinner, and spent an hour with me. He said I was not a bit too hard on Agassiz in my article. He said, as Huxley did, that while Agassiz deserves great credit as an indefatigable collector and observer, he is of no weight at all as a philosophical naturalist. And Spencer says to put him as high as Dr. Asa Gray or Jeffries Wyman is to put him too high, and Spencer "ought to know." This is the general opinion over here; they wonder why it is that Americans think so much of Agassiz. They all think Agassiz was in a way an obstruction to science in America. On the other hand, having lived in America, I see the American side of the case too, and know full well wherein Agassiz was of use to us, and could say a good thing about him, and perhaps I shall, though not just now, for I cannot let anything interfere with my book. Tyndall and Huxley were very much pleased with my article and Darwin said it was all true enough, but was a little too rough. Huxley said nothing about the tone, but Tyndall surmised that I had better have drawn it a little milder in one or two places. I have talked with lots of people and find the unanimous opinion to be that the great American is Dr. Gray. Over here they regard Gray as the greatest botanist in the world, even a little bigger than Hooker. But when you speak of Agassiz, there is apt to be a significant shrug of the shoul-ders, which says more than my article—and it is 'O yes, I believe the *Americans* think a great deal of him.''

I observe also that Darwin, Huxley, and Hooker all believe that Agassiz has never read the *Origin of Species!* And I am not at all sure that they are not right: *vide* my article. Tyndall had a talk with Agassiz and found that he could not state what Darwin's positions were. Tyndall said that Agassiz seemed utterly dazed and bewildered at the way the scientific world was moving away from him, his own son Alexander, included.

As you know, I wrote the Agassiz article in a great hurry, with Ethel sick at Petersham, and grandma Brooks interrupting me constantly in her excitement about your extreme fatigue from the care of Ethel. If I had the article in my hands I should just give it a little twist which would much improve it. It is a little too harsh.

Thursday the Reverend Moncure Conway gave a dinner party in honour of the "Mythmaker." At the party were: Ralston, Dr. Haffer, "Ph.D., Mas.D.," who is writing a book on Wagner, Froude the historian, Prof. W. Kingdon Clifford, and a Mr. Sergeant Tebbs, barrister-at-law. We had a delightful evening. Of course you want to know what I think of Froude, whose name, by the way, rhymes with "prude" and not with "proud". Well, he was very cordial to me —though, as I was the "guest of the evening," why shouldn't he have been?—but on the whole I didn't quite like him. He appears like a man who doesn't believe in anything, not even himself, a man in whom no one could safely confide; a bitter, hollow-hearted man. I find that Ralston has the same opinion of him. It seems rather wicked for me to say so, for his manner to me was very kindly. There are two men, so far, that I don't take to any more than *ile* takes to water—although they have both treated me well—Max Müller and Froude.

Conway is a fearful radical, but an honest man, I think; and his wife seems cordial and genial. Mr. Tebbs is a keen-eyed and jovial lawyer—a pleasant type of man. Clifford is a thoroughly good fellow, and, as I said before, an eminent mathematician. I liked him much. At the musical Dr. Haffer appeared to take a fancy to me and invited me to come to lunch at his house, and see Dr. Bridges, the great Positivist, you know; I shall go. You see I am running across everybody here; and you see I am getting feasted and toasted quite to my heart's content. . . .

London, England, December 15, 1873

Dear Abby:

Last Wednesday Fred Rogers called, along with Edward M. Tucke, of Lowell, Mass.! All America seems to be over here. Saturday I went with Tucke out to dine at a Mr. Sherman's in Norbiton Hall, Surrey. Queen Elizabeth used to stop at the house, which was built about Henry IV's time, around 1400. It is a princely place —truly magnificent. The dinner was superb and I am to go out again Saturday and take a drive to Richmond and Hampton Court. Tucke, I suppose, sailed for the U.S. this morning.

Thursday, Dec. 11th, I went to a great dinner of the Royal Society, as Huxley's guest. Saw Hooker, Williamson the chemist, Galton, Clifford, Maskelyne, Pritchard, Simpson, Sir John Hay, Crookes, Stokes, and others. Crookes performed some exquisite experiments on heat, and Huxley read a paper on a newly discovered crustacean. There were also papers by Stokes and Crookes. Galton—who wrote "Hereditary Genius"—had just been reading the October *North American,* and was loud and eloquent in his admiration of my article. Of all Americans, he said, I was the one he wanted to get a look at. Huxley hadn't seen the article yet, but grew very much interested in the conversation, and said he should lose no time in studying it up. It is a new idea to all of 'em. My "violent" friendship with Huxley began that evening. He attracted me wonderfully the first time I met him at Spencer's, but now I quite lost my heart to him.

Yesterday, Sunday, was a wonderful day not soon to be forgotten. First I "preached" at South Place Chapel to an audience of over 500, including many of the *élite* of London. Conway read from St. Paul and the Mishkat-al-Masalish and we had beautiful music to hymns by Longfellow and Emerson. You could have heard a pin drop at any time while I was speaking. Afterward I met, among others, Alexander Ellis the Chaucer man, and Darwin's oldest son. Conway says he calls it a success of the first water. I felt in good trim and, I think, spoke with more animation than usual. I had just been fixing up the lecture and liked it. I have no doubt it was a success; there could be no mistaking that. There will be a letter about it in the *Cincinnati Commercial.*

In the afternoon I went to the Lewes's and drank a cup of tea with them. Lewes was very jolly and told heaps of droll stories. Mrs. Lewes was also jolly, but as before, there were such a lot of folks there I couldn't get enough talk with either of them.

From there I went for my first Sunday evening at Huxley's where we had what he calls a "tall tea," i.e. on Sundays they dine early, and have an old-fashioned tea with meat at 6.30. We had delicious chicken and bacon, and it was good. Huxley's house is the nearest to an earthly paradise of anything that I have seen. He has seven of the loveliest children that ever lived. Miss Jessie, aged sixteen, who sings sweetly; Marian, aged fourteen, who also sings sweetly and draws wonderfully; two little girls, aged eleven and ten, who played a four-hand sonata of Beethoven, and did it well; two dear little boys—well, that is only six. I think I didn't see the seventh. Such a charming flock! And Mrs. Huxley is a sweet, motherly woman. They had four or five young lady nieces and cousins there, so there were a gang of us. After tea, Huxley and I retired to his study, which is the cosiest I have seen in England, and had a smoke and the very best talk I ever had. Darwin is the only man I have seen that equals Huxley. Darwin is a perfect old dear, but Huxley is a younger man—not much over forty-five I think—and so I feel more at home with him. He gave me his last book, with his pothooks on the title-page. He is very much interested in my book *Cosmic Philosophy*, and hopes I will add the chapter on "Matter and Spirit," which I have been mulling for a year back. We had a splendid talk about the soul. Later on we went into the parlour and had a lot of music, and more delightful talk, and some wine and biscuits. I didn't kiss Miss Jessie or Miss Marian, but kissed all the younger fry, and showed them the pictures of my own children, which much interested them. When I left, Huxley said there would be a plate set for me every Sunday as long as I stay in London, and it will be my own fault if I don't come and use it; in which Mrs. Huxley joined. I must say that I never in my life met more warm-hearted and lovable people. Why, my dear, I am getting to where I almost don't want to leave London.

Leaving the Huxley's after 10, I went to a soirée of the Cosmopolitan Club, where I had been invited by Sir Frederick Pollock, who translated Dante. I saw Lord Arthur Russell and Lord Acton, who know Norton, J. R. Lowell, and so on; and I had a long talk with *Tennyson!* He was sitting on a sofa in the chimney corner, smoking an Irishman's black clay pipe about three inches long! Conway introduced me to him, and I sat down on the same sofa, and we had a very pleasant chat. There is nothing especially attractive about him, except that he was good-natured and easy in manner. Sir. F. Pollock walked halfway back to 67 Great Russell St. with me, and told me to make myself at home at the Club as long as I stay in London. I shall probably meet more celebrities there than anywhere else. What do you think of this *one day's* experience?

I am sorry to have a tussle with James Freeman Clarke, but now that he has begun it, I will give him back the *quid pro quo*. I don't believe in not noticing attacks on me, except when they are anonymous, or simply ridiculous, like Sanborn's which are always so obviously dictated by personal feeling that there is nothing in them to answer. George said that Agassiz told Ripley that I am a jackass. I call it a very scientific rejoinder. I wish he would say so in print, but of course he isn't such a goose.

Last week I spent one whole day in the British Museum, in spite of the British red-tape, studying astronomy. If Chauncey Wright calls Darwin sixty-five years old, he "ought to know." I don't know positively, but should put him from sixty-five to seventy.

ADAM BADEAU
THINKS POORLY OF
ENGLISH ARISTOCRACY

1870s

Adam Badeau was a young man of no particular education and no particular talents who, at the age of thirty, managed to get an appointment as aide to General Sherman. Sherman handed him over to General Grant; he became Grant's trusted aide-de-camp, was made a lieutenant colonel and military secretary and, like Boswell and Johnson, clung to that attachment for the rest of Grant's life. In 1870 Grant, now President, appointed him consul general in London, a position which he held until 1881. In 1884 he was living with Grant, helping him write his famous *Memoirs;* eventually he himself produced a capital three-volume study, the *Military History of U. S. Grant,* and another book on *Grant in Peace.* His *Aristocracy in England* is a characteristic product of the man whose simple and homespun qualities commended themselves to the simple and homespun Grant.

The Caste System

If the influence of the aristocracy is vulgarizing upon the aristocrats themselves, rendering them often arrogant, supercilious and rude, it is still more so with their inferiors, debasing the spirit and

From Adam Badeau, *Aristocracy in England* (New York, 1886), pp. 155–164, 246–255.

degrading the behavior to an extent incomprehensible to an American, in persons who in other respects are neither abject nor servile. When one considers the character and history of the race, the grovelling of an Englishman before a lord is one of the marvels of modern times. There is nothing like it in any civilized nation on the globe. Neither the peasant of France or Spain, nor the private soldier of Germany, nor the lazzarone of Naples, nor even the emancipated Russian serf manifests in the presence of a superior that conviction of the existence of a caste composed of his "betters," which marks the educated Briton of the middle class. The sentiment is really more remarkable in the educated than in the ignorant, for in the latter it can be excused or comprehended; but the prostration of spirit and manner, the uncovering of the whole being, without any purpose or aim of sycophancy or interest, in a man or woman of culture and refinement and character, because of the presence of a person of rank transcends explanation. The very word "betters" has a meaning that is shocking to think of.

A woman of rank once asked me what, of all I had seen in England, struck me most forcibly. I had no doubt whatever, and answered: "The distinction of classes, the existence of caste." "But," she inquired, "do you really mean to say that in America the great merchant's daughter does not look down on the little grocer's daughter?" "Perhaps," said I, "the great merchant's daughter does look down, but very certainly the little grocer's daughter does not look up;" and the whole company was horrified at the idea of a country where the little grocers' daughters "don't look up."

This, indeed, is the difference between English and American life. In England everybody looks up. The most accomplished scholars, the men of science and letters, the artists, the great lawyers and physicians, even the politicians born without the pale, all look up to the aristocracy.

Mr. Gladstone and Mr. Disraeli, undoubtedly the two greatest statesmen England has produced since the days of Fox and Pitt, who have swayed the destinies and moulded the political character of the country for nearly a quarter of a century, each sprang from the middle class, and neither ever freed himself altogether from his awe of the aristocracy. Gladstone has done more to transmute liberal ideas into realities than any other Englishman that ever lived; yet not long ago he used these words: "So far as a man in my station can be supposed to understand or enter into the feelings of one of the rank of a duke;" and Disraeli, although he made himself a peer, could not get over his admiration and reverence for a born nobleman. His own adherents made this weakness their butt. Even after he had negotiated the treaty of Berlin, had snatched Constantinople from the grasp of Russia, and received the Order of the Garter from the Queen, I heard Tory wits, both men and women, laugh at his fondness for dukes, and declare that he was never so happy as when seated between duchesses, no matter how ugly or old.

For it is not enough to belong to the nobility; you must inherit the title to feel like an aristocrat. The law lords are always slightingly spoken of as new creations; people tell you how they are descended from barbers and tailors; and any duke with proper sentiment would rather his daughter were married to a stupid country squire of ancient family than to one of your modern Lord Chancellors. It is not till the blood of two or three generations has washed away the stain of plebeian origin that they take their place without uneasiness among the peers.

It is not only the chiefs in politics who are affected by the feeling of caste. In 1874, when Mr. Gladstone withdrew for a while from public affairs, the Liberals were obliged to select another leader. Mr. Forster was then by all odds their strongest and ablest man, but they had also Sir William Harcourt, Mr. Bright, Mr. Childers, Mr. Goschen, and others distinguished for intelligence and accomplishment. Yet the Marquis of Hartington, possessed of no striking qualifications of character or capacity, only the heir to a dukedom, was preferred. Had it not been for his rank he would never have been thought of; but all, it was said, could submit to his preeminence without humiliation. No one could object to a leader of so exalted rank and inconspicuous intellect; while if Forster or one of the others became chief, it would be a reflection on the abilities of those who were not preferred. And this was in the Liberal party of England!

Literature hurries after politics to bend before the lords. Froude and Lecky have written with all their force and eloquence on the "Uses of the Aristocracy" and the "Landed Gentry," to which they do not belong. They are as able and accomplished as any men in England to-day, and at least the intellectual equals of any living peer; but they want some one above them—some one "to kotow to." . . .

Not many years ago a statue of Mr. Peabody was erected in London, the work of our gifted countryman, Story. The Prince of Wales was present at the unveiling, and Mr. Motley, then Minister to England, delivered the address. It was an impressive circumstance—the commemoration by Englishmen of the munificence and charity of an American, who had bestowed his munificence on Englishmen. The presence of the heir to the throne and of the American Minister made the incident international; but the American artist was not invited. The city authorities of London looked upon him as a stonecutter, or at best as a tradesman who had sold them the result of his labor. Mr. Motley had to make a persistent application before they consented to include the sculptor in the ceremonies of which his own work was not only the principal ornament, but the occasion. In the eyes of the London citizen an artist is not an aristocrat; he is no better than one of themselves. . . .

The feeling of which I write extends to every sphere; it permeates England. The reverence that Gladstone and Disraeli showed is parodied in the sentiment of the servants, who regard the lords as beings of a different race from themselves. Even when the great people condescend, the servants never allow their own heads to be turned. . . .

This persistent humility is common with the class, and is manifested even toward republicans. I once found it convenient to assign to my valet a room in a part of the house near my own, and thought he would be pleased with the situation; but he told me respectfully he didn't like it at all. He was a servant, not a gentleman; he didn't want to be treated like a gentleman, nor to live in a gentleman's apartments. It was not proper.

They sometimes show this same appreciation of propriety in a different way. A cook, some time ago, took service with a physician who was a baronet. She knew her master's title, and did not suspect his occupation, but as soon as she discovered the reality she gave warning. She had only been used, she said, to living with the gentry.

I could fill pages with proof of the reverence for rank which many of the English besides Lecky and Froude defend, declaring that it exalts and refines the people who pay it: we all need something to venerate, they say. But the question is whether rank is the thing. In England, however, there is no question. The greatest nobles feel themselves honored by attendance on royalty, and their servants are conscious of no degradation in the duties they perform lower down, while the culture and genius of England are proud to pay both homage to the Queen and obeisance to the lords. To Americans this feature of caste is the most curious in the entire national character. That in the country of Carlyle and Bright, of Huxley and Mill, where the last results of modern thought and material civilization are soonest reached and often widest spread, where law and freedom are at least as universal in their prevalence as in America—this relic of barbarism should still survive, wrought into the very nature of the people—is as wonderful as if amid the congregations of Westminster Abbey or St. Paul's one should suddenly stumble on the worship of Isis or of Jove. . . .

"The English Nature Is Coarse" and "Sport Renders It Still More So"

One-third of the soil of England is devoted to the pleasures of the aristocracy, the principal of which is sport. The story is told of the foreigner who stayed at a country-house where every morning the men of the party exclaimed: "'Tis a fine day! Let's go out and kill something." The picture is not exaggerated. Many Englishmen of fortune seem to suppose they are sent into this world to hunt foxes and shoot grouse and deer. This is the object of their existence and the occupation of their lives. Among the aristocracy the man who does not shoot is an anomaly, almost a monstrosity. There must be something wrong about him.

All the arrangements of the upper classes—political or social, in town or country—are made with reference to sport. The fashionable season and the parliamentary season are determined by the game laws; country-house parties in winter and tours to the Continent in summer depend upon what are called "close times." Courtships are carried on, marriages are postponed, to suit the convenience of sportsmen. Great political revolutions are precipitated or deferred, questions of peace or war are taken up or let alone because ministers want to go to Scotland, because grouse-shooting begins in August, and fox-hunting is not over till February. The gravest crises in the history of a government are neglected when legislators are anxious to be off to the moors, and the sessions of Parliament cannot be held till the frost is out of the ground and the foxes begin to breed.

Estates are purchased and houses built because of the proximity of the covers; properties are valuable or insignificant according to the amount of game. Scores of fortunes are lost through the excessive love of sport. Every circumstance and event of English high-life revolves around this pivot, and the results are as visible as those of religion. Sport enters into politics, it colors literature, it controls society. It affects dress, manners, etiquettes, and entertainments, the relations of master and servant, man and wife, father and son; the characteristics of whole classes in the State. It is one of the principal causes and results of aristocracy to-day.

On the 12th of August the sportsman's year begins. Grouse-shooting dissolves Parliament, and all who have moors, or invitations to them, make haste to the north. There is some good shooting in the south, but the best grouse-moors are in the opposite direction. Parties of twelve or twenty are common, but the genuine sportsmen often go off in smaller numbers. In Scotland there are hundreds of small shootings let for the season at prices varying from forty pounds to four thousand, according to the extent and quality of the game; but the great proprietors of course reserve the best for themselves. On many estates there are small shooting-boxes, or still simpler cabins called shielings, plainly furnished, where half a dozen men can go without ladies, and devote a few days or weeks to their favorite pastime.

More often, however, society is combined with sport. At a great house the party is usually large. The men sally out each morning "to kill something," and sometimes the ladies accompany them. Of late years a few of these are shooters themselves. This is, of course, when the game is driven to the guns; at such times the bags made are enormous, hundreds of birds often falling to a single sportsman. The labor is less, and the glory, but the boasting is prodigious.

The shooters go out soon after breakfast—by ten o'clock always, and earlier when they are very much in earnest. The dresses are rough, necessarily; the boots heavy-soled, for tramping over the moors; the knickerbockers coarse, and in Scotland many wear the kilt. Lunch is taken on the moors, and by two o'clock it is very acceptable. Sometimes a cart comes out from the house with a hot lunch, and the ladies accompany it on ponies or in little carriages; but if the game is far from the road the gillies carry cold meat and claret in hampers. Whiskey each man takes for himself. The gamekeepers and gillies and beaters make quite a procession, with the extra guns and the game-bags. They load for the gentry, and sometimes bring in the birds, and beat, and drive, and take as keen an interest in the sport as their masters, or the dogs, which also form an important part of the company. The fresh air, the mountain mist, the purple heather, the glimpses of scenery, the exhilaration of the exercise, all make the pastime more than fascinating, even for those who have less than an Englishman's passion for "killing things."

In Scotland deer-stalking is another favorite form of the amusement. It is much more laborious, the sportsmen must walk farther, must lie on the hillside often for hours, must watch more warily, and shoot perhaps more skilfully, but the glory of bringing home a stag is great enough to compensate. The deer-forests, as they are called, contain no trees; they are simply great stretches of broken land, probably once wooded, but now bare and bleak for miles and miles; with little lochs scattered among the hills, their sloping banks covered with masses of bracken, the haunt and the browse of the red deer. These vast expanses devoted to stalking make up a large part of the estates of the Scotch nobility. Hundreds of thousands of acres are included in the deer-forests of some half a dozen dukes and earls.

A party of stalkers returning over the hills after a long day's sport, and standing out against the red evening sky, makes a picture that the stranger is sure to remember. Most of them are in Highland dress, with plaids and sporrans, feathers in their bonnets and daggers in their hose; their legs are bare, and their guns are at their shoulders. The stag is slung over a pony in the middle of the group, his antlers attesting his age. They shout and wave their bonnets and plaids as they approach, and those who have remained at home are sure to go out to meet them at the gate, to listen to the story of the day's exploits, to count the branches on the antlers, and accompany the party to the larder or the butchery, where the stag is weighed and divided. At night the man who has shot a stag is entitled to wear a red waistcoat at dinner.

A bath and a cup of tea refresh the jaded sportsman before the formal evening that follows. In Scotland, in the shooting season, dinner is often as late as nine, or even half-past nine; and in the long northern twilight candles are seldom needed before you sit down. The transformation in the appearance of the company when lights are brought in is sometimes startling. The rough garb of the sportsman has been exchanged for the habiliments of civilization, and the women are resplendent in jewels and lace. They take their finest diamonds to the wilds, and there is a peculiar fascination about the splendor and luxury of an aristocratic dinner, after the hardships and excitement of the forest and the moor.

The anglers have had more quiet pleasures, but they too boast at night of their successes, and the table groans under the results of the achievements of the day.

Partridge-shooting begins on the 1st of September, and is less arduous than grouse-shooting, and more of an English than a Scottish sport. Pheasants are not killed till October 1. This amusement also is principally a southern one, but every county in England has its pheasant preserves. The battues are enormous, and the covers like chicken yards. Game-keepers, indeed, are little more than stock-farmers, so far as pheasants are concerned; and many of the earnest shooters despise this phase of sport. The English themselves never call it "hunting;" they speak only of "shooting" pheasants. I should say butchering; for the pheasants are sold.

This is a feature of English sport that I never ceased to wonder at. These noblemen and gentlemen with their hundreds of thousands of acres and their hundreds of thousands of income, their estates and castles and retainers, their crowds of aristocratic guests—nearly all sell their game. Now and then they send a friend a brace of birds or a haunch of venison, but the game market is stocked by the nobility. To many of them it is a considerable source of revenue. I was once staying with a well-known nobleman while General Grant was President. I had been out with the shooters, and thought it would be pleasant to send the President a brace of pheasants from the spot where they had been killed. I mentioned to one of the guests that I meant to suggest this to our host, but he cautioned me not to commit the blunder. The matter was discussed by the entire party, and every man declared it would be improper to make the request. The game was marketable, and it would be indelicate to ask for it, even if I had shot the birds. Nobody seemed to think this strange. The high spirit of an aristocrat did not revolt at selling the game that his guests had killed; and the man who was lavish of his courtesies would have been amazed had I proposed he should pay this compliment to the head of a foreign State.

The devotion to sport that characterizes the English aristocracy is not elevating. It not only makes them indifferent to more serious occupations, taking the hereditary legislators from the affairs of state to which they are supposed to apply themselves, and often distracting them from their own more important interests; but the incessant practice is certainly brutalizing. To be forever planning and inflicting death and pain, even on animals, cannot be refining. The English nature is coarse in itself, but sport renders it still more so. They say, indeed, that they shoot and kill and torture because all this is necessary in order to procure food. But butchering is also necessary, yet gentlemen do not select the shambles for their pastimes. The Frenchman's criticism was fair. "Let us go and kill something," is the Englishman's idea of pleasure; and it is a coarse one. An American soldier once said something like this at an English table in my hearing, and one of the company insinuated that the sentiment was maudlin. But the American, who had been in forty battles, replied: "Oh! I believe in killing nothing but men."

Like everything else in England, this pleasure is a matter of privilege. Game is strictly preserved for the great. The unprivileged man may not carry a gun. Every Englishman loves sport, the peasant as well as the peer, but poaching is a criminal offence; and the poor man is sent for two months, six months, even a year, to gaol, for doing what gives the rich man his keenest gratification. Five thousand committals for poaching are made every year in England alone. The landlord is the magistrate, and decides upon the punishment after convicting of the crime. In this country of privilege, there is property even in the air; and the peasant who has no farm, no house, and no hope of ever owning either, no amusement, often no meat, may not shoot the rabbit that roots up his garden, or the wild bird that flies over the moor.

Nothing can be more fascinating for those who are fond of the pastime than the methods of aristocratic athletic pleasure; nothing more elaborate and imposing than its appliances and appurtenances. God's uplands and valleys themselves are the playground of the nobility. The broad domains, the stretching moors, the thick coverts, the lofty mountains, the purple heath-covered hills, rolling and billowy, like the waves of the sea, and, like them, extending to the horizon, are all reserved unbroken and undisturbed, for the amusement of the aristocracy; these are the stage on which the great disport themselves. When across some scene of stately natural grandeur or bewitching cultivated grace there passes a company of the masters of the soil, issuing perhaps from a great castle hoary with age and famous in history, with their guests and retainers, their horses and hounds, and guns and game, bent on exhilarating, manly pleasure; surrounded with all that makes life splendid and gay—one cannot but admire the taste and luxury and magnificence that come from centuries of privilege and generations used to caste.

But at the same moment another procession of starving, houseless hinds, a million in number, is marching to the almshouse.

RICHARD GRANT WHITE:

"ENGLISHMEN AS A MASS

ARE PHILISTINE"

1877

Richard Grant was one of the most perspicacious—and most prolific—of all the commentators on Britain. Born in New York City in 1821, he studied law and embraced music, but devoted his career to journalism and literary criticism. For a time music critic of the *New York Enquirer,* he became secretary to the Sanitary Fair—a kind of combination Red Cross and YMCA —during the Civil War and reported aspects of that war to the London *Spectator.* Meantime he turned more and more to literature and philology, published *Words and Their Uses* in 1870, edited a twelve-volume edition of Shakespeare, and contributed a steady stream of articles on language and literature to the *Atlantic Monthly* and other journals. *England Without and Within* presented impressions of England gathered on a visit there in 1876 and 1877.

The difference between the society of England and that of America down to the present time, or perhaps I should say until within the last twenty-five or thirty years, is due chiefly to what remained in the motherland—to certain immovable material things which the English colonists could not bring away, and certain other

From Richard Grant White, *England Without and Within* (Boston, 1881), pp. 593–601.

movable immaterial things which they did not choose to bring away with them. The abandonment of these, on the one hand, and the circumstances of the country to which he came, on the other, effected the changes, really slight, which made the Englishman of this country differ from his kinsmen who remained in the old home. But Philistinism was a new development of the English national character, which took place after the great English colonization of "Virginia" was completed. In it the "American" has not part nor lot. It is to-day the one great distinguishing difference between two societies of men of the same blood and speech, having the same laws and literature and religion, in two countries. It is the only difference which goes down beneath clothes and cuticle. British Englishmen as a mass are Philistine; American Englishmen as a mass are not. In the American there is a nimble flexibility of mind, an apprehensive adaptability, which reminds us of the Englishman of the Elizabethan era. He is at once more logical and more imaginative than his British kinsman; but at the same time less stable, less prudent, less sagacious. There are Philistines of a sort, in the United States, not a few of them; but they wear their Philistinism with a difference.

That Philistinism is rare and mild in its manifestations among us, we Yankees may reasonably be glad; but that the bird which broils upon our ugly coins should therefore plume himself and thank God in his heart that he is not as other brutes are, even as that poor British lion, is not quite so clear. For after all it must be confessed that the country under the protection of that roaring beast, although it is so entirely given over to the domination of this strange *ism* that it may truly be called Philistia, and although its people are often troubled at home and baffled abroad, is yet, on the whole, the happiest, and in many important respects the most admirable and respectable, in the world. John Bull himself confesses that he is a rude creature, who in some places welcomes a stranger by "'eaving arf a brick at 'im," and who beats his wife in most places; and yet England is the country of all Europe in which human life is safest. Dreydorf, in his work on the Jesuits in the German Empire, published in 1872, shows with emphasis that while in Rome there is one murder for 750 inhabitants, in Naples one for 2750, in Spain one for 4113, in Austria one for 57,000, in Prussia one for 100,000, in England there is but one for 178,000. And although John Bull may beat his wife, he wrongs women in what is generally regarded as a more grievous way very little when we compare his sins with those of other men in that respect. The same work shows that while for 100 legitimate births there are in Rome 243 illegitimate, in Vienna 118, in Munich 91, and in Paris 48, there is in London only one. This makes the proportion of suffering and wrong of this kind as follows: England 1, France 12, Germany 25, Austria 30, Italy 60. France is twelve times and Italy sixty times worse than England in this respect!

And England is of all countries in Europe, and I am inclined to think of all countries in the world, the one in which there is, if not the most freedom, the greatest degree of the best kind of freedom—that which is enjoyed by him who respects the freedom and the rights of all other men. There is no other country in the world in which the people are so little at the mercy of great corporations and of powerful individuals, and only one, if there be one, in which the poor man is so sure of the protection of the law against the rich, and the rich man is equally sure of justice if his adversary be poor.

What position in the world is so enviable as that of an English gentleman! What character, on the whole, more admirable than that of an English gentleman who is recognized among his fellows as worthy of his class! He is not always quickly apprehensive and alert of mind; he is sometimes over-confident; he is often very illogical; he blunders abroad and blunders at home; but his want of logic does not always show a want of sense. Sagacity is sometimes better than syllogism; and he is wise in remedying real evils in an utterly illogical way. In his difficulties he generally wins through by stoutness of heart and steady nerve, and fixed purpose to do what he thinks is his duty. He has a singular capacity of suffering when he sees that he must suffer, and a grand ability to die in silence when he sees that he ought to do so. Other men are as brave as he, some perhaps more dashing and brilliant in feats of arms—Frenchmen, Germans, even Spaniards and Portuguese; but the calm, steady beat of the English heart in the face of danger is like the swing of a pendulum that obeys only the one great law of the universe. English armies have been beaten; but they have rarely, if ever, been routed. They have left their lost fields with ranks as nearly unbroken and with as firm a step as the most exacting soldier could expect or hope for in his overpowered and retreating comrades. At Fontenoy and at Corunna there was no panic. And at Balaklava, when "it was not war," it was at least cool, unquestioning obedience to orders, in the retreat as well as in the charge. . . .

If Englishmen are a little loftily conscious of English prowess and English stability, they have the right to be so—a right given to them by such fields (not to mention others of minor fame) as Crecy, where Edward III's men were less in number than one to two of their opponents; and Agincourt, where Henry V's were not one to four;

and Plassy, where Clive's one thousand Englishmen had such heart to spare to their two thousand auxiliaries that together they put more than ten times their number to flight, although the enemy had almost as many cannon as the little British force had field-officers. Andrew Borde, a Sussex physician, who had seen the world of his day as few men then saw it, published in 1542 a book called *The Boke of the Introduction of Knowledge,* in which there are rude wood-cuts representing men of various nations, each of which has a motto or saying attached to it. That uttered by the Englishman is,—

> I do feare no man, all men fearyth me;
> I overcome my adversaries by land and sea.

Boastful, indeed, and therein not uncharacteristic: but true, and therein also characteristic. Borde says, "I think if all the world were set agaynst England it might never be conquered, they being trew within themselfe." We know that this opinion of our fore-fathers and our kinsmen has been sustained by the event. But from that time to the present, of what other people in the world, who are not of English race, could this be truly said?

The bearing of all this upon our present subject is that the rise and the progress of Philistinism in England were strictly contemporaneous with her assumption of her position as a power of the first class in the world, in wealth, in strength, in empire, in glory. India was won for Britain by her middle classes; and Philistinism marched steadily forward from the victories of Marlborough to those of Wellington.

And, moreover, see the attitude of England now, and of Englishmen, towards the agitators and revolutionists—agitators and revolutionists, however just may be their cause or great their provocation—who are threatening and striving to dismember the empire. Englishmen as a race do not like Irishmen as a race, on either side of the ocean; and Irishmen have now been doing all that deeds and words could do to inflame English hatred against them. But England has stood, although indignant, considerate, not without sympathy, and reluctant to strike. The very leaders of what is legal treason, and who are on trial for their crime, take their seats in Parliament, with no man to molest them or make them afraid. Mr. Parnell, indicted traitor in Dublin, sits as a member of Parliament in Westminster, and has all the privileges and immunities of his representative function. He is as safe in the House of Commons, and, what is more, as safe in the streets of London, as if he were John Bright or Mr. Gladstone. He and his colleagues are heard patiently until they deliberately undertake to obstruct the action of Parliament, and there is not a word uttered in speech or in print to excite personal ill-will against them. This is a noble attitude, and it is one peculiarly English. . . .

England has behaved to us too often rather as a mother-in-law than as a mother-in-blood, and some Englishmen have an unhappy mastery of the art of being personally offensive; but that is a poor and petty spirit which cannot see and admire greatness because it has received slight. And what wrong has England ever done us since we were an independent nation? She has scoffed and sneered and been insolent; and, as Plutarch says, men will forgive injurious deeds sooner than offensive words. But after all, is it not better to forgive even offensive words when they were spoken less in malice than in overweening conceit and utter ignorance? England is the cradle and the home of Philistinism, and never has the Philistine temperament of her dominant, although not her ruling, class been more manifest than in her attitude, until lately, towards her younger brother in "America." It has been quite like that of Mr. Anthony Trollope's Marquis of Brotherton towards his younger brother. And this went on all the while that we were, to all intents and purposes, but another English nation. Now, when we are being year by year more and more a mixed people, she is changing her tone, because we have fought a big war and are paying a big debt. Alas, that it is so! But *we* at least can afford to be good-natured, and to smile, not merely in rueful scorn, as we take the hand that would have been so much more welcome and so much more honored if it had been offered when we were weaker and poorer.

Yet we may trust England in this matter. It is not that she is snobbish, and is ducking to us merely because she has found out that we are strong and rich; it is that our war and its consequences have partly opened her Philistine eyes, have taught her something, although yet a very little, about "America." Her ignorance was ridiculous, but it is not unpardonable, nor quite incomprehensible. After living a while in England, one begins to discover how it is that it is so much farther from London to New York than it is from New York to London. He who cannot see that must be very dull or very ignorant,—himself a Philistine, indeed.

England is not perfect, for it is upon the earth, and it is peopled by human beings; but I do not envy the man who, being able to earn enough to get bread and cheese and beer, a whole coat, and a tight roof over his head,—chiefest need under England's sky,—cannot be happy there. He who is of a complexion to be surly because another man is called my Lord, while he is plain Mister,—she who frets because another woman may go to court, while she may only queen it at home,—can easily find occasion there to grumble or to pine. They whose chief aim is to rise in life do find there, not barriers indeed, but obstacles; to overcome which they must have *can* and *will* largely in their composition, as it is thought that they should have who rise. But they who are sufficient unto themselves, and who can take what life and the world offer with little concern as to what others may be thinking about them, may find in England the means and conditions of a sound and solid happiness. I never met a well-educated, wellbred Yankee, who had lived in England long enough to become familiar with her people, who found himself at all out of place there, or who was dissatisfied with any of his surroundings. As to Philistinism, the chief mark of distinction between the people of the two countries, one becomes used even to that, and finally forgets it. I confess, as I bid farewell to thee, Philistia, dear motherland, that while I was within thy borders I, a Yankee of the Yankees, felt at times as if I were a Philistine of the Philistines.

1880-1890

EDWIN WHIPPLE:
THE ENGLISH MIND IS
"COARSE, STRONG, MASSIVE,
STURDY, PRACTICAL"

1880s

Edwin Whipple, now almost completely forgotten, was one of the most highly esteemed critics and lecturers in the country. Born and schooled in the old seacoast towns north of Boston, he abandoned a business career for literature, and as early as 1848 published a two-volume collection of his critical essays. He lectured widely on the lyceum circuit, and gave the Lowell Institute lectures on the age of Elizabeth. Motely called him, somewhat widly, "one of the most brilliant writers of the century"; if not brilliant he was perspicacious and judicious. He died in 1885, leaving unpublished a two-volume biography of Dickens.

That pyramidal organism, with John Bull at the base and Shakespeare at the apex, which we call the English mind, is unexcelled, if not unequalled, in modern times for its sturdy force of being, its muscular strength of faculty, the variety of its directing sentiments, and its tough hold upon existence. No other national mind combines such vast and various creativeness, and presents so living a synthesis of seemingly elemental contradictions, which is at the same time marked

From Edwin Whipple, *Character and Characteristic Men* (Boston, 1884), pp. 166–183.

by such distinctness of individual features. That imperial adjective, English, fits its sedition as well as its servility, its radicalism as well as its conservatism, its squalor as well as its splendor, its vice as well as its virtue, its morality and religion as well as its politics and government. The unity of its nature is never lost in all the prodigious variety of its manifestation. Prince, peasant, Cavalier, Roundhead, Whig, Tory, poet, penny-a-liner, philanthropist, ruffian—William Wilberforce in Parliament, Richard Turpin on the York road—all agree in being English, all agree in a common contempt, blatant or latent, for everything not English. Liberty is English, wisdom is English, philosophy is English, religion is English, earth is English, air is English, heaven is English, hell is English. And this imperious dogmatism, too, has none of the uneasy self-distrust which peeps through the vociferous brag of corresponding American phenomena; but, expressing its seated faith in egotism's most exquisite *non sequiturs*, it says stoutly, with Parson Adams, "A schoolmaster is the greatest of men, and I am the greatest of schoolmasters"; and, moreover, it believes what it says. The quality is not in the tongue, but in the character of the nation.

This solid self-confidence and pride of nationality, this extraordinary content with the image reflected in the mirror of self-esteem, indicates that the national mind is not tormented by the subtle sting of abstract opinions or the rebuking glance of unrealized ideals, but that its reason and imagination work on the level of its Will. The essential peculiarity, therefore, of the English Mind is its basis in Character, and consequent hold upon facts and disregard of abstractions. Coarse, strong, massive, sturdy, practical—organizing its thoughts into faculties, and toughening its faculties into the consistency of muscle and bone—its whole soul is so embodied and embrained, that it imprints on its most colossal mental labors the stern characteristics of sheer physical strength. It not only has fire, but fuel enough to feed its fire. Its thoughts are acts, its theories are institutions, its volitions are events. It has no ideas not inherent in its own organization, or which it has not assimilated and absorbed into its own nature by collision or communion with other national minds. It is enriched but never overpowered by thoughts and impulses from abroad, for whatever it receives it forces into harmony with its own broadening processes of interior development. Thus the fiery, quick-witted, wilful and unscrupulous Norman encamped in its domains, and being unable to reject him, and its own stubborn vitality refusing to succumb, it slowly and sullenly, through long centuries, absorbed him into itself, and blended fierce Norman pride and swift Norman intelligence with its own solid substance of sense and humor. By the same jealous and resisting, but assimilative method, it gradually incorporated the principles of Roman law into its jurisprudence, and the spirit of Italian, Spanish, and German thought into its literature, receiving nothing, however, which it did not modify with its own individuality, and scrawling "England, her mark," equally on what it borrowed and what it created.

A national mind thus rooted in character, with an organizing genius directed by homely sentiments, and with its sympathies fastened on palpable aims and objects, has all the strength which comes from ideas invigorated but narrowed by facts. General maxims disturb it not, for it never acts from reason alone, or passion alone, or understanding alone; but reason, passion, understanding, conscience, religious sentiment, are all welded together in its thoughts and actions, and pure reason, or pure conscience, or pure passion, it not only neglects, but stigmatizes. Its principles are precedents buttressed by prejudices, and these are obstinately asserted from force of character rather than reasoned out by force of intellect. . . .

We have heard, lately, many edifying and sonorous sentences quoted from English jurists about the law of God overriding the law of man; but it is not remembered that when an English jurist speaks of the law of God, he really means that fraction of it which he thinks has become, or is becoming, the law of England. To make a true Englishman responsible for any maxim which is essentially abstract, *in*organic, *un*precedented, and foreign to the interior working of the national mind, is to misconceive both his meaning and his nature. No great English humorist—that is, no man who sees through phrases into characters—has ever blundered into such a mistake. The true localizing principle is hinted by Goldsmith's braggart theologian: "When I say religion, I of course mean the Christian religion; and when I say Christian religion, I would have you know, sir, that I mean the Church of England!"

Now it is evident that a national mind thus proud and practical, thus individual and insular, making, as it does, the senses final, and almost deifying rank and property, would naturally exhibit in its manners and institutions a double aristocracy of blood and capital. Hence results the most hateful of English characteristics—the disposition, we mean, of each order of English society to play the sycophant to the class above it, and the tyrant to the class below it; though, from the inherent vigor and independence of the Englishman's nature, his servility is often but the mask of his avarice or hatred. The best representative of this unamiable combination of arrogance and meanness is that full-blown Briton . . . Lord Chancellor Thurlow, who could justly claim the rare distinction of being the greatest bully and the greatest parasite of his time. . . .

The leading defect of English manners, however, is consequent on their chief merit. Being the natural expression of the national mind, all the harshness as well as all the honesty of the people is sincerely expressed in them; and they press especially hard on the poor and the helpless. In the mode of conducting political disputes, in the ferocity and coarseness of political and personal libels, and in the habit of calling unpleasant objects by their most unpleasant names, we perceive the national contempt of all the decent draperies which mental refinement casts over sensual tastes and aggressive passions. The literature of the nation strikingly exhibits this ingrained coarseness at the foundation of its mind, and its greatest poets and novelists are full of it in their delineations of manners and character. Chaucer and Shakespeare humorously represent it; Ben Jonson and Fielding, the two most exclusively English of all England's imaginative writers, are at once its happy expounders and bluff exponents; and Swift, whose large Saxon brain was rendered fouler by misanthropy, absolutely riots in the gutter. This robust manhood, anchored deep in strong sensations and rough passions, gives also a peculiar pugnacity to English manners. No man can rise there who cannot stand railing, stand invective, stand ridicule, "stand fight." Force of character bears remorselessly down on everything and everybody that resists it, and no man is safe who cannot emphasize the "me." This harshness is a sign of lusty health and vigor, and doubtless educates men by opposition into self-reliance; but woe unto those it crushes! . . .

We now come to a most delicate topic, which can hardly be touched without offence, or avoided without an oversight of the most grotesque expression of the English Mind. The determining sentiments of the people are to war, industry, and general individual and material aggrandizement,—to things human rather than to things divine; but every true Englishman, however much of a practical Atheist he may be, feels a genuine horror of infidelity, and always has a religion to swear by, and, if need be, to fight for. He makes it—we are speaking of the worldling—subordinate to English laws and customs, *Anglicizes* it, and never allows it to interfere with his selfish or patriotic service to his country, or with the gratification of his passions; but he still believes it, and, what is more, believes that he himself is one of its edifying exponents. This gives a delicious unconscious hypocrisy to the average national mind, which has long been the delight and the butt of English humorists. Its most startling representative was the old swearing, drinking, licentious, church-and-king Cavalier, who was little disposed, the historian tells us, to shape his life according to the precepts of the Church, but who was always "ready to fight knee-deep in blood for her cathedrals and palaces, for every line of her rubric, and every thread of her vestments." Two centuries ago, Mrs. Aphra Behn described the English squire as "going to church every Sunday morning, to set a good example to the lower orders, and as getting the parson drunk every Sunday night to show his respect for the Church." ... The cry, raised generally by cunning politicians, that "the Church is in danger," is sure to stir all the ferocity, stupidity, and ruffianism of the nation in its support. Religion in England is, in fact, a part of politics, and therefore the most worldly wear its badges. Thus all English warriors, statesmen, and judges are religious men, but the religion is ever subordinate to the profession or business in hand. . . . Perhaps the quaintest example of this combination of business and theology is found in that English judge, who was condemning to death, under the old barbarous law, a person who had forged a one-pound note. Lord Campbell tells us that, after exhorting the criminal to prepare for another world, he added: "And I trust that, through the mediation and merits of our blessed Redeemer, you may *there* experience that mercy which a due regard to the credit of the paper currency of the country forbids you to hope for *here.*" Indeed, nothing could more forcibly demonstrate how complete is the organization of the English Mind than this interpenetration of the form of the religious element with its most earthly aims; and therefore it is that the real piety of the nation, whether ritual or evangelical, is so sturdy and active, and passes so readily from Christian doctrines into Christian virtues. In its best expressions it is somewhat local; but what it loses in transcendent breadth and elevation of sentiment it gains in practical faculty to perform every-day duties.

JANE ADDAMS
SEES A LONDON OF
"HIDEOUS HUMAN NEED AND SUFFERING"

1883

Jane Addams of Hull-House has some claim to be considered the greatest woman in American public life. Born in 1860 of affluent parents, she obtained an innocuous education at Rockford College, in Illinois, then a kind of girl's finishing school. She hoped to study medicine, but illness put an end to that and left her with no clear outlet for her energies and her philanthropic instincts. In 1883 she and her lifelong friend, Ellen Starr, went abroad on what was to have been a typical tour of Europe. It was in London that Jane Addams first caught an impression of the wretchedness of large segments of mankind; it was in Spain, of all places, that she got the notion of setting up a settlement house in the midst of the Chicago slums to tackle the problem of poverty head-on. On her return to London she studied Toynbee Hall and other settlement houses, but did not in the end borrow much from them; what she created at Hull-House was something unique. It was in 1889 that she bought the old Hull-House, on Halstead Street in Chicago, in a neighborhood swarming with the poor from Italy, Poland, Ireland, and Russia; within a decade it was the most famous private address in America. She gathered about her one

From Jane Addams, *Twenty Years at Hull-House* (New York, 1910), pp. 66–71, 262–265.

of the most remarkable groups of co-workers in the country, women animated by a vision of social justice and prepared to work for it in the humblest as in the most exalted capacities: Dr. Alice Hamilton, Edith and Grace Abbott, Julia Lathrop, Florence Kelley, and others, all of whom made a mark on history. There—with the support of Chicago philanthropists fascinated by her accomplishments—she inaugurated a series of far-reaching experiments in education and social reform. She gave an impetus to the settlement-house movement everywhere in the country, anticipated John Dewey in teaching arts and music and drama to children, encouraged immigrant mothers to retain or recover their folk arts, set up fresh-air camps for the children of the slums, and found time to persuade the Illinois legislature to establish the first juvenile courts, to pass effective labor legislation, and to work for municipal reform. Soon scholars from the University of Chicago and the University of Wisconsin, and indeed from all parts of the country, were beating a track to Hull-House: John Dewey, John R. Commons, Richard Ely, Sophia Breckenridge, and others. Somehow she found time to campaign for federal child-labor legislation and to persuade President Roosevelt to create a Children's Bureau in Washington; somehow, too, she found time to write *Twenty Years at Hull-House,* one of the classics of American literature. Later in life, after she felt she had done what she could at Hull-House, she devoted her energies to campaigns for women's rights and for peace, and in 1931 was awarded the Nobel Peace Prize.

We present here excerpts from reflections on two visits to London separated by more than a decade.

The long illness left me in a state of nervous exhaustion with which I struggled for years, traces of it remaining long after Hull-House was opened in 1889. At the best it allowed me but a limited amount of energy, so that doubtless there was much nervous depression at the foundation of the spiritual struggles which this chapter is forced to record. However, it could not have been all due to my health, for as my wise little notebook sententiously remarked, "In his own way each man must struggle, lest the moral law become a far-off abstraction utterly separated from his active life." . . .

One of the most poignant of these experiences, which occurred during the first few months after our landing upon the other side of the Atlantic, was on a Saturday night, when I received an ineradicable impression of the wretchedness of East London, and also saw for the first time the over-crowded quarters of a great city at midnight.

A small party of tourists were taken to the East End by a city missionary to witness the Saturday night sale of decaying vegetables and fruit, which, owing to the Sunday laws in London, could not be sold until Monday, and, as they were beyond safe keeping, were disposed of at auction as late as possible on Saturday night. On Mile End Road, from the top of an omnibus which paused at the end of a dingy street lighted by only occasional flares of gas, we saw two huge masses of ill-clad people clamoring around two hucksters' carts. They were bidding their farthings and ha' pennies for a vegetable held up by the auctioneer, which he at last scornfully flung, with a gibe for its cheapness, to the successful bidder. In the momentary pause only one man detached himself from the groups. He had bidden in a cabbage, and when it struck his hand, he instantly sat down on the curb, tore it with his teeth, and hastily devoured it, unwashed and uncooked as it was. He and his fellows were types of the "submerged tenth," as our missionary guide told us, with some little satisfaction in the then new phrase, and he further added that so many of them could scarcely be seen in one spot save at this Saturday night auction, the desire for cheap food being apparently the one thing which could move them simultaneously. They were huddled into ill-fitting, cast-off clothing, the ragged finery which one sees only in East London. Their pale faces were dominated by that most unlovely of human expressions, the cunning and shrewdness of the bargain-hunter who starves if he cannot make a successful trade, and yet the final impression was not of ragged, tawdry clothing nor of pinched and sallow faces, but of myriads of hands, empty, pathetic, nerveless and workworn, showing white in the uncertain light of the street, and clutching forward for food which was already unfit to eat.

Perhaps nothing is so fraught with significance as the human hand, this oldest tool with which man has dug his way from savagery, and with which he is constantly groping forward. I have never since been able to see a number of hands held upward, even when they are moving rhythmically in a calisthenic exercise, or when they belong to a class of chubby children who wave them in eager response to a teacher's query, without a certain revival of this memory, a clutching at the heart reminiscent of the despair and resentment which seized me then.

For the following weeks I went about London almost furtively, afraid to look down narrow streets and alleys lest they disclose again this hideous human need and suffering. I carried with me for days at a time that curious surprise we experience when we first come back into the streets after days given over to sorrow and death; we are bewildered that the world should be going on as usual and unable to determine which is real, the inner pang or the outward seeming. In time all huge London came to seem unreal save the poverty in its East End. During the following two years on the continent, while I was irresistibly drawn to the poorer quarters of each city, nothing among the beggars of South Italy nor among the saltminers of Austria carried with it the same conviction of human wretchedness which was conveyed by this momentary glimpse of an East London street. It was, of course, a most fragmentary and lurid view of the poverty of East London, and quite unfair, I should have been shown either less or more, for I went away with no notion of the hundreds of men and women who had gallantly identified their fortunes with these empty-handed people, and who, in church and chapel, "relief works," and charities, were at least making an effort towards its mitigation.

Our visit was made in November, 1883, the very year when the *Pall Mall Gazette* exposure started "The Bitter Cry of Outcast London," and the conscience of England was stirred as never before over this joyless city in the East End of its capital. Even then, vigorous and drastic plans were being discussed, and a splendid program of municipal reforms was already dimly outlined. Of all these, however, I had heard nothing but the vaguest rumor.

No comfort came to me then from any source, and the painful impression was increased because at the very moment of looking down the East London street from the top of the omnibus, I had been sharply and painfully reminded of "The Vision of Sudden Death" which had confronted De Quincey one summer's night as he was being driven through rural England on a high mail coach. Two absorbed lovers suddenly appear between the narrow, blossoming hedgerows in the direct path of the huge vehicle which is sure to crush them to their death. De Quincey tries to send them a warning shout, but finds himself unable to make a sound because his mind is hopelessly entangled in an endeavor to recall the exact lines from the *Iliad* which describe the great cry with which Achilles alarmed all Asia militant. Only after his memory responds is his will released from its momentary paralysis, and he rides on through the fragrant night with the horror of the escaped calamity thick upon him, but he also bears with him the consciousness that he had given himself over so many years to classic learning—that when suddenly called upon for a quick decision in the world of life and death, he had been able to act only through a literary suggestion.

This is what we were all doing, lumbering our minds with literature that only served to cloud the really vital situation spread before
our eyes. It seemed to me too preposterous that in my first view of
the horror of East London I should have recalled De Quincey's
literary description of the literary suggestion which had once
paralyzed him. In my disgust it all appeared a hateful, vicious circle
which even the apostles of culture themselves admitted, for had not
one of the greatest among the moderns plainly said that "conduct,
and not culture is three fourths of human life."

For two years in the midst of my distress over the poverty which,
thus suddenly driven into my consciousness, had become to me the
"Weltschmerz," there was mingled a sense of futility, of misdirected
energy, the belief that the pursuit of cultivation would not in the end
bring either solace or relief. I gradually reached a conviction that the
first generation of college women had taken their learning too
quickly, had departed too suddenly from the active, emotional life
led by their grandmothers and great-grandmothers; that the contemporary education of young women had developed too exclusively the power of acquiring knowledge and of merely receiving
impressions; that somewhere in the process of "being educated"
they had lost that simple and almost automatic response to the
human appeal, that old healthful reaction resulting in activity from
the mere presence of suffering or of helplessness; that they are so
sheltered and pampered they have no chance even to make "the
great refusal." . . .

Our first few weeks in England were most stimulating. A dozen
years ago London still showed traces of "that exciting moment in the
life of the nation when its youth is casting about for new enthusiasms," but it evinced still more of that British capacity to perform the hard work of careful research and self-examination which
must precede any successful experiments in social reform. Of the
varied groups and individuals whose suggestions remained with me
for years. I recall perhaps as foremost those members of the new
London County Council whose far-reaching plans for the better-
ment of London could not but enkindle enthusiasm. It was a most
striking expression of that effort which would place beside the
refinement and pleasure of the rich, a new refinement and a new
pleasure born of the commonwealth and the common joy of all the
citizens, that at this moment they prized the municipal pleasure
boats upon the Thames no less than the extensive schemes for the
municipal housing of the poorest people. Ben Tillet, who was then
an alderman, "the docker sitting beside the duke," took me in a

rowboat down the Thames on a journey made exciting by the hundreds of dockers who cheered him as we passed one wharf after another on our way to his home at Greenwich; John Burns showed us his wonderful civic accomplishments at Battersea, the plant turning street sweepings into cement pavements, the technical school teaching boys brick laying and plumbing, and the public bath in which the children of the Board School were receiving a swimming lesson—these measures anticipating our achievements in Chicago by at least a decade and a half. The new Education Bill which was destined to drag on for twelve years before it developed into the children's charter, was then a storm center in the House of Commons. Miss Smith and I were much pleased to be taken to tea on the Parliament terrace by its author, Sir John Gorst, although we were quite bewildered by the arguments we heard there for church schools *versus* secular.

We heard Keir Hardie before a large audience of workingmen standing in the open square of Canning Town, outline the great things to be accomplished by the then new Labor Party, and we joined the vast body of men in the booming hymn

> When wilt Thou save the people,
> O God of Mercy, when!

finding it hard to realize that we were attending a political meeting. It seemed that moment as if the hopes of democracy were more likely to come to pass on English soil than upon our own. Robert Blatchford's stirring pamphlets were in every one's hands, and a reception given by Karl Marx's daughter, Mrs. Aveling, to Liebknecht before he returned to Germany to serve a prison term for his *lèse majesté* speech in the Reichstag, gave us a glimpse of the old-fashioned orthodox Socialist who had not yet begun to yield to the biting ridicule of Bernard Shaw although he flamed in their midst that evening.

Octavia Hill kindly demonstrated to us the principles upon which her well-founded business of rent collecting was established, and with pardonable pride showed us the Red Cross Square with its cottages marvelously picturesque and comfortable, on two sides, and on the third a public hall and common drawing-room for the use of all the tenants; the interior of the latter had been decorated by pupils of Walter Crane with mural frescoes portraying the heroism in the life of the modern workingman.

While all this was warmly human, we also had opportunities to see something of a group of men and women who were approaching the social problem from the study of economics; among others Mr. and Mrs. Sidney Webb who were at work on their Industrial Democracy; Mr. John Hobson who was lecturing on the evolution of modern capitalism.

We followed factory inspectors on a round of duties performed with a thoroughness and a trained intelligence which were a revelation of the possibilities of public service. When it came to visiting Settlements, we were at least reassured that they were not falling into identical lines of effort. Canon Ingram, who has since become Bishop of London, was then warden of Oxford House and in the midst of an experiment which pleased me greatly, the more because it was carried on by a churchman. Oxford House had hired all the concert halls—vaudeville shows we later called them in Chicago —which were found in Bethnal Green, for every Saturday night. The residents had censored the programs, which they were careful to keep popular, and any workingman who attended a show in Bethnal Green on a Saturday night, and thousands of them did, heard a program the better for this effort.

One evening in University Hall Mrs. Humphry Ward, who had just returned from Italy, described the effect of the Italian salt tax in a talk which was evidently one in a series of lectures upon the economic wrongs which pressed heaviest upon the poor; at Browning House, at the moment, they were giving prizes to those of their costermonger neighbors who could present the best cared-for donkeys, and the warden, Herbert Stead, exhibited almost the enthusiasm of his well-known brother, for that crop of kindliness which can be garnered most easily from the acreage where human beings grow the thickest; at the Bermondsey Settlement they were rejoicing that their University Extension students had successfully passed the examinations for the University of London. The entire impression received in England of research, of scholarship, of organized public spirit, was in marked contrast to the impressions of my next visit in 1900, when the South African War had absorbed the enthusiasm of the nation and the wrongs at "the heart of the empire" were disregarded and neglected.

THOMAS BAILEY ALDRICH:
"SMITH" AND BROWN'S HOTEL

1883

Thomas Bailey Aldrich was born and raised in the seaside town of
Portsmouth, New Hampshire, which he immortalized in his most successful
book, *The Story of a Bad Boy* (1870). Pretty much self-educated, he drifted
into journalism, reported the Civil War for the *Illustrated News,* and produced
some harmless poetry. After the war he moved to Boston, which was Paradise
enow for him; in time he rose to the very pinnacle of Olympus, as editor of the
Atlantic Monthly. Over the years he wrote scores of short stories, of which
"Marjorie Daw" was the most famous, half a dozen novels—including an
early example of the mystery novel, *The Stillwater Tragedy*—and many
essays on travel. Though Aldrich himself was at once prim and conservative,
he proved to be a good editor, and during his regime the *Atlantic* flourished.
This essay on Smith, and on the famous hotel which still stands on Dover
Street in the heart of Mayfair, is a good example of his pleasant but not very
consequential writing; "Ponkapog" was an imaginary village in eastern
Massachusetts, and Pesth the most exotic place imaginable.

From Thomas Bailey Aldrich, *From Ponkapog to Pesth* (Boston, 1883), pp. 167–194.

507

In London there is a kind of hotel of which we have no counterpart in the United States. This hotel is usually located in some semi-aristocratic side street, and wears no badge of its servitude beyond a large, well-kept brass door-plate, bearing the legend "Jones's Hotel" or "Brown's Hotel," as the case may be; but be it Brown or Jones, he has been dead at least fifty years, and the establishment is conducted by Robinson. There is no coffee-room or public dining-room, or even office, in this hotel; the commercial traveller is an unknown quantity there; your meals are served in your apartments; the furniture is solid and comfortable, the attendance admirable, the *cuisine* unexceptionable, and the bill abominable. But for ease, quietness, and a sort of 1812 odor of respectability, this hotel has nothing to compare with it in the wide world. It is here that the intermittent homesickness you contracted on the Continent will be lifted out of your bosom; it is here will be unfolded to you alluring vistas of the substantial comforts that surround the private lives of prosperous Britons; it is here, above all, that you will be brought in contact with Smith.

It was on our arrival in London, one April afternoon, that the door of what looked like a private mansion, in D—— Street, was thrown open to us by a boy broken out all over with buttons. Behind this boy stood Smith. I call him simply Smith for two reasons: in the first place because it is convenient to do so, and in the second place because that is what he called himself. I wish it were as facile a matter to explain how this seemingly unobtrusive person instantly took possession of us, bullied us with his usefulness, and knocked us down with his urbanity. From the moment he stepped forward to relieve us of our hand-luggage, we were his—and remained his until that other moment, some weeks later, when he handed us our parcels again, and stood statuesque on the door-step, with one finger lifted to his forehead in decorous salute, as we drove away. Ah, what soft despotism was that which was exercised for no other end than to anticipate our requirements—to invent new wants for us only to satisfy them! If I anywhere speak lightly of Smith, if I take exception to his preternatural gravity (of which I would not have him moult a feather), if I allude invidiously to his lifelong struggle with certain rebellious letters of the alphabet, it is out of sheer envy and regret that we have nothing like him in America. We have Niagara, and the Yosemite, and Edison's Electric Light (or shall have it, when we get it), but we have no trained serving-men like Smith. He is the result of older and vastly more complex social conditions than ours. His training began in the feudal ages. An atmosphere charged with machicolated battlements and cathedral spires was necessary to his perfect development—that, and generation after generation of lords and princes and wealthy country-gentlemen for him to practice on. He is not possible in New England. The very cut of his features is unknown among us. It has been remarked that each trade and profession has its physiognomy, its own proper face. If you look closely you will detect a family likeness running through the portraits of Garrick and Kean and Booth and Irving. There's the self-same sabre-like flash in the eye of Marlborough and Bonaparte—the same resolute labial expression. Every lackey in London might be the son or brother of any other lackey. Smith's father, and his father's father, and so on back to the gray dawn of England, were serving-men, and each in turn has been stamped with the immutable trade-mark of his class. Waiters (like poets) are born, not made; and they have not had time to be born in America.

As a shell that has the care of inclosing a pearl like Smith, Jones's Hotel demands a word or two of more particular description. The narrow little street in which it is situated branches off from a turbulent thoroughfare, and is quite packed with historical, social, and literary traditions. . . .

Overhead there are suites of apartments identical with our own, and I believe they are occupied—by serious-minded families of phantoms; they come and go so softly. There is no loud talking on the staircase, no slamming of doors, no levity of any description among the inmates of this hostelry. Whoever comes here finds his nature subdued to the color of his surroundings, like the dyer's hand. The wildest guest shortly succumbs to the soothing influence of Smith. He pervades the place like an atmosphere, and fits it so perfectly that, without jarring on the present, he seems a figure projected out of that dusky past which has lured me too long, and will catch me again before we get through. . . .

Smith's respect for you, at least its outward manifestation, is accompanied by a deep, unexpressed respect for himself. He not only knows his own place, but he knows yours, and holds you to it. He is incapable of venturing on a familiarity, or of submitting to one. He can wrap up more pitying disapprobation in a scarcely perceptible curl of his nether lip than another man could express in a torrent of words. I have gone about London a whole forenoon with one of Smith's thin smiles clinging like a blister to my consciousness. He is not taciturn, but he gives you the impression of unconquerable reserve. Though he seldom speaks, except to answer an inquiry, he has managed in some occult fashion to permeate us with a knowledge of his domestic environment. For the soul of me, I cannot say how I came by the information that Smith married Lady Hadelaide Scarborough's first maid twelve years ago, nor in what manner I got hold of the idea that Lady Hadelaide Scarborough's first maid rather stooped from her social status when she formed a matrimonial alliance with him. Yet these facts are undeniably in my possession. I also understand that Smith regards Mrs. Smith—who quitted service at the time of this *mésalliance*—as a sort of fragment (a little finger-joint, if that will help convey my meaning) of Lady Hadelaide herself. . . .

Smith has been very near to Royalty. To be sure, it was fallen royalty, so I shall waste no capital letters on it. It fell at Sedan, and picked itself up in a manner, and came over to London, where Smith had the bliss of waiting upon it. "The Hemperor was a very civil-spoken gentleman," observed Smith, detailing the circumstances with an air of respectful patronage, and showing that he had a nice sense of the difference between an English sovereign and an uncurrent Napoleon. . . .

I suppose it was in the course of nature that we should have fallen under the domination of Smith, and have come to accept him with a degree of seriousness which seems rather abject to me in retrospect. Without acknowledging it to ourselves, we were affected by his intangible criticism. I would not have had it come to his ears for a five-pound note that I had a habit of eating a chop in a certain snuffy old coffeehouse near Temple Bar, whenever lunchtime chanced to catch me in that vicinity.

O plump head-waiter at The Cock,

to which I most resorted, I should have been ashamed to have Smith know that I had the slightest acquaintance with you, though Tennyson himself has sung your praises! Nor would I have had Smith get wind of the low-bred excursion I made, one day, up the Thames, in a squalid steamer crowded with grimy workingmen and their frouzy wives and their children. I hid in my heart the guilty joy I took in two damaged musicians aboard—a violin and a flageolet. . . . When I returned to the hotel that night, Smith stood rebukefully drying the *Pall Mall Gazette* for me before the parlor fire. . . .

As to Smith's chronic gloom, it really had nothing of moroseness in it—only an habitual melancholy, a crystallized patience. We doubtless put it to some crucial tests with our American ideas and idioms. The earlier part of our acquaintanceship was fraught with mutual perplexities. It was the longest time before we discovered that *ay ill* meant Hay Hill Street, Smith making a single mouthful of it, thus—*ayill.* One morning he staggered us by asking if we would like "a hapricot freeze" for dessert. We assented, and would have assented if he had proposed iced hippopotamus; but the nature of the dish was a mystery to us, and perhaps never, since the world took shape out of chaos, was there a simple mould of apricot jelly looked forward to in such poignant suspense. . . .

You break from your abstraction to the consciousness that you are a stranger in your native land. The *genius loci* does not recognize you; you are an altered man. You are an American. Yet a little while ago the past of England was as much your past as it is Smith's, or that of any Briton of them all. But you have altered, and forfeited it. Smith has not altered: he is the same tall, efficient serving-man he was in the time of the Plantagenets. He has that air of having been carefully handed down which stamps so many things in England. . . . There, indeed, Nature seems careful of the type. The wretched woman who murders Kathleen Mavourneen in the street under your window shares this quality of permanency with Smith. She, or one precisely like her, has been singing ballads for ages, and will go on doing it. Endless generations of American tourists, lodging temporarily at Jones's perpetual Hotel, will give her inexhaustible shillings, and Smith will carry them out to her on his indestructible waiter. The individual Smith may occasionally die, but not the type, not the essence. My mind can take in Macaulay's picture of the New Zealander sitting on a broken buttress of London Bridge, and cynically contemplating the débris—"a landscape with figure," as the catalogues would put it—but I am unable to grasp the idea of the annihilation of anything so firmly established by precedent as Smith. I fancy that even out of the splintered masonry his respectful, well-modulated chest voice would be heard saying (through sheer force of habit), "Will you 'ave a look at the hevening paper, sir?" or, "If you please, sir, the 'ansom is at the door!"

CLAUDIUS PATTEN

DEPLORES THE SORRY STATE OF

PUBLIC EDUCATION IN ENGLAND

1884

Since 1870, when the national school system of England was established, a common school education is placed within the reach of every child in the kingdom. English parents, of the artisan class, who have had schooling experiences in both old and New England, have assured me that their children made better progress in their studies in England than in the United States. And they furthermore claim that the allotment of studies is more satisfactory in England than here to the parents of children who wish their boys and girls to acquire a practical education—an education adapted to their position and prospects in life. I found that reading, writing, arithmetic and history were taught in the common schools of the kingdom, while other branches of education were left almost entirely to schools of another class. The national schools were met, at their start, by a decided opposition from the Established Church. And even to this day they are under the ban of this church.

Quite recently a prominent Church of England divine openly

From Claudius Patten, *England as Seen by an American Banker* (Boston, 1885), pp. 214–224.

expressed his alarm and his regret over the fact that the education of the children of England had so largely fallen into the hands of a school system which considered it no part of its duty to teach the pupils the religion of the Established Church of England. The "high" wing of the English Church is particularly hostile to the national schools. The leading men in this branch of the Church loudly lament what they term the encroachments of infidelity and scepticism through the influence of the secular teaching of the national schools.

But these opponents of England's national schools have a school system of their own which is entirely after their heart. Their pet schools are established under their National Society for promoting the education of the children of the kingdom in the principles of the Established Church; and, in the schools under this organization, more pupils are to-day being taught than in the national schools.

The national Church schools have in charge 2,385,374 pupils; the national board schools, 1,298,746; the Roman Catholic schools, 269,231; the Wesleyan, 200,909. There is one fact, relative to this school question, which seemed novel to me. I visited in England common schools of the various classes, and often met with their teachers and the pupils out of school. I also gave no little time to the study of the educational system of the country. I found that these common, nominally free schools, which have been in many points modelled after the common schools of the United States, are almost entirely patronized by the children of the humble classes of the country—by the very poor, by the agricultural laborers, and by the artisans. The kingdom is full of private schools which are supported by the patronage of the classes other than those I have named, and vast numbers of children are sent to private schools on the Continent, single lists of which, to the extent of five thousand, I have seen advertised in London papers.

I have spoken of the national, Church and other common schools of England, which are mainly filled by the children of the humbler classes, as being modelled after our own free schools. But it ought to be stated that the children are charged a small school-fee. This, although a penny or two a week, becomes quite a burden to a poor man, having, as is so commonly the case with England's poor, a large number of school-needing children. This fee is remitted, to be sure, when parents are willing to say they cannot pay it, but England's poor laborers are proud, and, therefore, very reluctant to acknowledge themselves paupers; for the claim for the return of the school-fee amounts to this. I observed that the school boards often found themselves placed in a singular position in this matter of school-fees. They were obliged to instruct teachers to send pupils home whose school-fees were not paid. And, at the same time, if the parent is found not keeping his children in school, he is liable to be summoned into the police court.

I was interested in seeing the throngs of little children, all of the poorer classes, tramping along the London sidewalks, books in hand, on their way to the board schools, which are what we should term the common schools of the city. Yet they differ from our common or free schools in several points, one of which is the practice just mentioned, of making a small tuition charge against each pupil.

A little note about one of these board schools will be interesting as illustrating the methods and machinery of all of them. It stands in the heart of one of the poorest districts of London, and its buildings, made of stone and brick, have cost seventy-five thousand dollars, and will accommodate twelve hundred children, each of whom pay four pence a week tuition. Opposition to this tuition-fee often crops out most decidedly, and many of the parents say they wish they had the ragged schools again, for those cost them nothing.

At the time I was in London, the metropolis was going through with elections of members of the school board, and the exciting discussions over the question of the merits of the various persons who presented themselves as candidates for these positions incidentally led to an active canvass of the whole board school question. I noticed that one of the charges oftenest made against the board schools was that they did not pay sufficient attention to instruction of a technical character, an objection which had a decidedly home-like flavor. Candidates for positions on the board adopted the style of appealing to electors through advertisements in the leading papers. . . .

Only a small proportion of the expense of running the common schools of England is paid by the school-fees. The London school board pays, for instance, a million and a quarter sterling annually for the expenses of its schools, and of this amount it receives only about one hundred thousand pounds sterling in the way of annual school-fees. The school-teachers of both sexes in these schools are paid very small wages, and occupy a much more humble position socially than the same class in the United States. I found them quite often bearing the appearances of overwork, close confinement, and not over-generous living. I could not but notice the significance of an incident or two bearing upon this question of the social position of the common-school teacher in England. In one case, I heard that one of these teachers, who had for thirty years been an instructor in a parochial school, which had been rotated out of existence by the establishment of national schools, had taken to the road as a beggar, and had been arrested for asking alms. In another case which I happened to hear of, a male school-teacher got into court through marrying in haste, and somewhat irregularly, a tap-room bar-maid.

England's school-teachers are very much better paid than formerly, yet in some portions of the kingdom their remuneration seems small to an American. There, as here, the best salaries are paid to teachers in the largest cities and towns, and London heads the line. Its board schools divide their teachers into six classes, made up of the trained and untrained. The salaries of the male teachers range from sixty to one hundred and fifty-five pounds a year, and of the women from fifty to one hundred and twenty-five pounds. It will be observed that there are no such discrepancies between the male and female teachers as exist with us.

Many Londoners grumble over what they term the exorbitant salaries paid the city school-teachers, and at the meetings of the London school board speeches are made, sounding much like those we hear in our school boards, denouncing the extravagance of paying school-teachers so much more than hard-working shop-keepers' assistants are able to earn. I think the teachers in the London board schools work very hard—much harder than teachers here. The scholars are almost entirely children of the humblest classes. Many of them come to school in a ragged and half-starved condition. I have known of instances where the board school-rooms were thrown open at an early hour in order to give destitute children food, warmth and shelter. Lunches are, in many cases, provided at school for the poor children at public expense. It will readily be inferred from these facts that the teachers must have to do a deal of disagreeable "police" work. . . .

The village school-master in England has "no sort" of a social position. Another school incident, that came under my observation, illustrated the influential position of the vicar of a parish in the matter of school affairs. One of these clergymen was brought into court in connection with an assault case growing out of his peremptory dismissal of the parish school-master. The vicar and the lord of the manor generally rule in an English village.

In the rude, barn-like school-houses in England's rural districts, I found over-crowding and poor ventilation quite common. Then, again, there, as well as here, the cramping, confining school regulations, necessary in order to attain any approach to successful results from teaching under such unfavorable circumstances, render the situation of the pupil most uncomfortably restricted and entirely unnatural.

As a consequence there was heard, in many quarters, a clamor about overworked scholars, and a deal of talk about various sorts of diseases, and troubles with the eyes, such as chronic weaknesses and near-sightedness. But the more advanced thinkers were found arguing with much force that these school debilities came from causes other than over-study. And, as far as school pressure was concerned, it was proved conclusively that the standard of Great Britain was, age for age, the lowest in Europe. This last is a most interesting fact, since I had been led to look upon England as occupying a foremost position in educational matters. Mismanagement and under-feeding at home are, it is claimed, leading causes of the ill-health of English school-children.

I was much interested in my many visits to rural school-houses by the resemblance of their interiors to the old-fashioned school-rooms of New England. While we have progressed into more convenient and more attractive school-buildings, the English school-houses, having been built of stone and brick, and built to last hundreds of years, often remain just as they were long before the landing of the Pilgrims. The extreme plainness, even roughness, of the finishings and furnishings of these old school-houses surprised me. Yet the associations clustering around these buildings were more interesting than any thing else about them, for the traveller has pointed out to him the very seats—rough benches of oak—upon which once sat and studied men whose names to-day are identified with the literature, the politics, the wars of a time which appears very remote to us. . . .

Corporal punishment, once more common in America than at present, was one of those old England notions that we imported, and which is still in high favor in the mother-country. I found the teachers in the national schools quite liberal in the use of the rod. Once in a while I would hear of instances where irate parents prosecuted teachers for what they deemed unwarrantable punishment of their children. In one case, I noticed that a prosecuting parent won his case; not because the child got a very severe whipping, but because the rod was applied by an under-teacher when the head-teacher was the only one legally allowed to do the strapping. In looking over the reports of these cases, I received the impression that the justices were generally inclined to support the whippers.

HENRY JAMES: ENGLISH SCENES

1877, 1888

Probably no other American—certainly none of remotely comparable distinction—wrote so much about England, or saw so deeply into English character and society as Henry James. He was a member of the most famous literary family in our history—son of Henry James, Sr., and brother to William James the philosopher—and was himself perhaps the most distinguished of nineteenth-century American novelists. His introduction would be almost an impertinence. From childhood exposed to almost continuous travel, and educated by tutors or at foreign schools, Henry James never put down roots in America and with the passing years found himself increasingly alien to his native country. In 1877, when he was thirty-four, he decided to make England his permanent home, and he lived there—though with frequent visits to the Continent and the United States—until his death in 1916, and became, in the last year of his life, a British citizen. Yet James was by no means an uncritical admirer of England and things English; his somewhat ambivalent attitude is well expressed in a casual sentence from a letter to Charles Eliot Norton: "considering that I lose all patience with the English about fifteen times a day,

From Henry James, "An English Easter," *Lippincott's Magazine*, July, 1877, pp. 50–54; "English Hours," *Century Magazine*, December, 1888.

and vow that I renounce them forever, I get on with them beautifully and love them well." Although after his disastrous visit to the United States in 1903 (out of which came the difficult *American Scene*) James abandoned any expectation of returning to his native land, it cannot be said that he was ever fully at home in England, neither in London with its welcoming clubs nor in the country houses which he habituated, nor in his own beloved Lamb House, in Rye. "It's a complex fate being an American," James wrote—it is a phrase well worn by quotation—but added that "one of the responsibilities it entails is fighting against a superstitious valuation of Europe." James himself was successful in this: in his early novels and stories—*Roderick Hudson* (1877), *The American* (1877)—he pursued the story of American innocence and Old World corruption, and even in the later novels, such as *The Ambassadors* and *The Wings of the Dove*, where he tended to abandon the concept of American innocence, he did not abandon the theme of Old World corruption.

The first of these selections interpreting that city which James loved most passionately and in which he laid so many of his best novels and stories, appeared in 1877, the second in 1888. Both reappeared in his book on *English Hours*, with illustrations by his friend Joseph Pennell.

"A Country of Curious Anomalies"

It may be said of the English as is said of the council of war in Sheridan's farce of *The Critic* by one of the spectators of the rehearsal, that when they *do* agree their unanimity is wonderful. They differ among themselves greatly just now as regards the machinations of Russia, the derelictions of Turkey, the propriety of locking up the Reverend Arthur Tooth for his Romanizing excesses, the histrionic merits of Mr. Henry Irving, and a good many other matters; but neither just now nor at any other time do they fail to conform to those social observances on which Respectability has set her seal. England is a country of curious anomalies, and this has much to do with her being so interesting to foreign observers. The English individual character is very positive, very independent, very much made up according to its own sentiment of things, very prone to startling eccentricities; and yet at the same time it has beyond any other this peculiar gift of squaring itself with fashion and custom. In no other country, I imagine, are so many people to be found doing the same thing in the same way at the same time—using the same slang, wearing the same hats and cravats, collecting the same chinaplates, playing the same game of lawn-tennis or of "polo," flocking into the same skating-rinks. The monotony of this spectacle would soon become oppressive if the foreign observer were not conscious of this latent capacity in the performers for the free play of character; he finds a good deal of entertainment in wondering how they reconcile the traditional insularity of the individual with this perpetual tribute to custom. Of course in all civilized societies the tribute to custom is being constantly paid; if it is less observable in America than elsewhere the reason is not, I think, because individual independence is greater, but because custom is more sparsely established. Where we have customs people certainly follow them; but for five American customs there are fifty English. I am very far from having discovered the secret; I have not in the least learned what becomes of that explosive personal force in the English character which is compressed and corked down by social conformity. I look with a certain awe at some of the manifestations of the conforming spirit, but the fermenting idiosyncrasies beneath it are hidden from my vision. The most striking example, to foreign eyes, of the power of custom in England is of course the universal church-going. In the sight of all England getting up from its tea and toast of a Sunday morning and brushing its hat and drawing on its gloves and taking its wife on its arm and making its offspring march before, and, for decency's, respectability's, propriety's sake, making its way to a place of worship appointed by the State, in which it respects the formulas of a creed to which it attaches no positive sense and listens to a sermon over the length of which it explicitly haggles and grumbles—in this great exhibition there is something very striking to a stranger, something which he hardly knows whether to pronounce very sublime or very puerile. He inclines on the whole to pronounce it sublime, because it gives him the feeling that whenever it may become necessary for a people trained in these manoeuvres to move all together under a common direction, they will have it in them to do so with tremendous force and cohesiveness. We hear a good deal about the effect of the Prussian military system in consolidating the German people and making them available for a particular purpose; but I really think it not fanciful to say that the military punctuality which characterizes the English observance of Sunday ought to be appreciated in the same fashion. A nation which has passed through the mill will certainly have been stamped by it. And here, as in the German military service, it is really the whole nation. When I spoke just now of paterfamilias and his *entourage* I did not mean to limit the statement to him. The young unmarried men go to church; the gay bachelors, the irresponsible members of society. (That last epithet must be taken with a grain of allowance. No one in England is irresponsible, that perhaps is the shortest way of describing the country. Every one is free and every one is responsible. To say what it is people are responsible to is of course a great extension of the question: briefly, to social expectation, to propriety, to morality, to "position," to the classic English conscience, which is, after all, such a considerable affair.)

The way in which the example of the more comfortable classes imposes itself upon the less comfortable may of course be noticed in smaller matters than church-going; in a great many matters which it may seem trivial to mention. If one is bent upon observation nothing, however, is trivial. So I may cite the practice of keeping the servants out of the room at breakfast. It is the fashion, and so, apparently, through the length and breadth of England, every one who has the slightest pretension to standing high enough to feel the way the social breeze is blowing conforms to it. It is awkward, unnatural, troublesome for those at table, it involves a vast amount of leaning and stretching, of waiting and perambulating, and it has just that vice against which, in English history, all great movements have been made—it is arbitrary. But it flourishes for all that, and all genteel people, looking into each other's eyes with the desperation of gentility, agree to endure it for gentility's sake. Another arbitrary trifle is the custom of depriving the unhappy visitor of a napkin at luncheon. When it is observed that the English luncheon differs from dinner only in being several degrees more elaborate and copious, and that in the London atmosphere it is but common charity, at any moment, to multiply your guest's opportunities if not for ablution at least for a "dry polish," it will be perceived that such eccentricities are the very wantonness and pedantry of fashion. But, as I say, they flourish, and they form part of an immense body of prescriptive usages, to which a society possessing in the largest manner, both by temperament and education, the sense of the "inalienable" rights and comforts of the individual, contrives to accommodate itself. I do not mean to say that usage in England is always uncomfortable and arbitrary. On the contrary, few strangers can be unfamiliar with that sensation (a most agreeable one) which consists in perceiving in the excesses of a custom which has struck us at first as a mere brutal invention, a reason existing in the historic "good sense" of the English race. The sensation is frequent, though in saying so I do not mean to imply that even superficially the presumption is against the usages of English society. It is not, for instance, necessarily against the custom of which I had it more especially in mind to speak in writing these lines. The stranger in London is forewarned that at Easter all the world goes out of town, and that if he has no mind to be left as lonely as Marius on the ruins of Carthage, he, too, had better make arrangements for a temporary absence. It must be admitted that there is a sort of unexpectedness in this vernal exodus of a body of people who, but a week before, were apparently devoting much energy to settling down for the season. Half of them have but lately come back from the country, where they have been spending the winter, and they have just had time, it may be supposed, to collect the scattered threads of town-life. Presently, however, the threads are dropped and society is dispersed, as if it had taken a false start. It departs as Holy Week draws to a close, and remains absent for the following ten days. Where it goes is its own affair; a good deal of it goes to Paris. Spending last winter in that city I remember how, when I woke up on Easter Monday and looked out of my window, I found the street covered, overnight, with a sort of snow-fall of disembarked Britons. They made, for other people, an uncomfortable week of it. One's customary table at the restaurant, one's habitual stall at the Théâtre Français, one's usual fiacre on the cab-stand, were very apt to have suffered pre-emption. I believe that the pilgrimage to Paris was this year of the usual proportions: and you may be sure that people who did not cross the Channel were not without invitations to quiet old places in the country, where the pale, fresh primroses were beginning to light up the dark turf and the purple bloom of the bare tree-mosses to be freckled here and there with verdure. In England country-life is the obverse of the medal, town-life the reverse, and when an occasion comes for quitting London there are few members of what the French call the "easy class" who have not a collection of dull, moist, verdant resorts to choose from. . . .

But nothing is more striking to an American than the frequency of English holidays and the large way in which occasions for change and diversion are made use of. All this speaks to Americans of three things which they are accustomed to see allotted in scantier measure. The English have more time than we, they have more money, and they have a much higher relish for holiday taking. (I am speaking of course always of the "easy classes.") Leisure, fortune and the love of sport—these things are implied in English society at every turn. It was a very small number of weeks before Easter that Parliament met, and yet a ten days' recess was already, from the luxurious Parliamentary point of view, a necessity. A short time hence we shall be having the Whitsuntide Holidays, which I am told are even more of a festival than Easter, and from this point to midsummer, when everything stops, it is an easy journey. . . . A large appetite for holidays, the ability not only to take them but to know what to do with them when taken, is the sign of a robust people, and judged by this measure we Americans are rather ill-conditioned. Such holidays as we take are taken very often in Europe, where it is·sometimes noticeable that our privilege is rather heavy in our hands. Tribute rendered to English industry, however (our own stands in no need of compliments), it must be added that for those same easy classes I just spoke of things are very easy indeed. The number of persons available for purely social purposes at all times and seasons is infinitely greater than among ourselves; and the ingenuity of the arrangements permanently going forward to disembarrass them of the superfluous leisure is as yet in America an undeveloped branch of civilization. The young men who are preparing for the stern realities of life among the gray-green cloisters of Oxford are obliged to keep their terms but one half the year; and the rosy little cricketers of Eton and Harrow are let loose upon the parental home for an embarrassing number of months. Happily the parental home is apt to be an affair of gardens, lawns and parks. . . . .

London is ugly, dusky, dreary, more destitute than any European city of graceful and decorative incident; and though on festal days . . . . the populace is massed in large numbers at certain points, many of the streets are empty enough of human life to enable you to perceive their intrinsic hideousness. A Christmas Day or a Good Friday uncovers the ugliness of London. As you walk along the streets, having no fellow-pedestrians to look at, you look up at the brown brick housewalls, corroded with soot and fog, pierced with their straight stiff window-slits and finished, by way of a cornice, with a little black line resembling a slice of curbstone. There is not an accessory, not a touch of architectural fancy, not the narrowest concession to beauty. If I were a foreigner it would make me rabid; being an Anglo-Saxon I find in it what Thackeray found in Baker street—a delightful proof of English domestic virtue, of the sanctity of the British home. There are miles and miles of these edifying monuments, and it would seem that a city made up of them should have no claim to that larger effectivenss of which I just now spoke. London, however, is not made up of them; there are architectural combinations of a statelier kind, and the impression moreover does not rest on details. London is picturesque in spite of details—from its dark-green, misty parks, the way the light comes down leaking and filtering from its cloudy skies, and the softness and richness of tone which objects put on in such an atmosphere as soon as they begin to recede. Nowhere is there such a play of light and shade, such a struggle of sun and smoke, such aërial gradations and confusions. To eyes addicted to the picturesque this is a constant entertainment, and yet this is only part of it. What completes the effect of the place is its appeal to the feelings, made in so many ways, but made above all by agglomerated immensity. At any given point London looks huge; even in narrow corners you have a sense of its hugeness, and petty places acquire a certain interest from their being parts of so mighty a whole. Nowhere else is so much human life gathered together and nowhere does it press upon you with so many suggestions. These are not all of an exhilarating kind; far from it. But they are of every possible kind, and this is the interest of London. Those that were most forcible during the showery Easter season were certain of the more perplexing and depressing ones; but even with these was mingled a brighter strain. . . .

"To Live with Her Successfully Is an Education of the Temper"

It is, no doubt, not the taste of every one, but for the real London-lover the mere immensity of the place is a large part of its savour. A small London would be an abomination, as it fortunately is an impossibility, for the idea and the name are beyond everything an expression of extent and number. Practically, of course, one lives in a quarter, in a plot; but in imagination and by a constant mental act of reference the accommodated haunter enjoys the whole—and it is only of him that I deem it worth while to speak. He fancies himself, as they say, for being a particle in so unequalled an aggregation; and its immeasurable circumference, even though unvisited and lost in smoke, gives him the sense of a social, an intellectual margin. There is a luxury in the knowledge that he may come and go without being noticed, even when his comings and goings have no nefarious end. I don't mean by this that the tongue of London is not a very active member; the tongue of London would indeed be worthy of a chapter by itself. But the eyes which at least in some measure feed its activity are fortunately for the common advantage solicited at any moment by a thousand different objects. If the place is big, everything it contains is certainly not so; but this may at least be said, that if small questions play a part there, they play it without illusions about its importance. There are too many questions, small or great; and each day, as it arrives, leads its children, like a kind of mendicant mother, by the hand. Therefore perhaps the most general characteristic is the absence of insistence. Habits and inclinations flourish and fall, but intensity is never one of them. The spirit of the great city is not analytic, and, as they come up, subjects rarely receive at its hands a treatment drearily earnest or tastelessly thorough. There are not many—of those of which London disposes with the assurance begotten of its large experience—that wouldn't lend themselves to a tenderer manipulation elsewhere. It takes a very great affair, a turn of the Irish screw or a divorce case lasting many days, to be fully threshed out. The mind of Mayfair, when it aspires to show what it really can do, lives in the hope of a new divorce case, and an indulgent providence—London is positively in certain ways the spoiled child of the world—abundantly recognises this particular aptitude and humours the whim.

The compensation is that material does arise; that there is a great variety, if not morbid subtlety; and that the whole of the procession of events and topics passes across your stage. For the moment I am speaking of the inspiration there may be in the sense of far frontiers; the London-lover loses himself in this swelling consciousness, delights in the idea that the town which encloses him is after all only a paved country, a state by itself. This is his condition of mind quite as much if he be an adoptive as if he be a matter-of-course son. I am by no means sure even that he need be of Anglo-Saxon race and have inherited the birthright of English speech; though, on the other hand, I make no doubt that these advantages minister greatly to closeness of allegiance. The great city spreads her dusky mantle over innumerable races and creeds, and I believe there is scarcely a known form of worship that has not some temple there (have I not attended at the Church of Humanity, in Lamb's Conduit, in company with an American lady, a vague old gentleman, and several seamstresses?) or any communion of men that has not some club or guild. London is indeed an epitome of the round world, and just as it is a commonplace to say that there is nothing one can't "get" there, so it is equally true that there is nothing one may not study at first hand.

One doesn't test these truths every day, but they form part of the air one breathes (and welcome, says the London-hater—for there be such perverse reasoners—to the pestilent compound). They colour the thick, dim distances which in my opinion are the most romantic town-vistas in the world; they mingle with the troubled light to which the straight, ungarnished aperture in one's dull, undistinctive housefront affords a passage and which makes an interior of friendly corners, mysterious tones and unbetrayed ingenuities, as well as with the low, magnificent medium of the sky, where the smoke and fog and the weather in general, the strangely undefined hour of the day and season of the year, the emanations of industries and the reflection of furnaces, the red gleams and blurs that may or may not be of sunset—as you never see any *source* of radiance you can't in the least tell—all hang together in a confusion, a complication, a shifting but irremovable canopy. They form the undertone of the deep, perpetual voice of the place. One remembers them when one's loyalty is on the defensive; when it is a question of introducing as many striking features as possible into the list of fine reasons one has sometimes to draw up, that eloquent catalogue with which one confronts the hostile indictment—the array of *other* reasons which may easily be as long as one's arm. According to these other reasons it plausibly and conclusively stands that, as a place to be happy in, London will never do. I don't say it is necessary to meet so absurd an allegation except for one's personal complacency. If indifference, in so gorged an organism, is still livelier than curiosity, you may avail yourself of your own share in it simply to feel that since such and such a person doesn't care for real richness, so much the worse for such and such a person. But once in a while the best believer recognises the impulse to set his religion in order, to sweep the temple of his thoughts and trim the sacred lamp. It is at such hours as this that he reflects with elation that the British capital is the particular spot in the world which communicates the greatest sense of life.

The reader will perceive that I do not shrink even from the extreme concession of speaking of our capital as British, and this in a shameless connection with the question of loyalty on the part of an adoptive son. For I hasten to explain that if half the source of one's interest in it comes from feeling that it is the property and even the home of the human race—Hawthorne, that best of Americans, says so somewhere, and places it in this sense side by side with Rome—one's appreciation of it is really a large sympathy, a comprehensive love of humanity. For the sake of such a charity as this one may stretch one's allegiance; and the most alien of the cockneyfied, though he may bristle with every protest at the intimation that England has set its stamp upon him, is free to admit with conscious pride that he has submitted to Londonisation. It is a real stroke of luck for a particular country that the capital of the human race happens to be British. Surely every other people would have it theirs if they could. Whether the English deserve to hold it any longer might be an interesting field of inquiry; but as they have not yet let it slip, the writer of these lines professes without scruple that the arrangement is to his personal taste. For, after all, if the sense of life is greatest there, it is a sense of the life of people of our consecrated English speech. It is the headquarters of that strangely elastic tongue; and I make this remark with a full sense of the terrible way in which the idiom is misused by the populace in general, than whom it has been given to few races to impart to conversation less of the charm of tone. For a man of letters who endeavours to cultivate, however modestly, the medium of Shakespeare and Milton, of Hawthorne and Emerson, who cherishes the notion of what it has achieved and what it may even yet achieve, London must ever have a great illustrative and suggestive value, and indeed a kind of sanctity. It is the single place in which most readers, most possible lovers, are gathered together; it is the most inclusive public largest social incarnation of the language, of the tradition. Such a personage may well let it go for this and leave the German and the Greek to speak for themselves, to express the grounds of *their* predilection, presumably very different.

When a social product is so vast and various it may be approached on a thousand different sides, and liked and disliked for a thousand different reasons. The reasons of Piccadilly are not those of Camden Town, nor are the curiosities and discouragements of Kilburn the same as those of Westminster and Lambeth. The reasons of Piccadilly—I mean the friendly ones—are those of which, as a general thing, the rooted visitor remains most conscious; but it must be confessed that even these, for the most part, do not lie upon the surface. The absence of style, or rather of the intention of style, is certainly the most general characteristic of the face of London. To cross to Paris under this impression is to find one's self surrounded with far other standards. There everything reminds you that the idea of beautiful and stately arrangement has never been out of fashion, that the art of composition has always been at work or at play. Avenues and squares, gardens and quays, have been distributed for effect, and to-day the splendid city reaps the accumulation of all this ingenuity. The result is not in every quarter interesting, and there is a tiresome monotony of the "fine" and the symmetrical above all, of the deathly passion for making things "to match." On the other hand the whole air of the place is architectural. On the banks of the Thames it is a tremendous chapter of accidents—the London-lover has to confess to the existence of miles upon miles of the dreariest, stodgiest commonness. Thousands of acres are covered by low black houses of the cheapest construction, without ornament, without grace, without character or even identity. In fact there are many, even in the best quarters, in all the region of Mayfair and Belgravia, of so paltry and inconvenient, especially of so diminutive a type (those that are let in lodgings—such poor lodgings as they make—may serve as an example), that you wonder what peculiarly limited domestic need they were constructed to meet. The great misfortune of London to the eye (it is true that this remark applies much less to the City) is the want of elevation. There is no architectural impression without a certain degree of height, and the London street-vista has none of that sort of pride.

All the same, if there be not the intention, there is at least the accident, of style, which, if one looks at it in a friendly way, appears to proceed from three sources. One of these is simply the general greatness, and the manner in which that makes a difference for the better in any particular spot; so that, though you may often perceive yourself to be in a shabby corner, it never occurs to you that this is the end of it. Another is the atmosphere, with its magnificent mystifications, which flatters and superfuses, makes everything brown, rich, dim, vague, magnifies distances and minimises details, confirms the inference of vastness by suggesting that, as the great city makes everything, it makes its own system of weather and its own optical laws. The last is the congregation of the parks, which constitute an ornament not elsewhere to be matched and give the place a superiority that none of its uglinesses overcome. They spread themselves with such a luxury of space in the centre of the town that they form a part of the impression of any walk, of almost any view, and, with an audacity altogether their own, make a pastoral landscape under the smoky sky. There is no mood of the rich London climate that is not becoming to them—I have seen them look delightfully romantic, like parks in novels, in the wettest winter—and there is scarcely a mood of the appreciative resident to which they have not something to say. The high things of London, which here and there peep over them, only make the spaces vaster by reminding you that you are, after all, not in Kent or Yorkshire; and these things, whatever they be—rows of "eligible" dwellings, towers of churches, domes of institutions—take such an effective gray-blue tint that a clever water-colourist would seem to have put them in for pictorial reasons.

The view from the bridge over the Serpentine has an extraordinary nobleness, and it has often seemed to me that the Londoner twitted with his low standard may point to it with every confidence. In all the town-scenery of Europe there can be few things so fine; the only reproach it is open to is that it begs the question by seeming—in spite of its being the pride of five millions of people—not to belong to a town at all. The towers of Notre Dame, as they rise in Paris from the island that divides the Seine, present themselves no more impressively than those of Westminster as you see them looking doubly far beyond the shining stretch of Hyde Park water. Equally delectable is the large river-like manner in which the Serpentine opens away between its wooded shores. Just after you have crossed the bridge (whose very banisters, old and ornamental, of yellowish-brown stone, I am particularly fond of), you enjoy on your left, through the gate of Kensington Gardens as you go towards Bayswater, an altogether enchanting vista—a footpath over the grass, which loses itself beneath the scattered oaks and elms exactly as if the place were a "chase." There could be nothing less like London in general than this particular morsel, and yet it takes London, of all cities, to give you such an impression of the country. . . .

I feel as if I were taking a tone almost of boastfulness, and no doubt the best way to consider the matter is simply to say—without going into the treachery of reasons—that, for one's self, one likes this part or the other. Yet this course would not be unattended with danger, inasmuch as at the end of a few such professions we might find ourselves committed to a tolerance of much that is deplorable. London is so clumsy and so brutal, and has gathered together so many of the darkest sides of life, that it is almost ridiculous to talk of her as a lover talks of his mistress, and almost frivolous to appear to ignore her disfigurements and cruelties. She is like a mighty ogress who devours human flesh; but to me it is a mitigating circumstance—though it may not seem so to every one—that the ogress herself is human. It is not in wantonness that she fills her maw, but to keep herself alive and do her tremendous work. She has no time for fine discriminations, but after all she is as good-natured as she is huge, and the more you stand up to her, as the phrase is, the better she takes the joke of it. It is mainly when you fall on your face before her that she gobbles you up. She heeds little what she takes, so long as she has her stint, and the smallest push to the right or the left will divert her wavering bulk from one form of prey to another. It is not to be denied that the heart tends to grow hard in her company; but she is a capital antidote to the morbid, and to live with her successfully is an education of the temper, a consecration of one's private philosophy. She gives one a surface for which in a rough world one can never be too thankful. She may take away reputations, but she forms character. She teaches her victims not to "mind," and the great danger for them is perhaps that they shall learn the lesson too well.

It is sometimes a wonder to ascertain what they do mind, the best-seasoned of her children. Many of them assist, without winking, at the most unfathomable dramas, and the common speech of others denotes a familiarity with the horrible. It is her theory that she both produces and appreciates the exquisite; but if you catch her in flagrant repudiation of both responsibilities and confront her with the shortcoming, she gives you a look, with a shrug of her colossal shoulders, which establishes a private relation with you for evermore. She seems to say: "Do you really take me so seriously as that, you dear, devoted, voluntary dupe, and don't you know what an immeasurable humbug I am?" You reply that you shall know it henceforth; but your tone is good-natured, with a touch of the cynicism that she herself has taught you; for you are aware that if she makes herself out better than she is, she also makes herself out much worse. She is immensely democratic, and that, no doubt, is part of the manner in which she is salutary to the individual; she teaches him his "place" by an incomparable discipline, but deprives him of complaint by letting him see that she has exactly the same lash for every other back. When he has swallowed the lesson he may enjoy the rude but unfailing justice by which, under her eye, reputations and positions elsewhere esteemed great are reduced to the relative. There are so many reputations, so many positions, that supereminence breaks down, and it is difficult to be so rare that London can't match you. It is a part of her good-nature and one of her clumsy coquetries to pretend sometimes that she hasn't your equivalent, as when she takes it into her head to hunt the lion or form a ring round a celebrity. But this artifice is so very transparent that the lion must be very candid or the celebrity very obscure to be taken by it. The business is altogether subjective, as the philosophers say, and the great city is primarily looking after herself. Celebrities are convenient—they are one of the things that people are asked to "meet"—and lion-cutlets, put upon ice, will nourish a family through periods of dearth.

This is what I mean by calling London democratic. You may be in it, of course, without being of it; but from the moment you *are* of it—and on this point your own sense will soon enough enlighten you—you belong to a body in which a general equality prevails. However exalted, however able, however rich, however renowned you may be, there are too many people at least as much so for your own idiosyncrasies to count. I think it is only by being beautiful that you may really prevail very much; for the loveliness of woman it has long been noticeable that London will go most out of her way. It is when she hunts that particular lion that she becomes most dangerous; then there are really moments when you would believe, for all the world, that she is thinking of what she can give, not of what she can get. Lovely ladies, before this, have paid for believing it, and will continue to pay in days to come. On the whole the people who are least deceived are perhaps those who have permitted themselves to believe, in their own interest, that poverty is not a disgrace. It is certainly not considered so in London, and indeed you can scarcely say where—in virtue of diffusion—it would more naturally be exempt. The possession of money is, of course, immensely an advantage, but that is a very different thing from a disqualification in the lack of it.

Good-natured in so many things in spite of her cynical tongue, and easy-going in spite of her tremendous pace, there is nothing in which the large indulgence of the town is more shown than in the liberal way she looks at obligations of hospitality and the margin she allows in these and cognate matters. She wants above all to be amused; she keeps her books loosely, doesn't stand on small questions of a chop for a chop, and if there be any chance of people's proving a diversion, doesn't know or remember or care whether they have "called." She forgets even if she herself have called. In matters of ceremony she takes and gives a long rope, wasting no time in phrases and circumvallations. It is no doubt incontestable that one result of her inability to stand upon trifles and consider details is that she has been obliged in some ways to lower rather portentously the standard of her manners. She cultivates the abrupt—for even when she asks you to dine a month ahead the invitation goes off like the crack of a pistol—and approaches her ends not exactly *par quatre chemins*. She doesn't pretend to attach importance to the lesson conveyed in Matthew Arnold's poem of "The Sick King in Bokhara," that,

> Though we snatch what we desire,
> We may not snatch it eagerly.

London snatches it more than eagerly if that be the only way she can get it. Good manners are a succession of details, and I don't mean to say that she doesn't attend to them when she has time. She has it, however, but seldom—*que voulez-vous?* Perhaps the matter of notewriting is as good an example as another of what certain of the elder traditions inevitably have become in her hands. She lives by notes—they are her very heartbeats; but those that bear her signatures are as disjointed as the ravings of delirium, and have nothing but a postage-stamp in common with the epistolary art.

If she doesn't go into particulars it may seem a very presumptuous act to have attempted to do so on her behalf, and the reader will doubtless think I have been punished by having egregiously failed in my enumeration. Indeed nothing could well be more difficult than to add up the items—the column would be altogether too long. One may have dreamed of turning the glow—if glow it be—of one's lantern on each successive facet of the jewel; but, after all, it may be success enough if a confusion of brightness be the result. One has not the alternative of speaking of London as a whole, for the simple reason that there is no such thing as the whole of it. It is immeasurable—embracing arms never meet. Rather it is a collection of many wholes, and of which of them is it most important to speak? Inevitably there must be a choice, and I know of none more scientific than simply to leave out what we may have to apologise for. The uglinesses, the "rookeries," the brutalities, the night-aspect of many of the streets, the gin-shops and the hour when they are cleared out before closing—there are many elements of this kind which have to be counted out before a genial summary can be made.

And yet I should not go so far as to say that it is a condition of such geniality to close one eye's upon the immense misery; on the contrary, I think it is partly because we are irremediably conscious of that dark gulf that the most general appeal of the great city remains exactly what it is, the largest chapter of human accidents. I have no idea of what the future evolution of the strangely mingled monster may be; whether the poor will improve away the rich, or the rich will expropriate the poor, or they will all continue to swell together on their present imperfect terms of intercourse. Certain it is, at any rate, that the impression of suffering is a part of the general vibration it is one of the things that mingle with all the others to make the sound that is supremely dear to the consistent London-lover—the rumble of the tremendous human mill. This is the note which, in all its modulations, haunts and fascinates and inspires him. And whether or no he may succeed in keeping the misery out of the picture, he will freely confess that the latter is not spoiled for him by some of its duskiest shades. We are far from liking London well enough till we like its defects; the dense darkness of much of its winter, the soot on the chimney-pots and everywhere else, the early lamplight, the brown blur of the houses, the splashing of hansoms in Oxford Street or the Strand on December afternoons.

There is still something that recalls to me the enchantment of children—the anticipation of Christmas, the delight of a holiday walk—in the way the shop-fronts shine into the fog. It makes each of them seem a little world of light and warmth, and I can still waste time in looking at them with dirty Bloomsbury on one side and dirtier Soho on the other. There are winter effects, not intrinsically sweet, it would appear, which somehow, in absence, touch the chords of memory and even the fount of tears; as for instance the front of the British Museum on a black afternoon, or the portico, when the weather is vile, of one of the big square clubs in Pall Mall. I can give no adequate account of the subtle poetry of such reminiscences; it depends upon associations of which we have often lost the thread. The wide colonnade of the Museum, its symmetrical wings, the high iron fence in its granite setting, the sense of the misty halls within, where all the treasures lie—these things loom patiently through atmospheric layers which instead of making them dreary impart to them something of a cheer of red lights in a storm. I think the romance of a winter afternoon in London arises partly from the fact that, when it is not altogether smothered, the general lamplight takes this hue of hospitality. Such is the colour of the interior glow of the clubs in Pall Mall, which I positively like best when the fog loiters upon their monumental staircases.

In saying just now that these retreats may easily be, for the exile, part of the phantasmagoria of homesickness, I by no means alluded simply to their solemn outsides. If they are still more solemn within, that does not make them any less dear, in retrospect at least, to a visitor much bent upon liking his London to the end. What is the solemnity but a tribute to your nerves, and the stillness but a refined proof of the intensity of life? To produce such results as these the balance of many tastes must be struck, and that is only possible in a very high civilisation. If I seem to intimate that this last abstract term must be the cheer of him who has lonely possession of a foggy library, without even the excitement of watching for some one to put down the magazine he wants, I am willing to let the supposition pass, for the appreciation of a London club at one of the empty seasons is nothing but the strong expression of a preference for the great city—by no means so unsociable as it may superficially appear—at periods of relative abandonment. The London year is studded with holidays, blessed little islands of comparative leisure—intervals of absence for good society. Then the wonderful English faculty for "going out of town for a little change" comes into illimitable play, and families transport their nurseries and their bath-tubs to those rural scenes which form the real substratum of the national life. Such moments as these are the paradise of the genuine London-lover, for he then finds himself face to face with the object of his passion: he can give himself up to an intercourse which at other times is obstructed by his rivals. Then every one he knows is out of town, and the exhilarating sense of the presence of every one he doesn't know becomes by so much the deeper.

This is why I pronounce his satisfaction not an unsociable, but a positively affectionate emotion. It is the mood in which he most measures the immense humanity of the place, and in which its limits recede furthest into a dimness peopled with possible illustrations. For his acquaintance, however numerous it may be, is finite; whereas the other, the unvisited London, is infinite. It is one of his pleasures to think of the experiments and excursions he may make in it, even when these adventures don't particularly come off. The friendly fog seems to protect and enrich them—to add both to the mystery and security, so that it is most in the winter months that the imagination weaves such delights. They reach their climax perhaps during the strictly social desolation of Christmas week, when the country-houses are crowded at the expense of the capital. Then it is that I am most haunted with the London of Dickens, feel most as if it were still recoverable, still exhaling its queerness in patches perceptible to the appreciative. Then the big fires blaze in the lone twilight of the clubs, and the new books on the tables say "Now at last you have time to read me," and the afternoon tea and toast, and the torpid old gentleman who wakes up from a doze to order potash-water, appear to make the assurance good. It is not a small matter either, to a man of letters, that this is the best time for writing, and that during the lamplit days the white page he tries to blacken becomes, on his table, in the circle of the lamp, with the screen of the climate folding him in, more vivid and absorbent. Those to whom it is forbidden to sit up to work in the small hours may, between November and March, enjoy a semblance of this luxury in the morning. The weather makes a kind of sedentary midnight and muffles the possible smoky cavern; it gives the idea that literature is a thing of splendour, of a dazzling essence, of infinite gas-lit red and gold.

GEORGE W. SMALLEY

DESCRIBES THE PASSING

SHOW IN LONDON

1888

George Smalley was the dean of newspaper correspondents in London. A graduate of Yale—where he had rowed against Harvard—he read law with George Frisbie Hoar, afterward Senator from Massachusetts, and was close to Wendell Phillips and his circle of New England reformers. He reported the Civil War for the *New-York Tribune,* and after that war was sent abroad by Greeley to report the Austro-Prussian War. Then he was assigned to London, where he set up a network of European services for the *Tribune.* He remained in London until 1895, going everywhere, seeing everything, and knowing everybody; when he returned to America it was in the reverse role of American correspondent for the London *Times.* He felt more at home in London than in New York, however, and in 1905 returned to London and remained there for the rest of his life. Something of a Tory, something of a snob, he remained, nevertheless, thoroughly American in his point of view. We have here two samples from his many *London Letters,* which first appeared in the *Tribune.*

From George W. Smalley, *London Letters, and Some Others* (New York, 1891), I, pp. 161–167, II, 101–106.

Lord Randolph Churchill:
Showed His Party the Road

I give him the name by which he is most commonly referred to. In these busy times, people seldom say Lord Randolph Churchill. They say Lord Randolph; often, with a kind of affectionate brevity, Randolph. Affection, however, is not the feeling just now shown most freely to him by his party. It is a little startling to see him rise in the House of Commons without a solitary cheer from those about him. Those who frequent the House are used to this spectacle. I went down on Monday for the first time this year, and the incident had all the force of novelty. A Suakim debate was on. I cannot suppose that the American public takes a deep interest in Suakim, and it is not a subject upon which I am going to enter. But I apprehend we all have an interest in Lord Randolph; even those who think him the spoiled child of politics. There is only one more striking figure in the House to-day. Lord Randolph is sometimes reproached with having held different opinions on the same subject at different times. It may be so, but, if it be true of him, it is ten times truer of that other and older figure who sits surrounded by his shattered and divided legions.

Divided also from his former associates and colleagues is the still young leader of the Tory Democracy. He has renounced his central place on the Front Bench. He sits at the corner of the second bench; above the gangway, however, not below. The gangway is a Rubicon which he has yet to cross, though, after last night, there are people who hint that he may in time cross not only the gangway but the floor of the House. That is mere unprofitable guesswork. The future may take care of itself; to-day is quite interesting enough to those who care for the high lights of current politics. There at the corner of his bench sits Lord Randolph; his hat on, his head sunk, not much of him visible above the shoulders except the historical moustache, at which he is pulling in the historical fashion. . . .

It is known he is going to speak on Suakim, and there is a strong muster of Tories, gloomily wondering "What Randolph will do next." The scene, if we had time to look at it, is striking for more reasons than one. No less a person than Mr. John Morley opens fire on the Government, crowded together in a thin black line on the Front Bench; then, and often during this eventful evening, hurriedly consulting among themselves; a group of clustering and agitated heads. Mr. John Morley is hardly at his best; has not yet, I think, learned to be ever at his best in the House of Commons. There is still something about him which suggests the student rather than the debater. When a man's mind has run for a quarter of a century in one channel, it is not so easy all at once to turn the full force of the stream into another. He is clear, forcible, fluent enough—master of himself and his ideas; not quite master of his audience.

The occasion is great enough to bring Mr. Gladstone down to the House, and to put him on his legs; but does not rouse him to a great effort. His voice is neither clear nor strong; many and many a sentence do not reach to the bench under the gallery where I sit. The Tories, who will believe anything and say anything of Mr. Gladstone, tell you that this indistinctness is calculated. He prefers they should suppose him incapable of rising to the old level; intending, for his part, when the right moment comes, to rise as high as ever, and be heard in the remotest recesses of the House and the country. . . . Mr. Stanhope, Secretary for War, on whom the answer to Mr. Gladstone devolves, is resonant, business-like, direct . . . As he nears the end you may see Lord Randolph take off his hat and put it under the seat, and you know that he means to follow the Secretary for War.

The House by this time is full, surprisingly full for the fag end of an autumn sitting. The Tory benches are well covered above and below the gangway, and they maintain a grim silence as Lord Randolph is seen to be on his feet, and Mr. Courtney—for the House is in committee—calls on him. The Opposition cheer, and the cheer is a cordial one. Whatever may be their private sentiments about the orator, they more than guess that he is going to make himself disagreeable to the Government, and that is enough for them. The nervousness, if it be nervousness, which is denoted by the continuing movement of the forefinger to the upper lip, has ceased. . . . There is not a trace of embarrassment; the stranger would never guess that he stood alone, surrounded by enemies, or at least by opponents; by men once his supporters, now angry, suspicious, resentful.

If he were still Leader of the House he could not be more at his ease, more sure of himself, more ready to meet all comers. The foes at his back seem to give him no concern, and if he has friends in front, their friendship is not of a kind which calls for expressions of gratitude. Slight as the figure is, the stamp of energy on it is as impressive as the stamp of elegance; and both are impressive. It is a Democratic age, but the story of all ages, or of many ages, is the same; the Democrat prefers the Patrician for leader. The voice has the ring of authority in it. The House is silent as death. The faces on the Treasury Bench are the faces of men who wonder what is coming, and are getting ready to meet it. The scene, like so many scenes in the House, is dramatic, and the yellow light that floods the Chamber from the ceiling adds to the illusion, and to the theatrical character of it. Mr. Gladstone looks eagerly across the table. Mr. Morley, Sir George Trevelyan, Sir William Harcourt, are all alert. The one unmoved personage in the Liberal phalanx is Lord Hartington.

Almost the first sentence that Lord Randolph utters is a debating sentence: "When I recall the language in which I attacked the Government of the right honourable gentleman opposite (Mr. Gladstone) for engaging British military forces in the Soudan, I cannot refrain from expressing regret and alarm at what appears to be a recommencement of a course which I then so strongly denounced, and still at the present moment denounce." I quote it not because I am going to follow the speaker in his argument, for I am not, but as a good specimen of the right way of saying things to the House of Commons. The truth is, the two men most unlike each other are the two men who have taken almost identical views on the Soudan business—Lord Randolph and Mr. John Morley. This single sentence is a reminder to the House of all the disasters that befell Mr. Gladstone's policy in Egypt, and a warning to the present Ministry that they are entering upon the same road. That is what I call a debating manner, and a House of Commons manner.

Still more striking is the passage in which he pays off part of his debt to Lord Salisbury. The question I mentioned above was a question as to Lord Salisbury's statement in the House of Lords that the retention of Suakim was of no advantage to Egypt. That was a private opinion said Sir James Ferguson, who is Lord Salisbury's mouthpiece in the Commons. "Such an answer," now said Lord Randolph, "is flippant. To say that a declaration by the Prime Minister, made in a debate in the Lords, after full notice, is a mere private opinion, is a preposterous proposition. I should like to know what would have been the concentrated fury of honourable and right honourable gentlemen on this side of the House if the member for Midlothian had ever taken up such an attitude." The hit was palpable, but what followed went further home. Nothing has of late brought so much Radical criticism on Lord Salisbury as his calling Mr. Naoroji a black man. "I protest," proceeded Lord Randolph, "against the idea that Ministerial utterances, on Ministerial responsibility, are to be treated as private opinions when it is convenient. I can quite understand that the opinion of the Prime Minister the other day as to the colour of people in India is a private opinion which does not bind his colleagues, and which need not bind them, but is truly a private opinion—and perhaps a temporary opinion." The House, or rather the Opposition, received this with shouts of laughter and cheers. Tory faces grew blacker than Mr. Naoroji's. It was not a mere sally of wit, it was an illustration perfectly germane to the question at issue, and that was what made it so effective.

As he proceeds the speech becomes closer in argument, and more and more evidently hostile in purpose. I have heard him in the House, especially in earlier days, when his tone was one of mere banter, and when sincerity was not the thing that most impressed his hearers. He has more styles than one. To-day his style is serious enough to suit the dullest, yet point after point is made with a clearness and rhetorical force to which the dullest cannot be insensible. The voice, though not very various or deep, is what the French call a carrying voice; it penetrates everywhere without apparent effort. At times it is sibilant with passion; at all times there is meaning in every tone. He leans slightly forward, is sparing of gesture, cares little, apparently, for mere oratorical ornament. But the lips open and shut with an unusual degree of muscular energy, and the eyes have a light in them which burns. He watches the House as closely as the House watches him. He speaks for half an hour. When he sits down he is again cheered from the Liberal side, and again the silence of those about him is unbroken.

The English, said Montesquieu, like a man to be a man. There is in that phrase a hint of the source, or of one source, of Lord Randolph's power. He is without a party in the House, without any considerable following, but he is a man to be reckoned with from sheer force of character and courage, even more than from his extraordinary abilities. It is far too soon to sum up a career which, perhaps, has hardly more than begun. There is much, if you like, to be said against him, but what does it avail? Here is the one man among the English Tories who has shown capacity for leadership, in something more than a party sense. He it was who saw the meaning of the new suffrage; who perceived that if the Tory party had any hope of a future less sterile than the past, it lay in coming to terms with the new masters of this country. To struggle against the new Democracy was hopeless, but to win over the new Democracy was not hopeless. He it was who taught his party how they might become the popular party. He showed them the road. He set up the guidepost. It is hardly too much to say that he gave them power, and brought them into office with a fair prospect of a long tenure of office. They have shown their gratitude in the way we all know. Well, the day will come when the Tory Ministry will again be in difficulties, and must again appeal to the country. Then, if not before, they will bethink themselves of the discarded colleague who has the ear of the country.

The American Girl in England

The subject was once dealt with by a British Mother, a lady clever enough and with character enough to have been an American . . . The American invasion was in full tide of success and this lady was asked what she thought of American girls. "They are sad poachers," was her answer. She had expressed in four words what the average British Mother who belongs to the Classes had been thinking for years.

In America, I suppose, the solicitudes of the British Mother must seem excessive. They can hardly be understood in a country whose social organisation is so unlike that of England. The American girl asks little or no help from her mother in choosing a partner for life. The English girl has always been dependent upon her mother to get her a husband. You do not hear in London of a girl's coming out. You hear of her being brought out. If the girl does not marry during her first or second season, it is the mother who is pitied. "Lady X. has hacked those daughters of hers about London the last three years, and got rid of only one of them." That is the sort of remark you may hear. It is brutal in form but the Englishman is too often brutal in form; perhaps secretly prides himself on being so; is ashamed of seeming so good a fellow as he really is. Brutal or not, it expresses a truth. Lady X. has started out on a campaign and failed. She has toiled, schemed, and intrigued to find husbands for her girls, and has not found them. Perhaps the very men she had fixed on for her own offspring have married Americans. Do you wonder that she is sore? The girls seem to have less interest in the business than the mother. . . . Their rôle is passive. The mothers would be horrified if they saw their daughters thinking and acting for themselves. So, I suppose, would the eligible young men; perhaps not the ineligible, for their chances would be improved if the girls were given their heads, and if by chance they knew what to do with them when they had been given. It is of the average girl I speak; any one who knows London knows many who have little in common with the average.

No doubt there has been a change of late but the change is itself due, in some degree, to American influence. The English girl has been encouraged to copy her American cousin. All copies are mistakes, and this is a greater mistake than most others. Their only use, as La Rochefoucauld says, is to bring out the faults of the original. And it is the faults, not the merits, that are copied. Probably the American girl has faults. I speak of her as a type, not as an individual; the individual is always charming. Nor is the American girl, as girl, very well known here. It is after she has ceased to be girl and become a wife, and the wife of an Englishman, that she has been most studied in London. It is not in London or on English soil that she has done most of her poaching. If you were content with superficial causes, it might be enough to trace the causes of the American conquest to the new passion of the young Englishman for American travel. Twenty years ago hardly anybody went; the young Englishman of position who had seen "the States" was the exception. Now he is, if not the rule, common enough to make a rule for himself. He goes to America, sees the American girl, is captured or captures her, and brings her back to the old home. If you run down the list you will find that most Anglo-American matches have been made on American soil; with some notable instances to the contrary.

Opportunity is much but it is not everything. If the travelling Briton had not found the American girl attractive, he would not have married her. Why did he find her attractive—more attractive than the girl he left behind him? . . . The British Mother . . . will give you a dozen reasons offhand. If she happen to be in a bad temper she will declare they are forward hussies. She would give her fingers if her own girls knew how to be forward in the same sense. Very likely she will tell you that her own girls are as pretty, as well-bred (she will say better), as well-dressed, as well-taught, as well as a dozen other things, as the Americans. It is not all quite accurate but we can afford to admit it, and the retort is the more crushing, "Why then do the young Englishmen prefer the Americans?"

Each has his own reason, good unto him, but the reason which underlies all the others is social, not personal. The relations between the sexes in youth are ten times more natural, genuine, and right in America than in England. Life does not begin with the English girl on her coming out. She is still in the nursery or the school-room, is still the bread-and-butter miss, still the nonentity, still the shy, silent, unformed creature she was. She is not sure of herself, or of anybody else. She has no conversation, or none that does not require drawing out, and the young Englishman is not good at drawing out. She knows that she has been taken to market, and her sensations on entering society cannot be very different from those of the white slave on the auctionblock in the East. She has been taught to be timid. Opinions, ideas, initiative of her own, the meeting on equal terms with youngsters in black coats and white ties, any kind of frank or friendly intercourse, any knowledge of the world or of life—all these things are to her forbidden. She is what her mother and governess have made her; as her mother before her was made by her mother and governess. Her incapacities are hereditary; her notions are purely conventional; Mrs. Grundy is the Deity who rules over her Universe. She is monotonous, and men like variety. She is a chrysalis, and to a chrysalis even a butterfly is preferable. She is the raw material of a charming woman, and it is not every young Briton who feels himself competent to complete her education or willing to let others complete it. He often hung back, long before he heard of America. When he went there he found a girl who had everything the English girl had, and something beside. The American did meet him on even terms—as a rule much more than even, for she is as superior to the average young Englishman as to the average English girl. Her intelligence, quickness, freshness, animation, fulness of character, often her brilliancy, always her individuality, were perfectly novel to him and perfectly delightful. Is it so wonderful that he liked her better than her doll-cousin in this damp island and married her? . . .

"But the American girls have the most money," growled the British Mother on one occasion. Sometimes they have, and when they have it is again the social system in which they live that bestows it on them. If English fathers persist in sacrificing their daughters to their sons, what else can be expected? In the great families, of course, the younger sons fare not much better, as a rule, than the daughters. If there is a title the estate must be kept together to support it. If there is none, it must be increased in hopes the title may come. In the middle classes, with whom this particular marriage question concerns itself but little, the rule still is to give more to the male than to the female progeny, save when the upper middle class daughter is to be bartered for a title. Primogeniture or not, few of the great families would be as great as they are had not eldest sons from time to time married fortunes acquired in trade. But what remains to the others? A duke's daughter with   10,000 is thought rather well off. Anybody with twice that is a good match; and a girl with half a million is a prize for which a generation of young patricians compete. The growl about money is therefore merely a growl. The English have money enough; they could give it to their daughters if they liked; perhaps, as a last resource against the flowing tide from America, they will enlarge their portions. There would be one result, and one only. They would have then to invent a fresh reason to account for the continuing attractiveness of the American girl.

BRET HARTE:

"NOWHERE . . . IN THE WHOLE WORLD
CAN YOU FIND A CLASS
LIVING SO ENTIRELY
FOR THEMSELVES"

1889

Bret Harte was in his day the most popular writer in America, and his fame in Britain equaled his fame at home. Born in Albany, he moved, at the age of eighteen, to California, dabbled at mining, and then settled down to journalism in the new, bustling city of San Francisco, where in the sixties he became editor of the lively *Overland Monthly*. It was to this magazine that he contributed those stories of the mining West that won him instant and widespread attention: "The Luck of Roaring Camp," "Tennessee's Pardner," "The Outcasts of Poker Flat," and others of the same genre. Riding the wave of success he moved east, contracted with the *Atlantic Monthly* to supply monthly stories or articles at an unprecedented sum, and—detached from his milieu—promptly went into a literary decline from which he never really recovered. By 1878 he had run dry; President Hayes rescued him with a minor consular job at Crefeld, in Germany, and from there he had the good luck to be transferred to Glasgow. The remainder of his life was passed in England, mostly in London, where he eked out a living by writing potboilers of one kind or another. Though he managed to keep his family in America until

The Letters of Bret Harte, Geoffrey Bret Harte, ed. (Boston, 1926), pp. 341–345.

almost the end of his life, he did maintain a desultory correspondence with them: here is one family letter of more than family interest.

Trewsbury, Cirencester
September 15, 1889

... I have been here four weeks now, but during that time until the last three or four days have been steadily at work and have really seen but little of the country. I have written to the girls some descriptions of certain things which I thought might interest them. I can add very little for you, I fear. This is the usual English country house like the others I have described, and the impression one gets is nearly the same that was very truthfully and characteristically expressed by one of our countrymen to an Englishman, "You're too d——d comfortable over here." Nothing can be truer. The spectacle one ever has of a privileged class with nothing to think about but their own amusement, who apportion their lives with a certain kind of ridiculous formality to the regular habit of hunting, shooting, and race-going, who even arrange the meetings of Parliament so that the duty of governing the country shall not disturb their sacred institutions—is a little too d——d comfortable—to be even *manly.* There is no ambition—no endeavour—but of the most pitiable, trivial kind. Nowhere, I believe, in the whole world can you find a class living so entirely for themselves and in themselves as the English better class. Of course, there are some exceptions—men who travel about, men who devote themselves to higher pursuits; but they never entirely break away from their habits: the Prime Minister, the great politician, the great lawyer, must have his shootings, his game preserves, with all the costly wasteful accessories and paraphernalia. For it is a most singular thing that that *simplicity* which is the hall mark—the distinguishing trait—of the aristocracy is utterly wanting in their peculiarly English sports. They not only go about them "sadly," as Froissart said, but with a ridiculous show and even vulgar ostentation; they cannot shoot over these great preserves except in great parties, specially invited, and their proceedings are as vulgarly published as the Court Circular, not only how many brace they shot but *who* shot and what Lord So-and-So did; their costume is extravagantly ridiculous, their luncheons are feasts and as much of a feature of this "manly exercise" as their gamekeepers and beaters. Once a year all England—I mean all fashionable society—flock to see their schoolboys—*not rehearse their studies,* oh, no!—but *play their games!* The Eton and Harrow cricket matches thrill the fashionable parents as no examination of studies ever could or would do—for there are no public examinations that are fashionable; to be the mother or father or sister of a great cricketer or football player is a prouder distinction than to be related to a prize scholar. This is tacitly impressed upon them in their childhood; in their adolescence at Oxford and Cambridge they are as tacitly taught that it is "better form" to be good oarsmen at a regatta to which all fashionable society flock, than to win prizes or take degrees at college, honours which fashionable society coldly ignores. What wonder that the average Eton or Harrow boy can't write a decent English letter? But what can one think of Americans who worship this sort of thing—and send their children here to have an English education!

There has been a good deal of visiting from the neighbours, who have very beautiful seats (not the only ones they have—for there is one family of three who have as many places in other counties) and they are very hospitable. Our nearest neighbour is a Lady Elizabeth Biddulph, of very old family, whose daughter is a "Maid of Honour" to the Queen. She is plain, but very well educated; talks well and plays and sings well—which I am told is essential to those who "wait" on royalty. One thing strikes me about these people—and my knowledge of them is gathered from another "Maid of Honour" I know, and an "Equerry," who is a very charming "Warrington" sort of fellow, and also is one of my London friends—and that is, that they are one and all exceedingly gentle and singularly diffident in their opinions; sympathetic without being at all excited about anything and certainly never visibly *astonished* at anything. It may seem a dreadful thing to say, but their manner is that of persons who might be in the habit *of living with mad people*, or attending some kind of a reformatory. Of course, I don't dare to say such a thing "out loud" to any one; although these very people are themselves by no means always reverent or subdued in their own passing allusions to their duties.

This reminds me of another queer thing I have noticed among the best society people, which I do not remember to have heard spoken of before. They recognize and put up with a certain degree of eccentricity of conduct, dress, or behaviour among themselves that is simply astounding and seems utterly inconsistent with not only any sense of the hideous or annoying, but utterly inconsistent with their own canons of "form."

I have met people who acted like lunatics or idiots—and who indeed *were* in all but legal restraint and harmfulness. I have met people in drawing-rooms who were so outrageously absurd that I pitied their host and hostess until I saw that *they never seemed to notice it*. Once when I ventured to say to a lady, whom I know very well, that it was rather strange—she said simply, "Oh, it's only Lord A," or "Lady B," or "Sir So-and-So—*we all know him!*"—as if it were all-sufficient—as indeed it seemed to be. I once dined at a table of distinguished people, when our host, half through dinner, calmly went to sleep and *snored*—and, what was sublimer still, was not awakened by his brother peer at his side! I sat next to a man at another dinner, who wore a star, and who only had three words, "Ah! Ho! Hum!" The "Ah" was interrogative, the "Ho" confidential, the "Hum" contemplative. He said these three words continually through dinner—*and never said anything else!* Again, we were all assembled in a certain drawing-room before dinner, when there glided into the room, unannounced by the footman, the most extra-ordinary apparition I ever beheld in a dream or on the stage. She was hideously painted in pink and *yellow*, like a waxen mask; she had bright yellow ringlets, like golden sausages clustered round her forehead, and larger ones that depended nearly to her waist; a woman evidently of *sixty*, she had a baby waist and sash to her brocade dress, and the whole of this astounding figure was covered by a lofty headdress of ribbons and lace and tinsel like a grate ornament. I was speechless with alarm. I thought she was a family lunatic who had escaped from her room. I felt myself blushing for our hostess. But no one seemed concerned. The next moment she was introduced to me by a name and title that I had often heard and saw continually in the society news. Everybody knew her, everybody was accustomed to these vagaries; the mere possibility of her appalling anybody outside that sacred circle never occurred to them, and they *didn't care!*

1890-1900

ALICE JAMES
IS NOT ENTHUSIASTIC
ABOUT ENGLAND

1890-91

All members of the Adams family seem to have looked at England through the same bifocal spectacles: dangerous and corrupt when seen at a distance, but attractive and even amiable on closer view. Each member of the James family—Henry James, Sr., his sons William and Henry, and his daughter Alice—had quite individual views of Britain. The elder Henry looked at it through transcendentalist and Swedenborgian spectacles and found it wanting morally and spiritually, but respected its practical force. William James was sure that Cambridge, Massachusetts, was the center of the universe and the pleasantest place in the world and was unable to understand why anyone would bother to live in England, or anywhere but New England. Henry James's views were more complex than those of other members of his family, perhaps more complex than those of any American who has ever written on England, and were set forth at immense length in a dozen novels, volumes of stories, and essays. Alice brought a sharp and on the whole unsympathetic eye to focus on England; what she saw entertained her but did not greatly please her.

From *Alice James: Her Brothers, Her Journal,* Anna Robeson Burr, ed. (New York, 1934), pp. 90–91, 137–138, 186, 200–203.

Alice James was the youngest of the James family, and the only daughter. No less gifted than her brothers, she became an invalid at sixteen and thereafter lived almost wholly within herself, a kind of Emily Dickinson among the Jameses. After her father's death she lived briefly with William, then went, with her companion Katherine Loring, to London, staying at times with her beloved brother Henry, at times in her little house near Holland Park. She felt that England did not appreciate Henry; she herself saw little of England except nurses and doctors. As Henry later wrote, "I feel in reading (her Journal) that inevitably she simplified too much, shut up in her sick room, exercised her wondrous vigor of judgment on too small a scrap or what really surrounded her." But William wrote that "her life was a triumph"—a triumph certainly over illness and the certainty of early death.

"The Civility of All Classes"

June 13 [1889]. I went out again today, and behaved like a lunatic, "sobbing," à la Kingsley, over a farmhouse, a meadow, some trees and cawing rooks. Nurse says there are some people down-stairs who drive everywhere and admire nothing. How grateful I am that I actually see, to my own consciousness, the quarter of an inch that my eyes fall upon; truly the subject is all that counts! . . .

Imagine hearing that some one here in Leamington, whom I had never seen, had said that I was "very charitable." I felt as if all my clothes had been torn off, and that I was standing on the steps of the Town Hall, in the nude, for the delectation of the British Matron. This calumny arose, I suppose, from my having given a sixpence to the Brookses before No. 9 was born.

Mr. Howells' letter made me so happy by saying that mine had made father and mother seem living to him. No greater happiness can come than finding that they survive, or can be revived, in a few memories.

June 14. Nurse met Becky Brooks and her hanger-on in front of the pump-room. She had Eliza, the excrescence, of course, on one side, and was dragging, by a red scarf pinned around his neck, an unfortunate dog with her other hand; four of the others were tugging at the scarf, so that Becky's slender person of ten was upholding five others. When asked where the dog came from, she said, "The woman 'as wants to lose it gave it us; we's 'ad it all hafternoon." I think the dog must be sufficiently lost by now!

What one never loses a sense of, and never fails to adore in

England, is the civility of all classes, not only to their betters, but to each other. Of course there are hideous manners in "society" and in the slums, but in the middle region, amidst the wise, the rational, and the humble—among those that count, in short—civility, I'm sure, is the rule. Then these creatures that come from the hard, gritty, ragged interchange which passes for manners at home, actually don't perceive the difference. Heaven forbid that I should begin upon those that see not; it's too tragic! But one must be just; the poor things have had nothing to perceive all their days; when suddenly brought face to face with all this complexity, what can they do but seek refuge in blindness? . . .

The All-Pervasive Pharisaism
of The English

February 17 [1890]. I find myself, as the months pass, more and more oppressed by the all-pervasive sense of pharisaism in the British constitution of things. You don't feel it at first, and you can't put your finger upon it in your friends; but as the days go by you unfold it with your Standard in the morning, and it rises dense from the Pall Mall Gazette in the evening; it creeps through the cracks in the window frames like the fog, and envelopes you through the day. I asked H[enry] once how it struck him from his wider and varied field, not wanting my view to become cramped upon conclusions drawn from my centimetre of observation; he said that he didn't think that it could be exaggerated. It's woven of a multiplicity of minute details and incidents which elude you in the telling, but which seem to exist in the texture of things, and leave a dent in the mind as they file past. A monarchy to which they bow down in its tinsel capacity only, denying to it a manly movement of any sort! A boneless church, broadening itself out, up to date; the hysterical legislation over a dog with a broken leg, whilst society is engaged in making bags of four thousand pheasants, or gloating over foxes torn to pieces by a pack of hounds; the docility with which the classes enslave themselves to respectability or nonrespectability, as the "good-form" of the present may be; the "sense of their betters" in the masses; the passivity with which the workingman allows himself to be patted and legislated out of all independence; then the profound irreconcilable in the bone and sinew conviction that outlying regions are their preserves, for they alone of the human races massacre savages out of pure virtue. It would ill become Americans to reflect upon the treatment of aboriginal races; but I never heard it suggested that our hideous dealing with the Indians was brotherly love masquerading under the disguise of pure "cussedness." . . .

"The Demoralization of English Society"

November 9 [1890]. Harry came in the other day quite sickened from a conversation he had been listening to, which he said gave him a stronger impression of the demoralization of English society than anything he had ever heard. He had been calling upon a lady whom he knows very well, and who is very well connected; two gentlemen were there, one young, the other old; one of them asked about one of the sons who has just failed in an exam, for one of the services, when she said he had just had an offer of a place, their opinion of which she would like to have. Pulitzer, the ex-editor of the *New York World,* had applied to the British Embassy in Paris to recommend him a young man of good family, to act as his secretary, write his letters, etc.—but chiefly to be socially useful in attracting people to the house; to act in short, evidently, as a decoy duck to Pulitzer's gilded salons. A certain young man had fulfilled the functions for three years, and had just been married to an American, Pulitzer having given him a "dot" of 30,000 pounds, and it was presumable that his successor would fare equally well. The Englishmen both thought it would be a "jolly" life. She then turned and asked H. what he thought. "I would rather sweep the dirtiest crossing in London." At which rejoinder, staring amazement, H. asked if she knew Pulitzer's history—. Oh, yes, she knew all about him, and her only anxiety was that the son, who was a complete failure, might fail in getting the enviable berth. The snobling, it appears, has a strong taste for medicine, but thinks it a social disgrace to be a doctor, conceiving a social tout to a Pulitzer to be a nobler form of man.

Christmas Festivities in The Servant's Hall

January 23 [1891]. Before the year waxes older, I must recount our novel festivities at Christmas. Little Nurse has an exemplary habit of telling me all her experiences, great and small; and since I have been here she has afforded me infinite amusement by psychological revelations of the steward's room. She is allowed to report all mental eccentricities of the lady's maid, the chef, the steward, the waiter, etc., but the line is supposed to be rigidly drawn at all gossip about the "ladies," though I must confess that curiosity often gets the better of my high tone, and I listen, with great receptivity, to the shortcomings of Mrs. Jones, Brown, and Robinson; for, alas! I am sorry to say that the lady's-maid's mind, like mine, finds the recital of humanity's shortcomings more succulent than that of its treatment more than accounts for our preoccupation with the deviation therefrom.

In this way a wide social range was vicariously opened out to us—beginning by a servants' ball in the hotel on Christmas night, tapering down through a party at "Cousin Val's," a bootmaker who has been to Marlborough House to measure the illustrious foot of Royalty, and ending on Saturday night with a comprehensive gathering at the Sweep's at Hampstead, where the exalted Assistants from Marshall and Snelgrove's watched from the other side of the room the inspirations of a carter and a ploughboy.

The Nursling, knowing that she did not shine as a dancer, and being in no way inclined to obscurity, disguised herself for the ball, very successfully, as an old hag, and sang and acted one of those dreary compounds of "Charing," "Betsey Waring," "damp-attics," "roo-matics," known as a comic song. We have long had it impressed upon us that she "knew" music and drawing, but her histrionic genius has lain fallow; so we were much surprised and delighted at its unexpected blossoming. One day, when I told her how anxious I was about the first night of *The American,* she asked, "Should you have felt very badly if I had failed on Christmas night, Miss?" adding, "I never should have held up my head in this hotel again if I had."

The ladies and gentlemen being invited to honour the occasion, K. put on her mouse-coloured velvet gown and went down just before Nurse's song. She was received at the door by one of the "gentlemen" in the office, who escorted her to a chair, when Jennie, our chambermaid, came up with enthusiasm to greet her, and introduced another housemaid. Jessie, our second housemaid, sat beside her, while our three waiters interchanged conversational amenities with her from time to time, all as if they were friends and hosts, till one's heart was melted to hear about it. These aesthetic decencies so wrap about the iniquities, and so explain and justify their long continuance, that one has flaccid moments of shivering at the raw edges that will be laid bare as democracy sweeps its pope's-head through the festooning cobwebs, and crumbles the sickly-hued mould into dust. Jennie said to Nurse with delight the next morning: "Fancy Miss Loring shaking hands with me before the whole room." Let us pray that our unconscious benefactions outweigh our unconscious cruelties!

This, by the way, allies K. with the Countess of Portsmouth, who says she always shakes hands with the village school-mistress, because she thinks it's "the best plan." Think of the swindle of being so placed!—rigid with the framework of the Personage, and ne'er a shady corner from the cradle to the grave for the limbering and rejoiceful somersault. But I must get on with my festivities.

Cousin Val's party seemed commonplace with the trail of Royalty and a professional comedian upon it, Ivan Berlin, more woolly than terrible; but real life was found in perfection at the Sweep's, who lives in a little cottage in one of the hollows of Hampstead Heath.

The party consisted of about twenty (ten having fortunately failed), who were placed, in order to fill in, on stools close together round the walls of the little sitting-room, against which they couldn't lean, however, because they were dripping with wet, there being no fire, for fear of too much heat at this frigid season. Upon her stool, Nurse sat from five in the evening until six the next morning, save at the moments when she burst into song, the essence of the occasion being uninterrupted vocalization and an all-night sitting. Nurse at one moment raised the tone by making to the Marshall and Snelgrove contingent a literary allusion to the clammy hands of Uriah Heep; "The others wouldn't have known to what we referred, Miss." They seemed to be differentiated by special songs, one recalcitrant young woman being besought at frequent intervals through the watches of the night to sing "Joanna in her Shroud," which turned out to be "Joe in the Copper"; and the Sweep coming to Nurse to tell her that a young woman was about to sing one of her songs, and "what could he do about it?"—as if there were a vocal copyright. Over the evolutions of the carter and a gallon of beer, we must sadly draw a veil, but the ploughboy, pitted with small pox, with features fashioned in one of the least kindly moods of Providence, seemed the rarest flower of benignancy. So preoccupied was he with the welfare of the guests, and making the occasion "go off," that Nurse thought he must be related to the hosts. The last note of a song had hardly died before he would exclaim: "If no one else is going to sing, I know another"; and perched on his stool, his eyes tight shut, clinched hands, and heels tucked under him, he would drone out by the yard, ditties to the refrain of "My com-*ryde* died for me," and the like. Think of the joy in life of this lowly lad, his soul rapturous with song, all instinct and fluid with the grace of hospitality, as compared, for instance, with Lord Wharncliffe, whose ancestral exigencies are such that he turns his back upon his guests, however fair they may be, and takes his own sister, without a grimace, in to dinner, four days in succession. A lady staying with this unfortunate bondsman, pathetically remarked: "Having no title, I had to go in to dinner every day with the same gentleman, and *that* gentleman Mr. Smalley too."

HENRY WHITE
IS IMPRESSED BY THE G.O.M.
AND HIS WIFE BY THE QUEEN

1893-94

Born to wealth, educated in France and England, young Henry White was rapidly on the road to becoming an idler and a dilettante when he was saved by a fortunate marriage to Margaret Rutherford of New York, who insisted that he make something of himself. He did. Choosing—he was in a position to choose—a diplomatic career, he obtained first a post in Vienna and then in London, which was his social and his spiritual home. In time he came to be the senior figure in the American Embassy in London; he knew everybody, he went everywhere, he was a veritable Henry James of diplomacy. Theodore Roosevelt called him, with pardonable exaggeration, "the most useful man in the diplomatic service," and appointed him Ambassador to Italy and later to France. When the retirement of Roosevelt put a temporary end to his diplomatic career he retired to Washington, where he built a splendid mansion and entertained in the grand manner. President Wilson, who wanted a not too partisan Republican for his Peace Mission in 1919, appointed White to that post, and on his return to the United States White campaigned for the League of Nations.

From Allan Nevins, *Henry White, Thirty Years of American Diplomacy* (New York, 1930), pp. 87–91.

Gladstone, the Grand Old Man himself, is seen usually at second hand in the correspondence of the Whites; but three or four times they sat at dinner with him. One meeting is of special interest. The Right Honorable Arthur Peel, who was Speaker of the House of Commons for eleven years following 1884, used to give Mrs. White admission to the gallery of the House at practically all times, and she often attended. Her report of the debates interested her young son, and he asked many questions. As White years later wrote:

One day Miss Julia Peel very kindly asked him whether he would like to come down to her gallery (her mother had died shortly before) and hear a debate. Of course he accepted the invitation with alacrity, and it was arranged that on a certain day I should take him to Miss Peel's gallery and leave him there; and that I should call for him at the Speaker's house in the Palace of Westminster about half past five o'clock, after he had taken tea with her. This arrangement was carried out, and when I went to take the boy home I was surprised and interested, upon entering the Speaker's library, to find Mr. Gladstone addressing himself to Jack with considerable earnestness on the subject of dogs; the Speaker, who was a very tall and imposing man, standing before a fire in the great fireplace in his robes and wig—a very striking and picturesque scene.

It seems that when Jack had been brought down from the gallery for tea, the Speaker, who had heard of a favorite fox terrier of his called Spot, had asked him about his pet, which started a conversation on dogs, and something was said by the boy which aroused Mr. Gladstone's interest. Mr. Gladstone had the singular faculty of turning his mind abruptly and with great earnestness to any question, however insignificant or unimportant, which might suddenly occur in conversation, and on which he differed from an opinion expressed by some one else. On these occasions, of which I was several times a witness at dinner parties and elsewhere, he would often discourse at considerable length and with great eloquence. It was in the midst of just such an occasion that I entered the Speaker's library. The interesting part of it to me was not only that Mr. Gladstone should be talking to my youthful son in such an earnest and eloquent manner, but more particularly that a casual remark made by a little fellow of his tender years should have aroused the great British statesman as it did, and I shall never forget the scene. I have no recollection of the question at issue, but I remember Jack's asking one or two questions, which only seemed to increase Mr. Gladstone's interest and eloquence.

In another letter White describes how the G. O. M. was once his table companion:

> Last night Mr. Gladstone sat next to me and made himself most agreeable. He told me among other things that he always told Mrs. Gladstone all his state secrets and that she had never even hinted at the knowledge. He also said that one of his rules through life had always been never to talk over and if possible never to think of exciting or disagreeable things late at night or in bed, but always to wait for the morning, and it had now become second habit. Then he talked about his correspondence. In the course of his career to the Queen alone he had written 2,000 letters, and his yearly average of letters received, not counting those of special departments during office, is about 20,000. Besides all the writing done by his secretaries, he writes by hand (only letters) about four hours a day; and yet he reads everything and leads all his political life besides.

Now and then White, in his visits to the House of Commons, would witness an incident of dramatic value. One is recorded in a letter of April 22, 1893, to a friend:

> The Grand Old Man, who rose at ten minutes to twelve and spoke for more than an hour, was in his best form; he seemed as fresh and combative and full of gesture as I have ever seen him. One specially interesting incident took place. A few days ago Austen Chamberlain made what everybody seems to think a brilliant maiden speech, some of the arguments of which Mr. Gladstone dealt with; but in referring to the speech he praised it and said, turning round with emphasis to the elder Chamberlain, "I can only say that the speech must have been *very* dear to a father's heart." The effect of this was like an electric shock to Joseph Chamberlain, who started and buried his eyes in his hands, and shortly afterwards I saw him brushing away the tears of emotion which could not be kept back. I can give no idea of the manner and gesture of Mr. Gladstone in saying these words; but they of course produced more effect, coupled with Joe's emotion, than the words themselves.

Encounters with royalty in these years were rare and unimportant. Twice or thrice the Prince of Wales, later Edward VII, dined with the Whites, but they formed no novel impression of him. Of Queen Victoria they had mere occasional glimpses. The most extended record of her preserved in the Whites' papers is a bit of reminiscence by Mrs. White, referring to a visit which they paid in October, 1897, at Balmoral. They drove over from Braemar, being invited for dinner at 8:45 in the evening. Mrs. White writes:

I wore my black brocade Worth dress, with tulle sleeves and a big yoke on one side, a diamond and pearl chain, and diamond collar with a row of pearls; an aigrette in my hair. Lady Lytton said I looked nice! She took me into the household drawing-room where they all assemble, and from the door of which on the passage one makes one's obeisance to the Queen as she passes into the dining-room leaning on the arm of her Indians and followed tonight by Princess Beatrice, Prince Christian, and the Hohenlohes. I curtsied to the Queen and kissed her hand and she said she hoped I was not tired after the long drive. She looks wonderfully well; not so red as she used and a little thinner, and such a happy, peaceful expression; but very stiff and lame, walking with real difficulty and apparently shorter than ever. She is tiny! But her dignity is wonderful. It almost amounts to being abstract, so little is it helped by her personal appearance. I sat at dinner between Fritz Ponsonby, so nice and clever, and Joseph Chamberlain. Princess Hohenlohe looked so fresh and pretty in pink satin trimmed with fur and diamonds. The Queen sat between Prince Christian and Hohenlohe. For the most part they talked German together, and neither continuously nor much. Harry was placed between Princess Beatrice and Lady Lytton; he made Princess Beatrice talk quite glibly. After dinner we went to the drawing-room. I forgot to say that the Queen's two Indians looked very splendid in gold and scarlet at dinner, and waited on her chiefly, but also on everyone. A chair was put near the center table for the Queen, and next it a magnifying glass and one or two little objects that I did not make out.

First Lady Lytton went to talk to her, and during that time Princess Beatrice, Princess Hohenlohe, and I, standing near the fireplace, all talked together. By and by Lady Lytton came over for me and I went around and stood by the Queen and had the longest talk I have ever had with her and the easiest except for the physical effort of leaning down to her, I being standing and tall and she being seated and so short. I think I must have stood there quite twenty-five minutes. The Queen first asked me exactly where Carrie Fergie is. She said she didn't know the house. I told her it was the last house on the left on the Spittal Road, near the Black Gate leading into her forest. "Oh no, that is not my gate; it is Farquhar's." Then she said, "I understand that you have been a sufferer for some time and you came here for your health five years ago; I hope this place is doing you good." I told her a little about my poor health and how it had to my everlasting disappointment prevented me from attending her Jubilee at St. Paul's, and how bitterly sorry I was to have missed that great occasion.

I then told her that there had been much rejoicing in America over her Jubilee, in spite of some Jingo propensities, and she laughed and said: "Yes, they have always had a kind personal feeling for me, and I don't know why." Then I told her that the President had wanted to send Harry to Spain as minister, but that I had rather prevented this because I wished to stay in England, and I asked her if she thought I had done wrong. She said: "Oh no. Where one is happy one is best." I told her I had just been reading her letters and Tennyson's in the Memoir by his son, and asked her about Tennyson. "I have the book," she said, "but have not read it. Tennyson was a very gruff man in manner and was often misunderstood through this, but he was always very kind to me. He was like a person who had never been contradicted or disciplined, but he had noble thoughts."

Browning she said she had seen only once and thought his poetry very difficult to understand. She preferred Mrs. Browning's writings, and thought the "Sonnets from the Portuguese" very beautiful. Then she asked me if there was any new or coming poet in America, to take the place of Longfellow, Lowell, and the others. I told her I feared so far there was no one. We talked of golf. She said she had never really seen a game; that she had always been particularly stupid at mastering games, but she had seen people walking about with sticks in the distance, and it looked very dull. . . . And by and by the Queen gave her little bow and smile which means dismissal, and I retired to talk to Princess Beatrice and the others.

Then she talked to Harry. She told Lady Lytton she thought I had such a pleasant voice and speech (I suppose this she does not expect from Americans) and that she thinks me very pretty! Before she left the room I again kissed her hand.

RICHARD HARDING DAVIS
FOLLOWS AN ENGLISH ELECTION

1894

Richard Harding Davis, best remembered as a leading journalist, came rightly by his lifelong passion for writing; his mother was one of the first (and best) of realistic novelists—her *Life in the Iron Mills* is a literary landmark —and his father was editor of the *Philadelphia Public Ledger.* He studied at Lehigh University and at the recently opened Johns Hopkins, then turned to journalism. He reported, at one time or another, the Spanish War in Cuba, the Spanish-American War, the Boer War, the Russo-Japanese War, and the First World War. For a time on the *New York Sun,* he became in 1890 managing editor of *Harper's Weekly,* and for that lively journal he provided a long series of impressions of foreign nations. It was from one of these journalistic forays that he quarried the material for *Our English Cousins.* Davis also wrote a number of novels, the once widely read Gallegher stories, and some twenty-five plays.

I suppose the elections I saw in England at the last general election were considered legal enough, but I sometimes used to doubt it. I had been brought up properly to recognize that no man

From Richard Harding Davis, *Our English Cousins* (New York, 1894), pp. 51–77.

can hope to be elected without the support of enthusiastic young men with capes and oil lamps, and a brass-band to every fifty men, and every third band playing "Marching through Georgia." I saw nothing of this in England, and so I waited patiently to hear that the votes had been thrown out and that some one in authority had ordered a recount. As this did not happen I am forced to believe that a brass-band is not necessary at an election, though I still think it makes it a little more sure. It is like being married at the Mayor's office instead of being married with ushers and bridesmaids and rice. I suppose one is just as legal as the other, but I should be as sorry to go to Congress without having had a band play "See the Conquering Hero" as to be married without at least six ushers wearing my scarf-pins.

A general election in England is conducted by the entire people. There may be a Central Committee somewhere, as there is at home, but its work is not so conspicuous to the stranger as is the work of the first chance acquaintance he makes. Recall the most enthusiastic politician of your acquaintance during the late campaign, and multiply him by the whole population of Great Britain, and you obtain an idea of what a hold politics has on the people of England. By this I mean all the people, the voters and the non-voters, the gentleman who has thirteen votes in different counties and the young women of the Primrose League who have none, the landlord whose gates bar at his pleasure the oldest streets in London and the lodger who pays a few shillings for the back room.

Every class works for its party and for its candidate in its different way. Its way may be to address mass-meetings under the folds of the union-jack or to humbly address envelopes, but whatever his way may be, every one helps. As soon as Parliament ends, this interest, which has been accumulating less actively for some time, becomes rampant, and members fly north and south, taking their wives with them to sit upon the platforms, and their daughters to canvass the division, and their friends to make speeches, and the London season puts up the shutters until it is over. In London itself the signs of the times are various and many. You can see it in the crowds about the newspaper bulletin-boards, in the desertion of the Row in the morning, in the absence of the white light which had been burning over Westminster, in the placards on the hoardings, and in the carts and broughams filled with voters driving in elegance to the polls. The sandwich men on Piccadilly have changed their announcements of new plays and Van Beer's pictures and somebody else's catsup to "Vote for Bings," and you look down an irregular line of "Vote for

Bings" like the ghosts in Richard III, until you decide that no matter who the rival candidate may be, you will *not* vote for Bings. The under-butler, in undress livery, tells you that her ladyship has gone to the country to help Sir Charles in his canvass, and will not be back for a fortnight; and men you ask to dinner write you a week later from Ireland to say they have been attending the Ulster Convention, and speak of it as a much more important event than your dinner; and your chambers are invaded by Primrose Dames, who cause your landlady to look upon you with suspicion, and who seem to take it as a personal grievance and as an intentional slight on your part that you are an American and not entitled to a vote.

So I, personally, left London and followed the campaign through the fortunes of one candidate. And as his canvass resembled that of others, more or less, I will try to show through it what an English election is like. My Candidate's fortunes were very pleasant to follow, because his canvass was conducted with much picturesqueness in the form of rosettes and outriders, and was full of incident and local color, the local color being chiefly red. . . .

My Candidate stood for a county division where his people had been known for hundreds of years, and where he had been known for at least thirty, where the game-keeper remembered having handed him his first breech-loader, where the hunting set who follow the Duke of Rutland's hounds spoke of him as a "clinker" across country, and where the head of the family was the Lord Lieutenant of the county, and the owner of a great mansion which was familiarly particularized for seventy miles around as "the House." And while all this and all that pertained to it did not make his calling and election sure, it did make his efforts to render that election sure of peculiar interest to the visiting American.

My first intimation that I was to follow My Candidate's fortunes was an invitation delivered by himself in person during a luncheon in town, into the third course of which he plunged uninvited to ask if I would like to go down to a political meeting of his that night and have my head broken. Mr. Oscar Wilde was also included in the invitation because he happened to be there, but he showed a lack of proper sporting spirit, and, pleading an engagement, returned to the consideration of the fourth course. My host let me off, and My Candidate took me in a train to some place, where a carriage met us, and carried us the rest of the way to a village with a queer name. In that way was I pitchforked into English politics. That night we spoke at the school-house. I say "we" because for the few weeks which followed I cast my lot in with the Conservative party and My Candidate, and though I did not speak but once, on which unhappy occasion I turned all the conservatives of sixty years' standing into rabid Radicals I always considered myself in the plural number.

We had a small audience. It was as large as the school-house could hold, but it was small, and it was phlegmatically and delightfully Conservative. The farmers and their wives sat on the front row, with the young ladies from the rectory and the local political agent. Back of these were the agricultural laborers, who correspond as a political factor to our sons of honest toil, and who wore suits of white corduroy and red ties, and who surprised one by looking exactly like the agricultural laborers in the *Chatterbox* of our childhood and in the *Graphic* Christmas numbers of to-day. They had red, sunburnt faces, and a fringe of whiskers under the chin, and hair that would not lie down. When they were Conservatives they were nice and sober and clean-looking, and kept their lips closely shut while they observed us with bovine admiration and approval; but when they were Radicals, they, by some curious mental process, became strikingly unintelligent and boorish-looking, and expressed their only interest in the proceedings by howling "boo" or "yah." My Candidate addressed the loyal electors of the village in a happily keyed conversational tone. He made, on the whole, a most satisfactory and clever speech, and I learned for the first time how to say "hear, hear!" in such a way as to convey the sound of "'ere, 'ere!" and the idea of marked approval and deep conviction at the same time. And even after I had heard him deliver the same speech at four villages a night for a fortnight I still preserved my admiration for it, and, as I recall it even now, I remember it fondly as a satisfactory and clever oration. . . .

The next place received us calmly, although we came into it at a gallop, and with the Candidate's dog barking excitedly from the carriage window. Old women, who could not vote, dropped us courtesies from the cottage half-doors; and their daughters, who could not vote either, waved their aprons, and ran by the wheels to wave their hands in the windows; but their good men, who *had* votes, kept their hands in their pockets and their pipes in their mouths, and scowled uncomfortably over the hedges, as though instinct told them to touch their caps, and the Radical political agent had told them they must do nothing so foolish. Our local agent, with a union-jack in his button-hole, received us thankfully, for the gentleman then speaking had been trying for the last hour to hold the meeting together until we came, and was getting more hoarse as the crowd grew more noisy, and it had become a necessity of night or

Blücher. Then the local agent, who is always a young man with smooth hair and strong lungs, suddenly began to jump up and down and to cheer frantically, as though he had just discovered the Candidate's arrival, and the meeting turned to look, and the speaker said, "Thank Heaven!" and dropped into his chair, breathing heavily. The Candidate's speech was a little longer this time, because of doubtful spirits in the audience who had to be converted, and on account of their numerous interruptions. It struck me as a very noisy meeting, and I waited with some impatience to see the noisiest one put out as an example and a warning to the others; but no one was at all put out, not even the Candidate. That was my first experience of a mixed political meeting in England, and of the great and most curious institution of "heckling." Later in the campaign I was not so anxious to see the noisiest one put out as to ascertain at just which point in the proceedings it would be wisest for us to get out ourselves. . . .

The Briton's vote is a very precious thing to him, and he wants to know exactly who is going to get that vote, and why he thinks he should get it. So he goes to the meeting at which the candidate is announced to speak and asks him. This is called "heckling"; it is a Scotch word, and in Scotland is carried out with the careful and deliberate consideration which marks that people. . . .

Sometimes the privilege of heckling is conducted in good faith, but more frequently it is not. It has one great advantage, it teaches the unfortunate candidate to think while he is on his legs, and to keep his wits and his temper.

There was a man with a blue necktie. He was a most unpleasant gentleman, and he rose to ask questions at irregular moments with a pertinacity of purpose and a confident smile which no amount of howling on the part of the good Conservatives could dismay.

"Mr. ——, sir," he would say, "I 'ave a question I would like to put to you, sir. Did you, sir, or did you not, vote for the Impecunious School-masters Bill as presented on July 2, 1890?"

Now it was not at all likely that any of the Radicals present had ever heard of the bill before, or cared twopence about it if they had, but they saw the fiendish purpose of the question, and they howled accordingly, a triumphant, mocking howl, quite long and loud enough to drown any possible answer in case the Candidate had one to make, and sufficiently exasperating to make him forget it if he had. But the Candidate would smile easily, and raise his hands imploringly for silence, and then turn his head over his shoulder with a quick aside to his political agent, or to one of the other speakers, and whisper, fiercely, "Quick! look it up! what bill does the ass mean?" and then smile encouragingly on the heckler, while the political agent would thumb over a Speaker's Hand-book, and whisper back, hidden by the Candidate's figure: "Introduced by Lord Charing, seconded by Paddington; lost on second reading, 64 to 14. You voted *for* it. It was a bill to subsidize county school-teachers." Then the Candidate, who had probably been taking tea on the terrace when the bill was introduced, and who had voted with his party at the division, and returned in time to say, "Two lumps, please," would smile cheerfully, and ask the heckler if he would be so good as to repeat his question, which the heckler judged was a subterfuge to gain time, and would repeat it in a more triumphant and offensive manner than before.

"Impecunious School-masters Bill? Oh yes," the Candidate would say. "Introduced by Lord Charing, I believe. Oh yes, a very excellent bill; seconded, if I am not mistaken, by Mr. Paddington," and then, turning to the political agent, "Am I right?" to which the political agent, after a moment's consideration, nods a decided assent. "I voted for that bill." All the Conservatives cheered, and the gentleman with the blue necktie sat down, rather red in the face, and scanning the notes, with which the Radical political agent who had sent him there had furnished him, with dawning distrust. . . .

As heckling is the thing the American can't understand or admire, so the Corrupt Practices Act and its workings is the feature of an English election which appeals to him as its greatest triumph and glory. It is quite safe to say that bribery, as we know it, is unknown in England. The laws are against it, the sentiment of the people is against it, and the condition of things at the present time is against it. The Corrupt Practice Act places the conduct of an election in the hands of one person, the political agent, who is made responsible for, and who must furnish an itemized account for, every penny spent during the campaign. Every voter of the opposition is virtually an auditor of that account, and proof of corruption in the slightest degree, if corruption has degrees, not only sends the political agent to jail, but loses the candidate his election.

It is interesting to remember that after this general election Mr. Frank C. James, the Conservative who was elected in Walsall, was deprived of his seat by the courts because he provided hat-cards or favors for his adherents. That is, if an English candidate should supply his friends with the buttons which are worn over here by the adherents of different men and parties he would be looked upon as a corrupt and bribe-giving miscreant, and lose his chance of sitting in the Lower House. Mr. Nathaniel George Clayton also lost his seat; his offence consisting in his having given a check to a Conservative, who used the money to organize a picnic. This was held by the court to come within the provisions of the act prohibiting treating. It is of no use to say to this that we also have laws to punish corruption. We have, and every one knows how seldom they are enforced, and how little public sentiment there is back of them to put them in motion.

In England there is as little possible reward for services rendered after the election as there is actual bribery for services rendered before the election. Indeed, the most remarkable thing to me about the English elections was the number of women and men who worked for the different candidates with no other incentive than the desire to see their man and their party win. The shopkeepers, after a long day behind the counter, worked in the committee-rooms until two in the morning, folding and mailing circulars and other campaign matter. The women of the village, led by the rector's wife, directed forty-five thousand envelopes in one week; and the ladies from the Castle rose early and canvassed the town in rain and storm to fill in the little slips with which the political agent had furnished them, and which they forwarded to him at headquarters before they went to sleep at night. Gentlemen of many clubs deserted these clubs to travel in open dog-carts over rough roads to speak at noisy, heated meetings, to sleep in strange inns, and to eat when and where they might. No fly-by-night theatrical company or travelling tinker works harder or suffers more privations than does the political speaker at an English election. And for what? Not to get office, because the Member of Parliament has none to give. Not to gain notoriety, for his speeches are not reported; and certainly not to make himself popular, for he is lucky if he gets out of town with his carriage windows and his head unbroken. He is not a very bright speaker, the average English gentleman. He hems and hesitates, and deals largely in figures which the Chancellor of the Exchequer, were he present, might be able to contradict, but which the agricultural laborer imbibes unquestioningly. But he deserves the greatest possible honor for the trouble he takes and for the spirit which leads him to take that trouble, and which shames the busy American gentleman who thinks he has served his country well and sufficiently if he remembers to register and who then pairs off with some one else that they may both spend Election Day in the country.

JOHN CORBIN:

"THE SUPERIORITY OF
ENGLISH SPORTSMANSHIP"

1894

America inherited much of her sport and her ideas of sport and sportsmanship from England but, on the whole, without the class characteristics which English sport retains to this day. American baseball is the moral, or social, equivalent to English cricket, but vastly more informal and casual; as few Americans had well-groomed lawns, lawn tennis gave to clay court (or cement court) tennis; as American private schools played a distinctly subordinate role in American education, they did not nourish a special kind of football, e.g., rugger, as did the English public schools and the ancient universities. It is inconceivable that any American public figure, military or otherwise, could announce that the battle of Gettysburg was won on the playing fields of Exeter or of Yale. English ideals of sportsmanship have always had a special glamor for Americans, however, and these ideals are still solemnly invoked on ceremonious occasions though they are more and more rarely practiced. John Corbin studied at Balliol just as Logan Smith was leaving the place, and like Smith applied himself thereafter to literature. He was on the editorial staff of the Harper and Bros. Publishing house, dramatic critic for the *New York Times,* and an amateur historian. His first book, in

From John Corbin, *An American at Oxford* (Boston, 1902), pp. 145–156.

1898, was a series of rather superficial essays on *Schoolboy Life in England;* this was followed two years later by *An American at Oxford.* Toward the close of his life he turned to history, producing in 1930 a book on *The Unknown Washington.*

    The prevalence of out-of-door sports in England, and the amenity of the English sporting spirit, may be laid, I think, primarily, to the influence of climate. Through the long, temperate summer, all nature conspires to entice a man out of doors, while in America sunstroke is imminent. All day long the village greens in England are thronged with boys playing cricket in many-colored blazers, while every stream is dotted with boats of all sorts and descriptions; and in the evenings, long after the quick American twilight has shut down on the heated earth, the English horizon gives light for the recreations of those who have labored all day. In the winter the result is the same, though the cause is very different. Stupefying exhalations rise from the damp earth, and the livelong twilight that does for day forces a man back for good cheer upon mere animal spirits. In the English summer no normal man could resist the beckoning of the fields and the river. In the winter it is sweat, man, or die. . . .

    It is perhaps because of the incessant call to be out of doors that Englishmen care so little to have their houses properly tempered. At my first dinner with the dons of my college, the company assembled about a huge sea-coal fire. On a rough calculation the coal it consumed, if used in one of our steam-heaters, would have raised the entire college to inconvenience. As it was, its only effect seemed to be to draw an icy blast across our ankles from mediaeval doors and windows that swept the fire bodily up the chimney, and left us shivering. One of the dons explained that an open fire has two supreme advantages: it is the most cheerful thing in life, and it insures thorough ventilation. I agreed with him heartily, warming one ankle in my palms, but demurred that in an American winter heat was as necessary as cheerfulness and ventilation. "But if one wears thick woolens," he replied, "the cold and draught are quite endurable. When you get too cold reading, put on your great-coat." I asked him what he did when he went out of doors. "I take off my great-coat. It is much warmer there, especially if one walks briskly." . . .

    In a sportsman it would be most ungracious to inveigh against English weather. The very qualities one instinctively cures make possible the full and varied development of outdoor games, which

Americans admire without stint. Our football teams do day labor to get fit, and then, after a game or so, the sport is nipped in the bud. To teach our oarsmen the rudiments of the stroke we resort to months of the galley-slavery of tank-rowing. Our track athletes begin their season in the dead of winter with the dreary monotony of wooden dumb-bells and pulley-weights, while the baseball men are learning to slide for bases in the cage. In England the gymnasium is happily unknown. Winter and summer alike the sportsman lives beneath the skies, and the sports are so diverse and so widely cultivated that any man, whatever his mental or physical capacity, finds suitable exercise that is also recreation.

It is because of this universality of athletic sports that English training is briefer and less severe. The American makes, and is forced to make, a long and tedious business of getting fit, whereas an Englishman has merely to exercise and sleep a trifle more than usual, and this only for a brief period. Our oarsmen work daily from January to July, about six months . . . the English 'varsity crews row together nine or ten weeks. Our football players slog daily for six or seven weeks; English teams seldom or never "practice," and play at most two matches a week. Our track athletes are in training at frequent intervals throughout the college year, and are often at the training-table six weeks; in England six weeks is the maximum period of training, and the men as a rule are given only three days a week of exercise on the cinder-track. To an American training is an abnormal condition; to an Englishman it is the consummation of the normal. . . .

Because of these differences of climate and of temperament, no rigid comparisons can be made between English and American training; but it is probably true that English athletes tend to train too little. Mr. Horan, the president of the Cambridge team that ran against Yale at New Haven, said as much after a very careful study of American methods; but he was not convinced that our thoroughness is quite worth while. The law of diminishing returns, he said, applies to training as to other things, so that, after a certain point, very little is gained even for a great sacrifice of convenience and pleasantness. Our American athletes are twice as rigid in denying the spirit for an advantage, Mr. Horan admitted, of enough to win by.

The remark is worth recording: it strikes the note of difference between English and American sportsmanship. After making all allowances for the conditions here and abroad that are merely accidental, one vital difference remains. For better or for worse, a sport is a sport to an Englishman, and whatever tends to make it anything else is not encouraged; as far as possible it is made pleasant, socially and physically. Contests are arranged without what American undergraduates call diplomacy; and they come off without jockeying. It is very seldom that an Englishman forgets that he is a man first and an athlete afterwards. Yet admirable as this quality is, it has its defects, at least to the transatlantic mind. Even more, perhaps, than others, Englishmen relish the joy of eating their hearts at the end of a contest, but they have no taste for the careful preparation that alone enables a man to fight out a finish to the best advantage. It is no doubt true, as the Duke of Wellington said, that the battle of Waterloo was won on the playing-fields of England; but for any inconsiderable sum I would agree to furnish a similar saying as to why the generals in South Africa ran into ambush after ambush. . . .

The signal fact is that our young men do what they do with the diligence of enthusiasm, and with the devotion that inspires the highest courage. It is not unknown that, in the bitterness of failure, American athletes have burst into tears. When our English cousins hear of this they are apt to smile, and doubtless the practice is not altogether to be commended; but in the length and breadth of a man's experience there are only two or three things one would wish so humbly as the devotion that makes it possible. Such earnestness is the quintessence of Americanism, and is probably to be traced to the signal fact that in the struggle of life we all start with a fighting chance of coming out on top. Whatever the game, so long as it is treated as a game, nothing could be as wholesome as the spirit that tends to make our young men play it for all it is worth, to do everything that can be done to secure victory with personal honor. In later years, when these men stand for the honor of the larger alma mater, on the field of battle or in the routine of administration, it is not likely that they will altogether forget the virtues of their youth.

The superiority of English sportsmanship arises, not from the spirit of the men, but from the breadth of the development of the sports, and this, climate aside, is the result of the division of the university into colleges. The average college of only a hundred and fifty men maintains two football teams—a Rugby fifteen and an Association eleven—an eight and two torpids, a cricket eleven, and a hockey eleven. Each college has also a set of athletic games yearly. If we add the men who play golf, lawn and court tennis, rackets and fives, who swim, box, wrestle, and who shoot on the ranges of the gun club, the total of men schooled in competition reaches eighty to one hundred. A simple calculation will show that when so many are exercising daily, few are left for spectators. Not a bench is prepared, nor even a plank laid on the spongy English turf, to stand between the hanger-on and pneumonia. A man's place is in the field of strife; to take part in athletic contests is almost as much a matter of course as to bathe. Of late years there has been a tendency in England to believe that the vigor of undergraduates—and of all Englishmen, for the matter of that—is in decadence. As regards their cultivation of sports at least, the reverse is true. Contests are more numerous now than ever, and are probably more earnestly waged. What is called English decadence is in reality the increasing superiority of England's rivals.

Quite aside from the physical and moral benefit to the men engaged, this multiplication of contests has a striking effect in lessening the importance of winning or losing any particular one of them. It is more powerful than any other factor in keeping English sports free from the excesses that have so often characterized our sports. From time to time a voice is raised in America as of a prophet of despair demanding the abolition of inter-university contests. As yet the contests have not been abolished, and do not seem likely to be. Might it not be argued without impertinence that the best means of doing away with the excesses in question is not to have fewer contests, but more of them? If our universities were divided into residential units, corresponding roughly to the English colleges, the excesses in particular contests could scarcely fail to be mitigated; and what is perhaps of still higher importance, the great body of non-athletes would be brought directly under the influence of all those strong and fine traditions of undergraduate life which centre in the spirit of sportsmanship.

PRICE COLLIER:

IN ENGLAND EVERYTHING

IS DONE FOR THE MEN

1895

Price Collier was one of the most widely read of American commentators on the foreign scene. Son of a Unitarian clergyman, Collier attended the Harvard Divinity School and on graduation in 1882 held pastorates in Massachusetts for the next decade. In 1895 he went to England and the Continent; while there he became foreign editor of the then powerful *Forum*, a magazine of opinion, and thereafter devoted himself to writing and editorial work. Among his widely read books were *America and Americans from the French Point of View* (1897), and *Germany and the Germans from the American Point of View*. His book on England and the English, one of the most perceptive in the travel literature of the day, appeared in 1913. With his insatiable curiosity about foreign countries and peoples, his perspicacious intelligence, and his access to highly placed sources of information, Collier was a kind of precursor of John Gunther.

From Price Collier,*England and the English from an American Point of View* (New York, 1913), pp. 115–148.

English Home Life

On entering an Englishman's house the first thing one notices is how well his house is adapted to him. It seems to have grown up around him, as in so many cases it has, and to have taken on the folds of his character, as a coat often worn moulds itself to the figure of its owner. On entering an American's house, the first thing one notices is how well he adapts himself to his house.

In England, the establishment is carried on with a prime view to the comfort of the man, and this applies to rich and poor alike and to all conditions of society. In America the establishment is carried on with a prime view to the comfort and the exigencies of the woman. Men are more selfish than women, consequently the English home is, as a rule, at any rate from a man's point of view, more comfortable than the American home; barring of course our innumerable mechanical contrivances for heating, bathing, ventilation, cooking and so on, of which even now, not only the average English house is quite barren, but also the houses of the wealthy, both in town and country. But here again it is the woman and the servants who keep house who suffer, not the man. . . .

An Englishman is more at home in his own house than an American, first because he is by all the inmates recognized as the absolute master there, and because he spends more of his time there. He leaves it later in the morning, returns to it earlier in the day, and gives more of himself to it than does an American. An Englishman is continually going home, an American is continually going to business. Ages of social laws, and vast accretions of social distinctions have made the Englishman who can stay at home more important than the Englishman who must go to business; consequently, all Englishmen assume that they are much at home, and little at business, whether they are or not, for by so doing they loom larger on the social horizon.

The Englishman is forever planning and scheming to get home, and to stay at home, and to enjoy the privileges of his home; while the American is more apt to devote his energies to make his business a place to go to, and in which to spend himself. Here again the social lever plays its part, for in America a man is the more distinguished from his fellows the more business he has on his hands, and he, too, assumes a busy-ness sometimes out of proportion to the reality. . . .

Americans staying any time in England, whether men or women, are impressed by the fact that it is the country of men. Likewise the English, both men and women, who visit America are impressed by the fact that America is the country of women. Possibly we might deduce from this that Americans make the better husbands, and the English the better wives. But this is much too subtle a subject, and one providing too many exceptions to discuss. One may perhaps say tentatively, without much fear of contradiction, that Englishwomen take it for granted that their husbands' pleasure and comfort, and even amusements, should take first place; while the American man rather delegates the part of pleasure, comfort, and amusement to his wife, and she, perhaps, has come to look upon this often as her privilege, and sometimes, alas, as her right. Whatever the reason, the general average of home life is more comfortable in England than in America. Whether it be a matter of political economy, of free trade for example, or not, all the requirements for comfortable living are indubitably cheaper in England than in America.

People having incomes varying from $1,500 to $15,000 a year can and do live more comfortably in England than with us. In the view of the Frenchman, however, the English require more than the French. Taine writes that where a Frenchman eats a sheep and a half in a year an Englishman eats four sheep; and goes on to say: "Possess £ 20,000 in the funds here or else cut your throat. . . .

In the case of people with say less than $1,500 a year, or more than $20,000 a year, they do not profit so materially by the difference in prices, for the reason that luxury is everywhere expensive, and genteel poverty everywhere equally distressing; or even more distressing in this country where for so many months in the year the landscape looks like a charcoal drawing over which a damp sleeve has been drawn.

Nothing gives more conclusive proof of the truth of these comparisons than to notice how the English and the Americans respectively go about it to enconomize. In a large establishment in England the horses for the wife's brougham and victoria would go before the husband's hunters, while the reverse of this would be true in an American establishment compelled to make similar sacrifices. It is the husband, rather than the wife, who is looked to to advertise the family prosperity in England. It would be a very rare case indeed in America where the wife would not have more and greater variety of clothes than her husband, but this is much less true in England. Even poor men in England have more clothes than well-to-do men in America. An income of $5,000 a year in England would mean four times the amount of clothes that the possessor of the same income in America would think necessary. On the other hand, the percentage of any given income, from $3,000 to $20,000, expended by the wives and daughters for clothes, would be half to two-thirds less in England than with us. A man servant of some kind in the establishment is far more common in England than with us, and he among other things takes care of the master of the house, who is thus more easily capable of dealing with a large wardrobe and has more leisure to employ as he prefers.

Both for the reason that such service is much cheaper here, and also for the reason already given, that the man is the important person, the men are more cared for than the women, and a man servant is a common appanage of men in this country whose incomes would be deemed, and would be, as a matter of fact, quite inadequate for such an expense in America.

The last things that an Englishman willingly parts with are the appurtenances and conveniences which permit him to have his friends around him at his own table, or at his club; and this applies up and down through all but the lowest class. With us, on the contrary, the great mass of my countrymen, outside of a comparatively few dwellers in our large cities, would scarcely miss not having people to dine with them at their own table. An Englishman forced to economize would move out of a big house into a small one in order to keep certain conveniences, such as servants, a certain standard of living and a certain personal dignity, which make for his personal comfort; while an American would try to the last to stick to his big house, but cut down the number of servants and other personal conveniences by which he does not set so much store.

If one were training a race-horse to win an important event, the last thing one would economize upon would be comfortable stabling and the quality of his grooms and his feed. One is continually reminded of "training," in seeing how the hard-worked Englishman, whether in politics, business, literature, the civil service or in a profession cares for himself, and is cared for in his own house. Everything bends to make him and to keep him "fit."

Such men as the leading statesmen, diplomats, barristers, journalists, bankers, business men generally, and prelates; in short, the dignified, responsible and great ones of the earth are, so to speak, regularly groomed, and kept in condition, physically and mentally, for their arduous duties. They take frequent holidays; everything that paid service can do—and such service is astonishingly cheap here—from keeping their clothes to attending to their correspondence and their engagements, they are relieved of. . . .

We are not concerned for the moment with the comparative merits of these methods of life; they serve merely to illustrate the dominant theme. They all go to show that domestic economy in England is devised for, and directed to the aim of making the men as capable as possible of doing their work. The home is not a play-house for the women and their friends; nor a grown-up nursery for the mother and the children, but a place of rest and comfort in which the men may renew their strength. It is possibly fair to deduce from this that house-keeping as a rule in England has a more definite aim and consequently more system, and less waste of energy, and money, than is the case in the majority of American houses.

However awkward and flamboyantly dressed the Englishwoman may appear upon the boulevards of Paris; however dull she may appear when ranged alongside of her American cousin in a drawing-room, in her own house she has few superiors—unless it be in France—as a domestic business manager.

She gains this ability by previous years of training. It is the exception, rather than the rule, where both the boys and girls in an English household do not receive an allowance. It is true that no-thing permits of so many shades of meaning as the word "allowance" when thus used. It may mean anything, from a good-natured pater-nal promise to pay, which is irregularly fulfilled, to a light advance fund for gloves and bon-bons, to be followed each month, or each quarter, by the infantry and heavy artillery of dressmakers' and milliners' bills. Those who have suffered in adolescence from the one, and in maturity from the other, know what a multitude of interpretations lie between these extremes. The British interpreta-tion is, however, serious and fixed. Girls and boys alike are held pretty strictly to account and are obliged to live upon a certain fixed sum. Women coming into the management of establishments of their own are already trained to the business aspect of the situation. They have also a tremendous advantage over their American cousins, as an aid to wise expenditure, in public opinion. Nobody, from the King down, is either ashamed or afraid to be economical. Here either a man or a woman is thought to be a fool or a vulgarian who is not careful of expenditure; while in America our Negro, Irish, and other foreign servants have been clever enough to make it appear that economy is mean, and as a nation we suffer accordingly. We are fools enough to be fooled by these underlings who, driven from their own countries, come prepared to exploit ours.

Not so in England. Money is not so easily made, nor has it such earning power in England as in America, and as a consequence it is much more carefully cherished. And money buys more in England than in America. It is by no means true, as prevalent opinion leads one to believe, that money plays a greater rôle in America than in England. The "almighty dollar" receives no such obsequious homage in its native lair as does the "sovereign" in its own house of worship. Everybody takes tips in England, from the Prime Minister to whom an earldom is given, or the radical who is made a knight, down to the railway porter content with threepence. The typical American boy abroad, described by Mr. Henry James, whose frequently repeated war-cry is, "My dad's all-fired rich!" has many even more vulgar prototypes in England. The methods English men and English women will stoop to, and the humiliations they will suffer, in order to make or to get money, are not merely not practised in America, but are quite unknown there. For the very reason that money gives so much of comfort, and standing, and opportunity here, the struggle to get it is unparalleled anywhere else in the world. To have money here, no matter what the other advantages of birth or ability may be, is to add a thousand-fold to their value, while to be without it is a heart-breaking handicap. . . .

The fact that the English house is so ostensibly, and first and foremost, conducted with the aim of making the men comfortable, makes it easy to understand and to give the reasons for the greater economy practised therein. Men suffer from a far more severe strain of competition in England than with us, and economy always, whether it be economy of method, of time, or of money, is just so much saved from the imperative, for the voluntary. There is no possibility of great exertion without frequent periods of rest. This is taken into account here. In England men have more avocations, more amusements, more interests outside of the daily round of pressing business than with us. These avocations demand leisure, and economy is the mother of leisure. The percentage of men —although much less than it was twenty-five years ago—who aside from their engrossing pursuits of business or profession, devote themselves to some hobby, if one may call it so, is overwhelmingly greater than with us. . . . The number of men who raise horses, or dogs, or pigs, or sheep, or cows; who are players at cricket, golf, tennis, or rowing; who collect books, prints, or autographs, Japanese curios or odd bits of porcelain; who are studying an ancient or a modern language; who make a business of doing a bit of travelling every year; who climb mountains, or explore new countries; who go in for hunting, shooting, fishing, botany, or geology; who study some branch of archeology, or dig for the roots of a genealogical tree, is astonishingly large. Indeed the man of even moderate means who is without some such, more or less important, recreation is, one may almost say, the exception. Of course I am speaking now of men of serious pursuits. The idle club lounger is no more a stranger here than with us, and even less worth classifying. To know something about many things, and everything about something, is a good educational ideal, besides giving breadth, variety, and a saline interest to life. An Englishman's holiday is looked forward to, planned for, and provided for with some care; while all too often in America a holiday to a busy man over thirty-five is a white elephant, which he ends by turning over to his wife and daughters as a mount. . . .

The young and the old are much more together than with us. At a dinner in town, at a house party in the country, there is no dividing people by their ages. Fathers and sons, uncles and nephews, are much more at home with one another than with us, and see much more of one another, and have apparently more in common. In the Row of a morning, at the cricket-games, at the shooting and fishing and racing, at the billiard-table after dinner, the youngsters between twenty and thirty not only mingle with, but are the boon companions of, their elders. It is generally noted how much more a man of the world the English boy is than the American boy. He probably does not know as much, he certainly is not so sharp and quick, but he is far more of a man, speaking of course very generally and leaving room for exceptions. This is due to the fact that the English boy spends so much of his time with his elders. A common ground of meeting and conversation is of course sport, and in that realm prowess and experience, and not age, mark the differences between men. Here a man is merely as old as his handicap at the games he plays; and the number of "scratch" men over forty is greater than in any other country in the world. . . .

Of all nations in the world, with perhaps the exception of our own, England has had the reputation, at least, of demanding that success should be accompanied by virtue. At any rate since the days of those torpid Teutons, the Georges, this has been the case. But the strife has become so keen that even this imperative consideration is sometimes lost sight of. So long as a statesman keeps within legal bounds, he is judged rather by the power he wields than by his reputation at the club, or in his house. It may be said of course that genius always, everywhere, has been permitted a certain license, but that is not the point at issue here. The English people would never consent to be ruled by a genius, or to permit genius to be in power amongst them. Anything that is not ostentatiously, and plainly to the naked eye, commonplace, they distrust to a man. There is an easily recognized difference between power and genius; the one repres-

enting the result of organization, the other the result of temperament; and even to the former there is to-day accorded a liberty in the
realm of morals, which the great mass of the English people permit,
because they are forced to do so by exigencies of this keen competi-
tive strife. They are driven to employ their able men both at home
and abroad without too much scrutiny of their private morals. They
have been, and are, great soldiers, sailors, statesmen and pro-consuls
in England whose private lives would not endure examination. I
forbear illustrating this point. Only an Englishman would criticise
the statement, and, if he be well-informed, there are too many
examples to make it worth debating.

It may be said, without fear of successful contradiction, that if the
private life of every public man in England were submitted to the
same scrutiny that follows his public performances, there would be
more reversals of judgment than would result from the same kind of
criticism applied to public men in America. A country which is
preëminently a man's country must necessarily suffer from a man's
code of morals. Divorce is bad, to be sure, but no one who knows
England and the Continent and the arrangements—often enough
open—which take the place of the American divorce-court, would
for a moment wish to exchange the latter for the former. No man
could hold a position of supreme public trust in America whose
private life has been of the character of male sovereigns of England
for an hundred years. And be it remembered that they give the lead
to their subjects. . . .

The reasons why economy is more general in English than in
American households are scarcely more important than the results
of such economy. The best and all-sufficient result is that economy
gives leisure. System and regularity and lack of worry give men more
time to sleep, more time to eat, more time to play, and more time and
a better preparation for work. In America our first distinguished
men were from the South, where men had most leisure; and after
that from prosperous New England. And, say what one may—and
there is much to be said—in praise of the hard taskmaster, poverty, it
must be granted that the larger part of the distinguished work of the
world has been done, and is done, by men who have had, or who
have made for themselves, leisure. The man who voluntarily permits, or who is forced by circumstances to permit, things to get into
the saddle and ride, necessarily lacks the confidence and the mastery
which marks off the men who ride from the men who are ridden. . . .

English men spend more of their time with men, either for
business or pleasure, or the occupation of their leisure in other ways,

than do Americans. The American woman expects more, demands more, receives more attention, from the American man, than does the English woman from the English man. It begins in the nursery, and continues through the school age; the male animal is the favored one. More is done for him, more is expended upon him, and the household focuses its energies upon his development rather than upon that of the female. The result is the assumption of rights and privileges by the male, as over against the female, from childhood to, and through, maturity. This is a delicate thing to define, but all the more valuable as a contribution to the study of the English, because it is subtle and not easy of definition. There is an atmosphere in every household which predisposes the girls to look up to the boys, and most English women never recover from it, even where the one to whom they are expected to do reverence is openly unworthy of it.

As over against the French methods of bringing up their boys, as though they were girls, the results are in themselves sufficient comment upon which is the better system. An American may approve of the results in the bearing of the men themselves, but he is none the less tempted to wonder sometimes if the English woman is not here and there deprived of a little of all she has a right to inherit. But, to put it bluntly, this is no affair of ours. The American girls are marrying English men, and the English women are not marrying American men; and therefore comments upon the situation may be looked upon as acts of supererogation. To state the case at all demands the explanation that this is one of the prime factors in the development of the English man and in making him what we find him.

England is not only a man's country, but the English man is preëminently a man's man. The prizes here go to the soldiers, the sailors, the statesmen, the colonizers, the winners of new territory and the rulers over them, the travellers and explorers, the great churchmen and successful school-masters, to those, in short, with masculine brains and bodies. The feminine, the effeminate, and the Semitic prowess, is rewarded it is true—more of late years than ever before, be it said—but it is not the ideal of the nation. . . .

When we emphasize, therefore, certain peculiar features of their home life here, it is seen now at a glance not only that certain facts are true, but that they must be true. There would be no England without them.

That Englishmen are such hardy explorers, such persistent settlers of the waste places of the earth, attests their love of home.

They go, not because they wish to go, but because they hope to return with enough to establish a home in England.

Neither English men nor English women like the unattached and nomadic existence of the hotel and the boarding house. The proportion of Americans who could have a modest home, but who prefer the flat and stale unprofitableness of hotels and boarding houses, is, as compared with English people of the same income, vastly greater. And perhaps no one cause of the stricter economy of English households is more potent than this. To have a house and a bit of garden of one's own, an English man or woman will submit to the utmost economy of expenditure, and the most rigorously accurate system of accounts. It may be a social prejudice or an ingrained habit of the British stamp of mind, but whatever it is, there can be no doubt, that the Englishman's ideal of life is to be a free man and master of the castle of his own house.

CHARLES TUCKERMAN:
THE ENGLISHMAN
MAKES ALLOWANCES
FOR FOREIGNERS

1890s

Nephew of the famous Reverend Joseph Tuckerman, and connected with everybody in Boston, Charles Tuckerman cut a wide swath in society and literature. Born in the shadow of Boston State House, a student at the Boston Latin School and at Harvard College, Tuckerman was early caught up in travel, politics, and literature. He knew everyone, and his *Personal Recollections* contain portraits of Lincoln, Grant, Johnson, Sumner, Bancroft, and other more famous men—more famous, that is, than Tuckerman. As a young man he spent four years in China; as a middle-aged man he was the first American Minister to Greece; as an older man he was an expatriate, living most of his time in Italy.

The first thing I missed in England was the *politesse*—I refer to manners only—which, as a rule, distinguishes all classes of society in Southern Europe, and which, although often carried by the latter to an annoying extent, seems to me preferable to the phlegm and

From Charles K. Tuckerman, *Personal Recollections of Notable People at Home and Abroad, With Other Papers* (New York, 1895), I, pp. 18, 274–293.

brusquerie of a certain class of Englishmen. In France, Italy, and the Orient, the touch of the hat—frequently its entire removal—on meeting and parting, and on entering and leaving a shop, café, or club-house; the apology for anything that looks like the slightest intrusion, such as entering a railway-carriage where there are other passengers, or whenever an individual passes in front of another: these little courtesies—which I have heard an Englishman call "foreign monkey-tricks"—seem to me manly traits, indicating a proper regard for the feeling of others. No doubt much of it is mere veneering, and the same people might cut away in an emergency and offer no assistance, where an Englishman would be at your side in an instant as a friend in need. Still, the polish of external life is an immense factor towards the establishment of sympathetic relations between man and man. The eternal "*pardon*" of the foreigner, when a man passes to his seat between rows of packed travellers in a railway-carriage, gets to be a bore long before the journey is over; but I prefer this to the burly middle-class Englishman who shoves his way between one's knees, and very likely treads on one's toes, with a grunt or a growl which means, "It's *your* fault, and it can't be helped." So, too, how depressing it is to find one's only travelling companion for hours, not only dumb, but apparently utterly unconscious of your existence! He may take an opportunity of a side inspection of his companion to see if he is respectable, or safe to be shut up with, and if found to be so will "button himself up body and soul," as Washington Irving said, and straightway ignore your existence. Yet this is better than the impertinent loquacity and interrogations of the American traveller of the same class, who, with no object but harmless curiosity and his nature overflowing with *bonhomie,* succeeds in extracting from his travelling companion the particulars of his private life, where he came from, where he is going and why, before they reach the first station. ... English and American traits of character are nowhere more clearly noticeable than in the conversations between such travellers when thrown together on a journey. As a rule, the Englishman will talk altogether about himself and his own affairs, not asking a question, nor seeming to care who his companion may be. The American, on the contrary, sinks his individuality in his eagerness to obtain every possible information respecting persons and things about him. When two such travellers part company, the Englishman, very likely, exclaims to himself: "What a rum lot these Yankees are, to be sure! Awfully intelligent, but, bless me, how very inquisitive! I wonder who he is. I'd give a shilling to know." He would give a good many shillings before he would venture to ask for the information he desires, however discreetly, from the traveller himself; for to ask questions he has been taught from childhood to regard as a breach of good manners. His American companion, at parting, probably says to himself: "Singular people, these John Bulls! They'll tell you all about their personal affairs—for which I don't care a rap—and never ask a question, or express any interest whatever in yourself." . . .

A good many of the side-thrusts at foreigners proceed from a habit of criticism rather than from acrimonious feeling, and I must admit that the Englishman slurs his own countrymen behind their backs much more frequently than he does the stranger in the land. As to open political aspersions, they exceed anything I have ever observed in our own or other countries, and are so general and frequent that, although trenching upon the grossest personality, the victim seldom takes notice of them beyond retaliating by similar abusive epithets. Take a few examples: "Lord Grey declared that the three greatest rascals in the world were Lord Castlereagh, Lord Brougham, and Talleyrand." O'Connell said that "Mr. Disraeli was probably a descendant of the impenitent thief who was crucified on the cross." Another critic of the then Prime Minister declared him to be "the greatest political charlatan the world has produced." As to Mr. Gladstone, we know what epithets were applied to him by all who opposed his policy. Whenever a strong public measure is proposed or carried out, one may be sure of hearing the Prime Minister accused by the Opposition of "dragging England in the mire," an expression which was made use of in the days of Pitt and Fox, Sir Robert Peel and Palmerston. England, one might suppose, must be in a very miry condition by this time if there were any grounds muddy enough for such sweeping vituperation. . . .

An Englishman of the higher class makes it a *sine qua non* to ascertain "who's who" before giving the stranger, however respectable in appearance, the slightest excuse for claiming his acquaintance. If the latter be a foreigner, the Englishman is less particular, and may even go so far as to give him the honour of a familiar *tête-à-tête* if thrown together by themselves, as in the foreigner's case there is less fear of being bored by him afterwards. But if the stranger be one of his own countrymen, then he must indeed be guarded, lest by opening the door to personal acquaintanceship—even on a crack —he may be recognising an individual whose social status is below his own. Gradations are so marked in English society, and so jealously regarded, that conventionalism is rudely shocked by the trespass of a single barrier. I remember a certain titled English lady, on board of a Mediterranean steamer, who pushed exclusiveness to such a degree that she kept in her own cabin during the entire voyage, although the sea was as smooth as glass, coming out only at night to pace the deck on the arm of her son, an official in the Civil Service. This young man once asked me for a light for his cigar, which led to a conversation, when, discovering my nationality, he was at once transformed from a stiff, conceited prig to one of the pleasantest of companions. The next day he brought me an invitation from the *grande dame,* his mother, to visit her in her private cabin. The lady explained that she was delighted to make the acquaintance of an American on board "with whom she could converse," as she made it a rule never to make chance acquaintances with her own countrymen, "they were so apt to bore one by renewing it in England." Yet this lady was not snobbish or pretentious, but gifted with high breeding and with the most charming affability; she was simply carrying out the system of social self-preservation to which she had been educated from her youth upwards.

When the Englishman knows his man and desires his acquaintance, whether for companionship or friendship, the warmth of his nature reveals itself gradually—as a Chinaman strips off his silk robes, one after the other, with the approach of summer—and extends a confidence that is as rugged and enduring as his life. When he offers to you his hospitality he means it, and without flourish of compliment. Live or travel with him for months, and he may never let you know by a single complimentary phrase that he cares a pin's head for you; but if it comes to a test of his friendship in the hour of need, you will not find a sturdier heart of oak than beats beneath his undemonstrative and possibly unpolished exterior. Half his mannerism, or want of mannerism, is generally attributed to "shyness," but I confess I have no sympathy for this national infirmity.

1900-1910

ELIZABETH PENNELL
REMEMBERS
AUBREY BEARDSLEY
AND THE *YELLOW BOOK*

c. 1900

Around the turn of the century American artists and men of letters were more and more integrally part of the cultural life of London than at any other time in our history. London seemed to be the artistic and the literary capital of the Western world; it was where the action was. Whistler and Henry James had both left Paris for London some years earlier (Whistler was to return to Paris, but perforce), and they were joined there by the great painter John Sargent, and by the two leading illustrators of their day, Edwin Abbey and Joseph Pennell. If Henry James did not dominate the literary scene he permeated it, and it is worth remembering that the *Yellow Book,* which some claim to be considered characteristic of the *fin de siècle,* was edited by an American, Henry Harland. Elizabeth Robins of Philadelphia had married Joseph Pennell in 1884, and that year they moved to London, where they remained until 1921. Pennell was the fashionable illustrator of current books as Abbey was of classics; there is no happier combination of expatriate American talents than Henry James's *English Hours,* with almost a hundred illustrations by Pennell. Elizabeth and Joseph Pennell formed a team of

From Elizabeth Pennell, *Nights: Rome, Venice, London, Paris* (Philadelphia, 1916), pp. 177–187.

writer-illustrator who together pictured much of England, France, and even America. They wrote, too, the biography of James McNeill Whistler. In their house in Chelsea they maintained a kind of artist-writer salon, and much of the *Yellow Book* may be said to have been conceived in their hospitable if somewhat hectic quarters.

Harland was not original in wanting to set up a pulpit for himself—the originality was in the design for it. The *Yellow Book* was not like any other quarterly from which any other young man or group did his preaching.

Harland shared his pulpit. He would not have found the same design for it without Beardsley, nor would our Thursday nights, where a good deal of that design was thought out and talked out, have been the same without Beardsley. I would find it hard, even had there been no *Yellow Book,* not to remember Harland and Beardsley together. For it was from Mrs. Harland that we first heard of the wonderful youth, unknown still, an insignificant clerk in some Insurance Company, who made the most amazing drawings—it was she who first sent him to us that J. might look at his work and help him to escape from the office he hated and from the toils of Burne-Jones and the Kelmscott Press in which he was entangled.

He came, the first time, one afternoon in the winter dusk—a boy, tall and slight, long narrow pale clean-shaven face, hair parted in the middle and hanging over his forehead, nose prominent, eyes alight, certain himself of the worth of his drawings, too modest not to fear that other artists might not agree with him. The drawings in his little portfolio were mostly for the *Morte d' Arthur,* with one or two of those, now cherished by the collector, that have a hint of the Japanese under whose influence he momentarily passed. J. enjoys the reputation, which he deserves, of telling the truth always, no matter how unpleasant to those to whom he tells it. Truth to Beardsley was pleasant and his face was radiant when he left us. J. has also the courage of his convictions, and all he said to Beardsley he repeated promptly to the public in the first number of *The Studio,* a magazine started not as a pulpit but as a commercial enterprise —started, however, at the right moment to be kindled into life and steered toward success by the enthusiasm and the energy of the Young Men of the Nineties.

Beardsley was bound to become known whether articles were written about him or not. But J.'s was the first and made recognition come the sooner. The heads of many young men grow giddy with the first success; at the exultant top of the winding stair that leads to it, they no longer see those who gave them a hand when they balanced on the lowest rung. But Beardsley was not made that way. He kept his head cool, his eyesight clear. He never forgot. Gratitude coloured the friendship with us that followed, even in the days when he was one of the most talked about men in London. He knew that always by his work alone he would be judged at Buckingham Street, and to J. he brought his drawings and his books for criticism. He brought his schemes as well, just as he brought the youth not only of years but of temperament to our Thursday nights. He came almost as regularly as Henley and Henley's Young Men, adding his young voice to the uproar of discussion, as full of life as if he too, like Harland, grudged a minute of the years he knew for him were counted. In no other house where it was my pleasure to meet him did he seem to me to show to such advantage. In his own home I thought him overburdened by the scheme of decoration he had planned for it. In many houses to which he was asked he was amiable enough to assume the pose expected of him. The lion-hunters hoped that Beardsley would be like his drawings. Strange, decadent, morbid, bizarre, weird, were adjectives bestowed upon them, and he played up to the adjectives for the edification or mystification of the people who invented them and for his own infinite amusement. But with us he did not have to play up to anything and could be just the simple, natural youth he was—as simple and natural as I have always found the really great, more interested in his work than most young men, and keener for success.

I like to insist upon his simplicity because people now, who judge him by his drawings, would so much rather insist upon his perversity and his affectation. How can you reconcile that sort of thing with simplicity? They will ask, pointing to drawings of little mocking satyrs and twisted dwarfs and grotesques and extravagant forms and leering faces and a suggestion of one can hardly say what. But it might as well be asked why the mediaeval artist delighted to carve homely, familiar scenes and incidents, and worse, in the holiest places, to lavish his ingenuity upon the demons and devils above the doors leading into his great churches; why a philosopher like Rabelais chose to express the wisest thought in the most indecent fooling; why every genius does not look out upon life and the world with the same eyes and find the same method to record what he sees. Some men can only marvel with Louis Stevenson at the wide contrast between the "prim obliterated polite face of life" and its "orgiastic foundations"; others are only reconciled to it by the humour in the contrast or by the pity invoked by its victims. What makes the genius is just the fact that he looks out upon life, that he feels, that he uses his eyes, in his own way; also, that he invents his own methods of expression. Beardsley saw the satire of life, he loved the grotesque which has so gone out of date in our matter-of-fact day that we almost forget what it means, and no doubt disease gave a morbid twist to his vision and imagination. But, above all, he was young, splendidly young: young when he began work, young when he finished work. He had the curiosity as to the world and everything in it that is the divine right of youth, and he had the gaiety, the exuberance, the flamboyancy, the fun of the youth destined to do and to triumph. Already, in his later work, are signs of the passing of the first youthful stage of his art. It is suggestive to contrast the conventional landscapes with the grinning little monstrosities in some of the illustrations for the *Rape of the Lock;* the few drawings for his *Volpone* have a dignity he had not hitherto achieved.

Nobody can be surprised if some of the gaiety and exuberance and fun got no less into his manner towards the people whose habit is to shield their eyes with the spectacles of convention. Beardsley had a keen sense of humour that helped him to snatch all the joy there is in the old, time-honoured, youthful game of getting on the nerves of established respectability. Naturally, so Robert Ross, his friend, has said of him, "he possessed what is *called* an artificial manner"; that is, his manner was called affected, as was his art, because it wasn't exactly like everybody else's. I have never yet come across the genius whose manner was exactly like everybody else's, and shyness, self-consciousness, counted for something in his, at least at the start. He had only to exaggerate this manner, or mannerism, to set London talking. It was the easier because rumours quickly began to go about of the darkened room in which he worked, of his turning night into day and day into night like Huysmans's hero, and of this or of that strange habit or taste, until people began to see all sorts of things in him that weren't there, just as they read all sorts of things into his drawings that he never put into them, always seeking what they were determined to find. To many there was uncanniness in the very extent of his knowledge, in his wide reading, in his mastery of more than one art, for, if he had not been an artist, he most assuredly would have been a musician or a writer. Added to all this, was the abnormal notice he attracted almost at once, the diligence with which he was imitated and parodied and the rapidity with which a Beardsley type leaped into fashion.

Of course Beardsley enjoyed it. What youth of his age would not have enjoyed the excitement of such a success? It would have been morbid at his age not to enjoy it. He never seemed to me more simply himself than when he was relating his adventures and laughing at them with all the fresh, gay laughter of the boy—the wonderful boy—he was. Arthur Symons wrote of him, I have forgotten where, that he admired himself enormously. I should say that he was amused by himself enormously and was quite ready to pose and to bewilder for the sake of the amusement it brought him. He was never spoiled nor misled by either his fame or his notoriety.

It was so Beardsley's habit to consult J. that he would have asked advice, if Harland had not, for *The Yellow Book* which went through several stages of its preliminary planning in the old Buckingham Street chambers. Among the vivid memories of our Thursday nights one is of Harland taking J. apart for long, intimate discussions in a corner of the studio, and another of Beardsley taking him off for confidences as intimate and long, and my impression in looking back, though I may be mistaken, is that each had his personal little scheme for a journal of his own before he decided to share it with the other. It was characteristic of the friendliness of both that they should have insisted upon J. figuring in the first number. As vivid in my memory is the warm spring morning when Beardsley, his face beaming with joy, called to give me an early copy of this first number, with a little inscription from him on the fly-leaf—I have just taken down the volume from the near book shelf—"To Mrs. Pennell from Aubrey Beardsley" I read, as commonplace an inscription as ever artist or author wrote, but, reading it, I see as if it were yesterday the sunlit Buckingham Street room where I used to work, William Penn curled up on my desk, and, coming in the door, the radiant youth with the gay-covered book in his hands. . . .

I am not sure what the *Yellow Book* means to others—to those others who buy it now in the thirteen volumes of the new edition and prize it as a strange record of a strange period, from which they feel as far removed as we felt from the Sixties. But to me, the bright yellow-bound volumes mean youth, gay, irresponsible, credulous, hopeful youth, and Thursday night at Buckingham Street in full swing.

CECELIA BEAUX:
A VISIT WITH THE DARWINS
IN CAMBRIDGE

c. 1900

Cambridge, as Noel Annan has explained, has long been dominated by half a dozen great academic families, all almost inextricably interconnected and all with an astonishing ability to maintain their distinction generation after generation. Among these the Darwins have played one of the leading roles, and Miss Beaux's recollection of a visit at Newnham Grange, on the banks of the Cam, gives us something of that feeling of intimacy that we get from *Period Piece* by that other Philadelphia lady, Gwen Raverat. Like so many distinguished painters of her generation, Cecelia Beaux studied at the Philadelphia Academy of Fine Arts before moving to Paris to study at the Académie Julian. In 1891 she set up an atelier in New York and speedily became a fashionable painter; contemporaries regarded her as fully the equal of Chase and Sargent, an estimate which has not held up. Whatever the future may think of her portraits of Theodore Roosevelt, Clemenceau, and others, it cannot but be grateful to her for her charming autobiographical *Background with Figures,* from which we take this account of a visit to Cambridge sometime in the first decade of the new century.

From Cecelia Beaux, *Background with Figures* (Boston, 1930), pp. 179, 181–190.

Upon the dual origin which was the birthright Nature had awarded me, France had absorbed and fixed a pursuing lover, but one who remembered the keen onset of an unexpected emotion felt on her approach during a night of fog on her other parent shore. Hidden by night, and a heavy veil besides, the name if not the sight of England had sounded—one of those oracular messages straight from the sources of destiny that pierce and settle in the heart and are never withdrawn from it. Lost as I was in the very present claims of the *cours,* and my abandonment to the magic of even the little I then knew of France, the name had caught me a second time when an English girl at the *cours,* half demented with homesickness, had cried out, in a broken voice, "England! . . . England! . . ." The others had laughed, and teased her; I did not. I seemed to know her pain and love, and what caused it.

During the early spring days of our second year in Paris, I heard from an old friend in Cambridge, an American girl who had married George, the eldest of the sons of Charles Darwin. She demanded a visit, and soon, as the gay season in Cambridge was approaching. Her husband was at that time Plumian Professor of Mathematical Astronomy, Fellow of Trinity, and as I had always known, one of the leading men in the University. They, with their four children, lived at Newnham Grange, through whose garden the Cam, hidden by high banks and big trees, pursued its quiet and narrow way. . . .

My first waking in the big, chintz-hung guest-room at Newnham Grange is one of the jewel-set markers of memory. It was a near-by cuckoo-clock that woke me (I found out later that it was the fellow himself), and a pink-calico-clad houri came next, pulling aside curtains and arranging the bath. The sun poured in, and through its beams I could see across a meadow and under huge trees. Another window was hung, without, by a rich drapery of lilac wistaria, in full bloom, and when I sprang from my bed and put my head out, there was a cherry tree full of 'ripe ones,' just outside, also bird song; and a robin, making the best of the feast, superseded the cuckoo, and children of English voice and speech were in the garden below.

My friend Maud had discovered that for brittle-nerved Americans the day began too soon if it opened by family breakfast downstairs. She did not ask me if I shared her opinion, and, although her husband had a slightly contemptuous smile on the subject, we, in our separate nests, had trays with full English menus, and descended when we pleased before luncheon: a life-saving plan. Workers, by nature, cannot be agreeable all day, even when they have been kindly presented with the luxury of idleness. One must be a professional visitor to have a steady appetite for conversation. The English manage, by becoming monosyllabic, and without reproach. I watched the very nice-looking little wife of one of the most agreeable of the young professors, and saw that she did not speak at all during the whole evening (it was a dinner). She fell to my lot before the men came in, and I could glean nothing but "yes" and "no," even by varied effort; but she did not seem either shy or embarrassed, or to feel that she was failing in an obligation.

I soon gave up trying to express all I felt. I knew myself to be a plant whose roots were expanding in a deep warm soil, its own, but never felt before. Beauty, native and homogeneous—not a jarring or irrelevant passage anywhere—was always present. Mr. Darwin left his protected study and library, where I soon observed that he was steadily concealed, and led me about great courts, and by charming bridges over the still waters where undergraduates floated with dog and book. Strange that, under the stately towers, gateways, and walls of Gothic elegance, the England I already knew could circulate and look at home. Was this because it was all a slowly accumulated inheritance, without break, from a germ literally prehistoric? To one nurtured on the intimate account (it seemed to be almost contemporaneous) of Thackeray, Leech, and Du Maurier, a familiar figure was to be met at every corner. But in the general summing-up of what one might call essential England, in such a place, especially in silent, deep-shaded courts and alleys, Tennyson was above all present. His lines they were that kept rising in my mind, and I continually heard also fragments of Matthew Arnold's deep-toned elegies. From the old bells of Great Saint Mary's, I heard the Westminster chimes (that is, they are so called) for the first time, and have suffered in hearing them, since then, calling for such different reason, from the many stories of commerce.

As these fragments of experience are those of a light-hearted young person, perhaps she may be pardoned for a few impressions *sur place*—

> They have had people to dine both evenings. For the first, there were two men only, both very distinguished scholars; Mr. Robertson Smith, the Librarian who contains the whole British Encyclopaedia, and a Mr. Middleton of Middleton, a Professor and Lecturer on the Fine Arts. They look middle-aged, but are not. Mr. R. S. is like a little Scotch terrier, with every hair of him a telephone wire into storehouses full of facts. You only have to take off the

receiver, and it comes pouring out in a monotonous voice, nothing about him moving but his lower jaw. Mr. M. is long, narrow, gentle, bald, and has much more temperament and no less "larnin'." I wore my blue dress, and had my gold combs in my hair, otherwise "no jewels." I looked rather nice. Mr. Middleton knew it and observed me furtively during dinner. But Mr. R. S. would just as leave I had been bound in calf.

Luncheon to-day with Mr. Middleton. Mr. Darwin went with us. Maud appeared in white muslin and lace, white hat and feathers —an English beauty, if she *is* American, with her grand braids of golden hair and splendid blue eyes. I was sorry for her that her visiting friend had nothing effective to wear. In a corner of the Great Court of Kings, we found Mr. M.'s rooms. There was one other man, a Mr. Wilfrid Blunt, well known in politics here; had much to do with Araby Bey in the East; great Home-Ruler, has been in prison for four months for having been thought to have stirred up insurrection in Ireland. His meekness, Mr. M., received us very graciously, in his little rooms full of early Italian and Renaissance reproductions, etc. The luncheon was very informal, the men guests and host waiting on the table. They put the finished dishes on the hearth-rug, with the elegance of established custom in a refined *milieu.* (By these simplifications, "Fellows," who are never well off are able to entertain in their rooms very delightfully.)

After luncheon Mr. M. showed us his collection, and we all talked very learnedly. Mr. W. B. thought he knew something about Art, too, and condescended to a remark now and then. Then we all went to King's Chapel.

Here my feeble pen refused to lisp platitudes, and does still. It was the custom at Newnham to go to King's Chapel for Sunday morning service, and to Trinity for evensong. This made Sunday for me the best of days at all points. I had heard scarcely any music since leaving America, and this in itself would have fixed my happiness, even without the satisfaction of all the rest. Our party was Maud, the three older children, and myself, Mr. D. accompanying, but, as a Fellow and much besides, occupying a different throne. But we, too, as his family and adherents, were also among the chosen—we might pass under the great dividing Gothic screen where was the organ (or part of it), leaving the congregation in the *anti-chambre* of the chapel. The *élite,* who were about the number to fill the choir-stalls, might take their places in these, under high black-oaken canopies, behind reading-desks of the same, and turn the leaves of enormous in-folio prayer-books which lay upon them. But the most lofty and beautiful of all Gothic in England, and the succession of nearly as lofty windows, with glass, not brilliant, but satisfying to the limit of desire in design and tone, were subduant to any pride of place an inter-loper might feel in finding herself as near to occupying a Bishop's throne as she would ever come.

How delightful the walk home, joined by one's new friends among the Fellows, to be escorted to the Backs, and the Fellows' Garden of Trinity. How seldom are Peace and Novelty found hand in hand, especially when both are wrapt in beauty. At Newnham there was no retirement after this, for the rest of the day. Guests to luncheon, callers all the afternoon. Tea, in such weather, in the garden, under the copper beech, which hung over the river. Having come directly from an *atelier* in Paris, and being rather full of all which this implied, I began by expanding upon what, even in new and fascinating scenes, I could not forget. But I soon found that a polite silence followed any mention of French Art, and the Lecturer on the Fine Arts had never heard of Bastien Le Page, or any other contemporary artist just across the Channel. But I had little time for any but instant impressions. I had expected to find a kind of static calm in England, but every one, including myself, seemed to be busy. In spite of the telephone, Maud was constantly writing and posting notes. They would be delivered in an hour or two. Bicycles continu-ally flew by the windows which gave on the road, and were generally pedalled by undergraduates, but bulging scholastic gowns, mortar boards, and flying grey beards were to be seen as often, and were equally fearless and hurried: and, of course, there were all the girls from Girton and Newnham Colleges, whom one should honor for their preoccupation with matters more important than the fit of shirts and shirt-waists.

Even old ladies going out to tea might be met wheeling steadily in black lace and floating veils. Another swift goer was the butcher's cart. The pony never trotted other than briskly, and I enjoyed the sharp patter of his hoofs on Silverton Bridge. Pedestrians also stepped forth eagerly, as if just starting on a ten-mile walk, and were generally in pairs and very importantly conversing.

Noteworthy functions followed each other swiftly. The dinner at the Vice-Chancellor's Lodge soon occurred. The D.'s said it would be dull, but that I should see one of this kind. The Vice-Chancellor's "Lodge" was Pembroke College, historic with a poignant signifi-cance, for Bishop Ridley had been led from it to the fires of Smith-field.

It was a big house; dark carved oak, everywhere. Many menservants were standing about, but not in livery, and before I had time to notice this, I observed a *distingué*-looking young person at the top of the staircase, saying to myself, "At least, there is one young one, and I hope he will fall to my lot." But, alas, as we passed him he murmured to Mr. Darwin, "This way please, sir." Our host and hostess were a nice, comfortable-looking couple, the Vice-Chancellor` a small, stout, elderly gentleman, with a high collar and wearing bands with his otherwise worldly, evening coat.

Every one [my letter says] looked very proper, and there were no frumps, though some of the coiffures were very queer. The men were mostly elderly, but they gave me the only youngish one, a Scotchman, very clever and talkable, and as I had on my other side an eccentric and jolly professor of anatomy, I had a "monstrous good time." Of course, it was a huge table. (Maud told me there were thirty-seven guests), and covered with massive silver and flowers. Among other fruits, one muskmelon was offered with the faintest shade of importance. Its seeds remained as Nature had made them, but it did not blush for this informality, and had a very delicate flavor. When the "cloth" (which means long strips of damask linen laid along the edge of the table) were removed, the rich dark mahogany shone out, with resplendent age-old *patine*. Two servants then carried about a massive silver ewer, and a basin of equal proportion and richness, one of the men assisting with a long damask napkin. Each guest held a corner of his own serviette in the trickling stream from the ewer, and wiped his hands and lips, but the male guests also dipped their fingers in the basin, and touched the backs of their ears. This was far more picturesque than finger-bowls, and more delicate than the French *rinse-bouche*. I made as if it was no more a novelty to me than to the other guests, whose conversation flowed on uninterruptedly, but soon I could not refrain from asking Mr. Neil what it meant. "An old custom," he said, "only surviving at formal functions at Pembroke, and dating from times when, in order to continue drinking, men were glad to cool their blood by external applications of cold water." This was being "Wet," indeed, and a suggestion for Anti-Prohibitionists.

I was very proud in being taken to call on Mrs. Darwin, the wife of Charles, and mother of many sons, of whom my host was the senior. She was very old and received me in a wheeled chair, but had lost nothing of what had made her a fitting mate for such a man. She instantly reminded me of my own grandmother, and I realized how straight the line was of my English birthright, and how close. She had the same grand sort of sweetness, and the long lines of forehead and nose, accented by the same bands of hair, and even a similar bonnet, though it must be admitted that Mrs. Leavitt's *chapeau* was a little more elegant than Mrs. Darwin would have concerned herself with. She inquired if I had done any sketching in England, and would have been surprised if I had told her that I had not thought of it, being too much occupied with *looking*. Every one expected that I would have drawings to show, and could not believe that I had brought no "examples" with me, but soon I had done a little something, and vindicated in some degree this omission. I did a pastel of Maud in the garden, in her white hat, under the copper beech. What charming mornings we spent! George Duckworth, a beautiful and fascinating youth, and an adherent of Maud's, sat by us, reading aloud, while I stood working on the little picture. I also did a drawing of Billy, the youngest boy. All this prolonged my visit, but brought demands that I should return and undertake commissions, which I was fain to do.

Much restored by a little work, I entered with renewed vivacity into the functions and gaieties of the short Cambridge season. Maud urged me to come back for the "Long" if I must return to Paris. I had begun to feel the reality of opening friendships, and the work I might do was full of allure to me. Work and play seemed here at their best—how could I resist them! . . .

My good friends in Cambridge had made a tempting plan for my return. I was to have "the Mill," which was an antique structure by the water, on the edge of the garden at Newnham Grange, and far outdating it in age. This was to be my studio. Two ladies wished to pose for me, one of them being Mr. Darwin's sister-in-law, the other a Mrs. Goodheart, a neighbor and friend. I knew them both. Each, though not having actual beauty, was an exquisite type of character and grace. I longed to try what was so new to me in type, and also bearing the stamp of a remote civilization and breeding. Mrs. Goodheart was breaking through an ironclad plan in order to accomplish the sittings at all, and should begin at once. With a brimming beaker of hope and energy, I rushed back in a week, my cousin with me, sailing postponed, all plans changed. It was to be England for as much time as the work, or rather the adventure, required.

I insisted on our taking lodgings, as we were two, and this in itself turned out rather fun also. Ashton House was a small brick dwelling in a shady street, only a stone's throw from Newnham. It is difficult to refrain from recounting the details of our life in lodgings. For the pen of Dickens, it was a worthy subject, and as at Newnham, the procession which I had thought invented by him, Thomas Hardy, and Leech, passed my window continually. "Yesterday being market day, carriers' carts full of people were abundant, also Leech's greengrocers, and the well-known butcher's boy balancing his familiar tray, and holding sweet converse with the white-capped maids opposite, who stand down in the area looking up and grasping the railings just as in the pictures." My early intimacy with *Punch* (which has never waned) has made me familiar with England in the social grade which has been immortalized by many of her best writers and draughtsmen. The policeman is an old friend, Leech having *seen* him in the full-flavored essence of his humanity. The women are almost never so charming as Du Maurier made them, and I saw no queenly governesses and nursemaids, but his well-born girls from twelve to fourteen are often visible, and always lovely, and dressed with the greatest freedom and simplicity, and as unconscious as "Alice." The English got the start of the rest of the world in this, and girls at that age always held themselves well.

JACK LONDON:

"HERE . . . IS
WHERE THE BLOOD
IS BEING SHED"

1903

Jack London was, in his day, one of the three or four most popular writers in America; he remained, long after his day, the most popular of American writers in the Soviet Union. A waif, a vagabond, a hobo, an "oyster pirate," a jailbird, London managed, somehow, to discover that he had literary talent and to exploit that talent to the hilt. Without formal education he did manage one year at the University of California, but abandoned that experience in favor of participation in the Klondike gold rush. All these childhood and youthful experiences provided him with an inexhaustible body of copy for his later stories and novels. He made his reputation with a story in the *Atlantic Monthly* in 1899; in the next four years he managed to bring out eight volumes of stories and novels, among them the fantastically popular *Call of the Wild*. In 1902, London, now a figure of world renown, visited England to see for himself what was the lot of the poor in that country; his report, *The People of the Abyss,* confirmed the worst suspicions of all who looked on

From Jack London, *The People of the Abyss* (New York and London, 1903), pp. 250–262, 283–288.

England as the land of privilege. With prosperity there came a slackening of London's powers and abilities, yet before his untimely death at the age of forty he had written some fifty volumes of novels, stories, travel, and social criticism.

The Precariousness of Life

What do you work at? You look ill.
It's me lungs. I make sulphuric acid.

You are a salt-cake man?
Yes.
Is it hard work?
It is damned hard work.

Why do you work at such a slavish trade?
I am married. I have children. Am I to starve and let them?

Why do you lead this life?
I am married. There's a terrible lot of men out of work in St. Helen's.

What do you call hard work?
My work. *You* come and heave them three-hundredweight lumps with a fifty-pound bar, in that heat at the furnace door, and try it.
I will not. I am a philosopher.
Oh! Well, thee stick to t' job. Ours is t' vary devil.
—*From interviews with workmen by Robert Blatchford*

I was talking with a very vindictive man. In his opinion, his wife had wronged him and the law had wronged him. The merits and morals of the case are immaterial. The meat of the matter is that she had obtained a separation, and he was compelled to pay ten shillings each week for the support of her and the five children. "But look you," said he to me, "wot'll 'appen to 'er if I don't py up the ten shillings? S'posin', now, just s'posin' a accident 'appens to me, so I cawn't work. S'posin' I get a rupture, or the rheumatics, or the cholera. Wot's she going' to do, eh? Wot's she going' to do?"

He shook his head sadly. "No 'ope for 'er. The best she cawn do is the work'ouse, an' that's 'ell. An' if she don't go to the work'ouse, it'll be worse 'ell. Come along 'ith me an' I'll show you women sleepin' in a passage, a dozen of 'em. An' I'll show you worse, wot she'll come to if anythin' 'appens to me and the ten shillings."

The certitude of this man's forecast is worthy of consideration. He knew conditions sufficiently to know the precariousness of his wife's grasp on food and shelter. For her the game was up when his working capacity was impaired or destroyed. And when this state of affairs is looked at in its larger aspect, the same will be found true of hundreds of thousands and even millions of men and women living amicably together and coöperating in the pursuit of food and shelter.

The figures are appalling; 1,800,000 people in London live on the poverty line and below it, and another 1,000,000 live with one week's wages between them and pauperism. In all England and Wales, eighteen per cent of the whole population are driven to the parish for relief, and in London, according to the statistics of the London Cóunty Council, twenty-one per cent of the whole population are driven to the parish for relief. Between being driven to the parish for relief and being an out-and-out pauper there is a great difference, yet London supports 123,000 paupers, quite a city of folk in themselves. One in every four in London dies on public charity, while 939 out of every 1000 in the United Kingdom die in poverty; 8,000,000 simply struggle on the ragged edge of starvation, and 20,000,000 more are not comfortable in the simple and clean sense of the word.

It is interesting to go more into detail concerning the London people who die on charity. In 1886, and up to 1893, the percentage of pauperism to population was less in London than in all England; but since 1893, and for every succeeding year, the percentage of pauperism to population has been greater in London than in all England. Yet, from the Registrar General's Report for 1886, the following figures are taken:

Out of 81,951 deaths in London (1884)—

In workhouses	9,909
In hospitals	6,559
In lunatic asylums	278
Total in public refuges	16,746

Commenting on these figures, a Fabian writer says: "Considering that comparatively few of these are children, it is probable that one in every three London adults will be driven into one of these refuges to die, and the proportion in the case of the manual labor class must of course be still larger."

These figures serve somewhat to indicate the proximity of the average worker to pauperism. Various things make pauperism. An advertisement, for instance, such as this, appearing in yesterday morning's paper: "Clerk wanted, with knowledge of shorthand, typewriting, and invoicing; wages ten shillings ($2.50) a week. Apply by letter," etc. And in today's paper I read of a clerk, thirty-five years of age and an inmate of a London workhouse, brought before a magistrate for non-performance of task. He claimed that he had done his various tasks since he had been an inmate; but when the master set him to breaking stones, his hands blistered, and he could not finish the task. He had never been used to an implement heavier than a pen, he said. The magistrate sentenced him and his blistered hands to seven days' hard labor.

Old age, of course, makes pauperism. And then there is the accident, the thing happening, the death or disablement of the husband, father, and breadwinner. Here is a man, with a wife and three children, living on the ticklish security of twenty shillings ($5.00) per week—and there are hundreds of thousands of such families in London. Perforce, to even half exist, they must live up to the last penny of it, so that a week's wages, $5.00, is all that stands between this family and pauperism or starvation. The thing happens, the father is struck down, and what then? A mother with three children can do little or nothing. Either she must hand her children over to society as juvenile paupers, in order to be free to do something adequate for herself, or she must go to the sweat-shops for work which she can perform in the vile den possible to her reduced income. But with the sweat-shops, married women who eke out their husband's earnings, and single women who have but themselves to support, determine the scale of wages. And this scale of wages, so determined, is so low that the mother and her three children can live only in positive beastliness and semi-starvation, till decay and death end their suffering.

To show that this mother, with her three children to support, cannot compete in the sweating industries, I instance from the current newspapers the two following cases. A father indignantly writes that his daughter and a girl companion receive 17 cents per gross for making boxes. They made each day four gross. Their expenses were 16 cents for carfare, 4 cents for stamps, 5 cents for glue, and 2 cents for string, so that all they earned between them was 42 cents, or a daily wage each of 21 cents. In the second case, before the Luton Guardians a few days ago, an old woman of seventy-two appeared, asking for relief. "She was a straw hat maker, but had been compelled to give up the work owing to the price she obtained for them—namely, 4½ cents each. For that price she had to provide plait trimmings and make and finish the hats.

Yet this mother and her three children we are considering, have done no wrong that they should be so punished. They have not sinned. The thing happened, that is all; the husband, father, and bread-winner, was struck down. There is no guarding against it. It is fortuitous. A family stands so many chances of escaping the bottom of the Abyss, and so many chances of falling plump down to it. The chance is reducible to cold, pitiless figures, and a few of these figures will not be out of place.

Sir A. Forwood calculates that—

> 1 of every 1400 workmen is killed annually.
> 1 of every 2500 workmen is totally disabled.
> 1 of every 300 workmen is permanently partially disabled.
> 1 of every 8 workmen is temporarily disabled 3 or 4 weeks.

But these are only the accidents of industry. The high mortality of the people who live in the Ghetto plays a terrible part. The average age at death among the people of the West End is fifty-five years; the average age of death among the people of the East End is thirty years. That is to say, the person in the West End has twice the chance for life that the person has in the East End. Talk of war! The mortality in South Africa and the Philippines fades away to insignificance. Here, in the heart of peace, is where the blood is being shed; and here not even the civilized rules of warfare obtain, for the women and children and babes in the arms are killed just as ferociously as the men are killed. War! In England, every year, 500,000 men, women, and children, engaged in the various industries, are killed and disabled, or are injured to disablement by disease.

In the West End eighteen per cent of the children die before five years of age; in the East End fifty-five per cent of the children die before five years of age. And there are streets in London where, out of every one hundred children born in a year, fifty die during the next year; and of the fifty that remain, twenty-five die before they are five years old. Slaughter! Herod did not do quite so badly—his was a mere fifty per cent bagatelle mortality.

That industry causes greater havoc with human life than battle does no better substantiation can be given than the following extract from a recent report of the Liverpool Medical Officer, which is not applicable to Liverpool alone:

> In many instances little if any sunlight could get to the courts, and the atmosphere within the dwellings was always foul, owing largely to the saturated condition of the walls and ceilings, which for so many years had absorbed the exhalations of the occupants into their porous material. Singular testimony to the absence of sunlight in these courts was furnished by the action of the Parks and Gardens Committee, who desired to brighten the homes of the poorest class by gifts of growing flowers and window-boxes; but these gifts could not be made in courts such as these, *as flowers and plants were susceptible to the unwholesome surroundings, and would not live.*

Mr. George Haw has compiled the following table on the three St. George's parishes (London parishes):

	Percentage of Population Overcrowded	Death Rate per 1000
St. George's West	10	13.2
St. George's South	35	23.7
St. George's East	40	26.4

Then there are the "dangerous trades," in which countless workers are employed. Their hold on life is indeed precarious—far, far more precarious than the hold of the twentieth-century soldier on life. In the linen trade, in the preparation of the flax, wet feet and wet clothes cause an unusual amount of bronchitis, pneumonia, and severe rheumatism; while in the carding and spinning departments the fine dust produces lung-disease in the majority of cases, and the woman who starts carding at seventeen or eighteen begins to break up and go to pieces at thirty. The chemical laborers, picked from the strongest and most splendidly built men to be found, live, on an average, less than forty-eight years.

Says Dr. Arlidge, of the potter's trade: "Potter's dust does not kill suddenly, but settles, year after year, a little more firmly into the lungs, until at length a case of plaster is formed. Breathing becomes more and more difficult and depressed, and finally ceases."

Steel dust, stone dust, clay dust, alkali dust, fluff dust, fibre dust—all these things kill, and they are more deadly than machine-guns and pom-poms. Worst of all is the lead dust in the white lead trades. Here is a description of the typical dissolution of a young, well-developed girl who goes to work in a white lead factory:

Here, after a varying degree of exposure, she becomes anaemic. It may be that her gums show a very faint blue line, or perchance her teeth and gums are perfectly sound, and no blue line is discernible. Coincidently with the anaemia she has been getting thinner, but so gradually as scarcely to impress itself upon her or her friends. Sickness, however, ensues, and headaches, growing in intensity, are developed. These are frequently attended by obscuration of vision or temporary blindness. Such a girl passes into what appears to her friends and medical adviser as ordinary hysteria. This gradually deepens without warning, until she is suddenly seized with a convulsion, beginning in one-half of the face, then involving the arm, next the leg of the same side of the body, until the convulsion, violent and purely epileptic form in character, becomes universal. This is attended by loss of consciousness, out of which she passes into a series of convulsions, gradually increasing in severity, in one of which she dies—or consciousness, partial or perfect, is regained, either, it may be, for a few minutes, a few hours, or days, during which violent headache is complained of, or she is delirious and excited, as in acute mania, or dull and sullen as in melancholia, and requires to be roused, when she is found wandering, and her speech is somewhat imperfect. Without further warning, save that the pulse, which has become soft, with nearly the normal number of beats, all at once becomes low and hard; she is suddenly seized with another convulsion, which she dies, or passes into a state of coma from which she never rallies. In another case the convulsions will gradually subside, the headache disappears and the patient recovers, only to find that she has completely lost her eyesight, a loss that may be temporary or permanent.

And here are a few specific cases of white lead poisoning:

Charlotte Rafferty, a fine, well-grown young woman with a splendid constitution—who had never had a day's illness in her life—became a white lead worker. Convulsions seized her at the foot of the ladder in the works. Dr. Oliver examined her, found the blue line along her gums, which shows that the system is under the influence of the lead. He knew that the convulsions would shortly return. They did so, and she died.

Mary Ann Toler—a girl of seventeen, who had never had a fit in her life—three times became ill and had to leave off work in the factory. Before she was nineteen she showed symptoms of lead poisoning—had fits, frothed at the mouth, and died.

Mary A., an unusually vigorous woman, was able to work in the lead factory for *twenty years,* having colic once only during that time. Her eight children all died in early infancy from convulsions. One morning, whilst brushing her hair, this woman suddenly lost all power in both her wrists.

Eliza H., aged twenty-five, *after five months* at lead works, was seized with colic. She entered another factory (after being refused by the first one) and worked on uninterruptedly for two years. Then the former symptoms returned, she was seized with convulsions, and died in two days of acute lead poisoning.

Mr. Vaughan Nash, speaking of the unborn generation, says: "The children of the white lead worker enter the world, as a rule, only to die from the convulsions of lead poisoning—they are either born prematurely, or die within the first year."

And, finally, let me instance the case of Harriet A. Walker, a young girl of seventeen, killed while leading a forlorn hope on the industrial battlefield. She was employed as an enamelled ware brusher, wherein lead poisoning is encountered. Her father and brother were both out of employment. She concealed her illness, walked six miles a day to and from work, earned her seven or eight shillings per week, and died, at seventeen.

Depression in trade also plays an important part in hurling the workers into the Abyss. With a week's wages between a family and pauperism, a month's enforced idleness means hardship and misery almost undescribable, and from the ravages of which the victims do not always recover when work is to be had again. Just now the daily papers contain the report of a meeting of the Carlisle Branch of the Docker's Union, wherein it is stated that many of the men, for months past, have not averaged a weekly income of more than $1.00 to $1.25. The stagnated state of the shipping industry in the port of London is held accountable for this condition of affairs.

To the young working-man or working-woman, or married couple, there is no assurance of happy or healthy middle life, nor of solvent old age. Work as they will, they cannot make their future secure. It is all a matter of chance. Everything depends upon the thing happening, the thing with which they have nothing to do. Precaution cannot fend it off, nor can wiles evade it. If they remain on the industrial battlefield they must face it and take their chance against heavy odds. Of course, if they are favorably made and are not tied by kinship duties, they may run away from the industrial battlefield. In which event, the safest thing the man can do is to join the army; and for the woman, possibly, to become a Red Cross nurse or go into a nunnery. In either case they must forego home and children and all that makes life worth living and old age other than a nightmare.

A Vision of the Night

All these were years ago little red-colored, pulpy infants, capable of being kneaded, baked, into any social form you chose.
—*Carlyle*

Late last night I walked along Commercial Street from Spital-fields to Whitechapel, and still continuing south, down Leman Street to the docks. And as I walked I smiled at the East End papers, which, filled with civic pride, boastfully proclaim that there is nothing the matter with the East End as a living place for men and women.

It is rather hard to tell a tithe of what I saw. Much of it is untellable. But in a general way I may say that I saw a nightmare, a fearful slime that quickened the pavement with life, a mess of unmentionable obscenity that put into eclipse the "nightly horror" of Piccadilly and the Strand. It was a menagerie of garmented bipeds that looked something like humans and more like beasts, and to complete the picture, brass-buttoned keepers kept order among them when they snarled too fiercely.

I was glad the keepers were there, for I did not have on my "seafaring" clothes, and I was what is called a "mark" for the creatures of prey that prowled up and down. At times, between keepers, these males looked at me sharply, hungrily, gutter-wolves that they were, and I was afraid of their hands, of their naked hands, as one may be afraid of the paws of a gorilla. They reminded me of gorillas. Their bodies were small, ill-shaped, and squat. There were no swelling muscles, no abundant thews and wide-spreading shoulders. They exhibited, rather, an elemental economy of nature, such as the cave-men must have exhibited. But there was strength in those meagre bodies, the ferocious, primordial strength to clutch and gripe and tear and rend. When they spring upon their human prey they are known even to bend the victim backward and double its body till the back is broken. They possess neither conscience nor sentiment, and they will kill for a half-sovereign, without fear or favor, if they are given but half a chance. They are a new species, a breed of city savages. The streets and houses, alleys and courts, are their hunting grounds. As valley and mountain are to the natural savage, street and building are valley and mountain to them. The slum is their jungle, and they live and prey in the jungle.

The dear soft people of the golden theatres and wonder-mansions of the West End do not see these creatures, do not dream that they exist. But they are here, alive, very much alive in their jungle. And woe the day, when England is fighting in her last trench, and her able-bodied men are on the firing-line! For on that day they will crawl out of their dens and lairs, and the people of the West End will see them, as the dear soft aristocrats of Feudal France saw them and asked one another, "Whence came they?" "Are they men?"

But they were not the only beasts that ranged the menagerie. They were only here and there, lurking in dark courts and passing like gray shadows along the walls; but the women from whose rotten loins they spring were everywhere. They whined insolently, and in maudlin tones begged me for pennies, and worse. They held carouse in every boozing ken, slatternly, unkempt, bleary-eyed, and tousled, leering and gibbering, overspilling with foulness and corruption, and, gone in debauch, sprawling across benches and bars, unspeakably repulsive, fearful to look upon.

And there were others, strange, weird faces and forms and twisted monstrosities that shouldered me on every side, inconceivable types of sodden ugliness, the wrecks of society, the perambulating carcasses, the living deaths—women, blasted by disease and drink till their shame brought not tu'pence in the open mart; and men, in fantastic rags, wrenched by hardship and exposure out of all semblance of men, their faces in a perpetual writhe of pain, grinning idiotically, shambling like apes, dying with every step they took and each breath they drew. And there were young girls, of eighteen and twenty, with trim bodies and faces yet untouched with twist and bloat, who had fetched the bottom of the Abyss plump, in one swift fall. And I remember a lad of fourteen, and one of six or seven, white-faced and sickly, homeless, the pair of them, who sat upon the pavement with their backs against a railing and watched it all.

The unfit and the unneeded! Industry does not clamor for

them. There are no jobs going begging through lack of men and women. The dockers crowd at the entrance gate, and curse and turn away when the foreman does not give them a call. The engineers who have work pay six shillings a week to their brother engineers who can find nothing to do; 514,000 textile workers oppose a resolution condemning the employment of children under fifteen. Women, and plenty to spare, are found to toil under the sweat-shop masters for tenpence a day of fourteen hours. Alfred Freeman crawls to muddy death because he loses his job. Ellen Hughes Hunt prefers Regent's Canal to Islington Workhouse. Frank Cavilla cuts the throats of his wife and children because he cannot find work enough to give them food and shelter.

The unfit and the unneeded! The miserable and despised and forgotten, dying in the social shambles. The progeny of prostitution—of the prostitution of men and women and children, of flesh and blood, and sparkle and spirit; in brief, the prostitution of labor. If this is the best that civilization can do for the human, then give us howling and naked savagery. Far better to be a people of the wilderness and desert, of the cave and the squatting-place, than to be a people of the machine and the Abyss.

STARK YOUNG:

"THE GRACE AND SURENESS
OF LIVING"

c. 1904

Stark Young, one of the most distinguished novelists of his generation, was a man of wide interests and varied talents. A Southerner, but with New England antecedents, he studied at the University of Mississippi and later at Columbia University, and then spent a year or two at Oxford. He returned, about 1905, to teach English literature and drama at the University of Mississippi, the University of Texas, and eventually at Amherst College, where he was a colleague of Robert Frost. In the twenties he abandoned teaching for criticism; he was for many years dramatic critic for the *New Republic,* and learned Russian in order to translate Chekhov. He is best remembered, no doubt, as author of *So Red the Rose,* one of the best novels to come out of the South in his generation.

It was during this London visit, so enriched by Mrs. Prothero's hospitality, that I had my first chance to realize what English kindness and friendship may be. For example, there was Edmund Gosse,

From Stark Young, *The Pavilion* (New York, 1951), pp. 134–138.

at that time without the Sir: for all his fame, with one of his books—*Father and Son*—crowned by the French Academy, and so on, this knighthood was said to have been delayed by resentment in certain high quarters because of his sharp tongue and on occasion, to, put it mildly, even sharper manners, as reported to me by Lady Gregory, Julian Huxley, and various others, and with extra sharpness on his part by Maurice Hewlett, when I went to lunch with him at his table with its seventeenth-century green velvet cover under the fine linen that the nuns at Asolo had woven and its Savona majolica and Murano glass. He did say to me, "Though I am told the old viper can be kindness personified at times; for example he has done everything imaginable for that wretched creature Arthur Symons." But I never saw anything in Mr. Gosse but a warm and lively relaxation into friendship and an air of taking me under his wing.

I had been given a letter of introduction to Mr. Gosse by Madison Cawein, the Kentucky poet of whose work he had edited a volume of selections for a London publisher. I sent the letter to Mr. Gosse and was invited to call at the House of Lords, where he was Librarian, a handsome post, I gathered, somewhat like that of the Poet Laureate, with not much specified to be done. At any rate I called and was delighted, among other things, with the knowledge of my own country that he seemed so ready to express—I was to learn later that he prided himself on his geography—and was charmed with his talk and even more with his face: the fine skin, the clear, straight nose that Sargent recorded in the portrait, and the eyes forever youthful, impish, and truly if shyly passionate. That was the beginning of a friendship that lasted, for the most part in letters, of course, until his death. When presently he asked me to dinner I heard from Mrs. Gosse that his practice was first to invite bearers of introductions to the House of Lords Library before getting any further involved, and that it was always a relief to her when he did not detest them.

Afterwards Mr. Gosse had a kind of literary party for me, mostly of artists and writers and people of their world; and all during the evening he would come to whisper in my ear—with a combination of affection towards me and malice towards all—who this was and that was, and who had been in love with what lady, who was the author of this or the author of that, and so on. Another time at dinner he put me opposite the painter Sir Alfred East, the president of the Royal Academy, whose noble, gentle face showed that he lived in a dream. I remember Sir Alfred's saying that London was the most beautiful city in the world, and how Mrs. Joseph Pennell—the Pennells were great figures in London at the time—on his left said that what he meant was not a city but a cityscape, the way we say landscape, and that she had seen exactly the same thing in Brooklyn. Towards the end of dinner Sir Alfred East looked across the table at me and said, "Young man, why haven't I seen you before?" And when I said modestly how could I have known he wanted to see me? and said alas, I was leaving next morning for Paris, where I was engaged for the evening, he said that his studio was not far from my station, he would expect me and engage to be there. I went by the studio, therefore, and found that he had a water-color laid out and signed for me.

I had a letter of introduction from Professor Baker of Harvard to Lady Gregory, with whose one-act pieces the players from the Abbey Theatre were then delighting London. As an extension of her hospitality she sent me to an evening at the house of Rothenstein, the painter, where Yeats read from the poems, in English, of Tagore, which had never as yet been published, and Tagore himself broke his stillness now and then to make some comment. From that occasion not only Yeats but various other literary contacts arose, none of them, as I remember, and do indeed hope, coming from any forward or vulgar pushing from my side, but rather from their generous responses.

I had been some time before that last dinner at Mr. Gosse's to see the Bakst drawings that were being shown at one of the leading galleries, the name of which I cannot for the moment recall, though I do remember Sir Alfred East's saying that the drawings were very clever and very vulgar. I knew what he meant and I thought that that was exactly right for him and that the drawings were exactly right for Bakst. It was the year when the Diaghileff Ballet after a startling and revolutionary advent in Paris had burst on London. I had gone to every one of the ballet performances, and the drawings absorbed me beyond words, so much so that long after the noon hour had passed and the gallery emptied of visitors I was there still, and the director came up to me and said, as if he had been some cousin in Mississippi, "But my dear young man, you have had no lunch. I said I had never seen drawings in this particular style before and had forgotten all about lunch. "In that case," he said, "you must come down to my place in Surrey for this week-end. I will show you some fine Constables, and some Hogarths, and I will see that you eat your lunch, is that a contract between us?"

I remember, too, how riding up to London on the top of the coach from Devonshire I shared an umbrella with an old lady whose name long ago escaped me and has taken on the aspect of her gentle nature and the lovely passing landscape, against the drizzling rain, and that somehow or other we were presently talking of Francis Thompson, in whose poems with all their Gothic and Catholic and stained-glass complexities I was much absorbed at the time, and I was quoting various lines from "The Hound of Heaven":

> "Yea, faileth now even the dream
> The dreamer, and the lute the lutanist"

and I remember, too, saying:

> "And a voice beat
> More instant than the Feet—
> 'All things betray thee who betrayest me.'"

After these quotations she said simply that if I felt so about Francis Thompson I must come and stay at her house in London and meet him. I would also meet their friend the fine poet Alice Meynell. I was sailing in a day or two and so could not accept her invitation, but the gesture was a gracious one.

These were only some of the friendly gestures made me, for which I had none too much to offer in return, only a degree of youth, perhaps, and a warm interest. I have thought often of this British kindness and response, cordial but without gush, capable of intimacy but not prying, so beautifully well-bred and yet so close, so sweetly (and at its base so sombrely) and so tenderly and so persistently a part of the long line of our lives. And I have thought of a certain sense of security, the ample grace and sureness of living, that must lie behind such a ready following through of one's personal inclination.

WILLIAM DEAN HOWELLS
TAKES SOME LONDON FILMS

1905–09

William Dean Howells was, all in all, the most influential literary figure of his generation—and it was a very long generation. Born in a little Ohio River town in 1837 and—like Whitman, Mark Twain, and even Henry James —without any formal education, he became in time the dean of American letters. Editor, critic, novelist, dramatist, interpreter of his own country and of Europe, Howells dominated the American literary scene as has no other figure in our cultural history. He learned literature at his father's typesetting box; he learned something of frontier life from the history of his family—a history which has its echoes in such novels as *The Leatherwood God;* he saw something of the truth of urban life as reporter on a Columbus newspaper. A campaign biography of Lincoln won him the favorable attention of that successful candidate, and he was appointed consul at Venice. Out of this came his first characteristic book, *Venetian Life*—an interpretation of Venice which, after a century, holds its own. Returning to the United States in 1865, he settled down in Boston, whose literary chronicler he was to be, as assistant

From William Dean Howells, *London Films* (New York, 1905), pp. 100–114; *Seven English Cities* (New York, 1909), pp. 159–192.

editor of the *Atlantic Monthly,* and by 1871 this frontier lad without any education was editor in chief of the most powerful literary journal in the country. In 1891 he moved to New York—historians of American literature have dated the decline of Boston and the rise of New York as a literary center from that symbolic event—where he was, for the rest of his life, editor of Harper's "Easy Chair." Meantime he was turning out books in almost endless profusion. Jane Austen was his favorite novelist, but he was, in a sense, the Balzac of American society; certainly no other novelist, before or since, has made a more faithful transcript of American society than Howells. He portrayed Boston in *The Rise of Silas Lapham;* New York in *A Hazard of New Fortunes;* the New England village and the summer resort in gentle novels like *Their Silver Wedding Journey,* and less gentle ones like *The Son of Royal Langbrith;* and the frontier in *New Leaf Mills* and *The Leatherwood God.* He wrote uptopian romances, stories of international society, novels of economic protest. Perhaps more important, in the long run, he sought out young writers like Frank Norris and Stephen Crane and Hamlin Garland, and encouraged them, and he "discovered" European writers like Tolstoy, Zola, Ibsen, Björnson, and others. He was one of the first to recognize the genius of Henry James and promised to devote "half of every number" of the *Atlantic* to him; he was one of the first to recognize the genius of Mark Twain, and drew what is still the most penetrating portrait of him in our literature, *My Mark Twain.* He traveled widely and wrote widely of travel, but not until fairly late in life did he come to accept and understand England. Passionately devoted to his own country and his own society, he was for long put off by the British class society; a Socialist, highly critical of the capitalist economy, he was put off by British industrialism. But his attitude was ambivalent, for he had been, from boyhood, deeply immersed in English literature, and as he says in the second essay we give here—from *Seven English Cities,*—"England is . . . to the American always a realm of faery." Like Cooper, Hawthorne, and James, Howells was confronted with the problem of retaining an American identity vis-à-vis England and in many ways he managed better than any of them. Certainly his comments and observations are no less perspicacious than those of his peers.

Battersea: the Lowly and the Lowlier

The resort of the poorer sort of pleasure-seekers is eminently Battersea Park, to which we drove one hot, hot Sunday afternoon in late July, conscience-stricken that we had left it so long out of our desultory doing and seeing. It was full of the sort of people we had expected to find in it, but these people though poor were not tattered. The Londoner, of whatever class is apt to be better dressed than the New-Yorker of the same class, and the women especially make a bolder attempt than ours, if not so well advised, at gayety. They had put on the best and finest they had, in Battersea Park, and if it was not the most fitting still they wore it. The afternoon was sultry to breathlessness; yet a young mother with a heavy baby in her arms sweltered along in the splendor of a purple sack of thick plush; she was hot, yes; but she had it on. The young girls emulated as well as they could the airy muslins and silks in which the great world was flitting and flirting at the same hour in the closes of Hyde Park, and if the young fellows with these poor girls had not the distinction of the swells in the prouder parade they at least equalled them in their aberrations from formality.

There was not much shade in Battersea Park for the people to sit under, but there was almost a superabundance of flowers in glaring beds, and there were pieces of water, where the amateur boatman could have the admiration of watchers, two or three deep, completely encircling the ponds. To watch them and to walk up and down the shadeless aisles of shrubbery, to sit on the too sunny beaches, and to resort in extreme cases to the tea-house which offered them ices as well as tea, seemed to be the most that the frequenters of Battersea Park could do. We ourselves ordered tea, knowing the quality and quantity of the public English ice, which is so very minute that you think it will not be enough, but which when you taste it is apt to be more than you want. The spectacle of our simple refection was irresistible, and a crowd of envious small boys thronged the railing that parted us from the general public, till the spectacle of their hungry interest became intolerable. We consulted with the waiter, who entered seriously into our question as to the moral and social effect of sixpence worth of buns on those boys; he decided that it would at least not form an example ruinous to the peace of his tea-house; and he presently appeared with a paper bag that seemed to hold half a bushel of buns. Yet even half a bushel of buns will not go round the boys in Battersea Park, and we had to choose as honest a looking boy as there was in the foremost rank, and pledge him to a just division of the buns intrusted him in bulk, and hope, as he ran off down an aisle of the shrubbery with the whole troop at his heels, that he would be faithful to the trust. . . .

Perhaps poverty has everywhere become shyer than it used to be in the days before slumming (now itself of the past) began to exploit it. At any rate, I thought that in my present London sojourn I found less unblushing destitution than in the more hopeless or more shameless days of 1882–3. In those days I remember being taken by a friend, much concerned for my knowledge of that side of London, to some dreadful purlieu where I saw and heard and smelled things quite as bad as any that I did long afterwards in the overtenanted regions of New York. My memory is still haunted by the vision of certain hapless creatures who fled blinking from one hole in the wall to another, with little or nothing on, and of other creatures much in liquor and loudly scolding and quarrelling, with squalid bits of childhood scattered about underfoot, and vague shapes of sickness and mutilation, and all the time a buying and selling of loathsome second-hand rags. In the midst of it there stood, like figures of a monument erected to the local genius of misery and disorder, two burly figures of half-drunken men, threatening each other with loud curses and shaken fists under the chin of a policeman, perfectly impassive, with eyes dropped upon the fists which all but stirred the throat-latch of his helmet. When the men should strike, I was aware that it would be his instant duty, as the guardian of the public peace, to seize them both and hale them away to prison. But it was not till many years afterwards that I read in his well-remembered effigy the allegory of civilization which lets the man-made suffering of men come to the worst before it touches it, and acts upon the axiom that a pound of prevention is worth less than an ounce of cure.

I would very willingly have seen something of this kind again, but, as I say, I happened not to see it. I think that I did not see or hear even so much simple drunkenness in London as formerly, but again this may have been merely chance. I fancied that formerly I had passed more gin-palaces, flaring through their hell-litten windows into the night; but this may have been because I had become hardened to gin-palaces and did not notice them. Women seemed to be going in and coming out of such places in draggle-tailed processions in those wicked days; but now I only once saw women drinking in a public house. It was a Saturday night, when, if ever, it may be excusable to anticipate the thirst of the morrow, for all through the Sunday idleness it cannot be slaked enough. It was a hot night, and the bar-room door stood open, and within, fronted by a crowd of their loudly talking, deeply drinking menkind, those poor silly things stood drooping against the wall with their beer-pots dangling limply from their hands, and their mouths fallen open as if to catch the morsels of wit and wisdom that dropped from the tongues of their admired male companions. They did not look very bad; bad people never do look as bad as they are, and perhaps they are sometimes not so bad as they look. Perhaps these were kind, but not very wise, mothers of families, who were merely relieving in that moment of liquored leisure the long weariness of the week's work. I may have passed and repassed in the street some of the families that they were the mothers of; it was in that fortnight of the great heat, whose oppressiveness I am aware of having vainly attempted to share with the reader, and the street children seemed to have been roused to uncommon vigilance by it. They played about far into the night, unrebuked by their mothers, and the large babies, whom the little girls were always lugging, shared their untimely wakefulness if not their activity. There was seldom any crying among them then, though by day the voice of grief and rage was often lifted above the shout of joy. If their mothers did not call them in-doors, their fathers were still less exacting. After the marketing, which took place in the neighboring avenue, where there began to be a tremendous preparation for it in the afternoon, father and mother alike seemed to have renounced their domestic cares and to have liberated their offspring to the unrestricted enjoyment of the street.

As for drunkenness, I say again that I did not see much of it, and I heard less, though that might have been because I did not look or listen in the right places. With that, as with everything else in London, I took my chance. Once I overheard the unseen transports of a lady in Mayfair imaginably kept by the offices of mutual friends from assaulting another lady. She, however, though she excelled in violence, did not equal in persistence the injured gentleman who for a long, long hour threatened an invisible bicyclist under our windows in that humbler quarter already described as a poor relation of Belgravia. He had apparently been almost run down by the hapless wheelman, who, in a moment of fatuous truth, seemed to have owned that he had not sounded the warning bell. In making this confession he had evidently apologized with his forehead in the dust, and his victim had then evidently forgiven him, though with a severe admonition for the future. Imaginably, then, the bicyclist had remounted his wheel and attempted to ride off, when he was stopped and brought back to the miserable error of his confession. The whole ground was then gone over again, and again pardon with warning was given. Even a glad good-night was exchanged, the wheelman's voice rising in a quaver of grateful affection. Then he seemed to be riding off again, and then he was stayed as before by the victim, whose sense of public duty flamed up at the prospect of his escape. I do not know how the affair ended; perhaps it never ended; but exhausted nature sank in sleep, and I at least was saved from its continuance. I suppose now that the almost injured person was, if not drunk, at that stage of tipsiness when the sensibilities are keenest and self-respect is most alert. An American could not, at least, have been so tedious in his sober senses, and I will not believe that an Englishman could.

It is to be considered, in any view of the comparative drunkenness of the great Anglo-Saxon race, which is the hope and example of the human race in so many things, that much if not most of our American drunkenness is alien, while English drunkenness is almost entirely native. If the inebriety of the spirited Celt, which in the early years of his adoption with us is sometimes conspicuous, were added to the sum of our home-born intoxication, there could be no doubt which was the greater. As it is, I am afraid that I cannot claim to have seen more drunken men in London than in New York; and when I think of the Family Entrance, indicated at the side-door of every one of our thousands of saloons, I am not sure I can plume myself on the superior sobriety of our drinking men's wives. As for poverty—if I am still partially on that subject—as for open misery, the misery that indecently obtrudes itself upon prosperity and begs of it, I am bound to say that I have met more of it in New York than ever I met during my sojourns in London. Such misery may be more rigidly policed in the English capital, more kept out of sight, more quelled from asking mercy, but I am sure that in Fifth Avenue, and to and fro in the millionaire blocks between that avenue and the last possible avenue eastward, more deserving or undeserving poverty has made itself seen and heard to my personal knowledge than in Piccadilly, or the streets of Mayfair or Park Lane, or the squares and places which are the London analogues of our best residential quarters. . . .

Of course, the statistics will probably be against me—I have often felt an enmity in statistics—and I offer my observations as possibly inexact. One can only be sure of one's own experience (even if one can be sure of that), and I can do no more than urge a fact or two further in behalf of my observation. After we returned to London, in September, I used to stroll much among the recumbent figures of the unemployed on the grass of Green Park, where, lulled by the ocean roar of the omnibuses on Piccadilly, they drowsed away the hours of the autumnal day. These fellow-men looked more interesting than they probably were, either asleep or awake, and if I could really have got inside their minds I dare say I should have been no more amused than if I had penetrated the consciousness of as many people of fashion in the height of the season. But what I wish to say is that, whether sleeping or waking, they never, any of them, asked me for a penny, or in any wise intimated a wish to divide my wealth with me. If I offered it myself, it was another thing, and it was not refused to the extent of a shilling by the good fellow whose conversation I bought one afternoon when I found him, sitting up in his turfy bed, and mending his coat with needle and thread. I asked him of the times and their badness, and I hope I left him with the conviction that I believed him an artisan out of work, taking his misfortune bravely. He was certainly cheerful, and we had some agreeable moments, which I would not prolong, because I did not like waking the others, or such of them as might be sleeping.

I did not object to his cheerfulness, though for misery to be cheerful seemed to be rather trivial, and I was better pleased with the impassioned bearing of a pair who passed me another day as I sat on one of the benches beside the path where the trees were dropping their listless leaves. The pair were a father and mother, if I might judge from their having each a babe in their arms and two or three other babes at their heels. They were not actually in tatters, but anything more intensely threadbare than their thin clothes could not be imagined; they were worse than ragged. They looked neither to the right nor to the left, but stared straight on and pressed straight on rather rapidly, with such desperate tragedy in their looks as moved me to that noble terror which the old-fashioned critics used to inculcate as the high effect of tragedy on the stage. I followed them a little way before I gained courage to speak to the man, who seemed to have been sick, and looked more miserable, if there was a choice, than the woman. Then I asked him, superfluously enough (it might have seemed in a ghastly pleasantry, to him) if he was down on his luck. He owned that he was, and in guarantee of his good faith took the shilling I offered him. If his need had apparently been less dire I might have made it a sovereign; but one must not fly in the face of the Providence which is probably not ill-advised in choosing certain of us to be reduced to absolute destitution. The man smiled a sick, thin-lipped smile which showed his teeth in a sort of pinched way, but did not speak more; his wife, gloomily unmoved, passed me without a look, and I rather slunk back to my seat, feeling that I had represented, if I had not embodied, society to her.

I contribute this instance of poverty as the extremest that came to my knowledge in London; but I do not insist that it was genuine, and if any more scientific student of civilization wishes to insinuate that my tragedy was a masquerade got up by that pair to victimize the sentimental American stranger, and do him out of one of his ill-got shillings, I will not gainsay him. I merely maintain, as I have always done, that the conditions are alike in the Old World and the New, and that the only difference is in the circumstances, which may be better now in New York, and now in London, while the conditions are always bad everywhere for the poor. That is a point on which I shall not yield to any more scientific student of civilization.

"England Is . . . Always a Realm of Faery"

Nothing is so individual in any man as the peculiar blend of characteristics which he has inherited from his racial ancestries. The Englishman, who leaves the stamp of the most distinct personality upon others, is the most mixed, the most various, the most relative of all men. He is not English except he is Welsh, Dutch, and Norman, with "a little Latin and less Greek" from his earliest visitors and invaders. This conception of him will indefinitely simplify the study of his nature if it is made in the spirit of the frank superficiality which I propose to myself. After the most careful scrutiny which I shall be able to give him, he will remain, for every future American, the contradiction, the anomaly, the mystery which I expect to leave him. . . .

Loyalty, like so many other things in England, is a convention to which the alien will tacitly conform in the measure of his good taste or his good sense. It is not his affair, and in the mean time it is a most curious and interesting spectacle; but it is not more remarkable, perhaps, than the perfect acquiescence in the aristocratic forms of society which hedge the King with their divinity. We think that family counts for much with ourselves, in New England or in Virginia; but it counts for nothing at all in comparison with the face value at which it is current in England. We think we are subject to our plutocracy, when we are very much out of humor or out of heart, in some such measure as the commoners of England are subject to the aristocracy; but that is nonsense. A very rich man with us is all the more ridiculous for his more millions; he becomes a byword if not a hissing; he is the meat of the paragrapher, the awful example of the preacher; his money is found to smell of his methods. But in England, the greater a nobleman is, the greater his honor. The American mother who imagines marrying her daughter to an English duke, cannot even imagine an English duke—say, like him of Devonshire, or him of Northumberland, or him of Norfolk—with the social power and state which wait upon him in his duchy and in the whole realm; and so is it in degree down to the latest and lowest of the baronets, and of those yet humbler men who have been knighted for their merits and service in medicine, in literature, in art. The greater and greatest nobles are established in a fear which is very like what the fear of God used to be when the common people feared Him; and, though they are potent political magnates, they mainly rule as the King himself does, through the secular reverence of those beneath them for their titles and the visible images of their state. They are wealthy men, of course, with so much substance that, when one now and then attempts to waste it, he can hardly do so; but their wealth alone would not establish them in the popular regard. His wealth does no such effect for Mr. Astor in England; and mere money, though it is much desired by all, is no more venerated in the person of its possessor than it is with us. It is ancestry, it is the uncontested primacy of families first in their place, time out of mind, that lays its resistless hold upon the fancy and bows the spirit before it. By means of this comes the sovereign effect in the political as well as the social state; for though the people vote into or out of power those who vote other people into or out of administration, it is always—or so nearly always that the exception proves the rule —family that rules, from the King down to the last attache of the most unimportant embassy. No doubt many of the English are restive under the fact; and, if one had asked their mind about it, one might have found them frank enough; but, never asking it, it was with amusement that I heard said once, as if such a thing had never occurred to anybody before, "Yes, isn't it strange that those few families should keep it all among themselves!" It was a slender female voice, lifted by a young girl with an air of pensive surprise, as at a curious usage of some realm of faery.

England is in fact, to the American, always a realm of faery, in its political and social constitution. It must be owned, concerning the government by family, that it certainly seems to work well. That justifies it, so far as the exclusion of the immense majority from the administration of their own affairs can be justified by anything; though I hold that the worst form of graft in office is hardly less justifiable: that is, at least, one of the people picking their pockets. But is the universal make-believe behind all the practical virtue of the state that constitutes the English monarchy a realm of faery. The whole population, both the great and the small, by a common effort of the will, agree that there is a man or a woman of a certain line who can rightfully inherit the primacy amongst them, and can be dedicated through this right to live the life of a god, to be so worshipped and flattered, so cockered about with every form or moral and material flummery, that he or she may well be more than human not to be made a fool of. Then, by a like prodigious stroke of volition, the inhabitants of the enchanted island universally agree that there is a class of them which can be called out of their names in some sort of title, bestowed by some ancestral or actual prince, and can forthwith be something different from the rest, who shall thenceforth do them reverence, them and their heirs and assigns, forever. By this amazing process, the realm of faery is constituted, a thing which could not have any existence in nature, yet by its existence in fancy becomes the most absolute of human facts.

It is not surprising that, in the conditions which ensue, snobbishness should abound; the surprising thing would be if it did not abound. Even with ourselves, who by a seven years' struggle burst the faery dream a century ago, that least erected spirit rears its loathly head from the dust at times, and in our polite press we can read much if we otherwise see nothing of its subtle influence. But no evil is without its compensating good, and the good of English snobbishness is that it has reduced loyalty, whether to the prince or to the patrician, from a political to a social significance. That is, it does so with the upper classes; with the lower, loyalty finds expression in an unparalleled patriotism. An Englishman of the humble or the humbler life may know very well that he is not much in himself; but he believes that England stands for him, and that royalty and nobility stand for England. Both of these, there, are surrounded by an atmosphere of reverence wholly inconceivable to the natives of a country where there are only millionaires to revere.

The most curious thing is that the persons in the faery dream seem to believe it as devoutly as the simplest and humblest of the dreamers. The persons in the dream apparently take themselves as seriously as if there were or could be in reality kings and lords. They could not, of course, do so if they were recently dreamed, as they were, say in the France of the Third Empire. There, one fancies, these figments must have always been smiling in each other's faces when they were by themselves. But the faery dream holds solidly in England because it is such a very old dream. Besides, the dream does not interfere with the realities; it even honors them. If a man does any great thing in England, the chief figure of the faery dream recognizes his deed, stoops to him, lifts him up among the other figures, and makes him part of the dream forever. After that he has standing, such as no man may have with us for more than that psychological moment, when all the papers cry him up, and then everybody tries to forget him. But, better than this, the dream has the effect, if it has not the fact, of securing every man in his place, so long as he keeps to it. Nowhere else in the world is there so much personal independence, without aggression, as in England. There is apparently nothing of it in Germany; in Italy, every one is so courteous and kind that there is no question of it; in the French Republic and in our own, it exists in an excess that is molestive and invasive; in England alone does it strike the observer as being of exactly the just measure.

Very likely the observer is mistaken, and in the present case he will not insist. After all, even the surface indications in such matters are slight and few. But what I noted was that, though the simple and humble have to go the wall, and for the most part go to it unkicking, in England they were, on their level, respectfully and patiently entreated. At a railroad junction one evening, when there was a great hurrying up stairs and down, and a mad seeking of wrong trains by right people, the company's servants who were taking tickets, and directing passengers this way and that, were patiently kind with futile old men and women, who came up, in the midst of their torment, and pestered them with questions as to the time when trains that had not arrived would leave after they did arrive. I shuddered to think what would have at least verbally happened to such inquirers with us; but, there, not only their lives but their feelings were safe, and they could go away with such self-respect as they had quite intact. . . .

The single-mindedness of the English is beautiful. It may not help to the instant understanding of our jokes; but then, even we are not always joking, and it does help to put us at rest and to make us feel safe. The Englishman may not always tell the truth, but he makes us feel that we are not so sincere as he; perhaps there are many sorts of sincerity. But there is something almost caressing in the kindly pause that precedes his perception of your meaning, and this is very pleasing after the sense of always having your hearer constantly on to you. When, by a chance infinitely rarer than it is with us at home, one meets an Irishman in England, or better still an Irishwoman, there is an instant lift of the spirit; and, when one passes the Scotch border, there is so much lift that, on returning, one sinks back into the embrace of the English temperament, with a sigh for the comfort of its soft unhurried expectation that there is really something in what you say which will be clear by-and-by.

Having said so much as this in compliance with the frequent American pretence that the English are without humor, I wish to hedge in the interest of truth. They certainly are not so constantly joking as we; it does not apparently seem to them that fate can be propitiated by a habit of pleasantry, or that this is so merry a world that one need go about grinning in it. Perhaps the conditions with most of them are harder than the conditions with most of us. But, thinking of certain Englishmen I have known, I should be ashamed to join in the cry of those story-telling Americans whose jokes have sometimes fallen effectless. It is true that, whenever the Celt has leavened the doughier Anglo-Saxon lump, the expectation of a humorous sympathy is greater; but there are subtile spirits of Teutonic origin whose fitness we cannot deny, whose delicate gayety is of a sort which may well leave ours impeaching itself of a heavier and grosser fibre.

No doubt you must sometimes, and possibly oftenest, go more than half-way for the response to your humorous intention. Those subtile spirits are shy, and may not offer it an effusive welcome. They are also of such an exquisite honesty that, if they do not think your wit is funny, they will not smile at it, and this may grieve some of our jokers. But, if you have something fine and good in you, you need not be afraid they will fail of it, and they will not be so long about finding it out as some travellers say. When it comes to the grace of the imaginative in your pleasantry, they will be even beforehand with you. But in their extreme of impersonality they will leave the initiative to you in the matter of humor as in others. They will no more seek out your peculiar humor than they will name you in speaking with you.

Nothing in England seeks you out, except the damp. Your impressions, you have to fight for them. What you see or hear seems of accident. The sort of people you have read of your whole life and are most intimate with in fiction, you must surprise. They no more court observance than the birds in whose seasonable slaughter society from the King down delights. In fact, it is probable that, if you looked for both, you would find the gunner shyer than the gunned. The pheasant and the fox are bred to give pleasure by their chase; they are tenderly cared for and watched over and kept from harm at the hands of all who do not wish to kill them for the joy of killing, and they are not so elusive but they can be seen by easy chance. The pheasant especially has at times all but the boldness of the barnyard in his fearless port. Once from my passing train, I saw him standing in the middle of a ploughed field, erect, distinct, like a statue of

himself, commemorative of the long ages in which his heroic death
and martyr sufferance have formed the pride of princes and the
peril of poachers. But I never once saw him shot, though almost as
many gunners pursue him as there are pheasants in the land. This
alone shows how shy the gunners are; and when once I saw the trail
of a fox-hunt from the same coign of vantage without seeing the fox,
I felt that I had almost indecently come upon the horse and hounds,
and that the pink coats and the flowery spread of the dappled dogs
over the field were mine by a kind of sneak as base as killing a fox to
save my hens.

Equally with the foxes and the pheasants, the royalties and
nobilities abound in English novels, which really form the chief
means of our acquaintance with English life; but the chances that
reveal them to the average unintroduced, unpresented American
are rarer. By these chances, I heard out of the whole peerage, but
one lord so addressed in public, and that was on a railroad platform
where a porter was reassuring him about his luggage. Similarly, I
once saw a lady of quality, a tall and girlish she, who stood beside her
husband, absently rubbing with her glove the window of her motor,
and whom but for the kind interest of our cabman we might never
have known for a duchess. It is by their personal uninsistence
largely, no doubt, that the monarchy and the aristocracy exist; the
figures of the faery dream remain blent with the background, and
appear from it only when required to lay cornerstones, or preside at
races, or teas or bazars, or to represent the masses at home and
abroad, and invisibly hold the viewless reins of government.

Yet it must not be supposed that the commoner sort of dreamers
are never jealous of these figments of their fancy. They are often so,
and rouse themselves to self-assertion as frequently as our Better
Element flings off the yoke of Tammany. At a fair, open to any who
would pay, for some forgotten good object, such as is always engaging the energies of society, I saw moving among the paying guests
the tall form of a nobleman who had somehow made himself so
distasteful to his neighbors that they were not his friends, and
regularly voted down his men, whether they stood for Parliament or
County Council, and whether they were better than the popular
choice or not. As a matter of fact, it was said that they were really
better, but the people would not have them because they were his;
and one of the theories of English manliness is that the constant
pressure from above has toughened the spirit and enabled Englishmen to stand up stouter and straighter each in his place, just as it is
contended elsewhere that the aesthetic qualities of the human race

have been heightened by its stresses and deprivations in the struggle of life.

For my own part, I believe neither the one theory nor the other. People are the worse for having people above them, and are the ruder and coarser for having to fight their way. If the triumph of social inequality is such that there are not four men in London who are not snobs, it cannot boast itself greater than the success of economic inequality with ourselves, among whom the fight for money has not produced of late a first-class poet, painter or sculptor. The English, if they are now the manliest people under the sun, have to thank not their masters but themselves, and a nature originally so generous that no abuse could lastingly wrong it, no political absurdity spoil it. But if this nature had been left free from the beginning, we might see now a nation of Englishmen who, instead of being bound so hard and fast in the bonds of an imperial patriotism, would be the first in a world-wide altruism. Yet their patriotism is so devout that it may well pass itself off upon them for a religious emotion, instead of the superstition which seems to the stranger the implication of an England in the next world as well as in this. . . .

I was always regretting that I got at the people so little, and that only chance hints of what they were thinking and feeling reached me. Now and then, a native observer said something about them which seemed luminous. "We are frightfully feudal," such an observer said, "especially the poor." He did not think it a fault, I believe, and only used his adverb intensifyingly, for he was of a Tory mind. He meant the poor among the country people, who have at last mastered that principle of the feudal system which early enabled the great nobles to pay nothing for the benefits they enjoyed from it. But my other friend, the plumber, was not the least feudal, or not so feudal as many a lowly ward-heeler in New York, who helps to make up the muster of some captain of politics, under the lead of a common boss. The texture of society, in the smarter sense, the narrower sense, is what I could not venture to speak of more confidently. Once I asked a friend, a very dear and valued friend, whether a man's origin or occupation would make any difference in his social acceptance, if he were otherwise interesting and important. He seemed not to know what I would be at, and, when he understood, he responded with almost a shout of amazement, "Oh, not the least in the world!" But I have my doubts still; and I should say that it might be as difficult for a very cultivated and agreeable man-servant to get on in London society, as for an artist or poet to feel at home in the first circles of New York. Possibly, however, London society, because of its almost immeasurable vastness, can take in more of more sorts of people, without the consciousness of differences which keeps our own first circles so elect. I venture, somewhat wildly, somewhat unwarrantably, the belief that English society is less sensitive to moral differences than ours, and that people with their little *tâches* would find less anxiety in London than in New York lest they should come off on the people they rubbed against. Some Americans, who, even with our increasing prevalence of divorces, are not well seen at home, are cheerfully welcomed in England.

Perhaps, there, all Americans, good and bad, high and low, coarse and fine, are the same to senses not accustomed to our varying textures and shades of color; that is a matter I should be glad to remand to the psychologist, who will have work enough to do if he comes to inquire into such mysteries. One can never be certain just how the English take us, or how much, or whether they take us at all. Oftenest I was inclined to think that we were imperceptible to them, or that, when we were perceptible, they were aware of us as Swedenborg says the most celestial angels are aware of evil spirits, merely as something angular. Americans were distressful to their consciousness, they did not know why; and then they tried to ignore us. But perhaps this is putting it a little fantastically. What I know is that one comes increasingly to reserve the fact of one's nationality, when it is not essential to the occasion, and to become as much as possible an unknown quality, rather than a quality aggressive or positive. Sometimes, when I could feel certain of my ground, I ventured my conviction that Englishmen were not so much interested in Americans as those Americans who stayed at home were apt to think, but when I once expressed this belief to a Unitarian minister, whom I met in the West of England, he received it with surprise and refusal. He said that in his own immediate circle, at least, his friends were interested and increasingly interested in America, what she was and what she meant to be, and still looked toward her for the lead in certain high things which Englishmen have ceased to expect of themselves. My impression is that most of the most forward of the English sociologists regard America as a back number in those political economics which imply equality as well as liberty in the future. They do not see any difference between our conditions and theirs, as regards the man who works for a living with his hands, except that wages are higher with us, and that physically there is more elbow-room, though mentally and morally there is not. Save a little in my Unitarian minister, and this only conjectu. ally, I did not encounter that fine spirit which in Old England used to imagine the

New World we have not quite turned out to be; but once I met an Englishman who had lived in Canada, and who, gentleman-bred as he was, looked back with fond homesickness to the woods where he had taken up land, and built himself a personable house, chiefly with his own hands. He had lived himself out of touch with his old English life in that new country, and had drawn breath in an opener and livelier air which filled his lungs as the home atmosphere never could again. . . .

A thing that one feels more and more irritatingly in England is that, while with other foreigners we stand on common ground, where we may be as unlike them as we choose, with the English we always stand on English ground, where we can differ only at our peril, and to our disadvantage. A person speaking English and bearing an English name, had better be English, for if he cannot it shows, it proves, that there is something wrong in him. Our misfortune is that our tradition, and perhaps our inclination, obliges us to be un-English, whereas we do not trouble ourselves to be un-French, or un-Italian, for we are so by nature. The effort involved in distinguishing ourselves breeds a sort of annoyance, or call it no more than uneasiness, which is almost as bad as a bad conscience; and in our sense of hopeless perdition we turn vindictively upon our judge. But that is not fair and it is not wise; he does not mean to be our judge, except when he comes to us for the purpose; in his own house, he is civilly unaware of putting us to any test whatever. If you ask him whether he likes this thing or that of ours, he will tell you frankly; he never can see why he should not be frank; he has a kind of helplessness in always speaking the truth; and he does not try to make it palatable.

THE REVEREND
MONROE ROYCE:
THE PROSPERITY OF THE
FARMER AND THE MISERY OF
THE FARM LABORER

1905

Monroe Royce was an Episcopalian minister who spent most of his professional life as rector of American churches on the European Continent or in Britain, where he lived for some years after 1903. A graduate of Harvard College and of the Union Theological Seminary, he studied in Europe from 1880 to 1885, then rode circuit, as it were, to European cities. He was rector of the American Trinity Church in Paris, St. Paul's Church in Rome, St. James's Church in Florence; he founded the American Church in Munich and the American Circle in Nice, and was for a time rector of St. Mary's in London. "My chief purpose for employment as a clergyman in England," he confessed, "was the opportunity it might furnish me for studying the life and character of the British people." Royce was not really critical of English social institutions, and these animadversions on the deplorable lot of the farm laborers appear, almost fortuitously, in an otherwise cheerful chapter on village cricket. Yet it is interesting to note that Royce is saying pretty much what Moncure Conway had said a quarter of a century earlier.

From Monroe Royce, *The Notebook of an American Parson in England* (New York, 1918), pp. 90–98.

It is cricket that makes of one blood all sorts and conditions of Englishmen who dwell upon the face of the earth. . . .

All schoolmasters in England are cricketers, and their advancement depends as much, and frequently more, upon their ability to play the national game than upon their book-learning. The English country schoolmasters are decidedly inferior in learning and general culture to the American teacher of the same grade. I have been constantly astonished to discover the illiterate and grossly ignorant character of the low-grade country schoolmaster and mistress in England. It is true that they have to do only with children of their own stations in life, for none or practically none but the children of the masses are taught in the national country schools. The gentry, the middle class, the prosperous shopkeeper, and all who can possibly afford it have their own governess or send their children to private schools, for their primary education. Still it does seem hard, at least to a good American, that the children of the poor and the lowly should be hindered and not helped by their teachers in rising to higher things. . . .

Our squire—for he was as much ours as anybody's—not only looked his part to perfection but lived it out to perfection in every detail of life. He was a large landed proprietor and lived all the year round upon his estates; seldom going away beyond the day's return; and there was hardly a day when he could not be seen inspecting his fields, and cottages, and looking after the health and welfare of his people, as though they were his own immediate family. He was the most amiable of men, and there was not a man, woman, or child within the two or three parishes who did not regard him as their friend and protector. He knew all their many weaknesses, no one better, and yet his patience was always long-suffering and kind. If there must be a landed aristocracy with its inevitable dependents, I can conceive of no better landlord than this kindly, genial, hot-tempered, strictly conservative baronet. The truth is, as I learnt by personal observation and enquiry, the land belonging to this squire—something like 13,000 acres—brought him practically nothing, so that he actually kept up his estate, and worked hard day in and day out for the benefit of his tenants, the farmers being the chief beneficiaries. The English farmer I had known nothing about, previous to my residence in this parish, but supposed he was a worthy hard-working and ill-used person. I have completely changed my opinion. He may be more or less worthy, but he is neither hard-worked nor ill-used, so far as I have been able to judge. First of all he is the only person who gets a living out of the land. It of

course seems proper and just that he of all men should get a living
out of the land. But, with the farmer there is no such thing, or
seldom such a thing as the principle of live and let live. He gets his
land at a rate so low, as to leave the landlord no profit on the one
hand, and he gets his labour at a price so cheap as not to give the
labourer a reasonable living on the other hand. The agricultural
labourer is thus always kept at the door of the workhouse ready to go
in, in case of a day's sickness or loss of a day's work. From all I have
been able to learn, after some careful investigation, the farmer has
never been disposed even in his most prosperous days to give his
labourer a fair living wage; and the labourer does not regard him as
his natural enemy for nothing. He has tradition and experience to
fortify him in his belief that the farmer is always ready to screw him
down to the last farthing. When in trouble the agricultural labourer
never goes, as one would naturally suppose to the farmer, but to the
squire and it may be sometimes to the parson. But too often the
parson joins with the farmer unwittingly, of course, in oppressing
the labourer. And yet they, the farmer and the parson, cannot
understand why the labourers in such great numbers are quitting
the land for the town. This migration often ends in a much worse
state it is true. But the labourer sees in the town the possibility of
getting away from the small wage and the petty tyranny of the
farmer, and he is willing to risk almost any unknown thing in the
hope of finding something better than what he knows his present
condition to be. It is utter nonsense to say that the agricultural
labourer would quit the land where he was born, and has always
lived, to seek employment in the town, were it not for the poor wage
and the hard conditions imposed upon him by the farmer. He is not
an enterprising person, and would much prefer to accept a very
poor wage, with the security of home and the pleasure of his lifelong associations than to take a plunge into the unknown and
much-dreaded town. But he has no security either of a home or a
living wage. Everything rests upon the caprice of the farmer, and a
few days of idleness means that the labourer is thrown upon the
poor-rate and classed as a pauper, with the loss of his right to vote, as
well as all self-respect. There is no agricultural labourer in the world,
Russia not excepted, whose conditions are as bad as the English
farm-labourer. Whatever may be said in condemnation of the Russian Government, it at least protects the peasant, *i.e.*, the agricultural
labourer, from the landlord and farmer, for it gives him fixity of
tenure, which means a permanent home. The strength of a nation
rests upon the rural population, and it is obvious that to weaken the

peasant is to undermine the foundations of the national life and health. There has been a good deal of talk of late about turning the tenant farmer into the yeoman owner of the land. This of course would mean small holdings, and in that respect it would be a good thing provided the agricultural labourer is given a guarantee of a home, and a living wage. Otherwise his last state will be worse than his first, as the farmer will have him completely within his power, and can turn him out of house and home at his pleasure. I throw out these observations for what they may be worth. They are at least free from the influence of any entangling alliances with party politics. Land is going out of cultivation in England for the reason that the farmer will not pay the landlord a reasonable rent, nor the labourer a living wage, and he can well afford to do both. I know a case in point, where a farm of eight hundred acres is let at the rate of ten shillings per acre. This farmer has the best house in the parish, a very fine old manor-house in fact, fitted up with modern bathrooms, plumbing, etc., he drives the best horses in the parish; has rubber tyres on his dogcart, and altogether lives like a prosperous squire; whilst a real squire not two miles distant, who is a large landed proprietor is not able to keep a horse in his stables. There is not a farmer in four adjoining parishes so far as I know, who does not live in comfort and with more or less luxury, whilst eighty per cent. at least of the agricultural la-bourers are on the poor-rate for longer or shorter periods during the year. In considering the land question two things may be ac-cepted as absolute facts, namely the landlord is only too willing to let his land for cultivation, either in large or small lots if he can get a rental that will return him any reasonable margin of profit; and the agricultural labourer is only too willing to remain on the land provided he can be assured of a habitable home and a living wage. I have already said enough to express my belief that the farmer is the most universally prosperous man in England. There are many cases of course where he comes to grief, but they may be in most instances attributed to one of two causes, either his incapacity and want of industry, or his wish to play the part of a squire, which causes him to live beyond his means.

EDITH WHARTON:
AN AMERICAN FRANCOPHILE
VISITS
AN AMERICAN ANGLOPHILE

1906

Of that remarkable group of novelists who were providing, in the nineties and after, a literary portrait of America as faithful as that which the Edwardians were providing for England—William Dean Howells, Ellen Glasgow, Willa Cather, Grace King, Booth Tarkington, and others—Edith Wharton was closest to Henry James both in style and in philosophy. Born Edith Cadwalader Jones, of Knickerbocker aristocracy, and married to Edward Wharton of Boston, she turned to fiction as a relief from the stuffiness of her society and the inadequacy of her marriage. *The Custom of the Country, The House of Mirth, Hudson River Bracketed,* and others of the same genre did for New York what Ellen Glasgow was doing for Virginia and Howells for Boston. But Mrs. Wharton was far more than a local colorist; like James she cultivated the international novel (her first novel, *The Valley of Decision,* had been laid in Italy), and cultivated, too, international society; eventually she moved to France, where she maintained a great house and a salon outside Paris. Her many books and articles on interior decoration and gardening made her something of an arbiter of taste to the American rich. Always an admirer of

From Edith Wharton, *A Backward Glance* (New York, 1934), pp. 241–254.

James, in 1903 she formed an attachment to him which James reciprocated with a mixture of admiration and dependence. James, Mrs. Wharton wrote perceptively, "belonged irrevocably to the old America out of which I also came, and of which it might paradoxically be said that to follow up its last traces one had to come to Europe." The third figure in this pattern, Howard Sturgis, was the English-born son of Russell Sturgis of Boston, a banker who had made his home in London. Howard Sturgis, a product of Eton and Cambridge who wrote one Jamesian novel, *Belchamber,* did nothing in particular except entertain and hand embroider, and did it very well. At Qu'acre (Queen's Acre) on the edge of Windsor Park, he maintained a perfect little estate, and dispensed hospitality to old Etonians and Cantabrigians, and to friends like James and Wharton.

Not infrequently, on my annual visit to Qu'acre, I "took off" from Lamb House, where I also went annually for a visit to Henry James. The motor run between Rye and Windsor being an easy one, I was often accompanied by Henry James, who generally arranged to have his visit to Qu'acre coincide with mine. James, who was a frequent companion on our English motor-trips, was firmly convinced that, because he lived in England, and our chauffeur (an American) did not, it was necessary that the latter should be guided by him through the intricacies of the English country-side. Signposts were rare in England in those days, and for many years afterward, and a truly British reserve seemed to make the local authorities reluctant to communicate with the invading stranger. Indeed, considerable difficulty existed as to the formulating of advice and instructions, and I remember in one village the agitated warning: "Motorists! Beware of the children!"—while in general there was a marked absence of indications as to the whereabouts of the next village.

It chanced, however, that Charles Cook, our faithful and skilful driver, was a born path-finder, while James's sense of direction was non-existent, or rather actively but always erroneously alert; and the consequences of his intervention were always bewildering, and sometimes extremely fatiguing. The first time that my husband and I went to Lamb House by motor (coming from France) James, who had travelled to Folkestone by train to meet us, insisted on seating himself next to Cook, on the plea that the roads across Romney marsh formed such a tangle that only an old inhabitant could guide us to Rye. The suggestion resulted in our turning around and around in our tracks till long after dark, though Rye, conspicuous on its conical hill, was just ahead of us, and Cook could easily have landed us there in time for tea.

Another year we had been motoring in the west country, and on the way back were to spend a night at Malvern. As we approached (at the close of a dark rainy afternoon) I saw James growing restless, and was not surprised to hear him say: "My dear, I once spent a summer at Malvern, and know it very well; and as it is rather difficult to find the way to the hotel, it might be well if Edward were to change places with me, and let me sit beside Cook." My husband of course acceded (though with doubt in his heart), and James having taken his place, we awaited the result. Malvern, if I am not mistaken, is encircled by a sort of upper boulevard, of the kind called in Italy a *strada di circonvallazione,* and for an hour we circled about above the outspread city, while James vainly tried to remember which particular street led down most directly to our hotel. At each corner (literally) he stopped the motor, and we heard a muttering, first confident and then anguished. "This—this, my dear Cook, yes . . . this certainly is the right corner. But no; stay! A moment longer, please—in this light it's so difficult . . . appearances are so misleading . . . It may be . . . yes! I think it *is* the next turn . . . 'a little farther lend thy guiding hand' . . . that is, drive on; but slowly, please, my dear Cook; *very* slowly!" And at the next corner the same agitated monologue would be repeated; till at length Cook, the mildest of men, interrupted gently: "I guess any turn'll get us down into the town, Mr. James, and after that I can ask—" and late, hungry and exhausted we arrived at length at our destination, James still convinced that the next turn would have been the right one, if only we had been more patient.

The most absurd of these episodes occurred on another rainy evening, when James and I chanced to arrive at Windsor long after dark. We must have been driven by a strange chauffeur—perhaps Cook was on a holiday; at any rate, having fallen into the lazy habit of trusting to him to know the way, I found myself at a loss to direct his substitute to the King's Road. While I was hesitating, and peering out into the darkness, James spied an ancient doddering man who had stopped in the rain to gaze at us. "Wait a moment, my dear—I'll ask him where we are"; and leaning out he signalled to the spectator.

"My good man, if you'll be good enough to come here, please; a little nearer—so," and as the old man came up: "My friend, to put it to you in two words, this lady and I have just arrived here from *Slough;* that is to say, to be more strictly accurate, we have recently *passed through* Slough on our way here, having actually motored to Windsor from Rye, which was our point of departure; and the darkness having overtaken us, we should be much obliged if you would tell us where we now are in relation, say, to the High Street, which, as you of course know, leads to the Castle, after leaving on the left hand the turn down to the railway station."

I was not surprised to have this extraordinary appeal met by silence, and a dazed expression on the old wrinkled face at the window; nor to have James go on: "In short" (his invariable prelude to a fresh series of explanatory ramifications), in short, my good man, what I want to put to you in a word is this: supposing we have already (as I have reason to think we have) driven past the turn down to the railway station (which, in that case, by the way, would probably not have been on our left hand, but on our right), where are we now in relation to. . ."

"Oh, please," I interrupted, feeling myself utterly unable to sit through another parenthesis, "do ask him where the King's Road is."

"Ah—? The King's Road? Just so! Quite right! Can you, as a matter of fact, my good man, tell us where, in relation to our present position, the King's Road exactly *is?*"

"Ye're in it," said the aged face at the window.

It would be hard to imagine a greater contrast than between the hospitality of Queen's Acre and that of Lamb House. In the former a cheerful lavishness prevailed, and a cook enamoured of her art set a variety of inviting dishes before a table-full of guests, generally reinforced by transients from London or the country. At Lamb House an anxious frugality was combined with the wish that the usually solitary guest (there were never, at most, more than two at a time) should not suffer too greatly from the contrast between his or her supposed habits of luxury, and the privations imposed by the host's conviction that he was on the brink of ruin. If any one in a pecuniary difficulty appealed to James for help, he gave it without counting; but in his daily life he was haunted by the spectre of impoverishment, and the dreary pudding or pie of which a quarter or half had been consumed at dinner reappeared on the table the next day with its ravages unrepaired.

We use to laugh at Howard Sturgis because, when any new subject was touched on in our talks, he always interrupted us to cry out: "Now please remember that I've read nothing, and know nothing, and am not in the least quick or clever or cultivated"; and one

day, when I prefaced a remark with "Of course, to people as intelligent as we all are," he broke in with a sort of passionate terror: "Oh,
how can you say such things about us, Edith?"—as though my
remark had been a challenge to the Furies.

The same scruples weighed on Henry James; but in his case the
pride that apes humility concerned itself (oddly enough) with material things. He lived in terror of being thought rich, worldly or
luxurious, and was forever contrasting his visitors' supposed opul-
ence and self-indulgence with his own hermit-like asceticism, and
apologizing for his poor food while he trembled lest it should be
thought too good. I have often since wondered if he did not find our
visits more of a burden than a pleasure, and if the hospitality he so
conscientiously offered and we so carelessly enjoyed did not give
him more sleepless nights than happy days.

I hope not; for some of my richest hours were spent under his
roof. From the moment when I turned the corner of the grass-
grown street mounting steeply between squat brick houses, and
caught sight, at its upper end, of the wide Palladian window of the
garden room, a sense of joyous liberation bore me on. There *he*
stood on the doorstep, the white panelled hall with its old prints and
crowded book cases forming a background to his heavy loosely-
clothed figure. Arms outstretched, lips and eyes twinkling, he came
down to the car, uttering cries of mock amazement and mock
humility at the undeserved honour of my visit. The arrival at Lamb
House was an almost ritual performance, from those first ejacula-
tions to the large hug and the two solemn kisses executed in the
middle of the hall rug. Then, arm in arm, through the oak-panelled
morning-room we wandered out onto the thin worn turf of the
garden, with its ancient mulberry tree, its unkempt flower-borders,
the gables of Watchbell Street peeping like village gossips over the
creeper-clad walls, and the scent of roses spiced with a strong smell
of the sea. Up and down the lawn we strolled with many pauses,
exchanging news, answering each other's questions, delivering
messages from the other members of the group, inspecting the
strawberries and lettuces in the tiny kitchen-garden, and the chry-
santhemums "coming along" in pots in the greenhouse; till at
length the parlour-maid appeared with a tea-tray, and I was led
up the rickety outside steps to the garden-room, that stately and
unexpected appendage to the unadorned cube of the house.

In summer the garden-room, with its high ceiling, its triple
window commanding the grass-grown declivity of West Street, and
its other window looking along another ancient street to the Gothic

mass of the parish church, was the centre of life at Lamb House. Here, in the morning, James dictated to his secretary, striding incessantly up and down the room, and in the afternoon and evening, when the weather was too cool for the garden, sat with outstretched legs in his deep armchair before the hearth, laughing and talking with his guests.

On the whole, he was very happy at Rye, and in spite of the house-keeping cares which he took so hard the change was all to the good for a man who could never resist invitations, yet was wearied and irritated by the incessant strain of social life in London. At Rye, in summer at least, he had as many guests as his nerves could endure, and his sociable relations with his neighbours—among whom were, at one time, his beloved friends, Sir George and Lady Prothero—must have prevented his feeling lonely. He was very proud of his old house, the best of its sober and stately sort in the town, and he who thought himself so detached from material things tasted the simple joys of proprietorship when, with a deprecating air, he showed his fine Georgian panelling and his ancient brick walls to admiring visitors.

Like Howard Sturgis he was waited upon by two or three faithful servants. Foremost among them was the valet and factotum, Burgess, always spoken of by his employer as "poor little Burgess". Burgess's broad squat figure and phlegmatic countenance are a familiar memory to all who frequented Lamb House, and James's friends gratefully recall his devotion to his master during the last unhappy years of nervous break-down and illness. He had been preceded by a man-servant whom I did not know, but of whom James spoke with regard as an excellent fellow. "The only trouble was that, when I gave him an order, he had to go through three successive mental processes before he could understand what I was saying. First he had to register the fact that he was being spoken to, then to assimilate the meaning of the order given to him, and lastly to think out what practical consequences might be expected to follow if he obeyed it."

Perhaps these mental gymnastics were excusable in the circumstances; but Burgess apparently soon learned to dispense with them, and without any outward appearance of having understood what his master was saying, carried out his instructions with stolid exactitude. Stolidity was his most marked characteristic. He seldom gave any sign of comprehension when spoken to, and I remember once saying to my Alsatian maid, who was always as quick as a flash at the uptake: "Do you know, I think Burgess must be very stupid. When I speak to him I'm never even sure that he's heard what I've said."

My maid looked at me gravely. "Oh, no, Madam: Burgess is remarkably intelligent. *He always understands what Mr. James says.*" And that argument was certainly conclusive.

At Lamb House my host and I usually kept to ourselves until luncheon. Our working hours were the same, and it was only now and then that we went out before one o'clock to take a look at the green peas in the kitchen-garden, or to stroll down the High Street to the Post Office. But as soon as luncheon was despatched (amid unnecessary apologies for its meagreness, and sarcastic allusions to my own supposed culinary extravagances) the real business of the day began. Henry James, an indifferent walker, and incurably sedentary in his habits, had a passion for motoring. He denied himself (I believe quite needlessly) the pleasure and relaxation which a car of his own might have given him, but took advantage, to the last drop of petrol, of the travelling capacity of any visitor's car. When, a few years after his death, I stayed at Lamb House with the friend who was then its tenant, I got to know for the first time the rosy old town and its sea-blown neighbourhood. In Henry James's day I was never given the chance, for as soon as luncheon was over we were always whirled miles away, throwing out over the countryside what he called our "great loops" of exploration. Sometimes we went off for two or three days. I remember one beautiful pilgrimage to Winchester, Gloucester and beyond; another long day carried us to the ancient house of Brede, to lunch with the Morton Frewens, another to spend a day near Ashford with the Alfred Austins, in their pleasant old house full of books and flowers. Usually, however, to avoid an interruption to the morning's work, we lunched at Lamb House, and starting out immediately afterward pushed our explorations of down and weald and seashore to the last limit of the summer twilight.

James was as jubilant as a child. Everything pleased him—the easy locomotion (which often cradled him into a brief nap), the bosky softness of the landscape, the discovery of towns and villages hitherto beyond his range, the magic of ancient names, quaint or impressive, crabbed or melodious. These he would murmur over and over to himself in a low chant, finally creating characters to fit them, and sometimes whole families, with their domestic complications and matrimonial alliances, such as the Dymmes of Dymchurch, one of whom married a Sparkle, and was the mother of little Scintilla

Dymme-Sparkle, subject of much mirth and many anecdotes. Except during his naps, nothing escaped him, and I suppose no one ever felt more imaginatively, or with deeper poetic emotion, the beauty of sea and sky, the serenities of the landscape, the sober charm of villages, manor-houses and humble churches, and all the implications of that much-storied corner of England.

One perfect afternoon we spent at Bodiam—my first visit there. It was still the old spell-bound ruin, unrestored, guarded by great trees, and by a network of lanes which baffled the invading charabancs. Tranquil white clouds hung above it in a windless sky, and the silence and solitude were complete as we sat looking across at the crumbling towers, and at their reflection in a moat starred with water-lilies, and danced over by great blue dragon-flies. For a long time no one spoke; then James turned to me and said solemnly: "Summer afternoon—summer afternoon; to me those have always been the two most beautiful words in the English language." They were the essence of that hushed scene, those ancient walls; and I never hear them spoken without seeing the towers of Bodiam mirrored in their enchanted moat.

Another day was memorable in another way. We were motoring from Rye to Windsor, to stay, as usual, with Howard Sturgis, and suddenly James said: "The day is so beautiful that I should like to make a little *dètour,* and show you Box Hill." I was delighted at the prospect of seeing a new bit of English scenery, and perhaps catching a glimpse of George Meredith's cottage on its leafy hillside. But James's next words chilled my ardour: "I want you to know Meredith," he added.

"Oh, no, no!" I protested. I knew enough, by this time, of my inability to profit by such encounters. I was always benumbed by them, and unable to find the right look or the right word, while inwardly I bubbled with fervour, and the longing to express it. I remember once being taken to see Miss Jekyll's famous garden at Great Warley. On that long-desired day I had a hundred questions to ask, a thousand things to learn. I went with a party of fashionable and indifferent people, all totally ignorant of gardens and gardening; I put one timid question to Miss Jekyll, who answered curtly, and turned her back on me to point out a hybrid iris to an eminent statesman who knew neither what a hybrid nor an iris was; and for the rest of the visit she gave me no chance of exchanging a word with her.

To see Meredith and talk with him was a more important affair.

In spite of all reservations, my admiration for certain parts of his work was very great. I delighted in his poetry, and treasured two of his novels—"The Egoist" and "Harry Richmond"—and I should have enjoyed telling him just what it was that I most admired in them. But I foresaw the impossibility of doing so at a first meeting which would probably also be the last. I told James this, and added that the great man's deafness was in itself an insurmountable obstacle, since I cannot make myself heard even by the moderately deaf. James pleaded with me, but I was firm. For months he had been announcing his visit to Meredith, but had always been deterred by the difficulty of getting from Rye to Box Hill without going up to London; and I should really be doing him a great service by allowing him to call there on the way to Windsor. To this, of course, I was obliged to consent; but I stipulated that I should be allowed to wait in the car, and though he tried to convince me that "just to have taken a look at the great man" would be an interesting memory, he knew I hated that kind of human sight-seeing, and did not insist. So we deflected our course to take in Box Hill, and the car climbed the steep ascent to the garden-gate where James was to get out. As he did so he turned to me and said: "Come, my dear! I can't leave you sitting here alone. I should have you on my mind all the time; and supposing somebody were to come out of the house and find you?"

There was nothing for it but to comply; and somewhat sulkily I followed him up the narrow path, between clumps of sweetwilliam and Scotch pinks. It was a tiny garden patch, and a few steps brought us to the door of a low-studded cottage in a gap of the hanging woods. It was useless to notify Meredith in advance when one went to see him; he had long since been immobilized by illness, and was always there, and always, apparently, delighted to receive his old friends. The maid who announced us at once returned to say that we were to come in, and we were shown into a very small low-ceilinged room, so small and so low that it seemed crowded though there were only four people in it. The four were the great man himself, white of head and beard, and statuesquely throned in a Bath chair; his daughter, the handsome Mrs. Henry Sturgis (wife of Howard's eldest brother), another man who seemed to me larger than life, perhaps on account of the exiguity of the room, and who turned out to be Mr. Morley Roberts—and lastly a trained nurse, calmly eating her supper at a table only a foot or two from her patient's chair.

It was the nurse's presence—and the way she went on steadily eating and drinking—that I found most disconcerting. The house was very small indeed; but was it really so small that there was not a corner of it in which she could have been fed, instead of consuming her evening repast under our eyes and noses? I have always wondered, and never found the answer.

Meanwhile I was being led up and explained by James and Mrs. Sturgis—a laborious business, and agonizing to me, as the room rang and rang again with my unintelligible name. But finally the syllables reached their destination; and then, as they say in detective novels, the unexpected happened. The invalid stretched out a beautiful strong hand—everything about him was strong and beautiful—and lifting up a book which lay open at his elbow, held it out with a smile. I read the title, and the blood rushed over me like fire. It was my own "Motor Flight through France", then lately published; and he had not known I was to be brought to see him, and he had actually been reading my book when I came in!

At once, in his rich organ tones, he began to say the kindest, most appreciative things; to ask questions, to want particulars—but, alas, my unresonant voice found no crack in the wall of his deafness. I longed to tell him that Henry James had been our companion on most of the travels described in my modest work; and James, joining in, tried to explain, to say kind things also; but it was all useless, and Meredith, accustomed to steering a way through these first difficult moments, had presently taken easy hold of the conversation, never again letting it go till we left.

The beauty, the richness, the flexibility of his voice held me captive, and it is that which I remember, not what he said; except that he was all amenity, all kindliness, as if the voice were poured in a healing tide over the misery of my shyness. But the object of the visit was, of course, to give him a chance of talking with James, and presently I drew back and chatted with Mrs. Sturgis and Morley Roberts, while the great bright tide of monologue swept on over my friend. After all, it had been worth coming for; but the really interesting thing about the visit was James's presence, and the chance of watching from my corner the nobly confronted profiles of the two old friends: Meredith's so classically distinguished, from the spring of the wavy hair to the line of the straight nose, and the modelling of cheek and throat, but all like a slightly idealized bas-relief "after" a greater original; and James's heavy Roman head, so realistically and vigorously his own, not a bas-relief but a bust, wrought in the round by harsher but more powerful hands. As they sat there, James benignly listening, Meredith eloquently discoursing, and their old deep regard for each other burning steadily through the surface eloquence and the surface attentiveness, I felt I was in great company, and was glad.

"Well, my dear," James said to me, as we went out into the dusk, "wasn't I right?" Yes, he had been right, and I had to own it.

BOOKER T. WASHINGTON
VISITS THE LOWLY
OF LONDON

1909

Though his reputation is temporarily in eclipse, Booker T. Washington will probably survive as the greatest leader of and representative of the Negro race in America. Born in slavery, in 1856, Washington managed to get an education at the Hampton Institute in Virginia and, some years later, to found the world famous Tuskegee Institute in Tuskegee, Alabama. There he and his devoted associates set themselves the task of helping train Negroes to the opportunities and responsibilities of freedom, and of bridging the gap between the races which Reconstruction and the new populist governments had deepened. His famous speech at the Atlanta Exposition in 1893 brought him national prominence, and within a decade, certainly after the publication of his classic *Up from Slavery* (1901), he was widely regarded as the almost official spokesman for his race—a position shortly to be challenged by W. E. B. Du Bois. It is a reflection of the psychotic state of the American mind at that time that when Theodore Roosevelt invited Washington to lunch at the White

From Booker T. Washington, *The Man Farthest Down, A Record of Observation and Study in Europe*. With the collaboration of Robert E. Park (Garden City, N.Y., 1912), pp. 37–42, 45–46, 366–376.

648

House he created something like a national—or at least a Southern—crisis, but that Queen Victoria's invitation to Washington to have tea at Buckingham Palace a few years earlier had passed almost without comment in England. In 1909 Washington returned to England to study conditions among the poor and the working classes. John Burns was a leader and spokesman for the workingmen of England; we shall meet him again via William Allen White. Robert Park was a sociologist at the new University of Chicago.

Petticoat Lane

The first thing about London that impressed me was its size; the second was the wide division between the different elements in the population.

London is not only the largest city in the world; it is also the city in which the segregation of the classes has gone farthest. The West End, for example, is the home of the King and the Court. Here are the Houses of Parliament, Westminster Abbey, the British Museum, most of the historical monuments, the art galleries, and nearly everything that is interesting, refined, and beautiful in the lives of seven millions of people who make up the inhabitants of the city.

If you take a cab at Trafalgar Square, however, and ride eastward down the Strand through Fleet Street, where all the principal newspapers of London are published, past the Bank of England, St. Paul's Cathedral, and the interesting sights and scenes of the older part of the city, you come, all of a sudden, into a very different region, the centre of which is the famous Whitechapel.

The difference between the East End and the West End of London is that East London has no monuments, no banks, no hotels, theatres, art galleries; no history—nothing that is interesting and attractive but its poverty and its problems. Everything else is drab and commonplace.

It is, however, a mistake, as I soon learned, to assume that East London is a slum. It is, in fact, a city by itself, and a very remarkable city, for it has, including what you may call its suburbs, East Ham and West Ham, a population of something over two millions, made up for the most part of hard-working, thrifty labouring people. It has its dark places, also, but I visited several parts of London during my stay in the city which were considerably worse in every respect than anything I saw in the East End.

Nevertheless, it is said that more than one hundred thousand of the people in this part of the city, in spite of all the efforts that have been made to help them, are living on the verge of starvation. So poor and so helpless are these people that it was, at one time, seriously proposed to separate them from the rest of the population and set them off in a city by themselves, where they could live and work entirely under the direction of the state. . . .

I got my first view of one of the characteristic sights of the East End life at Middlesex Street, or Petticoat Lane, as it was formerly called. Petticoat Lane is in the centre of the Jewish quarter, and on Sunday morning there is a famous market in this street. On both sides of the thoroughfare, running northward from Whitechapel Road until they lose themselves in some of the side streets, one sees a double line of pushcarts, upon which every imaginable sort of ware, from wedding rings to eels in jelly, is exposed for sale. On both sides of these carts and in the middle of the street a motley throng of bargain-hunters are pushing their way through the crowds, stopping to look over the curious wares in the carts or to listen to the shrill cries of some hawker selling painkiller or some other sort of magic cure-all.

Nearly all of the merchants are Jews, but the majority of their customers belong to the tribes of the Gentiles. Among others I noticed a class of professional customers. They were evidently artisans of some sort or other who had come to pick out from the goods exposed for sale a plane or a saw or some other sort of second-hand tool; there were others searching for useful bits of old iron, bolts, brass, springs, keys, and other things of that sort which they would be able to turn to some use in their trades.

I spent an hour or more wandering through this street and the neighbouring lane into which this petty pushcart traffic had overflowed. Second-hand clothing, second-hand household articles, the waste meats of the Saturday market, all kinds of wornout and cast-off articles which had been fished out of the junk heaps of the city or thrust out of the regular channels of trade, find here a ready market.

I think that the thing which impressed me most was not the poverty, which was evident enough, but the sombre tone of the crowd and the whole proceeding. It was not a happy crowd; there were no bright colours, and very little laughter. It was an ill-dressed crowd, made up of people who had long been accustomed to live, as it were, at second-hand and in close relations with the pawnbroker.

In the Southern States it would be hard to find a coloured man who did not make some change in his appearance on Sunday. The Negro labourer is never so poor that he forgets to put on a clean collar or a bright necktie or something out of the ordinary out of respect for the Sabbath. In the midst of this busy, pushing throng it was hard for me to remember that I was in England and that it was Sunday. Somehow or other I had got a very different notion of the English Sabbath.

Petticoat Lane is in the midst of the "sweating" district, where most of the cheap clothing in London is made. Through windows and open doors I could see the pale faces of the garment-makers bent over their work. There is much furniture made in this region, also, I understand. Looking down into some of the cellars as I passed, I saw men working at the lathes. Down at the end of the street was a bar-room, which was doing a rushing business. The law in London is, as I understand, that travellers may be served at a public bar on Sunday, but not others. To be a traveller, a bona-fide traveller, you must have come from a distance of at least three miles. There were a great many travellers in Petticoat Lane on the Sunday morning that I was there.

This same morning I visited Bethnal Green, another and a quite different quarter of the East End. There are a number of these different quarters of the East End, like Stepney, Poplar, St. George's in the East, and so forth. Each of these has its peculiar type of population and its own peculiar conditions. Whitechapel is Jewish; St. George's in the East is Jewish at one end and Irish at the other, but Bethnal Green is English. For nearly half a mile along Bethnal Green Road I found another Sunday market in full swing, and it was, if anything, louder and more picturesque than the one in Petticoat Lane.

It was about eleven o'clock in the morning; the housewives of Bethnal Green were out on the street hunting bargains in meat and vegetables for the Sunday dinner. One of the most interesting groups I passed was crowded about a pushcart where three sturdy old women, shouting at the top of their lungs, were reeling off bolt after bolt of cheap cotton cloth to a crowd of women gathered about their cart.

At another point a man was "knocking down" at auction cheap cuts of frozen beef from Australia at prices ranging from 4 to 8 cents a pound. Another was selling fish, another crockery, and a third tinware, and so through the whole list of household staples. . . .

While on one side of Bethnal Green Road the hucksters were shouting and the crowd was busy dickering and chaffering for food and clothes, I noticed on the other side of the street a wayside preacher. I went over and listened to what he had to say, and then I noted the effect of his words upon his hearers. He had gathered about him perhaps a dozen persons, most of them, however, seeming to be his own adherents who had come out to the meeting merely to give him the benefit of their moral support. The great mass of the people who passed up and down the street did not pay the slightest attention to him. There was no doubt about the earnestness and sincerity of the man, but as I listened to what he had to say I could find in his words nothing that seemed to me to touch in any direct or definite way the lives of the people about him. In fact, I doubted whether the majority of them could really understand what he was talking about.

Somewhat later, in another part of the city, I had an opportunity to listen to another of these street preachers. In this case he was a young man, apparently fresh from college, and he was making a very genuine effort, as it seemed to me, to reach and influence in a practical way the people whom the lights of the torches and the music had attracted to the meeting. I observed that the people listened respectfully to what he had to say, and I have no doubt they were impressed, as I was, with his evident desire to help them. It was only too evident, however, that he was speaking another language than theirs; that, in fact, one might almost say he belonged to a different race of people. The gulf between them was too great.

After listening to this man I thought I could understand in a way that I had not understood before the great success which the Salvation Army at one time had among the masses of the people of East London. In its early days, at least, the Salvation Army was of the people; it picked its preachers from the streets; it appealed to the masses it was seeking to help for its support; in fact, it set the slums to work to save itself. . . .

London Through the Eyes
of John Burns

What John Burns is doing, and the spirit in which he is doing it, will, perhaps, appear in the course of my description of a trip which I took with him through his own district of Battersea and the region adjoining it in order to see what the London County Council is doing there to make the life of the poor man better. I am sorry that I will not be able to describe in detail all that I saw on that trip, because we covered in a short time so much ground, and saw so many different things, that it was not until I had returned to my hotel, and had an opportunity to study out the route of that journey, that I was able to get any definite idea of the direction in which we had gone or of the connection and general plan which underlay the whole scheme of the improvements we had seen.

I think it was about two o'clock in the afternoon when we left the offices of the Local Government Board. Mr. Burns insisted that, before we started, I should see something of the Parliament Buildings, and he promised to act as my guide. This hasty trip through the Parliament Buildings served to show me that John Burns, although he had entered political life as a Socialist, has a profound reverence for all the historic traditions and a very intimate knowledge of English history. I shall not soon forget the eloquent and vivid manner in which he summoned up for me, as we passed through Westminster Hall, on the way to the House of Commons, some of the great historical scenes and events which had taken place in that ancient and splendid room. I was impressed not only by the familiarity which he showed with all the associations of the place, but I was thrilled by the enthusiasm with which he spoke of and described them. It struck me as very strange that the same John Burns once as "the man with the red flag," who had been imprisoned for leading a mob of workmen against the police, should be quoting history with all the enthusiasm of a student and a scholar. . . .

When he afterward told me that he had had very little education in school, because he had been compelled to go to work when he was ten years of age, I asked him how he had since found time, in the course of his busy life, to gain the wide knowledge of history and literature which he evidently possessed.

"You see," he replied, with a quiet smile, "I earned my living for a time as a candle maker and I have burned a good many candles at night ever since."

Mr. Burns had promised to show me, within the space of a few hours, examples of the sort of work which is now going on in every part of London. A few years ago, on the site of an ancient prison, the London County Council erected several blocks of workingmen's tenements. These were, I believe, the first, or nearly the first, of the tenements erected by the city in the work of clearing away unsanitary areas and providing decent homes for the working classes.

It was to these buildings, in which a population of about 4,000 persons live, that we went first. The buildings are handsome brick structures, well lighted, with wide, open, brick-paved courts between the rows of houses, so that each block looked like a gigantic letter H with the horizontal connecting line left out.

Of course, these buildings were, as some one said, little more than barracks compared with the houses that are now being erected for labouring people in some of the London suburbs, but they are clean and wholesome and, to any one familiar with the narrow, grimy streets in the East End of London, it was hard to believe that they stood in the midst of a region which a few years ago had been a typical London slum.

A little farther on we crossed the river and entered what Mr. Burns referred to as "my own district," Battersea, where he was born and where he has lived and worked all his life, except for one year spent as an engineer in Nigeria, Africa.

The great breathing place for the people of this region is Battersea Park, and as we sped along the edge of this beautiful green space, stopping to look for a moment at the refreshment booths on the cricket grounds, or to speak to a group of well-dressed boys going from school to the playgrounds, Mr. Burns interspersed his information about workmen's wages, the price of rents, and the general improvement of the labouring classes with comment on the historic associations of the places we passed. Where Battersea Park now stands there was formerly a foul and unwholesome swamp. Near here the Duke of Wellington had fought a duel with the Earl of Winchelsea, and a little farther up Julius Caesar, nearly two thousand years ago, forded the river with one of his legions.

It was a happy and novel experience to observe the pleasure which Mr. Burns took in pointing out the improvement in the people, in the dwellings, and in the life of the people generally, and to note, in turn, the familiar and cheerful way with which all sorts of people we met on the streets greeted him as we passed.

"Hello! Johnny Burns," a group of schoolboys would call as we went by. Once we passed by a group of some fifteen or twenty workingwomen sitting in one of the refreshment booths, drinking their afternoon tea and, apparently, holding a neighbourhood meeting of some kind or other. As they recognized the man who, as member of the London County Council, had been responsible for most of the improvements that had been made in the homes and surroundings in which they lived, they stood up and waved their handkerchiefs, and even attempted a faint and feminine "hurrah for John Burns," the member from Battersea.

There are 150,000 people in Battersea, but Mr. Burns seemed to be acquainted with every one of them, and when he wanted to show me the inside of some of the new "County Council houses," as they are called, did not hesitate to knock at the nearest door, where we were gladly welcomed. The people seemed to be just as proud of their new houses, and of Mr. Burns, as he was of them.

The houses which we visited were, some of them, no more than three or four rooms, but each one of them was as neat and wholesome as if it had been a palace. They were very compactly built, but provided with every sort of modern convenience, including electric lights and baths.

There were houses of five and six rooms intended for clerks and small business men, which rented for a pound a week, and there were cheaper houses, for ordinary labouring people, which rented for two dollars per week. These houses are built directly under the direction of the London County Council, and are expected to pay 3 per cent. upon the investment, after completion.

The London County Council was not the first to make the experiment of building decent and substantial houses for the labouring classes. Some thirty years before, on what is known as the Shaftbury Park Estate, 1,200 houses, which provide homes for eleven thousand people, were erected and the investment had been made to pay.

I looked down the long lanes of little vine-covered buildings which make up this estate. It seemed as if some great army had settled on the land and built permanent quarters.

These labour colonies were interesting, not merely for the improvement they had made in the lives of a large section of the people living in this part of the city, but as the forerunner of those garden cities which private enterprise has erected at places like Port Sunlight, near Liverpool; Bourneville, in the outskirts of Birmingham, and at Letchworth, thirty-four miles from London.

Not far from Battersea Park, and in a part of the city which was formerly inhabited almost wholly by the very poor, we visited the public baths and a public washhouse where, during the course of a year, 42,000 women come to wash their clothes, paying at the rate of three cents an hour for the use of the municipal tubs and hot water. Children pay a penny or two cents for the use of the public baths. The building is also provided with a gymnasium for the use of the children in winter, and contains a hall which is rented to workingmen's clubs at a nominal price.

What pleased me most was to see the orderly way in which the children had learned to conduct themselves in these places, which, as was evident, had become not merely places for recreation, but at the same time schools of good manners.

We passed on the streets groups of neatly dressed, well-bred looking boys, with their books slung over their arms, going home from school or making their way to the park. Mr. Burns was delighted at the sight of these clean-cut, manly looking fellows.

"Look at those boys, Mr. Washington," he would exclaim, as he pointed proudly to one or another of these groups. "Isn't that doing pretty well for the proletariat?"

Then he would leap out of the automobile, before the driver could stop, put his arm around the boy nearest him and, in a moment, come back triumphant with the confirmation of his statement that the boy's father was, as he had said, only a small clerk or a letter carrier, or, perhaps, the son of a common labourer, a navvy.

When I contrasted the appearance of these well-dressed and well-behaved boys with some of those I had seen elsewhere, with the children who attend the so-called "ragged" schools, for example, I understood and shared his enthusiasm.

From Battersea Park we went to Clapham Common and, as we were speeding along through what appeared to be a quarter of well-to-do artisans' homes, Mr. Burns nodded casually in the direction of a little vine-clad cottage and said:

"That is where I live."

Although Mr. Burns now occupies one of the highest positions in the British Government, in which he has a salary of $10,000 a year, he has not yet assumed the high hat and the long-tailed coat which are the recognized uniform in London of a gentleman. On the contrary, he wears the same blue reefer coat and soft felt hat, speaks the same language, lives in the same style, and is apparently in every respect the same man that he was when he was living on the $25 a week guaranteed him by the Battersea Labour League when he entered parliament. He is still a labouring man and proud of the class to which he belongs.

It was at Clapham Common, although Mr. Burns did not mention this fact, that he was arrested for the first time, away back in 1878, for making a public speech. It was somewhere in this region also, if I remember rightly, that Mr. Burns pointed out to us a private estate on which 3,000 houses of the cheaper class had been erected.

"And mind you, there is no public house," said Mr. Burns. Instead he showed us a brand-new temperance billiard hall which had been erected to compete with, and take the place of, the barrooms which have disappeared.

At Lower Tooting, an estate of some thirty-eight acres, the London County Council is building outright a city of something like

5,000 inhabitants, laying out the streets, building the houses, even putting a tidy little flower garden in each separate front door yard. It was as if the London County Council had gone to playing dolls, so completely planned and perfectly carried out in every detail is this little garden city.

Mr. Burns, who has all his life been an advocate of temperance, although he had once served as pot-boy in a public house, pointed out here, as he did elsewhere, that there was no public house.

In the building of this little paradise all the architectural and engineering problems had indeed been solved. There remained, however, the problem of human nature, and the question that I asked myself was: Will these people be able to live up to their surroundings?

It is fortunate, in this connection, that in Mr. Burns the inhabitants have a leader who dares to speak plainly to them of their faults as well as their virtues and who is able, at the same time, to inspire them with an ambition and enthusiasm for the better life which is opened to them. Engineering and architecture cannot do everything, but education, leadership of the right sort, may complete what these have begun.

At Warden Street and Lydden Road, on our way back to the city, we stopped to look for a moment at what Mr. Burns said was the most wretched part of the population in that quarter of the city. The houses were two-story dwellings, with the sills flush with the pavement, in front of which groups of lounging idle men and women stood or squatted on the pavement. A portion of the street was given up to gypsy vans, and the whole population was made up, as I learned, of pedlers and pushcart venders, a class of people who, in the very centre of civilization, manage somehow to maintain a nomadic and half-barbarous existence, wandering from one place to another with the seasons, living from hand to mouth, working irregularly and not more than half the time.

A little farther on we passed by the Price candle factory, "where I began work at a dollar a week," said Mr. Burns in passing. A group of workmen were just coming from the factory as we passed, and the men recognized Mr. Burns and shouted to him as he passed.

Then we drove on back across the Chelsea Bridge and along the river to the Parliament Buildings again. "Now," said Mr. Burns at the end of our journey, "you have seen a sample of what London is doing for its labouring population. If you went further you would see more, but little that is new or different."

WILLIAM ALLEN WHITE
BREATHES THE AIR
OF REVOLUTION
IN LLOYD GEORGE'S ENGLAND

1909

One of the most distinguished and beloved American journalists, William Allen White was a historian, biographer, novelist, politician, friend and adviser to statesmen and Presidents. As a young man he became editor of the obscure Emporia (Kansas) *Gazette* and made it, almost overnight, a national paper. He was the ideal provincial, and probably no other man of his time was so nearly the representative and the symbol of the Middle Border—deeply rooted in the soil of Kansas, but national and even cosmopolitan in the range of his mind and his interests. He wrote a series of novels of the Middle Border, of which *In the Heart of a Fool* is probably the best known; a classic of children's literature, *The Court of Boyville*; essays like "What's the Matter with Kansas?" and "Margaret White," which have made their way into scores of anthologies; a biography of Calvin Coolidge; a political history of the post-Civil War years; and one of the notable autobiographies of our literature. He was a "liberal" and a "progressive," but always a party regular; as Franklin Roosevelt once said—it was during a speech in Kansas—"There's my old friend Bill White who is with me three and a half years out of every

William Allen White, *Autobiography* (New York, 1946), pp. 411–419.

four." White was devoted to Britain and in the crisis of 1939 organized the Committee to Defend America by Aiding the Allies; here, too, as in politics, his timidity came to the fore, and the so-called "Century" group had to take the committee away from him and agitate, more successfully, for American intervention in time to do some good.

Edwardian England

My mother went to England as an army with banners. She could not forget the Irish famine, nor the failure to grant home rule. So she looked with a fishy eye on the glamorous scenes that we loved because they were a part of our racial heritage. For a week or ten days we put up in London at a smart, rather exclusive second- or third-class haunt of the decade's nobility and gentry—the Artillery Mansions. To get in, we had to be introduced. We had pleasant rooms with a fire in the grate in the evening even though it was midsummer. The children played in the courtyards around and in a fountain.

It was in England that we bade farewell to the lilacs, which came upon us first at Madeira in April. They tagged us into Italy and through Switzerland. We saw them in Germany in June, and saw the very ragged last of them in France, and then came upon what seemed to be hothouse lilacs—dark, dark purple flowers—in England.

Mr. Howells had given us a letter to Henry James and another to his brother-in-law, Larkin G. Mead, a dear old man, an expatriated American sculptor with the slang of the sixties still in his mouth. These two letters were the only social letters we presented. I had a sort of letter from President Taft to all embassies, suggesting courtesies, which I never used. I had no desire to make this a plug-hat trip. But at Henry James's invitation I did go on a pilgrimage to his home. He lived at Rye in Sussex—and lived most charmingly—in an old though modest house with a little walled garden back of it. It seemed to me that the house, the garden, and Henry James were all one. We two had luncheon together and a long talk about the United States and about American writers, most of whom I knew, men and women whose work he was enjoying. For an exile he was well informed about American books and writers. We talked after luncheon there in the walled garden under a spreading tree; then we walked about Rye and visited an old church. He told me its history charmingly. He talked, as he wrote, in long involved sentences with a little murmur—mum-mum-mum—standing for parentheses, and with these rhetorical hooks he seemed to be poking about his mind, fumbling through the whole basket of his conversational vocabulary, to find the exact word, which he used in talking about most ordinary matters. He seemed to creak with those murmuring parentheses, but he did talk well, and was altogether a joy. He was of middle height, high-domed, stocky though not chubby; and I fancy his mumbling, fumbling way of talking came because he lived alone so much, an old bachelor. He walked sturdily, with just the faintest swagger to his well set rounding shoulders. The afternoon I spent with him was one of the lovely experiences of that gorgeous summer.

I knew that *A Certain Rich Man* had been published that summer. Macmillan & Company in London brought out a small edition, and we had fancy bindings put on several copies for friend and kin. The company indicated mildly that the book was doing well in the United States, but said it more plainly by inviting us down to the home of one of the Macmillans. It was a typical English country home. The hostess was most scrupulously English in all her domestic arrangements, although she had been born and reared in Indianapolis. We had never seen the service in an English country house before—so many kinds of servants to do so many things. The English scorn of modern plumbing gave great respectability to servants, who did what plumbing did for folks in the United States. I remember a maid brought a shallow tin bathtub and large pitchers of hot water for Mrs. White's bath, and routed me out down a corridor to a stairway to where she said my bath was ready. I wandered about the place for four or five minutes and never could find the bathtub. Heaven knows what they thought of me, but that chambermaid had me cringing. She had come into my room where I undressed hastily, had taken my drawers out of my trousers where I had left them crinkled on the floor, found my undershirt, and put the two together folded neatly on the bed while I cowered under the bedclothes. They had unpacked our valise while we were in the garden an hour after we came, and scattered things about drawers and in closets so that we did not know where to find them. And some way I shuddered to realize that that maid knew everything about us—the undarned condition of our stockings, underwear, maybe buttons missing here and there, for we had been away from home three months and were not in the very pink of sartorial perfection. Sallie had great glee over my embarrassment before the maid and my reservations about letting her bounce me around in my nightgown.

But the Macmillans were exceedingly kind and did not realize our hardships. They had their notions of how life should proceed in a country house, and it went that way. And we, at least and in truth, were as interested in the strange maneuvers of the servants as they must have been amazed at our savage individualistic attitudes. But the talk was good and the house full of young boys from the British public schools and universities—Eton, Oxford, and maybe Cambridge—who were so much more intelligent than the college boys that I had known that I was amazed at what British civilization was doing for upper-class British youth. They talked politics, national politics. The sons and nephews of the family were nicely divided between the Tories and the Liberals, and you could hear them going at it at all hours. My collegiate experience in discussing American politics had been limited to losing five dollars on Blaine in 1884 after which I became, as I think most college boys in midwestern United States were, hermetically sealed to the issues of modern American politics, however we might delve into American history. We did not relate history with life. History stopped for us with the Civil War, or at most the panic of '73. But in England, and particularly there at the Macmillan home, I began to realize the uproar that Lloyd George was causing in that year 1909 with his budget bill. It provided for a tax on land. It carried with it heavy income taxes, for those days; and there was an implication that if the House of Lords held it up too long the powers of the Lords would be curtailed. And imagine discussing such things in a conservative English household a generation ago.

At the publishing house I was invited to luncheon by the Macmillans, and there I met Thomas Hardy. The luncheon was no great shakes—fine rare roast beef, boiled potatoes and cabbage, Yorkshire pudding and a savory dessert. But Hardy, who was then at the height of his fame, was something to write home about. He had a sandy, scrubby, wayward little mustache, blond gray, that had been spoiled too long to be taken in hand in his sixties. His was a ruddy pink skin. He had gorgeous blue eyes which opened sometimes like the lifting of a curfew. His hair was a dark graying brown. His voice was mousy, something almost like a senile tenor. I never knew a man so entirely unconscious of himself. At our luncheon table one of the guests told us that Hardy sat through the first operatic performance of "Tess" smiling, pleased as Punch, but like a wraith, quite disconnected from the world about him. When it was over he sat in the box and clapped his hands for the composer to come out, and then for the singer, and finally for all of the people in the cast. But no one called for him and it did not occur to him probably, that anyone

should call for him. He was just that dear. I remember nothing that
he said at that luncheon, for I did not write it down, but I do
remember that what he said was impressive and that the way he said
it was delightful. He carried conviction as much by his smile and his
mien as by his words, and I was charmed. Under direct examination
I tried to tell those at the table something about Kansas. But I must
have made a poor first of it, for they did not believe there was any
such country. I tried to tell them about Stubbs and the American
insurgents, but there I know they thought I was more than mildly
mad. And when I said that Kansas had lived submissively under state
prohibition for nearly thirty years without raising an issue in politics
worthy of a name, I could see that my reputation as a reporter was
wilting. But Hardy was greatly amused. He thought it excruciatingly
funny that the same people would endure prohibition whose ancestors one hundred thirty years before had arisen in rebellion against
the British government over the little matter of taxes. He strained
with inner mirth and would not let himself laugh—probably from
habit, but maybe because he wished to be polite to me. But I could
see that he was struggling terribly with his risibilities, and I saw the
humor of it too, and laughed perhaps as loudly as Hardy would have
liked to laugh. The luncheon was really more than a passing event. It
was an experience. I really wanted to see Kipling and Barrie, but
something happened to prevent our meeting. Perhaps they heard of
my desire in time to act. I should not blame them. For I was walking
through the vast menagerie of the world gawking wide-eyed and
perhaps serving myself too much.

But I did see one British politician whom I particularly wished to
see. It was John Burns, the labor leader. I bore a letter to him from
either Peter Dunne in New York, or Robert Hunter, who at that time
was considerable of a Socialist. He arranged for a luncheon—where,
I don't know. I can remember it was in a small room. With him came
two or three of the left-wing members of Parliament, men whose
names I cannot remember. But he was the soul of the company, a
most remarkable man. He must have been in his sixties. He seemed
old to me. He had a ruddy face and rugged, covered sparsely by
what might be called a scraggly beard, decently kept but thin. His
voice was gentle, not the roaring rabble-rousing trumpet that I had
expected; and his eyes were bright, lively, illuminating, a blue or
gray, which I cannot remember. He seemed to be as anxious to know
about American politics as I was to learn about English. I tried to tell
him of Roosevelt and about Taft, in whom I was beginning to lose
faith. And he told me much about Lloyd George, of whom he had

not the highest opinion. He felt that Lloyd George was what in the parlance of politics we called "a double-crosser"—a man who makes too many promises to too many people about too many different kinds of things. Of course Lloyd George was trying to assemble a parliamentary majority and stretch it as far to the right as he could, and as far to the left. John Burns knew this, and he was an uncompromising left-winger. And he hated palaverers, and Lloyd George was one. He was a hand-shaker and a back-slapper, an orator and a politician who liked to please perhaps better than to serve. Most politicians of that type get the notion that their own pleasure is their country's service, that in building up their own strength they are saving their country. From my talk with Burns at that luncheon I gathered that he regarded Lloyd George as just another politician. I knew enough about politics to bet Burns' picture of Lloyd George rather too exactly in my heart. Although the terminology Burns used was British, the political atmosphere in which he moved and spoke was universal. Politics from the days of Moses to the days of the second Roosevelt are the same old game. Issues change a little, but men and their weaknesses, the handles, levers and push-buttons by which politicians work and achieve their ends, are well worn through the ages of use.

I suppose I learned more of British politics during that hour or so with John Burns and his left-wing supporters than I had learned in the weeks that I was in London.

But I lost class at the Artillery Mansions when it became known that I was lunching with John Burns. Now that the American boarding house has passed with the coming of the hot-dog stand, the hole-in-the-wall café, the hamburger joint, the cafeteria, the automat, nothing in America remains like the Artillery Mansions. Of course they dressed for dinner there. Of course the meals, although varied, were essentially the same. The cooking was, from any American standard I knew, decent but terrible. The menus adhered scrupulously to an imitation of the table d'hôte of restaurants of a much higher grade. The guests ate in silence, murmured with their food, were exceedingly well bred—more proud of their breeding than they were of the scrimpy, almost stingy respectability of the ménage. I gathered from their uniforms at dinner that many of the men were retired army and navy officers, with an occasional retired Indian civil servant or a county agent in town for the week end, all with their women kind who seemed as lean, as circumspect, as tightly buttoned as the men. They all met in a large salon or parlor after dinner, floating like ice cakes from table to table, where there were magazines and most respectable newspapers, and where also the repressed murmur of softly modulated voices was a constant rebuke to any American. I was branded with the "scarlet letter" when it became known through the head clerk (whom I had asked to get Burns on the telephone) that I was consorting with a left-wing labor leader. If I had introduced smallpox I would have caused less panicky horror than I spread about me after coming back from my luncheon with John Burns. I felt that even the servants—who in America would have been for Burns—deprecated my social misadventure, but in sorrow rather than in anger. One of them, mentioning my transgression, exclaimed, "Ow, him!" and let it go at that. Class runs to the core of British society. It is not a matter of wealth or power. It is a matter of inward attitude of the poor and lowly, the rich and great alike. All these things I learned graciously, happily, but well at the Artillery Mansions.

Once when we were stopping there many years later I spoke of it to H. G. Wells, and he exclaimed, "Ow, there!" Then he caught himself and said that once he had luncheon there, and looked at me shrewdly to see whether I realized whither I had wandered. It was the British Empire on the half-shell. . . .

A few days before we left England, the children and their grandmother came up from Littlehampton, and we took them on another adventure. For days the newspapers were talking about the great parade that Lloyd George was backing, to demonstrate for his budget bill. The budget bill was, in its way, as revolutionary as the flight of Blériot, for it proposed a tax on land, a deep gouge in income tax on the rich. Moreover—and this is what crashed into the Artillery Mansions like a bomb—Lloyd George's supporters were saying that if the House of Lords opposed the budget, the Commons would take away its power of veto. Revolution was in the air. We were anxious to see the parade, so immediately after lunch one summer's day we hired a rattle-bang old taxi, all of us, and sallied forth. I never saw such a parade before. Organizations from all over England, Wales and Scotland were on the march—laboring men, farmers, farm workers, miners, clerks, the little people of England. They were singing as they marched. Bands were blaring, drums rolling, and it was almost orderly. They even kept step, many thousands of them. Hundreds of thousands were in line. For an hour we rode up and down alongside the procession where the police would let us cruise. I began to see old banners that I had seen in the Populist parade fluttering in the air. Among them were a lot of

Jeffersonian mottoes that gripped at our hearts. Pretty soon, in the midst of a battalion of Welsh miners who had bands fore and aft, came, on a purple banner lettered in gold, the Jeffersonian slogan I had heard in the days of the Greenbackers and the Grangers and that I had seen coming down Main Street at Eldorado, and Commercial Street in Emporia, when the Farmers' Alliance and the Populists appeared:

Equal rights to all; special privileges to none.

—*Thomas Jefferson*

How often my father had quoted that when he talked politics on his hundred forty-four feet of porches around the old White house in Eldorado. It was too much for me. I tapped my taxi driver on the shoulder and said:

"Wheel in there behind that banner if you can!"

He could, and did. And that taxi load of Kansans, old and young, rolled slowly into the line and followed the banner for half an hour. We had to stop sometimes. It was a slow pace for a taxi. But I thought of Stubbs and Bristow in Kansas, and of Roosevelt and his fight for seven years in Washington. And I knew that old Bob La Follette would have crowded into the taxi if he had been on the sidewalk. And we were all proud and happy to follow his Jeffersonian flag in the great British revolutionary parade. It was the high day of our trip thus far. Galleries, concerts, strange places and stranger people all paled in significance beside this stupendous parade that shocked upper-class Britain to its foundations. Blériot and Lloyd George were unsettling the footing stones of civilization. Indeed these two harbingers of danger—these two symbols of machine-age revolution that was coming—the revolution, indeed, that was presenting its heralds with trumpets—were waking up, slowly but inevitably, a dazed world. The revolution had appeared. How, few of us knew. I should have known, of course, that the Kansas rebels whom I had fought and who took me in, were a part of this Lloyd George uprising, but I did not realize the unity of the revolt. As we rode in the procession in a rattle-bang old hack, and as I closed my eyes and heard the same old tunes from the bands along St. James's Park that I heard in Kansas: "John Brown's Body," among others, and "The Marseillaise," "Where Has My Highland Laddie Gone?" and "America" set to the tune of "God Save the King," I was stirred to the very roots of my being. Sallie and I held hands and when I opened my eyes through my tears I saw hers. We felt that we were a part of something great and beautiful. We did not know exactly what, except that we knew the under dog had slipped off his leash and this was his time to howl. So in our hearts we gave voice for him and with him.

The children were delighted, their grandmother baffled, by the size and mass and emotional impact of the parade. I think she bragged a little around the hotel when we returned that evening. What with my luncheon with John Burns and the bad odor Americans carried in general, there with the nobility and gentry (junior grade), because of Selfridge's bad form, this countenance of the Lloyd George budget parade was just another evidence that Americans were essentially lower.

1910-1920

WALTER HINES PAGE
CHAMPIONS THE CAUSE OF
WARTIME ENGLAND

1914–18

Born in North Carolina before the Civil War, Walter Hines Page studied classics at Randolph-Macon College in Virginia and at the newly founded Johns Hopkins, then turned to journalism. Returning to North Carolina, he bought the *Raleigh State Chronicle* and made it one of the liveliest and most progressive newspapers in the South. In 1885 he moved to New York, where he joined the staff of the *Forum;* then he became assistant editor—and finally editor-in-chief—of the *Atlantic Monthly.* At the turn of the century he returned to New York to join the publishing house of Doubleday (which became Doubleday, Page), and founded *World's Work,* a magazine which served much the same function that *Foreign Affairs* has served in recent years. Active in educational, reform, and progressive circles, he was an ardent supporter of Woodrow Wilson's candidacy in 1912, and on his election Wilson returned to the literary tradition by appointing him Ambassador to the Court of St. James's. Before the outbreak of the First World War the President and the Ambassador were very close, but after the outbreak of the war, and particu-

From Burton J. Hendrick, *The Life and Letters of Walter Hines Page* (Garden City, N.Y., 1922, 1925), III, pp. 46–51, 163–165; II, 64–67; III, 265–269; II, 328–345.

larly after the sinking of the *Lusitania,* Page forfeited Wilson's confidence by a championship of the British cause, which went so far as to paralyze some of Wilson's diplomatic efforts to bring the warring nations to the peace table. Late in 1916 Page concluded that his usefulness was over and submitted his resignation; the dramatic turn of events which took the United States into the war changed the picture, and Page was allowed to stay on. Not surprisingly he was immensely popular with the British government—and people. In 1918, when ill health forced his retirement, Lloyd George wrote him, "That our people are now fighting side by side in the cause of human freedom and that they are manifesting an ever growing feeling or cordiality to one another is largely attributable to the exceptional wisdom and good will with which you have discharged your duties." Two months after his return to New York Page died. Burton J. Hendrick, who edited the *Life and Letters* in two volumes, and then added a third containing Page's letters to President Wilson, was himself one of the leading journalists of his day, and also a successful popularizer of history. In addition to these volumes on Page, Hendrick wrote biographies of Carnegie, Admiral William Sims, and the Adams family, and histories of Lincoln's War Cabinet and of the Constitution. Here Page's letters, taken from volumes published at different times, are arranged in chronological order.

To the President

American Embassy London
May 21, 1914

Dear Mr. President:

At this season, as you know, everybody comes to London; the King gives his levees and his courts and his balls and the rich and the high and the climbing exercise on the social ladder and trapeze; the ambassadors dine one another and other great folk; American ladies come over to be presented; hundreds of people drink Mrs. Page's tea every Thursday afternoon (on July 4th they come 3,000 strong) and we are supposed to have lots of fun; and the funny part of it is, we do! I hear more gossip, get more points of view, see more people, get closer to my colleagues than at any other time of year. I dine with everybody, from the King down—this whole Babylon goes on a tear! Mrs. House and Mrs. Hugh Wallace, for examples, forgetting republican simplicity, will be here to go with us to the Palace. Seriously, it's a fine show—to see once or twice. I am very, very sorry that McAdoo couldn't come. I had a place for your daughter in "the diplomatic circle," and she would have enjoyed it. I told Jessie[1] that

---

1. Mrs. Francis Bowe Sayre, the President's recently married daughter.

she made a bad mistake in marrying at the wrong time of year! I let the oldish ladies go hang: I like young ones about me. . . .

In spite of our "seasonable" gaiety, I do assure you (and it never leaves me) that there's a sadness in this Old-World life that in certain moods weighs heavily on a man who has been bred to a hopeful outlook on the future, and on a sympathetic man whatever his outlook. I have given you glimpses of what the aristocratic dowagers tell me: you'd expect this from old women of pampered families. But it tinges all English life. The Dowager Lady T. sat in a garden where I was spending Sunday twenty miles out of London—she's a vigorous, handsome, perfectly sincere fine lady of sixty, younger than many women at forty—and she said:

"What would you do and what would you wish your son to do if you were me? My husband's family has had a seat in the House of Lords for 600 years. My son sits there now—literally 'sits,' for a peer can now do nothing else. All their power has been taken away. They are robbing us of our property. When they can they will abolish the monarchy itself. The King knows that his house is doomed. England the Empire of which we have been so proud—their glory is in the past." Tears came into the old lady's eyes and she said,

"Let's walk and talk of something else."

The Duchess of S. told me last night again that if there should be a fight in Ulster she was ready in three hours to have nurses on the way and that the Duke would at once go and fight. (He's six feet four inches.)

"They are robbing us, these devils," and her great diamond necklace seemed to spit fire.

The Liberals, too are sad. A real victory is so hard to win. Sir Edward Grey carries a philosophic sadness in his manner. The Prime Minister talks like a man who would be glad to be relieved of the whole struggle and to get a little rest before he dies. Donald,[2] the editor of the really only Liberal morning paper in London, complains to me: "We can't get the fighting help we need. If a man puts up money for any of our causes, damn him, he wants a title in return." A member of Parliament brought in a bill the other day to abolish hereditary titles—amid general laughter: and a Conservative twitted him thus: "You're tired of making Liberal peers and have them become Conservative—eh?"

They're all sad—both sides. The machine that confers titles, gives social distinctions, confers orders, gives out sinecures, appoints men to livings and doles out many other such alms and uniforms,

2. Robert Donald, editor of the *Daily Chronicle*.

captures the ambitious women and the rich men; and the poor devil who can get none of these things pays the bill. If he knows that he is "worked," he can hardly hope for relief in his lifetime, and he goes sadly on, doing the best he can and drinking the King's health as an expression of pride in the Empire. Yet they are all a vigorous race. Else they'd be in real despair permanently. The mills of the gods and of Lloyd George grind slowly.

Yet all this sadness is hilarity in comparison with the note of weary resignation that I think I detect in such men as the very cultivated Greek Minister, the Rumanian Minister, the Austrian Ambassador, and especially the foxy but melancholy old Benchkendorff of Russia. They, I think, having got some glimpses of the free world, carry with them a real hopelessness. But even this English life would depress me if I had to adjust myself to it permanently.

I was talking about this the other night to Lady X. I said frankly that I thought the Englishmen ought to leave our American ladies alone—we need them ourselves!

"And what nationality do you suppose I am?" she asked.

"Great Heavens! are you, too, an American?" "Certainly.

"And you wouldn't have your children marry here?" she asked.

I told her, "No," because of the underlying sadness of it. The wife of the Argentine Minister (herself from Kentucky!) said to me afterward, "You are very, very right: all the sunlight falls on the New World."

It is weighted—heavily, all this Old World.

"Do you look at us through economic glasses?" asked Lord Milner.

"I do and—am sad."

"Well, you may be," said he. "My friend, keep your hopeful mood and pray that your country may never get old—as it will."

Heaven forgive me (and I hope you will, too) for so long a letter. But 'tis true, the sunlight falls on our New World. Here we are very gay but—in the shadow.

Always faithfully yours,
Walter H. Page

October 15, 1914

... Of course, I don't know what you know of this unprecedented fierceness or what is known about it in the United States. But if the British public do not yet realize it—are not yet conscious of all that is at stake—I fancy that few men 3,000 miles away realize it.

The simple truth is, it *is* unbelievable. I see indications that it is not in the least understood in many quarters. Take, for instance, the resolution passed by the Pan-American Union, which we received by telegraph to-day, asking for peace. "If England lives, who dies?" And, if England dies, who lives? That's their mood; and this resolution reads here like a Sunday-school resolution passed in Kansas requesting cruel Vesuvius to cease its eruption, which destroys villages of innocent people. This is a vast eruption—a world-changing clash of systems: not a "war," as we have hitherto understood the word, but a sort of crash of worlds. If England win, the world will be ruled by English institutions and ideas and ideals and those ideas and ideals that are English-sprung. If Germany win, the war lord will set out to bestride the world, and we shall have big armies and big navies indefinitely and periodical great conflicts. The Monroe Doctrine will be less than a scrap of paper—the mere faded breath of a dead man.

The men who have this colossal undertaking in hand feel its magnitude and seriousness. The two ablest of them show it in different ways. Grey, who had made it his life work to prevent it, grows a year older every month. Anderson, who went with me the other day to the Foreign Office to a conference on our shipping controversy, and who sees Sir Edward less often than I see him and consequently notices changes in his appearance more clearly, remarked as we came away that he had "a Lincoln look"; and so he has. Kitchener, the imperturbable, the man of colossal "cheek," affects an unnatural calmness—even an unconcern—while he works like a Titan. These men are lonely, sad, remote, feigning their old-time joy in life and work, and keeping up, as far as they can, their old-time manner, when all the while they are conscious that life means something different from what it ever meant before. You can see as you talk with them that their manner and speech are merely reminiscent of their old selves: they have entered a new stage of responsibility; they have a new measure of life, of hope, of work; and they are perfectly capable of yawning, after you have gone, and saying to themselves, "Oh, well, what does it matter now? What does anything matter?" Then you can imagine them shaking themselves together and taking a new turn at the wheel, with a grim, weary smile—at life. For death is a daily piece of news to them—the death of kinsmen, of friends, of companions, and they wonder whether they may not live to see the death of England and the eclipse of English civilization. They think not in terms of mere "war," but in terms of the possible death of civilization—a million men, perhaps, already dead, many of them rotten, unburied, in France and Austria. Red Cross and coffins and quiet graves or affectionate farewells—there are not enough of these to count: shells and acres of bloated human bodies, careless of sun or rain, giving only stench—a hundred miles of them in each of three places—and inviting pestilence. All this for the clash of systems! I myself, as detached from it as a man here can be, often find myself, when I ought to be in bed, sitting alone silently looking into the dying fire, not only thinking but dumbly brooding on it, wondering in what world I live. For it is not the same world it was last July—nothing is the same. All one's measures and centres of reference are different; and the people you meet have changed; and all talk somehow seems hollow. You wonder yourself if you mean what you say, for you are all the time readjusting yourself to some great shock of things that has hitherto seemed incredible. . . .

Summer, 1915

The truth is, in their present depressed mood, the United States is forgotten—everything's forgotten but the one great matter in hand. For the moment at least, the English do not care what we do or what we think or whether we exist—except those critics of thing-in-general who use us as a target since they must take a crack at somebody. And I simply cannot describe the curious effect that is produced on men here by the apparent utter lack of understanding in the United States of the phase the war has now entered and of the mood that this phase has brought. I pick up an American paper eight days old and read solemn evidence to show that the British Government is interrupting our trade in order to advance its own at our expense, whereas the truth is that the British Government hasn't given six seconds' thought in six months to anybody's trade—not even its own. When I am asked to inquire why Pfister and Schmidt's telegram from New York to Schimmelpfenig and Johann in Holland was stopped (the reason is reasonably obvious), I try to picture to myself the British Minister in Washington making inquiry of our Government on the day after Bull Run, why the sailing boat loaded with persimmon blocks to make golf clubs is delayed in Hampton Roads.

I think I have neither heard nor read anything from the United States in three months that didn't seem so remote as to suggest the captain of the sailing ship from Hongkong who turned up at Southhampton in February and had not even heard that there was a war. All day long I see and hear women who come to ask if I can make inquiry about their sons and husbands, "dead or missing," with an interval given to a description of a man half of whose body was splashed against a brick wall last night on the Strand when a Zeppelin bomb tore up the street and made projectiles of the pavement; as I walk to and from the Embassy the Park is full of wounded and their nurses; every man I see tells me of a new death; every member of the Government talks about military events or of Balkan venality; the man behind the counter at the cigar store reads me part of a letter just come from his son, telling how he advanced over a pile of dead Germans and one of them grunted and turned under his feet—they (the English alone) are spending $25,000,000 a day to keep this march going over dead Germans; then comes a telegram predicting blue ruin for American importers and a cheerless Christmas for American children if a cargo of German toys be not quickly released at Rotterdam, and I dimly recall the benevolent unction with which American children last Christmas sent a shipload of toys to this side of the world—many of them for German children—to the tune of "God bless us all"—do you wonder we often have to pinch ourselves to find out if we are we; and what year of the Lord is it? What *is* the vital thing—the killing of fifty people last night by a Zeppelin within sight of St. Paul's on one side and of Westminster Abbey on the other, or is it making representations to Sir Edward Grey, who has hardly slept for a week because his despatches from Sofia, Athens, Belgrade, and Salonika come at all hours, each possibly reporting on which side a new government may throw its army—to decide perhaps the fate of the canal leading to Asia, the vast British Asiatic empire at stake—is it making representations to Sir Edward while his mind is thus occupied, that it is of the greatest importance to the United States Government that a particular German who is somewhere in this Kingdom shall be permitted to go to the United States because he knows how to dye sealskins and our sealskins are yet undyed and the winter is coming? There will be no new sealskins here, for every man and woman must give half his income to keep the cigarman's son marching over dead Germans, some of whom grunt and turn under his feet. Dumba is at Falmouth to-day and gets just two lines in the newspapers. Nothing and nobody gets three lines unless he or it in some way furthers the war. Every morning the Washington despatches say that Mr. Lansing is about to send a long note to England. England won't read it till there comes a lull in the fighting or in the breathless diplomatic struggle with the Balkans. London and the Government are now in much the same mood that Washington and Lincoln's administration were in after Lee had crossed the Potomac on his way to Gettysburg. Northcliffe, the Lord of Yellow Journals, but an uncommonly brilliant fellow, has taken to his bed from sheer nervous worry. "The revelations that are imminent," says he, "will shake the world—the incompetence of the Government, the losses along the Dardanelles, the throwing away of British chances in the Balkans, perhaps the actual defeat of the Allies." I regard Lord Northcliffe less as an entity than as a symptom. But he is always very friendly to us and he knows the United States better than any Englishman that I know except Bryce. He and Bryce are both much concerned about our Note's coming just "at this most distressing time." "If it come when we are calmer, no matter; but now it cannot receive attention and many will feel that the United States has hit on a most unhappy moment—almost a cruel moment—to remind us of our sins."—That's the substance of what they say.

Overwork, or perhaps mainly the indescribable strain on the nerves and vitality of men, caused by this experience, for which in fact men are not built, puts one of our staff after another in bed. None has been seriously sick: the malady takes some form of "grip." On the whole we've been pretty lucky in spite of this almost regular temporary breakdown of one man after another. I've so far escaped. But I am grieved to hear that Whitlock is abed—"no physical ailment whatever—just worn out," his doctor says. I have tried to induce him and his wife to come here and make me a visit; but one characteristic of this war-malady is the conviction of the victim that he is somehow necessary to hold the world together. About twice a week I get to the golf links and take the risk of the world's falling apart and thus escape both illness and its illusions. . . .

London, December 31, 1915

My Christmas guess, of no particular value, but as good as anybody else's, is that the war will end next summer or autumn —sooner only if some decisive military event give the Germans a good excuse to make terms. We live in a censored world here—in a sort of fog; but there are too many signs of impending German disaster to doubt its coming: this in spite of the extraordinary series of bad failures by the Allies—the Dardanelles failure, the Balkan failure, two military failures in France when the German line was actually broken. These failures have singularly little effect on the English, whose slow stupidity one curses with the more vehemence and whose cool endurance one admires with the more confidence the more one sees of them. The upshot of it is they are invincible, but they bungle their work so that a victory is far, far more costly than it ought to be. They think that the all-around changes they have just made in their military commands are great improvements. I can form no opinion about that; but anybody can see that some sort of change was desirable.

There is great dissatisfaction, too, with the Government; but there's no way to change it except by the voluntary resignation of the Ministers. The Prime Minister will not resign (his wife said the other day that "nobody but God could put Herbert out"); and Sir Edward Grey's resignation will not be accepted by him. It is against these two that the fiercest criticism continues to beat—against Asquith because the war doesn't go forward fast enough and because he doesn't seem to deal frankly with the people, and against Grey for the diplomatic failure to secure the Balkan States to the Allies. But during those months the English were thinking chiefly of keeping the Germans out of Calais and of holding the German line in France till the Russians should threaten—Berlin! The story goes about now that the Turks offered to permit the British to go through the Dardanelles for the payment of a sum that is small in comparison with what the Dardanelles failure cost. The answer they got was that the English do not do things in that way. The Navy and Army regard Sir Edward Grey, who is supposed to be responsible for this answer, as a visionary statesman—"too much of a gentleman," as old Lord Fisher said of Mr. Balfour.

Of course, we who are onlookers here have long ago passed the place where we can be surprised by any event; but unless new and disastrous things happen in the Balkans or beyond, I have good hope that Sir Edward will not be driven out of office till the war end. He will then go because his eyes demand rest. Else he may go blind. I lay stress on this because his continuing in office is of prime importance to us. He sees more nearly eye-to-eye with us than (I think) any other member of the Cabinet. He has to yield to his associates, who reflect and represent British opinion about the uses of sea power; and especially does he have to yield to the military and naval group and to the lawyer group. But he has softened many a blow. The diplomatic corps here share my estimate of him. Within the last few days Allied and neutral diplomats alike have expressed to me the greatest alarm lest he should resign in disgust at the criticism of him which comes from half the points of the compass. I don't think the diplomats now in service command great weight or brains. I fear that one has a tendency to lessen his list of great men as he sees them at close range. But, as nearly as I can judge, the group in London make a higher average by a good deal than the group at any other capital. Imperiali, the Italian Ambassador, dined with me three nights ago, and I could get him to talk about nothing else than Sir

Edward. Merry del Val, the Spaniard, gave me a call lasting a whole working morning, to express his alarm. The Minister from X . . . danced all around the room muttering his fear, "God knows we have a hard enough time now. But with Curzon, who can tell what we should suffer?" And it's Curzon they talk about for the Foreign Office if a change should be made.

Those of us who have so far fought thro' this war have long ago got past the least trace of awe of noble lords, or vice-gerents, or royalty; but you don't want—for steady intercourse—to deal with a fellow who has an air of ordering all mundane things; you're afraid you'll be tempted some day to say what you think of him, which wouldn't be diplomatic. In India Curzon quarrelled with Kitchener—which I secretly hold to his credit. For nobody seems able to work with Kitchener. For twenty years he ordered savages and dependent nations about. The people believe him great and the Government used him most effectively. His name raised a great army, Lord Derby actually doing the work. Thus, you see, we live not in an ordered world, but in a world of ragged hopes and fears. I fancy that History, in one of her vagaries, will set down these plausibilities for facts—that Asquith was England's greatest Prime Minister and that Grey failed in the great war as Secretary for Foreign Affairs—both wide of the truth.

I've heard nothing lately about the British reply to our long Note. I know they are looking up facts for a reply, and I'll ask when I see Sir Edward next—in a day or two. But I think I have written you that I do not expect any important concession to our demands. The navy party has public opinion squarely behind it; they are going to do all they can to starve out Germany and settle the bill with neutrals after the war. There isn't much feeling against us on the score of our protests against British action. Feeling flares up when provoked by any event; but nobody has time or feelings to spare from the demands of the war. Then, too, so long as the *Lusitania* controversy is unsettled, our Notes and protests are regarded by the public—I will not say by the Government—as formal. Austria is no longer thought of by the British as an independent power—only a German satrapy, like Turkey or Bulgaria. Consequently, the English conception of the *Ancona*[3] controversy is that it is an incident. Only Germany is regarded as a real power here. Any Englishman who speaks quite frankly will say something like this: "We caught and destroyed

3. The *Ancona* was sunk by an Austrian submarine in the Mediterranean, November 7, 1915. American lives were lost.

between seventy and eighty German submarines so that their activity off the English and Irish coast had to be discontinued. The American controversy gave them a convenient way to 'come-down.' Rather than confess an English victory they pretended to give in to the American Government. Of course the American Government had to accept their come-down; but of course also it wasn't worth the breath it took to utter it. The real test is the *Lusitania:* will they disavow that?"

Such is the public feeling here as the year ends. Men take only a languid interest in anything but the war. The eternal wrangle about the Government's inefficiency goes on all the time. You may look out the window anywhere at any time of day and see recruits drilling in the streets and convalescent wounded taking an outing. God knows how many hospitals there are in London and all over the kingdom or how many maimed lie in them. On Christmas day I saw 1,000 in one hospital—cheerful fellows in the main, singing Christmas songs. . . .

To ARTHUR W. PAGE

American Embassy
London, December 23, 1917

Dear Arthur:
I sent you a Christmas cable yesterday for everybody. That's about all I can send in these days of slow mail and restricted shipping and enormously high prices; and you gave all the girls each $100 for me, for the babies and themselves? That'll show 'em that at least we haven't forgotten them. Forgotten? Your mother and I are always talking of the glad day when we can go home and live among them. We get as homesick as small boys their first month at a boarding school. Do you remember the day I left you at Lawrenceville, a forlorn and lonely kid?—It's like that.

A wave of depression hangs over the land like a London fog. And everybody on this tired-out side of the world shows a disposition to lean too heavily on us—to depend on us so completely that the fear arises that they may unconsciously relax their own utmost efforts when we begin to fight. Yet they can't in the least afford to relax, and, when the time comes, I dare say they will not. Yet the plain truth is, the French may give out next year for lack of men. I do not mean that they will quit, but that their fighting strength will have passed its maximum and that they will be able to play only a sort of second part. Except the British and the French, there's no nation in Europe worth a tinker's damn when you come to the real scratch.

The whole continent is rotten or tyrannical or yellow-dog. I wouldn't give Long Island or Moore County for the whole of continental Europe, with its kings and itching palms.

. . . Waves of depression and of hope—if not of elation—come and go. I am told, and I think truly, that waves of weariness come in London far oftener and more depressingly than anywhere else in the Kingdom. There is no sign nor fear that the British will give up; they'll hold on till the end. Winston Churchill said to me last night: "We can hold on till next year. But after 1918, it'll be your fight. We'll have to depend on you." I told him that such a remark might well be accepted in some quarters as a British surrender. Then he came up to the scratch: "Surrender? Never." But I fear we need in some practical and non-ostentatious way—now and then to remind all these European folk that we get no particular encouragement by being unduly leaned on.

It is, however, the weariest Christmas in all British annals, certainly since the Napoleonic wars. The untoward event after the British advance toward Cambrai caused the retirement of six British generals and deepened the depression here. Still I can see it now passing. Even a little victory will bring back a wave of cheerfulness.

Depression or elation show equally the undue strain that British nerves are under. I dare say nobody is entirely normal. News of many sorts can now be circulated only word of mouth. The queerest stories are whispered about and find at least temporary credence. For instance: The report has been going around that the revolution that took place in Portugal the other day was caused by the Germans (likely enough); that it was a monarchical movement and that the Germans were going to put the King back on the throne as soon as the war ended. Sensation-mongers appear at every old-woman's knitting circle. And all this has an effect on conduct. Two young wives of noble officers now in France have just run away with two other young noblemen—to the scandal of a large part of good society in London. It is universally said that the morals of more hitherto good people are wrecked by the strain put upon women by the absence of their husbands than was ever before heard of. Everybody is overworked. Fewer people are literally truthful than ever before. Men and women break down and fall out of working ranks continuously. The number of men in the government who have disappeared from public view is amazing, the number that would like to disappear is still greater—from sheer overstrain. The Prime Minister is tired. Bonar Law in a long conference that Crosby and I had with him yesterday wearily ran all round a circle rather than hit a plain proposition with a clear decision. Mr. Balfour has kept his house from overwork a few days every recent week. I lunched with Mr. Asquith yesterday; even he seemed jaded; and Mrs. Asquith assured me that "everything is going to the devil damned fast." Some conspicuous men who have always been sober have taken to drink. The very few public dinners that are held are served with ostentatious meagreness to escape criticism. I attended one last week at which there was no bread, no butter, no sugar served. All of which doesn't mean that the world here is going to the bad—only that it moves backward and forward by emotions; and this is normally a most unemotional race. Overwork and the loss of sons and friends—the list of the lost grows—always make an abnormal strain. The churches are fuller than ever before. So, too, are the "parlours" of the fortune-tellers. So also the theatres—in the effort to forget one's self. There are afternoon dances for young officers at home on leave: the curtains are drawn and the music is muffled. More marriages take place—blind and maimed, as well as the young fellows just going to France—than were ever celebrated in any year within men's memory. Verse-writing is rampant. I have received enough odes and sonnets celebrating the Great Republic and the Great President to fill a folio volume. Several American Y.M.C.A. workers lately turned rampant Pacifists and had to be sent home. Colonial soldiers and now and then an American sailor turn up at our Y.M.C.A. huts as full as a goat and swear after the event that they never did such a thing before. Emotions and strain everywhere!

Affectionately,

W.H.P.

Probably January, 1918

The disposition shown by an endless number of such incidents is something more than a disposition of gratitude of a people helped when they are hard pressed. All these things show the changed and changing Englishman. It has already come to him that he may be weaker than he had thought himself and that he may need friends more than he had once imagined; and, if he must have helpers and friends, he'd rather have his own kinsmen. He's a queer "cuss," this Englishman. But he isn't a liar nor a coward nor any sort of "a yellow dog." He's true, and he never runs—a possible hero any day, and, when heroic, modest and quiet and graceful. The trouble with him has been that he got great world power too easily. In the times when he exploited the world for his own enrichment, there were no other successful exploiters. It became an easy game to him. He organized sea traffic and sea power. Of course he became rich—far, far richer than anybody else, and, therefore, content with himself. He has, therefore, kept much of his mediaeval impedimenta, his dukes and marquesses and all that they imply—his outworn ceremonies and his mediaeval disregard of his social inferiors. Nothing is well done in this Kingdom for the big public, but only for the classes. The railway stations have no warm waiting rooms. The people pace the platform till the train comes, and milord sits snugly wrapt up in his carriage till his footman announces the approach of the train. And occasional discontent is relieved by emigration to the Colonies. If any man becomes weary of his restrictions he may go to Australia and become a gentleman. The remarkable loyalty of the Colonies has in it something of a servant's devotion to his old master.

Now this trying time of war and the threat and danger of extinction are bringing—have in fact already brought—the conviction that many changes must come. The first sensible talk about popular education ever heard here is just now beginning. Many a gentleman has made up his mind to try to do with less than seventeen servants for the rest of his life since he now *has* to do with less. Privilege, on which so large a part of life here rests, is already pretty well shot to pieces. A lot of old baggage will never be recovered after this war: that's certain. During a little after-dinner speech in a club not long ago I indulged in a pleasantry about excessive impedimenta. Lord Derby, Minister of War and a bluff and honest aristocrat, sat near me and he whispered to me—"That's me." "Yes," I said, "that's you," and the group about us made merry at the jest. The meaning of this is, they now joke about what was the most solemn thing in life three years ago.

None of this conveys the idea I am trying to explain—the change in the English point of view and outlook—a half century's change in less than three years, radical and fundamental change, too. The mother of the Duke of X came to see me this afternoon. hobbling on her sticks and feeble, to tell me of a radiant letter she had received from her granddaughter who has been in Washington visiting the Spring Rices. "It's all very wonderful," said the venerable lady, "and my granddaughter actually heard the President make a speech!" Now, knowing this lady and knowing her son, the Duke, and knowing how this girl, his daughter, has been brought up, I dare swear that three years ago not one of them would have crossed the street to hear any President that ever lived. They've simply become different people. They were very genuine before. They are very genuine now.

It is this steadfastness in them that gives me sound hope for the future. They don't forget sympathy or help or friendship. Our going into the war has eliminated the Japanese question. It has shifted the virtual control of the world to English-speaking peoples. It will bring into the best European minds the American ideal of service. It will, in fact, give us the lead and make the English in the long run our willing followers and allies. I don't mean that we shall always have plain sailing. But I do mean that the direction of events for the next fifty or one hundred years has now been determined.

To the President

London, March 7, 1918
. . . The danger that the present government is in here, comes, it seems to me, not mainly from the split in public opinion that I have described, but from the personal enemies of Mr. Lloyd George and his Government. They make the most of the dismissal of Jellicoe and of Robertson and of the appointment of Beaverbrook and North-cliffe and of the closeness of the Government to agitating newspapers—whether the newspapers run the Government or the Government runs the newspapers doesn't matter: they are, their enemies say, too closely intertwined.

It is certain that Lloyd George keeps power mainly if not solely because he is the most energetic man in sight. Many who support him do not like him personally. But nobody doubts his supreme earnestness to win the war, and everybody holds that this is the only task now worth while. This feeling has saved him in both recent political "crises." After the last one, he remarked to me with an exultant manner: "They don't seem to want anybody else—yet, do they?" His dismissal of Robertson has been accepted in the interest of greater unity of military control, but that was a dangerous rapids he shot; for he didn't handle the boat very tactfully. The previous dismissal of Jellicoe has now just come up, rather bitterly, in the House of Commons. Whether these two incidents are quiescent, it is hard to tell. From the inside I hear that both were necessary because of the inability both of the great sailor and of the great soldier to work in administrative harness with other people. It may very well be true that the place for both is in fight, not in administration. Such surely was the case with Kitchener.

Yet there is a certain danger to the Government also because some of them are thought to be wearing out. Parliament itself—I mean the House of Commons—is thought to be going stale: it has had an enormously long life. The Prime Minister, though a tough and robust man, has increasingly frequent little breakdowns. Bonar Law seems and is very weary. Mr. Balfour's health is not uniformly robust, and his enemies call him old and languid. But, just when this criticism finds a voice, he makes a clearer statement than anybody else has made and the threatened storm passes. Still, the Government, like all other governments in Europe now, is overworked and tired.

But I believe British opinion to be sound, and British endurance is only having its first real test. The people here are forever accusing one another, especially those in authority, of weakness. They have always done so. It is a sort of national vice, which it is well to remember in all outbursts of dissatisfaction. I form my opinion from what I know and see of two opposite and widely separated sections of society. Labour—there has been grave trouble with Labour since the beginning of the war—in its recent manifesto stood quite firm and resolute. The "lower classes" are undoubtedly in favour of a fight to a finish. The Tommy is made of as good fighting material as there is in the world. He knows enough to be bulldoggish and not enough to have any philosophic doubts. I was much impressed a little while ago with the reasons that Lord Derby gave me for regarding the present British Army as the best that the world has ever seen. I reminded him, when he had enumerated his reasons, that all that he had said suggested to me that for those very reasons there would soon be a better army. He was gracious enough not to dispute my contention.

The aristocracy—the real aristocracy—too are plucky to the last degree. That's one virtue that they have supremely. They do not wince. They seem actually to remember the hard plight that Napoleon put them in. They licked him. Hence, they can lick anybody. The separation of this island from the Continent and the ancient mixture here of the breeds of men produced a kind of man that stands up in a fight—no doubt about that—whether he be a bejewelled and arrogant aristocrat and reactionary or a forgotten and neglected Hodge of the soil.

I was at a dinner of old Peers at the Athenaeum Club—a group of old cocks that I meet once in a while and have come to know pretty well and ever to marvel at. I think every one is past seventy—several of them past eighty. On this occasion I was the only commoner present. The talk went on about every imaginable thing —reminiscences of Browning, the years of good vintages of port, the excellence of some court opinions handed down in the United States by quite obscure judges—why shouldn't they be got out of the masses of law reports and published as classics?—wouldn't it have been well if the King had gone and spent his whole time at the front and on the fleet,—what's an English King for anyhow?—then a defense of Reading; and why should the Attorney General or the Lord Chief Justice be allowed out of the Kingdom at all at such a time?

"Call in the chief steward.... Here, steward, what's that noise?"

"A hair raid, milord."

"How long has it been going on?"

"Forty minutes, milord."

"I must be deaf," said the old fellow, with an inquiring look at the company. Everybody else had heard it, but we've learned to take these things for granted and nobody had interrupted the conversation to speak of it. Then the old man spoke up again.

"Well, there's nothing we can do to protect His Excellency. Damn the air raid. Pass the port."

Then the talk went on about the ignorance and the commonness of modern British governments—most modern governments, in fact. French statesmen—most of 'em common fellows, and Italians and Germans—ach! What swine! "Think of that fellow Von Kühlmann. I lent him a valuable book and the rogue never returned it. Did you know Kühlmann?"

"But," turning to me, "you are to be congratulated. You have a *gentleman* for your President. How do you do it? That breed seems to be out of a job in most countries."

Not one of those old fellows drove to the club. They can't get gasoline and they have no horses. Nor can cabs be got after ten o'clock. When the firing and bomb dropping had ceased, the question arose whether it was safe to walk home. My car had come and I took five of them in it—one on the front with the driver. As each got out at his door he bade me an almost affectionate good-night. One of them said, "By our combined forces the God of our Fathers—not the barbarous Prussian Gott—will see us through."

There's no sham about these old masters of empire. They feel a proprietary interest in the King, in the Kingdom, in everything British. Every man of them had done some distinguished service and so have the sons of most of them; and at least half of them have lost grandsons or sons in the war, to which they never allude. An enemy might kill them if he could get to them, but change them or scare them or make them surrender—never. Take 'em all in all, for downright human interest, I don't know where you'd find their equals. Take them as mere phenomena of human society and of a social system—well, that's another story. But they, and their like, are not going to give up in this war.

Well, a little before that, I met once a week for three or four weeks at dinner about a dozen Labour leaders, who good-humouredly wrangled with one another and with me, they being of a disputatious turn. It's a pretty good world to them, on the whole; but economic society is organized with gross injustice and their misfortune is that they must set it right. On many things they can't agree with one another; but on one thing they are of like mind: the employer wasn't fair before the war and he isn't fair now. The war brings no reasons to their minds why they should surrender. Let *him* surrender, rather. *But* they wouldn't desert the country. They'll beat the hog of an employer, but they'll keep up the war, and a larger measure of democracy will follow. Most of these men are keen-minded, able, pugnacious and, like all breeds of the John Bull stock, *tenacious*. They have a case—I'm disposed to think, a good case —which they urge most often by bad methods. They *will* have a larger measure of democracy. The first concrete form that it has taken is the new Franchise Act which doubles the number of voters. There is now an approximation to one vote for every man over twenty-one and for every woman over thirty. Other such concrete changes will come—perhaps a Labour government, certainly a Labour government if all Labour holds together. One of these fellows goes on a crutch from a war wound. They are not for a peace that will soon end in another war.

As I make it out, it is chiefly in political and philosophic circles that hopelessness finds a home. Lord Lansdowne belongs to both these groups, to one by temperament, the other by training. I ran across him a fortnight ago. He had, for an old man who is far from well, an almost unseemly gaiety of spirit, and he insisted on talking almost wholly about agriculture. I had sent to our Agricultural Department for certain of its publications, which greatly interested him. I almost forgive him his vagueness, cut bias of political thought because of his sound agricultural knowledge. . . .

GEORGE SANTAYANA:

"HE CARRIES HIS ENGLISH

WEATHER IN HIS HEART"

c. 1920

"The remarkable thing about my career," wrote Santayana, "is that I should have spent the better part of my life in the United States and written my books in the English language while retaining my Spanish nationality and sentiment, and living in the English-speaking world as a sort of permanent guest, familiar, appreciative and I hope discreet, and still foreign. This is no less true of me intellectually than it is socially." Santayana was born in Madrid of Spanish parents in 1863; as a boy he was taken to Boston, where his mother lived with the children of a former marriage, and he graduated from Harvard College in 1886. After study at the University of Berlin, Santayana returned to Harvard to join the most distinguished department of philosophy that has ever flourished in America—a department which included Josiah Royce, William James, George Herbert Palmer, Hugo Munsterberg, and not least Santayana himself. Where Munsterberg became very much part of the American scene, Santayana remained a foreign though not an alien observer. His observations can be read in the wonderful *Character and Opinion in the United States,* one

From George Santayana, *Soliloquies in England* (London, 1922; New York, 1923), pp. 3–6, 29–32.

of the classics of our literature, and in his semiautobiographical novel, *The Last Puritan*. Though he lived a life of contemplation and of travel, Santayana was prodigiously productive: a five-volume study of *The Life of Reason*, four volumes on *Realms of Being;* two volumes of *Soliloquies in England*, a volume of sonnets, a large novel, and three volumes of autobiography, *Persons and Places*. Though a sceptic, Santayana never formally left the Catholic Church; for the last twenty-seven years of his life he lived in a convent in Rome, taken care of by English nuns and adoring disciples.

We should none of us admire England to-day if we had to admire it only for its conquering commerce, its pompous noblemen, or its parliamentary government. I feel no great reverence even for the British Navy, which may be in the junk-shop to-morrow; but I heartily like the British sailor, with his clear-cut and dogged way of facing the world. It is health, not policy nor wilfulness, that give true strength in the moral world, as in the animal kingdom; nature and fortune in the end are on the side of health. There is, or was, a beautifully healthy England hidden from most foreigners; the England of the countryside and of the poets, domestic, sporting, gallant, boyish, of a sure and delicate heart, which it has been mine to feel beating, though not so early in my life as I could have wished. In childhood I saw only Cardiff on a Sunday, and the docks of Liverpool; but books and prints soon opened to me more important vistas. I read the poets; and although British painting, when it tries to idealize human subjects, has always made me laugh, I was quick to discern an ethereal beauty in the landscapes of Turner. Furgueson's *Cathedrals of England*, too, and the great mansions in the Italian style depicted in the eighth edition of the *Encyclopaedia Britannica*, revealed to me even when a boy the rare charm that can envelop the most conventional things when they are associated with tender thoughts or with noble ways of living.

It was with a premonition of things noble and tender, and yet conventional, that after a term at the University of Berlin I went to spend my first holidays in England. Those were the great free days of my youth. (I had lived familiarly in Spain and in the United States: I had had a glimpse of France and of Germany, and French literature had been my daily bread: it had taught me how to think, but had not given me much to think about. I was not mistaken in surmising that in England I should find a *tertium quid*, something soberer and juster than anything I yet knew, and at the same time greener and richer.) I felt at once that here was a distinctive society, a way of living fundamentally foreign to me, but deeply attractive. At first all gates seemed shut and bristling with incommunication; but soon in some embowered corner I found the stile I might climb over, and the ancient right of way. Those peaceful parks, and those minds no less retired, seemed positively to welcome me; and though I was still divided from them by inevitable partitions, these were in places so thin and yielding, that the separation seemed hardly greater than is requisite for union and sympathy between autonomous minds. Indeed, I was soon satisfied that no climate, no manners, no comrades on earth (where nothing is perfect) could be more congenial to my complexion. Not that I ever had the least desire or tendency to become an Englishman. Nationality and religion are like our love and loyalty towards women: things too radically intertwined with our moral essence to be changed honourably, and too accidental to the free mind to be worth changing. My own origins were living within me; by their light I could see clearly that this England was pre-eminently the home of decent happiness and a quiet pleasure in being oneself. I found here the same sort of manliness which I had learned to love in America, yet softer, and not at all obstreperous; a manliness which when refined a little creates the gentleman, since its instinct is to hide its strength for an adequate occasion and for the service of others. It is self-reliant, but with a saving touch of practicality and humour; for there is a becoming self-confidence, based on actual performance, like the confidence of the athlete, and free from any exorbitant estimate of what that performance is worth. Such modesty in strength is entirely absent from the effusive temperament of the Latin, who is cocky and punctilious so long as his conceit holds out, and then utterly humbled and easily corrupted; entirely absent also from the doctrinaire of the German school, in his dense vanity and officiousness, that nothing can put to shame. So much had I come to count on this sort of manliness in the friends of my youth, that without it the most admirable and gifted persons seemed to me hardly *men:* they fell rather into an ambiguous retinue, the camp followers of man, cleverer but meaner than himself—the priests, politicians, actors, pedagogues, and shopkeepers. The *man* is he who lives and relies directly on nature, not on the needs or weaknesses of other people. These self-sufficing Englishmen, in their reserve and decision, seemed to me truly men, creatures of fixed rational habit, people in whose somewhat inarticulate society one might feel safe and at home. The low pressure at which their minds seemed to work showed how little they were alarmed about anything: things would all be managed somehow. They were good company even when they said nothing. Their aspect, their habits, their invincible likes and dislikes seemed like an anchor to me in the currents of this turbid age. They were a gift of the gods, like the sunshine or the fresh air or the memory of the Greeks: they were superior beings, and yet more animal than the rest of us, calmer, with a different scale of consciousness and a slower pace of thought. There were glints in them sometimes of a mystical oddity; they loved the wilds; and yet ordinarily they were wonderfully sane and human, and responsive to the right touch. Moreover, these semi-divine animals could talk like men of the world. If some of them, and not the least charming, said little but "Oh, really," and "How stupid of me," I soon discovered how far others could carry scholarly distinction, rich humour, and refinement of diction. I confess, how-ever, that when they were very exquisite or subtle they seemed to me like cut flowers; the finer they were the frailer, and the cleverer the more wrong-headed. Delicacy did not come to them, as to Latin minds, as an added ornament, a finer means of being passionate, a trill in a song that flows full-chested from the whole man; their purity was Puritanism, it came by exclusion of what they thought lower. It impoverished their sympathies, it severed them from their national roots, it turned to affectation or fanaticism, it rendered them acrid and fussy and eccentric and sad. It is truly English, in one sense, to fume against England, individuality tearing its own nest; and often these frantic poses neutralize one another and do no harm on the whole. Nevertheless it is the full-bodied Englishman who has so far ballasted the ship, he who, like Shakespeare, can wear grace-fully the fashion of the hour, can play with fancy, and remain a man. When he ceases to be sensual and national, adventurous and steady, reticent and religious, the Englishman is a mad ghost; and wherever he prevails he turns pleasant England, like Greece, into a mem-ory. . . .

What is it that governs the Englishman? Certainly not intelli-gence; seldom passion; hardly self-interest, since what we call self-interest is nothing but some dull passion served by a brisk intelli-gence. The Englishman's heart is perhaps capricious or silent; it is seldom designing or mean. There are nations where people are always innocently explaining how they have been lying and cheating in small matters, to get out of some predicament, or secure some advantage; that seems to them a part of the art of living. Such is not the Englishman's way: it is easier for him to face or to break opposi-

tion than to circumvent it. If we tried to say that what governs him is
convention, we should have to ask ourselves how it comes about that
England is the paradise of individuality, eccentricity, heresy,
anomalies, hobbies, and humours. Nowhere do we come oftener
upon those two social abortions—the affected and the disaffected. . . .

Let me come to the point boldly; what governs the Englishman is
his inner atmosphere, the weather in his soul. It is nothing particularly spiritual or mysterious. When he has taken his exercise and is
drinking his tea or his beer and lighting his pipe; when, in his garden
or by his fire, he sprawls in an aggressively comfortable chair; when,
well-washed and well-brushed, he resolutely turns in church to the
east and recites the Creed (with genuflexions, if he likes genuflexions) without in the least implying that he believes one word of it;
when he hears or sings the most crudely sentimental and thinnest of
popular songs, unmoved but not disgusted; when he makes up his
mind who is his best friend or his favourite poet; when he adopts a
party or a sweetheart; when he is hunting or shooting or boating, or
striding through the fields; when he is choosing his clothes or his
profession—never is it a precise reason, or purpose, or outer fact
that determines him; it is always the atmosphere of his inner man.

To say that this atmosphere was simply a sense of physical
well-being, of coursing blood and a prosperous digestion, would be
far too gross; for while psychic weather is all that, it is also a witness to
some settled disposition, some ripening inclination for this or that,
deeply rooted in the soul. It gives a sense of direction in life which is
virtually a code of ethics, and a religion behind religion. On the
other hand, to say it was the vision of any ideal or allegiance to any
principle would be making it far too articulate and abstract. The
inner atmosphere, when compelled to condense into words, may
precipitate some curt maxim or over-simple theory as a sort of
war-cry; but its puerile language does it injustice, because it broods
at a much deeper level than language or even thought. It is a mass of
dumb instincts and allegiances, the love of a certain quality of life, to
be maintained manfully. It is pregnant with many a stubborn assertion and rejection. It fights under its trivial fluttering opinions like a
smoking battleship under its flags and signals; you must consider,
not what they are, but why they have been hoisted and will not be
lowered. One is tempted at times to turn away in despair from the
most delightful acquaintance—the picture of manliness, grace, simplicity, and honour, apparently rich in knowledge and humour
—because of some enormous platitude he reverts to, some

hopelessly stupid little dogma from which one knows that nothing can ever liberate him. The reformer must give him up; but why should one wish to reform a person so much better than oneself? He is like a thoroughbred horse, satisfying to the trained eye, docile to the light touch, and coursing in most wonderful unison with you through the open world. What do you care what words he uses? Are you impatient with the lark because he sings rather than talks? and if he could talk, would you be irritated by his curious opinions? Of course, if any one positively asserts what is contrary to fact, there is an error, though the error may be harmless; and most divergencies between men should interest us rather than offend us, because they are effects of perspective, or of legitimate diversity in experience and interests. Trust the man who hesitates in his speech and is quick and steady in action, but beware of long arguments and long beards. Jupiter decided the most intricate questions with a nod, and a very few words and no gestures suffice for the Englishman to make his inner mind felt most unequivocably when occasion requires.

Instinctively the Englishman is no missionary, no conqueror. He prefers the country to the town, and home to foreign parts. He is rather glad and relieved if only natives will remain natives and strangers strangers, and at a comfortable distance from himself. Yet outwardly he is most hospitable and accepts almost anybody for the time being; he travels and conquers without a settled design, because he has the instinct of exploration. His adventures are all external; they change him so little that he is not afraid of them. He carries his English weather in his heart wherever he goes, and it becomes a cool spot in the desert, and a steady and sane oracle amongst all the deliriums of mankind. Never since the heroic days of Greece has the world had such a sweet, just, boyish master. It will be a black day for the human race when scientific blackguards, conspirators, churls, and fanatics manage to supplant him.

1920-1948

SAMUEL ELIOT MORISON:

OXFORD, "THE MOST

HUMANE AND INTELLIGENT

GROUP OF PEOPLE

I HAVE EVER KNOWN"

1925

Though Professor Smythe had lectured on the American Revolution at Cambridge in the 1860s, American history had, in general, been ignored by both Oxford and Cambridge. After the First World War Lord Harmsworth set up the first chair of American History at Oxford University, and Samuel Eliot Morison, a young teacher at Harvard, was appointed the first incumbent of that chair: in the three years which he held the chair he gave it character and distinction, and the indelible stamp of his personality. A descendant of generations of Eliots, Otises, Morisons, and other New England families, S. E. Morison was to become, in time, the very symbol of Boston Back Bay and of Harvard. The successor to Francis Parkman among American historians, Morison made distinguished contributions to many fields of history: the history of Puritanism, the history of Harvard University, the history of New England Federalism among them. His most extensive and most creative work was in the field of maritime and naval history. As a young man in his

From S. E. Morison, "An American Professor's Reflections on Oxford," *The Spectator,* November 7, November 14, 1925, pp.. 811–866.

mid-twenties he wrote the classic maritime history of Massachusetts; as a veteran historian in his eighties he produced a new *Discovery of America;* in between he wrote the fifteen-volume history of U. S. Naval Operations during the Second World War.

The Liberty of Oxford.

They are not long, the days of wine and roses.

Dowson's verse keeps running through my head, beating time with the engine that drives me every moment farther from Oxford and nearer to America. I must hasten to jot down impressions, before the rush and stress of American academic life blurs them into a dream of grey walls and green fields, vivid youths on motor-cycles, and modest maidens on push-bicycles, dinners in hall and evenings in common-room, the Friday luncheons that fell on Mondays, and the history luncheons where everything but history was discussed. Unfortunately, even impressions have to be generalized on paper; and Oxford is the most complex, the most unsystematic, the most paradoxical, and the most difficult of institutions to generalize.

No other university is at once so hospitable and so indifferent to new individuals, disciplines, and subjects. The undergraduate body is the most varied in the world as to nationality, race and colour; yet no one manages to resist some trace of the "Oxford manner." The faculties include specialists on almost every branch of knowledge; but if the specialists want pupils, they must conform to regulation and tradition. A newcomer either remains isolated, within a little wall which he alone does not see, or he is absorbed into the tepid current of donnish life, and the world knows him no more, unless through his books. A reforming Commission is lost if it comes to Oxford and accepts the gracious hospitality of the colleges. For no sensible man who knows Oxford would wish greatly to change it. Rather must he be chiefly concerned to preserve the many things of worth and beauty that time has tested, and spared.

To an American sojourner, the note of freedom is dominant at Oxford; not merely the corporate freedom that the University enjoys within the State, and the colleges within the University, but freedom of the individual within either. All three are closely interrelated. Almost all university and college business, of the sort that in American universities is settled by presidential or decanal fiat, in Oxford is referred to a number of boards and committees. The time consumed is well worth the loss in efficiency, for the system gives everyone an official finger in many pies, and an opportunity to air his views. The universal craving to mind other people's business is thereby satisfied; and Oxford harmlessly employs in administrative activity the "nosey" and talebearing sort of individuals that are the pest of American faculties. Collegiate autonomy seems at times almost anarchical to one who is used to the modern centralized university; but the history of Oxford, as of the United States, shows that federalism permits a more varied and wholesome life than centralization. Nowhere in America or on the Continent would it be possible for organizations so diverse as Ruskin College, the women's colleges, Ripon Hall, Campion Hall, Manchester College, and the Catholic Workers' College, to share the benefits of a great University without losing their individuality. Oxford and Cambridge, alone of modern universities, are really universal.

The keystone in this arch of liberty, and the most enviable and precious thing in all Oxford's rich inheritance, is the self-government of the University; its almost complete control by the resident and teaching M.A.s. The University is poor, but gifts or endowments purchased at the price of the thinnest wedge of outside control would be too dearly purchased. Yet there is no reason why gifts should be so purchased; and in view of the many wealthy men among Oxford graduates, it seems to an American scandalous that the British taxpayer should be called upon to help support the University, or that institutions like St. Edmund Hall should want funds.

Oxford and, apparently, all the British universities are happily free from the unreasoning and malicious criticism that every American university has to bear from Press and public. They are not expected to be all things to all men; nor is admission to their colleges demanded as a right. It matters not whether this sound attitude of the British public be due to appreciation or indifference; the universities are left free to serve the nation as their own members think best. University extension work in America too often takes the form of advertisement, or of a sweet sop to a nagging public; in England, it is performed by those who are interested, for the benefit of the few who want it. Within the University there is not only complete freedom of speech, but complete privacy. A professor need never fear, as in America, lest one day's classroom witticism appear the following day in a screaming headline. Nobody outside Oxford knows, and nobody within Oxford cares, if a certain professor be Communist or Fascist. . . .

About the tutorial method of preparing candidates for the honour schools, I leave Oxford less enthusiastic than when I viewed it from afar. Tutoring is admirably fitted for teaching *literae humaniores*, for which it was devised; but more modern subjects, such as the promising new school of philosophy, politics and economics, are somewhat refractory to one-man teaching. Tutoring tends to become mere cramming, both with facts and with clever answers to "spotted" questions; the college tutors, in supplanting the paid coach, have not eliminated his defects. In some of the honour schools, the system neither affords a good general education, nor produces scholars.

The Oxford "first" has an admirable command of language, and a brilliant style that comes of writing to impress clever people. He can make less knowledge go further, and write what he has to say far better, than the *summa cum laude* men of American universities. But he has seldom gone to the bottom of anything, or approached it so near as an American B.A. who has done an honours thesis. Full of self-confidence, he is ready to bring up any subject in the world for you in two weeks; inordinately proud of the things he does not know, the humbling process takes at best a long time, and, if he becomes a fellow at Oxford, sometimes never takes place. There is something to be said for catching your tutor young, but there are too many college fellows who took a first, won a prize essay, and have done nothing since. Interested only in winning good classes for their pupils, or writing cramming books to help the process, they thwart the efforts of more scholarly or ambitious colleagues to provide something more than academic honours for the better sort of student. Travelling fellowships are wanted so that colleges can afford to send their candidates for tutorships abroad for two or three years, and to require evidence of ability to do research, before they appoint.

Professors, Libraries, and the Study of History.

The college fellows at Oxford are underpaid but not overworked in comparison with the younger members of American university staffs. An American instructor is lucky to get an hour's recreation a day; his terms extend to thirty or thirty-five instead of twenty-four weeks of the year; he gets no extra pay for examining; and instead of dining he merely eats. Those Oxford fellows who have the taste and ability for research, manage to find the time; and the quality of their contributions to human knowledge is so high and distinctive that one wishes there were more of them. Further, unless a don have a taste for writing or research, his soft routine is apt to pall after ten or fifteen years. Few suspect how many of those, around the age of forty, are wishing to be anywhere but Oxford.

If the life of the Oxford don seems enviable to the harried and hard-worked young American instructor the life of an Oxford professor is ideal beyond the dreams of his American colleagues. He really has time to study his subject, and it rests wholly with his own taste and conscience whether he do even that. But he is curiously un-co-ordinated with the University. The statutory Commission has wisely proposed to provide every professor with a seat in the governing body of some college. There will remain, in many faculties, an underlying antagonism between professors and tutors that no parliamentary commission can dissolve. For Oxford is essentially a master's university; and the professor, after some centuries of trial, has not yet found his place. New blood comes into the professoriat, when it is already old blood, which will not mingle with that which has already been dyed an Oxford blue. Hence, a professor who comes up with an unbecoming zeal to teach his subject in other fashion than writing books about it must struggle for years against prejudice and vested interest to almost certain defeat; or he may ignore the undergraduates and write books, which is what the University expects of him. There are a few brilliant exceptions, like Sir William Osler, who manage to teach and do research and many things beside; and there are others who do practically nothing but potter about. Recent and well-deserved promotions of tutors to professorial chairs point out one way to end the ancient feud, which makes the most conspicuous waste of energy and talent that I have noticed in Oxford.

Professors might also be used more than hitherto in directing post-graduate research. In some of the sciences, research appears to be well organized and admirably guided; in the humanities it is, for the most part, wholly unorganized, and lamentably guided. Owing to political pressure, Oxford recently and reluctantly established a D.Phil. degree; an *ersatz* Ph.D. The candidate merely chats with a "supervisor" twice a term for two or three years, submits his dissertation, and wins or loses on the opinion of two examiners, who have no accepted standard. A new university statute offers some promise of seminars, and a real training in method, but the statute was so emasculated in passage, through the efforts of those who do not believe in research, that it is little more than a promise. The faculty boards may, if they wish, establish seminars and advanced study courses; and it is to be hoped they may, for it would be a pity if the Oxford D.Phil. proved in the end to be an inferior article to the American Ph.D.

Among the other discouragements to scholarship at Oxford must be counted the libraries. They are hopelessly un-co-ordinated and so decentralized that it requires years to learn what books on one's own subject may be found there. Conditions in general, and no one in particular, are to blame for this situation. . . .

Cecil Rhodes, in his notebook, expressed the wish that Oxford dons might annually repeat to their pupils his economic credo once a year. Fortunately, there is no danger lest Oxford dons repeat homilies to their pupils at stated intervals, or post up pious maxims in hall. If Cecil Rhodes really expected his scholars to be indoctrinated with some form of political orthodoxy, he chose the wrong university for his experiment. Oxford has outlived many dogmas, and outgrown the fashioning of dogmas. Few persons there are even a little afraid—and the theologians are not the least afraid—of new ideas; and nobody runs after them because they are new, which they seldom are. There is something in the discipline and genius of the place that makes it superior to propaganda, and zealous only in the search for truth. A don is apt to be a radical in respect of his own subject, and conservative in respect of those things he does not profess to have studied.

Yet some concession in the matter of content might well be made to the imperial vision of men like Rhodes and Beit, by giving undergraduates more opportunity to study the history of the Dominions and the United States. Chairs have been established for that purpose, and professors appointed; yet Imperial and American history are still peripheral to the appropriate honour schools. There is nothing in the statutes, but everything in fact, to discourage an undergraduate from spending time on tracing the history of the British race overseas. In modern history, for instance, he must spend so much time on the Anglo-Saxon and Norman kings, on whom he is certain to be examined, that he has no time for Lord Durham and Abraham Lincoln, on whom he is certain not to be examined. America and the Dominions lose by this, for their history much wants writing by the literary historians that Oxford occasionally produces. Possibly the undergraduates of to-day and rulers of to-morrow might also benefit by some knowledge of the history and problems of the Dominions and the United States.

If these suggestions have any value, they will in the end be adopted. For Oxford, with all her diversity, has a sort of inner and corporate wisdom that enables her to ignore unsound advice, to adapt herself to the needs of successive eras, and to save all that is waiting before.

The voyage is nearing its end, and America lies just below the horizon. To-morrow I shall once more taste Walt Whitman's "joy of being toss'd in the brave turmoil of these times." But there will be many moments when I shall regret the soft and sheltered days within Oxford walls, the conversation and the company of the most humane and intelligent group of people I have ever known. My days of wine and roses are over.

CHARLES RUMFORD WALKER:

THE RELIGION OF

SOCIALISM ON THE CLYDE

1926

A graduate of Yale College in 1916, Charles Rumford Walker returned, after service in the A.E.F., to journalism; he was for a time assistant editor of the *Atlantic Monthly*, and associate editor of the *Bookman* and the *Independent*. His interests were, from the beginning, in what might be called the sociology of industry—the impact of industry and technology on society and particularly on the working classes. In the 1940s he became director of research in technology and industrial relations at Yale University and a fellow of Berkeley College, Yale. His writings include a novel, *Bread and Fire,* and economic studies of *American City, Steeltown; Man on the Assembly Line;* and *Modern Technology and Civilization.* This visit to Clydeside came in the midst of the Great Depression in England, which hit the shipping yards with particular severity, and at a time when the brief triumph of Ramsay Mac-Donald had inspired hope among the working classes of the ultimate triumph of socialism.

From Charles Rumford Walker, "Those Wild Men of the Clyde," *Atlantic Monthly,* May, 1926, pp. 701–704.

Glasgow, the Reddest spot in the British Isles! Yes, but before Glasgow is Socialist, or Communist, she's Scotch. I was traveling with the London correspondent of the *Wall Street Journal*—what a companion for an invasion of the Red Clyde! We got off the train and into a taxi that had no meter and only the remnants of an engine. The car coughed its way up a hill to Armstrong's Hotel, and the driver demanded two shillings and sixpence. Wall Street protested. "No other taxi in England," said he, "would charge over a shilling for that ride." "Aye," said the driver, "but this is no England."

Right you are. Glasgow is "no England," but Scotch, and all the movements in it, labor and political, whatever else they are, are Scotch too. The city blocks and the residences, almost wholly stone, have more sturdiness and respectability in them than anything in Boston or Main Street. The better pubs are oaken chapels for the worship of Scotch whiskey. The shops are full of substantial Scottish goods at Scottish prices. "No New Yorker," said a lady of my acquaintance, "could afford to live in Glasgow." (She was charged twenty-five shillings for a small cambric handkerchief.) Every other block is an insurance company, and every third is a church. Bookstores are very thickly sprinkled over the town: we noted a Presbyterian bookshop, a theosophical, a Catholic, and a Socialist. The Scotch nationalize everything. In the Roman Catholic shop they were booming a Scottish Jesuit who had written a book. Religion is everywhere. I looked into a tobacco shop, and filling the window was, "Dr. White's Presbyterian Mixture," with a picture of the church on the can!

The Prime Minister of Great Britain slipped up to Glasgow the other day and made a tour of the slums, "incog." There has been a "rent war" on for months in Glasgow, and this is the other side of the picture.

If you will walk through the streets of Bridgton, which is the constituency of Jimmy Maxton, most popular of the Clyde M. P.'s, you will begin to understand the political atmosphere of Glasgow. Or if you go through Clydebank and Dumbarton, which year after year send Davy Kirkwood, the noisy and eloquent opponent of royalty, to the legislative halls of the House of Commons. The odd thing is that the slums are as sturdy and Scotch as the shops, the churches, or the pubs. Dark and unsanitary, they are built solidly of stone, like Roman walls or the Cloaca Maxima. They are likely to last as long.

For a time these sturdy stone buildings, smoked over with soot from factory chimneys and steel mills, will deceive the American visitor. Compare this firm construction, he is led to say, with the rotten jerry-built shacks of our own Pittsburgh! But the proof of the house is in the living. One toilet for five families, a floor that has been damp for a hundred and fifty years, rooms that for a century have been lit by lamps and not by sunlight. And, in large numbers of houses that do not suffer from these defects, the evil fact of over-crowding. Houses in Clydebank, pleasant enough from the outside, are often packed to the windowpanes—if there are any—with humanity. For every room, or for every two rooms, a family. Because of the so-called "rent strikes" of Glasgow the Government instituted an inquiry; evidence showed the need for a hundred and fifty thousand new houses in the Clyde region.

I was in Bridgton at twelve o'clock on Saturday, when the whistle blew, and I found myself among the crowds ejected from a boiler factory, a carpet mill, and a laundry.

Here were folk by no means broken either by industry or by poverty. Hardy Scots, shod well and clothed decently. Most of the laundry girls had silk stockings, like any American stenographer. But these hurrying eddies of men and girls were in sharp contrast to the silent pools of unemployed that lounged along the same street. The latter were sallow and hungry and broken. They looked like scarecrows that have been out in the rain too long. Their eyes, which I hated to look at, were dead or neurotic. Their faces had lost character along with their clothes. My Wall Street companion pointed to an open market in an empty lot, and we moved over to it. These little markets are good places to visit if you want to find out about the people of a neighborhood. The quality and variety of the goods will show you what the people use, and the prices are an index of purchasing power. This was Wall Street's suggestion.

There were things laid out on tables and troughs which I didn't believe could draw a farthing from anyone. The rags and the remnants of trousers and shirts, the remains of utensils, old clocks, in a great mélée. And a row of shabby toy dogs, which a desperate little man, in an exhausted voice, was trying to sell to unsympathetic paupers. A number of people wandered about, but almost no one made a purchase. A sallow and degraded group, however, had gathered before an ex-soldier in a sombrero, who had something to sell to make men strong. It was a salve. "I am going to ask you," said the giver of health and strength, "to refrain from using soap for seven days." I looked about me and I knew the right note had been struck. The Bridgton slum audience opened their ears and their hearts to the man in the sombrero.

In the environs of Glasgow is a network of coal mines; not far from the mines sprawl steel mills, and along the Clyde itself stretch the greatest shipyards of the world. For seven miles the sprouting skeletons of ships rise among their supporting poles and runways; webs of railway tracks cover the banks; and against the sky loom those vast steel spiders, the cranes that seize and move the limbs of ships. An army of men live along the bank—an army that is many divisions too large, for with the drop in production after the war there was no industry in Great Britain to take them in. Unemployment figures for the United Kingdom stand well over a million.

The same is true for the steel mills. Follow the highway through Dumbarton and Clydebank, and you will come to Motherwell, which is a little Scotch Pittsburgh. Here, in one works which boasts thirty-two furnaces, nine are at work. And while the plant has a capacity for giving employment to eight thousand men, I found four thousand employed.

Upon the foundation of bad housing, unemployment, and a fighting Scotch temperament, are built the Red movements of the Clyde. There are "antiparliamentary rallies" held by the Communist Federation at the Ross Street Unitarian Church. And every Saturday the Communists hold a whist drive and social at Bakunin House.

The so-called Labor College movement, which believes in education as "a weapon in the class struggle *and no more than that,*" finds its stronghold in Glasgow. The number of classes in Great Britain last year was 1048, the number of students 25,071, and of these, according to a rough estimate given me by the Bridgton M. P., over 10,000 are Scotch. "The subjects we study in our classes," to quote from *Plebs,* official organ of the movement, "are means to an end, and that end is the creation and development of a militant, informed, working-class consciousness."

But you are going to get a wrong impression of this movement and of the Clyde if you just read figures and aims. Especially if you're an American. The only thing to do is to visit a class and listen. Picture to yourself a Scotch working-class town, filled with stone houses of workingmen, surrounded by mines and by steel mills. In a respectable stone building a schoolroom, with rows of sloping desks. And behind the desks, not fifty school-children, but fifty miners, steel-workers, machinists, laundry girls. Men and women from twenty-five to forty, with tough, hardy bodies, and earnest, intelligent Scotch faces. Pipes are lighted. The lecture begins.

"One of the few things I learned in college—one of the very few—was an experiment in psychology." The lecturer is a graduate of Glasgow University. "Take three basins of water, one hot, and one cold, and one tepid. Put your right hand into the cold water, and your left hand into the hot." ("Note," said a Right Wing Scotch Socialist, "that it's his *left* hand that's in hot water.) "Keep them submerged for three minutes, and then plunge both into the tepid water. To your right hand the water is hot, to your left hand it is cold." The class gave a serious smile to this and moved their feet. "This shows you, in one way only, how difficult it is to get at facts. How much more difficult in the social and industrial field, where prejudice, passion, privilege, and exploitation rule. . . . But," he went on, "the Labor colleges are the only group getting at the truth, because they believe first of all in taking the capitalistic bias out of education. That sort of education is the only really scientific kind. That sort of education starts with the great scientific truth, set down first by Karl Marx, of capitalist exploitations."

The class went wild over this, with a deep rumble in its throat, and terrific applause.

"I want to protest," the speaker resumed, "against the attempt, the world over, to suppress the work of Karl Marx. . . . Why is it," he added, in a soft and burning voice, "that English gentlemen in English universities refuse to credit him with the scientific truths he has discovered or even to mention his name? It is because, if the scientific work of Marx were disseminated through the world, the present system of capitalism, with its enrichment for them and its load of wretchedness and exploitation for the workers, would be utterly swept away!"

Following the lecture, discussion; following that, questions; and following that, tea! The ladies brought it in, with bread and cakes, and the miners and steel-workers ate and drank lustily at their desks. . . .

I couldn't help thinking, as I turned the afternoon over in my mind, that this thin, impassioned Scotch lecturer, with his long arm and lean finger raised over his excited students, was a seventeenth-century Calvinist—model 1925. Here was Scotch passion for theology, Scotch skill in dialectic, and Scotch attraction to a hell-and-damnation ethics. In an hour's talk the speaker said much that was true, but he marshaled his facts around a philosophy; he drove a passion into his words that made the thing not a student's gathering but the preparation for a holy war. Which he would, of course, be the first to admit. Certainly, a holy war against Capitalism. . . .

Every year in Glasgow the Socialist faithful gather together to preach and to pray in memory of Saint Keir Hardie. I went to this year's prayer meeting. The church was St. Andrew's, the largest public hall in Glasgow. Father and Mother and the kids were there, sitting row on row and in the encircling gallery, up to five thousand. A long bank of flowerpots supplied a fence of flowers, behind which sat the elders, Chairman Rankin, the Calvinistic frame of J. Maxton, and the archepiscopal stomach of George Lansbury, Labor M. P., editor and Socialist agitator. Behind these the choir boys and choir girls. And, in lieu of a hymn book or church notices, posters, yellow and black and red.

After an organ recital, Rankin opened the service with exhortation and prayer—I'd call it that, all right. He put down a little political economics as a foundation, saying the present Government functioned upon the misery of the working classes, and so on; and noted—an excellent point, I thought—that under the Conservatives (the last Government was Socialist, you know) unemployment had jumped from 1,270,000 to 1,400,000. But he swung into straight gospel preaching right soon—the gospel of Socialism. Capitalist miseries, he said, were making "the army of pale, propertyless people plod on to the full clear light of Socialism." The New Jerusalem became the day when a Labor Socialist majority would sit in the British House of Commons! He used personal religious experience to vivify the thing. One night, when sleeping in the open, he said that he found himself on a sudden in the presence and novelty of dawn. It was like something that Socialism was doing to the world to-day. His words put me in mind of the revelation of Saint John.

"The new light and the new day," he ended, on a ringing note of ecstasy, "are not far away!"

Then, while we were still breathing heavily, he switched over to a few words introducing Jimmy Maxton, and sat down.

Instantly the five thousand Glasgow worshipers deafened the taut air with applause; they swayed in their seats, and smiled up happily and reverently at Jimmy. The new preacher began with an invocation of Saint Keir Hardie, and then passed by degrees to what I should call Socialist moral theology.

"The Scotch have always been known," he said, "for their thrifty ways, for hardy and simple lives. Now, as everyone knows, I've never been an advocate of flabby livin'. I've never preached that it was better for the Scotch workman to be restin' in the lap of luxury than to be livin' hard. But it's one thing," he said, his voice cutting our ears like a drill, "to live with simplicity and thrift yourself, and it's another to compel people to live simply and thriftily *for your benefit.*" There was hot lava in this, which flowed, I knew, from experience taken in his own body and nerves. "Our simplicity of life," he went on, "has enabled the ruling class to keep us in single-room apartment houses. . . . I say, it is an evil thing to exploit a man's worst failings for your profit, but it is a damnable thing to take a man's best characteristics and pervert them to his undoing and your own wealth!"

I thought this the saltiest Socialism I had found in Britain. One remembered the slums of Bridgton, and the men with dead faces in unemployment queues. If it were not the whole loaf of truth, it was a large slice.

The preacher didn't let his congregation gloat much over their own misery. He told them promptly the misery was their own fault. They had been backsliders, lazy and shiftless, lacking energy, lacking faith in the religion that could save them—Socialism. He beat and flayed them for their Socialist sins, for their supineness in action, their trade-union laxity, their social heresy, their little faith. And they cheered him for these scourgings louder than for his curse on the capitalist. They were Presbyterians, and had the conviction of sin in their hearts!

The preacher ended on a note that had in it both a thrill and a threat.

"I gather," he said, "that the press is well pleased at the moderation shown at Liverpool (annual Conference of the Labor Party). I want to issue a warning. While the masses are ready to move forward on even keel, ready to go along constitutional paths . . . if they are hindered and blocked in carrying out fundamental changes, *they will take those means that lie most ready to hand.*"

And those means, as Jimmy has repeated many times to me and to others, are the general strike, and whatever of revolution may follow.

This statement was greeted with an immense demonstration. . . .

To me the most interesting of all the Wild Men is Jimmy Maxton, who in the past three years has raised himself from the obscurity of a Bridgton schoolmaster to be chief of the Clydesiders. And not only that, but leader of the Left Wing movement, in Parliament and out, for Great Britain. Jimmy's personality would attract followers and worshipers, without or despite his politics. He breathes good will and a rare kindliness; he ties you to him with a hundred courtesies and rich-hearted trifles. He's just what a Tory wouldn't expect a Red leader to be.

To begin with his face: it'll make you turn and look a third time, as though at the weird mask of a showman. He is a dark Scot. All the angles of his face are bone angles, chiseled. It's like an expressive carving out of wood, or a death mask, a little shrunken; but it can smile with incomparable charm, and the eyes burn with a number of things, including tenderness and indignation. The body-frame is nothing—I doubt if Jimmy weighs a hundred and ten pounds—but he must stand six feet in his socks, and he can play cricket, run races, dance all night, or make speeches, as the hour asks. I've seen him do all four in the same day.

There are three sides to Jimmy that I have experienced with some intimacy; there may be more—I don't know. The first, James Maxton, parliamentarian, politician. I watched him for a week as chairman of a cliquey group of Independent Laborites in summer-school session. He gave every man his due of talk, only choking the windbags, and those gently. He prodded and was silent; he led discussions from the arid and foolish to the lively and practical. He summarized, clarified. He used sentiment and passion like sugar and salt, where they would do the most good. And I've heard him doing the same thing in the House of Commons as far as they'd let him.

There is, secondly, Maxton—lovable genius of friendship. I gave you some scrap of an idea how Jimmy mixes and how Jimmy clowns at a Socialist sociable. But it goes deeper than that—fifty times. It's more than the mere mixing-gift. He has talent for those thoughtful rememberings that make you love your king more than if he gave you a half of his kingdom. He told me where to go for heather, that I might bring some back to a Scotch girl in Boston. He offered to take me out to Loch Lomond himself, in his second-hand Ford car. And with a subtle and vigilant kindness he kept saving me embarrass-ment and calamity through my whole invasion of Scotland. These things and bigger ones he is doing twenty-four hours a day for everyone he meets. And his constituency in Bridgton, who know he is using up his health in their service, bring their children out when he comes by, to have him touch and talk to them! As if he were really king of Bridgton Slums!

I think, however, the real reason he is the most popular man in the British Labor movement is the way he can dance the "eightsome reel." You'd think so if you saw him. He reels with all the abandonment with which he agitates. Black hair in the wind, his white teeth ashining, he goes to it a little like a panther cat. With enormous grace and rhythm. Spectators, Scotch or English, go wild.

Thirdly, there is the side that makes Jimmy a seer and a prophet of the Lord. His father was a Conservative and a schoolmaster. But in his father's school, which Jimmy attended, he found boys who by permission of the law went to work at ten years of age, for twelve hours a day, for three days a week, in the Glasgow calico mills. "They worked from six in the morning till six at night," Jimmy told me. "Then the next day they had to face up with the rest of us, who went to school every day. I remember noticing the breakdown of their minds." That, to begin with, bit into his own mind and helped to mould the emotional side of his personality. Later he lost his wife through lack of proper medical care—one of the fruits of an enforced poverty. He spent two years in prison for opposing the war, and while still there was asked by his present constituency to represent them in Parliament. He was elected M. P. for Bridgton in 1922. Though not born a Socialist, Jimmy both acquired his Socialist religion and had it thrust upon him by the world in which he lived. And, like most religions, it rests for Jimmy ultimately not upon reason but upon the soul's conviction. "You may prove me all wrong," I heard him tell Hartley Withers, the famous Anti-Socialist, "but I *know* that Socialism is true."

His views and policy, which are roughly those of the Left Wing all over Britain, in Parliament and out, are as follows:

Socialism is the only hope of the working classes for a good life. Capitalism is breaking down in England much more rapidly than even Socialists a few years back believed possible. Witness the complete breakdown of the coal industry and the partial breakdown of a dozen others. Observe the rising political power of the workers: the Labor Party growing from nothing to the second party of Britain in twenty-five years! An equal advance is observable in economic power. Last August the miners, dockers, and railway men brought the Government to its knees. Winning a ten-million-dollar subsidy for coal! The grand crisis, when it comes, will have been forced by the capitalist exploiters, by British Fascists. It may mature in a few years, or even in a few months, but whenever it comes we must be prepared; and the weapon ready to our hands is not gunpowder but industrial action. The general strike, if wisely and properly used, will accomplish our purposes. We must then take over the government, take over the industries, and run both in the new Socialist State for the benefit of the whole people.

That is a brief statement of Left Wing belief, erring I believe, if at all, by understatement.

Although the come-back of Ramsay MacDonald last fall has put a smothering blanket upon the loud advertisement of this policy, the policy remains—the Left Wing's answer to economic misery, awaiting time and the torch of opportunity. If England begins to get her markets back and some of her million and a quarter at work again, the policy of the Left Wing will become smoke without flame. If neither of those things happens, the movement may well kindle and blaze upon the dry leaves of economic wretchedness.

JAMES TRUSLOW ADAMS:
LONDON "HAS MANAGED
TO KEEP ITSELF
GREEN AND HOMELIKE
AND BEAUTIFUL"

1927

James Truslow Adams—not one of the Massachusetts Adamses—was a stockbroker turned historian. After studying at Yale he served briefly in military intelligence during the First World War, then as consultant to the Versailles Peace Conference. On his return to America he abandoned business for history, and produced, in rapid succession, three capital volumes on New England history—*Founding of New England, Revolutionary New England,* and *New England in the Republic.* Later volumes, such as a biography of the Adams family and a study of the slavery struggle, *America's Tragedy,* consolidated his position as one of the most popular of scholarly historians. In 1931 he wrote *The Epic of America,* for long a standard popular history. An ardent but not uncritical Anglophile, he made many long visits to England. In his later years Adams grew increasingly conservative and increasingly alienated from his own society.

From James Truslow Adams, "Home Thoughts from Abroad."*Atlantic Monthly,* October, 1927, pp. 434–438.

Coming from the Continent, a "citizen of the world" feels at once that he has come from the backwaters into a great centre of human interest. London is not only in sheer extent and population the largest city in the world, so that Paris and even New York, in the restricted limits of its only interesting portions, seem quickly exhaustible in comparison, but it is the centre as yet of the greatest and most widely scattered empire the world has ever seen. The dweller in it feels that he is at the crossroads of all the world's chief highways. One can survey the world from here as from no other one centre. France, it is true, has a scattered empire also, but the average Frenchman has, for the most part, as little interest in the world at large as has the American of the Middle West. . . .

Here . . . that world is, so to say, in the air and not the ether, and one does not have to make a special effort or acquire exceptional apparatus to share in it. There are certain types of the stay-at-home smaller business Englishman who are as hopelessly narrow and provincial as Babbitt. But, even if one is not a Joshua to fell the walls of high society or the higher political circles, one is more apt here to meet all the time people who have just come from China or the Cape, or almost any part of the world, than one is at home to meet strayers from Dayton or Houston or Los Angeles. Moreover, if one picks up a dozen English magazines on the news stand and contrasts them with a dozen American ones, the wider range of interests at once becomes apparent. Of course, there are reasons for this. The main business of England, both in merchandising and banking, is international. The larger business man has a direct interest in almost all quarters of the globe. Again, speaking broadly, there is scarcely a family of the better-magazine-reading classes which has not a member of it living in some remote corner of the Empire or of the world outside. Cape Town, Calcutta, and Peking are not merely far-off foreign cities which creep into the news occasionally as centres of political disturbance, but places where "Tom" or "Dick" or "Harry" is stationed.

Another and perhaps one of the chief charms of London is that, if it is the greatest of all great cities, it is also the most homelike and, one might almost say, rural. The low sky line, and the fact that the architectural unit for most of the town yet remains the small house as contrasted with the vast "apartment houses" and skyscrapers of American cities, account for part of this "homey" atmosphere for a generation which still feels that a home means a house and not a slice of some costly communal barracks. Then there are the parks everywhere, affording not only the welcome relief of lawns and trees, but opportunities for cricket and golf and tennis within walking distance of one's house almost wherever it may be. Apart from the innumerable larger parks there are the endless "squares" and "gardens," so that one may walk only a few minutes in almost any direction without the eye encountering the restful green of trees and shrubs. Cheek by jowl with the busiest thoroughfares there are village-seeming streets or quiet nooks which are as retired and peace-bringing as any cathedral close. One steps out of Piccadilly to find one's self surrounded by the flowers and country atmosphere of the Albany, or one passes from the confusion of High Holborn under an archway to rest in the charming old-world garden of Staple Inn, where the lilacs and iris bloom and a fountain splashes with the cool serenity of the garden sanctuary of some country house. Again, one may pass from the Strand, busiest of the streets of men, under another archway to the perfect sylvan peace of the Temple, where lawns stretch to the river and boys and girls are playing tennis and one feels a brooding calm under the shade of almost immemorial trees. One of the loveliest rural views in England is looking up the water in St. James's Park, only three minutes from what, with the Abbey and Parliament Buildings, may be called the very centre of Empire. Starting there, one may walk for miles over grass and under the trees, keeping all the time in the heart of London. I know in America no country club to compare in sheer rural beauty with Ranelagh, with its superb gardens, its flowers, water views, tennis courts, golf course, and polo grounds, yet this, like Hurlingham, is not an hour or so out of town by train, but on one of the busiest arteries of traffic within the city itself.

All these open spaces, all this green and the scent of flowers, give one the impression that everywhere the country is overflowing into the city. One hears the syrinx rather than the riveter, and Pan and Flora yet hold the field against Midas and Vulcan. Nowhere in London, with the exception of the Mall and perhaps one or two other instances, do we find any such planned architectural vistas as so delight the French. London, vast as a primeval forest, has just naturally grown without elaborate city planning, but unlike New York and the larger American cities it has managed to keep itself green and homelike and beautiful. Nature has not been banished, but welcomed in a thousand nooks and corners prepared for her to enter. The difference seems to depend on national taste and a different scale of values. In America the sole "value" of a piece of city real estate is considered to be what it will yield when built upon, and every inch is made to produce as much as possible by building on it. Here—although, Heaven knows, London land is costly enough —open spaces, irises and daffodils, hawthorns and lawns, have their values also for the human life of the town. It is this sense of human values, in private properties as well as public parks, maintained in spite of the need and lure of money in the world's most densely populated city, which again gives one a sense of its civilized attitude toward life.

Yet another element in its civilization is the almost perfect quiet that reigns in it. As contrasted with the insane tooting of horns day and night in Paris and New York one rarely hears a motor, and although these warm days the parks are filled with children and older persons of all grades of society, walking about or playing games, one never hears any such "cat-calling," yelling, and general racket as one would in American city parks with such masses of people. . . .

Perhaps the highest test of whether a city or a people is civilized is just this one of how far it has gone in learning what things can and cannot be done in order to attain to the most perfect balance between expression and restraint. This, of course, is most obviously manifested in the nature and character of the laws, in the speed and impartiality with which they are enforced, and in the attitude of the people at large to them. One feels here that, whether by centuries of training or by some political instinct, this people can govern itself as no other can. There are comparatively few laws interfering with the liberty of the individual to do as he likes, but they are enforced with a swiftness, an impartiality, and a completeness that leave an American green with envy. . . .

It may be said that good enforcement of the law might also be had under an autocracy, but what strikes one here as a test of civilization is not merely the enforcement of law by the authorities, but the attitude of the people themselves toward it in a democracy. Take the case of the regulation of the liquor traffic. We tried it ourselves at home for years; but, on the one hand, the authorities proved themselves too incompetent and venal to enforce any laws regulating the saloon, and, on the other, the people as a whole were too lawless to make the problem a small one. From this we went on to prohibition, with the resulting farcical but no less disgraceful mess we are in to-day. Over here, ever since the war, the traffic has been regulated by permitting sales only at certain hours of the day, and it is illuminating to see how the law is everywhere enforced by the people themselves. The hours vary slightly in different towns so that not infrequently in the past five years I have found myself asking for a drink in a public house or hotel a few minutes ahead of the particular opening time in that locality. In all these years I have never yet witnessed a single case in which the law has been infringed by the fraction of a second on my behalf or that of anyone else. As a result, the law has been entirely successful. The possibility of prohibition, with all its evils, has been put off indefinitely, and on the other hand drunkenness has ceased, as far as my observation has gone. I have seen only one case of even semi-intoxication, that of a man who had that afternoon received a decree of divorce and was either drowning his sorrows or celebrating his luck, I never knew which. Over the Whitsuntide holiday some two hundred and fifty thousand persons went to Blackpool, and there was not a single instance of drunkenness or disorderly conduct.

I have mentioned the charm of the flowers in London, but the children, dainty and flowerlike, are no less charming, and these warm days the parks and squares and streets are full of them. As great numbers of the boys of the better classes are away at school, the girls are most in evidence, with their skirts so short as to be mere flounces on the bottom of abbreviated waists. One can study childish legs from ankle to hip here by the thousand, and one comes to the conclusion that they are among the most beautiful things the world has to offer. These youngsters, arrayed in a way to make Main Street gasp, have also a gentleness, a modesty, and a quietness of demeanor that are equally beyond the ken of that thoroughfare. . . .

As one looks at the beautiful English landscape, more beautiful in its well-tended charm and utter peacefulness than any other I know in the whole world, a sudden nostalgia will come over one for a rough, neglected bit of some Vermont hillside or the familiar ugliness of some fishing village on the shore. One murmurs to one's self, "Beautiful, beautiful," in Devon or Warwickshire, and then may unaccountably be seized with a sudden desire to "muss it all up." All Englishmen have to some extent this love of the wild and the unfinished, and perhaps those of us whose families have been in America for centuries . . . have 'gone native' a bit, have become a little more uncivilized, a little savage. Something revolts in us at living too continuously too perfect, too orderly, too civilized a life.

MARGARET THORP:

"CIRCUMSTANCES CANNOT

BE ALTERED: THE HUMAN

BEING MUST ALTER"

1934

Margaret Thorp is a scholar and journalist, best known for her fascinating study of six "strong-minded" women called *Female Persuasion*. Like most American visitors to England, from Lydia Smith to the present, she is impressed by the reluctance of the English to make any concessions to technological or practical advances in domestic economy.

It was not until the Daily General caught a chill and vanished for a week to her home in Kentish Town that I grasped the great principle which lies motionless at the base of English domestic economy. I had made before only a cursory examination of the far too small kitchen in our sixteenth-century flat. Now I learned that one cannot wash dishes very expeditiously, or very clean, when the tap sheds cold water only; that, the cupboard space being limited, most of the cooking utensils were kept in the oven and had to be extricated and set about the floor whenever one desired to bake; that

From Margaret Farrand Thorp, "Domestic Manners of the English," *Atlantic Monthly*, September, 1934, pp. 371–373.

717

the sink fell away abruptly in the opposite direction from the drain, and water ran out only when personally conducted.

Cold water is a great fact of nature, and after all there is a geyser in the bathroom; but I purchased some hooks from the indispensable Woolworth, screwed them into every available bit of woodwork, and cleared the oven for its legitimate purposes; then I sent—we live in one of the Inns of Court—for the Bureau of Works. They arrived with admirable promptness and gazed upon the sink. They considered it for long minutes in silence and at last announced judicially that it would be quite impossible to tilt it in the right direction because to do so might crack the pipe; after all, it had been like this for years; and—this was not said, of course, but implied—better men than I had had their dishes washed there and eaten off them in silence. The Bureau of Works went away.

And then at last I comprehended the principle on which the English home is founded; circumstances, material things, cannot be altered; therefore the human being must alter, adapting herself and enduring as best she may. The English housewife's attitude toward her work is consequently quite different from that of the housewife in America or on the Continent. It does not occur to her that there might be anything beautiful in her profession, that it might be done with grace, with finesse; it requires all her moral energy to get it done at all. You do not feed the starving with golden-brown meringues or *omelettes aux fines herbes.* To think of cooking or homemaking as an art would be in her eyes French and decadent, uncomplimentary adjectives both. Neither has she the American impatience or ingenuity which invents labor-saving devices and sells them, which declines to do by hand what can be done better by an electric switch, which tiles its bathrooms and curves its curners to make cleaning painless and then invents a vacuum cleaner to reduce the painlessness by half.

Right here that rugged individualism, gazed at so wistfully by the overstandardized American, plays the Englishwoman an ill turn. You can use, for instance, in Springfield, Massachusetts, the electric toaster you bought in Springfield, Illinois, but move so much as across the street in London and you may have to reëquip your establishment from wireless to basement. Consequently the woman who wants to enjoy any other occupation cannot, as the unhappy American phrase is, "do her own work." She must have servants and she must exact of them tasks not unlike those imposed by the witches in fairy tales.

Perhaps an ethnologist will one day draw for us the precise line between carrying water in a sieve and ministering to the brass cans and hot-water bottles in a five-story London house; between picking grains of rice out of the ashes and washing dishes with a geyser. Not that the mistress has any witch-like qualities; she is probably exceedingly sympathetic and charming to her maids in all relations of life which do not impinge upon unalterable material things. She will pay the expenses of a long illness, celebrate her parlor maid's engagement, or send advice and blankets to the butler's sister's baby, but Tudor floors must be scrubbed and Queen Anne sinks borne with. I shall not soon forget the tone of terrified amazement with which I was told in a certain cathedral town of the young wife of a newly appointed dean who had cut the deanery in halves, literally, and rented part of it because she refused to ask her maids to travel through eleven rooms every time they went from the kitchen to the front door.

And the servants themselves, of course, are for the most part quite unaware that they are being "put upon." Tradition is very strong, and they share the attitude of their employers toward the facts of domestic life. Our little Daily General thinks our socialism just another idiosyncrasy of Americans, like our fondness for salt and sauces. Some of the Socialists' ideas are quite good, she tells us, but she is a Conservative. Each of my American friends who keeps house in London has related to me with tears in her eyes how she has tried to prevent her maid from going down upon her knees to scrub the hall and doorstep, how she has presented her with varieties of long-handled mops, in vain. There is something peculiarly degrading to the American eye in the endless line of chars and housemaids kneeling upon the cold stone which one must pass each morning in every London street, but if they were aware of our sympathy they would receive it with wide-eyed incomprehension, or perhaps indulgence.

The complete picture of the great principle is to be seen, I think, in an advertisement I chanced on the other day in an 1850 newspaper. It would be lettered differently to-day, but the spirit continues. The demand was for a housemaid who, it was desired, should be under thirty-five years of age, a good churchwoman, and so forth and so forth. "Her principal duties," the paragraph concluded, "will be in the kitchen, but skill in cooking is of small consideration compared with good principle."

The same countenance with which she approaches the sink the housewife turns toward food. Meat and vegetables are axiomatic, given, not to be altered, merely encompassed as a part of the essential duty of keeping fit. It is such human foibles as desire for variety and flavor which must be subdued by a strong will. You may heat comestibles—though even that is a little cowardly; I have had an Englishman give me six solemn reasons for the superiority of cold toast—but it is absurd to attempt to carry them very far from their natural state. Those French vegetables, peas and beans, the cook boils guiltily, soothing her conscience by presenting them always a little raw. For the attempt to alter nature's data is more than foolish; it is dishonest.

Gissing has an eloquent, and perfectly serious, chapter in *Henry Ryecroft* on the admirable honesty of English cooking which never attempts, like its deceitful colleague across the Channel, to disguise with sauces the pristine quality of the food it touches, never mixes ingredients or adds elaborate flavorings, but contents itself with bringing out the fundamental rightness of the British joint or vegetable marrow. That is the secret of the national passion for potatoes; treat a potato as you will, it continues triumphantly to announce its honest origin. To be on the very safe side, however, the English prefer their potatoes boiled, and without butter. They have an uncanny ability, too, to turn all their other vegetables into cabbage, that safe and solid norm. Nothing is more indicative of the strength of the national character than the appearance of Italian broccoli after it has grown for a year or two in an English garden.

Sauces, of a very definite or completely tasteless nature—horseradish or bread sauce—are admitted, but they must be kept as far as possible from the meat until the final moment of mounting upon the devouring fork. An English sauce always reminds me of the small boy who was asked to draw a picture of a cruel man. In the centre of the paper appeared the conventional head, body, and legs. "That," he explained, "is the man, and that," pointing to a small spiral in the upper left-hand corner, "is his cruelness."

When she does dare to compose a mixture—to construct, for instance, a "sweet,"—the English cook goes quite mad. The things which she combines in her panic have no conceivable real relationship. It never occurs to her to consider how they will taste. (You cannot persuade her to taste a dish, anyhow; she boils the fish for the proper length of time, and if it is not done then that is its own fault.) So she produces for your delight such anomalies as tinned apricots arranged with whipped cream to resemble poached eggs couched on pieces of cake-toast; assorted chips of fruit crowded into a glass and smothered with a glue-like custard; gingerbread and treacle; puddings of spaghetti and sugar flavored with vanilla.

Neither will she stoop to enlist the suggestive power of pretty names. A French cookbook instructs you to bake a crust till it is as golden as a sunset sky, to beat the eggs to a snow, to introduce a bouquet of savory herbs—the meanest action is bathed in a poetic glow. The British manual talks flatly of suet and drippings, of stale bread crumbs and of grease, while British menus bear such realistic titles as Brown Gravy Soup, Gooseberry Fool, Treacle Sponge, Cold Shape.

This is, as you see, all in exact accord with the housewife's creed: *Non mensa flectat, sed mens.* Circumstances cannot be altered; man must bend or endure.

And the creed extends far beyond the table. I went into a shop in Oxford Street the other day, seeing in the window some frocks of a charming flowered print. When I tried one on, however, its lines proved to be fantastically wrong. Mildly I suggested that perhaps they had not given me the proper size. "Oh no, madam," the saleswoman assured me, "the beauty of that frock is that it fits all sizes."

The more closely one studies this point of view in the breakfast room, the sewing room, or the kitchen, the more thoroughly one understands the ways of the whole race. Even as they cook the dinner, so do they muddle through their battles and their economic crises. The Englishman makes no attempt to change the menacing circumstances about him, be they financial, political, or military; he merely stands solidly in their midst munching an underdone potato.

MARGARET HALSEY
PREFERS THE ENGLISH
UNGENTRY TO THE GENTRY

1937

A graduate of Skidmore College, in upstate New York, Margaret Halsey married Professor Henry Simon and in 1936–37 went with him to England, where he was a visiting professor at Exeter. Her entertaining but malicious account of her experiences in provincial society expresses faithfully enough the frustrations and confusions felt by most American wives when they try to adapt themselves to the somewhat inflexible standards and habits of English society. *With Malice Toward Some* was for a time almost required reading for the hundreds of American academics who flowed over to England as Fulbright Scholars. Miss Halsey followed it up with a series of volumes in the same genre, including *Some of My Best Friends are Soldiers* and *Color Blind*.

Exeter, September 7, 1937. . . . What makes a visiting American feel most helpless and lonely in England is, I think, neither the food nor the climate nor the damp houses nor the relentless subservice of the lower classes nor the spectacle of English gentlemen being conscientiously banal under the impression that it represents a

From Margaret Halsey, *With Malice Toward Some* (New York, 1938), pp. 149–237.

magnificent discipline. What makes an American realize sinkingly that this, by God, is alien corn is the relative scarcity of laughter. You can get a kind of whinnying sound out of the well-bred English merely by saying that it is raining, and the English who are not well-bred have a superlative gift for catching the humor of a situation. But when it comes to humorous language, American similes and metaphors land with a morbid thump in the midst of a puzzled silence. The only way to make the English laugh, as laughter is understood in the United States, is to jab them with your elbow and say out of the corner of your mouth, "That's funny." Then they all look nervously around at each other and allow you two decibels of politely acquiescent mirth.

September 8. Henry is busy, and I have been going dutifully about, either with or without him, to lunches and teas and dinners. It is not especially stimulating, and I am glad I will be eight miles away in Yeobridge this winter. At the moment I feel, with my invitations, like a shopper whose arms are breaking under a load of packages which will not be any fun to open on getting home. A small college, I begin to suspect, is a small college the world over. The one in Exeter is more subdued and serious and less silly than American institutions customarily are. The students are better mannered and less flauntingly adolescent and all the activities connected with the establishment are pursued with a great deal of dignity. There are no fraternities, and athletics are purely for exercise. But the faculty has the same proportion of people who think they are too good for their jobs, the same handful who actually are too good and do not think so, and the same round of liturgical entertainments with which the professors and their wives fight off the consciousness of mediocrity.

Clean-Up Day

Yeobridge, October 18.

1. It seems to me one of the principal differences in the feeling-tone of English and American life comes from the fact that Americans are prone to favor you with their opinions and to do it, moreover, in the manner of an office boy favoring letters with stamps at five minutes to five, whereas the English think of an opinion as something which a decent person, if he has the misfortune to have one, does all he can to hide.

2. I sometimes wonder what living in Yeobridge would be like if we did not have Phyllis. In spite of her suppliant Yes-Adams and No-Adams, she contrives to make the callers seem, in contrast, a collection of faded daguerreotypes. You can get your teeth into Phyllis, and unless I am greatly mistaken, she can be trusted to return the compliment.

3. Two things I have not seen in England: (a) people working at enjoying themselves and (b) people enjoying themselves. Every schoolboy knows that Americans do not enjoy themselves. But they do have a concept of enjoyment and, indeed, put themselves through a whole variety of tortures in its name. In England, on the other hand, there appears to be no concept of enjoyment at all, except among the poor. They, if one can trust passing glimpses of cheap excursions, have the knack of having fun. But the better-off English, so far as I can see, seem totally unable to conceive of any pleasure beyond the ghostly satisfactions of doing one's duty. The phrase "sense of duty," as a matter of fact, takes the place of the ominous American "sense of humor," except that an Englishman described as having a sense of duty really does have one.

4. Our English acquaintances would be utterly incredulous if it were pointed out to them that they are consistently and unendurably insulting to Americans, but it happens to be true. As always, one must make a distinction in favor of the so-called lower classes, who, if they do not regard being an American as a pleasant and interesting attribute, at least succeed in giving that impression. But the people we meet as equals have been trained from childhood to patronize Americans as Americans are trained from childhood to clean their teeth, and they do it just as automatically. They have been saying, as if it were the ultimate in compliments, "Of course, you aren't like other Americans" for so long that they are no more conscious of the affronting implication than they are of the chairs they are sitting on. There are luminous exceptions, of course, like Mr. Primrose, but generally speaking it is impossible for an American to get through an afternoon or evening in the company of English people without hearing at least half a dozen unmistakable hints that culturally speaking, his compatriots are running neck and neck with the anthropoid apes.

And however unconsciously and without deliberation these hints are thrown out, the effect on the visiting alien is disastrous. He can remind himself until he is blue in the face that the English would be more courteous to Americans if they were less desperately jealous of the United States, which is after all a tribute. It is, but it is not a tribute you would pick out if you had your choice of a better one. And the relentless and unceasing intimations of American inferiority, unimportant enough singly, have nevertheless a powerful cumulative effect. After a while you begin to find yourself as incapable of forming calm, unbiased judgements of England as a hay fever sufferer is of pronouncing with detachment upon the August countryside. It is not the criticism. Nobody with any pretensions to good sense objects to fair criticism. It is that the English do not criticize America for criticizable things. If they have ever heard of lynching, of municipal corruption, of the violence attendant upon American strikes, no syllable of reference to such shortcomings ever passes their lips. They have just one big blanket indictment of America. It isn't England. What can you do with people like that, except to go home and raise hell in a diary?

October 26. . . . In middle-class England a woman is offered a drink with the same degree of frequency with which she is offered deadly nightshade, and at English dinners, when it gets on for ten o'clock and you are numb with cold and half hysterical from hearing about English weather, the gentlemen all have whiskey-and-soda and the ladies, God bless them, have tea! A woman who wants hard liquor at an English dinner has to ask for it, and then her host (nice and warm himself, of course, in woolen clothes, long sleeves and the radiation from a quantity of port) glances questioningly at her husband, as who should say, "She's a little minx, but I don't believe a tiny bit would hurt her." It is a discouraging state of affairs, for (quite aside from the cold storage dining) probably no class of people in the world could do more handily with a little of the stimulation and release of alcohol than well-bred Englishwomen. However, a visiting American does better to refrain from proselyting, to do her drinking in large batches (if possible) on the maid's day out, and on other occasions to remain silent and stoically let the pleurisy fall where it may.

November 12th. Most of the Yeobridge gentlefolk have visited the paper factory at one time or another, and derived great comfort therefrom. The factory is a small one, planked down in the middle of the English countryside, with trees and hedgerows coming right up to the railway siding. It is a setup which pleasantly confirms the gentry in their conviction that the plight of the oppressed classes is greatly exaggerated. However, not much import can be attached to a manufacturing plant in Devon. The principal industry of the country seems to be not paper or even (in spite of the pastures and sheep and red cows) grazing, but providing a haven, very beautiful and rather cheaper than the rest of England, for retired military men and the relicts of the clergy. Though half-dissolved little Devon has hardly any other resemblance to Connecticut, there is about it the same proportioned, exquisite, useless air that Connecticut villages achieve when they have been taken over by well-off New Yorkers.

Inside the factory, the country-club-cum-museum note disappears immediately. We went first through a hot, steamy, unbearably smelly place where South American grass was being boiled up into pulp, and then we followed the pulp through an endless series of moving belts, all of which looked exactly alike to me, although they were not supposed to. The floor around the belts was splashed with puddles, some of them over my instep, and the factory hands wore shoes with soles inches thick. Mr. Higginson, who had his character on virtuous side out, went with us, but the workmen explained the processes and Mr. Higginson had little to say. Some of the workmen were very young, with bright blond hair and extremely red cheeks, and some of them were seamy and intensely middle-aged, but they all looked deep-dyed English. They attended us politely but with a sort of cynical good humor; the factory has a great many visitors and the workmen know spurious enthusiasm when they see it.

Just as we were leaving, I saw two little boys sweeping an immense, dusty litter down a long corridor. They must have been fourteen, which is the age for leaving school in England, but they were small enough to be taken for nine or ten. They glanced at us apathetically and then went drearily on with their sweeping. I touched Mr. Higginson on his pin-striped sleeve and asked him how many boys of that age were employed in the plant, but either he did not hear me over the noise of the machinery or he pretended not to. There is a curious distinction, incidentally, between English and American conservatives. It lies in their hearing. If an American reactionary has his attention called to living conditions, he answers with great heat that those people spend all their money on radios and fur coats. The British Tory, on the other hand, smiles radiantly and replies, "We *have* been having frightful weather, haven't we?" That is the principal difference, I think, between the two civilizations—Americans make an unconscionable noise and clatter in their running away from life, whereas the English have been running away from it for so long, they do not even know that it is there.

November 13th. A long letter from Mr. Primrose, splendidly un-disappointing. Clearly, he is having a good time, though he suffers horribly from the hot rooms and judging by his account, expects to come back to England clad in nothing more than a spoonful of gravy. But he notes with surprise and pleasure that an English accent goes a long way in America (which is not exactly the fate of an American accent in the Stepmother Country), and though he left England to the accompaniment of loud choruses of his countrymen exclaiming that he would not be able to stand the pace in New York, he says he likes the pace. He likes the music in New York—he thinks, as Henry does, that there is more of it and it is better than in London—and he likes American food and American coffee. Between English and American students he notices the same differences that Henry does. And about the things he does not like, he writes calmly and rationally and without a single trace of It-isn't-Englishness.

Lovely, human Mr. Primrose. He is the only person we have met in England not in the "lower classes" who actually seems to be alive. Some of the more advanced Englishmen are interested in vitality, and they examine it curiously and kindly—leaning down for the purpose from a rarefied height where there is none. Most Britishers, however, from our experience of them, are not only not interested in it, but when they meet a person who has some, they promptly penalize him for offside play.

November 18th. There are times when living in England makes you feel, momentarily, that back in New York you never really had any adequate idea of comfort. It gets dark now around four o'clock, and I take a last look at the racing clouds and the sodden garden and the solitary red rose thrashing hopelessly around in the wind, and then I draw the curtains. Henry, if he has come home early, pokes the fire. Phyllis brings in tea, in a silver teapot, and Henry and I sit around the hearth eating toast and strawberry jam and wallowing in well-being.

It occurred to me today, as I sat stirring my third cup of tea, that this relaxed, late-afternoon atmosphere extends over a good deal of English life. An American living in England is constantly fetching up with a whang against the caste system; against a corrosive envy of the United States; against the worn-outness of an old country; and against that death-in-life which the Britons, with characteristic understatement, like to call English reserve. In the irritation resulting from these collisions, the American tends to overlook the fact that he can read his English newspapers in the relative peace engendered by an absence of race riots, lynchings, Vigilantes, rackets, wholesale murders, police brutalities and Roman holidays like the Hauptmann execution. It is not, I think, that the English are more fair-minded than other nations, but that their unfairness is so placid. British injustice is a leisurely inequity, arrived at by due process of law and free from any hoyden impulses to take people out and string them up on trees. A good deal in England makes the blood boil, but there is not nearly so much occasion as there is in America for blood to run cold.

MARY ELLEN CHASE:
SPRING IN ENGLAND

1937

Mary Ellen Chase was, like Margaret Halsey, academic, but it would be difficult to find a greater contrast between two views of the same country than we have here between Miss Chase's affectionate understanding and Miss Halsey's exasperated amusement. Mary Ellen Chase was, in a sense, Sarah Orne Jewett's successor as the interpreter of maritime Maine; some of her Maine stories and biographies are classics—*Mary Peters* and *Silas Crockett* among the novels, *A Goodly Heritage* and *Jonathan Fisher* among the biographies. In 1926 the Scottish-born William Allan Neilson, one of the great educators of America, called Miss Chase to Smith College, and there she remained for many years, teaching English literature and Biblical literature. Her book, *In England Now* was in part the product of two years' study at Cambridge University in the mid-thirties.

This year I followed upon the heels of the spring in France from late March until mid-April. The lilacs and cherries, quinces, magnolias and Judas trees of Provence had dropped their blossoms

From Mary Ellen Chase, *In England Now* (New York, 1937), pp. 205–219.

when on Easter morning in the green fields and gardens of Isère they were in full flower. Two days later in the small dark valleys of the Jura the close purple buds of the lilacs were only just flushing with violets, the fruit trees by the small swift streams only just showing their white petals. The Isère poplars shimmered in full leaf in the spring sunlight, which in Flanders had brought but the first hint of green to their upright branches. Late March starred the high fields of La Grande Chartreuse with primroses; mid-April gave them to the Flemish dikes at the same hours when cowslips had taken their places on Carthusian slopes. And during the bleak days following Easter in Reims one must perforce be content with the less secure immortality of the innumerable leaves carved in stone on the walls and capitals of her cathedral.

One could not thus follow the spring in England. Primroses, it is true, come a bit earlier on the high, green banks of Devonshire and at the foot of Somerset hedges than they do in the Midlands and the north, thanks to the milder Channel winds and brighter sunlight of the south. They are sold on dark March days in London for two-pence a bunch and taken home by thousands of city workers to brighten dingy, fog-swept rooms. Yet this little world of England is in herself too small to afford the variations of France, her valleys too shallow, her mountains and hills too low, her climate in general too similar from Northumberland to Kent; and although the snowdrops in the gardens of the south may be some days earlier than those farther north, the long, slow coming of the English spring is rela-tively the same within the four hundred miles of quiet country between the Sussex marshes and the Tweed.

The arrival of spring in most of America is sudden, bursting upon us one April day when we are sick to death of sodden snow, cold March winds, reluctant trees. We wake one morning to a new warmth in the air, to the sound of dripping eaves, and to a sun whose heat by noon has opened our coats and made us call excitedly to friends on the streets that spring is really here. Following a night of warm rain, dandelions glow in the new grass; orchards bloom and fade in one short week of sudden warmth; song sparrows give place to thrushes before we are aware.

This is not England's way. Her tardy spring does not appear in any such vivacious manner, has none of the swift, breath-taking qualities of that at home, although it is prodigal beyond words when it is once upon her. It begins its leisurely unfolding in late January, braving some of the worst weather this island can produce; it saves its completeness for the entire month of May when the whole land slowly spreads itself in bloom. One can, therefore, watch minutely its beginnings, its retardings, its progress step by step, for literally four months of the new year. For this reason it is in England the most rewarding of seasons, dilatory and unhurried, spacing its surprises comfortably and well.

By the last week of January the snowdrops and the aconites have reared their heads in garden plots everywhere. Sometimes stiff with frost in the morning, sometimes buried in a night's wet snowfall, by noon they are limber and jaunty enough and apparently quite unharmed. In January on the high Northumberland fields above the sea the gulls follow the farmer's plough in great clouds of white as he turns a darker earth than the warm reds that mark the soil of the Midlands and the south. By February in and above the fields of winter grain or of stubble the skylarks are singing. On a day of warmth and sunlight they fill the air with music, now almost a high monotony like that which at home is made by the high shrilling of crickets in autumn, now, when they leave the ground to shoot upward and out of sight, a sudden crescendo of unimaginable variation falling in trills and quavers from sky to earth. By February, too, the blackbirds and thrushes have abandoned their mid-winter silence and the minor notes of their November songs for full-throated calls and carollings from the blackthorn hedges, just beginning to show their first faint traces of white. The backs of the Cambridge colleges in February are royal with the gold and purple of thousands upon thousands of crocuses. They carpet the green lawns of Trinity and King's, follow the quiet backwashes of the river, catch and hold and scatter the sunlight of rare warm mornings.

In March the ewes are put out into the meadows to await their lambs. This certain sign of awakening life is more encouraging to those who watch than in the new but reluctant growth of the hedgerows, which seem to change little from day to day. Enclosures are built for them, and the rectangular, box-like lambing-hut of the shepherd, lumbering along the country roads, takes up its stations in the centre of the fields. The shepherds, I am told, receive the sum of ninepence for each lamb brought to a sufficiently secure maturity; and like Gabriel Oak they work early and late at their lonely midwifery. March and April midnights in the country are filled with the bleatings of ewes and new lambs; and if one lives fortunately near a lambing meadow as I have for two years past, there is small want of entertainment for six weeks on end. Lambs in every stage of life lie or stagger, frisk or leap, suck or sleep from early dawn until late twilight, the stout long-legged lambs of Northamptonshire and

Huntingdon, the smaller ones of Somerset and Wilts. There is more than the picturesque or the amusing in this pastoral scene which is enacted every spring; for these long meadows throughout England have to no small extent contributed to her history for well-nigh a thousand years. Slowly the spring comes on its way, retreating before days of cold rain and weeks of blustering wind. But the vanguards tenaciously remain as an earnest—snowdrops, aconites, and crocuses, early blossoming plums, the frail lavender flowers of the rosemary, the first green of the hedges. By April there is a larger hope. Now the king-cups open in the marshes; the cowslips, "paigles" as the country people call them, fill the meadows and the hands of country children; celandines blossom by the streams and ditches; and "lords and ladies" begin to sit under their canopies of green. Daffodils by thousands take the place of crocuses along the Cambridge backs beneath the sweeping willows; ladies' smocks silver the fields everywhere, now as by the Avon three centuries ago. The flat bulb lands of Lincolnshire, glowing with yellow, purple, and scarlet beneath the pale sky, vie with Holland in their wealth and brightness.

In the gardens of old cottages and of new council houses men and women dig in the evenings which, now that the time has changed, afford light until nine o'clock. These small gardens are one of the most wholesome and beautiful features of English village life. There is literally no house, however mean, without its wallflowers, tulips, forget-me-nots, and pansies. Conversation is exchanged over gates and hedges, comparisons made; swappings take place between this garden and that, superfluous roots and seedlings from one going to people the bare spaces of another. Men engaged all day in various trades and jobs like to turn in the evening to a bit of gardening; and the effect all summer throughout rural England not only amply repays them for their labour but helps to make imperishable that sentiment which has for so long surrounded the English village.

At five o'clock one mid-April morning one is suddenly awakened by the cuckoo, calling from far across the fields, invisible in his covert. And now, one says, spring *has* come. There is no longer any question. The cuckoo is everywhere accepted as the proof. As the days advance, he is the most ubiquitous of birds. From one place or another, always baffling the seeker, he calls from dawn till dark. Warm mid-days are his delight and drowsy afternoon. Taught by Wordsworth and other English friends of his charm, I had long counted him one of the major reasons for watching a spring in England. But I have seen days when, encompassed by a quite substantial and un-faery-like world of work, I have many times cried with Wordsworth, "O blessed bird!" although the emotion that fills me and the connotation within my harassed words are far different from his own!

Now spring hastens on toward her fulfillment. There is no stopping her. The dingy market-places of the county towns glow with flowers: daffodils at fourpence a bunch, poet's narcissus at sixpence, anemones like those at Epidaurus, forget-me-nots, tulips, hyacinths, and pansies to be bought for a song; stout seedlings of every description to bring summer gardens more quickly into bloom; bunches of purple-pointed asparagus for romantic natures, sick of cauliflower, cabbage and brussels sprouts; English strawberries grown under glass for those who can afford them; spruce lettuces to take the place of the inert and sluggish January variety; onions and radishes, and jaunty bundles of fresh watercress. There is spring in the cries of the vendors: "'Ere you are, ladies! Daffodils to cheer your 'eart. Who'll take 'ome a bunch at tuppence, for mother or for sweet'eart, or the old?" A young boy selling cowslips is not behind his elders in the rhythm of his cries: "Cowslips, fresh cowslips, the sign o' spring! Picked early in the meadows by me own 'and!"

Now the orchards and hillsides, woodlands and spinneys and copses come into their own. Apples in Kent and Dorset are white and crimson with bloom, heavy with the sound of bees; the blackthorn and wild plum edge the fields everywhere with drifts of white; the spotless, pendant blossoms of the cherry literally hang it branches with snow, the white, clinging snow of a New England April; the gorse blows in mounds of yellow on heath and moorland, and the early heather begins to show its first faint traces of violet. Trees put out their flowers, red, green, and yellow, waiting for the first days of May to form and shape their leaves.

Spring is on the streets of city, town, and village. On London squares and corners the flower-carts shed brightness. Undergrounds and buses carry blossom-laden people homeward from their work; for the English carry flowers less self-consciously than any other people in the world. Late April brings out the blue and the white tricycles of the ice cream vendors, those good-natured blue-or-white-coated men, treadling behind the succinct sign which says, "Stop Me and Buy One." The fish-and-chips peddler, rattling through the villages in the early evening, gives an extra pennyworth of sizzling chips to the small boys who leave their cricket to encircle his smoking van. There is an added lilt in the cry of the North

Country boot-mender as he trundles past in his swaying cart: "Boots? Boots? Is owt wrong with your boots?" Men now drink their evening ale and beer not within the public-house but without, sitting with their pipes and mugs on the benches beneath the sign of *The Blue Boar, The Sow and Pigs, The Black Duck,* or *The Green Man.* And those misguided minds who think the English an unsentimental race have but to note how in the hours between tea and supper lovers sit beneath the hedges, or later, with arms about each other's waists, start for the cinema, there to see the supplement, the complement, or the consummation of their own seasonal heart-stirrings!

But it is May which completes the long travail of the spring. There is nothing elsewhere that I know even remotely resembling this month in England. By May the spring is at its full. The wonder is that it is held so long in its completeness, that its flood tide does not diminish. It is now that the English climate is justified, now that the soaking, driving rains of January, February, and March absolve themselves. Old Thales, had he lived in England, might have been amply bolstered up in his contention that the beginning of all things lies in water! In England such miracles are not instantaneous but long drawn out, thanks to a climate which has no early heat to wither and consume what her slow spring has taken so long to bring to birth.

Lilacs in May hang over garden walls and hedges in veritable weeks of bloom, even while quinces, forsythia, lauristinus, pink flowering currants, and Judas trees retain their April freshness. The splendour of apples and cherries, plums and pears, in this island is not a short but a long perfection. Now comes the red and the white may in close masses of starry flowers, making the whole land rejoice; now comes, too, the laburnum, golden chains, the children call it, to hang its clusters over thousands of hedges and transform a pale grey day into sunshine. Horse-chestnuts, Whitsun trees, lift their pyramids of white and rose, touched indeed by Pentecostal flames. From the crannies of old walls everywhere throughout the south, from the sea wall of St. Ives in Cornwall, above the high, narrow lanes of Devonshire, the valerian blossoms, a mass of rose and white lasting far into July. The purple spikes of veronica catch their own reflection in the shining mirror of their leaves; wallflowers are persistent tongues of fire in every garden; and along the wide avenues of great country houses like that of Longleat in Wiltshire the rhododendrons begin to show their pink, white, and purple.

Not behind the gardens in their array are the common hedgerows everywhere. For they flaunt the Union Jack in the red of wild crane's bill, the blue of the speedwell, and the white of stitchwort. Bluebells carpet the ground of Madingley Wood, and above them on still, warm midnights the nightingale sings until dawn. The roadsides are tangled with the frail white of Queen Anne's lace; the green of the fields is lost in the white and crimson of the low English daisy and the yellow of buttercups; and over the ploughed lands the spring crops stretch in orderly rows, straight and level in the east, climbing the high, patchwork hills of Cornwall, billowing over the undulating fields of the Midlands and of Kent.

It is for these, one thinks that the people of this island endure her climate, knowing that in this sure and certain coming of the Holy Ghost they are saved indeed. And not alone are they in the country vouchsafed a new and abundant life. Into the outlying residence districts of London with their rows upon rows of indiscriminate, ugly houses, even into the dreary lines of brick and stone that stretch in all directions from the textile and mining centres of England, May penetrates in some degree. Now it is that that desire, so dear to the Englishman, to name his home is in a measure understood. To insist upon a name rather than a number, to call one's cottage or one's villa, so exactly like its dull and miserable neighbour, *Hazelmere, Lilycroft, Woodville, Fernmead, Glendale, Highfields* (all of which names I have seen in the outskirts of London) seems in December and January only absurd or pathetic, only at best to emphasize that sense of individuality so stubbornly characteristic of all Englishmen everywhere. But when a warm May evening brings out the plumber from *Lilycroft* and the joiner from *Fernmead,* each to dig in his six square feet of frontal space, when the black knobs of the slow planes are at last tufted with a new green, and the thin, undernourished branches of a sickly fruit tree bear a few struggling blossoms, when the sun streams through the greyness upon boys on the pavement with their tops and marbles and roller-skates, then it is that *Hazelmere* and *Lilycroft, Woodville* and *Fernmead, Glendale* and *Highfields* assume a new significance in the imagination. Their absurdity fades, even their pathos is transcended, in the understanding that, stronger even than this innate sense of his own rooftree, is the Englishman's insistence upon the countryside as his birthright. It is this birthright which triumphs over brick and mortar, city dumps and railway tracks, which places flowers in tubs from Mayfair to Southwark, which decorates even the bare spots between the chimney-pots on the roof of Stepney and Shoreditch, Lambeth and Bethnal Green. The name of *Lilycroft,* one suddenly knows, must have been engendered on some clear May evening over a high tea of eggs and kippers and steaming cups of Lyons' at tuppence the packet!

VINCENT SHEEAN:

"A FOOLISH WAY

TO GOVERN,

BUT IT WORKED"

1939

Vincent Sheean, a leading American journalist, was for many years European correspondent for the powerful *Chicago Tribune*. A prolific novelist, biographer, and essayist, he is best known for his biographies of Gandhi and of Nehru, and of Verdi—*Orpheus at Eighty*—and for his moving tribute to his friend Elinor Wylie. Married to the daughter of Forbes Robertson, he had the opportunity to know England well and became deeply devoted to her. The book from which this excerpt is taken, *Not Peace but a Sword,* describes England on the eve of the Second World War, a war which he helped the American people understand.

Pall Mall, to the right, is where the clubs are. (Not all of them, we say hastily, not all.) We don't see much of them from the top of the bus; in fact we are rapidly turning our backs to them as we wheel into Cockspur Street for Trafalgar Square. But we can hardly catch even a glimpse of those solemn gray exteriors, all Regency or early Victorian, without thinking of the extraordinary form of life they

From Vincent Sheean, *Not Peace but a Sword* (New York, 1939), pp. 723–726, 733–736, 740–741.

736

sequestrate and fertilize. The club would not be possible, I suppose, without the university; it is the university which trains Englishmen of the upper classes to believe that they must shelter themselves from their womenfolk in order to read a newspaper. Hence these huge, comfortable monasteries where you can eat a very bad lunch and drink magnificent wine with it, in the best English tradition, and sit over your coffee afterwards in a lounge where everybody talks in a discreet undertone, and all the papers published in London, daily and weekly, are to be seen if somebody else hasn't got what you want first. These are the political clubs, the clubs which date from the nineteenth century; the purely aristocratic clubs are further away, in St. James's, and do not come within the purview of the Thirteen Bus. There is an exception even to this rule: for that club up the way (next to the Athenaeum) is aristocratic enough, and nonpolitical, having been founded "for gentlemen who have made the Grand Tour."

The Grand Tour . . .

Well, at that, the men in those clubs do have some idea of what is going on. They know exactly where Tunis is, and the Ebro, and Slovakia, and the Ukraine. They have at times an absolutely terrifying plenitude of information, combined with a set of opinions fully worked out and not susceptible of modification. Their information is of the sort you get in a *Times* supplement, import and export, balance of trade, alignment of political parties, architectural monuments, etc., etc. They don't actually know how the people feel about anything, but they don't want to. Their interest in the people is of a purely electoral or philanthropic nature; they want them to vote this way or that, and they are quite willing to contribute to funds to keep them from starving to death outright. They also support the "voluntary" hospital system of England, which, although very bad, is regarded with the utmost pride by a class which appreciates its own virtue before everything else. They take an unflagging interest in all public affairs, which to them are mere shop talk; for they are the governing class of England.

Americans often do not know what the governing class of England is. Sometimes they think it is the aristocracy; sometimes they think it is the democracy (although not often); sometimes they think it is the rich. Such clues as I have been able to obtain lead me to think that the English governing class is recruited from the public schools and the universities, which is a purely economic selection only slightly mitigated by the system of university scholarships offered to promising students of the ordinary schools. But this economic selection (which is basic) is supplemented by an intricate machinery of social selection as well. A man may come of the most respectable family, pass all his examinations handsomely at Oxford or Cambridge, and still not get into the Foreign Office if he has the bad luck to offend in any one of a number of ways. He may be forced into the Treasury; or, if the Treasury will not have him, into the Colonial Office or the India Office or the Admiralty or the Home Office. When you see what did get into the Foreign Office, you marvel that anybody could ever have been refused for it; but they say people are refused all the time. One man I know had his eye on the Treasury all through Cambridge, and then landed in the Colonial Office, to his bitter disappointment. Some day he will no doubt be exercising the powers of empire over some godforsaken tribe of blacks which never will be able to understand why, at times, his eyes grow misty and his arm of justice falters; for how can the Senegambian know about Pall Mall and Whitehall?

It does seem a foolish way to govern, but it worked remarkably well during the great imperial period of which the present time is the dregs. The men who made the empire were, of course, seldom from the governing class: they were the traders, merchants and adventurers who came from all classes and expressed in their way the bursting vitality of a people too big for their island. The governing class came along afterwards and wielded the scepter. H. G. Wells once said that they had all been brought up by governesses, which may indeed be true; I never knew a governess. But it seems to me that their chief limitations come rather from this lifelong habit of secluding themselves in quiet rooms with deep carpets among other men exactly like themselves. It starts in school (without the quiet or the deep carpets), is fixed by the university, and continues throughout the lives of hundreds of men who might otherwise—in spite of the economic and social prejudices of their class—achieve a fairly comprehensive view of the material which is, after all, what they deal with, the existence of the population. They can tell you almost anything in the way of statistical, political, geographical, historical or ethnological information, but they don't seem to realize why it matters. To expect any collection of such men to solve a problem involving the passions of a people would be idiotic, you might say; and yet the Runciman mission was sent to Czechoslovakia.

All the English governing class is not in Pall Mall clubs, of course; nor does everybody in the clubs belong to the governing class. But all those men from the Foreign Office and the Home Office and the rest of it, with their parliamentary cousins, their womenfolk and their friends—the people who have the habit of their company

—make up what can be called, fairly accurately, the governing class. It is a thing distinct from the aristocracy, although members of the aristocracy often belong to it; and it is certainly distinct from "society," an institution which exists in England (as elsewhere) for enjoyment or display. I think it has no exact counterpart in any other country, for it does not fit into an exact economic or social category. Like the B.B.C., it is and it is not an organ of the state. This ambiguity and lack of definition characterize so much of the structure here that foreigners are sometimes (like the bewildered French writer) inclined to put it all on to climate, and say that England as a whole lives in a fog.

But even if it were true, it is a fog from which all those gentlemen in the clubs in Pall Mall have emerged at some time or other. They have surveyed the foreigner in his habitat; they have made the Grand Tour. . . .

Every newspaper in the world has some kind of representation in Fleet Street, even if it is only through the press associations of the various countries. The great London daily papers have their presses on the side streets between here and the river; the principal ones (except the *Times*) are in or near Fleet Street itself. None of them, except the black-and-clear-glass palace of the *Daily Express,* strikes us as particularly noticeable architecturally. It is a street of higgledy-piggledy late nineteenth-century buildings, mostly, some high and some low, some imposing and some shabby, all dirty, all busy at nearly every hour of the day. The life of the place goes on in the street, in the pubs, in the eating places as much as in the offices themselves. Nearly every kind of human being is to be found hereabouts engaged somehow in the production or distribution of newspapers. There are elegant ladies and gentlemen of high degree employed to collect gossip about their friends and relations; there are millionaires who like to own newspapers because of the power it gives them, and there are millionaires who made their money out of the papers; there are innumerable varieties of journalists and editors, special writers and tipsters and hangers-on; there are the printers themselves, and there are thousands of workers in distribution.

But what is it that they write, print and distribute?

The inquiry could occupy us far longer than it will take for the Thirteen Bus to pass through the street and climb Ludgate Hill. They write, print and distribute newspapers of a wider range than can be found anywhere else in the world except New York. The worst American press is probably worse than the worst English; but the best American press is, I think, better than the best English. That is, our best newspapers will suppress nothing and garble nothing in a moment of great crisis, so long as they are not directly subjected to an official censorship. By reason of its ownership or its relations with the government, the English press has no such independence. This has been shown very clearly in two recent crises which profoundly disturbed the whole country: the first was the abdication of Edward VIII, the second the triumph of Hitler in September, 1938. In the first of these instances the English press, having been silent as the grave about the whole business, suddenly began (on whose signal?) to thunder at the King because of his intention to marry, and by means of a crisis of the most sudden and trumped-up nature, forced an abdication. In that whole affair the press acted simply as an organ of the government of the day. Again in September, when very much graver matters were being decided, the press as a whole, seized by the panic fear of war, followed the lines of policy decided upon (or stumbled into) by the government of the day, and actually saluted Neville Chamberlain as the savior of the world's peace when he returned from Munich. Generations which will have to bear the frightful consequences of that unnecessary surrender may never understand, as they pore over the press of the months just past, how such things could be written, printed and read.

Along there on the left side of the street, as we whisked by, I caught sight of a white shaft let into the wall of the church of St. Dunstan-in-the-West. It was surmounted by a marble head, and the inscription beneath it said that it was a memorial to Northcliffe.

That, perhaps would supply a clue to the relations of the press and government in England: a serious study, which should some day be possible, of the life of Alfred Harmsworth, Lord Northcliffe. H. G. Wells has given us some very illuminating pages on the subject in his autobiography. He taught some of the Harmsworth children (not Alfred) in school, and had seen, in those far-off days, the first copies of the school newspaper, written and printed by Alfred a year or so before. Decades later Wells came again into relations with Alfred Harmsworth when the *Daily Mail* had become a market for a writer's work, and through an association of some years he was able to get an idea, not only of the tangle of publications over which Harmsworth was lord, but also of the curious unbalanced man, irresponsible, uninformed, violent and despotic, who wielded that immense power. Northcliffe was, of course, a journalistic genius, in that he was always thinking of some new trick or gadget for catching the public's fancy and making money out of increased circulation and advertising; but that sort of genius can scarcely compensate for an ignorant and irresponsible use of colossal power. Wells tells us that the war-time cabinet, to keep Northcliffe and his younger rival, Beaverbrook, quiet, invented ministries for them; and there is a funny scene in the book, where Northcliffe, seated solemnly in a drawing room at Crewe House as minister of propaganda, says to Wells (in effect): "You are a believer in social revolution. We two are here. Isn't that social revolution enough for you?"

The government is quick to grant peerages to the owners of newspapers, quick to give them any sort of honor, distinction or privilege they may fancy, and to see that they have no cause to complain of the social or political system. Alfred Harmsworth at a smart London dinner party, surrounded by a gaggle of duchesses, could hardly have been expected to retain his independence of judgment, even if he had possessed the powers of intelligence or the education to make a sound judgment on any serious question. He was not, apparently, much taken in by the purely social aspects of his bewildering success, but its ramifications in political power were too much for him; he governed his realm by whim, by fantasy, held everything else of no account, and came to grief in the end because his mind could not stand the strain.

SHIPPING MAGNATE
FALLS TO
DEATH

That is what the new poster says, flourished by the boy down on the corner of Fleet Street and Ludgate Circus; it is just out, with the ink still wet, and covers over the anti-French scuffle in Rome and the new French troops in Tunis. The shipping magnate (if I bought the newspaper I might find out that he was a bookkeeper in a shipping firm) had apparently fallen or been pushed from a window, and it is possible to imagine fifty reasons why this event should have taken place, but not one of them fully explains why the event is more interesting than the anti-French scuffle in Rome or the new French troops in Tunis.

That is what they are interested in, there is no doubt: that is why most people buy most newspapers, to find out about the shipping magnate who falls to death, to see the West End thru' a Keyhole. The sober journals of opinion (so-called) do not circulate widely, and the most unsober the journal the more people it finds to share its insobriety. Northcliffe was among the first to discover the depth and width of this phenomenon, and his monument is not the *Times* (which he did, indeed, own for a while toward the end, out of sheer vainglory) but the popular press of London. That, and a queer legend of Fleet Street, and a shaft of white stone at St. Dunstan-in-the-West. . . .

Down on the right, off Queen Victoria Street, is the *Times* newspaper, an institution unique in its sensitiveness to the mood of the governing class. It is scarcely a newspaper at all; it is rather a mirror in which the governing class, and indeed, to make it more specific, the governing clique, can admire themselves. It is an eminently satisfactory mirror because the picture it presents is always flattering under any circumstances. It also has the magic property of leading devotees onward—few mirrors can predict and make their predictions come true and thereafter cause the accomplished fact to be gazed upon with ecstatic admiration. Yet this is what the *Times* newspaper accomplished in the autumn of 1938. It was the *Times* newspaper that first tipped us off to the impending vivisection of Czechoslovakia, in a leading article of unexampled slyness and perfidy (September 6, 1938). The governing class was not altogether pleased with that, and there was quite a row for a while, but as event followed event, and Mr. Neville Chamberlain took airplane after airplane, the *Times* newspaper upheld and carried him like a full Wagnerian orchestra under a shaky soprano, until the goal was reached at last. Hitler had been temporarily appeased by the offering of the flesh and blood of others, and the *Times* could proclaim, as it did on October 1, 1938, "A New Dawn," to the universal satisfaction of its readers.

And let it be clear: if you want to know how those people's minds work you must read the *Times* every day for a long while. It is absolutely indispensable. You must read it all, the dramatic criticisms, the reviews of books, the news from America, the news from India and the colonies, the news of Spain, China and the whole continent of Europe, the correspondence columns. Not even the smallest letter from a clergyman in the country who has heard the first cuckoo should be disregarded. The transaction between the *Times* and the mind of the British upper class is so continuous, intimate and hereditary that it is almost impossible to tell, under ordinary circumstances, which originates and which replies in the flow of communication between them. Yet at important periods, such as this last autumn, you can feel the slight tug of discreet leadership, in which the *Times* reveals (without at all displaying) its conscious direction. Once a crisis is past, the *Times* and its readers subside into their normal state of exchange, in which the editorial comment tells the reader exactly what he already thinks in words which seem to him exactly what he would have used if he could have thought of them; the correspondence columns are filled with the usual debates over dates, places or quotations; conscience funds are started for the victims of the last crisis; and the upper class is enabled again to contemplate its own virtue in the mirror which the *Times* faithfully presents every morning at breakfast.

J. FRANK DOBIE:
"THERE IS SOMETHING OF
THE MARTYR IN THEIR
RESISTANCE TO CHANGE"

1942

A Texan who at one time ran a cattle ranch of 200,000 acres, J. Frank Dobie was described by a contemporary journalist as "the Southwest's most raucously successful cultural historian." From 1933 on a professor of English literature at the University of Texas, Dobie made his reputation in part as a historian of the frontier—*Coronado's Children, Apache Gold and Yaqui Silver, The Voice of the Coyote,* and others—and as one of the most famous raconteurs in the country. After Henry Commager had established a beach-head in American history at Cambridge University in 1941, Dobie was invited over to teach history and to spread an understanding of America among the Cambridge undergraduates and the service groups who were exposed to Cambridge for some time during the war. "He was not," it was observed, "precisely the Action type of scholar," but with his Texas accent, his inexhausti-ble fund of stories, his ten-gallon hat, his good will and good humor and good scholarship, he was an immense success. After his return to Texas, Dobie became something of a firebrand in university and state politics, a rallying center for those who looked with misgivings on the growing power of the oilmen and the professional politicians in Texas affairs.

From J. Frank Dobie, *A Texan in England* (Boston, 1945), pp. 102–109.

The conservatives motivated by taste, particularly taste in architecture, and by "The Old Squire" sentiment for old names, oid fields, old ways, are an integral part of the British soil. There is something of the martyr in their resistance to change—often also something of the bull—and a good deal of sheer inertia. When the love for an old hall by a college of dons dooms charwomen to carry coalscuttles up and slopjars down three flights of stairs, the conservatism has a flavor not idyllic. Yet kitchen help in my college almost struck last winter over the installation of a plate washer. After I had dined with a Foreign Office man in one of the largest clubs of much beclubbed London, we went into the big loungeroom for coffee. A middle-aged woman, black-dressed, brought it, one of her hands bandaged and in a sling supporting the tray. What was the matter with her hand? my host asked. Strain from carrying trays from the kitchen in the basement up to the ground floor, more than fifty round trips every evening, sometimes a hundred. A doctor had advised rest; she could not take off, for there was no one else to carry the trays. At home she had a family in a nine-room house to look after.

"How easy it would be, or would have been, in normal times," my host commented, "to build a dumb-waiter to carry the trays up and down."

In some of the coal mines of England and Wales miners continue in wretched forms of physical drudgery elsewhere done away with by improved machinery. Yet the miners themselves, it seems, are more averse to new machinery than the mine-owners are. On icy days I have seen women on their knees scrubbing with a hand brush flagstones that could be easily and quickly cleaned with hose and stiff broom. In a country where the Society for the Prevention of Cruelty to Animals is as familiar as the strains of "God Save the King" and as highly regarded for its humaneness as the King is for his kindness, there seems to be no particular sentiment for installing machinery to alleviate human drudgery. No doubt the surplus of population and, consequently, of labor in normal times is partly responsible. Putting the laborer out of a job with a gadget may be more inhumane than keeping the laborer on her knees. Very likely the laborer does not pine to get off her knees. The manager of the Duke of Bedford's estate at Woburn told me that he offered, this year, to install running water in nineteen rent houses at a cost of a few pennies a month, and that only one renter wanted the running water. Some of the others resented the proposal as a landlordly attempt to raise their rents, which are astoundingly cheap. In Mexico if a gringo asks why the hard way of doing a thing is not remedied by an easier way, the invariable answer is, *"No es costumbre."* Watching a boy in an English field lead a horse hitched to a plow guided by a man, I have imagined that if I asked the man why he did not use plow lines and drive the horse himself, thus saving the use of the boy, he might reply, like the Mexican, "It's not the custom."

The Englishman wants his customs, like his buildings, his machinery, the operations of his institutions, his Church, to stay established. He will pay high for a highly complicated engine designed to get the last ounce of energy out of every drop of oil and every lump of coal, and he will be willing to stand the high cost of maintaining such an engine, rather than install a simpler and cheaper engine of American or German type that wastes a small amount of fuel but costs little to maintain and may be inexpensively discarded for another model to meet changing conditions. Something in him pulls powerfully strong for permanence. Having put up a building, he may add to it and go on adding to it, but he hates to raze it to make way for a structure of entirely new design. The official plan for restreeting the great area demolished by German bombs around Saint Paul's in London is being opposed by conservative architects because the proposed thoroughfares, designed for heavy motor traffic, will not, in the manner of the old alleys too narrow for traffic, invite businessmen to go out bareheaded into the open and transact big business with the casualness of ancient merchants upon the Rialto.

In the parks of London rolls of barbed wire still make the ground hideous and obstruct walking. Most people want the wire taken away and men half idle in military camps could easily take it away; but the Responsibles seem to feel that what is once put should stay put.

"These people," wrote Ambassador Walter Hines Page to President Wilson in 1914, "are *set.* They naturally shrink from changing anything; they instinctively resent change. A naval man told me that after breech-loading guns were invented, they kept the muzzle-loaders ten years; arguing meantime that no breech-loading guns could possibly be accurate." How did they ever come to start the Machine Age, to make the Industrial Revolution?

It is significant that R.A.F. development of radar to the highest stages of effectiveness in the world has been in a field of science unhampered by tradition, precedents and inherited achievements. In this field caution against discarding the old, lest something good be lost, could not slow down the rush into the new.

"What," Abraham Lincoln asked, "is conservatism? Is it not adherence to the old and tried, against the new and untried?"

> Be not the first by whom the new are tried,
> Nor yet the last to lay the old aside.

Few reform bills have been debated, not alone in Parliament but in print and private conversation, so long, steadily and earnestly as the Education Bill finally made into law in the summer of 1944. The new plan calls for nothing like the French Revolution plan to sweep away all extant gods in order to set up the new Goddess of Reason. It aims to extend education rather than to channel it, to care better for the needs of drudging millions, to project, with modifications, the present multiform system, rather than to melt it all up like so much artwork in gold and silver to be remolded into uniform bars. As the Headmaster of the famous Harrow School has said: "It is in accordance with variety in the needs and capabilities of children and with the English tradition that within the educational system of the country there should be a variety in types of school, in educational methods and freedom to experiment. The vitality of our education depends largely on this variety and freedom." The state is to send poor boys to the so-called public schools, which have so long borne the reputation of being exclusive, but the public schools are to retain their prestige. The state is to support many church secondary schools and by virtue of support to assume stronger direction over them; yet in a way they remain church schools. Compulsory education has long been a fact, but the scholastic age limit has been advanced, and now the need for trained teachers will give women larger representation in the teaching profession than the males have up to the present conceded.

While the scientific age has been accepted in Britain as thoroughly as it has been accepted in America, it has been accepted more critically and less defiantly, because there is no strong Fundamentalist cult in religion, based on ignorance. More critically, for in accepting science, British conservatism has clung to classical ideals. British universities have not relegated Latin and Greek to the status of Sanskrit as those languages are being relegated by American universities. The Matthew Arnold ideal of infusing the scientific world with sweetness and light, of keeping machinery from becoming Frankenstein by tempering its driver with Hellenism, does not prevail, but it persists.

The most talked-of lecture at Cambridge during my year's residence has been one delivered on "Plato and Modern Education," by an Oxford classicist, Sir Richard Livingstone. This age, he argues, needs as no other age has needed "a sense of values by which to judge and use the gifts of material civilization." Plato's "concern was to impart values." Yet, "as for sermonizing, a sense of values is perhaps best imparted by those who feel them intensely but never mention them." We cannot improve on Plato's idea: "When the child goes to school, 'the works of great poets are put into his hands, and he learns them by heart,' that he may see what human greatness is and desire to imitate it."

Quotations from Homer and Horace no longer flavor debates in Parliament, but the classics are emphatically taught in the secondary and in the public schools, and all students who enter the great universities have passed examinations in the classics. The classics are going on in the direction of total eclipse, but they are not likely to be booted out any time soon in order to make way for a smattering of Spanish useful for automobile salesmen in South America. Reforms, no matter how drastic, are not likely to trade off the whole classical tradition for a Dismal Swamp of "Education" courses designed by their "unctuous elaboration of the obvious" to stultify any mind subjected to them—courses politically useful, however, to the professors who give them, for thus they are kept in jobs, and politically useful also to the students who take them because the Education monopolists have manipulated laws to bar even the humblest job in most American public schools to any applicant who has not spent his or her golden youth in massing Education credits. . . .

The elements of materialism and of idealism may be of about equal weight in Uncle Sam and John Bull. They are not blended in each according to the same chemical formula. Tennyson's Northern Farmer, who always heard the hoof-beats of his horse saying "Proputty, proputty, proputty," would hardly have sold the hawthorn hedges off his land for any other kind of property. An American agriculturist visiting in England recently advised against hedges as taking up too much soil space; barbed wire fences would take up less space and serve just as well to separate fields. He seemed to overlook the material fact that hedges afford protection for animals and for tender plants against harsh winds. He took into no account how hedges shelter and feed the wonderful bird life of England and how the more birds there are in the hedges, the fewer bugs in the garden. He left out the country's deep-seated and for centuries established appreciation of the charm, the graciousness and the loveliness that hedges give the landscape.

HENRY STEELE COMMAGER:
ENGLISH TRAITS,
ONE HUNDRED YEARS LATER

1948

This essay was originally written to commemorate the centenary of Emerson's *English Traits;* it reaffirmed, what Emerson himself had asserted, that English Traits are deeply engrained and not easily changed. Henry Commager, then a professor at Columbia University, went to England in the autumn of 1941 to inaugurate the teaching of American history at Cambridge, and in 1947 became Pitt Professor of American History there; he was subsequently Harmsworth Professor of American History at Oxford. This essay appeared in its original form in *The Nineteenth Century;* it is here reprinted in a somewhat changed version.

National character is everywhere wonderfully tenacious, but nowhere is it more tenacious than with the English, who have, after all, something of a patent on tenacity. This is the first and most obvious of English traits—the stability and permanence of the English character. Come hell or high water, the Englishman remains

Henry S. Commager, "English Traits, One Hundred Years Later," *The Nineteenth Century,* July 1948 imperturbably English. He is, it would seem, less affected by the currents and cross-currents of history than people of any other nation; he is less affected, too, by passing fashions whether of literature or of dress or of food. Nothing will make him false to his word or discourteous to his guest; nothing will keep him from his tea or change his cooking.

For more than a century and a half—from John Adams to John Winant—Americans have been busy describing the English. That they have so largely repeated each other is a comment not on their lack of originality but on a persistence of national traits almost monotonous. It makes, perhaps, for dullness, but there is this to be said about England: you can count on her, you can set your sights on her, you can almost set your watch by her. "What kind of people do they think we are?" asked Churchill at a fateful moment in history, and those who forgot what kind of people the English were—the Germans and the French, for example—paid heavily for their failure.

Yet what is interesting about all this is that while the underlying character has remained palpably the same, that character itself is no simple thing, but wonderfully complex and even paradoxical. "England is the land of mixture and surprise," wrote Emerson, and the mixture has perplexed most of the interpreters. For the English character is not only stable and uniform, but various and heterogeneous; it is at once obvious and elusive, and almost every generalization must be not so much qualified as confounded.

A materialistic people—who can doubt it?—the English have produced more than their share of mystics and poets, of idealists and transcendentalists, more than their share of the Donnes and Herberts, the Blakes and Shelleys, the Wordsworths and Coleridges, the Foxes and Penns. The greatest colonizing people of modern times, they confess the most passionate attachment to their own country, their own county, their own community: they are at once the most indefatigable globetrotters and gardeners. Their wealth and their wanderlust have enabled them to know the best of all other nations, but they remain true to their own: they carry their language with them wherever they go, and though every Englishman delights in French cooking, none permits his chef to imitate it.

A small nation, with a population highly mobile and highly urban, their differences in idiom and accent are the despair of foreigners; Vermonters and Texans can understand each other better than men from Devon and Lancashire, or from Glasgow and

London, and if the observation that the best English is spoken in Dublin is an exaggeration, it is interesting that it should be made: no one ever suggested that the best American was spoken in Toronto. A unified and harmonious people, the English have persisted in class distinctions, and divisions more ostentatious than those found in most other countries; while politically they have achieved as great a degree of democracy as any other people, they remain class-conscious, and until recently at least, it could be said that every Englishman is branded on the tongue with his class mark.

A peaceful people, tender and kind, they are, when aroused, the most belligerent of men, good friends and bad enemies, with the indomitable qualities of the bulldog. Allegedly without a sense of humor, or with a belated one, they have produced, after all, the greatest humorists of our time, and the nation which confessed Herbert Spencer boasted, at the same time, Gilbert and Sullivan. The most law-abiding people, they write the best of all detective and mystery stories and their literature is stained with violence. Monuments of conformity—no sin is more grievous than to do what is not done—they are at the same time passionate individualists, and the nation where nonconformity is a term of rebuke is that in which eccentricity flourishes unrestrained.

II

This is all paradox, and it is perhaps an additional paradox that the English character, though sometimes paradoxical, is rarely puzzling and unreliable. The broad traits are clear enough; they persist through the years, they run through all classes of society. The qualities that tend to unify the English are far stronger than those which divide them. What, then, are the traits which have persisted?

They are a law-abiding people. Probably no other people confess the same deep respect for the law, no other conform so instinctively to the rules and regulations of government or of any organization that has authority. They do not smoke where smoking is forbidden, or walk on grass in defiance of signs, nor do they dabble in the black market or try to evade payments on their income tax, or get out of place in a queue. Property is safe, women and children are safe, life is safe, and the critic George Orwell suggested that the trait which most sharply distinguished the English from all other people was their habit of not killing one another. Nor does all this rest upon law, or upon the police force: the whole of society is one vast law-enforcement agency and public opinion is fiercely hostile to law-breakers and rule-breakers.

That the English pay a price for this trait cannot be doubted. They are, if anything, too law-abiding and acquiesent. They do not revolt readily enough against bad laws and troublesome regulations, but where law is concerned, they take the attitude that theirs is not to reason why. They have come, indeed, to find security in regulations: where an American regards a regulation as a challenge and a "don't" sign as an affront, the Englishman takes a positive pleasure in abiding by rules and regulations, and is lost without them. It is sometimes hard to avoid the feeling that the Englishman likes standing in queues, and that a single Englishman forms a queue automatically.

The English have a highly developed sense of justice and right. No phrase is more commonly used, by the ordinary people, than "it's right" or "it's not right," and that pretty much concludes the matter. They want to know where they stand, and they usually do. They believe in fair play, on the playing field and in the law courts and in business. They have little patience with subtlety or cleverness: they do not want rights that can be argued about. They hate all chicanery, all evasiveness, and all slipperiness. They are upright and down-right, foursquare and simple and staunch. They carry their sense of justice over into the political realm—in large matters of national or international politics, in small matters which have their day as questions in the House, they are at once just and heartless; and in matters outside the law they are philanthropic but not charitable.

They believe that every man should have his due, but neither more nor less, and they have contrived a complex and rigid system to see that each has his due—and no more nor less. The English instinct for observing laws should make most controls superfluous, but much of English life seems organized on the basis of suspicion rather than trust, and an expensive and pernicious system of checks and controls permeates life. Few Englishmen cheat on their railway tickets, yet where in America a single functionary looks at a ticket, in England there are no fewer than three who perform this unnecessary service. When you ride on a bus or in a subway, you must be ready to prove that you have paid for your ride. Accounts are kept scrupulously; some shops even note down the number of pound notes; the crossed cheque is an English invention, and a man could as easily burgle the Bank of England as cash a cheque where he is not known.

The insistence that every man have his due extends from formal arrangements, like food rationing, to informal relationships, like gratuities: it is the enemy not only of favoritism, but of carelessness. Before he will admit you to his libraries or schools, before he will trade with you even, the Englishman wants to know who you are and what claims you have on him, and he will make clear, too, what claims he has on you.

In all this the English are at once the most courteous and the most discourteous of people, and the combination has confused observers for two centuries. It is the courtesy that is instinctive and pervasive, displaying itself formally in the ease of all social relationships and the quiet efficiency of all public ones, and informally in a thousand little acts of thoughfulness. It is in part the product of training and habit—no children are more courteous than the English; it springs from respect for the individual; it is inspired by natural kindliness. It is to be found alike in individuals, in organizations, and even in crowds; it is habitual but rarely, as with the French, ostentatious.

The discourtesy is a more complicated matter, a mixture of suspicion, indifference, and arrogance, and it is, as often as not, calculated. Its explanation, like that for so many English traits, can be found in the class structure and class-consciousness of English society, and the danger to that structure from anything incomprehensible or inharmonious. Once an individual is placed, whether as publican or gentleman, as charwoman or lady, all is smooth, but the social sport, whose position and whose claims threaten the structure of the class society, is subject to endless rebuffs. For until he has presented acceptable credentials, the stranger is suspected of asking more than his due, usurping a position which is not his by right, making claims which may be unfounded. Nowhere is the accredited visitor received more hospitably, nowhere is the unaccredited stranger—one whose dress or accent betrays a dubious position—so coldly rebuffed.

III

The English are an intensely practical people, infatuated with common sense. They have produced few great speculative philosophers but many practical ones: Bacon and Locke, Bentham and Mill, Spencer and Huxley, are their typical products, not men like Spinoza or Kant. They like to see a program and they judge by results. In politics they have a wonderful feeling for the practical and the actual, an instinctive repugnance for the doctrinaire. They distrust all extremes: their Conservatives are liberal and their Liberals conservative, and even their socialism is a bundle of compromises. They will not waste their votes, and they will not waste their time on men or parties that are too sublte or fanatical and no people are less susceptible to demagoguery.

For all their open-mindedness and their tolerance, they are an intensely conservative people. They hate innovation, wrote Emerson, and their instinct is to search for a precedent. Even where they are forced to make changes, they change the substance rather than the form, and though English law is certainly as modern as American, the English judge still wears a wig and a King's Counsel takes the silk. Where to an American the fact that something has always been done a certain way is sufficient reason for changing it, to an Englishman it is sufficient reason for retaining it. When asked why Britain did not print an air-mail stamp instead of requiring two stamps to be pasted on every air-mail letter, one of the most unconventional of British scholars answered simply that they had never printed special stamps, and thought the answer conclusive.

Notwithstanding their conservatism the English are progressive and it is a peculiarity of the English character to achieve revolution through evolution. Those who speak in the House of Commons are still required to wear a hat, but what they say is rather more radical than anything that can be heard in the American Congress, and if top hats are still required at Eton, education there seems to produce men fit for the responsibilities of the new day. Oxford and Cambridge are still, to all appearances, aristocratic and even feudal institutions, yet they select their students on the basis of talent and each takes a larger percentage of its student body on scholarships than any American university. Everywhere this process of evolutionary adjustment can be seen: ostentatiously in the realm of politics, less spectacularly in the church, in education, in the relations of labour and industry, in the military.

For all their conservatism, their phlegm, they are the most adventuresome of people. What other nation boasts a comparable galaxy of explorers, mountain climbers, navigators, what other could maintain a Hakluyt Society? From the day of Drake and Frobisher to that of Doughty and Burton the English have led the way to the strange places of the earth always carrying with them their Englishness, even their afternoon tea, for while they are wonderfully adaptable in large matters, they make few concessions on the little ones. They penetrate every river, conquer every mountain, levy upon the whole globe for their collections of flora and fauna, or of esoteric lore; no other literature since the Icelandic sagas is so hectic and adventurous, and the adventurer of John Buchan's Richard Hannay are not wholly imaginative.

Although they are the greatest explorers and colonizers, and have spread the English language and laws throughout the earth, they are the most provincial of people. Even their patriotism is parochial rather than imperial, and it is as hard for Englishmen to sing the praises of things they do not know as it is easy for Americans of the prairie states to celebrate rocks and rills, or woods and templed hills. The English love their county rather than their nation, and every acre of England has its historian and its muse. The London *Times* and the Manchester *Guardian* give adequate attention to world news, but few other papers do, and English journalism, generally, is less cosmopolitan than American. In matters of language, too, they are parochial. They do not take readily to foreign languages, expecting foreigners rather to learn English, and they are still inclined to think the American language a sort of debased dialect of theirs.

IV

English conservatism and parochialism are not unconnected with self-satisfaction. On the whole the English approve of themselves, as well they may. Instinctively, rather than intellectually, they are sure that theirs is the best of societies, and their highest compliment is still that a thing is "so English." Recent events have, superficially, shaken this Gibraltar-like assurance of superiority but it persists in little things, subconsciously as it were. Thus English scholars acknowledge the achievements of Harvard or Columbia or the University of Chicago, but they know in their hearts that Oxford and Cambridge are better, and when they are not on guard their pens slip into the assertion that their higher education is the highest in the world. Most of them are still convinced that the *Times* is the greatest newspaper in the world and that if a book is not in the Bodleian it is not literature. It was equally characteristic that a recent edition of Muirhead's *London* should describe the library of the British Museum as along with the Bibliothèque Nationale the largest in the world, though there are three in the United States that are larger; that an Oxford don should gravely inquire if any American law library has as many law books as the library of his college; and that some passengers from Grimsby should refuse to touch any of the wonderful variety of fish prepared by the chef of a French Line boat because they knew no fish could compare with the fish of Grimsby.

The English have, needless to say, ground for complacency. It is true, as Emerson remarked, that they make well those things which are ill made elsewhere in the world. Though this, alas, is changing. It is not skill alone that accounts for the superiority but certain traits of character. They believe in durability and make things to last—boots and guns and houses, for example. They take pride in their work, and have infinite patience. They carry into affairs even of business their standards of integrity and propriety: if their books are not always exciting they are almost always well written; if their advertisements rarely lure, they do not outrage decency.

They are a thrifty people—thrifty of property, of speech, of their emotions. It is not merely that they prefer understatement to exaggeration; they suspect any public expression of emotion, verbal or by gesture. There is less public lovemaking in England than in either America or France, and less public manifestation of family affection. The English do not shout themselves hoarse at games, but are content with a "well played" and applaud the play rather than the team. They dislike a fuss and, above all, a scene; they will endure any discomfort rather than complain about it publicly, will waste an hour looking for a road rather than accost a stranger for information.

They are thrifty of the products of their minds, as well. They prefer, on the whole, a performance that is not too brilliant, a conversationalist who is not too clever. Churchill was suspect all his public life for his incomparable oratorical gifts. They distrust the ready speaker, the facile orator, the brilliant player, as they distrust men or women who are too well dressed. They resist styles, prefer old clothes to new, and have made tweeds and the umbrella national symbols.

The English love of privacy is proverbial, and has not been exaggerated. Even the shabbiest garden is concealed behind a hedge, and often the hedge is reinforced by a brick wall. Few households are so poor that they cannot afford curtains and draperies, carefully drawn at night—though few people have less to conceal. English houses do not have front porches or verandas, and when the Englishman sits out in his garden it is always at the back, not at the front of his house. Anyone who enters a first-class railway compartment is likely to be regarded as an intruder, and a stranger who strikes up a conversation is looked upon with suspicion unless he proves to be an American, when his ignorance of good manners is indulged. The instinct for privacy characterizes personal relations as well. Except in the novels the Englishman does not readily bare his soul; professional men are reluctant to let the stranger in on the secret of their profession and scholars to confess their scholarly pursuits. Christian names are less commonly used than in most countries.

They have created a masculine country—a society made for men and run for men; the contrast here with either France or America is striking. The English home belongs to the man, not the woman —belongs legally, as far as ownership is concerned, and psychologically, where furnishments and conveniences are concerned. England has few magazines designed primarily for women, and English banks are not fitted with special rooms where women can transact their business. The whole tone of English society is masculine: the importance of clubs, the role of the pub, the concentration of family money on the education of the sons.

There are no girls' schools with the standing of Eton or Harrow or Winchester, and it was only a few years ago that Cambridge University conceded degrees to women. Of some twenty-five Cambridge colleges, there are only three for women; and when it was observed, recently, that the number was scarcely sufficient, there was prompt agreement: there should be, said a young don, at least four. An American would have said, almost automatically, that there should be twenty. Yet it must be added that all this has nothing to do with politics, or with literature and the arts. There are more women M.P.s than congresswomen and for a generation now the best novelists have been women.

V

Not the most important, but the most pervasive and the most pernicious of English traits is class-consciousness. It is not political, it is only in small part economic; it is social and psychological and philosophical. Its persistence is a tribute to the tenacity of traditional ways of thinking and acting, for it has resisted, stubbornly and successfully, the whole twentieth-century movement of democratization. Originating with the privileged classes, it is retained by the unprivileged, and class sentiment today is stronger with the lower than with the upper classes, and strongest perhaps with the middle.

It reveals itself in a thousand ways, most of them insignificant in themselves, but cumulatively not only important but controlling. In England alone, or English-speaking countries, accent betrays class.

There are not only dialects for every section of England, but for each class, and the dividing lines are formidable. The terms "lady" and "gentleman" still have meaning, and have not yielded to the leveling process; other terms, too, confess a special class significance—"top drawer," for example, while the innocuous phrase "not quite" is loaded with dynamite when applied socially. The distinctions between officers and privates in the army, officers and ratings in the navy, are more decisive than in the American services, and even in the Second World War a public school accent was helpful in obtaining a commission.

Nowhere else have domestic servants played a comparable role, nowhere was the hierarchy of the domestic staff more implacable, nowhere was Thorstein Veblen's theory of conspicious waste more fully validated than in prewar England. The use of the phrase "master and servant" to cover the field of labor relations derives from common law, and there is a social as well as a professional distinction between solicitor and barrister.

The English have achieved a far greater degree of economic democracy than their American cousins, but the average Englishman still tends to stay in his class, and his father's class, in matters of work and trade or profession; the Alger stories have no true English counterpart. For all the self-respect of an English workingman or servant, the expectation of gratuities is widespread and curiously systematized: no foreigner can hope to comprehend its well-arranged intricacies but every English gentleman understands them intuitively.

Class distinctions extend even into the intellectual realm, where they are least justifiable. The intellectual preeminence of Oxford and Cambridge may be challenged, but never the social; it is interesting to note that though both are located in the provinces, it is the other universities—those at Manchester, Liverpool, and Birmingham—that are called provincial. Any man can get a good education at the provincial universities but if he has social ambitions he might as well cut his throat as go to them. (This was pre-York and pre-Sussex, both of which have achieved social prestige.) A comparable hierarchy prevails in the whole field of secondary education, and it is little exaggeration to say that half a score of public schools, along with Dartmouth and Sandhurst, dominate England socially.

The class distinctions in newspapers and journals is sharper than elsewhere: the *Times* and the Manchester *Guardian* appeal to a small and select audience, as does the *Spectator* or the *New Statesman*. Even religious affiliations have a class tincture: the Church of England is the church of the upper, and, perhaps, of the lower, classes, and the term "chapel" still has social connotations. Socially it was for long almost as embarrassing to be "chapel" as to have gone to a council school or to pay your own tailor in pounds, though none of this now applies. For England alone of all countries has had a special coin for social purposes. The guinea is fictitious, to be sure, but no fiction was ever more real, and the distinction between schools, doctors, writers, tailors, who were paid in aristocratic guineas and those paid in vulgar pounds was profound.

Logically, this pervasive class-consciousness should poison English society, but in fact it does no such thing. English social relationships seem, in defiance of all logic, easy and even happy. Ease, good nature, and good humor characterize English social life.

Crisis tests character. The English character is made for normal times and enables the English to jog along cheerfuly from day to day. But it is made for crisis, too. Honor, courage, tenacity, pluck, ability, practicality, fortitude, integrity—these have ever been English traits.

> Come the three corners of the world in arms,
> And we shall shock them. Nought shall make us rue,
> If England to itself do be but true

Wrote Shakespeare, over three centuries ago, and Emerson's memorable speech at Manchester concluded on the same note:

"Is it not true that the wise ancients did not praise the ship parting with flying colours from the port, but only that brave sailor which came back with torn sheets and battered sides, stript of her banners, but having ridden out the storm? And so, gentlemen, I feel in regard to this aged England, with the possessions, honours, and trophies, and also with the infirmities of a thousand years gathering around her, irretrievably committed as she now is to transitions of trade, and new and all but incalculable mores, fabrics, arts, machines, and competing populations—I see her not dispirited, not weak, but well remembering that she has seen dark days before; indeed, with a kind of instinct that she sees a little better in a cloudy day and that in storm of battle and calamity, she has a secret vigour and a pulse like a cannon. I see her in her old age, not decrepit, but young, and still daring to believe in her power of endurance and expansion."

Who that knows England today, struggling to pay for the grandeur and misery of victory, can doubt that she is at her best in adversity, or refuse to have faith in her power of endurance and expansion?

INDEX